THE CHRISTIAN CENTURIES

The Church in a
Secularised Society

THE CHRISTIAN CENTURIES

A New History of the Catholic Church

THE CHRISTIAN CENTURIES

Volume Five

THE CHURCH IN A SECULARISED SOCIETY

by

ROGER AUBERT
with P. E. Crunican, John Tracy Ellis,
F. B. Pike, J. Bruls, and J. Hajjar

*The French texts of Roger Aubert, J. Bruhls, and J. Hajjar
were translated by Janet Sondheimer*

The illustrations were selected and annotated by Peter Ludlow

—

PAULIST PRESS
NEW YORK/RAMSEY, N.J./TORONTO

DARTON, LONGMAN AND TODD
LONDON

Published in Great Britain by
Darton, Longman & Todd Ltd
89 Lillie Road, London SW6 1UD

ISBN 0 232 35608 4

Published in the United States of America by
Paulist Press
Editorial Office: 1865 Broadway, N.Y., N.Y. 10023
Business Office: 545 Island Road, Ramsey, N.J. 07446

ISBN 0–8091–0244–7

Library of Congress Catalog Card Number: 78–53496

First edition 1978

Printed in Great Britain by The Anchor Press Ltd
and bound by Wm Brendon & Sons Ltd, both of Tiptree, Essex

CONTENTS

PART ONE

The Catholic Church from the Crisis of 1848 to the War of 1914

PART TWO

Catholicism in the Anglo-Saxon World

PART THREE

Catholicism in Latin America

PART FOUR

From Missions to 'Young Churches'

PART FIVE

**The Eastern Churches
(J. Hajjar)**

PART SIX

The Half-Century leading to Vatican II

INTRODUCTION

This is volume five of Christian Centuries, though it is only the third to appear in English. Volumes three and four are being revised, for their English editions.

The enterprise was begun more than fifteen years ago. Professor Rogier who initiated the project, died on March 30, 1974 without the satisfaction of having seen it finished; and the same was true of the third co-editor Dom David Knowles, who passed away soon afterwards, on November 21 of the same year. Both however were able to read the entire text of volume V and offer suggestions in connexion with its final preparation [1]. Hence these are truly communal labours which we now present to the public. In later years Professor Rogier's state of health prevented him from carrying out (as had been his original intention) the editing of the greater part of this final volume, my own collaboration having in the first instance been only intended to cover the history of the Catholic Church in Europe under the pontificates of Pius IX and Leo XIII. It was at his request that I agreed to replace him. As a consequence, there have not only been some modifications to the original plan but also several years' delay, all the more regrettable since the other contributors had produced their manuscripts by the date originally stipulated. Despite the drawbacks inherent in this sort of work, they have been good enough to bring their contributions up to date before we eventually went to press; even so, there will inevitably be a few traces of adjustment left here and there.

This notwithstanding, we hope that this volume in its present form will prove useful to the reader. In it we have tried to trace the main lines of development of the Roman Catholic Church during those one hundred and twenty years from the accession of Pius IX on the eve of the great European crisis of 1848, to the closing of the Second Vatican Council (and a little further still in the contributions concerning America), while doing our best to remain true to the policy outlined in the Introduction to Volume One. A glance at the table of contents will show our resolute intention of breaking

---

1. My special thanks are due to the late Dom David Knowles for his general approval of my necessarily brief treatment of the development of Catholicism in England during the last century and a half, and for the finer distinctions here and there which he advised me to draw.

with the old habit of seeing the Church as a primarily European institution, by our having devoted a large amount of space to the English-speaking world beyond Europe and also, which is not so often done, to the Third World, be it the ancient Christianities of Latin America or the 'young Churches' of Africa and Asia today reaching maturity. We have also been at pains to break with the long established practice of Catholic historians by devoting most of our space to the daily life of the People of God, instead of concentrating on the more or less tumultuous relationships between Church and State, interspersed with sundry controversies between professional theologians. The first part, devoted to a general picture up to the First World War, and the final part, devoted to the half-century preceding and preparing the way for the Second Vatican Council, both open with chapters outlining the major religious policies of the various popes succeeding Pius IX to John XXIII with attention to the orientation of these pontiffs' varying personalities (for the role of these personalities was indeed of capital importance in such a period of intense centralisation). But they are followed by a whole series of chapters on the evolution of the Church in relation to the liberalising trends of the day and to the movements concerned with improving the lot of the working classes, on the evolution of those organs by which the centralisation of the Roman Church made itself felt, on the varying forms taken by lay Catholic Action over the last hundred years, on the emergence of new pastoral methods, on the various forms of Christian vitality within the Roman Church (devotion to the Blessed Virgin, cult of the Sacred Heart, Eucharistic devotion, liturgical movement, Biblical renewal and so forth) and on the slow awakening of the ecclesiastical sciences culminating in the modernist crisis and the subsequent development of Catholic thought – not merely confined to theology – during the inter-war period and the pontificate of Pius XII. On all these matters, as well as on the vicissitudes of the larger national Churches during the century in question, it has not been possible to go into detail and there is no question of our production's serving as a university textbook! Nonetheless we hope that even specialists in these subjects will be glad to have an over-all picture of the period, in which we have tried to emphasise the essentials and to show what a more sociological approach to church-history can reveal of what is new and even essential in the life of an organism, in which believers recognise the action of the Holy Spirit but which is nonetheless subject to the laws and contingencies governing any association of human beings.

What a general survey of this sort inevitably presents incompletely and occasionally schematically can however be to some extent remedied by recourse to the bibliographical references, which we have made more extensive and detailed than would be the case in a merely popular treatment. Some of the information, when particularly apposite, is indicated by a note in the text itself, but in most cases we have thought it more logical to concentrate the references, chapter by chapter, at the end of the volume. There, generally speaking, the reader will find the exact title and full bibliographical reference to books or articles alluded to in the body of the work. Readers, should bear in mind that for many of the subjects treated in this volume no adequate general work of reference as yet exists. Hence we have been obliged to refer the inquirer to a great many studies of more limited character. The main value of Volume Five we believe to be the presentation as an extended fresco of the principal results obtained to date from these works of detailed research.

A word in conclusion on two preoccupations governing the editors since the inception of the work: namely, to site the life of the Church of God squarely in the world of men, that is to say, in secular history; and never to forget the ecumenical factor. Many readers may doubtless think that these two aspects might have merited more extended treatment, but the authors have been obliged, often much against their wills, to impose severe limits on themselves, given the quantity of available material, becoming ever more abundant the further we progress towards the present day. We do however take the liberty of drawing the reader's attention to the Chronological Table at the start of the book, in which we have tried to draw an often stimulating parallel between successive political, social and cultural events on the one hand, and the evolution of the history of the Church in its various aspects on the other. Furthermore if, on the assumption that, had more space been available – which was not the case – more should have been devoted to ecumenical matters after the Second World War and to the increasingly similar problems now confronting the major Christian confessions, it should be remembered that the period running from Pius IX to Pius XII was probably the one in which confessional barriers were at their most impermeable ever as far as the Roman Catholic Church was concerned. This notwithstanding, even at the darkest moments – the First Vatican Council for instance, or the encyclical *Mortalium animos* – we have tried not to lose sight of their presence on the horizon of those 'separated brothers' to whom the Roman Church of today owes more than she would ever have suspected even a few years ago.

Louvain   Roger Aubert

ABBREVIATIONS

A.A.S.	*Acta Apostolicae Sedis*
A.S.S.	*Acta Sanctae Sedis*
C.H.R.	*Catholic Historical Review*
D.H.G.E.	*Dictionnaire d'histoire et de géographie ecclésiastiques*
D.T.C.	*Dictionnaire de théologie catholique*
Mansi	*Sacrorum conciliorum nova et amplissima collectio*
R.H.E.	*Revue d'histoire ecclésiastique*
R.H.E.F.	*Revue d'histoire de l'Eglise de France*
R.S.C.I.	*Rivista di storia della Chiesa in Italia*
R.st.Ris.	*Rassegna storica del Risorgimento*

CHRONOLOGY OF SOME IMPORTANT EVENTS

Political, Social, Cultural Events		*Church History*
In France: July Revolution. Louis Philippe King of France. Belgian independence.	1830	Death of Pius VIII. Blessed Virgin appears to Catherine Labouré.
	1831	Cardinal Cappellari becomes pope (Gregory XVI).
	1835	Lacordaire inaugurates the Notre-Dame Conferences.
Victoria Queen of England.	1837	
	1840	J. Jugan founds the Little Sisters of the Poor.
	1842	Rome re-establishes the episcopal hierarchy in Australia.
End of the anti-clerical dictatorship of Espartero in Spain.	1843	Foundation of a Benedictine monastery in Sydney, Australia.
Feuerbach's *The Essence of Christianity* (E.T. 1844).	1844	
Great famine in Ireland.	1845	Newman's conversion. Newman's *Essay on the Development of Christian Doctrine*.
	1846	Death of Gregory XVI. Cardinal Mastai-Ferretti becomes pope (Pius IX). Encyclical *Qui pluribus*, condemning liberalism. Vision at La Sallette.
	1847	In Switzerland: defeat of the *Sonderbund*. Restoration of the Latin Patriarchate of Jerusalem.
Revolution in Paris and Rome. Fall of Louis Philippe. Louis Napoleon President of the	1848	Encyclical *In suprema Petri* and the synodal Reply of the Eastern patriarchs.

French Republic. The king of Prussia grants freedom of worship. End of the 'Metternich era' in Austria. New Swiss Constitution. Karl Marx's *Communist Manifesto*.		Lacordaire and Ozanam found the *Ère nouvelle*. First *Katholikentag* in Mainz. Pope's flight to Gaeta.
Republic proclaimed in Rome. Intervention of a French expeditionary force. Pope re-established on his throne.	1849	*Civiltà cattolica* founded. National council of Melkites at Jerusalem.
Loi Falloux on education. Beginnings of Irish immigration into Canada.	1850	Re-establishment of the hierarchy in England. Suppression of the Church's temporal jurisdiction in Piedmont.
Louis Napoleon's *coup d'état*.	1851	Spanish Concordat. Manning leaves Anglicanism.
Napoleon III Emperor of France. Second Empire. Cavour Prime Minister of Piedmont. Comte's *Positivist Catechism*.	1852	First Plenary Council of Baltimore. Guatemalan Concordat.
Opening up of Japan to Europe.	1853	Encyclical *Inter multiplices*. Netherlands hierarchy re-established. Société chrétienne orientale founded in Rome.
Crimean War.	1854	Immaculate Conception proclaimed.
Death of Kierkegaard.	1855	Austrian Concordat.
	1856	Clement Bahouth Patriarch of the Melkites. Review *Les Études* founded. Feast of the Sacred Heart extended to the universal Church.
Indian Mutiny. Livingstone's *Missionary Travels and Researches in South Africa*.	1857	Günther condemned. Suppression of the Church's temporal jurisdiction in Mexico. Assassination of Bp Sibour in Paris.
England abolishes the East India Company.	1858	Lourdes visions. Russian Orthodox Church mission established in Jerusalem.
Italian War. Magenta. Solferino. Peace of Zurich. Darwin's *Origin of Species*.	1859	St John Bosco founds the Salesians. Bulgarian Church crisis. Reduction of the Papal States.

Unification of Italy under the aegis of Piedmont. Nice and Savoy joined to France. García Moreno in power in Ecuador.	1860	Provincial council of Cologne. Papal defeat at Castelfidardo. Anti-papal reaction in Canada.
American Civil War. Foundation of Kingdom of Italy. Victor Emmanuel King of Italy.	1861	*Osservatore Romano* founded. Charles Perin's *Wealth in Christian Societies.*
Garibaldi marches on Rome. Polish revolt. Bismarck Prime Minister of Prussia.	1862	The Vatican re-establishes diplomatic relations with Russia. Encyclical *Amantissimus humani generis Redemptor.* Ketteler's *Freedom, Authority and the Church.*
Lincoln abolishes slavery. Scott Act, in Canada. Renan's *Life of Jesus.*	1863	Ecuadorian Concordat.
First International. National Association founded in Ireland.	1864	Encyclical *Quanta Cura* with its appendix *Syllabus errorum.* Beatification of Marguerite-Marie Alacoque. Newman's *Apologia pro vita sua.*
End of the American Civil War. *Stories of a Russian Pilgrim.*	1865	Manning Archbishop of Westminster. China Inland Mission founded. Beginnings of the Salvation Army.
Break between Prussia and Austria. Austrian defeat at Sadowa.	1866	Second Plenary Council of Baltimore.
Canadian Confederation created. Garibaldi defeated at Mentana. Karl Marx's *Capital.*	1867	Anti-clerical laws in Italie. Bull *Reversurus.* Lord Halifax President of the English Church Union.
Spanish Revolution.	1868	
Civil interment of the positivist philosopher Sanz del Rio in Spain. Suez Canal.	1869	First Vatican Council opens (8 December).
Franco-German War, Sedan. Third Republic proclaimed. Occupation of the Papal State by Italian troops.	1870	Constitution *Pastor aeternus* defines Papal Infallibility. 'Catholic programme' in Canada. Newman's *Grammar of Assent.*
Paris Commune. Treaty of Frankfurt. German Empire proclaimed. Beginning of the *Kulturkampf.*	1871	'Old Catholic' Church created. Albert de Mun founds L'Oeuvre des cercles catholiques ouvriers.

In Germany, scholastic law, interdiction of the Jesuits.	1872	Madame Carré de Malberg founds the Daughters of St Francis de Salles.
	1873	The 'May laws' in Germany: Church life under the control of the State.
Disraeli Prime Minister in England. Restoration of the Bourbons in Spain.	1874	Austrian laws on church life. Beginnings of the Opera dei Congressi in Italy.
García Moreno assassinated in Ecuador. Law expelling all religious congregations from Prussia.	1875	Mgr Dupanloup obtains the freedom of higher education. Creation of Catholic universities in France.
Serbian War.	1876	Freedom of worship in Spain.
Russo-Turkish War.	1877	
Congress of Berlin.	1878	Death of Pius IX. Election of Leo XIII. Encyclicals *Inscrutabili Dei consilio* and *Quod apostolici numeris* of Leo XIII.
	1879	Encyclical *Aeterni Patris* (on Thomism). Serbian Church becomes autocephalous.
French law against religious congregations. Condemnation of the Knights of Labor in Canada. Public Instruction Act in Australia.	1880	First International Eucharistic Congress in Lille. Vatican archives opened to historians of all denominations.
Tsar Alexander II assassinated.	1881	Encyclical *Diuturnum illud.* Decree *Orientalium Ecclesiarum ritus.*
Scholastic laws in France: end of compulsory religious instruction. Amnesty for the bishops and re-opening of the seminaries in Poland.	1882	Apostolic Letter *In Supremo.* Beginning of Mercier's course in Thomist philosophy at Louvain. Assumptionists found *La Croix.*
Death of Karl Marx. Nietsche's *Thus Spoke Zarathustra.*	1883	A. Loisy begins teaching. Manning's *The Eternal Priesthood.*
	1884	Encyclical *Humanum genus* (against freemasonry). Third Plenary Council of Baltimore. Creation of the Union catholique d'études sociales.

Leopold II acquires the Congo. Hanging of Louis Riel in Canada.	1885	Encyclical *Immortale Dei*. Rumanian Church becomes autocephalous. Refusal to allow Albert de Mun to found a Catholic Party.
Boulangism in France.	1886	Albert de Mun founds the A.C.J.F. Portuguese Concordat.
Young Czech movement. The Brothers of Christian Schools found the Syndicat des employés du commerce et d'industrie. Re-opening of diplomatic relations between the Vatican and Russia.	1887	Colombian Concordat. Catholic university created in the United States. St Anselm's College opened in Rome. Excommunication of E. McGlynn. Rampolla Secretary of State.
William II Emperor of Germany. Cardinal Lavigerie's anti-slavery crusade.	1888	Encyclical *Libertas praestantissimum* (on the true meaning of liberty).
Foundation of the Association of Catholic Workers in the Netherlands. Foundation of Fribourg University in Switzerland. V. Soloviev's *La Russie et l'Eglise universelle*. Fall of Bismarck.	1889	A. Van Hoonacker's course at Louvain on 'The critical history of the Old Testament'. Separation of Church and State in Brazil.
Anti-slavery Act (Brussels Conference). Renan's *The Future of Science*.	1890	Encyclical *Sapientiae christianae*. Foundation of the Ecole biblique in Jerusalem.
'Second Christian Democracy' in France. The *Ralliement*.	1891	Encyclical *Rerum novarum* (on social questions).
First Christian unions in Austria. Death of Renan.	1892	Encyclical *Au milieu des sollicitudes*. Spanish College opened in Rome.
Abbé Daens founds the Christian Labour party in Flanders. Maurice Blondel's *L'Action*.	1893	Encyclical *Providentissimus* (on Holy Scripture). Jerusalem Eucharistic Congress. Apostolic Letter *Ad extremas* on the foundation of a seminary in India.
Franco-Russian alliance. Nicolas II Tsar. Establishment of mitigated universal suffrage in Belgium. Beginning of the Dreyfus Affair.	1894	Encyclicals *Praeclara gratulationis* and *Orientalium dignitas*. Americanist controversy. Leo XIII's message in favour of Christian unity. *Revue néo-scolastique* founded at Louvain.

Theodor Herzl's *The Jewish State.*	1895	Leo XIII's Letter *Ad Anglos* to the English people.
Italian defeat at Adowa. Padua Social Congress.	1896	Encyclical *Satis cognitum.* Bull *Apostolicae curae* declaring Anglican orders invalid. Loisy founds the *Revue d'histoire et de littérature religieuses.* Blondel's *Lettre sur les exigences de la pensée contemporaine en matière d'apologétique.*
Graeco-Turkish War. Dreyfus Affair. Leo Bloy's *La Femme pauvre.*	1897	Reunion of the four types of Franciscan observance. Death of St Teresa of the Child Jesus.
Fashoda conflict. Rudini's measures against the socialists and the 'Catholic movement'. Spanish-American War.	1898	Meletios, Metropolitan of Laodicea, becomes Patriarch of Antioch.
Boer War. Marc Sangnier leads the Sillon.	1899	Encyclical *Annum sacrum* (on devotion to the Sacred Heart). Apostolic Letter *Testem benevolentiae* of Leo XIII condemning Americanism. Plenary Council of Latin-American bishops in Rome.
Boxer Rising in China. Foundation in Germany of the Gesamtverband christlichen Gewerkschaften Deutschlands. Death of Nietsche.	1900	Constitution *Condita a Christo* on congregations of simple vows. Clergy Congress at Bourges. Launching of the *Dictionnaire de théologie catholique.* *Revue d'historie ecclésiastique* founded at Louvain.
In France: law on associations (against the congregations). Death of Queen Victoria.	1901	Encyclical *Graves de Communi* (on Christian democracy). Foundation of the Union d'études des catholiques sociaux.
	1902	Creation of the Biblical Commission in Rome. Loisy's *The Gospel and the Church.*
Death of Spencer. Foundation of B. Croce's *La Critica.*	1903	Death of Leo XIII. Election of Pius X. Loisy put on the Index. The Jesuit H. Leroy founds *L'Action populaire.*

●

The *Entente cordiale*. First Semaine Sociale in France. Publication of *La Pensée chrétienne*.	1904	International Marian Congress at Rome. Pius X dissolves the Opera dei Congressi.
France: law separating Church and State. Russo-Japanese War. Nicolas II's edict of toleration.	1905	Encyclical *Il firmo proposito*, first official charter of Catholic action. Decree on frequent communion. E. Le Roy's 'Qu'est-ce qu'un dogme?'. A. Fogazzaro's *Il Santo*.
In France, the Inventories. Publication of Duchesne's *Histoire ancienne de l'Eglise* begins. Review *Anthropos* founded.	1906	Encyclical *Vehementer nos* (against the separation of Church and State). Encyclical *Gravissimo officii*.
	1907	Modernism condemned in the decree *Lamentabili sane exitu* and the encyclical *Pascendi*.
Young Turks' democratic revolution. G. K. Chesterton's *Orthodoxy*.	1908	International Eucharistic Congress in London. Loisy excommunicated.
	1909	Pontifical Biblical Institute founded. Encyclical *Communium rerum*. First plenary council of Quebec province. Beatification of Joan of Arc.
Social revolution in Mexico. French law on workers' retirement. Portugal becomes republic. Péguy's *Le Mystère de la Charité de Jeanne d'Arc*. Claudel's *Cinq Grandes Odes*.	1910	Decree *Quam singulari* on infant communion. Sillon condemned. Encyclical on St Charles Borromeo. Edinburgh World Missionary Conference (Protestant).
Italo-Turkish War. Agadir incident. Chinese Republic proclaimed. Separation of Church and State in Portugal.	1911	Bull *Divino afflatu*. Foundation of the Catholic Foreign Mission Society of America (Maryknoll).
Balkan Wars. Universal suffrage in Italy. Claudel's *L'Annonce faite à Marie*.	1912	Decree *Tradita ab antiquis*. Encyclical *Singulari quadam* on trade unions.
The Patto Gentiloni in Italy (between Catholics and liberals). Unamuno's *The Tragic Sense of Life in Men and in People's* (E.T. 1921).	1913	*Annales de philosophie chrétienne*, 5th series, put on the Index, Laberthonnière forbidden to publish.
First World War. Death of Péguy.	1914	Pius X condemns the periodical *Action française*.

		Death of Pius X. Cardinal Della Chiesa becomes pope (Benedict XV). Foundation of the Croisade eucharistique.
Catholic Historical Review launched.	1915	
Pére de Foucauld assassinated. Louis Hémon's *Maria Chapdelaine.* Bremond's *Histoire littéraire du sentiment religieux.*	1916	
Russian Revolution. Allies capture Jerusalem. Catholic rising in Guadalajara, Mexico. Death of Léon Bloy.	1917	Promulgation of the code of canon law begun by Pius X. Benedict XV creates the Sacred Congregation for the Eastern Church. 1 August: Benedict XV offers to mediate between the belligerents. National Catholic War Council. Fatima apparitions. Pan-Russian synod. Foundation of the Pontifical Institute for Eastern Studies.
French landing in Syria. First World War ends.	1918	
League of Nations pact. Treaties of Versailles and Saint-Germain. Maurice Denis and Desvallières found the Ateliers d'art sacré.	1919	Encyclical *Maximum illud* (on missions). Benedict XV speaks in favour of Eastern Christendom.
Anglo-French agreement on the boundaries of Palestine. International Labour Office founded. Foundation of the International Confederation of Christian Trade Unions.	1920	Encyclical *Spiritus Paraclitus* (on Scripture). Encyclical *Pacem Dei munus.* Encyclical 'To All the Churches of the World' from the Orthodox synod of Constantinople.
Irish independence.	1921	Legion of Mary founded in Ireland. Malines Conversations begin between Catholics and Anglicans.
Mussolini in Rome.	1922	Death of Benedict XV. Cardinal Ratti becomes pope (Pius XI). Encyclical *Ubi Arcano.* Rome establishes apostolic delegation in China. Patriarch of Moscow arrested.
M. Barrès's *Une enquête au pays du Levant.* Completion of Notre-Dame du Raincy church.	1923	Encyclicals *Rerum omnium, Ecclesiam Dei* and *Studiorum ducem.* The patriarch of Moscow recognises the Soviet regime.

Kuomintang reorganised in China.		Seminary opened in the Cameroons.
Death of Lenin. Stalin.	1924	Karl Adam's *Das Wesen des Katholizismus*.
Locarno Pact. Exposition des Arts décoratifs in Paris. Ho Chi Minh founds the Indo-China communist party.	1925	Holy Year. Canonisation of the Curé d'Ars and St Theresa-of-the-Child-Jesus. Encyclical *Quas primas* (instituting the feast of Christ the King.) First ecumenical conference in Stockholm. Cardijn founds the J.O.C. Dom Lambert Beauduin founds Amay priory.
General Strike in England. Eisenstein's *Battleship Potemkin*.	1926	Death of Cardinal Mercier. Encyclical *Rerum Ecclesiae*. The first six Chinese bishops consecrated. International eucharistic congress in Chicago. Guérin inaugurates the French J.O.C. Dom Beauduin founds the review *Irénikon*. Condemnation of Action française.
Heidegger's *Existence and Being*.	1927	Lausanne ecumenical conference.
Sound in the cinema. Briand – Kellog Pact.	1928	Encyclical *Mortalium animos* (on ecumenism). Encyclical *Rerum orientalium* (on Eastern Christendom). Opus Dei founded in Madrid. Lagrange's *L'Evangile de Jésus-Christ*.
United States economic crisis. Lateran Treaty.	1929	Encyclical *Divini illius Magistri* (on education). Pontifical Institute of Medieval Studies founded in Toronto.
	1930	Encyclical *Casti connubii* (on marriage and the family). Dorothy Day founds the Catholic Worker Movement.
Republic proclaimed in Spain.	1931	Encyclicals *Quadragesimo anno* (anniversary of the Social encyclical *Rerum novarum*) and *Non abbiamo bisogno* (against fascism).
Bergson's *The Two Sources of Morality and Religion*.	1932	
Hitler comes to power. F. D. Roosevelt president of the U.S.A.	1933	Concordat with the German Reich.

6 February riots in Paris. Dollfuss assassinated in Austria. The 'long march' in China.	1934	Catholic Interracial Council, New York. End of Bulgarian schism.
Laval-Mussolini agreement. Italians in Ethiopia.	1935	Couturier founds the review *L'Art sacré*.
Popular Front victory in France. Spanish Civil War. Maritain's *Integral Humanism*. François Mauriac's *Vie de Jésus*. G. Bernanos's *Diary of a Country Priest*.	1936	Encyclical *Vigilanti cura* (on the cinema). First congress of Orthodox theology in Athens.
Sino-Japanese War. Sinarquist movement in Mexico.	1937	Encyclicals *Mit Brennender Sorge* (against nazism) and *Divini Redemptoris* (against communism). Ecumenical conferences at Oxford and Edinburgh. Congar's *Chrétiens désunis*. He founds the collection *Unam Sanctam*.
Austria annexed to Germany (the *Anschluss*). Munich agreement.	1938	Central office for Catholic Action set up in Rome. De Lubac's *Catholicisme*.
German-Soviet Pact. German troops enter Czechoslovakia. German invasion of Poland. Second World War begins.	1939	Death of Pius XI. Cardinal Pacelli becomes pope (Pius XII). Encyclicals *Summi pontificatus* and *Sertum laetitiae* (150th anniversary of the American hierarchy).
German invasion of Western Europe. Battle of Britain.	1940	Bultmann's 'Neues Testament und Mythologie'.
Germans attack Russia. Pearl Harbor. Death of Bergson.	1941	Mission de France founded.
	1942	Taizé community founded. L. Cerfaux's *La Théologie de l'Église suivant saint Paul*.
Stalingrad. Fall of Mussolini. Death of Maurice Denis. Sartre's *Being and Nothingness*.	1943	Encyclicals *Mystici Corporis Christi* and *Divino afflante spiritu*. Godin and Daniel's, *France, pays de mission?*
Liberation of Western Europe by the Allied armies.	1944	Encyclical *Orientalis Ecclesiae decus* (for the anniversary of the death of St Cyril of Alexandria).
German surrender. Hiroshima.	1945	Encyclical *Orientales omnes*. Boyer founds the Association inter-

Independence of the Philippines and Indonesia. United Nations Organisation created.		nationale pour l'unité spirituelle des peuples.
Fourth Republic in France. Perón president of Argentina.	1946	Synod of Lvov. Return of the Ukrainians to Orthodoxy proclaimed.
China and Egypt establish diplomatic with the Vatican. Camus's *La Peste*.	1947	Encyclical *Mediator Dei*. Cardinal Suhard's pastoral letter: *Essor ou déclin de l'Église*. Canonisation of Jean de Britto, a 17th-century missionary in India.
Communists seize power in Prague. Foundation of State of Israel. Berlin crisis. Yugoslavia breaks with Moscow.	1948	World Council of Churches founded in Amsterdam. Moscow Pan-Orthodox Conference. Athenagoras I as ecumenical patriarch.
People's Republic of China. NATO created.	1949	Holy Office decree against all collaboration with communist parties.
Korean War. Religious liberty in Portugal.	1950	Dogma of the Assumption. Voillaume's *Au coeur des masses*.
	1951	First world conference on the apostolate of the laity, in Rome. Mgr Willebrands founds the Catholic Conference for Ecumenical Questions. Tillich's *Systematic Theology*.
Neguib in power in Egypt. Eisenhower president of U.S.A.	1952	Lombardi launches his 'Towards a better world' movement in Italy.
Death of Stalin.	1953	Spanish concordat.
Algerian War begins. Nasser in power in Egypt. Geneva Agreements on Indo-China.	1954	Encyclical *Sempiternus Rex*. World Council of Churches' Second Assembly at Evanston. Worker-priests suspended. Pius X canonised.
Istanbul riots. Fall of Perón in Argentina. Death of Teilhard de Chardin. Death of Claudel. Ronchamp chapel built. Teilhard de Chardin's *The Phenomenon of Man* published.	1955	Apostolic letter organising Biblical circles. CELAM (Consejo Episcopal Latino Americano) created.
Poznan (Poland) rising. Hungarian rising. Suez crisis.	1956	A.C.J.F. crisis in France.

Khrushchev. Common Market (E.E.C.). Ghana independent (first State of black Africa).	1957	Encyclical *Fidei donum*. 'Faith and Order' conference at Oberlin, Ohio. Promulgation of the codification relating to the constitution of the Oriental Church and patriarchal and synodal rules.
French Fifth Republic: De Gaulle. Castro in power in Cuba. Second Berlin crisis. Brussels world exhibition.	1958	Death of Pius XII. Cardinal Roncalli becomes pope (John XXIII). Official reconciliation between Constantinople and Moscow. American bishops' pastoral letter on the curse of racism.
	1959	Announcement of an ecumenical council. World Council of Churches committee in Rhodes.
John F. Kennedy U.S. president. Independence for the Cameroons, Congo-Brazzaville, Gabon, Chad, Central African Republic, Togo, Ivory Coast, Dahomey, Upper Volta, Niger, Nigeria, Senegal, Mali, Madagascar, Somalia, Mauritania, Congo-Leopoldville.	1960	John XXIII creates a Secretariat for Christian Unity; president, Cardinal Bea. Pan-Orthodox Conference of Rhodes.
Berlin wall. First space flight by Gagarin. Hochhuth's *The Representative*.	1961	Encyclical *Mater et Magistra*. The Moscow patriarchate is admitted to the general assembly of the World Council of Churches in New Delhi.
Algerian independence. Cuban crisis between the U.S.A. and the U.S.S.R. MacLuhan's *The Gutenberg Galaxy*.	1962	Vatican II opens.
Kennedy assassinated. Johnson U.S. president.	1963	Encyclical *Pacem in terris*. Death of John XXIII. Cardinal Montini becomes pope (Paul VI). Vatican II, second session, begins. Paul VI announces his intention of making a pilgrimage to the Holy Land.
Fall of Khrushchev. Missionaries expelled from the Soudan.	1964	Paul VI meets Patriarch Athenagoras in Jerusalem. Vatican II, third session. Constitution *Lumen gentium* (on the Church).
American military intervention in	1965	Closure of the council debates.

Vietnam.		Constitution *Dei Verbum*. Holy Office reforms announced. Constitution *Gaudium et Spes*. Excommunication lifted between Rome and Constantinople.
Missionaries expelled from Burma.	1966	CELAM conference at Mar-del-Plata, Argentina.
Six-Day War, in Israel. Detroit race riots. Missionaries expelled from Guinea. Montreal World Exposition.	1967	Encyclical *Populorum progressio*. Pontifical pilgrimage to Constantinople and Ephesus. First synod of Catholic bishops in Rome. International theology conference at Toronto. Paul VI decides to re-structure the curia.
Warsaw Pact forces intervene in Czechoslovakia. Social crisis in France.	1968	Encyclical *Humanae vitae*. Martin Luther King assassinated. Institute for Ecumenical and Cultural Research opened at St John's University, Collegeville, Minnesota, U.S.A.
Man on the moon. De Gaulle's resignation. Pompidou president of French Republic.	1969	Second synod of Catholic bishops.
Salvador Allende elected in Chile. Death of Mauriac. Gierecz in power in Poland.	1970	Growth of a Catholic Pentecostal movement at Duquesne University, Pittsburgh, U.S.A.
Chinese People's Republic admitted to the U.N.	1971	Third synod of bishops. Mother Theresa of Calcutta founds a house in Harlem, New York. Ecumenical Institute for Advanced Theological Studies opened at Tantur, near Jerusalem.
Meeting between Mao Tse-tung and Nixon.	1972	Death of Patriarch Athenagoras. International conference of the Catholic Charismatic Renewal at Notre Dame University (U.S.A.).
Chilean *putsch*. October War in the Middle East.	1973	
Death of Pompidou. Giscard d'Estaing president of French Republic. Nixon resigns.	1974	Fourth synod of bishops. Youth Council at Taizé.

LIST OF ILLUSTRATIONS

(Explanatory captions are provided, where necessary, alongside
the pictures, together with sources and acknowledgments)

C.   THE CHURCH UNIVERSAL

A. The Church in Europe

1. Pope Pius IX (1846-1878). (*The Universe*, London)

A2. 16 July 1846: popular demonstration of affection in Rome, following Pius IX's amnesty for political prisoners. (Museo Centrale del Risorgimento, Rome. Photo: Guido Guidotti, Rome)

LA LIBERTÉ FAISANT LE TOUR DU MONDE .

A3. Pius IX as Liberator: an optimistic French representation of the Pope's early reforms. The Pope is seen in a chariot breaking away from the control of the ancient monarchies. He confers on those who had formerly been enslaved, the fruits of the French Revolution: Liberty, Equality and Fraternity, and in doing so performs the will of Christ. (Museo Centrale del Risorgimento, Rome. Photo: Guido Guidotti, Rome)

Strada di ferro da Gaeta a Roma.

A4. July 1849: the 'iron road' from Gaeta to Rome. Pius IX and his cardinals return from exile supported by French bayonets. (*Il Fischietto*, Rome, 24 July 1849; B.L. 4/1866)

A5. 17 July 1849: Pius IX's proclamation to his Roman subjects three years after the amnesty of July 1846. (Museo Centrale del Risorgimento, Rome. Photo: Guido Guidotti, Rome) In English the text reads as opposite:

PIVS PP. IX

AI SUOI AMATISSIMI SUDDITI

IDDIO ha levato in alto il suo braccio, ed ha comandato al mare tempestoso dell'anarchia, e dell'empietà di arrestarsi. Egli ha guidato le armi cattoliche per sostenere i diritti della umanità conculcata, della fede combattuta, e quelli della Santa Sede e della Nostra Sovranità. Sia lode eterna a LUI, che anche in mezzo alle ire non dimentica la misericordia.

Amatissimi Sudditi, se nel vortice delle spaventose vicende il nostro cuore si è saziato di affanni sul riflesso di tanti mali patiti dalla Chiesa, dalla religione, e da voi; non ha però scemato l'affetto, col quale vi amò sempre, e vi ama. Noi affrettiamo co'Nostri voti il giorno che Ci conduca di nuovo fra voi, e allorquando sia giunto, Noi torneremo col vivo desiderio di apportarvi conforto, e con la volontà di occuparci con tutte le Nostre forze del vostro vero bene, applicando i difficili rimedii ai mali gravissimi, e consolando i buoni sudditi, i quali mentre aspettano quelle istituzioni, che appaghino i loro bisogni, vogliono, come Noi lo vogliamo, veder guarentita la libertà e la indipendenza del Sommo Pontificato, così necessaria alla tranquillità del mondo Cattolico.

Intanto pel riordinamento della cosa pubblica andiamo a **nominare una Commissione**, che munita **di pieni poteri**, e coadjuvata da un **Ministero, regoli il** governo dello Stato.

Quella benedizione del Signore, che vi abbiamo sempre implorata anche da voi lontani, oggi con maggior fervore la imploriamo, affinchè scenda copiosa sopra di voi: ed è grande conforto all'animo Nostro lo sperare, che tutti quelli che vollero rendersi incapaci di goderne il frutto pe'loro traviamenti, possano esserne fatti meritevoli mercè di un sincero e costante ravvedimento.

Datum Cajetae die 17 Julii anni 1849.

PIVS PP. IX

ROMA 1849.— DALLA TIPOGRAFIA DELL'REV. CAM. APOST.

A6. October 1849: Pius IX, supported by Louis Napoleon and assisted by other symbols of reaction, quenches the revolution which he had helped to inspire in 1848. (*Il Fischietto,* Rome, 4 October 1849; B.L. 4/1866)

POPE PIUS IX

To His Beloved Subjects

God has raised high his arm and has commanded the tempestuous sea of anarchy and godlessness to abate. He has guided the Catholic armies to uphold the rights of oppressed humanity, of the embattled faith, of the Holy See and of Our Sovereignty. Eternal praise to HIM, who even in his wrath does not forget mercy.

Beloved Subjects, in the frightful maelstrom of present events our heart is overflowing with anxiety as We contemplate so many ills suffered by the Church, by religion and by you; it bears you, however, no less affection now than it has always borne you in the past. By Our prayers We strive to hasten the day which will bring Us once more among you, and when it comes, We shall return with the keen desire to bring you comfort and with the will to devote Ourselves totally to your true interests, applying difficult remedies to the gravest ills and consoling Our good subjects who, while waiting for appropriate institutions to satisfy their needs, wish, like Ourselves, to see guaranteed the Supreme Pontiff's freedom and independence, so necessary to the tranquillity of the Catholic world.

Meanwhile, in an effort to restore order to public affairs, We intend to nominate a Commission which, furnished with full powers and assisted by a Ministry, will see to the government of the State.

Today, with even greater fervour, We implore that blessing of the Lord which We have always implored for you, even when far away, so that it may descend on you in abundance: and Our soul is greatly comforted by the hope that all who wilfully made themselves incapable of enjoying its fruits by their corrupt ways may be made deserving of it by sincere and steadfast amendment.

Given at Gaeta on the 17th day of July in the year 1849

— Signorina, sapreste insegnarmi dove si vota in Torino per il foro?
— Monsignore, ho inteso a dire che in Torino si fa tutto contro il foro.

Il Fischietto raccoglie per reliquie le lagrime di un Geremia che piange su d'una Gerusalemme non rovinata ma ricostrutta.

« E loro ordinò di nulla prendere pel cammino se non un bastone, e di non avere nè sacco, nè pane, nè monete nella loro cintura ». *Ev. S. Marco, cap. VII.*

A7-9 CHURCH-STATE RELATIONS IN ITALY, 1849-70: ANTI-CLERICAL PROPAGANDA

(Top) A7 a and b. 1850: Piedmont is lost — a satirical comment on the passing of the Siccardi laws which *inter alia* abolished separate church courts and clerical exemption from existing laws. (*Il Fischietto,* Rome, April 1850; B.L. 4/1866). In English the captions read:

a. Madam, may I ask whether the vote in Turin will be in favour of the courts? Monsignor, I understand that in Turin everybody is against the courts.

b. Il Fischietto catches the tears of a Jeremiah who weeps over a Jerusalem which has been built afresh rather than renovated.

(Bottom) A8. 1851: disciples old and new: a satirical comment on ecclesiastical wealth, a stock-in-trade of anti-clerical propaganda. (*Il Fischietto,* Rome, 18 December 1851). The caption beneath is Mark 6:8 – 'He charged them to take nothing for their journey except a staff: no bread, no bag, no money in their belts.'

ITALY IN ROME.

Papa Pius (*to* King of Italy). "I MUST NEEDS SURRENDER THE *SWORD*, MY SON; BUT *I KEEP THE KEYS!!*"

A9. 1870: *Punch* on the Italian annexation of Rome. (*Punch,* vol. 59, 1870; B.L. 744313)

THE POPE "TRYING IT ON" MR. JOHN BULL.

THE NEW OXFORD COSTUME.
AN UNDERGRADUATE GOING TO LECTURE.

(Top) A10. Pope Pius IX (1846-1878) 'trying it on' Mr John Bull. (*Punch*, vol. 19, 1850; B.L. 744313)

(Bottom) A11. The new Oxford costume. (*Punch*, vol. 19, 1850; B.L. 744313)

THE THIN END OF THE WEDGE.

DARING ATTEMPT TO BREAK INTO A CHURCH.

12. The thin end of the wedge: Rome gains a foothold at Westminster in London. (*Punch*, vol.
9, 1850; B.L. 744313)

A13. The Council in session. (Engraving; Museo Centrale del Risorgimento, Rome. Photo: Guido Guidotti, Rome)

A14. Sliding on thin ice: *Punch* on Papal infallibility. (*Punch,* vol. 57, 1869; B.L. 744313). The following piece of doggerel appeared on the page opposite the cartoon:

> Lo, now the end! About the marble chair
> From earth's wide ends the Church's fathers draw –
> Cardinals, Patriarchs, and all that wear
> The mitre, and own him their living God and Law,
>
> Summoned to curse whatever erst he blest,
> The faiths, the hopes, the charities to ban,
> That the new Pope's humanity confest,
> What time the natural manhood in him yearned to man.
>
> And him who this great circle has swept through,
> From zenith unto nadir of thought's zone,
> Whose 'true' to-day is next-day's most 'untrue',
> The Church has gathered here INFALLIBLE to own!

PUNCH, OR THE LONDON CHARIVARI.—November 1, 1873.

KAISER CHRISTIAN AND GIANT POPE.

"SO I SAW THAT CHRISTIAN WENT ON HIS WAY; AND SET A GOOD FACE ON IT, AND CATCHED NO HURT."—*Pilgrim's Progress.*

A15. A battle royal: *Punch* on the Kulturkampf. (*Punch,* vol. 65, 1873).

8. Jahrgang **Nummer 5**

SIMPLICISSIMUS

Abonnement vierteljährlich 1 Mk. 80 Pfg.
Billige Ausgabe

Illustrierte Wochenschrift

Reichspost-Beitungsliste: No. 7330
Bayr. Post-Beitungsliste: No. 797

(Alle Rechte vorbehalten)

Petri Fischzug

(Zeichnung von Th. Th. Heine)

A16. 1903-4: Pope Leo XIII successfully netting the crowned heads of Central Europe. *Simplicissimus*, the most accomplished satirical journal in Imperial Germany, registered increasing alarm about the possibility of a new, reactionary, anti-socialist coalition between Prussian conservatives and German catholics. (*Simplicissimus*, 8 Jrg., no. 5)

A17. Pope Leo XIII (1878-1903). (Süddeutscher Verlag, Munich)

A18. Pope Pius X (1903-1914) blessing pilgrims shortly before his death. (Süddeutscher Verlag, Munich)

A19-21 THE FIRST WORLD WAR

Left) A19. Pope Benedict XV (1914-1922). (Süddeutscher Verlag, Munich)

Above) A20. Cardinal Archbishop Piffl of Vienna blesses weapons in a ceremony at the Imperial Military Academy, Vienna. (Süddeutscher Verlag, Munich)

Below) A21. 1915: French military chaplains, complete with bicycles. (Süddeutscher Verlag, Munich)

A22. Broadcasting to the faithful. (Süddeutscher Verlag, Munich)

A23. Receiving the Latin text of one of the books of the Bible newly revised by monks whom he had commissioned to carry out the revision. (Süddeutscher Verlag, Munich)

A24-25 TWO CONCORDATS SIGNED

(Above) A24. January 1925: Cardinal Pacelli, later Pope Pius XII but at this time papal nuncio in Munich, and the Bavarian Prime Minister Dr Held conclude the concordat between the Holy See and the Bavarian government. (Süddeutscher Verlag, Munich)

(Below) A25. 1929: Cardinal de Gasperi, Secretary of State, and Mussolini sign the Lateran Treaty. (Museo Centrale del Risorgimento, Rome. Photo: Guido Guidotti, Rome)

A26. 19 March 1932: a priest leads schoolchildren to pay their last respects to Aristide Briand. (*L'Illustration*)

A27. September 1935: Pius XI between opposing forces in the Abyssinian crisis: an optimistic French comment. As the conflict deepened, papal impartiality became increasingly problematical. (*Sept,* issue of 6 September 1935)

A28. July 1933: the Concordat is signed. Seated from left to right: Mgr Kaas, formerly a Centre Party politician; Baron von Papen, German vice-chancellor; Cardinal Pacelli; Dr Buttmann of the German Ministry of the Interior; and an official from the German Embassy. (Keystone Press Agency, London)

A29. November 1933: Nazi exploitation of the Church's apparent approval of the new regime:
a poster used in the campaign preceding the referendum of 12 November. (Süddeutscher Verlag,
Munich). The text reads: 'A solemn moment during the stone-laying ceremony at the House of
German Art. The Papal Nuncio, Bajallo di Torregrossa, says to the Führer, 'For long I have not
understood you. But for long I have tried. Today I do understand you.'

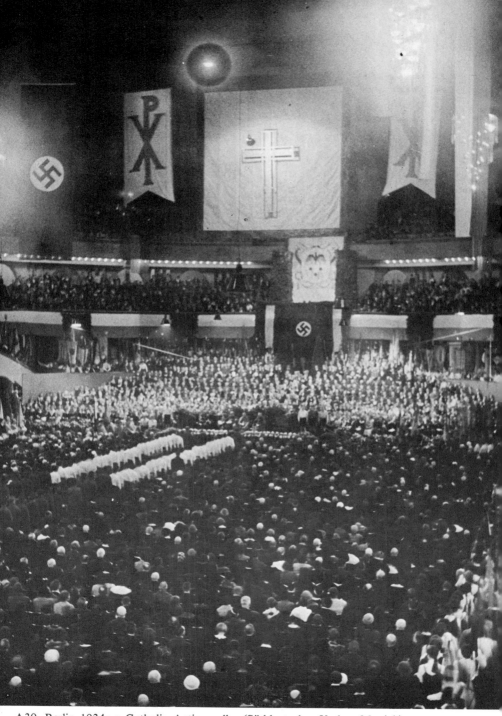

A30. Berlin 1934: a Catholic Action rally. (Süddeutscher Verlag, Munich)

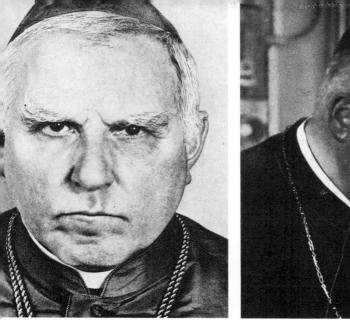

(Top left) A31. Bishop Clemens von Galen of Münster. (Süddeutscher Verlag, Munich)

(Top right) A32. Cardinal Faulhaber of Munich. (Süddeutscher Verlag, Munich)

(Bottom) A33. 1944: Father Delp, SJ on trial before the People's Court for his part in the July plot. (Süddeutscher Verlag, Munich)

(Above) A34. June 1947: Mass at the opening of the Auschwitz Camp Museum. (Keyston
Press Agency, London)

A35-36 POPE PIUS XII (1959-1958)

(Top right) A35. 19 May 1939: the new pope takes possession of the Lateran. (Süddeutsch
Verlag, Munich)

(Bottom right) A36. August 1943: praying with the people of Rome for an end to the bombin,
the city. (Keystone Press Agency, London)

7-40 CHURCH AND STATE IN SPAIN

(top left) A37. 1932: Jesuits ordered to leave Spain. (Süddeutscher Verlag, Munich)

(bottom left) A38. The Civil War, 1936-39: government supporters shoot at a statue of Christ Madrid. (Süddeutscher Verlag, Munich)

(top) A39. 1931: Spanish Army officers at Mass. (Süddeutscher Verlag, Munich)

(bottom) A40. General Franco with church dignitaries.

(Above) A41. 1942, Vichy: Marshal Petain; Cardinal Suhard, archbishop of Paris; Cardinal Gerlier, archbishop of Lyons; and Pierre Laval, at a military parade on 29 October. (Paul Popper)

A42-43 POST-WAR CHRISTIAN DEMOCRACY IN FRANCE AND GERMANY

(Top right) A42. September 1958: Robert Schuman lays the foundation stone of a new European Village in the Saarland. (Paul Popper)

(Bottom right) A43. Konrad Adenauer praying during a visit to a Berlin refugee camp. (Paul Popper)

(Below) A44. February 1949, Budapest: the trial of Cardinal Mindszenty. (Associated Pre

(Top right) A45. 31 October 1956, Budapest: the release of Cardinal Mindszenty during Hungarian uprising; he is pictured here with his liberators outside his residence. (Associa Press)

(Bottom right) A46. 9 November 1955, Stalinogrod, Poland: consecration of the new cathed (Paul Popper)

47-48 POPE JOHN XXIII (1958-1963)

(Left) A47. December 1958; Rome: visiting the Regina Coeli prison. (Süddeutscher Verlag, Munich)

(Above) A48. 25 October 1962: praying for peace at the height of the Cuban crisis. (Süddeutscher Verlag, Munich)

(Left) A49. 11 October 1962: Vatican Council II, the solemn inauguration. (Süddeutscher Verlag, Munich)

(Above) A50. September 1971, Rome: Pope Paul VI (1963-) celebrating mass in the Sistine Chapel at the opening ceremony of the Synod of Bishops. (Süddeutscher Verlag, Munich)

B. The Church Outside Europe

B 1-8 THE MISSIONARY CHURCH: THE EXPERIENCE OF THE MILL HILL ORDER

(Below) B1. Martyrdom in India: the cover page drawing of one of the earliest numbers of the Order's journal, *St Joseph's Advocate,* showing the fate of Bishop Diaz and using it as a basis for an appeal for support. (*St Joseph's Advocate,* vol. 2, 1885)

(Top right) B2. Teaching Africans to till the ground. (*St Joseph's Advocate,* vol. 2, 1891)

(Bottom right) B3. A reading class in Uganda. (*St Joseph's Advocate,* vol. 5, 1908)

No. 5. { Australian Edition. } *WINTER QUARTER, 1884.* Price, 2d. ; Post free, 2½d. Ann. Subs., Post free, 10d.

HELP! HELP! HELP us to send Priests to the 900,000,000 HEATHEN.

BISHOP DIAZ IS LED OUT TO MARTYRDOM IN 1857.

Bottom left) B4. Agricultural pilot scheme in Jinja, Uganda. (*Mill Hill World,* vol. 11, 1969)

Top left) B5. A nun advises a young African on how to use an advanced printing machine. *Mill Hill World*)

Top right) B6. Medical work in a well equipped hospital. (Mill Hill World)

Below left) B7. 8 December 1939: The first African bishop, Joseph Kiwanuka of Uganda just after his consecration. (Father Nicholls)

Below right) B8. President Nyerere welcomed by Cardinal Rugambwa, with Archbishop Maranta on the right. (*Mill Hill World,* Vol. 10, 1968)

B9-16 CHURCH AND STATE IN THE UNITED STATES OF AMERICA

B9. *Harper's Weekly* on the ideal relationship. (*Harper's Weekly*, Februrary 1871)

B 10. The catholic threat to the Public (state) School, the principal instrument of racial integration. (*Harper's Weekly*, December 1871)

B11. Papal infallibility. (*Harper's Weekly*, December 1871)

B12. St Patrick's Day 1867: anti-Catholic sentiment was often confused with anti-Irish feeling. (*Harper's Weekly*, April 1867)

B13. St Patrick's Day 1948: Cardinal and President: Cardinal Spellman and President Truman with J. A. Coleman, President of the Sons of St Patrick. (Süddeutscher Verlag, Munich)

B14. 1953 Korea: Cardinal Spellman and the troops. (Süddeutscher Verlag, Munich)

315. January 1955, Vietnam: Cardinal Spellman's visit. (Süddeutscher Verlag, Munich)

316. 1968: the Berrigan Brothers leaving Balto County jail on their way to trial on charges of burning draft records. (Paul Popper)

B17-20 SOUTH AMERICA

(Above) B17. Brazil: a Franciscan celebrates mass in the Amazon jungle. (Süddeutscher Verlag, Munich)

(Left) B18. Peru: Franciscans in an urban setting in Lima. (Camera Press, Fred J. Maroon)

(Above) B19. Peru: Church, Army and State, presided over by General Juan Velasco Alvarado, celebrate the 150th anniversary of the country's independence. (Camera Press, Prensa Latina)

(Right) B20. Chile: a Christian Democratic rally in Quillota in support of its candidate, Eduardo Frei. (Camera Press, Lynn Pelham)

B21-24 AUSTRALIA

(Above left) B21. 1872: the Devil thrives on religious bigotry – fed by the *Protestant Standard* and the Roman Catholic *Freeman's Journal.* (*Sydney Punch,* 1872)

(Above right) B22. 1903, the elections: the 'Orange' candidate. Voice of the Animal: 'Gentlemen, what we want at the next Federal elections is that you should drop all questions about tariffs, promotion of local industries, transcontinental railways, old age pensions, settlement of the people on the land, debt consolidation, arbitrations, defence, and all matters relating to your own interests, and vote solely for Orange candidates.' (*The Bulletin,* 1903)

(Top right) B23. Phil May in Rome. (*The Bulletin,* 1891)

(Bottom right) B24. On the revival of state aid for independent schools. (*The Bulletin,* 1944)

AUSTRALIANS IN ROME

"WHEN DOES THE POPE BLESS THE DONKEYS MR SMITH"

"WELL I DON'T THINK HE EVER BLESSES ANYTHING ELSE."

WHO IS THIS BLOKE?
A NUT? A PROTTO?
A TYKE? - I'D BETTER BE
CAREFUL - HE MIGHT
HIT ME.

"What do you think of State Aid for Church Schools."

"Education should encourage a fearless spirit of enquiry"

C. The Church Universal

C1-3 LOURDES

(Below) C1. Pilgrims on the way by train, 1954. (Süddeutscher Verlag, Munich)

(Top right) C2. The grotto, with abandoned crutches displayed. (Süddeutscher Verlag, Munich)

(Bottom right) C3. International commerce. (Süddeutscher Verlag, Munich)

C4-5 POPULAR PIETY IN ITALY

(Top left) C4. August 1953, the Madonna's tears: a young Sicilian invalid reported that tears began to flow from the eyes of the Madonna above her bed. The house was immediately besieged by the pious and the curious. (Süddeutscher Verlag, Munich)

(Bottom left) C5. In an open field three women kneel at small confessionals erected near the spot where the Madonna is said to have appeared to a Roman girl in 1960. (Süddeutscher Verlag, Munich)

(Below) C6. 1932, Dublin: the Eucharistic World Congress. (Süddeutscher Verlag, Munich)

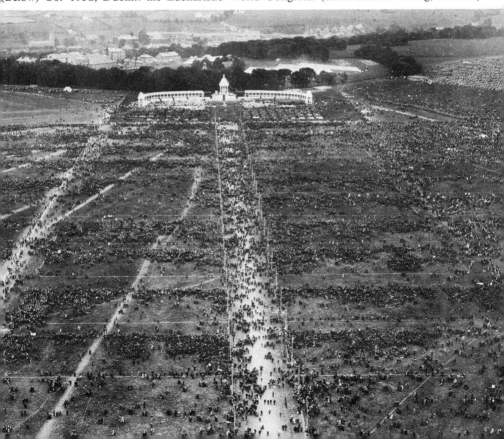

C7. October 1962, Rome: Pope John XXIII shakes hands with the Russian Orthodox Archimandrite Vladimir Kotlyarov. (Süddeutscher Verlag, Munich)

8. May 1967, Rome: Pope Paul VI greets the Armenian Patriarch Khoren; Cardinal Bea ands in the centre. (Associated Press)

(Below) C9. The Puseyite Moth and the Roman Candle. Cartoon from *Punch,* vol. 19, 1850

(Top right) C10. Cardinal Bea and the Archbishop of Canterbury. (Süddeutscher Verla Munich)

(Bottom right) C11. Pope Paul and the Archbishop. (Süddeutscher Verlag, Munich)

THE PUSEYITE MOTH AND ROMAN CANDLE.

" Fly away *Silly* Moth."

C12. The church militant: a detachment of German Catholic pilgrims marching away from an audience with Pius X shortly after the latter's Encyclical denouncing the Protestant Reformation. Date 26 May 1910. (Süddeutscher Verlag, Munich)

13. Pope Paul visits the World Council of Churches at Geneva. (WCC, Geneva)

(Top left) C14. An Evangelical pastor shares in a service at the German Katholikentag, 1968. (Süddeutscher Verlag, Munich)

(Bottom left) C15. Joint services in Amsterdam. (Süddeutscher Verlag, Munich)

(Below) C16. Plus ça change: Ulster, 1872. *Punch* cartoon on Protestant-Catholic riots in Belfast, 1872. *Punch,* vol 63, 31 August, 1872.

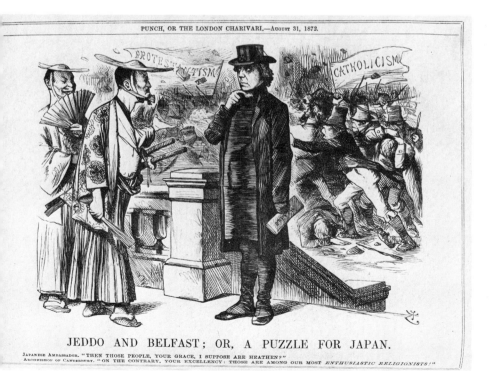

PUNCH, OR THE LONDON CHARIVARI.—August 31, 1872.

JEDDO AND BELFAST; OR, A PUZZLE FOR JAPAN.

Japanese Ambassador. "THEN THOSE PEOPLE, YOUR GRACE, I SUPPOSE ARE HEATHEN?"
Archbishop of Canterbury. "ON THE CONTRARY, YOUR EXCELLENCY; THOSE ARE AMONG OUR MOST *ENTHUSIASTIC RELIGIONISTS!*"

PART ONE

THE CATHOLIC CHURCH FROM THE CRISIS OF 1848 TO THE WAR OF 1914

1

THREE POPES:
PIUS IX, LEO XIII, PIUS X

POPE Gregory died on 1 June 1846 at the height of his unpopularity. His unwillingness to reorganise the Papal State on more modern lines was widely deplored. Dissatisfaction with him in Italy was heightened by his completely negative attitude towards patriotic aspirations to liberate the peninsula from Austrian misrule. It is therefore not surprising that when the cardinals gathered in conclave, and in a conclave in which the Italian element was overwhelmingly predominant, their choice should have been determined by the problems confronting the Roman State. There were some cardinals who favoured the election of the reactionary Cardinal Lambruschini, Secretary of State, in the hope that this would guarantee continued Austrian support in suppressing the revolutionary agitation which was steadily gaining ground. Others, conscious of the need for a departure from the previous regime, were in favour of a pope who would make some concession to the spirit of the times and who was also a native of the Papal State, which would make him appear less dependent on foreign influence. Passing over Gizzi, recently commended by Massimo d'Azeglio as the ideal candidate for the neo-Guelfs but regarded by many as too far advanced – wrongly, as A. Simon has well shown [1] – they plumped for Cardinal Mastai, who as bishop first of Spoleto and then of Imola had made himself acceptable to the liberal circles particularly active in those parts. At the first ballot Mastai secured fifteen votes to Lambruschini's seventeen. On the next day the votes of those who feared a Lambruschini victory were hastily transferred to Mastai, who emerged on the second morning of the conclave with the two-thirds majority.

The man who, as Pius IX, was to occupy the see of St Peter for the next

1. *Documents relatifs à la nonciature de Bruxelles, 1834-1838* (Brussels 1958), 51-91.

thirty-two years was still, at fifty-four, comparatively young. As a cleric he had been distinguished from his earliest days by his piety and pastoral zeal, and his diocesan priests were united in praising his geniality and open-heartedness. As pope he quickly became a contradictory figure: to some he appeared as little less than a saint, placed by providence at the head of the Church to guide her with a steady hand in repelling the repeated assaults of the devil; to others he appeared as a conceited autocrat, or else little more than a puppet, allowing himself to be manipulated by a clique of diehard reactionaries. Despite the continuing lack of a good critical biography, we are in a better position today than his contemporaries to assess the limitations and true greatness of this pope whose imprint on modern Catholicism has been so profound.

Pius IX suffered under a triple handicap. He was easily swayed by his emotions and this led him to act on whatever advice was the most recently tendered – though he could prove unshakable when he thought the true interests of the Church were at stake. Next, as with most Italian ecclesiastics of his generation, his intellectual training had been only superficial. This was compensated in part by a native shrewdness and common sense, but there were times when it prevented him from appreciating the relative character of certain propositions on which he was urged to pass judgment, or from grasping the true complexity of the problems before him, so that he was more inclined, for example, to regard the political convulsions affecting the Church as yet one further round in the great struggle between God and Satan than he was to subject them to any proper technical analysis. Lastly, he was surrounded by confidential advisers whose zeal and dedication did not compensate for their tendency to look at things with the intransigence of doctrinaires quite out of touch with the modern mind.

These limitations, which were especially unfortunate in a leader who would be required to take more and more decisions on his own, should not blind us to the positive aspects of the man and his work: his human qualities, his simplicity and kindness, his serenity in adversity, his gifts as an orator, his deep religious feeling and his obvious determination to fill the role, not of temporal ruler – the cares of which he was glad to leave to the capable Cardinal Antonelli (1806–76),[2] Secretary of State from 1849 to 1876 – but of priest and churchman, responsible before God for the defence of threatened Christian values.

Pastoral concern, not personal ambition or a leaning towards theocracy,

---

2. Giacomo Antonelli, 1806-76. A biography is still awaited, but see *Dizionario biografico degli Italiani*, III, 484-93. Shrewd, capable, but limited in outlook, as a diplomat he was more adept at finding ways round difficulties and covering them up than at thinking out new solutions. A man more of the world than of the Church, he was always careful to refrain from intervention in strictly religious questions.

lay at the root of his systematic encouragement of the movement towards Roman centralisation, just as it was pastoral concern that dictated his frequent and increasingly violent anathemas of liberalist principles. The steady progress of the ultramontane movement, to which the Vatican council gave its solemn seal of approval, is one of the most marked features of the pontificate. To people who appreciated the advantage of pluralistic local churches and dreaded the thought of an episcopate under the thumb of the Roman curia, the success of the movement became a source of regret and recrimination, well before the days of Vatican II. But if Pius IX gave the movement every encouragement, it was because to him it appeared an essential condition for the restoration of Catholic life in countries where the apostolic zeal of clergy and faithful was in danger of stifling under the weight of government interference, and as the best means of rallying the still vital forces of Catholicism to combat the mounting tide of anti-Christian liberalism.

Influenced by the type of traditional political philosophy current in Catholic circles in the middle of the nineteenth century, Pius IX was incapable of judging fairly between the principles of 1789 that were of positive value, and indeed in the long run prepared the way for a greater spiritualisation of the Church's apostolate, and those which represented a transposition into political terms of a rationalist ideology inherited from the Enlightenment. Confounding democracy with the 'Revolution' and the latter with the overthrow of all traditional values, and failing on the opposite tack to understand the historical impossibility of claiming from the State both protection for the Church and the full liberty for the Church he so greatly valued, Pius IX was unable to adapt himself adequately to the profound social and political changes which characterised the nineteenth century. And yet, at the back of this confusion and incomprehension there was a cloudy perception, clumsily expressed, of the need to bring before a society intoxicated with a scientific conception of progress the prior claims of what theologians called the 'supernatural order', the biblical vision of man and of the history of his salvation, a vision which stood in stark contrast to contemporary interpretations of history as a progressive emancipation of mankind from religious values. Such faith in man's potentialities left no room for a redeemer. To understand the grimness with which Pius IX fought liberalism (which he stigmatised as the delusion of our century), it is important to see this long-drawn-out battle as part and parcel of his untiring effort to restore the fundamental data of revelation to their central place in Christian thinking, an effort of which the Vatican Council was intended in his own mind to be the fulfilment.

Just as important – and still more important in terms of positive result – was the parallel effort by Pius IX to enhance the quality of ordinary

Catholic life. The most notable result of this long pontificate was undoubtedly its quickening effect on the current of popular devotion and clerical spirituality which had started to flow during the first half of the century. The movement derived its impulse from a variety of sources, but Pius IX made a quite distinctive contribution, both by his example and still more through his directives and encouragement; and it was precisely because he believed an intransigent attitude to be necessary to the success of this work of Christian renewal that he forced himself, despite his personal inclination towards conciliation, to insist with an unfortunate bluntness on a certain number of principles which made up the substance of his doctrinal teaching.

The thirty-two years of his pontificate were also notable as a time of external development and consolidation for the Church. Under the impetus supplied by the Vatican from the centre, missionary expansion, running parallel with Europe's colonial expansion, continued in all five continents while, at the same time, Catholic immigration stimulated the growth of new Churches in Canada, Australia, the United States and Latin America: 206 new dioceses and vicariates apostolic were created in the course of this pontificate. In the Old World, Churches doomed since the Reformation to a precarious existence were rehabilitated: in England and Holland through the restoration of the episcopal hierarchy and in Germany through increased contact with the Holy See, the benefits of which, in terms of the increased vitality of the German Church, were shortly to be demonstrated during the *Kulturkampf*.

If the local Churches now turned with increasing readiness to Rome, this was not solely in consequence of a systematic policy of centralisation in which the nunciatures and the Society of Jesus played a key role. The movement was in part spontaneous and it was further assisted by the immense prestige, exceeding that of any of his predecessors, which Pius IX enjoyed at 'grass roots' level: for his very misfortunes, from the Roman revolution of 1848 to the reiterated aggressions by the 'Piedmontese', won him a sympathy in the Catholic world in addition to the fascination exerted on the lower clergy and their flocks by his personal charm and virtues, which distance made to shine all the more brightly.

But among the governing classes the triumph of Ultramontanism, coupled with the pope's thundering denunciations of liberalism, gave rise to increasing disaffection, and the last years of the pope who at the time of his election was hailed as 'sent by God to accomplish the great task of the century, the alliance of religion with liberty' [3] were darkened by conflicts with most of the governments of Europe and America, driven to exasperation by

---

3. Ozanam to Guéranger, 29 January 1847 (quoted by Delatte in his *Dom Guéranger*, I, 410). For this early enthusiasm see R. Aubert, *Le Pontificat de Pie IX*, 20-1.

Rome's unyielding attitude towards the whole modern movement of ideas. Thus while in fact the Catholic Church had gained in inner strength and in numbers, the superficial view at the death of Pius IX (7 February 1878) seemed to show a situation even worse than at the death of Gregory XVI: for it was no longer merely in relation to the population of the Roman State and enlightened circles in Italy but in the eyes of a large body of opinion, in the old world as in the new, that the papacy appeared isolated and exposed to the growing hostility of all who were determined not to turn their backs on modern civilisation.

The conclave of February 1878 which opened in this threatening climate marks in many ways the start of a new epoch. The first point to notice is the added strength of the foreign cardinals, who on this occasion made up forty per cent of the Sacred College and nearly all of whom, thanks to the development of railways, were able to be present. Then there was the change, dating from the events of 1870, in the international position of the Holy See, which meant that the electors had in some ways greater freedom, in others less. The fact that the pope was no longer a head of a territorial State made it unnecessary to consider the internal political factors which had weighed so heavily at the previous conclave, nor was there much reason for the great powers to pursue their traditional rivalry. This was certainly all to the good. On the other hand, for the operation to take its normal course, it was now necessary to rely on the good will of the Italian authorities, about which there was room for doubt; but after some initial anxiety on this score it became clear that the government was determined to stick to the policy of non-intervention in keeping with the very clear wish expressed by France and Austria.

As far as the choice of candidate was concerned, one party among the curial cardinals, who either still hoped for a miracle or gambled on taking a deliberately pessimistic stand, believed that the immediate need was to keep up, as Pius IX had done, an unflagging condemnation of liberalism as the source of all evil, and for the rest to lie low and await the coming of better days. Their ideal pope was therefore a man of prayer and doctrine and as unlike a politician as a pope could possibly be. At the opposite extreme to these intransigents, whose counsels Manning described as 'ecclesiastical quietism', stood a handful of cardinals who thought the time might have come to turn over a new leaf and to start on the road to *conciliazione* with the new Italy, as moderate liberals had been urging for the past twenty years. But the majority of those who judged that the policy of Pius IX and Antonelli had failed would not go so far. They remained uncompromising on the issue of re-establishing the pope's temporal sovereignty, but thought the best way of enlisting the support of the great powers to this end was to restore to the Church the prestige she had lost in the eyes of the modern world, that is by adopting a conciliatory attitude over current politico-religious conflicts and by showing as much openness as possible towards all that was acceptable in the culture of the nineteenth century. This was the view, in particular, of most of the foreign cardinals. As representative of this new policy some suggested Cardinal Franchi, but at Rome he was considered too *politicante*. In any case there was someone else recently coming to the fore, Gioacchino Pecci, archbishop of Perugia. It was pointed out that, in addition to wide intellectual interests and the diplomatic experience acquired in his younger days as nuncio in Brussels (1844–6), Pecci had behind him the advantage of a long pastoral career, during which he had proved himself one of the best of the Italian bishops. This impressed those who thought the papacy ought to concentrate increasingly on its specifically religious tasks. Pecci's candidature had the ardent support of Cardinal Bertolini, who with Manning's help succeeded in winning most of the foreign cardinals to his cause. To many electors he was virtually unknown, but he made a favourable impression by the unruffled efficiency with which he discharged his duties as camerlingo, and it was also in his favour that with the exception of the last few months he had been out of Rome, and so was less identified than most with the decisions of the preceding pontificate. When the conclave opened, the die was already as good as cast and Cardinal Pecci was elected the following day (20 February 1878). He announced that he would take the name Leo in memory of Leo XII, a pope whom he had always admired for his interest in learning, his conciliatory approach to governments and his concern for closer relations with separated Christians.

The new pope was sixty-eight and in delicate health, which seemed to augur a fairly brief pontificate. In fact he was to govern the Church, and to govern it in highly individual fashion, for the next twenty-five years. He was a natural leader, possessing the clearness of vision, self-mastery and sense of the possible which make for positive achievement. If there was also an element of emotional coldness, this is a quality that is often needed to enable a leader to forge ahead without being too disturbed at the effect on individuals of decisions judged necessary for the common good.

The contrast between the attitudes of the new pope and those of his predecessor has often been exaggerated. That there was a new spirit at work was shown early on by the nomination of Newman as cardinal, and there had already been a foretaste of it in Pecci's pastoral letters of 1877 and 1878, with their favourable reference to themes dear to Dupanloup and Montalembert.[4] But in a number of spheres there was an obvious continuity with the preoccupations of Pius IX. Leo XIII was personally very devout, and for all his taste for diplomatic ploys he was to prove no less zealous

4. For a commentary see M. Spahn, *Leo XIII* (Munich 1915), 185-98.

than Pius IX in encouraging devotions to the Sacred Heart and to the Blessed Virgin. He was to renew the condemnations of rationalism and Freemasonry and to work for the rehabilitation of Scholastic philosophy and the ousting of Kant and Hegel as influences on Catholic intellectuals. In the sphere of Church-State relations Leo XIII kept up the vigorous opposition to secularising liberalism, and in the encyclicals in which he expounded the traditional doctrine of the Christian State he was not afraid to include several references to the *Syllabus,* to the great disappointment of those who had hoped, a little naively, for a 'liberal pope'. Another surprise in store for many was the still greater stress he placed on the Church's centralisation on Rome. Similarly with the Roman question: although he was willing during the early years of his pontificate to negotiate over the ways and means of restoring the temporal sovereignty, he stood no less firm than Pius IX on the principle. Here he was in some ways even more rigid than his predecessor, since he was much less moved by the grandeur of the Italian idea and the mystique of the Risorgimento. So from this point of view he was even more than Pius IX a man of the past and a pope of the old regime. If they wore their common intransigence with a difference, the underlying reason for it was the same: the conviction that the pope's complete political independence of Italy was essential to the religious independence of the Holy See and that this political issue had to be settled if the pope was to carry out his proper religious function. The primordial importance that Leo XIII, unlike his successor Pius X, attached to achieving an immediate legal settlement of the question meant that in his time, as under Pius IX, papal policy towards the great powers was largely determined by efforts to make the question an international issue, in the hope that the other powers would exert pressure on Italy. In the meantime Italian Catholics with liberal leanings found that the policy of *non expedit* was still in operation and was even reinforced.

Yet there is no denying that the pontificate of Leo XIII marked a turning-point, and that this was the result of the new direction he gave to papal policy. He carried out his policy with the help of his secretaries of State: Franchi[5] for the first six months, Nina[6] from 1878 to 1880, Jacobini[7] from 1880 to 1887 and above all Rampolla,[8] who held office for the

5. Alessandro Franchi, 1819-78; he combined intransigence over principles with great moderation in their application. Appointed 5 March, died suddenly 31 July.

6. Lorenzo Nina, 1812-85; a close friend of Franchi's, and like him conciliatory in his attitude to modern society. Leo XIII dismissed him after two years in office, following the rupture of diplomatic relations between Belgium and the Vatican.

7. Ludovico Jacobini, 1832-87; as nuncio at Vienna one of the main architects of the *détente* with Bismarck; beneath a somewhat insignificant exterior an executive of considerable skill and subtlety.

8. Mariano Rampolla, 1843-1913; formerly nuncio at Madrid; conscientious, erudite,

remaining sixteen years of the pontificate. But Leo XIII did not regard them in the same light as secretaries in the past, who were presumed to have a special competence and were left to run their department more or less independently; he expected them instead to be the agents of an overall policy, which he himself devised. This policy had as its general characteristics a more positive attitude towards liberal institutions, a more conciliatory approach to governments, a cordiality of reference to the salutary aspects of civilisation and true progress, and a more up-to-date conception of the ways in which the Church should seek to influence society.

While Leo XIII was prodigal in his advice to Catholics on the political attitudes he wanted them to adopt – paying scant regard to the legitimate autonomy the Church ought to concede to the citizen in this sphere – he did not follow Pius IX in encouraging the more intransigent to stress their separation from co-religionists who were willing to come to terms with institutions which did not conform to the right principles. On the contrary, he insisted that at the practical level there must be an end to the sterile theoretical debates over the ideal regime and an agreement among Catholics to make the best use of existing liberal institutions, in order to press home certain essential Catholic claims: the right of everyone to live according to his faith, the right of the young to a Christian education, respect for the sanctity and indissolubility of marriage, freedom to set up religious associations, a good understanding between Church and State and, never to be forgotten, the independence of the Holy See. Instead of disputing the freedom of the press, Catholics should exploit it for the benefit of the Church; and if the founders of democratic institutions had often proceeded from false principles, those institutions were not bad in themselves and Catholics should seek, by forming a common front with 'men of good will', to use them for salutary ends. Such was the theme which, with variations and differences as to detail, was to recur so frequently in the encyclicals Leo XIII addressed as occasion demanded to the episcopates of the various countries.

<hr>

energetic, 'warm-hearted and cool-headed' (Bülow). Rampolla was very conscious of the growing part played by the masses in the life of modern States, but much more intransigent than his predecessors in his attitude towards the new Italy. His enemies, of whom there were many, most of all in the curia, the Germanic countries and French monarchist circles, regarded him as a bad influence on the pope, but his role in fact seems merely to have been that of a deputy, devotedly applying himself, with the help of particularly well-chosen colleagues, to the implementation of his master's ideas. In this connection however we should note a comment made by C. Benoist: 'Towards the end of the reign the secretary of state seems to have been so much in tune with his master's thinking that he was able casually to suggest some project to Leo XIII and then allow it to lie dormant until such time as it revived in the Holy Father's mind of its own accord, to be relayed to Rampolla one morning as the pope's spontaneous invention' (*Souvenirs*, Paris 1932, I, 161).

Leo XIII's relations with governments show him transposing to the international scene the circumspect attitude he had displayed towards the Italian authorities when he was archbishop of Perugia: he avoided the heated protestations indulged in by his predecessor and made plain his preference for the methods of diplomacy. Since his first aim was to allay suspicions of the Church, he seized every occasion of revolutionary unrest (anarchist activity in the southern countries, socialism in Germany, Irish agitation in Great Britain, Polish agitation in Russia) to stress to governments the value of the Church as a moral support. It may be that this policy, which entailed closer alignment with the ruling bourgeoisie, helped to harden in their conviction those who accused the Church of being the opium of the people, but in the short term it achieved some remarkable results, most notably the calling off of the German *Kulturkampf*. Within the space of a few years, existing disputes with Switzerland and most of the Latin American republics had been settled, the tension in Russia eased, relations with Spain and Great Britain had started to improve and the relationship with the United States had become extremely cordial. But as J. E. Ward[9] has shown, the diplomatic skill of Leo XIII should not be overrated, and there were some important issues over which he met with defeat. In France his policy of *ralliement* was doomed to failure, while in Italy, despite his efforts, the Roman question remained in a state of deadlock, and after 1887 relations between the Vatican and the Quirinal were again to deteriorate.

But Leo XIII's true greatness was precisely that, notwithstanding his taste for politics – and may be it was even too pronounced – he was not an exclusively political pope; that, while he was a diplomat, he was also an intellectual who was sympathetic to the advance of learning and aware of how important it was for the Church to show an open attitude on this side, and that he was equally a pastor, caring for the internal life of the Church and for the spread of the Church's message throughout the world.

Whereas the stock reaction of Pius IX had been simply to proscribe lines of enquiry which struck him as inadmissible, with Leo XIII care was at last taken to give Catholics positive rulings. This change of atmosphere, much remarked on by his contemporaries, was to make possible, as Marrou has noted, the return of Catholics in strength to the field of scholarship and of historical scholarship in particular, in which they had long allowed themselves to be outdistanced.

It was this same concern for a resumption of the Church's dialogue with the world that led Leo XIII to tone down his predecessor's anathemas against the modern freedoms. If this was a field in which Leo XIII tended to remain a prisoner of his historical context, the perspectives he opened up

9. J. E. Ward, 'Leo XIII: the diplomat pope', *Review of Politics*, XXVIII (1966), 47-61.

contained nevertheless much that was relatively novel in the Catholic world of that date, in particular his views regarding the legitimate independence of the civil power, within its own order, in relation to the spiritual. This line of thought provided at once a growing-point for new ideas and where necessary a boundary to keep them in check. It is under this same double aspect that we must see Leo XIII's teaching on social justice. For all its relative timidity, the encyclical *Rerum novarum* was to prove that the papacy had at least come to grips with the working class question and was anxious to play an active part in its solution.

Among the motives, apart from sincere and indisputable conviction, which impelled Leo XIII to commit himself so definitely to this new path, must be mentioned his distress at the advance of socialism and hope of cutting away the ground beneath its feet, and equally his desire, now that the masses were well on the way to the universal franchise, to find support for the Church in that quarter to counterbalance the anti-clericalist policies often pursued by governments elected on a middle-class vote. And here we touch on another characteristic feature of the pontificate, the pope's constant and generous encouragement of all forms of Catholic organisation in which the laity played an activist role. It is not impossible that the idea first came to him, as Spahn suggests, when he was nuncio in Belgium and saw what was achieved by the Belgian and Rhineland associations of this type. However that may be, it is remarkable to observe this natural aristocrat showing a tendency to rely on the masses, increasingly as his reign advanced, for their support in exerting pressure on governments on behalf of the Church, and to find him, when there seemed real chance of success, actually mobilising Catholics to play their part in the parliamentary arena as the advance guard of the Church militant. Having had the realism to accept that in most countries the age of the Catholic princes was past, Leo XIII set out to rechristianise governments at their roots, hoping to find there new support for the Church. From this many-sided concern to see Catholics sharing the aspirations of their century, so that the Christian spirit might penetrate modern civilisation in all its forms, emerged in outline the great twentieth-century conception of Catholic Action: the idea of a capillary action on the part of the faithful, permeating the lives around them. His grasp of the realities of such a situation likewise accounts for the interest Leo XIII took in the Catholic minorities which were developing in regions outside the Catholic nations. Where his predecessors down to the middle of the nineteenth century seem to have cut their losses and concentrated solely on what were known in contemporary parlance as 'the Catholic crowns', Leo XIII was clearly aware of the important role that might be played in future by the flourishing Churches in countries not officially Catholic, in particular the United States.

In this last field Leo XIII admittedly did no more than underline a policy which had been broadly initiated under Pius IX, the restoration of an episcopal hierarchy to England (1851) and the Netherlands (1853) being among the first-fruits. In the field of Christian reunion, by contrast, he was a true innovator. To be sure, interest in Christian unity had also been manifest on several occasions during the previous pontificate. The changes in the Slav world and the Turkish empire brought about by the developments in the 'Eastern Question' had aroused hopes of progress on the Orthodox front, and the Oxford Movement and the crisis within German Lutheranism provoked by the rise of liberal Protestantism had aroused similar hopes regarding the Reformed Churches. Rome had certainly not been indifferent to the prospect of the return of populous communities in the Balkans and the Near East to unity with the Catholic Church, as is shown for example by the decision in 1862 to divide the Congregation de Propaganda Fide into two sections, one of which was to devote itself to the Churches of Eastern rite. But it was a return envisaged exclusively in terms of assimilation, which made all effort at *rapprochement* vain; indeed the trend was all the other way, for what with Cardinal Barnabò's thoroughgoing policy of centralisation and the Latinisation imposed at local level by most of the missionaries and apostolic delegates, by about 1870 many of the communities already united with Rome were in a state of crisis.[10] As for the attempts to make contact with the Anglicans, the attitude of the Holy See had been one of great reserve, and in the sixties, under the influence among others of Manning, even showed signs of hardening, as for example when English Catholics were forbidden to join the Association for the Promotion of the Union of Christendom.[11] All things considered, it is not surprising that the clumsy approaches made at the time of the First Vatican Council should appear to the modern historian as one of the most painful examples of missed opportunity in the whole tormented history of relations between separated Christians.[12]

If Leo XIII was still far from sharing our present ecumenical outlook, he at least saw the question in a new light. The reunion of the separated Churches with Rome was undoubtedly among his major preoccupations — to say with Fr Esposito that it was fundamental seems to me excessive — and this for a variety of reasons, from which the desire to raise the standing of the Holy See in the world was not entirely absent. He expressed his concern by measures more concrete than the uttering of pious wishes and the issue of

10. See chapter 17, 453-7.
11. See chapter 11, 215-16.
12. Cf. F. de Wyels, 'Le Concile du Vatican et l'Union', *Irénikon*, VI (1929), 368-79, 488-516 and 655-65, and J. Hajjar, 'L'épiscopat catholique oriental et le premier concile du Vatican', *Revue d'histoire ecclésiastique*, LXV (1970), 423-55 and 737-88.

general invitations to return. The opportunity provided by the Eucharistic Congress at Jerusalem in 1893 was used by Leo XIII to demonstrate that the Holy See was well disposed towards the Christian East and concerned to respect its liturgical traditions, and this intention of revoking the policy of Latinising the Uniate patriarchates was solemnly reaffirmed in the encyclical *Orientalium dignitas* and on several later occasions. [13] The systematically pro-Slav policy pursued by Rampolla in the Balkans is part of the same pattern; and the encouragement which towards the end of his life the pope gave to the negotiations set in train by the Abbé Portal and Lord Halifax, in the hope of effecting closer understanding between Rome and Canterbury, [14] is yet another indication of a state of mind which J. Hajjar has characterised as 'revivalist's optimism' — an optimism not without a dash of utopianism. It was with this unionist context in mind that the pope composed his encyclical *Satis cognitum* (30 June 1896), the most important statement in the field of dogmatic theology to appear during his pontificate. In the course of it he defines the image of the Church as willed by her founder as 'the body of Christ, living in his supernatural life', and while insisting all the time on the note of unity, he stresses the difference between unity and unicity and goes on to remark that the teaching office in the Church is exercised by the pope and the bishops in collegiality, the latter being in no sense mere vicars of the former — statements which the Anglican world greeted with favour.

During the last years of the pontificate the conservatives, now led by Cardinal Mazzella, succeeded in recovering a measure of influence over the aging pope, and this resulted in the adoption of a harder line, as illustrated by the condemnation of Americanism and the more reserved attitude towards Christian democracy. Like many another pope, Leo XIII lived too long. It should be said, too, that although by contrast with his predecessor Leo XIII appears so modern, his roots were in the old regime and he was never able to divest himself of a somewhat imperialistic conception of the Church's role, which at the dawn of the twentieth century could lead only to disappointment. This was especially so since by nature Leo XIII seems to have been one of those who have the gift for conceiving great designs but do not elaborate them in sufficient detail and pay too little attention to the means of carrying them out.

But for all his defects and limitations, there is no denying his superior qualities or that his policies, if not always so inspired as has sometimes been

13. See chapter 17, 462-70. For the Jerusalem congress see the doctoral thesis presented in 1971 to the Catholic University of Louvain by C. Soetens, *Le congrès eucharistique international de Jérusalem (1893) dans le cadre de la politique orientale du pape Léon XIII*, Louvain 1977.
14. See chapter 11, 216-19.

made out, were instrumental in winning for the Church and the Holy See a prestige they had not enjoyed since the first flush of Pius IX just before the 1848 revolution, together with the more substantial reward of an enhanced moral authority and hence an effective political power which was greater than the official power the Church had lost. The increase in the number of countries, including non-Christian countries, which had diplomatic representation at the Vatican, and above all the well-nigh unanimous homage paid to the pope on the occasion of the jubilee ceremonies of 1883, 1894, and 1902, provide some measure of the recovery that had taken place in the course of this 'glorious pontificate', which ended on 20 July 1903: and for all its wealth of immediate achievement, in the eyes of the present-day historian the pontificate of Leo XIII must appear richer still through the ripening possibilities which gradually matured in succeeding decades.

On the eve of the conclave for the election of Leo XIII's successor the Sacred College found itself far more divided than had been the case twenty-five years earlier. In the eyes of a fair number of cardinals the most fitting replacement for the pontiff who had so magnificently enhanced the prestige of the papacy was his Secretary of State, Cardinal Rampolla, the late pope's intimate confidant and for the past sixteen years collaborator with him in his great designs. The cardinals who thought in this way included the majority of those who wanted a continuation of Leo XIII's conciliatory policy in respect of modern attitudes and they were joined by a group of 'intransigents', who valued Rampolla as the implacable opponent of the official Italian regime. But there were many more who thought the time was right for a change, though they were not in agreement over the direction it should take. Some, and they too were swayed by 'political' considerations, wanted the Holy See to become less inflexible in its attitude to Italy, arguing that it was unrealistic to count on the kingdom's imminent collapse, and they thought it preferable for the Church to rely for support on Catholic Austria and the German Centre rather than on Orthodox Russia, whose growing influence in the Near East gave cause for apprehension, or on anti-clericalist France, the source of so much cruel disillusionment to Leo XIII. Others, more sensitive on the doctrinal score, were disturbed by the liberal infiltrations into exegesis and theology and likewise by the threat to the authority principle implicit in the democratic ideas fostered by the Secretary of State; they therefore counselled a return to the intransigence which had characterised the pontificate of Pius IX. And finally there were those who, along with many priests and faithful, thought the time had come to give pastoral questions priority and who hoped the choice would fall not on some high official of the Roman curia but on a man matured in the episcopal ministry.

Another complication was the renewed intrusion of the diplomatic factor.

This was because in the period which had elapsed since 1878 the great powers had again become aware of the importance to them of the Vatican as a potential source of moral support. But while the French government was naturally all in favour of Rampolla, Austria had against him his reservations on the subject of the Triple Alliance, his pro-Slav policy in the Balkans and his support of Christian democrats. Even so, Vienna was reluctant to invoke the old right of veto against him and the emperor's eventual decision to use it was due to the insistence of Cardinal Puzyna, archbishop of Krakow, who thought the election of Rampolla would be harmful to the Church and who blamed him moreover for sacrificing Polish interests in the pursuit of his pro-Russian policy. [15]

Thirty-eight Italian and twenty-four foreign cardinals [16] were present at the conclave, which opened on 1 August 1903. On the first day three candidates already stood out: Rampolla, who was clearly in the lead; Gotti, the Prefect of Propaganda, a Carmelite and in doctrinal matters a conservative, but reputed to be broad-minded over political questions involving the Church; and lastly Sarto, the patriarch of Venice, little known to the general public and the foreign cardinals but discreetly indicated by Leo XIII on several occasions as his possible successor and strongly supported by Italian cardinals not belonging to the curia. Then on the morning of 2 August came Puzyna's official announcement of the imperial veto, of which he had warned Rampolla and the camerlingo some days previously. The gesture seems in fact to have been unnecessary since the Secretary of State clearly stood no chance of securing the two-thirds majority. After a sterile display of protest, Rampolla's supporters asked him to name the candidate he wished them to vote for in his stead, but this he refused to do, arguing that he could not stand down without appearing to give way to Austria; but he was doubtless also aware that his influence was not strong enough to steer the election in the direction he wanted.

While Rampolla's supporters were engaged in fruitless agitation, Sarto found the number of his adherents steadily rising, first from twenty-one to twenty-four and then on the morning of 3 August to twenty-seven, by which time he had overtaken Rampolla, while Gotti had been as good as eliminated. For a moment it was feared Sarto would refuse to accept a responsibility for which he felt his powers unequal, but he eventually allowed himself to be persuaded and was elected on the morning of 4 August, securing fifty votes against ten which remained faithful to Rampolla. Serving clear notice of the direction he intended his pontificate should take, he an-

---

15. See principally Z. Obertyński, 'Kardinal Puzyna und sein Veto', *Festschrift Franz Loidl*, Vienna 1971, III, 177-95, especially 183-4; note Puzyna's statement (quoted 188): 'It was not that Austria used me but that I used Austria'.
16. Including for the first time in history an American.

nounced that he would bear the name Pius, in honour of the pontiffs of that name 'who in the last century battled with such courage against proliferating sects and errors'.

In the nineteenth and twentieth century it has not been uncommon for popes to have had some previous experience of diocesan responsibility, but in the whole history of the papacy one can think of few who, like Pius X, rose to the papal throne after working their passage through all the ranks of the pastoral ministry. Born in 1835 to a humble family in Venetia, educated at a seminary where it was said of him that he was the most remarkable pupil even the oldest masters could remember, Pius X started his career by serving as a curate in a rural parish and then as parish priest in a market town; he was next entrusted by the bishop of Treviso with important responsibilities in the administration of that diocese, including the spiritual direction of the seminarists. Appointed in 1884 bishop of Mantua, this upright and zealous priest proved that he had the practical gifts of a leader and within a few years he transformed an ailing diocese into a model one. In 1893 Leo XIII, who had not been slow to appreciate his qualities, made him a cardinal, promoting him at the same time to the patriarchal see of Venice. Despite the augmented scope of his responsibilities, Sarto remained at heart a pastor of souls, constantly urging his priests to greater zeal in such matters as preaching, catechising and frequent communion, encouraging laymen to involve themselves as much as possible in charitable activities, always on the strict understanding that control rested with the clergy, demanding from the clergy total obedience to their bishop's instructions in every last particular. But there is another point to notice. Intent as he was on erecting a barrier against the rising tide of socialism, whose assaults on the traditional foundations of society he found deeply disturbing, this assiduous reader of Cardinal Pie, who in his pastoral letters denounced liberal Catholics as 'wolves in sheep's clothing', was prepared to recommend at the level of local politics an alliance between the Venetian Catholics and the moderate liberals.

This past history made it reasonable to predict that the new pope would be more conciliatory than his predecessor towards the new Italy, and his pontificate was in fact to mark the beginnings of a slow improvement in relations between the Vatican and the Quirinal. But if what loomed largest in the eyes of journalists and Italian politicians were the new pope's intentions over the Roman question, in his own mind this was a relatively minor aspect of the situation. His approach to his office was very different from that of his predecessor. The subtle diplomatic and political ploys which had delighted Leo XIII held no appeal for Pius X, unwilling as he was to bend himself to the compromises such manoeuvres almost inevitably entail. He judged furthermore that Leo XIII's policy of seeking improved relations with governments and courts had ended in failure and he was firmly resolved to concentrate on the problems of the apostolate and the Christian life.

The contrast between the new pope and his predecessor was striking from every angle. First, in their physical appearance: Leo XIII was tall and slender, his complexion translucent, his manner to visitors cold and distant, his bearing solemn and majestic. Pius X was of medium height and rather stout, his complexion florid, his voice warm and gentle. He had a welcome for all, winning immediate sympathy by his ready smile with its hint of sadness, and he had no taste for pomp. At a more profound level, Leo XIII was an intellectual with extensive cultural interests and a penchant as a thinker for wide-ranging, speculative syntheses. Pius X followed the dictates of his heart, being filled with sympathy for the weak, but he was also practical-minded and careful of detail in everything he touched, alert to the danger of letting go the substance for the shadow. He had an instinctive distrust of progressive movements, whether in ideas or in society, and considered that his predecessor's policy of openness to the modern world, if perhaps not wrong in principle, had at least been hedged with insufficient safeguards and was likely in the short run to have injurious consequences. He therefore believed there was no alternative to some measure of reaction, and his pontificate wore from the outset an air of retreat and 'Catholic defence'. This is noticeable in three fields in particular. First, in the pope's relations with governments which, save in the special case of Italy, marked a return to the intransigence of the time of Pius IX, the pope's overriding concern being to claim for the Church complete freedom from the civil power without regard to the numerous conflicts which were the consequence; second, in his much more cautious attitude towards the Christian democracy, leading in the case of Murri's Italian Azione popolare and of Marc Sangnier's French Le Sillon to official condemnation, a severity of treatment in marked contrast to the indulgence shown towards the Action française; third, in the repression of modernism, to which we shall return in more detail in a later chapter.

Even in the pope's own lifetime, the energy – some would say the implacability – with which the campaign of reaction was mounted appeared to commentators in a very varying light, as it had done ever since. While some extol the saint-pope as the intrepid defender of orthodoxy and the rights of the Church, others criticise his inability to tackle from a new angle the serious problems confronting the Church and accuse him of attempting, by the application of increasingly authoritarian measures, to freeze the Church into reactionary and clericalist positions totally at variance with the movement of history.

Yet whatever judgment the future may pass on the work of Pius X as defender of the Church, it would be untrue to history to claim that the whole of his pontificate boils down to this one and much debated aspect. For the pope who appeared to his contemporaries so old-fashioned and conservative, as indeed he was from many points of view, was in reality one of the great reforming popes of history. He had taken as his motto *Instaurare omnia in Christo,* and to his way of thinking the restoration of the Christian society implied not only the passionate defence of the rights of Christ and his Church but an at least equally determined effort at the Church's positive reform, together with the launching of initiatives aimed at essentially pastoral ends, with the intention of deepening its interior life and encouraging the better use of its resources. Pius X brought to this task the experience of forty years spent in the various grades of the active ministry far from the curia, to which was added the clear-sightedness and drive he had already shown in the administration of his two dioceses, Mantua and Venice. By refusing to be halted by bureaucratic routine and by exerting his authority, he accomplished in a pontificate which lasted only eleven years a whole series of reforms, some of which had been urged for centuries and many of which were regarded at the time as revolutionary. To several of them we shall return: the decrees relating to frequent communion and to the communion of children, the reform of church music and the liturgy; his directions regarding the laity which, although inspired by a conception of it which seems today to be outdated, nevertheless made him a pioneer of Catholic Action in the modern sense of the term; his measures to improve the teaching of the catechism and the standard of preaching; the reorganisation of the seminaries to provide a better training for the clergy. But if the clergy as a whole, from the topmost rank of the hierarchy to the bottom, were to make their fullest contribution, there had to be some alteration to the law and institutions of the Church, to which no systematic thought had been given since the time of the Council of Trent. The task was enormous, especially when one thinks of the force of inertia confronting anyone who attempts to alter established usage. Pius X was not to be daunted.

Within a day or two of his election he made known his intention of arranging for the compilation of a new code of canon law, in which the legislation of the Church would be condensed and presented in systematic fashion, and in a form adapted to modern conditions. The opposition from certain circles in the Vatican was strong and went even to the length of an appeal to Friedberg, the Protestant author of a critical edition of the *Corpus juris canonici,* to demonstrate the impossibility of any such reform. Nothing came of it. The pope invoked the assistance of Gasparri, eminent canon lawyer and future cardinal, and after a labour of eleven years, to which the pope gave his personal attention and encouragement at every stage, at his death Pius X left the new code so nearly complete that his successor was able to promulgate it in 1917.

Another long overdue reform, the reorganisation of the Roman curia or, in other words, the central administration of the Church, Pius X had the satisfaction of carrying through from start to finish. Having passed through successive draftings and redraftings, three decrees were published in July 1908 which overturned a number of established practices and introduced greater clarity, not to mention greater equity, into the workings of a somewhat archaic administration. The Roman Congregations, which form the various departments of the Church's central government, found their functions re-allocated and redefined according to a more logical pattern. At the same time their procedures were speeded up, to make them better able to cope with the flow of business which, as a result of the centralisation of the Church over the past half-century, was daily increasing.

Great as was his personal share in the direction of affairs, Pius X obviously had to have collaborators. He was anxious to enlist as his colleagues men who shared his vision of a Catholic restoration. He chose for preference religious, whose participation in the work of the Roman Congregations increased at this period, or prelates he knew to be opposed to liberalism in all its forms: all worthy and hardworking but many of them narrow-minded, totally devoted to the Holy See but apt to be obtuse in their zeal, men who had little understanding of the Church's real situation or of minds outside the small world of Italian ecclesiastics. Not all the pope's assistants fitted this description, Mgr Gasparri being one of the notable exceptions. Among the collaborators of Pius X, special reference must be made to his personal secretary, Mgr Bressan, who on the testimony of Count Della Torre was more than once carried away by his somewhat excessive personal zeal, and above all to the three especially intransigent cardinals who in the eyes of many commentators were the evil geniuses of the pontificate: Vives y Tuto, the Capuchin who was so influential in the Holy Office; De Lai, the all-powerful Prefect of the Consistorial Congregation, who ruled the dioceses and seminaries with a dictator's rod of iron; and the Secretary of State, Merry del Val,[17] who was associated far more closely than the foregoing in the religious policies of the pontificate. Merry del Val, the priest of pious and austere habit, the refined and urbane aristocrat who was total in his dedication to the Holy See and blandly impervious in his opposition to all modern movements, possessed, it has been said, the positive

17. Raphael Merry del Val, 1865-1930; all the biographies are hagiographies, the least bad being P. Cenci's (Rome 1933) and J. M. Javierre's (2nd ed. Barcelona 1966); numerous documents and testimonies are given in *Romana beatificationis et canonizationis Servi Dei Raphaelis card. Merry del Val informatio,* Vatican City 1957; see too A. C. Jemolo, *Chiesa e Stato in Italia negli ultimi cento anni* (Turin 1948), 483-562. Son of a Spanish diplomat, while still very young singled out for advancement by Leo XIII. He commended himself to Pius X for a number of reasons: his great spiritual worth, his polyglot linguistic talent, his knowledge of diplomacy (in fact more theoretical than practical), his lack of Italian connections, which the pope thought would make him more independent.

and negative qualities of the Spaniard, though it has also to be said that he sometimes connived at manoeuvres involving delation which did no credit to the secretaryship of State. Thanks to his intimacy with the pope, who prized the efficiency and dedication of this colleague who shared so closely his views on the essential priorities, Merry del Val wielded considerable power, especially after the reform of the curia had added substantially to the fields of intervention open to the secretary's department. He has for that reason attracted much critical attention and some have saddled him, along with De Lai, with the prime responsibility for the increasingly reactionary character of the pope's decisions: this last judgment is certainly too extreme, since it appears from É. Poulat's recent edition of the Sodalitium Pianum dossier [18] that Mgr Benigni complained on the contrary of Merry del Val's excessive timidity in carrying out some of the pope's instructions and accused him of being misled by his diplomatic temperament into watering down decisions already taken, because of the opposition their harshness had aroused. But this having been said, and without succumbing to the hagiographical temptation of trying to exculpate Pius X from responsibility for the less agreeable aspects of his pontificate, it must still be allowed that the role of the pope's entourage was more important than he himself recognised: for one thing because several of his collaborators, carried away by their enthusiasm, implemented certain of his orders or made use of certain procedures in a way the pope did not intend; for another because the pope himself, in all good faith, took decisions on the basis of the one-sided and tendentious information supplied by his advisers. Since personal sanctity is no guarantee of superior judgment in ecclesiastical politics, it is inevitable that when a pope thinks it his duty to take sovereign decisions for the Church as a whole he will in most matters find himself dependent, to some degree at least, on his advisers and executives. But it should be noted that if some of Pius X's collaborators exceeded his intentions in the sense of being too rigid, there were others who sometimes interposed a passive resistance to his orders or at least tempered their harshness. Pius X was made painfully aware of this during the last months of his life, when the anti-integrist reaction started to assert itself even in Vatican circles, but the phenomenon was not new. Many of the reforming measures launched at the start of the pontificate had encountered latent opposition from the conservatives, who were just as hostile to changes adumbrated by the supreme authority as they were to the reformism of the progressives. Poulat had such instances in mind when he spoke of Pius X as being 'strong in will, weak in authority'. If this is perhaps going too far, it all goes to show that the problem of the relationship between Pius X and his collaborators is more complex than most of his admirers and

18. *Intégrisme et catholicisme intégral* (Tournai 1969), esp. 76-7.

detractors, from their opposite points of view, would have us believe.

Another complex and much debated question is that of the Holy See's attitude at the outbreak of the First World War. The story is often told that when an Austrian envoy asked the pope for his blessing on the emperor and his armies, Pius X replied: 'Tell the emperor that I could bless neither the war nor those who willed it; my blessing is on peace', adding: 'Let the emperor think himself fortunate not to receive the malediction of the Vicar of Christ'. Some hagiographers have gone further and claim that the pope contemplated the excommunication of Franz Joseph. The despatches of Bavarian and Austrian diplomats accredited to the Vatican tell a very different story. The Bavarian representative, writing on 26 July, reported: 'The pope approves of Austria taking severe measures against Serbia',[19] and the Austrian representative reported in the following terms a conversation he had with Cardinal Merry del Val the next day: 'He unreservedly approved the note addressed to Serbia and indirectly expressed the hope that the monarchy would refuse to give way. It is regrettable, he added, that Serbia was not humbled long ago.'[20] When this text was made public the cardinal challenged its accuracy but admitted he had said 'that Austria ought to stand firm and that she was entitled to the utmost in reparations'. To be sure, at the time he may have thought, along with many other diplomats, that the conflict could still be localised, but Vienna might personally take his words as a clear sign of encouragement. This attitude on the part of the Holy See is easy enough to explain. For one thing there was the high esteem in which the pope held the aged Franz Joseph, who had again recently, on the occasion of the Eucharistic Congress in Vienna, shown himself the exemplary Catholic prince by following the procession of the Blessed Sacrament on foot and in full dress uniform; more important, the break with France had left Austria-Hungary as the only remaining important Catholic state, and the Vatican in any case regarded every weakening of Austrian influence in the Balkans or in the Danube basin – and from this point of view the Serb provocations constituted a real threat – as a gift to Orthodox Russia, the chief adversary of Catholicism in the Near East.

Be that as it may, one thing is certain. Even if, at the moment when the Austrian ambassador came to inform him of the ultimatum to Serbia, Pius X declared himself ready to intervene as mediator and to urge both sides to show moderation, once hostilities had been declared he remained passive, his only gesture being the issue of a somewhat subdued exhortation to the nations, calling them to prayer. He was doubtless conscious of the enfeebled diplomatic position of the Holy See, which did not allow initiatives such as

19. *Bayerische Dokumente zum Kriegsausbruch*, III (Munich 1925), 206.
20. *Österreich-Ungarns Aussenpolitik. Diplomatische Aktenstücke*, VIII (Vienna 1930), 893-4.

Pius XII would attempt a generation later at the outbreak of the Second World War. Perhaps too it was quite simply that the worn-out old man no longer had the energy to raise a prophet's voice and to act when all hope seemed gone.

The fact is that for a year and more the health of the pope had been giving anxiety, and in the previous month he had entered his eightieth year. The end came almost without warning on the night of 19–20 August, and he died leaving his successor to tackle the new and difficult problems which would face the Church as a result of the war which had just begun.

2

THE CHURCH AND THE EUROPEAN REVOLUTIONS OF 1848

THE beginnings of the pontificate of Pius IX appeared to confirm the reputation of 'liberal' that was fastened on this enlightened conservative by the retrograde circles of Rome. One or two really quite modest gestures were enough to release a wave of enthusiasm throughout Italy, and with the renewed condemnation of basic liberal principles in the encyclical *Qui pluribus* (9 November 1846) passing unnoticed, it was not long before every demonstration, whether against the reactionary regimes or the grip of Metternich's Austria on the peninsula, was ringing to the cry *'Viva Pio Nono'*. The myth of the liberal pope acted as a catalyst on the disparate elements which, on the eve of 1848, made up progressive opinion in Italy. All of them, former enemies of the Church, Catholics converted to modern ideas, and patriotically-minded clergy, found themselves momentarily united in a common hope. Disappointment was to be all the greater when people were shortly confronted with the facts: the pope's actions did not live up to their expectations.

Disillusionment started over the question of internal reforms. Here Pius IX was circumscribed not only by the mounting opposition from most of the curial prelates but also by his own unwillingness, for all his sincere desire for improvements in the antiquated and police-ridden government of the Papal State and for a measure of administrative reform, to go beyond what might be described as 'ecclesiastical paternalism'. He feared that the surrender to laymen of any part of his priest-kingship would limit the independence of the Holy See and so hamper the fulfilment of its religious mission. As R. Quazza has shown,[1] even at the period of his most trusting collaboration with

---

1. R. Quazza, *Pie IX e Massimo d'Azeglio nelle vicende romane del 1847*, 2 vols, Modena 1957.

Massimo d'Azeglio the pope remained at heart the enlightened despot, unprepared at any price to transform the Papal State into a constitutional State on the modern pattern. Under the pressure of circumstances, skilfully manipulated by one or two who excelled in exploiting his love of popularity, he was nevertheless obliged, very much in spite of himself, to go some way in that direction, and with the fall of Louis Philippe in France he eventually had to decide to grant in haste the constitution his subjects had been demanding over the past months;[2] but this once again had all the appearance of a palliative, and hence did more to inflame than to appease public opinion, which now became increasingly impatient.

The pope's hesitant frame of mind, incapable of deciding between the advice coming to him from right and left and dominated by the unattainable ambition of acting in a way displeasing to none, inevitably also had its effect, and with yet more serious consequences, on his attitude towards the Italian movement. Although at the time of his election many had believed otherwise, he had in fact always regarded the neo-Guelfist programme as an empty dream and thought it would not be right for the pope, as spiritual head of all Christians, to fill the role of president in an Italian federation. But it is no less true that in the charged atmosphere of the times he found his generous impulses stirring in sympathy with efforts to free Italians from foreign domination. What has been called the 'miracle of 1848' rested in part on a misunderstanding, but for a few months the 'miracle' was a reality. He had only to utter some remarks in contrast to Gregory XVI's attitude of hostile reserve, for many Italians to become convinced that the new pope supported the nationalist programme in its entirety and was ready, as Gioberti desired, to head the crusade to expel Austria and to make the peninsula at long last a national unity. When on 10 February 1848, in the course of a speech which in his own mind was intended to damp down the war fever, Pius IX invoked God's blessing on Italy, the exultation reached a new peak, and, convinced that the pope was with them, clergy and faithful from the various parts of Italy came out during the next few weeks in considerable if not total support of the national uprisings.[3] But then came the allocution of 29 April,[4] which made it plain that, despite his sympathy with

2. Cf. A. Ara, *Lo statuto fondamentale dello Stato della Chiesa*, Milan 1966.
3. The support of the clergy, the higher clergy included, was massive in the north and considerable in the centre (save at Rome itself). In the kingdom of Naples, although the bishops in general continued to support the Bourbon monarchy, the lower clergy, secular and regular, were divided, but a fair proportion had been won over to the national cause. For a wealth of bibliographical information see *Rassegna storica toscana*, IV (1948), 277, n. 28. Even the Jesuits were not everywhere as reactionary in their attitude as is generally claimed (cf. G. De Rosa, *I Gesuiti in Sicilia e la rivoluzione del '48*, Rome 1963).
4. On the preliminaries of this allocution and its true bearing according to the ideas of Pius IX see G. Martina, in *Rassegna storica del Risorgimento*, LIII (1966), 527-82 and LIV (1967), 40-7.

the Italian cause, the pope would never agree to taking an active role in the war of independence against Austria, which in his eyes would conflict with his religious mission as father of all the faithful.

Serious economic difficulties, which bore heavily on the population, and the pope's incompetence, were enough between them to bring the crisis to a head. After the assassination of Pelegrino Rossi, the pope's chief minister, Pius IX yielded to the advice of conservatives who were fearful that he would commit himself to some ill-considered concessions, and on 24 November fled Rome in disguise to take refuge at Gaeta, in Neapolitan territory.

In January a republic was proclaimed at Rome, governed by a triumvirate with Mazzini at its head. It lasted only a few months; the pope had the diplomatic backing of the European powers and was restored to his throne following the intervention of a French expeditionary force led by General Oudinot. Although there was general agreement that there could be no return to the situation as it had been under Gregory XVI, the timid reforms proposed in the *motu proprio* of 12 September 1849 scarcely ventured beyond the recommendations formulated by the powers in their memorandum of 1831. But if the reforms were 'eighteen years behind the times' (Ghisalberti), they were all too progressive for a number of the cardinals who, with backing from the court in Naples, saw to it that the implementation of the reforms was preceded by a repressive operation, conducted in an atmosphere of such savage resentment that it fully justified Mgr Corboli-Bussi's description of the papal restoration as 'blundering and reactionary'.

But more important in the history of the Church than the retrograde character of the political restoration was the change in outlook noticeable from this time in Pius IX who, while in Gaeta – which became the 'Coblenz' of the Italian reaction – was preoccupied, unlike his entourage, with the religious reaction that was to dominate and determine the political reaction in its ideological aspects. We know how men can be marked by the loss of their cherished illusions and, to make matters worse, in this case the reactionaries surrounding Pius IX neglected no opportunity of reviving in his impressionable mind the bloody memories of the Roman revolution, dwelling in particular on the fate of Pellegrino Rossi, whose support for a general liberalisation of political institutions did not save him from assassination by the radicals. But going beyond the psychological, the episode also helped to confirm Pius IX in his theoretical convictions and in his long-standing distrust of the principles whose dangerous consequences were now clear for all to see. He was more than ever persuaded of a close connection between the principles of 1789 and the destruction of traditional values in the social, moral and religious order. As A. M. Ghisalberti has pointed out in connection with the pope's allocution of 20 April 1849, this realisation contained within it the germ of the full-blown *Syllabus*. The change of direction first became apparent on 30 May 1849 when the works in which Gioberti, Rosmini and Ventura had expounded their programme of reform were at the pope's request placed on the Index. With the foundation, on the initiative of a group of Jesuits headed by Fr Curci and with the pope's active encouragement, of the *Civiltà cattolica,* the new policy was provided with an organ for the dissemination of its doctrines and with a powerful agent of propaganda which reached well beyond the borders of Italy.

Among the first countries to be affected by the great wave of revolution which broke over Europe in 1848 was in fact France (end of February). For all the want of cordiality between the Church and Louis Philippe's government, Catholics were dismayed at the news of the proclamation of the republic, since the word conjured up unhappy memories of the outrages against the social and religious order which had characterised the first republic half a century before. But though there were some anti-religious demonstrations in the provinces, in general the *'quarante-huitards'* treated the Church with respect — in part because of a sentimental regard for Christianity left over from the Romantic movement, in part because of the favourably liberal impression created in its early days by the pontificate of Pius IX — and priests were even invited to bless the trees of liberty. On the Catholic side, there was comfort to be gleaned from Falloux's assurance that in the American republics religion was flourishing, as also from the reflection that the Revolution, by introducing universal suffrage into a country where the peasants were still in large part susceptible to clerical persuasion, guaranteed the Church a more effective political influence than she had had under the property franchise. The bishops and other Catholic leaders were therefore soon at one in preaching *ralliement* to the Republic, and the results of the elections to the Constituent Assembly were to provide speedy confirmation of their hopes.

But the socialist element in the 1848 revolution presented French Catholics with a problem of conscience more complex than simple acceptance of the republic: *ralliement* to the ideas of social reform was a far less obvious matter than *ralliement* to the new political regime. The true dimensions of the social problem as it affected the working class were still not understood by the great majority of Catholics, most of whom belonged to rural communities or to the provincial petty bourgeoisie. Under the July Monarchy only a tiny minority of clerics and laymen had come to realise that charity and moral exhortations were not enough and that the real need was for structural reforms. A few of this number, members of the circle round Fr Lacordaire and d'Ozanam, founded a newspaper which advocated a relatively advanced programme of reforms. This was *L'Ère Nouvelle,* which had the support of the archbishop of Paris. But the relatively favourable reception it met with at the outset, in particular from a younger section of the clergy, did not last. The disquiet of the great mass of Catholics, very sensitive on the issue of the maintenance of order and the intangibility of the 'sacred dogma of property', turned to panic after the June riots. From that moment, and for the next twenty years, the French Church, with a few rare exceptions, was back in the conservative camp, driven there by the conviction that religion and morality were threatened along with the traditional social order, a conviction confirmed by the happenings at Rome and, after the 'red peril', prepared for any compromise. This reaction was encouraged furthermore by the Orleanist bourgeoisie, which from now on was only too pleased to see the Church join with it in the defence of property. In combining with Thiers and Molé to form the 'great party of order', Montalembert and his friends were doubtless keeping the religious interest in view and they were in fact successful in securing substantial advantages for the Church, notably the *'loi Falloux'* (15 March 1850), in effect a belated victory for liberal Catholicism, which at last gave the Church freedom to engage in secondary education and at the same time ensured that the clergy had an appreciable influence in State schools. But if the Catholic leaders calculated correctly in the political arena, they were less sensitive to the long-term dangers of this pact between religion and the interests of capitalism. To make matters worse, by lending their solid support to the measures, each more anti-democratic than the last, by which the National Assembly sought during 1849 and 1850 to reduce the influence of leftist elements, French Catholics made themselves appear not merely anti-socialist but also anti-republican. This was an impression their attitude towards Louis-Bonaparte would only serve to confirm. That they voted for him rather than Cavaignac in the presidential election of December 1848 is doubtless to be explained by his promise of freedom in secondary education and of French support in the restoration of the pope's temporal power. But the closer he moved towards dictatorship, the more he seemed to grow in favour with the clergy, whose traditionalist wing had waxed still more sympathetic towards authoritarian forms of power. The eagerness with which the French Church, with very few exceptions, rallied to the *coup d'état* of 2 December 1851 was predictable right from the start.

This attitude seemed at first to pay. It was not that Napoleon III and his advisers were especially anxious to encourage the Church, but they appreciated the advantages of religion as a social and moral influence to counteract the effects of revolutionary propaganda and they hoped in addition that the clergy's co-operation with the regime would help to win over the legitimists, still a force to be reckoned with in some country areas. The government increased the State's financial contribution to the churches, more or less ignored the Organic Articles, suppressed the anti-religious tendencies of teaching in the State schools and went out of its way to associate the Church in the public mind with the official image of the State. The reaction against revolutionary excess was also to the benefit of the Church in that it encouraged the return to the fold of a growing section of the bourgeoisie, to whom the Church represented the sole effective bulwark of the existing social order. This steady recovery of influence over the governing class, which had been in process since the beginning of the century, enabled the clergy to count on the support of many highly placed officials, as well as on that of many *maires,* whose power was apt to be considerable under an authoritarian regime and whose favour therefore emphasised still further the good standing of the clergy in the eyes of authority.

Religion's recovery of prestige and the improvement in the material condition of the rural clergy, which except in the more 'Christian' regions had remained down to the middle of the nineteenth century at a fairly precarious level, soon had an impact on recruitment to the priesthood, which benefited in addition from the effects of the *loi Falloux.* For France as a whole the number of ordinations rose by more than a third, which makes the Second Empire stand out in this respect as a peak between a period of moderate growth under the July Monarchy and a period of progressive decline under the Third Republic.

At the same time the government turned a blind eye to the astonishingly rapid development of congregations of religious, who under the Second Empire enjoyed a period of great prosperity. This was particularly marked in the case of orders for women, membership of which rose from 34,208 in 1851 to 89,243 in 1861, while the numbers of men religious, which in 1851 stood at just on 3000, had risen by 1861 to 17,656.

This rapid growth in numbers supplied the Church with the teaching force it needed for the twofold task of penetrating the State schools and developing the church schools. The *loi Falloux* had made it possible for the *curés* to exercise control over the *instituteurs* in the State schools — a control many of the latter greatly resented — but, not content with this, the Church worked on local authorities, which were often controlled by known sympathisers, to secure the transfer of as many publicly provided schools as possible to the religious orders. At the same time advantage was taken of the very favourable legal provisions regarding gifts and bequests to multiply the number of Catholic schools and colleges.

The field of welfare work was another in which the government, while refusing to be ousted by the Church from its role as dispenser of public assistance, made wide calls on Catholics for their collaboration. The result was a rapid growth alongside the State refuges and hospitals of a variety of Catholic institutions nearly all of which, whether run by religious orders or by laymen, were associated with the Society of St Vincent de Paul or the Société d'économie charitable, in which Vicomte Armand de Melun was still, as under the July Monarchy, the moving spirit.

But this outwardly very favourable state of affairs should not deceive us. It was not only that, as the threat of revolution receded, the government came to resent the growing importance of the clergy as figures in public life. More seriously, the external brilliance of the institutional apparatus was but a partial reflection of the true state of religion, whether among the masses on the one hand or the intellectual élite on the other. Only the most perspicacious had started to suspect that there were two sides to the prosperity of the Church during the first decade of the Second Empire, but the time was at hand when the symptoms of the approaching religious crisis would start to spread.

France was not the only country where Catholics were able to profit from the events of 1848. In very different circumstances, and it may be said with more lasting results, the same was true in the German countries where the Catholics were in a minority, in particular Prussia and Holland.

Following the risings in Berlin and the Rhineland in March 1848, a National Assembly met at Frankfurt to work out a new constitution for the German Confederation. It soon became apparent to the delegates that the political changes made it necessary to review the constitutional position of the churches. The Bavarian Catholics still favoured the regime of the concordat, claiming that the royal protection it afforded had largely contributed to the religious renaissance in Bavaria since 1815, but the majority of Catholic delegates opted for independence, reckoning that the Church's freedom was ample compensation for the loss of government favours, and it was on this principle that the Assembly agreed. The Assembly's decisions, which it was intended should apply to all the German states, were soon to be nullified by the political events of early 1849; but in Prussia, the largest of the German States, the principles were actually put into practice. Under the constitution granted by the king of Prussia on 5 December 1848 Catholics were in effect guaranteed, along with freedom of worship, independence of the State, which meant free communication with their ecclesiastical leaders, non-interference in appointments to benefices, abolition of the *placet,* and rights of association, that is, liberty for the religious orders. The archbishop of Cologne was right to regard the granting of this constitution as 'an event of incalculable consequence', for the freedom it conferred was to encourage a rapid blossoming of the religious life, especially since the accompanying schools settlement, by strengthening the denominational character of State education, gave the clergy sufficient influence in State schools to make the erection of a system of private Catholic education seem pointless. So the Church had all the advantages of freedom without suffering the disadvantages of separation, and co-operation with the State was made all the easier by the government's choice of dedicated Catholics to staff the Catholic Affairs department (*Katholische Abteilung*) of the Ministry of Worship. On an objective view, and notwithstanding the nostalgia of survivors from the era of Catholic romanticism, there is no denying that, from the middle of the century, Catholicism appeared a more vital force in Protestant Prussia than it did in officially Catholic Bavaria.

The position in Bavaria was that the apathy of the faithful, to which their priests contributed by their fears of despotism on the part of the bishops liberated from government control, left the way clear in many fields for the administration to impose its arbitrary jurisdiction, just as in the eighteenth century. In Prussia, by contrast, where Catholics made up one-third of the population and in the Rhineland and Silesia formed the majority,[5] freedom was put to intelligent use. One principal result was the great progress made by the religious orders and congregations. Particularly significant is the case of the Jesuits. While Bavaria continued to exclude them, they established themselves as early as August 1848 in Cologne. Two years later they opened their first novitiate in Westphalia, and in less than ten years they were playing such a major role in all departments of German Catholic life that some people ended by finding their presence all too obtrusive.

German Catholics were fortunate to have as guides during these crucial years prelates of outstanding merit. At the start they had Cardinal Johann Geissel, archbishop of Cologne 1845–54, who while at the seminary in Mainz had acquired a noble ideal of the mission entrusted to the Church and the priesthood and at the same time a clear view of the conditions surrounding the exercise of that ministry in the modern world. If his theological education had been somewhat rudimentary, he made up for it by an admirably balanced judgment and 'a statesman's capacity to sum up a situation at a glance' (Goyau). Geissel ran his efficiently organised diocese on a highly centralised plan, and from his diocese and his province, whose cohesion was demonstrated by the council held in 1860 in Cologne, his influence gradually spread to the whole of northern and eastern Germany. After Geissel's death his role as mentor and moving spirit of the Catholic Church in Germany was inherited by a man fifteen years his junior and bishop of a smaller diocese. Wilhelm von Ketteler, from 1848 to 1877 bishop of Mainz. As a young man Ketteler had been in contact with Görres and his circle and this had left a lasting impression. He made it his life's goal to work for that

5. It is to be noted that although Catholics in Prussia increased slightly during the third quarter of the century in the regions with a Protestant majority, they declined a little in those regions where the majority was Catholic (from 55.95 per cent to 52.35 per cent in Westphalia and from 75.07 per cent to 72.27 per cent in the Rhineland between 1846 and 1880;cf. H. A. Krose, *Konfessionstatistik Deutschlands* (Freiburg-im-Breisgau 1904, Table 60 ff.).

penetration of all branches of human activity by the Christian spirit which had characterised the civilisation of the Middle Ages and which modern secularism was tending to obstruct. But he was more keenly aware than many of his contemporaries of the irreconcilable differences between the Middle Ages and his own epoch and of the need to invoke new methods, for which he believed the best formula could be found in post-Tridentine Catholicism. To aid him, Ketteler found in Mainz lieutenants who, although their views might not always coincide with his own, were already committed to the same ideal, exemplary and immensely energetic priests, almost too inflexible in their dedication to the Catholic cause, men such as Christoph Moufang, president of the seminary.

Under the influence of men such as Geissel, Ketteler and Moufang the evangelistic methods based on individual initiative and personal contact which had been advocated by the Sailer school during the first half of the century gradually gave way to a corporate Catholicism. Its outward expression took the form of parochial missions, which made considerable headway once the ostracism of the religious orders started to diminish, and Catholic associations *(Vereine)* of every description (to be dealt with more fully in a later chapter),[6] pending the day when, to the fury of opponents of 'political Catholicism', a breakthrough was made into the parliamentary arena. The more forward-looking were also quick to perceive the importance of the press, but this was a field which presented particular difficulties: in order to get round them a *Pressverein* was formed which gave its backing to a number of successful ventures, ranging from newspapers and magazines aimed at the popular market to the highbrow *Kölnische Blätter* (since 1869 the *Kölnische Volkszeitung*), launched in 1860.

Prussia was not the only Protestant country where Catholics benefited from the development of more liberal institutions following the upheavals of 1848. The same happened in Denmark, where the new constitution of 1849 proclaimed liberty of worship and so brought to an end three centuries of Catholic proscription, and especially in Holland.

Despite their numbers, a good third of the population, Dutch Catholics had until now been in an inferior position and, remarkably enough, they were still on a par with Catholics in mission countries, having no canonically constituted dioceses. It was the support given to the liberal party by the Catholic bourgeoisie of the northern provinces that had made possible the peaceful revolution which produced the new constitution of 1848. Despite efforts by Calvinist conservatives to preserve the character of their country as a 'Protestant nation', this constitution stated that before the law all religious denominations were equal and that all religious bodies were to be responsible for regulating their own internal affairs.

6. See chapter 7, 136-7.

It should have been obvious that the natural culmination of full legal emancipation was the reintroduction of a regular diocesan regime, something which had been on the agenda for the past thirty years and more. But the truth is that many of the clergy did not wish it, and it was chiefly laymen from the north who pressed Rome to give them full bishops, among other reasons because they realised that in future they would need the guidance of local authority over political questions affecting the interests of the Church. But although they agreed over the principle they differed as to the form, some preferring a concordatory solution, others, young liberals in particular, attaching more importance to the Church's independence of the State, even at the price of total separation. The conditions insisted upon by the government, which had to reckon with Protestant hostility to the establishment of dioceses in the north of the country, obliged the Holy See to resign itself to the latter solution and to decide unilaterally to re-establish the hierarchy. The bull of creation of 4 March 1853 unleashed from the Protestant side a wave of protest known as the *Aprilbeweging* but the new bishops, refusing to be deterred by the agitation, at once set about the reorganisation of the Dutch Church to meet the requirements of canon law. Directing their labours was Mgr Zwijsen (1794–1877), appointed archbishop of Utrecht, a zealous pastor, relatively limited in outlook but with a good sense and firmness that were valuable assets at this difficult period, even if he helped to intensify the 'ultramontane ghetto' atmosphere that Dutch Catholicism was to retain for more than half a century.

This isolation was especially marked at the cultural level and, notwithstanding the emergence among the urban bourgeoisie of a small band of Catholic intellectuals, the second half of the century, when compared with the ferment of the years around 1830, was noticeably a time of cultural regression. But if Catholics continued to hold aloof from most aspects of the nation's life, they were brought together among themselves in multifarious voluntary associations which covered all aspects of human existence and which did not cease to multiply and prosper, kept firmly under control – and here is a difference with the German *Vereine,* in which the role of the laity was extremely important – by a clergy, secular and religious, full of piety and zeal and steadily increasing in numbers.

3

THE CHURCH AND LIBERALISM

THE convulsions which in the course of 1848 shook the whole of Europe, not sparing even the papal throne, posed afresh and with new acuteness the great problem the Church had had to face for the past half-century: what attitude was to be adopted to the world born out of the intellectual and political revolution of the late eighteenth century, and in particular to the regime of civil and religious liberties symbolised by the *Déclaration des droits de l'homme et du citoyen.*

The violence which in many countries had been the outcome of the agitation set up by the liberal parties could not but harden in their conviction all those who believed there was a direct connection between the principles of 1789 and the destruction of traditional values in the social, moral and religious order. After 1848 many indeed were the pastors and faithful who saw no salvation outside an authoritarian Catholicism. Hypnotised by memories of medieval Christianity, which the Catholic romantics had presented in a highly idealised light, they wanted the Church to cling to or go back to the regime of external privileges and prestige within the bosom of an officially Catholic State, which would act as a shield against the buffetings of anti-Christian currents of opinion. The regime they wanted was one to which certain existing states in fact bore some resemblance; Spain under Isabella II, the Habsburg Empire, and until 1859, many of the Italian states. Those who thought in this way were more sensitive to the 'scandal of the weak' than to the 'scandal of the strong'; disturbed by the falling-off in religious observance, which (being moralists rather than sociologists) they put down to the errors freely disseminated by the wicked press, they believed that the faith of the modern common people ought to be protected by political institutions and that the masses, above all the rural masses, which at that time made up the great majority of Europe's population, would not so lightly desert a Church held in honour by authority. This anti-liberal

Catholicism, which took as its text the *Ensayo sobre el catolicismo, el liberalismo y el socialismo,* published by its Spanish author Donoso Cortes in 1851 and hastily translated first into French and then into German, had as its official organ the *Civiltà cattolica* of the Roman Jesuits, and in several countries the Society of Jesus, with some individual exceptions, helped to reinforce the impression that these were the only positions in keeping with Catholic orthodoxy.

But facing these hankerers after the old regime were other Catholics who claimed on the contrary that it was dangerous and deluding to go back to the ideas of the Restoration. They pointed out that since a considerable part of the governing class had in fact ceased to be *croyant,* it was living in a dream world to go on expecting the State to provide disinterested aid and protection. The most the Church could hope for was a benevolent neutrality. Some went even further. Sensitive to what was authentic in liberal values, they were ready to open themselves to a more modern conception of man, in which there was greater emphasis on individual rights and more respect for what we nowadays call 'the autonomy of the secular', not always perceiving the danger there can be in over-valuing this autonomy and claiming for man too great an independence of God.

Here then were two groups of Catholics destined to become increasingly at loggerheads, each as anxious as the other to serve the Church but holding opposing views of the best way to set about it. The optimists thought the Church ought to go out to meet the modern world, to baptise liberal institutions just as in the past she had baptised Graeco-Roman civilisation, the movement in the twelfth century for communal independence or the humanist aspirations of the Renaissance, and so draw a discreet veil over the anathemas of the encyclical *Mirari vos,* memory of which was starting to fade. But many others, who saw the modern world chiefly under the anti-Christian aspects of the Revolution, believed on the contrary that it was communications and shore up the defences in order to avoid all danger of contamination. What they wanted from the pope and the bishops was greater emphasis on the previous condemnations of liberalism and other modern errors. They remained indifferent to the risk, in so doing, of reinforcing the misapprehension which made many liberals sincerely imagine that if society was to be refashioned to meet the needs of the times the Church must first be shorn of all her influence.

The controversies among Catholics over the question of modern liberties reached their highest pitch in France, and were further embittered, in that country where politics are apt to become invested with religious and philosophical significance, by the issue of *ralliement* to the Empire.[1] On one

1. Montalembert and his friends, who could not forgive Napoleon III for having replaced

side were those who were proud to style themselves just 'Catholics', contrasting themselves with the 'liberal Catholics' and underlining their scrupulous loyalty to the Roman position. They took their cue from Dom Guéranger and still more from Mgr Pie, the arch-opponent of naturalism and its elimination of God and the Church from the affairs of this world, and the ardent promoter of the rechristianisation of institutions and of the State. Pie at least accepted that the realisation of the kingdom of God in its fullness would come only at the end of time.[2] Some of his more zealous disciples on the right were less inhibited. Ignoring their master's eschatological perspective, his circumspection when it came to individuals, the care he took as bishop of Poitiers not to enter into too precise a political engagement, they went further than he did in the temporalisation of the supernatural, not hesitating to advocate direct power for the Church and the pope over civil society and seriously expecting before long to see the Christian State of the Middle Ages incarnate in the person of the Comte de Chambord. These extremist views were circulated in the crudest form, often with a spicing of unfair comment about Catholics who thought differently. For this a number of journalists were responsible, the most prominent being Louis Veuillot. The bishops were on the whole guarded in their attitude towards this publicist who claimed to be more orthodox than themselves, but he soon became the oracle of the provincial lower clergy, who found his popular style and sweeping judgments very much to their taste, and through them his influence penetrated to a limited but still considerable number of the faithful. The result was that for some time to come their attitude towards the civil power was one of clericalist intolerance and systematic denigration.

Against these paladins of the absolute were ranged a large number of moderate, that is to say unconsciously liberal Catholics, among whom two small but very active groups stand out: the disciples of Mgr Maret, dean of the faculty of theology at the Sorbonne, who envisaged the concordat as the instrument of voluntary collaboration between the Church and a secularised society;[3] and the *Correspondant* circle, an academic and fashionable group

---

the parliamentary monarchy by an authoritarian regime which held constitutional liberties cheap, were incensed by the adulation heaped on the 'new Charlemagne' by many opponents of Catholic liberalism who hoped to obtain for the Church by imperial favour a privileged status which, by making it possible to invoke legal constraints, would make her mission easier to accomplish.

2. For the position of Mgr Pie (1815-80), bishop of Poitiers from 1849, see E. Catta, *La Doctrine politique et sociale du cardinal Pie*, Paris 1959, and the substantial modifications by J. Gadille, *La Pensée et l'Action politique des évêques français au début de la Troisième République* (Paris 1967), I, 48-59; on the extremists' position, see Gadille, *op cit.*, I, 59-72.

3. On this group, which has attracted less attention than the more sparkling but more superficial *Correspondant* circle, see X. de Montclos, *Lavigerie, Le Saint-Siège et l'Église* (Paris 1965), 130-2, 225-7, 287-323, and J. Gadille, *op. cit.*, I, 89-108 and 134-9; note also G. Bazin, *Vie de Mgr Maret*, 3 vols, Paris 1891-2.

which had certain lay anti-Bonapartists among its prime movers, Falloux, Cochin, de Broglie and above all Montalembert, men whose talents, social standing and past services to the Catholic cause made them influential even in circles which did not fully share their views and who benefited from the support and growing prestige of Mgr Dupanloup,[4] the eloquent and restless bishop of Orleans, who was denounced by the entire ultramontane press as the leading prelate of the 'Catholic liberal party'. In fact Dupanloup's liberalism was strictly relative, since at bottom his aim was still to reconstruct a Christendom which met the ends of the Church. Where he differed from his opponents was over means. He sought to work through institutions that were in tune with the spirit of the age, arguing that in contemporary circumstances these alone were feasible.

This was likewise the position of most of the Belgian bishops and of the canon law professors at the university of Louvain. They had no sympathy with the liberal ideology but were very conscious of the concrete advantages conferred by the liberal constitution of 1831. This constitution in effect guaranteed to the Church a degree of independence in relation to the civil power at that time almost unparalleled, and it also in practice enabled the Church, thanks to the influence of the Catholics in parliament, to recapture wide tracts of social territory, which the clergy defended inch by inch against the demands of the anti-clericalists for further secularisation. Such too was the position defended by Ketteler in his book *Freiheit, Autorität und Kirche,* published in 1862, which despite the reservations of certain conservative circles, notably the Austrian Jesuits, won approval from the majority of German Catholics, who were well aware that constitutional liberties had their advantages for the Church, especially in States with a non-Catholic majority.

But what impressed Rome was the fact — by about 1860 undeniable — that nearly always when liberals came to power they lost no time in introducing legislation not merely unfavourable to the Church but often frankly hostile, especially on the subject of education and the religious orders. Placed at the centre of Christendom, Pius IX feared that if he did not react it would discourage the handful of Catholic nations which remained more or less faithful to the system of protection and privileges he still regarded as the ideal. Having been obliged by force of circumstances to accept concessions in practice in several countries, he believed it all the more necessary to come out with a firm restatement of the principles.

The need to take up a position with regard to liberalism as a whole seemed all the more urgent since, in addition to the increasingly acrimonious debate surrounding the Christian concept of society, there were by this time

4. On Mgr Félix Dupanloup (1802-78), see *Dictionnaire d'histoire et de géographie ecclésiastiques,* XIV, cols 1070-1122; on his political theology, J. Gadille, *op. cit.,* I, 72-89.

other issues over which the Catholic élites of some important countries were divided. On the one hand, centring in Germany on Döllinger and in England on Acton and his journal *The Rambler,* there was the question of the freedom of Catholic scholars in relation to ecclesiastical authority, to which we shall return.[5] On the other hand, there was the Roman question, which had its repercussions everywhere but nowhere more strongly than in Italy.

After the Restoration of 1849 the Papal State had enjoyed a decade or so of outward tranquillity, and the lesser folk, in particular, seemed reasonably content with the paternalist government of the pope. In this he had the able assistance of Cardinal Antonelli, whose contribution in the way of material and administrative improvements has been too much neglected by liberal historians.[6] But discontent continued its rumblings among the educated middle class, exasperated as they were by this 'government of priests' which shelved urgently needed reforms and allowed the citizen no measure of political responsibility. This was a situation which Cavour, bent on the unification of Italy, had no difficulty in exploiting: after the war of 1859 he proceeded to the annexation of the Romagna (March 1860), pressing on after the defeat at Castelfidardo in September of the pope's small army (fielded by Mgr de Merode[7] and commanded by a Frenchman, General de Lamoricière) to the annexation of the Marches and Umbria. For ten years, thanks to the support of Napoleon III, who needed the political backing of his Catholic subjects and did not wish to provoke them, the pope kept his control of Rome and its surroundings, but in the eyes of many '*Italianissimi*' this was a temporary state of affairs, to be ended as soon as possible by the installation at Rome of the capital of the new kingdom: an event which duly came to pass once Italian troops, taking advantage of the Franco-Prussian war, had occupied the remnant of the Papal State (20 September 1870).

After in each case a momentary hesitation, the Vatican's reaction to the events of 1859 and 1860 was that the only attitude to take was a blank refusal to bow to the *fait accompli*. Antonelli, who did not sufficiently appreciate how much political conditions and ideas had changed in Europe over the past ten years, hoped that the policy which had succeeded at Gaeta, the appeal to the Catholic powers in the name of legitimacy and of the pope's inalienable rights over his territories, would once again suffice to rescue the pope's temporal power. But this made it necessary to stand firmly on the principle of international law without appearing to admit even the possibility of a compromise.

5. On Döllinger see 59, 66, 167-70: on Acton and his group, see 210-12.
6. See, despite its apologetic viewpoint, P. Della Torre, *L'Opera riformatrice e amministrativa di Pio IX fra il 1850 e il 1870,* Rome 1945; also M. Roncetti in *Bolletino della Deputazione di storia patria per l'Umbria,* XLIII (1966), 139-74.
7. On Mgr de Merode (1820-74) see L. Besson, *F. F. X. de Mérode,* Lille 1908; R. Aubert, *Revue générale belge* (May and June 1956), 1102-43, 1316-34; J. Martin, *Pio IX,* IV (1975), 3-27.

The position taken up by Pius IX had a somewhat different basis. Unlike his Secretary of State, he was still deeply in sympathy with the Italian cause, but independence for Italians in respect of Austria was one thing, unification achieved in the form of enforced centralisation under the aegis of anti-clerical Piedmont, leading to the disappearance of the Papal State, quite another. If Pius IX attached great importance to the temporal sovereignty, it was not on its own account but because he saw it as the indispensable guarantee of the pope's spiritual independence, and the chorus of protest which rose from the entire ultramontane press of Europe confirmed his view that the power at stake was one for which he was accountable to the Catholic world as a whole and not something he could dispose of as he pleased. Realists who tried to persuade him that sooner or later there must be negotiation found themselves up against a mystical trust in providence which was sustained by the pope's conviction that the political convulsions in which he found himself embroiled were merely one episode in the great struggle between God and Satan, a contest from which God would obviously emerge the victor. The conflict between liberal Italy and the temporal power became in his eyes a religious war. This meant that resistance to what he was increasingly disposed to describe as 'the Revolution' was no longer a question of balancing diplomatic or political forces but of resorting to prayer and trust in God. The quasi-mystical fervour with which some of the Risorgimento leaders threw themselves into the campaign against the Church's claims only served to strengthen his conviction that the question at issue was essentially religious.

Buoyed up in his hopes of a 'miracle' by the illusions of those around him and by the extravagant demonstrations of the swelling throng of pilgrims flocking to acclaim the 'pope-king', encouraged furthermore by the narrow sectarianism of those responsible for the direction of Italian policy, the aging pope tended more and more to join to his claims for the spiritual liberty of the Holy See a radical critique of liberal principles. Thus he revealed his incapacity to distinguish among the confused aspirations of his time what was of positive value from what was an inept concession to the passing whim or, as in some cases, a more or less unconscious compromise with ideologies which had little in common with the Christian spirit.

Such was the atmosphere surrounding the preparations for a general condemnation of 'modern errors', which after several trial efforts finally took the form of an encyclical, *Quanta cura*, accompanied by a list of eighty propositions judged to be inadmissible which appeared under the title *Syllabus errorum*.[8] A number of these propositions were manifest heresies or at least errors which the theological schools were unanimous in rejecting,

8. On the preparation of the *Syllabus* see G. Martina, 'Osservazioni sulle varie redazioni del "Syllabo" ', *Chiesa e Stato nell'Ottocento. Miscellanea in onore di P. Pirri* (Padua 1962), vol. II, 419-523 (supplemented in *Archirum historiae pontificiae*, VI (1968), 319-69).

and other propositions provided by their presence a salutary warning, too little heeded at the time, against Hegelian-inspired doctrines of State totalitarianism or the social abuses which stem from economic liberalism. But a section of both documents aimed explicitly at the liberal conception of religion and society: its claim for the monopoly of education by the State, its hostility towards religious orders, but equally its affirmation that each religion is as good as the next and that human societies ought in future to take no account of religion, from which followed the demand – advanced no longer as a practical solution to an existing state of pluralism but as an ideal in its own right and a mark of progress – for the secularisation of institutions, the separation of Church and State and complete freedom of worship and of the press. It was above all this section which struck the general public, all the more since some of the propositions, torn from their contexts, appeared highly disconcerting to the modern mind. Matters were not improved by the commentary offered in a section of the ultramontane press, whose contribution only served to deepen the misunderstandings between the two sides.

Many non-Catholics regarded the *Syllabus* at first sight as spectacular confirmation that Catholic doctrine and nineteenth-century ways of life and thought were fundamentally incompatible. There were many liberal Catholics, especially in France and Belgium, who believed they saw themselves condemned. In no time at all, however, people started to make the necessary distinctions and the storm soon died down, thanks in particular to a pamphlet produced by Mgr Dupanloup. This translation of the encyclical into modern language – with a dash of sweetening, it must be confessed – enjoyed an enormous success, extending even to America, and within a few days it swung opinion round, to the great displeasure of the anti-clericals and even more of Veuillot and his friends, who were especially piqued to find that, thanks to circumstances that Dupanloup knew how to exploit, the pamphlet came to have the appearance of a semi-official interpretation.[9]

Dupanloup's adroit intervention saved the liberal Catholics from having to beat the retreat which at first had seemed unavoidable, and as a result they were able to hold out until the accession of Leo XIII. But they had to shorten sail: not only because many of them were made aware by the pope's intervention that some of their contentions were exaggerated and lacking in precision, but above all out of a prudent wish not to provoke any further the aging pontiff, who was becoming more and more exasperated by the growing sectarianism of those who styled themselves liberals and was finding it

9. See R. Aubert, 'Mgr Dupanloup et le Syllabus', *Revue d'histoire ecclésiastique*, LI (1956), 79-142, 471-512 and 837-915. On reactions to the *Syllabus* see in particular E. Papa, *Il Sillabo di Pio IX e la stampa francese, inglese e italiano*, Rome 1968.

difficult to distinguish sufficiently clearly the differences between liberal Catholicism and liberalism based on rationalism and naturalism. While resigning himself in very many cases to toleration of the 'liberal hypothesis' because circumstances demanded it, he could not help showing his lack of sympathy with those who, as he thought, opted for it too eagerly. All his favours were reserved for those Catholics who continued, without reference to any change of outlook or even to what was locally expedient, to press the claims of the traditional 'Christian social order', and the encouragement that even the most fanatical of them received at Rome ended by convincing them that they had a genuine task to perform. [10] The fall from grace of the liberal Catholics was to mean that for the next fifteen years the forefront of the stage would be occupied by extremists, on one side the radical liberals, on the other the ultramontane intransigents, each as intolerant as the other and each with a burning desire to impose his ideology on the mass of his fellow-citizens.

The accession of Leo XIII was regarded by liberal Catholics as a victory for their point of view, and the future was to prove them by and large correct. That is not to say that Leo XIII can be regarded as a 'liberal'. He himself always repudiated the description and with good reason. Not merely (as pointed out in Chapter 1) was he to refer on more than one occasion to the authority of the *Syllabus;* he was also to reaffirm in varying circumstances the doctrinal substance of Pius IX's principal pronouncements on the subject of the Christian society. Whereas liberalism based its theory of the State on freedom, Leo XIII's political philosophy took as its starting-point the concept of authority. Far from being resigned to a progressive secularisation of institutions, his aim was on the contrary to rechristianise them, using for the purpose all the resources available under modern public law, and to restore the Church to the position she had held in past centuries as the spiritual mentor of mankind. But it was no less true that, in his anxiety to see the Church resuming her dialogue with the world and advancing cautiously along the paths of the future, Leo XIII did not confine himself to resolving the multiple disputes with governments that he had inherited from his predecessor and encouraging Catholics to exploit their constitutional liberties for the furtherance of their cause. He also made a great effort at the theoretical level to integrate liberal institutions into a Catholic conception of the State and of society. Of course, this was not to be done without precipitating a crisis of conscience for people who had been convinced by Pius IX's repeated anathemas against modern society that it was their religious duty to aim to return as completely as possible to the forms of the past – a crisis so acute that in certain convents prayers were even offered

10. See S. Louant, 'Charles Périn et Pie IX', *Bulletin de l'Institut historique belge de Rome,* XXVII (1952), 181-220.

that God would speedily deliver his Church from the 'Freemason pope'. A succession of incidents such as the ill-tempered resignation of the Belgian professor Charles Périn,[11] champion of the 'Christian social order' as conceived by Pius IX, the conduct of the Spanish journalist Nocedal and the outburst of Cardinal Pitra in 1885 [12] demonstrated that even intellectuals had their difficulties in adapting to the change of front asked of them by the new pope. Fortified by lengthy cogitations during the years he had spent out of the public eye, and influenced perhaps by his recollections of the constitutional experience of Belgian Catholics and rather more by his interest in the Church's position in the English-speaking countries, Leo XIII addressed himself throughout his pontificate in a series of encyclicals which attracted a great deal of attention, to formulating the Catholic theory of the relation between the temporal and the spiritual, between Church and State, in terms that were positive and adapted to modern conditions. By placing his condemnations of the naturalist and rationalist ideal of the atheistic State within the framework of broadly conceived and positive expositions of the ideal Christian society and the Catholic conception of liberty – which he was not afraid to describe as 'the most marvellous of God's gifts' – Leo XIII made his disavowals appear more reasonable since they were manifestly not the expression of a reactionary outlook but the logical application of a coherent doctrine. In addition, with his habitual sensitivity to the finer shades of meaning, he was prepared to admit to the text of his encyclicals (as in the celebrated encyclical *Libertas* (1888) in which he explained what was admissible in contemporary ideas regarding the freedoms of conscience, worship and the press[13]) the precise commentaries which Pius IX, afraid of detracting from the force of his anathemas, was too often content to supply orally. He also distinguished clearly the permanent from the variable. If he did not seek to go beyond the distinction, which no longer satisfies us today, between the thesis and the hypothesis, that is between the ideal society and the situations which have to be tolerated in practice, he did at least place more emphasis on the hypothesis, and made it clear that for our age this is the normal regime, whereas his predecessor, without denying that the regime of the hypothesis had in a great many cases to be accepted, never left off exhorting Catholics to see that its field of application was reduced as near as possible to the minimum. Again, while Pius IX during his last fifteen years only added fuel to the flames of the controversies which set liberal Catholics

11. See M. Becqué and A. Louant, 'Le dossier "Rome et Louvain" de Charles Périn', *Revue d'histoire ecclésiastique*, L (1955), 36-124.
12. See A. Battandier, *Le Cardinal Pitra* (Paris 1893), 695-737 and E. Lecanuet, *Les Premières Années du pontificat de Léon XIII* (Paris 1910), 285-94.
13. On the encyclical *Libertas* see C. de T'Serclaes, *Le Pape Léon XIII*, I (Lille 1894), 524-39, Lecanuet, *op. cit.*, 312-23, and G. Martina, in *Aspetti della cultura cattolica nell'eta di Leo XIII* (Rome 1961), 597-630.

and intransigents at loggerheads – the controversies over the legitimacy of constitutions founded on the application of the principles of 1789 – Leo XIII, as soon as he became pope, expressed his formal disapproval of these debates, which he judged to be sterile and pernicious. Citing the example of the early Church, he urged Catholics – save in Italy, where the Roman question gave the problem a different dimension – to take their part in public life, even in countries whose institutions were not in harmony with the Christian ideal.[14]

But the change was not only one of tone and emphasis. Leo XIII, while holding fast to the essentials in the teaching of his predecessors, was responsible for introducing a number of important definitions which marked the beginning of a shift to more modern points of view. In particular, unlike Pius IX, he did not stop short at affirming the rights of the Church but rounded off this aspect of Catholic teaching by undertaking to define the rights of the civil power, stressing its completeness within its own order and its legitimate independence in relation to ecclesiastical authorities. While never losing sight of the Church's spiritual omnipotence, which he stressed in terms we nowadays find too clericalist, he thus inaugurated in his encyclicals *Immortale Dei* (1885) and *Sapientiae christianae* (1890) a rehabilitation of the secular 'in which the theological scheme is considered in a new light with regard to history and law'. With the help of his Thomist-Aristotelian philosophy, Leo XIII propounded a theology of the State and of civilsociety which recognised their legitimate autonomy within their own order. These were relatively novel ideas in Catholic circles at that date, and that he expressed them – with circumspection to be sure but also with firmness – was among Leo XIII's greatest merits. Similarly, in the advice he gave to French and Spanish Catholics to 'rally' to the new regimes and renounce their attachment to a legitimism which ignored the march of history, Leo XIII transcended the mere opportunism of Gregory XVI and sketched out the beginnings of a theology of the Revolution.

Certainly, much was left unfinished in this first blueprint of a Christian public order adapted to a society which had finally done with the *ancien régime*. As Fr Murray has argued so convincingly in a series of important articles,[15] Leo XIII's teaching on this matter was inevitably affected by the historical context within which it was expressed, in the immediate context, that is to say, of the capture of political power in most European and Latin American countries by Freemasonry with the aim of eliminating the Church's influence from public life, and of the movement of so-called liberal

14. Mgr A. Simon has an apt comment: 'Leo XIII was not more clearsighted than Pius IX. It was the facts that had become clearer (*L'Hypothèse libérale en Belgique* (Wetteren 1956), 31).
15. See bibliography to chapter 3.

governments towards policies of hostile intervention in the affairs of the Church. It was also affected by the wider historical context of some four centuries of absolutist regimes – whether based on the divine right of kings or on the Jacobin conception of the State was immaterial – which had undoubtedly left their mark on Catholic political philosophy, even if the formulae it repeated remained in substance those of the Schoolmen. When the papal pronouncements are put back into their rightful historical perspective it becomes easier to grasp the contingent character of their formulation. Thus, to give but one example, by stating the authority-liberty problem in terms of *potestas*[16] rather than community, Leo XIII reveals himself as in reality untrue to the political teaching of the Middle Ages, and of St Thomas in particular, and beyond any doubt still subject to the absolutist tradition of the sixteenth and seventeenth centuries. He was in any case, by temperament quite as much as by training, the complete opposite of a democrat.

By assimilating and giving the stamp of official doctrine to what was most reasonable in the intuitions of Catholics of the preceding generation, and where they had been too hasty in their conclusions, redressing the balance with wisdom and caution, Leo XIII gave liberal Catholicism a wider hearing. A few years later, the polemicist Barbier's two-volume denunciation of liberal Catholicism, *Les progrès du libéralisme en France sous Léon XIII* (1907), appeared. A similar picture emerged elsewhere. Notwithstanding rearguard activity of the kind exemplified by the book entitled *El liberalismo es pecado* produced by a Spanish priest, F. Sarda y Salvany, in 1884, or the outburst of Cardinal Pitra, the new spirit penetrated to every country and gained ground from year to year. In addition, the move in many countries towards a more clear-cut political situation, allied with the pope's clarification of the doctrinal issues, gave rise to a realignment of forces. Thus in France, in Italy or in Belgium the Christian democrats, whose political programme was undoubtedly influenced by the principles of 1789, were in large part drawn from the 'intransigent' circles which for twenty years had campaigned so vigorously against the liberal Catholics and their counsels of *ralliement* to modern society.[17] Or again, to take a specific case which shows very strikingly how outlooks were changing, the programme of the Dutch Catholic party led by Mgr Schaepman, which entailed joint action with Protestants to combat the secularisation of society and of education in particular, can be termed at once anti-liberal and liberal, in keeping with the anathemas of Pius IX and the intransigents against 'social atheism', but implicitly accepting religious freedom and its consequences and recognising

16. Fr Murray has convincingly shown that the main focus of Leo XIII's political theology was always the 'prince', whose duty it was to mould society and make it virtuous from above, the citizen being regarded first and foremost as 'subject'.
17. For further details see chapter 8.

that beneath the confessional differences there lay a common Christian basis.

Nevertheless, if for some years and especially after 1885 there was a noticeable abatement in the controversies which for a generation had raged between Catholics on the subject of modern institutions and the Christian society, the fires were still smouldering beneath the ashes, all the more since, as the years went by, it became increasingly evident that beyond the question of constitutional liberties there loomed for Christian consciences a much wider question. This was what has been described as the 'formidable and many-layered question' of the behaviour to be adopted towards 'modern society' in all its facets, which had implications going beyond the merely political to impinge on the social, intellectual and even the spiritual spheres. It is not until we reach the pontificate of Pius X and the integrist offensive that we meet the full tide of the reaction against the new face of liberal Catholicism, but the later years of Leo XIII already provide a foretaste of the fresh battles to come, in the shape of the Americanist controversy, and in particular in the form it took in France. [18]

In 1894 the Abbé F. Klein had brought out in French translation, under the title *L'Église et le siècle,* a selection of the speeches of the American archbishop John Ireland, one of the Catholic world's most enthusiastic defenders of American democracy and an ardent champion of the greatest possible agreement between Catholicism and modern civilisation. Three years later Klein wrote a preface for a French version of the biography of Isaac Hecker, founder of the American Paulists, which urged the modern evangelist not to forget that the supernatural spirit gave no dispensation from the practice of the natural virtues, to remember to stress what were known as the 'active' virtues and to ascribe at least as much merit to the spirit of initiative and to the inspiration of the Holy Ghost as they did to passive submission to their superiors. This preface, which invited the clergy of Europe to draw inspiration from the new and somewhat rosily depicted missionary spirit of America, bore the characteristics of a manifesto. The liberal Catholics and Christian democrats applauded it to the echo, but people who had been upset by Leo XIII's political and social directives and for whom the attitudes of the United States clergy represented precisely what they feared to see replacing the traditional ideas, were loud in their protests, being well aware that the authoritarian system which to them contained the essence of religion was being eroded and threatening to break apart under the impact of two forces whose activity Fr Hecker and his apologists were so eager to commend: the Holy Ghost and its charismas on the one hand,

18. For the strictly American aspect of the crisis and its repercussions in Rome see chapter 14, 274-6.

religious subjectivity on the other. Following the lead of the Abbé Charles Maignen, author of a pamphlet entitled *Le Père Hecker est-il un saint?* (1898), they denounced admirers of liberty at any price, the natural virtues and the modern spirit as neo-Pelagians, on the one hand putting to effective use certain particularly vulnerable phrases lifted bodily from the *Vie de P. Hecker* and on the other making capital from the equivocal support the advocates of the new ideas received from people even more advanced in their views, who saw in 'Americanism' a chance to pave the way for a neo-Catholicism, radically altered in spirit and structure. For months the battle raged, filling the pages of newspapers and journals with its reverberations. It confirmed many unbelievers, who had been making vague gestures of *rapprochement*, in their belief that Catholicism was incompatible with the modern spirit, and added to this it might well be asked whether these dissensions did not check the impetus of the missionary apostolate and delay the formation of Catholic Action.

It was useless for Leo XIII to protest, in a public letter to the archbishop of Bourges (25 May 1899), that the encyclical which gave warning against the erroneous tendencies some people described as Americanism did nothing to alter his directives concerning the political and social deportment of French Catholics. The opponents of his policy, who like the liberal Catholics before them had been obliged over the past twenty years to shorten sail, sensed that the wind was beginning to turn in their favour again at Rome where, as the pope grew older, the intransigents were gradually regaining their ascendancy, pending their chance to set the tone openly in the next pontificate.

Banking with optimism on a trend favourable to the Church in the world which had issued from the intellectual revolution of the eighteenth century and from the political revolutions of the nineteenth, Leo XIII had pursued a policy of openness and presence. Pius X, whose natural inclination was reinforced by that of his entourage and of Merry del Val in particular, retreated on the contrary to positions of intransigence, fearing to see the Church betray her primordial mission by compromising over the manifestations of modern civilisation actively promoted by liberalism, in particular by the democrats who formed its pace-making wing: increased secularisation of institutions and of society, promotion of the masses at the expense of hierarchical élites, liberation of the mind, in the name of scientific progress, from authoritarian constraints.

To be sure, it would be wrong to see the attitude of the two popes as one of total contrast, and Pius X was careful, especially in his practical directives on political matters, to avoid at least in his early years giving the impression of dissociating himself from his predecessor. [19] For instance, for several years he showed himself quite well disposed – more so than his

Secretary of State – towards the political group formed by Jacques Piou under the name 'Action libérale populaire' which sought to defend French Catholicism against the anti-clericalist offensive by invoking the principles of 'liberty for all' and 'equality before the law'. He even addressed to Piou statements such as: 'The only defence of the Church in France is liberty', or again, 'The task is to build up a sound republic under the banner of Jesus Christ'. However, the increasing sectarianism of French public life was to lead him to side more and more with opponents of the *ralliement* policy, who had not ceased to warn that 'the Republic means war on the religious principle', and to conclude that, for all their good intentions, the liberal Catholics were playing ultimately into the hands of Freemasonry. The speech delivered on 19 April 1909 to French pilgrims who had come to Rome for the beatification of Joan of Arc was considered a strong pointer in this direction. [20]

But irrespective of possible changes in the matter of the best tactics for the defence of the Church in the political arena, what must be stressed is Pius X's fundamental hostility to liberalism, which like Pius IX he was very ready to regard as the meeting-point of all the heresies. There was one particular item in the liberal programme, made highly topical by events in France, which appeared to Pius X totally inadmissible: acceptance of the separation of Church and State.

Profoundly convinced that religion, politics and society formed a continuous whole and failing to perceive the distinction between administrative separation of Church and State into spheres of competence and the divorce of the nation from Christianity, Pius X looked on the separation as a sacrilege, 'a grave insult to God, as much the founder of human societies as the creator of individuals, to whom is owed in consequence the duty of public as well as of private worship'. [21] Leo XIII had expressed himself in much the same terms as regards the principles, but he had not failed to recognise the possible practical advantages to the Church of the liberal solution, for example in the case of Belgium, where he had enjoined Catholics such as Périn, who believed that loyalty to the teaching of Pius IX compelled them to press for a return to stricter union between the two powers, to keep silent. Pius X, on the contrary, was quick to censure publicly the

---

19. L. Dimier's attempt in 1904 to have the instructions in favour of *Ralliement* rescinded produced no immediate results. And as late as 1908 two works in which the Abbé E. Barbier attacked the political position Leo XIII prescribed for French Catholics were placed on the Index (details in E. Barbier, *Le Devoir politique des catholiques*, Paris 1910).
20. A development which certainly seems in part to have been influenced by a memorandum submitted by the Abbé E. Barbier, in full agreement with Mgr Turinaz, one of the leading episcopal opponents of *Ralliement*, to the pope in the spring of 1908 (cf J. Caron, *Le Sillon. . .*, 645-6).
21. The encyclical *Vehementer nos* of 11 February 1906.

pastoral letter on the theme of 'the Church and modern times' in which Mgr Bonomelli, the aged and *transigent* bishop of Cremona, suggested that, in view of the realities of the situation, the best course for the Church, to avoid a violent rupture made in anger, was to negotiate with the State on a friendly basis and agree a mutual separation, asking nothing further than the Church's freedom under the common law. [22]

There were other features of the liberal conception of society towards which Pius X showed he had the strongest possible reserves: its assertion of the absolute sovereignty of the people – which appeared to him, as to many theologians of his time, to be contrary to the biblical principle 'all power comes from God' – and the resultant slackening in the feeling for discipline and of respect for the hierarchical values which were so important in his eyes; its stress on the autonomy of the individual conscience and on the need for a generous toleration of all shades of opinion; and more generally its preference for an evolutionary conception of society, rather than a static one which refused to call in question traditional structures, confining itself to readjustments inside a framework taken to be immutable.

It is this background that helps to explain one of the acts of Pius X's pontificate which must have shown particularly the development of an unfavourable attitude in the Vatican towards the aspirations of modern democracy: the condemnation of the Sillon.

The Sillon movement originated with a group of students at the Collège Stanislas in Paris who in the early 1890s were seeking to reconcile Christianity and a society committed to the principles of 1789, along the line of a left-wing Catholicism which had three distinguishing features: unreserved adherence to the content of revelation as transmitted by the Church, acceptance of the historical process as a progress in which God is involved through his intervention in man's moral conduct, and sympathy with the *persona* of left-wing non-Catholics, with whom they felt an affinity of temperament while rejecting the rationalism on which they based their premises. From 1899 what had started as a thinkers' group was to be transformed into an activist movement. This was the work of Marc Sangnier (1873–1950), a fiery-souled *polytechnicien* who belonged by birth to the élite of the bourgeoisie, capable of exerting an astonishing and well-nigh hypnotic influence over his fellow-students. He effected the transformation by giving a new direction to the journal *Le Sillon* which had been founded by P. Renaudin in 1894 and by initiating a series of projects which, thanks to his devouring energy and burning eloquence, achieved a rapid and spectacular success: study circles for the study of social questions, which brought together young intellectuals and young workers on terms of completely equality (by

22. Cf C. Bellò, *Geremia Bonomelli* (Brescia 1961), 201-4.

1905 there were about two thousand, covering the entire country); institutes of popular education, set up in competition with the socialists, popular universities; public meetings to debate topical subjects; and the formation, with the help of H. du Roure, one of his most dedicated collaborators, of a corps of 'Young Guards' whose members underwent an admission ceremony after keeping a religious vigil at Montmartre and whose task was to police the frequently turbulent public meetings and to make propaganda for the movement. The latter, which thanks to the support of one or two strong local personalities had not been slow to spread to the provinces – in particular to Brittany, the North, Lorraine and the Midi, not forgetting the South-East where it joined forces with similar organisations already in existence for some years – soon took on the character of a crusade serving an ideal which recalled the old dream of the *Avenir*: to christianise modern democracy through the agency of laymen overflowing with the apostolic spirit, by striving in particular to win the working classes for the Church and to reconcile the Church to the Republic.

Although he had so much in common with the liberal Catholics and the Christian democrats, for example his complete faith in the virtues of the democratic ideal, Sangnier was determined to keep his distance from both: from the liberal Catholics, whether of the *Correspondant* circle or of the Action libérale populaire, because he judged them to be too cut off from the rising classes and 'incapable of making a clean enough break with the old conservative elements'; from the Christian democrats because they pressed exclusively for reforms of an institutional order when it seemed to him more urgent to undertake the moral education of people as individuals, with the aim of nurturing in them, with the indispensable assistance of spiritual forces, the true spirit of democracy, without which democratic institutions would be fatally flawed. (This was an aspect, it should be noted, in which, for all its assertions to the contrary, Sillonism marked itself out as being in the best tradition of the liberal Catholicism of the nineteenth century.)

This contrast between, on the one hand, an impetuous messianism which put its trust solely in the compellingly exultant effect of a charismatic spell and which was determined that the only bond must be that of man's common brotherhood, with no set organisation to stifle its creative spirit, and, on the other, a patient effort of the will, striving little by little to insinuate the Christian ideal into the complex structures of society and putting its trust therefore in organisation as a preparation for the assumption of full responsibilities in the affairs of the polity, was at the root of a first series of crises within the movement which occurred in 1905. These included the secession first of the Lyons and then of the Limoges groups, whose dissatisfaction was further increased by Sangnier's dictatorial and centralising methods, and later in the same year Sangnier's dismissal of one of his principal lieutenants, the less prophetically inclined Charles d'Hellencourt, effected by a miniature *coup d'état* which was followed shortly after by the voluntary departure of many of d'Hellencourt's supporters.[23] But these internal upheavals did little to diminish the powerful spread of the Sillon's influence. A more serious crisis was to start building up in 1906, the result of the Sillon's involvement in politics and the consequences this was to have for the movement's relations with the ecclesiastical authorities.

At an earlier stage, influenced by one or two Oratorian disciples of Fr Gratry, the Sillonists had envisaged forming a spiritual polity which, by gradually moulding the democratic polity from within, would transform it into a new Christendom. But in the light of experience they were gradually persuaded they must change their initial programme of 'Christianity via democracy' into one of 'Christianity as part of the democracy', since in the pluralism of a democratically based society Christians were offered opportunity to penetrate, to assert their views and to disseminate them in an atmosphere of mutual respect. This new trend, which first declared itself in 1906, led to the transformation of a confessional group with essentially apostolic aims into a movement increasingly involved in politics, taking its stand, at times in provocative terms, on the side of 'laicity' and calling on non-Catholics — members of Protestant youth organisations and even free-thinkers — to collaborate in creating a spiritually-based civilisation founded on values of Christian origin (what Sangnier called 'the greater Sillon').

This development was bound to disturb the representatives of ecclesiastical authority, anxious as they were to keep Catholic youth in a hothouse under their exclusive control. Even greater, then, was the problem posed by the participation of young priests and seminarists in a movement which intended to make its choices without reference to the episcopal hierarchy, especially since some of them, taking advantage of Sangnier's insistence on the autonomy of the civic conscience, were displaying independence of their superiors in other fields as well. Several bishops took counter-measures as early as 1907, and it was also at this stage that the Vatican, where Pius X had watched the beginnings of the movement with sympathy, started to feel uneasy. Many Catholics who had at first been captivated by the generous enthusiasm and masterful idealism of their young

---

23. J. Caron (*Le Sillon...*, 354-65) sees the 'd'Hellencourt crisis' primarily as the result of conflict along class lines between the educated upper bourgeois and aristocrats on the one side (Sangnier excepted) and the wage-earners from humble backgrounds and with no secondary education on the other. Without denying this aspect, M. Launay (*Revue historique*, CCXLV, 1971, 393-426) has shown, on the basis of fresh documents, that there was a deeper conflict going on between two conceptions of the nature of the Sillon, a conflict moreover symptomatic of a 'cleavage running right through the whole history of the Christian democratic movement in France'.

co-religionists felt injured at finding their conservative positions – and their in many cases monarchical convictions – so impugned by the increasingly insulting tone of the Sillon's attacks on Catholic attitudes to modern society and by its undiscriminating apologias for the democratic regime, which had a tendency to represent republican institutions as a necessary consequence of the universality of the Redemption and the Eucharist. These opponents – to whom were added former Sillonists who could no longer stomach Sangnier's dictatorial airs – found such incautious language, made the more objectionable by the arrogance which went with it, easy enough to attack. Starting with a severe warning from Cardinal Luçon in February 1909, a systematic campaign developed in the press. Some bishops, for example Mgr Mignot and Mgr Chapon, who still had faith in the Sillon and feared its condemnation would identify the Church once again with the forces of reaction, attempted a counter-offensive, but its chief result was to make clear to the public the division within the episcopate, which finally convinced Pius X of the need for the intervention that right-wing circles had been urging on him for the past year and more.

It took the form of a letter addressed on 25 August 1910 to the French episcopate.[24] On the basis of texts authentically Sillonist but subjected in many cases to 'a magnifying and simplifying effect' by being torn from their context or historical setting, this document singled out three types of error: modernist infiltrations; inadmissible claims to moral autonomy to the exclusion of the ecclesiastical hierarchy, a fault compounded by the ecleticism of the alliances formed with non-Catholics;[25] positions incompatible with the traditional Catholic doctrine of society and reminiscent of 'the doctrines of the so-called philosophers of the eighteenth century and of the oft-condemned doctrines of the Revolution and of liberalism', concerning in particular the origin and exercise of authority, the equality of man, and the need for radical change as the solution to the social problem, 'when all that is needed is to reinstate the structures broken up by the Revolution and to relate them, in the same Christian spirit which first inspired them, to the new environment created by the material advances of contemporary society: for the true friends of the people are neither revolutionaries nor innovators but traditionalists'.

24. *A.A.S.*, II, 1910, 607-33. On the sources which seem to lie behind this document (E. Barbier's book *Les Erreurs du Sillon*, an account drawn up by Abbé Desgranges, a pamphlet by an editor of *La Croix*, and certainly a scheme by the bishop of Chalons, Mgr Sevin), see J. Caron, *Le Sillon* . . ., 707-11;
25. As a practical solution, the pope wanted the splitting up of the movement into strictly confessional diocesan groups subordinate to the bishops and called 'Catholic Sillons'. Marc Sangnier and all his friends immediately submitted unreservedly, but the proposed solution caused the disappearance of what constituted the movement's originality and, while some sections vegetated for a few years, most of its adherents broke up.

The right-wing press was exultant. 'Never since the *Syllabus* of Pius IX', declared the *Action française* of 30 August, 'have the doctrines of the Revolution been condemned with such precision and such lucidity. And never before have the traditional doctrines been so vigorously reaffirmed.' Left-wing papers, on the other hand, had the satisfaction of pointing out how well the papal document confirmed the incompatibility they had always declared existed between the Church on the one side, and the Republic, democracy and progress on the other.

This conviction was strengthened moreover by the sympathetic interest that the Action française, a group on the extreme right, was currently attracting from a sizeable section of Catholic opinion, with the open support of some well-known theologians and half the French episcopate, including several cardinals. The Action française even had its supporters in Rome, among them Fr Billot, S.J., professor at the Gregorian, Fr Le Floch, superior of the French Seminary, Pie de Langogne of the Capuchins and the Cardinals Merry del Val and De Lai, who reckoned that by its relentless attacks on the 'persecutor Republic' and the freemason democracy the Action française was 'rendering a valuable service to the Church'.

Pius X himself made no secret of his sympathy with Action française: 'It is acting in defence of the principle of authority, in defence of order', was his reply to liberal Catholics who accused the writings of its founder, Charles Maurras, of purveying a pagan conception of the State which tended to make *raison d'État* the supreme value.[26] The pope was less sensitive than he might have been to the inconsistencies between Maurras's ideology with its basis in positivism and naturalism, and Christian principles, because Maurras's doctrine, served out piecemeal in articles on topics of current political interest, had never been the subject of a systematic exposition; and faced as he was with democracy as incarnated in the parliaments of France and Italy, which in his eyes epitomised disorder and anarchy, Pius X was on the contrary grateful to Maurras for propagating a counter-revolutionary idea of society based on the concepts of tradition and hierarchy, and for having established, at the instigation of Dom Besse, a 'chair of *Syllabus* studies'. He went even further, not hesitating to characterise the agnostic Maurras as 'the valiant defender of the Holy See and the Church',[27] scarcely noticing, it appears, that what Maurras was praising was the success of these institutions in having contained within barriers borrowed from the wisdom of ancient Rome the more explosive elements in the message of the

---

26. One of the most notable reviews is due to Father L. Laberthonnière, in *Annales de philosophie chrétienne*, June 1910.
27. But not 'of the faith', as C. Bellaigue has inadvertently written, and besides, has post-dated by a year this declaration, made 6 July 1913 (cf. A. Dansette, in *Études*, CCLXXIX (1953), 391-2).

'Hebrew Christ'. The Catholic democrats, who had long been denouncing the errors of the Action française, judged it wise after the condemnation of the Sillon to lie low; but early in 1913, with support from several bishops, they returned to the attack. At this point Maurras brought out in self-justification his book *L'Action française et la religion catholique,* and at the same time a number of prelates and other 'important people' petitioned the pope 'both orally and in writing' to block referral of the master's works to the Congregation of the Index, claiming that the allegations against them were a trap set by the demo-liberals. After a brief hesitation Pius X nevertheless decided that the Congregation should deal with the affair in full freedom, and on 26 January 1914 it condemned the works complained of, along with the fortnightly edition of the periodical *Action française* (though not the daily of the same name). The pope confirmed this sentence, which was unanimous, but decided that for the moment it should remain secret. [28] He judged that its publication would play into the hands of the modernists and the militant anti-clericals, by casting reprobation on the publicist who appeared to him one of their most effective opponents. Pius X died without having taken any further steps in the matter, and since news of the sentence had not been slow to leak out, it was easy to point the contrast between his attitude towards the democrats of the Sillon and his indulgence towards the anti-liberals of the Action française.

If it is true that the pontificate of Pius X was a painful period for liberal Catholicism, following as it did the sunny period of the days of Leo XIII and preceding the decisive breakthrough it achieved in the second quarter of the twentieth century, we should still not see the matter in too simple a light. The fact that its enemies, to all appearance more powerful than ever, did not cease to complain in accents of unfeigned alarm of its baleful presence in every domain is surely food for thought, especially since this disquiet, which the pope was ready to echo, far from being allayed by the measures taken at the time of the integrist reaction, increased with the passing years. On reflection, this at first sight paradoxical state of affairs should not surprise us. Given that liberal Catholicism represented an attitude of mind rather than a well-defined doctrine, it was natural that harsh measures, for all their momentarily damping effects, would be powerless to stifle it completely. We have only to look closer to discover that under the pontificate of Pius X liberal ferment in the Catholic world remained more plentiful and more active than our current historical writing is ready to allow. [29]

28. See the documents in *Index librorum prohibitorum,* 1930, pp. xxviii-xxxi; French translation in *Documentation Catholique,* XVII (1927), cols 129-39.
29. I draw my inspiration here from, É. Poulat, 'Un Problème: Catholicisme et Libéralisme en France sous Pie X', in *Les Catholiques libéraux au XIXe siècle'* (Actes du Colloque de Grenoble, 1971) (Grenoble 1974), 337-51. The very stimulating observations that he makes regarding France can be extended to the whole Western Church.

Take first the political scene. At the very moment when in France the rout of the *Correspondant* school seemed complete – the frustration of the attempt to celebrate the centenary of Montalembert in 1910 is but one of many indications – in Italy a gradual *rapprochement* was taking place between Catholics and moderate liberals, a *rapprochement* in which the Patto Gentiloni of 1913 was to stand out as a landmark – this was happening furthermore with the blessing of Pius X, who made no difficulties over accepting the distinction between thesis and hypothesis when it was a question of barring the road to socialism.

But much more important was the persistence and even the development of the liberal spirit in all domains that one finds among many Catholics. This was truest of all of the rising generation, who were coming more and more to the conclusion that history was irreversible and that an intelligent and loyal Catholic deserved to have something other than perpetual anathemas in his armoury. So thought a fair number of the professors at the university of Louvain, which during the early years of the century was in the full tide of its revival, who were assured of the enlightened support of Désiré Joseph Mercier, the new archbishop of Malines. In France, this opinion was shared by the several hundred priests who were responsible for the success of the ecclesiastical congresses held at Reims and Bourges; by the readers, writers and editors of the old-established *Annales de philosophie chrétienne,* now in the hands of Fr Laberthonnière and M. Blondel, of the new and flourishing *Revue du clergé française* or of the ephemeral but highly significant *Demain*, a weekly published at Lyons, or again of the host of little local journals of every type, whose capillary action cannot be ignored; by the many Catholics in the universities, who were less and less reluctant to declare themselves as such but were at the same time determined to keep pace with the times, thus P. Imbart de la Tour, A. Dufourcq, the Thureau-Dangins, father and son, the Brunhes brothers, Édouard Le Roy, J. Zeiller, P. Viollet; by the authors of the numerous books and pamphlets emanating from the publishing houses of Bloud et Gay, Gabalda and Vitte; and we should not omit from this category the bulk of the membership of the A.C.J.F., a movement born in a counter-revolutionary *milieu* but which, under the influence of its president, J. Bazire, had moved towards the liberal Catholic camp. Turning to Italy, such again was the opinion shared by the readers of Fogazzaro, by the group of young laymen connected with the Milanese journal *Il Rinnovamento* and by the young priests who openly or in secret were disciples of Murri. And it would not be difficult to continue the list. These people were not part of an organised movement, and the development of their opinions has been described as an example of 'spontaneous growth'. The personalities involved present some striking contrasts – one has only to think of the Abbés Frémont, Huvelin, Bremond and Klein. But all in their fashion bear witness that the ferment of the closing years of the nineteenth century, formed from as yet unparticularised aspirations and to a still extent largely unchannelled, was not stifled but merely restrained – and to some degree refined – by the anti-liberal reaction which set in with the pontificate of Pius X and which had in fact started – something too often forgotten – during the later years of Leo XIII. The seeds of many of the initiatives which were to come to fuller development during the two wars were sown during this difficult period.

4

PROGRESSIVE CENTRALISATION
ON ROME

THE pontificate of Gregory XVI had marked a decisive stage in the growth of the ultramontane movement. Benefiting from the Church's loss of influence in civil society and her consequent tendency towards introversion, the movement developed with an intensity that varied according to the country, under the pressure of internal forces which had first come into play during the Restoration period. A growing number of bishops and still more of priests and laymen involved in Catholic Action discovered the possible advantages of support from Rome for individual Churches which, left in isolation, were far more vulnerable to government pressures. There were also many who realised that there was something anachronistic about clinging to regional autonomies in a world where the problems were becoming increasingly supranational in character. Lastly, in France, there was the particular element represented by the lower clergy, who resented the discretionary power the Organic Articles gave to the bishops and saw great benefit in claiming protection from the Roman congregations against arbitrary episcopal decisions.

Yet in nearly every country there were pockets of resistance. This was so in England, where the Catholic community had a style of its own, authentic, but somewhat insular and individual; in Austria and Northern Italy, where traces of the Josephinist outlook persisted; in Germany; even in France, despite the irresistible pressures applied by Lamennais's disciples. Many theologians, not yet aware of theories of dogmatic development, did not understand how the pope could be recognised as having a more important position in the Church than the one he had occupied in the earliest centuries of her history. And most important of all, although people were becoming more and more convinced of the apostolic advantages of grouping Catholic energies around the Sovereign Pontiff, there were some who wondered whether it was appropriate that the concentration should take the form of a centralisation so thorough-going that the real authority of the bishops was inevitably diminished, and of a standardisation of discipline, the liturgy, and even of the forms of piety, which would make necessary the abandonment of venerable local customs and the adoption throughout the Church of a religious 'life style' analogous to that of Italy.

At Rome there had at first been some hesitation about offering too open encouragement to the ultramontane movement, which had started from below, because of fears of a head-on collision with governments, hostile in principle to greater papal intervention in the affairs of national Churches. However, around the middle of the century matters were judged sufficiently advanced for Rome to abandon this reserve. The later years of the pontificate of Gregory XVI had witnessed the beginnings of a development which gathered rapid momentum under the pontificate of Pius IX, encouraged by a phenomenon new in the Church's history, the pope's enormous popularity with the Catholic masses in all parts of the world. In every domain a noticeable and systematic effort was made by Rome after the crisis of 1848 to rally Catholic forces for the battle against 'revolutionary and anti-Christian' liberalism round a single command. The professors at the Gregorian gave fresh prominence to the classical theses concerning the pope's primacy and infallibility, as also to the thesis of the Church's 'indirect power' in civil society, and these ideas were popularised in telling fashion by the *Civiltà cattolica* and disseminated to seminaries throughout the world, carried there by students at the Gregorian whose numbers were steadily increasing as more and more national seminaries were opened in Rome. At the same time a campaign was launched against manuals still in use which had Gallican or Febronian tendencies, and several were placed on the Index. The proclamation in 1854 by Pius IX of the dogma of the Immaculate Conception can be seen as part of the same pattern since this event, which profoundly impressed the Catholic world, helped to bring the papal prerogatives to the forefront in no uncertain fashion. Intervention by nuncios in the internal affairs of national Churches became more frequent, and bishops were recalled to their lapsed duty of making regular visits *ad limina*. Priests who were loyal to the Roman ideas received all possible encouragement, some even being elevated to the prelacy to enhance their standing in face of the prejudices of less enthusiastic bishops. Anything likely to perpetuate regional differences in the life of the Church was frowned upon, ideas of summoning national councils were discouraged, Churches were exhorted to return to full observance of the canon law as taught at Rome and encouraged to bring cases of all types, even the most trivial, to the Roman curia. In the matter of episcopal appointments the pope took less and less notice of the recommendations sent in by the local higher clergy, letting himself be guided chiefly by the candidates' Roman education and their personal tractability.

In the East the new policies were too subversive of venerable traditions not to meet with active resistance,[1] but in Europe, although there were some who took them in bad part, they gained ground without too much difficulty, thanks usually to the combined influence of a bishop with strong personality, and Catholic movements among the masses and the religious press, not forgetting the highly effective role played by the Jesuits.

In Austria, where the Concordat of 1855 annulled the legislation of Joseph II and permitted the organisation of clerical education along the lines desired by the Holy See, it was the archbishop of Vienna, Cardinal Rauscher, who with the support of his colleagues Rudigier, Gasser and Fessler, all three of Tyrolean origin, saw to it that the Catholic societies were ultramontane in tendency. At the university of Vienna the Roman position was upheld by Schrader, who was a Jesuit, and by G. Phillips, the layman and canonist whose *Kirchenrecht* (seven vols, 1845-72), written in German, did much to familiarise the German-speaking countries with the more radical ultramontane positions. In Germany, where Mgr Ketteler succeeded to the dominant position held by Geissel of Cologne until his death in 1864, Mainz was more than ever the spearhead of the movement; active sympathisers grew in number from year to year and by degrees imposed their views and attitudes on the mass of the faithful, kept firmly in hand in the *Vereine*. As for France, after an attempt at reaction in 1852–3 which was rebuffed by the encyclical *Inter multiplices*, the victory of Ultramontanism was promoted by factors such as the government's benevolent neutrality at the start of the Second Empire, the success of Dom Guéranger's campaign for the restoration of the Roman liturgy, the shift towards Roman positions of the Sulpicians, the order which trained a large part of the clergy, and (to a large extent) the press campaigns of Louis Veuillot's *L'Univers*, which as a fighting organ resembled *L'Avenir* of twenty years earlier, with the difference that its success was more lasting.

The origins of the ultramontane movement can be traced to a justifiable reaction against the more debatable aspects of Gallicanism and Josephinism and more particularly to a concern to safeguard the Church's independence, in face of the regalian claims of governments, by invoking the Holy See as a support. But like all reactions it did not know where to stop, and the moderates gradually found themselves overtaken by extremists. Some of these extremists, with an irresponsibility hard to credit, were prepared to cast doubts not merely on the orthodoxy but even on the morality of ecclesiastics whose careers they thought it in the interest of their cause to

---

1. See part V, especially chapter 17, 454-7.

break. Their legitimate desire to counteract teaching which minimised the pope's prerogatives led them to propagate a simplistic ecclesiology in which, for example, the Church was presented as 'the society of the faithful governed by the pope', to the seeming neglect of the bishops' divinely appointed and equally essential role, or which declared that the teaching function of the bishops was limited to the transmission to the faithful of teaching handed down by the Holy See. With other extremists the tendency was to stretch papal infallibility to cover every kind of papal pronouncement, including those relating to the Church's involvement in politics, and to encourage forms of devotion to the pope which verged on 'idolatry of the papacy'. They would speak, for example, of the pope as being 'God's deputy among men', or as 'the Word Incarnate still dwelling among us'. These extravagant adulations, which Pius IX did too little to discourage, were given great prominence in the ultramontane press, and filled with disgust critics who failed to notice that, for all their unfortunate wording, these were at bottom the clumsy expression of popular faith. Inevitably these extravagances did much to reinforce the remaining strongholds of resistance, the chief centres of which were Munich and Paris.

In Germany, resistance to the advance of ultramontane ideas had been most stubborn in the university world. But there was always the possibility that it would remain passive in character, as was the case at Tübingen. What gave the resistance the character of an open conflict was the influence of the 'old master of Munich', the illustrious Döllinger, who had taken the lead in the movement reacting against the incursion of 'Romans' into Catholic scholarship as also into the direction of the German Church.[2] The publication of the *Syllabus* confirmed Döllinger in his double fear of a threat to Catholic academic freedom and the impending imposition of the medieval theocratic system as an article of faith, and this confirmation, combined with other events which the strength of his feelings magnified out of all proportion, led him to ask whether the ultramontane party was not in process of perverting not merely Catholic institutions but the religious ideal of Christianity. Given Döllinger's great prestige, it was natural that these apprehensions, whose sincerity none could doubt, should have been widely echoed by his many disciples. But the violence of the polemic against the 'papal system' as it developed served to antagonise the bishops, even those like Rauscher and Ketteler who were beginning to find certain aspects of Roman centralisation excessive. In Germany, in consequence, open opposition to Ultramontanism remained virtually confined to the universities.

In France, by contrast, a group with decidedly anti-ultramontane views grew up during the later years of the Second Empire inside the episcopate,

2. See below, chapter 9, 167-70.

representing the coalescence of two very different streams. One stream was made up of newly appointed bishops, reared in the traditions of moderate Gallicanism and indebted for their sees to Mgr Maret[3] and his good relations with Napoleon III. Their chief spokesman was Mgr Darboy, from 1863 archbishop of Paris, a great champion of episcopal autonomy against the 'meddlings' of the Roman congregations. To the other stream belonged the allies of Mgr Dupanloup. They had long had their differences with the Bonapartist bishops and had been formed in a very different theological climate, as is shown by their former enthusiasm for Ultramontanism as a guarantee of the independence of the Church in her dealings with the State. But with Ultramontanism now represented by men who favoured absolutism in the Church and in civil society their enthusiasm had departed, and they feared that the proclamation of the pope's infallibility in the terms desired by the neo-ultramontanes would reinforce the authority of the *Syllabus* or other comparable documents in which the views expounded on religious-political issues were incompatible with the modern outlook.

This revival of a Gallican front for which, paradoxically, the widespread success of the ultramontane movement was itself responsible, was to make for grave difficulties in the course of the ecumenical council which Pius IX, after prolonged hesitation and despite the reserves felt by one section of the curia, had decided to convoke for 8 December 1869.[4]

The intention of Pius IX in convoking the council was on the one hand to put fresh heart into the stand he had been promoting against naturalism and rationalism since the start of his pontificate, and on the other to adapt ecclesiastical law to the profound changes which had taken place in the world since the Council of Trent. But the announcement of the council made more pronounced the opposition between the two schools of thought within the Church which had been confronting one another over the past twenty years: liberal Catholics and neo-Gallicans on one side, ultramontanes and opponents of modern liberties on the other. The choice of the consultors whose task was to prepare the drafts of conciliar decrees (sixty out of the ninety-six consultors were Romans and nearly all were noted for their un-compromising ultramontane and anti-liberal views) was worrying to those who had hoped the council would provide an opportunity for bishops from the periphery to open the Church, at least in some degree, to the aspirations

3. Mgr Henri Maret (1805-84), dean of the faculty of theology at the Sorbonne and one of the few noteworthy theologians France produced in the nineteenth century. For his liberal and Gallican views, see G. Bazin, *Vie de Mgr Maret*, Paris 1891, 3 vols and R. Thijsman, in *Revue d'Histoire ecclésiastique*, LII (1957), 401-65.

4. The idea of summoning a council as a remedy for the troubles plaguing the Church had been suggested to Pius IX as early as 1849, but it was only towards the end of 1864 that he started confidential consultations on the subject with the curial cardinals and a few of the bishops. He made his intention public on 26 June 1867.

of the modern world. They thought that they detected signs of a scheme to prepare for the council in secret, removed from the arena of debate and taking into account only the viewpoint of the curia, and then to present the Fathers with ready-made proposals, to be accepted without discussion. An inopportune despatch from an anonymous French correspondent published on 6 February 1869 in the *Civiltà cattolica*, the journal run by the Roman Jesuits, seemed to confirm this prognosis by foreshadowing a definition of papal infallibility by acclamation, that is without opportunity for amendment or discussion by the Fathers. Reactions were particularly vehement in the German-speaking countries, even in circles none could suspect of systematic hostility towards Rome, and Döllinger published under the pseudonym 'Janus' an unrestrained attack on the papal primacy and Roman centralisation. Similar polemics, but couched in more moderate language, also filled the pages of the French press. With dramatic suddenness, the question of papal infallibility, which had figured scarcely at all in the council's initial programme, emerged during the course of 1869 as a burning issue.

From their own point of view, several governments were apprehensive about the decisions the council might reach regarding civil marriage, secular schooling or constitutional liberties, and they feared a move to reassert in all solemnity some of the medieval claims of the Church in relation to the civil power. The desire of certain bishops, favourably received at Rome, to make the *Syllabus* of 1864 the basis of the council's deliberations, could not but add to these apprehensions. And those inside the Church who dreaded an ultramontane triumph at the council worked as much as possible on these fears of governments, in the hope of stimulating the issue of admonitions and warnings through diplomatic channels.

The council opened on 8 December 1869 in the presence of some seven hundred bishops, a good two-thirds of those qualified to attend. They included 60 prelates from Churches of an Eastern rite, most of them natives of the Near East, and close on 200 Fathers from European countries: 121 from America (49 from the United States, 18 from Canada, 10 from Mexico, 6 from Brazil and so on), 41 from British India and the Far East but only 9 from the African missions, which were still in their infancy. It should be borne in mind, however, that many of these prelates from other parts of the world were of European origin, and that both Asia and Africa had yet to receive an indigenous bishop. In effect predominantly European, this assembly was just as predominantly Latin. True, there was a sizeable English-speaking contingent (but with the Irish element well to the fore) and some seventy-five German and Austrian prelates; but Frenchmen and Italians (most missionaries at this date tended to be of French origin) made up between them fifty-two per cent of the assembly (seventeen per cent

French, thirty-five per cent Italian), and there were in addition close on a hundred Spaniards and Latin Americans. It should also be noted that two-thirds of the consultors or experts and all the secretaries were Italian, as were the five presidents; only one important position, that of secretary general, went to a man who did not belong to the Roman curia, Fessler of Austria.

The controversies over the question of papal infallibility which had built up during 1869, and in particular an impolitic move by Mgr Dupanloup in the middle of November made the Fathers regroup, almost as soon as the council opened, along either side of an ideological line. Many Fathers, utterly out of sympathy with their generation's enthusiasm for liberalism, were far from dismayed at the prospect of a reiteration by the council of the classical doctrine regarding the relations between Church and State in an ideally governed Christian society; and many Fathers – often, but not always the same (Manning, Dechamps, Mermillod, not to mention the Americans, did not share this horror of liberal institutions) – were hoping for a formal definition of the pope's personal infallibility. Even if they did not approve of all the centralising measures of the Roman curia, it seemed to them natural to use the council as a means of cutting short the recently revived doctrinal controversies over the prerogatives specific to the Roman pontiff, controversies which as pastors, not very alive to the historical or theological issues, they considered completely sterile. In any case many of them were sustained in their convictions by extra-theological considerations, for example the veneration they felt for Pius IX or their anxiety to see the authority principle emphasised as strongly as possible in a world riddled with democratic aspirations, which in their eyes appeared a watered-down version of revolutionary anarchy and which they claimed had its prime source in Protestantism. Yet other bishops were impelled by the same mingling of doctrinal with non-theological considerations to regard such a programme as potentially disruptive of the Church's traditional constitution and an apparent threat to civil society's most legitimate aspirations. Some of the Fathers – and they were more numerous than history written with apologetic aims subsequently allowed – were still deeply attached to a conception of the Church's *magisterium* which made it impossible for the pope to pronounce on a matter of doctrine without ratification from the body of bishops. More common seems to have been anxiety to safeguard the second element in the divinely appointed structure of the hierarchy: many of the Fathers suspected that the projected definition of the pope's infallibility was part of a programme whose general tenor was in practice to nullify the episcopate. Furthermore, the way in which the question of infallibility had been presented in the leading ultramontane journals was enough to confirm in their beliefs those who were convinced that the pope was to be declared infallible in matters of faith in order to make people believe him infallible in everything else, that is to say, in concrete terms, in matters impinging to a greater or lesser degree on politics. If it indeed came to that, it was quite reasonable to expect a reaction from governments, with harmful effects on local churches. Beyond the question of immediate tactics, moreover, there was a question of principle which exercised all who believed that, politically speaking, the future lay with liberal institutions and that the Church had everything to lose by setting herself up as the champion of an autocratic authoritarianism.[5] There were also ecumenical considerations to take into account: the proposed definition would make the *rapprochement* with the Christians of the East a still more difficult undertaking, it would make for even greater aggressiveness in certain Protestant circles, and it ran the risk of provoking a new schism in German intellectual circles, where Döllinger's campaign had made a deep impression. The Fathers who took this general line were less numerous than the other group – hence the description of them as 'the minority' – but the more prominent of them were held in high esteem, either because of their theological learning or because of the eminence of their sees. Included in the minority were almost the entire episcopate of Austria-Hungary, led by Cardinal Rauscher, a noted patrologist and an ardent champion of the rights of the Holy See against Josephinist or liberal pretensions; all the great German sees; a notable number of French prelates, among them the archbishops of Paris and Lyons; several North American archbishops; the archbishop of Milan, the most heavily populated diocese in Italy; and three Eastern patriarchs.

In January the moment came for the two groups to reveal their numerical strengths. While the sessions in the *aula conciliaris* were taken up with interminable speeches on relatively non-controversial texts dealing with rationalism and its errors or with minor points of ecclesiastical discipline, a pressure group acting independently of the curia put into circulation a petition, which ended by amassing over 450 signatures, calling on the pope to place the question of infallibility on the council's agenda, a step the preparatory commission had not been prepared to take on its own account. The minority in great alarm hastened to collect signatures to a counterpetition, but although 136 names were secured, representing one-fifth of the assembly, Pius IX decided on 1 March to accede to the wish of the majority and arrange for the insertion of a passage defining papal infallibility into the schema of the dogmatic constitution on the Church, which had been distributed to the Fathers some weeks earlier.[6]

5. The extent to which the attitude of opponents, especially French opponents, of the definition of the papal infallibility was influenced by worries of a political-religious order is well brought out by J. Gadille, in the introduction to his edition of A. du Boijs, *Souvenirs du concile de Vatican*, Louvain 1968.

6. This schema was not without its merits, but even leading members of the majority

The affair of the petitions had made it necessary for the minority to organise its opposition, hitherto diffuse and scattered. Mgr Dupanloup had deluded himself in imagining that his mere appearance on the scene was enough to make him instantaneously the rallying-point for the various discontents. The true mainspring of the minority was in fact a layman and an Englishman, John Acton, who as historian shared the objections of his teacher, Döllinger, to the dogma now in preparation but who feared even more the indirect consequences of the definition for Catholicism's prospects in the future, in a society centred increasingly on the idea of liberty. It was Acton, well served by his international connections and his knowledge of languages, who from the start of the council was largely instrumental in bringing together the main leaders of the opposition, many of whom were scarcely known to one another; and it was Acton again, with his parliamentary flair, who instructed them in the possibilities of common action, suggested approaches to be tried, drew their attention to manoeuvres afoot in the opposite camp, provided them with historical dossiers to back up their objections, and all this apart from his role as intermediary between the leaders of the minority and a number of foreign governments.

For the opponents of the definition did not limit their efforts to persistent appeals to individual Fathers they hoped to win for their cause. Convinced of the harmful character for the Church of the definition in preparation and of the legitimacy of employing all available means to avert it, some of the minority thought it necessary to alert public opinion as a way of bringing external pressure to bear on the council authorities and several even tried to obtain the support of governments, in particular in Paris, since special weight would attach to an intervention from Napoleon III, whose military and diplomatic backing was essential to the continued existence of what remained of the pope's temporal power.

The agitation thus set going in the salons, in the press, in the chancelleries, was all on the fringes of the council. The assembly meanwhile continued on its prescribed course. But it soon became apparent that at the current rate of progress the chapter dealing with the pope's primacy and infallibility (chapter XI of the schema on the Church) would not come up for discussion at the earliest before the following spring. During March 1871, therefore, fresh petitions were got up, requesting that the celebrated chapter, which had all the council on tenterhooks, be taken out of turn and dealt with as soon as the assembly had finished its examination of the constitution on rationalism

regretted the flagrant imbalance between the passages devoted to the episcopate and to the papacy, and in the chapters on Church and State the viewpoint was markedly theocratic. See F. von der Horst, *Das Schema über die Kirche auf dem I. Vatikanischen Konzil,* Paderborn 1963, and C. Colombo, 'La Chiesa e la Società civile nel Concilio Vaticano I', *La Scuola cattolica,* LXXXIX (1961), 323-43.

(this constitution was formally approved on 24 April). Three out of the five presidents of the council were against the proposal, not wishing to exasperate the minority, but Pius IX, increasingly annoyed by the latter's campaign of opposition, decided in its favour. To mitigate any irregularity there might be in taking chapter XI before the rest, it was decided to expand this chapter into a little constitution on its own, devoted specifically to the pope.

The general debate on the text as a whole, which began on 13 May, in fact led straight into a discussion, growing at times quite heated, of the opportuneness of the definition. After about fifteen sessions the assembly moved on to the special debate, that is to the examination of the text in detail. The debate turned essentially on chapter four and its proposed definition of infallibility, already amended in the commission but still taking insufficient account of the role in the Church's teaching office belonging rightfully to the episcopate and exercised alongside and in conjunction with the pope. Fifty-seven speakers took the floor, to draw attention now to the theological arguments, now to the historical difficulties, as well as to the practical advantages or disadvantages of a definition at that particular moment. These often tedious debates at least provided an opportunity to tighten up certain formulations and to dispose of some objections. In the meantime, moreover, there had been a stepping up of negotiations behind the scenes. In fact, apart from the two extremes of the majority zealots and the out-and-out resisters, the great mass of the Fathers was composed fundamentally of people with moderate views, to whom this frenzied agitation was painful and distasteful. Far from wanting to see the enemy crushed, their one desire was to find a compromise formula which would prevent any dramatic disclosure to the world at large of the divisions in the assembly. Such in particular, as Mgr Maccarrone has well brought out, was the case with most of the Italians, who had played no part in the initial moves to bring infallibility on to the agenda. Thanks to their numbers, they furnished decisive support to the informal 'third party' which from the outset had been seeking, and in the end managed to make prevail, formulae which struck a balance between the ultramontane and anti-curialist extremes and left room for later amplification.

There is even reason to suppose that in the end a much larger portion of the minority would have rallied to this delicately-poised solution if Pius IX had not shown so much intransigence, for another result of Maccarrone's recent study is to reveal, on the basis of documents previously unknown, that as the discussion dragged on the pope intervened more than once on the side of the ultras. But whatever the pope's personal responsibility, it remains a fact that the eleventh-hour efforts to bring the opponents round met with no success, despite the good impression produced by the summary exposition presented by Mgr Gasser, acting as spokesman for the commission on theology, an official commentary which is still of prime importance for an understanding of the nuances of the conciliar text.[7] A last approach by the minority to Pius IX having yielded no result, some sixty bishops decided to leave Rome before the final vote to avoid having to vote *non placet* against the pope on a question concerning him directly. The other members of the minority were satisfied that the successive amendments to the text and Mgr Gasser's commentary disposed of their most fundamental objections and they decided in consequence to approve the definitive text. The latter was formally carried on 18 July with the virtually unanimous agreement of those present.

Events made it impossible to carry on with the council, which so far had completed only a minute part of its initial programme (there were still fifty-one schemas to be voted on, most of which had not even been distributed). After the Fourth Session the council's work proceeded at snail's pace, the summer heat and the outbreak of the Franco-Prussian war having caused the great majority of the Fathers to leave Rome. The subsequent annexation of the remnant of the Papal State to the kingdom of Italy forced Pius IX to conclude that the freedom of the council was no longer assured and on 20 October he declared the council adjourned *sine die*.

The end of the debates was not followed by an immediate calming of the storm, but although some of the minority bishops such as Hefele and Strossmayer hesitated for some months before submitting, in the end no one refused. Many soon came to see that to evade the issue would endanger the principle of ecclesiastical authority in the eyes of the faithful. They also had to admit on reflection that the nuances introduced into the definition, together with Mgr Gasser's commentary, met the essentials of their concern. By contrast, as the more clear-sighted had predicted, not a few intellectuals and theologians in the German-speaking countries persisted in their opposition and preferred to break with Rome, Döllinger, who had not thought to go beyond a kind of prophetic protest, invoked the lessons of history as a warning against any systematic organisation of schismatic communions. But the process had already started, in a way impossible to reverse. With the aid of bishops belonging to the Little Church of Utrecht, a new Christian confession, which took the name 'Old Catholicism', came to join the other Churches separated from Rome.[8] But it was apparent before too long that the danger was not as great as had first been feared. Most of the younger clergy were ultramontane in their sympathies, and the launching at this moment of the *Kulturkampf* gave priests and faithful an incentive not merely to close the ranks but to look more than ever to Rome, centre of the universal

---

7. Mansi, LII, cols 1204-30. See G. Thils, *L'infaillibilité pontificale* (Louvain 1969), Pt II, esp. 191-221.
8. On the Old Catholic schism and its subsequent development see V. Conzemius, *Katholizismus ohne Rom. Die Altkatholische Kirchengemeinschaft*, Zurich 1969.

Church, for the support which seemed all the more desirable in the now perilous situation of their national Church.

At the accession of Leo XIII the Holy See, meaning the pope assisted by the Roman Congregations, had become the true nerve centre of the Catholic Church in a way it had not been even in the medieval heyday of papal power. Contrary to what the Fathers of the Council had imagined, the disappearance of the pope's temporal power had been a contributory factor, as Mgr V. Martin has pointed out: 'The doctrinal exaltation of the supreme power at the Vatican Council, with the political events which followed soon after and which enhanced the respect of clergy and faithful for the person of the pope, turning it indeed into something more akin to an emotional attachment with a colouring of mystical love and admiration, helped to make the Vatican more than ever the point on which all Catholics fix their gaze.' [9] And if Leo XIII was at pains to eliminate a note of rather puerile polemic which friends of Louis Veuillot sought to inject into the pilgrimages in homage to the Holy Father, he nevertheless encouraged the development of these manifestations, as a highly effective way of exalting the papacy. Towards the end of the century, again with the aim of making the pontifical sovereignty known and respected throughout the world, he took the step of appointing a papal legate to preside at religious ceremonies of international importance (the first occasion was the Eucharistic Congress held at Jerusalem in 1893).

Certainly, from some points of view Leo XIII may seem to have retreated from positions held by Pius IX: he encouraged the practice of holding bishops' conferences, in which the previous regime had been quick to detect a whiff of Gallicanism; he took care to avoid anything in the nature of a snub to national episcopates[10] and refrained in particular, which his predecessor frequently had not, from lending Rome's support to priests in difficulty with their bishop; he even found it possible to promote to the prelacy priests and religious who had sided openly with the opposition at the time of the Vatican Council. But let there be no mistake: though there may have been proof of greater flexibility, in all its essential aspects the process of centralisation was even more pronounced.

It was at Rome that detailed plans were drawn up for the Third Plenary Council of Baltimore (1884), and if in the event no Roman prelate was sent to preside, Mgr Gibbons was appointed to act as president as the delegate of the Sovereign Pontiff. The first assembly of the South American episcopate was held in the Vatican, and the pope himself presided. Leo XIII was in any case lavish with his directives to national episcopates and he did not shrink

9. *Dictionnaire de théologie catholique*, XI, col. 1895.
10. For a highly characteristic example see R. Rémond, *Les Deux Congrès ecclésiastiques de Reims et de Bourges* (Paris 1964), 112-13.

from direct intervention in the conflicts involving religion and politics which were raging in several countries, his intention being to fix the line to be followed by faithful and clergy even at the risk of upsetting some who on the eve of 1870 had been among the most ardent proponents of Ultramontanism, such as the French legitimists or the leading lights in the German *Zentrumpartei*. One result was a substantial reinforcement of the role of the nunciatures, which received official definition in a note from the Secretary of State of 13 April 1885.[11] A Spanish journalist named Nocedal had declared, in connection with a reprimand addressed by the nuncio at Madrid to a bishop too closely involved with the Carlist camp, that 'the authority of a bishop is superior in scale and scope to that of the apostolic nuncio', whose role was alleged to be purely diplomatic. The Roman note, which was clearly to be taken as an expression of the pope's own views, had an importance beyond the Spanish case and was destined to become a *vade mecum* for all papal diplomats. By way of rejoinder it declared that the nuncios were not mere representatives accredited to governments, but the Holy See's natural channels of communication with the faithful and the bishops, and the Holy See's delegates in those affairs which the pope, whose role as universal pastor for the whole Church had been solemnly reaffirmed at the First Vatican Council, saw fit to confide to their authority. Since matters which affected the relations between Church and State were of concern to the Church as a whole, they pertained in quite special fashion to the competence of the Supreme Head of the Church, and hence to that of his delegates the nuncios, whose authority in this respect it would be wrong to claim as inferior to that of the bishops.

Less concerned than Leo XIII to guide the Churches in their political options but more concerned than he to keep every diocese of the world under a tight control which should also stimulate their religious life, Pius X underlined in his own way the developing character of the nunciatures. His policy was to replace career diplomats by bishops or former heads of a religious order and he made it their prime duty to report to the Holy See on the state of the dioceses, to supervise the teaching given in the seminaries, to visit religious houses, and so on. As part of the same pattern, the visits of bishops *ad limina,* obligatory since the time of Pius IX, now had to be made on dates strictly laid down, and the bishops were required in addition to submit regular and very detailed reports to the Consistorial Congregation, as indeed were the superiors of religious houses. The choice of superiors was increasingly controlled from Rome, and the policy inaugurated under Leo XIII[12] of encouraging the transfer of mother houses to Rome was taken up

11. Text in *A.S.S.,* XVII (1884-5), 561 ff.
12. Of particular significance was the obligation laid on the Benedictines in 1893 to establish a primate in Rome, notwithstanding the obvious reluctance of those who remained attached

with renewed vigour, being spurred to greater success by government hostility to the religious congregations in France, where many had hitherto had their headquarters. The reform of the curia, which was referred to in an earlier chapter,[13] by concentrating the government of the Church in a few hands, added particular weight to the interventions of the Roman congregations in the affairs of the Catholic world as a whole. In particular, the consistorial Congregation was from now on made responsible for handling the nominations to bishoprics and received precise instructions on how the candidates' dossiers were to be compiled, while on his side the Secretary of State found his office increasing in importance as a result of the reform. The new code of canon law was soon explicitly to affirm that by the expression 'Holy See' should be understood not just the pope but equally the Roman congregations (Canon 7). Insensibly, the tendency to attribute in practice the same authority to the Congregations as to the infallible *magisterium* had in fact begun to creep in at the end of the previous pontificate, and the growing insistence of Pius X at the time of the anti-modernist reaction, on the need for unconditional obedience not simply to the strict orders of the Sovereign Pontiff but even to expressions of his will, conveyed it might be by members of his entourage,[14] could not but confirm in their view all those people, growing more numerous since the Vatican Council, who were disposed to identify the Holy See with the Church, in fact at least if not in law.

to the tradition of the autonomous monastery.
13. See chapter 1, 19-20.
14. A telling example is to be found in the pope's allocution of 18 November 1912, quoted by É. Poulat, *Intégrisme et Catholicisme intégral* (Tournai 1969), 458.

5

THE LOCAL CHURCHES OF
CONTINENTAL EUROPE

1. FRANCE

WE HAVE already seen that the Catholic Church in France derived
considerable advantages from its alliance with the Second Empire regime.[1]
This alliance, after a cooling off in the early 1860s due in large part to
the Roman question,[2] was resumed in 1867 as the two powers were brought
together again by their common fear of the republican opposition. The fall
of the Empire in September 1870 was deeply upsetting to the Catholics,
all the more so when it was followed by displays of anti-clericalism, particularly in Paris and Lyons, more violent than any since the days of the Great
Revolution. But as happened in 1848, the very excesses of the Commune
produced a swing to the right, and the Catholic majority in the National
Assembly elected early in 1871 proved to be more solid than any in
French history. With a 'moral order' government in power the clergy's
influence in the State's main services – the army, public welfare, education
– was assured, and in 1875 Mgr Dupanloup was able to crown his success
of 1850 by securing the extension of the principle of freedom in education
to higher education, as a result of which a number of Catholic universities
came into being. This extension of Catholic education to all levels, possibly
the most important occurrence in the history of French Catholicism in
the third quarter of the century, had its ambivalent aspect. As A. Latreille
has remarked: 'It gave the Church an opportunity consistently denied her
since the Revolution. Conversely, in the long run it was bound to nourish
as nothing else the suspicion in which the Church was held', to which
we might add that it also contributed over the next few generations to the

1. Chapter 2, 28-30.
2. For details see J. Maurain, *La Politique ecclésiastique du Second Empire* (Paris 1930),
chapters 13-21 and on education J. Rohr, *Victor Duruy, ministre de Napoléon III*, Paris
1967.

emphasis on the dechristianisation of education in the State schools.

The increase in religious vocations, which Charles Pouthas sees as the characteristic feature of French Catholicism at the beginning of the Third Republic and the continued development of Catholic social organisations, which under the stimulus of the Assumptionists at last attained some degree of regional and even national co-ordination, bear witness that his outwardly imposing Church was not just a façade and that it conserved a strong fount of Christian vitality. But the smooth running of the institutional machine and the achievements of a small if noteworthy spiritual élite did not bring about any true and far-reaching rechristianisation of society. This is the conclusion to emerge more and more clearly from sociological investigations of religious history along the lines opened up by Gabriel Le Bras.

True, there were regions such as the West, the Massif Central and the Jura in which the Christian tradition remained unbroken down to the end of the century, regions where even among the men the level of religious observance remained high, sustained by an increasingly dense network of church schools. And there were dioceses which after a serious falling away under the July Monarchy had been partially and temporarily reclaimed, thanks to the systematic efforts of enterprising bishops such as Dupanloup of Orleans or Parisis of Arras who made use of religious orders which specialised in parochial missions. But this work of recovery affected chiefly the bourgeoisie of the smaller towns and the inhabitants of backsliding rural parishes in countrysides still predominantly Christian. Elsewhere desertions among the men became even more pronounced. Worst of all was the situation in the Paris basin, in the Charentes and in the south-east in Provence, where there was a further decline from the already low pre-1848 level of observance; and the nearer we come to the end of the century, the wider the spread of the bad patches. In general it can be said that from the time of the Second Empire a large part of rural France was already in a state of religious indifference, and that where religious observance continued it did so from motives that had more to do with social conformity than with profound conviction. Thus when republican governments laid greater stress on anti-clericalism, the old conformism gave way to the new and church-going went out of fashion. Around 1900 it became clear to a few more discerning priests that France was becoming a 'mission field'.[3] What made the outlook all the bleaker was that the urban proletariat, greatly swollen in numbers since the middle of the century, had grown up on the fringes of the Church,[4] feeling sociologically and psychologically out of place in the

3. The Abbé Calippe writing in *La Demócratie chrétienne* (October 1902), 370. See also the quotations given in É. Poulat, *Le 'Journal d'un prêtre d'aprés-demain'* (Tournai-Paris 1961), 39-44.

4. For figures showing the sharp decline in baptisms in Marseilles, Lyons and Paris see F.

traditional Catholic environment and disposed to regard the clergy as allied with the forces of conservatism. It is true there were exceptions. In the northern and eastern parts of the country, where the more privileged sectors of the working class were chiefly concentrated, the existence of flourishing Catholic voluntary organisations made it possible to build up a 'Christian sub-sector' which at the end of the century provided the main membership of the first Christian trade unions.

Although the Church was clearly losing ground with the masses, the 1850s and 1860s saw the return to the fold of part of the middle class, and at the start of the Third Republic the Church was in consequence quite well represented in the army, the judiciary and the higher civil service. But a fair number of those who reverted to churchgoing might more aptly be described as clericalists rather than as true Christians; and although in some quarters, especially in the provinces, religion was now accepted as an outward sign of respectability, the spread of rationalist positivism in place of romanticism in intellectual circles led to their increasing estrangement from the Christian faith[5] while the masonic lodges became definitely established as centres for the propagation of a secularist ideal, the aim of which was no longer merely to free society from the 'clerical yoke' but to liberate the human spirit from the bonds of 'religious obscurantism'.

The church authorities in France were disturbed by the situation but, with rare exceptions, seemed incapable of dealing with it in any adequate fashion. Instead of subjecting their evangelism to a searching re-examination they were content to institutionalise the methods that had proved themselves in previous decades; and to judge from the bishops' pastoral letters and from the sermons, no attempt was made to instil a critical spirit into the clergy or to initiate them into the new techniques of scientific scholarship. The seminaries, in which the standard of instruction was often at the level of one long catechism, all in Latin, turned out priests who, although unquestionably the most virtuous in Europe, were trained to minister to the *bien pensants* in their churches and works of perseverance rather than to seek contact with the indifferent masses and to meet the needs of the rising social classes. Another source of weakness was the quarrel, which became more acrimonious after 1848, between those who thought with Montalembert, Dupanloup and Maret that a more open attitude towards the modern world would win the Church the ear of the new élites, and those who retorted with

---

L. Charpin, *Pratique religieuse et formation d'une grande ville*, Paris 1964, in particular pp. 61-6, and for the Toulouse region, *Revue géographique des Pyrénées et du Sud-Ouest* (XIV), 1943, 48-78.

5. P. Duployé (*La Religion de Péguy*, Paris 1965, pp. 13-17) has described Péguy's work as in sum 'a chronicle of unbelief in France in the late nineteenth century' which 'records in full why it was that the majority of his generation ceased to be Christians'.

Louis Veuillot and a large number of the clergy that concessions to modern liberties lay at the root of the decline in religious observance. To crown it all, in the early years of the Third Republic the most prominent Catholics, with bishops well to the fore, were implicated in blundering attempts to restore a monarchical regime, at the very moment when the Republic stood out in the eyes of the new classes in society as a symbol of progress and the guarantee of their total emancipation.

The failure in 1877 of the policy Dupanloup had prescribed for the defence of religion and society led to the replacement of the 'Republic of the Dukes', which had encouraged religion as a social influence, by the 'Republic of the Republicans' which concentrated from the outset on a policy of systematic secularisation. This marks the beginning of a difficult period which, with alternations of acute conflict and relative calm, was to last until the outbreak of the First World War.

The middle-class republicans who were now in command were swayed by motives at once ideological and practical. If their legalism, linking up with the old tradition of parliamentary Gallicanism, made them want to crush the powerful church establishment for the benefit of the State as sole master, still more did their positivism, with its faith in reason and progress, impel them to hasten the supersession of the theological era by scientific civilisation. They were equally convinced that the strength of the royalist opposition was connected with the influence exerted by the clergy and in particular with their hold over the schools. After its period of quiesence under the Second Empire, the tussle between State and Church as competing agents of education was resumed with a vengeance, and because of the role played by the religious congregations in education, State education included, the offensive launched in 1880 by Jules Ferry had a double objective. The outcome was the closure (in some cases only temporary) of 261 houses for men, the Jesuits being the especial target, and the school laws: of 28 March 1882, which abolished the obligatory character or religious instruction, and of 30 October 1886, which defined the schools' neutrality in much more restrictive terms and started the exclusion of men and women religious from State schools. The secularisation of education, a key move in the secularisation of society, was accompanied by measures intended to do the same for the other great public services: the abolition of army chaplains, the removal of religious symbols from law courts and hospitals, the suppression of public prayers at the reassembly of the Chambers, the transformation of public assistance into a purely secular service, and so on.

The effect on Catholic opinion of this rapid succession of laws and decrees hostile to the Church was traumatic, all the more since they were accompanied by certain deplorable and well-publicised occurrences – the desecration of crucifixes, forced entry into religious houses and the like. But historians who concentrate on Paris have sometimes failed to notice that reactions to the religious conflict were in fact very varied, depending on the mood of the department and the behaviour, in one place obtusely sectarian, in another prudently restrained, of the local authorities. The tension was kept up by the religious press, which denounced the 'persecution' with a crudeness that today seems astonishing, and in particular by the Assumptionists, who in 1882 added to their popular weekly Le Pèlerin a daily, La Croix, which was soon printing 150,000 copies.

But even while the agitation was still at its height – politically it had little effect[6] though psychologically it helped to deepen the gulf between the 'two Frances' – more and more of the bishops became persuaded that the change was irreversible. Without disavowing their political theology, they sought ways of adapting to the situation, encouraged by the Holy See, whose weight was all on the side of conciliation. Following the precepts of Rome rather than the example of the Belgian episcopate in a similar situation, the French bishops refrained from any formal condemnation of the neutrality prescribed for the schools. With co-operation from leading Catholics they tried to palliate the effects of secularised State education by expanding the 'free' sector, which at this period attained its apogee. Between 1887 and 1898 the numbers in Catholic secondary institutions rose from 50,085 to 67,643 (in 1898 representing 41 per cent of the total as against 19 per cent in 1854) and between 1880 and 1898 ten new schools were founded in Lyons alone; between 1887 and 1898 three thousand 'free' primary schools opened their doors.

The bishops nevertheless had to recognise, with Cardinal Guibert, that in three communes of the country out of four it was impossible to establish and maintain a second school. Realising they could no longer fall back on institutions, some of the bishops began to pay more attention to properly pastoral work. In 1882 Perraud went so far as to invite fervent Christians to turn themselves into true 'lay deacons', to work for the rechristianisation of the country.

The retreat of these bishops to more realistic positions and their relative disengagement from politics occurred at a time of fresh developments in the parliamentary scene. With the failure of Boulangism in 1889 the opportunistes or moderate republicans came to power, and they regarded it as dangerous, both internally and externally, for the young Republic to make an open break with the Church. Leo XIII, whose interest in the position of the French Church was stimulated by the importance of its contribution in the mission field and by his hopes of French aid in resolving the Roman question, had for some time been convinced that the only solution for the

6. J. Gadille has called attention to a frequent contradiction between religious observance and voting Republican.

Catholics was to coalesce in a single conservative party which united all up-right people under the banner of religious liberty and enable them to press for the amendment of the anti-clerical legislation by constitutional means. He judged the moment had come for him to urge French Catholics to aban-don the increasingly chimerical idea of restoring a Christian monarchy and to place themselves squarely on the constitutional ground of the Republic. A new nuncio, Ferrata, was charged with this delicate mission; and the efforts of Jacques Piou to move closer to the left centre were given spectacular en-dorsement by the famous toast which, on the pope's formal instructions, was proposed at Algiers by Cardinal Lavigerie on 12 December 1890. [7] The pope made his intentions more precise a couple of months later in the en-cyclical *Au milieu des sollicitudes* (16 February 1892). Unfortunately, the mass of French Catholicism with all their strongly emotional reflexes, were opposed to the desire for progress manifested by many of their leaders in the hierarchy, and though for a few years hopes were raised by the 'new spirit' on the government side and by the entry on the scene of a new generation which had some leanings towards Christian democracy, the blundering con-duct of Catholics over the Dreyfus affair [8] fatally compromised the policy known as *ralliement*. As we now see more and more clearly, it was a policy almost bound to fail. Its failure was not merely due to the lack of systematic preparation of Catholic opinion, a point too much neglected by Leo XIII, or to the unduly conservative tendencies of the Catholic group responsible for promoting it in parliament. The success of the policy sup-posed above all a fundamental change in Catholic mental attitudes towards the State's secularism, matched by an inverse movement of Republican opi-nion towards a less dogmatic conception of the Revolution, two conditions which were far from being met at the dawn of the twentieth century and which were even less likely to be met at the level of relations between parish priests and teachers in State schools than at the level of relations between bishops and politicians.

The new anti-clerical offensive developed in two stages. Waldeck-Rousseau directed his first blow at the Assumptionists, particularly vulner-able because of the involvement of their press in political disputes. His next objective was to regulate the status of religious congregations as a whole (in twenty years their total membership had risen from 160,000 to close on 200,000), in a way that would make it easier for the State to control

7. The documents relating to this episode (apart from those in the Vatican Archives which are still inaccessible) have been brought together by X. de Montclos in his *Le Toast d'Alger*, Paris 1966. They make it clear that Leo XIII chose deliberately to make his views public through the archbishop of Algiers without committing the Holy See too deeply.

8. In addition to the general accounts given by Lecanuet and A. Latreille (*Histoire du catholicisme en France*, III, 489-96) see P. Sorlin, *La 'Croix' et les 'Juifs'*, Paris 1967, open to argument on some points but very enlightening.

their influence on society. But the parliamentary committees went further than he intended, and the law of 1 July 1901 was applied by his successor, Combes, with a systematic malevolence which led in the spring of 1903 to the inhuman dispersion of 30,000 religious and to the voting of a complementary law (7 July 1904) directed specifically at the Brothers of the Christian Schools, and described as 'the most outrageous measure against freedom in education ever passed in public law'. But this was still only one step more along the road towards final rupture between France and the Vatican. The citation to Rome, in contradiction of the provisions of the Organic Articles, of two bishops with republican leanings whose administration of their dioceses had attracted criticism,[9] provided Combes with legal grounds for repudiating the Concordat and in November 1904 he introduced a bill providing for a very rigorous separation of the churches from the State, which after much impassioned debate became law on 9 December 1905.[10] The original text of the law sought to give the State continued control over the Church without involving any expenditure of public funds, but the diplomacy of Briand and the fair-mindedness of Louis Méjean, the liberal Protestant who was his principal adviser, saw to it that this was replaced by a regulation more acceptable to Catholics. If the religious affairs budget (35 million gold francs) was abolished, freedom of worship was guaranteed, and if the vast patrimony of the Church, reassembled during the last century under the auspices of the Concordat (and calculated by Caillaux to be worth 411 million) was declared State property, opportunity was provided for part of it, in particular the churches, presbyteries and seminaries to be vested free of charge in 'Religious Associations' composed of elected members of the confession in question – a solution which Protestant and Jewish communities lost no time in accepting.

Pius X, who had kept silent throughout the debates on the law, once the vote had been taken issued the encyclical *Vehementer nos* (11 February 1906) in solemn condemnation of the principle of separation and followed it on 6 August 1906 with the encyclical *Gravissimo officii* forbidding the French Church to take advantage of the 'Religious Association' plan, which because it did not accord the leading role *ex officio* to the bishop was out of keeping with the Church's hierarchical constitution. Intransigents in the curia and among French Catholics were jubilant. Acting on the naive hope that the worse the Church's situation became the greater would be the revul-

---

9. As regards Mgr Geay, bishop of Laval, the study by M. Denis, *L'Église et la République en Mayenne 1896-1906*, Paris 1967, enables us to appreciate the true complexity of the situation in which the prelate, without discredit to his personal integrity, found himself involved. The case of Mgr Le Nordez, bishop of Dijon, given notoriety by A. Billy's novel *Introibo*, still awaits its historian.

10. Text in A. Coutrot and F. Dreyfus, *Les Forces religieuses dans la société française* (Collection U) (Paris 1965), 330-5.

sion against the left bloc, they had been the instigators of the pope's refusal to accept Briand's compromise device. But to most of the bishops, accustomed by Leo XIII to policies of conciliation, the rejection came as a shock, and their dismay was shared by some of the priests and the faithful, who concluded that Rome had little inkling of the true state of affairs in France and who judged it would be reasonable to give the new law a fair trial, especially since the practical disadvantages of the Concordat were increasingly apparent. Three times over (in March and September 1906 and in January 1907) a plenary assembly of the French episcopate – the first attempt in a century at concerted action – tried to find a formula for the 'Religious Association' which met both the legal requirements and those of canon law, while at Rome a number of lay notables (in particular a group of Academicians nicknamed 'the green cardinals') pointed out for the pope the dangers of a totally negative attitude. But an attempt at negotiation failed and Pius X remained unyielding. The government was in a very delicate position. Having taken the required inventory of church property, which in regions where religion still had a stronghold was met with displays of popular violence,[11] the government was supposed to proceed on the expiry of the term allowed by the law to the closing down of churches. Faced with this absurd situation and knowing that the majority of the population, if it approved the separation, would not approve of persecution, the government resigned itself to leaving the churches in the hands of the clergy, who were reduced to the position of 'occupiers without legal title', and to authorising the conduct of services without the completion of any preliminary formality. In short, Pius X's intransigence, if it encouraged the mass of Catholics to join the camp of the Action française, which held out all along for total resistance, also had the effect of constraining the government to a more liberal course than it might have adopted had not Rome stood so firm.

Still more interesting to contemplate than the legal situation is the actual situation of the French Church just after the separation. A very distinct change had set in during the decade or so preceding the separation, and those who expected the new law to be the death of the Church were surprised and disappointed to discover that the freedom the new law conferred enabled this change to bear fruit. On top of this, the climate was steadily growing more propitious. The successes of the anti-clericals in securing the secularisation of institutions necessarily robbed it of much of its sting and

11. As. J.-M. Mayeur has shown in his informative article 'Géographie de la résistance aux inventaires', *Annales, Économies, Sociétés, Civilisations*, XXI (1966), 1259-72, the agitation was in fact confined to certain regions and was not as widespread as the newspapers made out. However, if in some regions the agitation was stimulated by royalist gentry or by the young men of the Action française, in others it was a case of spontaneous outbursts by country people in defence of a religion which was part and parcel of their everyday lives.

the spiritual revival which occurred around the turn of the century brought benefit to Catholicism.

The new generation of priests had been encouraged by Leo XIII's directives to work with a clear conscience for the reconciliation of the Church with the age. While the Assumptionist press still turned out rodomontades in the style of Louis Veuillot, the younger clergy, unimpressed, went to sit at the feet of new masters, Georges Fonsegrive, for example, perceptive author of the *Lettres d'un curé de campagne* (1894) and the *Journal d'un évêque* (1896) and enterprising editor of the *Quinzaine* (1893–1907), in which he set out to 'acclimatise French Catholics to the modern environment' as created by scientific progress, the rise of democracy and the quest for social justice. During the 1890s a Pentecostal wind swept over the French Church leaving in every part of it signs of a true leaven at work, to which the two clergy congresses organised by the Abbé Lemire at Reims (1896) and at Bourges (1900) bear notable witness. [12] The great bubbling up of invention and experiment in the social, the intellectual and the pastoral sphere, where the promoters were more numerous than in the small and very active groups associated with the *abbés démocrates* and more recently with the Sillon, [13] will receive attention in later chapters.

What has to be stressed here is the way the freedom bestowed on the French Church by the law of separation worked on these movements as an extraordinary ferment of renewal. The Church was at last in a position to apply herself to the pastoral problems posed by urban civilisation. More churches were built in Paris between 1906 and 1914 than throughout the entire century under the Concordat, and this despite the confiscation of the greater part of the Church's wealth. More directly, the clergy were no longer dogged by the nagging control of officials and the laity were less grudging in their assumption of responsibility, now they no longer saw the priest living like a little lord at the State's expense. The separation speeded up the process by which French Catholicism, like society as a whole, moved out of the era of the individual into that of the group. With the *maire* and the prefect powerless to object, Catholic organisations had a free rein. Congresses and associations sprang up on all sides, following the model of Catholic Germany whose experience in this field was relayed to the French public by the young Georges Goyau. More specifically, between 1905 and 1914 the whole of France was provided with a network of diocesan and parochial

12. There is a good study by R. Rémond, *Les Deux Congrès ecclésiastiques de Reims et de Bourges*, Paris 1964, which draws attention to the significance of the project: 'As we read through the documents we come face to face with the secular clergy as a vital force and with the nature of their preoccupations. This normally silent body made its voice heard, perhaps for the first time since the Revolution, and here lies the great novelty of the enterprise' (p. viii).
13. The Sillon is treated above, chapter 3, 48-52.

associations in which an important place was reserved for the laity; and if the laymen still seemed to be there chiefly as auxiliaries of the clergy, their presence was none the less symptomatic and a pointer to future developments. The failure, except in one or two regions, of the campaign against the inventories helped to hasten on such developments in that it opened the eyes of many Catholics to the fact that, from now on, practising Catholics would form a minority in an increasingly secular France. It was vital to emerge as quickly as possible from the ghetto atmosphere in which Catholicism, encumbered by its monarchism and by the clericalism, of the *moines ligueurs,* had been enveloped between the fall of the 'Republic of the Dukes' and the Combist ministry.

Certainly not all the consequences of the separation crisis were favourable to the Church. It has already been said that the stand taken by Pius X helped to reinforce the influence on French Catholicism of the Action française. One result of this was to foster nationalistic tendencies within French Catholicism, but this was not all. Action française sympathisers who had the ear of circles in Rome made life hard for the Christian democrats, and they had a hand in whipping up witch-hunt during the anti-modernist reaction. Moreover, since the Holy See was now free to choose bishops as it wished, there was scope for Action française sympathisers to influence episcopal appointments. There is no doubting that the chosen candidates were priests of piety and zeal, but they tended by disposition to be more militant than conciliatory and they were expected by Rome to act as its mere lieutenants in a campaign to repress anything that smacked however remotely of modernism. Here was the germ of a new division in the French Catholicism, already sorely tried by the controversies aroused first by liberal Catholicism, then by *Ralliement* and most recently by Christian democracy. Again, if the Church was impoverished as a result of the separation, that is not to say it became the Church of the poor: quite the contrary, since the clergy were now more than ever dependent on landed proprietors and industrialists to subsidise the church school and to swell the proceeds of the *denier du culte,* the average Catholic being very slow to acquire the habit of making his contribution. The confiscation of the seminaries, the material difficulties of the clergy, who were reduced to living on the income from often quite meagre fees, the fall in prestige of the country *curé* contrasted with the rise in the social scale of the village schoolmaster, the abolition of the seminarist's exemption from military service, all contributed to an appreciable decline in recruitment to the priesthood: for France as a whole the number of ordinations fell from 1,518 in 1904 to 1,114 in 1909 and by 1914 it had dropped to 704, while in certain dioceses seminary admissions fell by more than 75 per cent in the space of ten years; even the more Christian parts of the country were affected. To make matters worse, the fall in recruitment coincided with a crisis in the clergy brought about by the modernist movement, which led to a fair number of defections from a none-too-numerous intellectual élite. Further, if members of religious orders were still available in reasonable numbers to assist the diocesan clergy (the men in the lawful capacity of secular priests, the women as teachers, which was allowed so long as they ceased to wear the habit of their order), recruitment was becoming very difficult since it had been necessary to remove most of the noviciates to foreign soil. Lastly, while it may be true that what has been called dechristianisation was already well under way before the separation — the Abbé Naudet's reference to France as a mission field was made as early as 1895 — the separation undoubtedly speeded it up. If the majority of Frenchmen still retained what Clémence calls 'habits of worship', at least at the most solemn moments of human existence, if the removal of the bogey of clericalism encouraged an atmosphere of toleration and in some instances — as in the Isère — was even instrumental in recovering some of religion's lost ground, the reports of the mission preachers are nevertheless almost unanimous in recording the advance of religious indifference, [14] which was so pronounced among the men that some of the missioners were now starting their sermons with the words 'My dear sisters. . .' The beginnings of a decline in observance were even apparent in regions as Christian as Brittany, which had hitherto held out, and among women and girls, in particular pupils of the *lycées* and women students. [15] In 1914 a government minister, Viviani, was to boast of what had been achieved as a result of the 'anticlerical campaign' pursued with such unremitting vigour by republican governments, declaring: 'We have extinguished in the firmament lights that will never be rekindled'.

Yet against this deterioration, which at the level of the masses became more and more marked, can be set the beginnings of a revival among the intellectual élites. The critique of scientism and materialism, broached in the

14. These impressions are borne out by the statistics. To cite an example, on which we should not be too hasty to generalise: at Limoges the number of children not baptised stood in 1899 at 2.5 per cent, by 1904 it had risen to 19.2 per cent and by 1914 to 33.9 per cent. The number of civil burials at Limoges quadrupled in ten years (G. Le Bras in *Revue d'histoire de l'Église de France*, XIX (1933), 498-9.

15. After the Separation the teaching in the State schools was subjected to more virulent attack, the impulse for which came from Rome (cf J.-M. Mayeur, *L'Abbé Lemire* (Paris-Tournai 1968), 407-8). But as Y. Hilaire has remarked in commenting on G. Cholvy's valuable *Géographie religieuse de l'Hérault*, Paris 1968: 'The "Godless school" does not appear to have exerted the dechristianising influence often claimed for it. Secularism seems to have been the line adopted only by a minority of teachers in the period 1907-14, although this was a time when the anti-religious campaign was well to the forefront. Religious observance did not lose ground in the Carrigues, which was a region with few Catholic schools. In places where Catholic schools were well established in the community they continued to hold the fort for Christianity, but where this was not so they were unable to dent the surrounding indifference or hostility. The environment at the receiving end of ideas plays a decisive role' (in *Revue d'histoire de l'Eglise de France*, LVI (1970), 179-80).

first place by J. K. Huysmans, Bourget or Brunetière, followed up by philosophers such as Boutroux or Bergson, led to the generation of Claudel, Péguy and Psichari.[16] Religion as a phenomenon was arousing new interest among the younger members of the middle class. By 1912 the group founded by P. Poyet at the École normale supérieure and known as the *'Talas'* (people who *'vont-à-la-messe'*) numbered about one third of the students. The progress of the A.C.J.F., the success of the Sillon and the launching of various other equally active movements were all signs of vitality in a Catholicism which continued to lose in quantity but to gain in quality. The groups in question were often as yet very small, but they were harbingers of a change which following the First World War would not be slow to make itself felt.

2. ITALY

The unification of Italy was brought about in 1860 by assembling under the aegis of Piedmont a number of principalities which in ecclesiastical and religious matters, as in political, administrative and cultural, possessed very varying traditions. The real unity of the Church, as of the State, was therefore yet to be accomplished, and there was a further hindrance in that a sizeable section of the higher clergy and of the clerical world in general clung for some time to the hope that the constitution of the new unitary kingdom was only provisional. It is typical, for example, that the bishops kept to their regional groupings, contact between the regions being few and far between, and that in so far as they concerned themselves with matters outside their region their interest was more with the universal Church than with national questions, on which they never took a common stand.

But if regional differences went deep – the lack of adequate local studies makes their precise nature still too little known – there were certain problems all regions had in common. First the Roman question, which for decades was to absorb most of the energies of the Italian Catholic world and so divert attention from other pressing problems, at a cost that would later prove high. Second the problem of liberalism, or to be more precise, the difficulties created for the Church by the change from the accustomed status of State religion to the regime increasingly common in Western Europe since the beginning of the century under which the Church was obliged to exercise her ministry within the framework of the common law.

This development, which the ecclesiastical authorities were to find very hard to accept, began in Piedmont some ten years before the unification and in response to pressure from a middle class which had become increasingly opposed to ecclesiastical privilege, although in matters of faith and obser-

16. See for example R. Griffiths, *The Reactionary Revolution. The Catholic Revival in French Literature, 1870-1914*, London 1966.

vance it was still much more loyal than its counterpart in France. The first measures, introduced under Massimo d'Azeglio's moderate administration and consisting in particular of the Siccardi laws (April 1850) which abolished the Church's secular jurisdiction and imposed limits on mortmain, were not at all outrageous and they had the approval, despite Rome's objection to them on principle, of a large section of Catholic opinion, driven to exasperation by the misapplied rigidity of Fransoni, archbishop of Turin. But the blunders of the Piedmont government, the ultra-conservatism of the Roman canonists, impervious to the changing spirit of the times, and the Machiavellianism of Cardinal Antonelli, who thought it clever to exploit the Fransoni affair to suit his own political game but to the long-term detriment of the religious interests at stake, all helped to embitter a situation which was further aggravated by Cavour's alliance with the anti-clerical left, whose support he needed to carry through his Italian policy. This was the background to the start on the secularisation of the schools, which was followed by the voting, after a last-minute hesitation on the part of the king, of the law of 22 May 1855 which suppressed a large number of religious houses. The creation of a united Italy had the effect of extending this legislation on the Church to the new kingdom as a whole and its speedy implementation in the former papal provinces was made all the more painful to the Vatican by the fact that Ricasoli, the Tuscan who succeeded Cavour on his death in 1861, held reforming opinions and was thought, wrongly as it happened, to be bent on making the country Protestant.

Nevertheless, despite the official rift and the growth of a Catholic opposition – more noisy than effective – there were still possible grounds for a *rapprochement*. On the Italian side there were many moderate liberals who, although determined that the Church's role in the national life should be tailored to fit the requirements of a modern State, were anxious to find a basis for understanding with Rome, whether from motives of religious conviction or traditional sentiment, or because they regarded the Church's influence over the people as a guarantee of social order. On his side Pius IX was very much alive to the religious effects of the conflict, the most serious of which was the disruption to diocesan life following the arrest of priests in dispute with the civil authorities and the expulsion of recalcitrant bishops. By 1864 no less than 108 sees out of 225 were vacant, the government having refused legal recognition to the priests nominated by Rome as replacements. The first attempt at compromise, made in 1865, was wrecked by a twofold opposition, from the anti-clerical left in Florence, the new capital, and from fanatical opponents of the new Italy in Rome. Two years later, when the parties concerned had well-founded hopes of reaching an agreement, it was in fact radicalism that carried the day, for in the positivist climate that set in around 1866 anti-clericalism became more aggressive in character, denouncing the Catholic religion as the great obstacle on the road to progress. So it came about that Ratazzi's second cabinet secured approval for the law of 15 August 1867, which was patently Jacobin in inspiration. It was to have a powerful effect on the kingdom's ecclesiastical policy for many years to come, all the more when after the occupation of Rome in 1870 certain sectarian elements obliged the king and his government, in sheer self-defence, to tighten up the provisions specifically aimed at the Church, in spite of the relatively moderate character of the Law of Guarantees of 13 May 1871 which tried to provide for the independence of the sovereign pontiff in his new situation. True, there was some relaxation during the early years of Leo XIII's pontificate, but after the failure of an attempted *rapprochement* between the Vatican and the Quirinal in 1877 a new phase of sectarianism was ushered in which Crispi's administration, the mood of which was plainly indicated by the homage paid to the memory of the victim of the Inquisition, Giordano Bruno.

But let us not exaggerate. In practice the anti-clerical legislation was often applied with flexibility and moderation. [17] This was especially the case at the local level, not merely inasmuch as the relationship made famous by Don Camillo and Peppone corresponds to an authentic Italian tradition but also because in many areas Catholics succeeded in gaining control of the organs of local government and used it to further the interests of the Church, thus substituting a new *temporalismo* for the old. Again, from the psychological angle, the Church's loss of a landed patrimony was an advantage in that it enhanced the Church's credibility in the eyes of the faithful, and the economic disadvantages were mitigated by the conservation, as it appears, of a considerable liquid capital and by contributions from wealthy Catholics who were moved by the Church's change in circumstances to dip more deeply into their pockets. Regarding the laws aimed at the religious orders, it should not be forgotten that several of the older orders, particularly in the south, had been in decay for generations past, so that the legislation nationalising monastic property merely stressed, albeit in brutal fashion, the elimination of much dead wood. In other cases the stringency of application again varied greatly according to the circumstances. The authorities were willing, for example, to turn a blind eye to convents for women religious and to orders in process of developing their missionary activities, which the government valued as a means of counteracting French influence in the Near East. The newer congregations, especially those like the Salesians which had charitable or social objectives, emerged relatively unscathed and

17. To quote just one example: Crispi brought in several measures designed to secularise welfare organisations (this the law of 17 July 1890), but for all his show of anti-clericalism, he was not bold enough to disrupt the centuries-old system of Catholic hospitals (cf. A. Cherubini, 'Per una storia dell' assistenza pubblica in Italia', *Previdenza sociale*, 1964, 549 ff. and 1203 ff.).

in some cases flowered perceptibly, thanks to the benign effects of the new climate in which liberty under the law replaced the hampering restrictions of the old jurisdictionalism. It will be obvious that the liberal attack on the religious orders inevitably had also its disadvantageous side. The closure of chapels and convents had ill effects on popular piety and in the long run the disappearance of many educational institutions run by religious had damaging long-term consequences in terms of Catholic cultural life. In the older orders many superiors, instead of thinking out what had to be done to adapt to the new situation set their sights more than ever on the past and were determined, come what may, to reconstruct the pattern as it had been before the storm. And it may be asked whether the genuine success which between 1870 and 1914 attended the efforts to restore the religious orders was not vitiated in part by its strong undercurrent of triumphalism, which the troubles of the period only helped to accentuate.

The clergy who were to set the tone in the last third of the century passed their formative years in this time of tension, in which liberalism figured as the oppressor of Christian values – and also as the tool of Freemasonry, though this was only to come true in the time of Leo XIII; [18] and it was in this same climate that Italian Catholic action was born.

Under the joint impact of a fall in vocations and of frequent apostasies the Italian clergy was rapidly diminishing in numbers (by over twenty-five per cent between 1871 and 1901), although even so the provision remained generous, with in 1881 one diocesan priest to every 270 of the faithful. But of greater significance was the change in its character. A large number of priests without parochial functions disappeared following the government's suppression of the foundations they had served and a new type of pastor was appearing, a distinct improvement on the old in respect of morals and piety and in close touch with the people, but ill-equipped for encounters with the intellectual world of the bourgeoisie. The blame for this weakness attaches to the very low standard of seminary education in which, despite warnings from one or two clear-sighted bishops, there was to be no improvement until a beginning was made, and then it was inadequate, with the reform introduced in 1907 by Pius X. Liberal tendencies and aspirations to a democratic reform of the Church, as still held by a fair number of priests surviving from the generation of 1848, were discouraged, sometimes quite ruthlessly, by an episcopate whose character was also changing. The difference in the episcopate became most marked after 1871, when Pius IX was able to fill the numerous vacant sees without reference to the government's *exequatur*. The qualities now looked for in a bishop were rigid

18. From the 1880s Freemasonry under Lemmi its Grand Master formed the spearhead of the anti-clerical movement in Italy. For some indication of its role see R. F. Esposito, *La Massoneria e l'Italia dal 1880 ai nostri giorni*, 4th edn Rome 1969.

intransigence in respect of modern ideas (a requirement which after the interlude of Leo XIII became even stiffer under Pius X), unquestioning obedience to orders from Rome, often at the expense of cultivation and independence of mind, pastoral zeal – many of the bishops came to their sees from the past parochial ministry – and piety. Outstanding personalities in this episcopate (which numbered over 250) were few, but they were not completely lacking. One has only to think of a Pecci, a Riario Sforza or an Arrigoni in the older generation, of a Bonomelli, a Scalabrini or a Capecellatro under Leo XIII, of a Ferrari or a Maffi in the early years of the new century. It is unfortunate that with a few exceptions the pastoral letters of the period are so much coloured by the circumstances in which they were written, which gives them an air of being exclusively on the defensive in face of the epidemic of official secularism.

This same touchy and defensive spirit prevailed in the 'Catholic movement' which from 1894 took shape round the Opera dei Congressi under its president Giambattista Paganuzzi.[19] Catholics who accepted the *faits accomplis* and were ready to emulate the Belgian Catholics in attempting to fight the Church's battles from inside the framework of the liberal State – known earlier as the *conciliatoristi* but later more commonly as the *transigenti* and in any case a far from homogeneous group – had believed at the accession of Leo XIII that the order *Ne eletti ne elettori,* which had kept Italian Catholics out of active politics for close on twenty years, was about to be rescinded. They were quickly disillusioned, and the growing stress on anti-clericalism in official circles during the 1880s finally put paid to their chances. Save in the south of the country, the forefront of the stage was to be occupied for many years to come by the *intransigenti,* who had been galvanised into action by the *Syllabus* and its anathemas against liberal society and who were fortified in their opposition by the frequent encouragement of Cardinal Rampolla. Refusing to accept the new state of affairs as permanent, the *intransigenti* aimed to create outside the framework of existing political institutions a large-scale militant movement whose first objective, as the indispensable preliminary to the rectification of the political situation, would be to make the Christian spirit once more paramount in society. At bottom this programme rested on a mistaken analysis of the relative strengths of the various forces currently confronting one another in Italian society, just as it ignored the ineluctable trend which had set in during the past century towards the secularisation of institutions. There is no denying that the *intransigenti* clung to an outdated political theology, not to mention their mediocrity in other cultural spheres, which was in large part responsible for the isolation of Italian Catholicism which persisted well into

19. For further details see chapter 7, 139-43, and chapter 8, 159-63.

the twentieth century. But it would be wrong to regard them as belated legitimists or simple reactionaries. Thanks to the new studies initiated by F. Fonzi we can now appreciate their merits,[20] which the liberal school of historians totally ignores. First let us mention their personal qualities of dedication and self-sacrifice in what they believed to be God's cause: for before any political inspiration 'Catholic action' was a religious movement, which bore witness that, despite the superficial character of the religion of many Italians and despite the scepticism and indifference so widespread in the intellectual world, there was still, and especially in the north, a substantial reserve of Christian vitality, sustained in particular by the many confraternities and tertiary orders which flourished throughout this period. But there is still more on the credit side: the leaders' instinct for organisation at the local level, which makes them pioneers in Italy in this field, the awareness they had of the importance of bodies which stood midway between the individual and the centralising State, their interest in the popular press; and above all the concern of one wing of the movement that the 'iron law' of liberal economics should be opposed by a Catholic view of society which paid attention to moral values and to the rights of individuals, and the corresponding concern that the Church should not be seen by the toiling masses to be compromised with the ruling capitalist bourgeoisie. Special mention must be made in this connection of Don David Albertario, the clerical journalist whose polemical flights recall the excesses of Louis Veuillot but who succeeded in persuading Italian Catholics to descend from their apocalyptical 'wait and see' perch of the Pius IX era and to organise for action, and who awakened them to the problems posed by the condition of the peasantry.

But the revival of such issues, just at the time when the wounds opened by the Risorgimento were healing and the Roman question was receding into the background, was itself enough to sow the seeds of a serious crisis which was to split the movement into two contrary wings. When in May 1898 the prime minister Rudini ordered the closing down of many of the committees affiliated to the Opera dei Congressi, aiming with one blow at both the Catholic and the socialist movement, the conservative element felt vindicated in its doubts regarding the progressive social tendencies which, under pressure from a group of younger members, had developed in the move-

20. At the risk however of sometimes neglecting the merits of the *transigenti*, for example their concern not to lose contact with modern culture or with unbelievers, and their work for students. The contrast at every point – theological and philosophical, aesthetic and literary, political, social, attitude towards the temporal power, attitude towards the Jesuits – between the *transigenti*, continuators of the liberal Catholic tradition of 1848 and the *intransigenti*, remotely descended from the promoters of the traditionalist Catholic revival under the Restoration, is well brought out by F. Fonzi: see (among other authorities) his remarks in *Convivium* (1949), 958-60.

ment in recent years. Alarmed at the prospect of being bracketed with socialists, the great majority of Catholics and above all of the clergy were prepared to make overtures to the moderate liberals, who by contrast with the socialists now stood out as champions of the established order. This marked the first step in the direction of the tacit conciliation which took place a decade or so later, following the gradual merging of this stream with that of the former *transigenti,* the two being brought together by their common concern for defending the social order.

But this shift to the right provoked the socially more progressive wing of the Catholic movement, under its leader Don Romolo Murri, to forge ahead on its own, in the name of the logical demands of Christian democracy. Brushing aside the restraints of the old guard and the *non expedit* they urged an immediate descent into the political arena, adopting a position on the autonomy of the Christian in temporal matters and on the separation between the domain of the Church and the domain of the State no different from that of the *transigenti,* but differing from Catholic liberals of the old type in claiming to base their rejection of the confessional State not on any hypothesis of what was expedient in the circumstances but on the inherent demands of the Christian faith.[21] The warnings Leo XIII issued on the subject of Murri's Lega democratica nazionale, followed by Pius X's increasingly patent repudiation of it, brought about the rapid dwindling of this wing into a small minority group. The great majority of young Christian democrats followed the lead of the brilliant Milanese lawyer Filippo Meda and made their way back to the main body of the Catholic forces, which on the eve of the First World War, with the blessing of Pius X, were about to re-enter political life under the banner of the *clerico-moderatismo* which characterised the Giolitti era.

3. GERMANY

The political fragmentation of Germany down to 1870 meant that, as in Italy down to 1860, the separate States retained their individual characteristics, in church affairs as in others,[22] but the general pattern of development was nevertheless everywhere much the same.

After the decade or so of fair weather for Catholics following the crisis of 1848, during the 1860s the climate started to change. A resurgence of confessional self-awareness, promoted in educated circles by converts such as K. Jarcke and G. Phillips and in popular circles by the missions preached by the Jesuits, gave Protestants the impression of a successful offensive under way (in fact the proportion between the two confessions remained stable, the

---

21. For R. Murri and political modernism in Italy see pp. 161-2, 196, 202-3.
22. For examples of the petty harassment of Catholics in some of the smaller German principalities see G. Goyau, *L'Allemagne religieuse,* IV, 33-6.

percentage of Catholics in the population being 35.4 in 1822, 34.2 in 1858 and 36.2 in 1871, that is after the annexation of Alsace-Lorraine). The State governments were made less favourably disposed by the strengthening of Roman influence in Germany, to which the opponents of Ultramontanism gave strident publicity, and by the demands for the Church's freedom being voiced in States where the position was less favourable than in Prussia.

Tension was increased by the growing trend in favour of a united Germany centred on Prussia rather than Austria and from which Austria would be excluded, for among the most ardent supporters of Prussia's ambitions were the liberals of the *Nationalverein* in whose eyes Austria stood condemned, especially since the concordat of 1855, as a clerical and feudal stronghold of Ultramontanism. The news of Austria's defeat at Sadowa was therefore felt by Catholics as a bitter blow, in spite of all that Ketteler, in his pamphlet *Deutschland nach dem Krieg von 1866,* could do to urge them to accept the inevitable with no private reservations and to demonstrate that 'in love for the German fatherland they were second to none' while also insisting on Prussia's dissociation from any movement which interpreted her 'German vocation' in an anti-Catholic sense. But these realistic views wounded too many susceptibilities to win immediate acceptance, and the dissatisfaction voiced by many Catholics appeared to their enemies sufficient justification for an accentuation of anti-clerical policies, in particular in relation to the schools.

The threat first became concrete after 1866 in the Grand Duchy of Baden where Jolly, the minister, with covert encouragement from Bismarck and invoking the 'logic of secularism' declared his intention of 'honouring afresh and under new forms the fundamental conception of Josephinism', that is under forms adapted to the modern parliamentary system. The Church's perilous situation had the effect of crystallising certain trends which had been developing in German Catholicism since the middle of the century: the movement towards closer understanding between the bishops of the different German States, leading in 1867 to the decision, on Ketteler's suggestion, to meet in annual conference at Fulda; the more militant mustering of Catholic forces on the occasion of the *Katholikentage*; the expansion of the Church's social undertakings in an effort to cement the loyalty of the masses; and greater stress on activity in the political arena.

The Catholics of Prussia, with Ketteler's approval, concluded that the best way to defend their threatened liberties was by a resumption, with refinements, of the tactics of the 1850s and the formation of a political party which would not to be exclusively confessional but open to all who were concerned to defend Christian traditions against the threat of secularisation. This *Zentrumpartei,* well supported by its journal the *Germania,* came out with a relatively advanced social programme and was led by some notable personalities, among them Ludwig Windthorst, as a tactician second to none. The effect was to convince Bismarck, who was much concerned to consolidate the moral unity of the new empire, that he was witnessing the formation of a State within a State, indebted for its support to the masses 'made fanatical by the Church' and placing the interests of Catholicism above those of Germany, a conviction made all the stronger by his existing grievances over the support given by the clergy of the eastern provinces to the Poles in resisting Germanisation and by his awareness that in the Rhineland and Bavaria yearnings for Austria were still strong. He tried to bring about the dissolution of the new party by exerting pressure on the church authorities and, to show them he meant business, having thrown his weight behind the Old Catholics, he identified himself with the *Nationalverein* programme directed against confessional schools and the religious congregations, which were accused of encouraging Catholic dependence on 'a power alien to the German nation'. Next, having broken off diplomatic relations with the Vatican, he instructed Falk, the *Kultusminister,* to draft a set of laws subjecting every department of church life (clerical education, appointment and dismissal of parish clergy, excommunication of the faithful and so on) to the control of the State, measures deemed to be necessary in defence of modern civilisation (the expression *Kulturkampf* was first employed on 17 January 1873 by the liberal deputy Ludwig Virchow). These laws, the *Maigesetze,* were voted through between 11 and 14 May 1873, amendment having been made to the articles of the 1850 constitution which gave the churches complete liberty in the conduct of their affairs, and despite the reservations expressed by many conservatives they received reinforcement over the next few years from measures providing for exceptions or suppressions (notably the law of 31 May 1875 expelling from Prussia all religious congregations with the exception of those caring for the sick).

Since the different States which made up the new German *Reich* had been left with control of ecclesiastical policy within their own territories, the Prussian example was not always slavishly followed. In Württemberg, thanks to Mgr Hefele's conciliatory attitude, the effect was minimal and the same applied to Oldenburg, in this instance thanks to the broad-mindedness of the Grand Duke. In Bavaria the minister in charge of religious affairs was Lutz, who had been among the instigators of the *Kulturkampf* – he was behind the voting on 16 January 1871 of an imperial law restricting freedom to preach, the so-called pulpit clause – but in face of growing Catholic opposition, stirred up by Prussian example, he became more cautious, as befitted one who in reality was more a Josephinist of the Montgelas type than a true enemy of the Church. But Saxony, Hessen and above all Baden committed themselves wholeheartedly to the Bismarck line.

After a moment's hesitation the bishops, spurred on by the dynamic Ketteler, made plain their refusal to submit to the control the State claimed to impose; and as though to confound the pessimists who had assumed that priests with doubts over Ultramontanism were lacking in Catholic solidarity, the lower clergy came out almost to a man in support of the bishops' resistance, despite the threat of increasingly heavy penalties – fines, imprisonment, expulsion.[23] The year 1876 found all the sees in Prussia vacant, and at one time nearly a quarter of the parishes were without a pastor. But although Bismarck, who assumed personal responsibility for this trial of strength, had declared right at the start that he would never go to Canossa, the episcopate had no intention of surrendering, being sustained by the virtually unanimous support of the Catholic masses who had reacted with a vigour which Bismarck, with his total lack of sensitivity to popular forces, had failed to foresee. Peasants in the Rhineland, in Westphalia, in East Prussia, in south Germany, artisans and unskilled workers in the industrial towns of the west and of Silesia – the broad sociological base of German Catholicism at this period – came out in spontaneous defiance of the liberal champions of bourgeois capitalism. Furthermore, having for some twenty years enjoyed the benefit of active working men's associations which kept them in close touch with the Church, and being kept up to the minute by a rapidly developing Catholic press,[24] the Catholic masses had a very clear idea of the religious issues at stake. So it came about that the Centre party, which Bismarck had aimed to destroy, found itself making spectacular gains at every fresh election. Mention should also be made of a fact too often forgotten but to which G. Wolf has recently drawn attention, namely that Falk's programme of systematic secularisation encountered increasing opposition from Protestant circles, taking their lead from Rogel, the court chaplain.

Bismarck, who did not subscribe to the ideology of the liberals' campaign but had merely used it to further his political ends, was too much of a realist not to bow before the facts, especially in view of the new threat presented by the steady advance of socialism. The accession early in 1878 of a pope of more conciliatory outlook than Pius IX, and from whom Bismarck hoped for support over the Polish question, prepared the way for a compromise.

23. Studies of the *Kulturkampf* have tended to concentrate on the parliamentary and diplomatic aspects rather than on its impact in everyday life. There is need for more studies in the nature of G. Bettner's *Die Ost- und Westpreussischen Verwaltungsbehörden im Kulturkampf*, Heidelberg 1958, which shows that in the Polish parts of East Prussia, where the population was predominantly Catholic, the local authorities were often able to avoid the injection of bitterness into the conflict, which in Westphalia and the Rhineland by contrast tended to be particularly venomous.

24. Between 1871 and 1881 the number of Catholic dailies increased from 126 to 221; cf. H. J. Reiber, *Die Katholische deutsche Tagepresse unter dem Einfluss des Kulturkampfs*, Gorlitz 1936.

But the going was not easy. Bismarck, for his part, was prepared to surrender only the minimum of the State's claims, and the Centre party, flushed with success, refused to make certain concessions which the Vatican and several bishops were prepared to accept, as the price of bringing to an end the disruption of church life in Germany and the tendencies to indiscipline and demagogy which were developing among the younger clergy. The secret negotiations initiated through the nuncios at Munich and Vienna having produced no result, at the end of two years Bismarck resolved on unilateral action. A first and provisional law of normalisation was voted on 14 July 1880 and with its passage, although there had been no formal declaration of an armistice, the *Kulturkampf* lost much of its sting. Two more *Novelle* of 31 May 1882 and 11 July 1883 pointed still more clearly towards *détente,* since they left the authorities free to refrain from the application of the most objectionable provisions of the *Maigesetze,* although the legislation itself remained unaltered. In the meantime, however, negotiations with the Vatican had been resumed, following the re-establishment of diplomatic relations in April 1882. On the Roman side, because of the absence through illness of the Secretary of State, Jacobini, the negotiations were increasingly dominated by Mgr Galimberti, a great admirer of Germany. The dominating influence on the German side proved to be the new bishop of Fulda, Mgr Kopp, who found the intransigence of the Centre and of some of his fellow bishops excessive. Another further important factor was the self-delusion of Leo XIII, who persuaded himself that a show of reasonableness over the resolution of the *Kulturkampf* would win him Germany's support over the Roman question. The outcome was the Peace Laws (*Friedengesetze*) of 21 May 1886 and 27 April 1887 which finally abolished the *Kulturexamen* for future priests, removed the possibility of appeal from episcopal decisions to civil tribunals, freed the exercise of the priestly office from all State control and allowed the religious congregations to reorganise (with the exception of the Jesuits, who were to remain excluded from Germany until 1917). In return, while the pope remained adamant on the issue of clerical education, and although he was to continue his protests to the Bavarian government over the exercise of the royal *placet* and its other similarly regalian measures,[25] there was one point in the legislation of 1873 on which, despite objections from the Centre party, he gave way: the obligation placed on the bishops to declare every appointment, and the right of the government to object in individual cases.

25. See in particular the encyclical *Officio sanctissimo* of 22 December 1887, addressed to the Bavarian bishops, and on subsequent developments, E. Soderini, *Il pontificato di Leone XIII*, III, 498-519. Under Pius X the Vatican was still receiving complaints that the Bavarian episcopate was too much a 'court episcopate'. This no doubt explains why the repeated efforts of the Munich government to secure the nomination of a Bavarian cardinal met with no success until 1914 (cf H. Philippi, *Historisches Jahrbuch*, LXXX, 1961, 185-217).

Windthorst had been excluded from the negotiations between Rome and Berlin and was disappointed with a solution which, as one compromise followed another, made it impossible for the Centre to realise its goal of returning to the situation of 1870. But the government's concessions were substantial, since for the first time the chancellor had accepted a revision of the law which was not left to the good will of the authorities to implement. Besides, the fears of the Centre proved groundless since the government's right of objection was very rarely invoked and furthermore, thanks partly to the persistent efforts of the Catholic deputies and partly to William II's anxiety to keep the Vatican from moving over into the Franco-Russian camp,[26] the next few years saw the recovery of some of the ground which under the compromise of 1887 had been left to the enemy. The one exception was the eastern provinces where, down to the fall of the Empire, the State's arbitrary control continued, exercised against a body of clergy which, from the bishop of Posen down, persisted in its passionate and systematic defence of Polish rights to resist Germanisation.

The Catholic victory, if not complete, was undeniable, all the more so in view of the fact that the fifteen-year long conflict had served to galvanise the Catholics into action, to consolidate their internal unity and to cement, especially in the south, their bonds with Rome. At the conclusion of a struggle which had had its grim moments, even if the situation was never as desperate as Catholic historians of the traditional school have sometimes made out, a *modus vivendi* was reached which, because in essentials it met the requirements of both parties, was to endure for close on half a century.

From that moment, that is from the end of the century, although liberal and nationalist hostility towards 'political Catholicism' was not completely extinguished and was indeed to flare up again from time to time, as over the unfortunate affair of Pius X's 'Borromeo Encyclical' in 1910,[27] Catholics started to feel at home in the prosperous empire of William II, so much so that it has been asked whether their too profound immersion in the established social and national order was not responsible for the reluctance many were to feel in giving wholehearted adherence after 1918 to the democratic Weimar Republic. It was difficult, in any case, for Catholics not to succumb to the materialistic outlook of the newly prosperous bourgeoisie, for although top posts in the civil service and in big business were still largely

26. William II's position with regard to Catholicism was complex. He distrusted the Centre party, which was too democratic in its orientation for his taste, but he admired Catholicism as a power structure, declaring to Cardinal Rampolla in 1903: 'There are now only two forces on earth, the army and the papacy' (Archives du Ministère des Affaires étrangères de Bruxelles, *Saint-Siège*, XXIII, 5 mai 1903).

27. Published on the occasion of the tricentenary of St Charles Borromeo, hero of the Counter-Reformation, the encyclical expressed itself on the subject of Luther and Protestantism in terms the reverse of ecumenical.

the preserves of liberals and Protestants, the proportion of Catholics in the new middle-class professions and above all in the tertiary sector of the economy was steadily growing.[28] If in the years just before the war there were young Catholics who joined 'back to nature' movements such as the Jugendbewegung and the Wandervogel in protest against the artificiality of urban life, there were by contrast a great many Catholics who were happy to integrate with the bourgeois culture of their day, almost without noticing that the urban proletariat, one of the forces behind the Catholic movement of the preceding generation, was becoming increasingly detached from the Church. 'Twenty years ago Cologne was the German Rome; today not more than twenty per cent of the workers so much as make their Easter duty,' an outside observer noted in 1912.[29] These developments were reflected in the Centre party, which under the leadership of a new generation of politicians who were more chary of embracing social reform, men such as Peter Spahn and Georg von Hertling, was drawing away from the socialists. If we omit the brief interlude of 1907-9, when Chancellor Bülow, infuriated by the Centre's criticisms of aspects of his colonial policy, relegated it to the opposition, the party was taking an increasing share in the responsibilities of government.

The Catholics nevertheless had their troubles. The ending of the religious struggle had been followed by a crisis of re-orientation, one effect of which was to encourage centrifugal tendencies within the body of Catholicism, divergence over political, economic and social issues becoming all the more likely once the necessity for presenting a front against a common enemy was removed and the distinction between conservatives and progressives was clearer cut. In addition, the Centre party was faced with a difficult choice. It could remain as circumstances had made it, a party based on the defence of Catholic freedoms, or it could expand to transform itself into a political party with no confessional ties. This was the solution advocated in 1906 by a Catholic deputy, Julius Bachem, in a challenging article entitled 'we must come out of our tower', sparking off in so doing a heated controversy which became entangled with the debates on interconfessionalism currently raging in the trade union movements.[30] Despite Pius X's undisguised preference for the 'confessional' line, which had vigorous champions in Cardinal Kopp and Mgr Korum, bishop of Trier, both of whom were eager to see the Centre party more submissive to episcopal directives, it was the other view, whose main champions were to be found in Cologne and

28. The changes in the social stratification of German Catholicism between 1850 and 1914 are the subject of an interesting chapter in C. Bauer's *Deutscher Katholizismus. Entwicklungslinien und Profile* (Frankfurt 1964), 28-53.
29. Fr. Poels quoted in *Journal de Bruxelles*, 29 February 1912.
30. For more details on this conflict between what were known as the *'Kölner'* and the *'Berliner'* schools, see chapter 8, 155-6.

München-Gladbach, that eventually prevailed. But this *Zentrumstreit*,[31] which was at its height in 1912, weakened the position of the Catholics as it at the same time falsified the position of the pope who left the chancellor as arbiter between the major Catholic party and himself instead of keeping Leo XIII's position as arbiter between the government and the Centre party.

There was yet worse. If internal dissensions did not prevent the Catholic group from becoming an increasingly decisive factor in the nation's political and social affairs, so vital indeed that organisations like the influential Volksverein für Katholische Deutschland[32] came under sporadic attack from Protestants of the Evangelical League, the cultural state of German Catholicism around the year 1900 was far less satisfactory. The phenomenon is not be explained simply by the fact that for a long time Catholics had belonged to the depressed classes in the community, for the state of affairs was worse than in the middle of the century, since when the social level of Catholics had tended to rise. Also to be taken into account, apart from the official bias in favour of Protestants each time a university chair or other important position had to be filled, are the effects of the Old Catholic schism in draining off much talent from intellectual circles and, more important still, the retreat of the Catholics as a group into their own shell, in a mood of reaction against modern culture induced by the resistance to the *Kulturkampf.* This was the weighty debit side of a struggle which from so many other points of view had proved beneficial, and it would be many decades before the *Görresgesellschaft,* a society founded in 1877 to encourage young Catholic intellectuals, was able to work it off. The isolated voices raised in protest – they have been grouped together under the misleading label *Reformkatholizismus*[33] – did nothing to dent the prevailing conformism, and the almost unanimous outcry from Germany's Catholic press against A. Ehrhard's penetrating and courageous work on 'Catholicism and the twentieth century' is sadly typical. To be sure, Catholic historical scholarship fared quite well, with representatives as distinguished as Ludwig Pastor (though to find a chair he had to go to Austria), F. X. Kraus, A.

31. See E. Deuerlein, 'Verlauf und Ergebnis des "Zentrumstreites" ', *Stimmen der Zeit,* CLVI, 1955, pp. 103-26. The principal documents are printed in L. Bergstrasser, *Der politische Katholizismus* (Munich 1923), II, 332-87.
32. Founded October 1890 on the initiative of Windthorst, by the Abbé Hitze (one of the most progressive leaders of the German Catholic social movement) and by F. Brandt, who became its first president, and much indebted to the dynamism of A. Pieper, its general secretary. Its aim was to unite all the forces of Catholicism in Germany (workers, peasants, middle classes, intellectuals) in building up a democratic society based on Christian principles. The headquarters at München-Gladbach housed one of the largest collections of books dealing with the social sciences. Activities included the organisation of public meetings and the production of propaganda leaflets. In 1914 membership of the Volksverein stood at over 850,000. Cf. K. H. Brüls, *Geschichte des Volksvereins,* I, *1890-1914,* Münster 1960.
33. See chapter 10, 199.

Ehrhard, H. Finke, S. Merkle and M. Grabmann, and in the field of social theory there were worthwhile contributions from two Jesuits, V. Cathrein and H. Pesch, whose writings commanded an international audience; but contributors in other fields usually stuck to the writing of highly conventional textbooks, conceived from an apologetic standpoint, and rather than attempt creative work they preferred to dwell on the Church's services to culture in the past. Literary criticism became the monopoly of the clergy who, through the influential *Borromäusverein,* slanted output towards the needs of parochial libraries. There can be no doubt that Catholic literature suffered under this regime, in which moralising considerations led all too often to a neglect of the aesthetic.

Around the turn of the century, however, there were signs of a change. The most notable was the foundation by K. Muth in 1903 of the review *Hochland,* which soon became a rallying-point for young Catholics who saw the need to emerge from their isolation and to break right away from the baroque and romantic tradition in order to take up a positive attitude towards twentieth-century culture. But the bitter controversy (*Literaturstreit*) which subsequently raged round this brave *avant-garde,* unleashed by the traditionalists who took their stand with the Austrian R. von Kralik and his review *Der Gral* (1906 on), shows that on the eve of the First World War the battle was still far from won.

4. AUSTRIA

In Austria, as in Germany, the year 1848 marked the beginnings of a revival. It started with the liberal and reforming group centred on Günther,[34] who looked for the regeneration of the Church through the renewal of Christian vitality from within rather than from external support, but its realisation took a much more traditional form, being the work of Cardinal J. O. Rauscher (1797-1875), from 1853 archbishop of Vienna and the principal negotiator of the 1855 Concordat. This agreement, which satisfied the chief requirements of the ultramontanes, took too little account of the principles underlying the modern State to be lasting, but it at least had the advantage of handing back to the Austrian Church a real measure of autonomy in relation to the government bureaucracy, still imbued with Josephinism.

Clear-headed and energetic, Rauscher was for twenty years the undisputed leader of the Austrian episcopate. More concerned to promote a Christian character in institutions than to foster pastoral initiatives, he was lukewarm in his encouragement of the Catholic association movement which was making good progress in Germany, and sought in any event to preserve it from lay control. He devoted himself in particular to the

34. See W. Simons, 'Vienna's first Catholic political movement: the Güntherians, 1848-1857', *Catholic Historical Review,* LV (1969), 173-94, 377-93, 610-26.

reorganisation of public education, including the universities, in a way that gave the Church control. But despite the efforts of apostolically-minded priests more sensitive to the aspirations of their contemporaries, of whom J. E. Veith (1787-1870) is an outstanding example, and not forgetting the influence in high society of the Jesuits (readmitted to the country in 1852) and the parochial missions preached by the Redemptorists, the Catholicism of the Habsburg Empire remained a superficial affair; and this despite an external grandeur which was at its most ostentatious in Hungary, where in many respects the Church was to retain down to 1918 the trappings of the *ancien régime*. Understandably, there was little reaction from the mass of Catholics – save in the Tyrol, where the spirit of the Enlightenment had impinged scarcely at all on the tradition set by the Counter Reformation – when in 1867 the liberal government which came to power after Sadowa introduced its programme in respect of civil marriage and the secularisation of the schools, or when after the vote on the papal infallibility the government made its unilateral repudiation of the Concordat, or again in 1874 when it passed three laws regulating the Austrian Church in a manner similar to that envisaged in Bismarck's legislation. These laws were admittedly less radical in their stipulations than their German counterparts, and in application they proved milder still, following personal interventions from the Emperor Franz Joseph, who moreover used his veto to kill a fourth law, aimed at the suppression of the monasteries. What has been described as the Hungarian *Kulturkampf* was in reality less a tightening of the State's control than the implementation of a liberal Catholic programme, aimed in particular at promoting religious toleration and facilitating mixed marriages [35] but without detracting from the more than comfortable economic situation of the clergy (around one million hectares of landed property, diocesan revenues estimated at about nine million gold francs . . .). The devotion of the bishops to the monarchy made them anxious to avoid weakening the regime by internal discords. This factor, combined with the bishops' long tradition of taking for granted that the Church acted in close alliance with the State, helped to avert religious strife in the lands of the Dual Monarchy.

The decades following the return of the conservatives to power in 1879 were in many ways a golden age for Austrian Catholicism. They witnessed the expansion of the religious congregations and of Catholic charitable in-

---

35. It should be noted that the confessional position was more complicated in the Hungarian part of the Dual Monarchy than in the Austrian (each enjoyed a wide measure of autonomy under the terms of the compromise of 1867): around 1895 the Austrian part contained some 22,000,000 Catholics against 1,500,000 Protestants; the Hungarian part contained only 11,000,000 Catholics (of whom about 2,000,000 were of an oriental rite) against 3,700,000 Protestants, socially and culturally extremely influential, 2,750,000 Orthodox and 800,000 Jews. Cf. J. G. Strossmayer, *Beiträge zur Konfessionellen Situation Oesterreich-Ungarns in ausgehenden XIX. Jht.*, Salzburg 1962.

stitutions, the introduction in 1890, on the initiative of H. Abel, the 'apostle of Vienna',[36] of Marial congregations for adults, the organisation of parochial missions and efforts to adapt pastoral work in the big cities to the changing situation, a greater emphasis on the confessional character of the primary schools, the strengthening of the Catholic press (much to be desired in an officially Catholic country where all the leading newspapers were in anti-clerical hands), and the foundation of moderately active social organisations, some of which, owing their inspiration to Baron Vogelsang, were paternalistic in tone, while others were more democratic in style, being directed by K. Lueger, founder of the new Christian social party. In the years just before the First World War there was a feeling in Europe, and more particularly in the Vatican, that Austria, the bastion of the Roman Church on the frontier with the Orthodox world, was destined to succeed France as the major Catholic power, a prediction which gained in credibility with the participation of Franz Joseph and his court in the international Eucharistic Congress held in Vienna in 1912.

But if the façade was brilliant, there was no dearth of problems lurking behind. Tension, often acute, between the higher clergy and the Christian social party, which in its early days had received discreet backing from the nunciature and whose policies were now advocated, often in a way that smacked of demagogy, by a section of the younger clergy; the spread of an irreligious socialism in working-class circles and the emergence of anti-clerical leanings among the peasants of Galicia, who had their eye on the Church's vast estates and who accused the higher clergy of betraying their national cause; intensification of freemason activity and the growing hold of the liberal outlook on the mind of the bourgeoisie; the rise of the *Los-von-Rom* movement[37] with its denunciation of Catholicism as a *'deutschfeindliche Macht'*, and the parallel revival in Bohemia of the Hussite movement; nationalist stirrings among the clergy of the Slav parts of the Empire and in Transylvania.[38] To all this must be added the character of the Austro-Hungarian episcopate[39] which, with one or two exceptions, for example Mgr O. Prohaszka, from 1905 bishop of Szekesfehérvar, lacked the lustre of the preceding generation; the want of energy displayed by many of

36. See G. Leb, *P. H. Abel. Ein Lebensbild*, Innsbruck 1926.
37. Launched in 1897 it had the effect over the next ten years of making several thousand Catholics desert Catholicism for Protestantism or Old Catholicism. Cf. *Die Religion in Geschichte und Gegenwart*, 3rd edn, IV, cols 452-5.
38. In the context of rapprochement with Russia, Leo XIII and still more Rampolla had given support to certain claims put forward by Slav populations, especially in Croatia, and for a time there had been a distinct cooling off in relations between Vienna and the Vatican. But the accession of Pius X brought a marked change in Rome's attitude on this point.
39. On recruitment to the episcopate, which was controlled by the imperial government, see the well-documented study by E. Saurer, *Die politischen Aspekte der österreichischen Bischofsernennungen, 1867-1903*, Vienna 1968.

the clergy – in 1894 Mgr de T'Serclaes described them as 'steeped in lethargy' and twenty years later things were little different – and the relaxation of discipline among the religious, who were in any case less numerous than in the countries of Western Europe;[40]· lastly, the paucity of lay involvement in Catholic enterprises, although Austrian laymen needed to look no further than to their German neighbours for inspiration. Despite the undeniable improvement in comparison with the difficult years which had followed the repudiation of the Concordat, and with due credit to the sincere devotion to the Catholic Church so faithfully evinced by the aged Franz Joseph, the situation was in truth far less satisfactory than can have appeared at first sight to the casual observer.

5. SPAIN

Equally deceptive in appearance was Catholic Spain, though here again one can point to real improvement in comparison with the critical situation which developed under the pontificate of Gregory XVI and again at the end of the pontificate of Pius IX.

The *détente* inaugurated by the ending of Espartero's anti-clerical dictatorship in 1843 was consolidated in 1851 by a concordat which restored the Church to a preponderant position in the State, making possible the systematic reinstatement of church structures. The restoration was made all the smoother by the attitude, considerably more benign than Catholic historians generally allow, of the moderate liberal government in power and by the backing of Queen Isabella II, especially once she had as her confessor and adviser on ecclesiastical affairs the zealously apostolic S. Antoine-Marie Claret (1807–70). But if for twenty years or so the Church seemed in a prosperous situation, it was one which rested on somewhat flimsy foundations. Wide sectors of the population were certainly still profoundly attached to the Church, but the clergy – still very plentiful, to the tune in 1868 of one priest for every 380 inhabitants, in other words twice as many as in France – were too easily content with a religion compounded of rites and daily routines and made little effort to adapt to the changes which had taken place in the realm of ideas since the now distant days of the 'golden age' (the Catalan theologian Jaime Balmès was an exception, but he died all too young in 1848). In the anti-liberal atmosphere of the Pius IX era the hierarchy, in particular, became set in an increasingly conservative mould, and if the bishops did not in general share the Carlists' antipathy for the constitutional regime, their attitude towards modern aspirations was basically defensive, which not unnaturally made the episcopate appear a mainstay

40. In the Hungarian part of the Empire in 1903 there were 2,200 male religious and 5,112 female religious, whereas in anti-clerical France, with a population only four times as large, there were close on 40,000 male religious and over 150,000 female.

of reaction. Consequently from about 1860 the number of intellectuals alienated from the Church started to grow; and it is not surprising that the provocatively ostentatious defence of their position by spiritual heirs of the Carlists, ranged round Nocedal's *Pensamiento español* and fanatically anti-modern, brought the latent anti-clericalism of the liberal bourgeoisie to life. The revolution of 1868 put an end to the detested regime of Queen Isabella and her minister Narvaez, and from that date until the re-establishment of the Bourbon dynasty in 1875 anti-clericalism had a free rein.

But the period of revolutionary excess was followed by a return to order under the moderate liberal administration of Canovas del Castillo, and once again the fears of the ecclesiastical authorities were put to sleep. There was an immediate return to the Concordat of 1851. Under the constitution of 1876 Catholicism was once again recognised as the religion of the State (but despite vehement protests from the clergy and even from Pius IX, the constitution also conceded the principle of freedom of worship). In addition to the eighty per cent of the secondary schools and the high proportion of urban primary schools already run by the Church, the Church regained control of public education, the universities included; the seminaries were gradually placed on a more regular footing, and with the foundation by the Jesuits in 1890 of the university of Comillas and the opening in 1892 of the Spanish College in Rome, they were guaranteed a supply of teachers formed in the Roman tradition. The religious congregations, especially those for woman, found themselves again in a more favourable position and in 1877, after four decades of uncertainty, they at last secured a legal status (only to have it challenged in 1901, and again and more seriously in 1910, under the administration of Canelejas, but without any serious consequences).[41]

As interesting extensions of the institutional restoration we may note ventures such as the foundation, not without difficulty in some cases, of a number of scholarly journals: the *Ciudad de Dios* (1899), the *Razón y Fe* (1901), the *Estudios franciscanos* (1907), the *Ciencia tomista* (1910). Further positive contributions include the scholarly work of Menendez Pelayo (died 1912), according to Canon Jobit one of the few intellectual 'greats' to remain loyal to the Church; the influence in the social field of Rodriguez de Capade, professor at the university of Madrid, and of Jesuits such as A. Vicent and G. Palau; the widespread following which another Jesuit, P. Tarin, commanded among the masses; and the foundation in 1909 by one of his young colleagues, Fr Angel Ayala, assisted by a lay mis-

41. Pius X's rejoinder to the 'padlock law' was to recall the nuncio from Madrid, but two years later relations were resumed and little had actually been done to curb the activity of the orders and congregations. Besides, the influx of religious expelled from France provided some justifiable reason for apprehension. At the beginning of the twentieth century the number of religious was again almost equal to what it had been in 1835, but with the proportion between men and women reversed: 10,500 and 40,000 instead of 31,000 and 22,000.

sionary, A. Herrera, of the Associación católica de propagandistas which foreshadowed the Catholic Action movements of the inter-war period.

But alongside the bright spots were a number of more ominous features. The most serious was not the deep division separating Catholics over the political issue, to which contemporary observers and recent historians so often call attention. Ranged on one side of this division were the Carlists, backed by a large number of the lower clergy, who could see no salvation for the Church other than through the installation, if necessary by force, of a totally Catholic government and who lived pending this event like *émigrés* in their own country, withdrawn into their own self-enclosed group, served by a press which imparted to the religious polemic a virulence unknown in the rest of Europe. On the other side were the Catholics who, with encouragement from Leo XIII[42] and the majority of the bishops, had come to terms with the regime and to some extent with liberal institutions, having recognised that systematic opposition would place the throne itself in jeopardy and stimulate revolutionary intrigues, an attitude which incidentally helped to identify the Church even further with the forces of social reaction. But the terms of this controversy were too anachronistic to keep it going for long. Far more serious for the future was a marked change of attitude which manifested itself both in educated circles and among the masses. Burnings of churches and physical assaults on priests and religious during the republican episode had already given warning of a chasm opening up between the proletariat of the large towns and the Church. The rift did not stop there. It spread to Catalonia, where in 1909 there were violent disturbances following the execution of a revolutionary, Francisco Ferrer, and even to the countryside, where a fiercely anti-clerical form of anarchism began to develop. [43] Among the liberal bourgeoisie, if there was no general lowering in the standards of family life, there was a distinct tendency among one section towards an anti-clericalism inspired not simply by political and economic motives but by an anti-Christian rationalism. Positivist philosophy was introduced into Spain by J. Sanz del Rio, whose civil obsequies in 1869 were attended, symptomatically, by a demonstration. He had a worthy successor in Fr Giner de los Rios, the founder in opposition to the clericalised universities of the Institución libre de enseñanza, which was essentially though not exclusively anti-religious. But more important still and highly typical of the trend is the fact that almost all the generation of 1898 of which Miguel de Unamuno was such a shining light had been educated in Catholic colleges.

42. It was for this purpose that he sent to Spain one of his most outstanding nuncios, the future Cardinal Rampolla. Similarly, having won over to his viewpoint the Augustinians, who had great influence in Spain, he persuaded the general of the Jesuits to intervene in order to bring over the Society of Jesus, which down to the end of the century had supported Nocedal's integrist movement.

43. See G. Brenan, *The Spanish Labyrinth*, 2nd edn (Cambridge 1950), 87-197.

According to Fr Oromi, 'what made young intellectuals give up their belief in Catholic dogma was not moral depravity, which from laziness or the desire to make history simple is the answer too often given, but sheer intellectual deprivation, from which Spanish Catholicism has suffered to quite an extreme degree in recent centuries'.[44] Several decades had yet to go by before Cardinal Goma spoke out against a 'religion based on the shifting sand of superstition, sentiment, habit and ignorance', and equally before it was realised that the failure to adapt religious teaching to all levels of understanding meant that the Spanish people though bombarded with sermons was still not evangelised.

The situation was worse still in Portugal, where the ruling liberal bourgeoisie harassed the Church by frequent interventions and was more inclined than its Spanish counterpart to persecute the religious congregations, where Freemasonry was better organised and where the clergy, to add to the difficulties, left a great deal to be desired. The brutal separation of Church and State in 1911 was merely an epiphenomenon, indicative of a gravely compromised situation.

6. BELGIUM

Though the doctrinaires were scarcely willing to admit it, the situation was very much better in Belgium, the country whose liberal constitution had caused such perturbation at Rome in the time of Gregory XVI. The work of Catholic restoration, put vigorously in hand immediately after independence, was successfully continued by an episcopate persuaded of the extreme importance of Catholic schooling and aspiring to an ever tighter control of every department of church life. The bishops were assisted by a clerical force adequate in numbers and remarkable for a realistic approach to the apostolate, but whose meddlings in politics left room for charges of clericalism. The diocesan clergy could count on the close collaboration of the religious congregations, membership of which rose from about 12,000 in 1846 to 58,351 in 1910, and of an élite of influential laymen, who served the Catholic cause as faithfully in the parliamentary arena as in the voluntary organisations which were set up to keep the masses in contact with the Church.

Although Catholics found it quite natural that the Church, under the aegis of constitutional liberties, should regain in fact if not in law a voice in the management of institutions and in civil society, the liberals soon decided that this situation could not continue and started to agitate for the restoration of independent secular authority in all domains, in particular that of education. This reaction reached its climax in the 'schools' war' of

44. Quoted by P. Lain-Entralgo, *La generación del Noventa y ocho* (Madrid 1945), 123-4.

1878–84, embittered on the one hand by the anti-religious rather than merely anti-clerical tendencies which had developed among the new generation of liberals, and on the other by the campaign mounted by the ultramontanes, with backing from Pius IX and a number of recently appointed bishops, against 'the liberties of perdition'. But first Leo XIII's counsels of moderation and then the electoral defeat of the liberals in 1884, which put the Catholic party in power for the next thirty years, had the effect of making these controversies appear less important than the social question. So far as the agrarian aspect was concerned, this presented little difficulty, the foundation of the Boerenbond in 1890 signalising an important advance, but progress in the industrial field was slower and beset with obstacles, since the bishops' main preoccupation was with preserving the unity of the Catholic party, which they regarded as the Church's most important defence, with the result that even after the encyclical *Rerum novarum* they were chary of offering much encouragement to the beginnings of Christian democracy. [45]

Around the middle years of the century another problem had started to rear its head. In parallel with the development among the convinced core of Catholics of a certain mystique of religious defence, and notwithstanding serious efforts to improve the quality of the Catholic press, there was the spectacle among the rank and file of a slow but steady spread of religious indifference, especially marked in the Walloon districts but extending even into Flanders and, accompanying it, a deterioration in the standards of family life. [46] Even in country districts, where religious observance was more or less stable, the influence of 'freethinkers', backed by Freemasonry, was tending to supersede the traditional authority of the *curé*. As for the big industrial centres, where parochial organisation had not kept pace with the times, the decline went beyond a steady falling off in Sunday and Easter duties and extended to loss of contact with the Church even at the most solemn moments of human existence. An example (though not one on which we should be too hasty to generalise) is provided by Seraing, on the outskirts of Liège: on the eve of the First World War civil burials stood at sixty-four per cent, civil marriages at forty-six per cent, unbaptised children at twenty-three per cent. [47] The first decade of the new century nevertheless witnessed a great effort to stem the tide by giving new shape to Catholic organisations, for example the Catholic congress of 1909, the launching by Fr Rutten, O.P. of the first Catholic trade unions (membership of which rose

---

45. For more details regarding these problems and the controversies to which they gave rise see chapter 8, 153-4.

46. From 1880 to 1910 the divorces rose from 214 to 1089 and the birthrate coefficient fell from 31.13 to 22.40.

47. L. de Saint-Moulin, 'Contribution à l'histoire de la déchristianisation. La pratique religieuse à Seraing depuis 1830', *Annuaire d'histoire liégeoise*, X (1967), 33-126.

between 1904 and 1914 from ten thousand to a hundred thousand), the success of the eucharistic societies, the beginnings of the pastoral liturgical movement associated with Mont César, soon to have imitators in all parts of the world, and the new direction given to youth organisations and student study circles under the influence of D. J. Mercier, newly-appointed archbishop of Malines. Another unmistakable sign of vitality was the growing share taken by Belgian Catholics in missionary work overseas.

7. THE NETHERLANDS

The history of the Catholic Church in the Netherlands in the second half of the nineteenth century shows some parallels with developments in Belgium. As we have already seen,[48] Dutch Catholics, in a minority compared with the Protestants,[49] reaped an early benefit from the introduction of liberal institutions. This made Dutch Catholics so confident that in 1857 many joined the liberals in voting for a school law which eradicated the Protestant bias still very evident in public primary schools and introduced for the first time in Europe a completely neutral type of school. But in Holland, even more than in Belgium, Catholic collaboration with the liberals owed more to tactical considerations than to any change of outlook and, as in Belgium, though with a few years' delay, deep divergences of viewpoint were not slow to reappear. The exaggerations of the anti-clerical polemic launched at the time of the *Syllabus* strengthened the position of Catholics like J. W. Cramer, a Dutch disciple of Veuillot, who in his paper the *Tijd* stressed the incompatibility between the Catholic *Weltanschauung* and the principles of 1789. Besides which, the example of liberal Protestantism, which in the Netherlands assumed a distinctly radical air, confirmed many Catholics in their belief that there were dangers to the faith in giving too eager a welcome to modern ideas. As in Belgium, the final break came over the schools question. Discovering that the neutral teaching was becoming in practice more and more irreligious, the bishops, from the time of the provincial council of 1865, started to press the right of Catholic children to be educated in Catholic schools. Faced with the liberals' refusal to satisfy this demand and with the voting in 1878 of a law which appeared ominous for the future of free education, the Catholics decided that, in order to resist the threat, they must form a confessional political party. The idea had been mooted by the *Tijd,* invoking the precedent of the German Centre Party, as early as 1877,

48. Cf. chapter 2, 32-3.
49. In 1850 they formed 38.15 per cent of the population. In consequence of numerous defections following emigration from the country to the towns, in 1890 they formed no more than 35.39 per cent. Over the next twenty-five years, however, the percentage slowly increased (37 per cent in 1914), while between 1900 and 1920 the percentage of Protestants fell from 60 to 52, the result of a lower birthrate and more importantly of the rise in the percentage of 'non-confessionals', which increased during this period from 2 to 9 per cent.

and it was to be put successfully into effect by a young priest, Herman Schaepman (1844-1903). A great admirer of Leo XIII, he succeeded in giving the Catholic party a popular base and furthermore, despite the protracted opposition of a section of his co-religionists, he had no hesitation in allying himself in the political arena with believing Protestants, thus avoiding the isolation which condemned the ultramontanes of Latin countries to the voicing of sterile protests. The shift among the liberals towards a rationalist and positivist viewpoint in place of the spiritual conception which had been uppermost in the middle of the century was in effect leading Calvinists and Catholics to discover they had a common subsoil which could serve as a base, not indeed for the ecumenical dialogue, for which no one was yet prepared, but at least for a Christian coalition in defence of religious rights. This unnatural alliance, as many people at first considered it, was to play an important part in Dutch life over the next few decades and lead in particular to the introduction of a set of school laws fairer than any in Western Europe (for primary schools in 1889, for secondary schools in 1905).

At the same time Dutch Catholicism was rapidly making good its backwardness in social matters, thanks to the work of men such as A. Ariëns, founder in 1889 of the Association of Catholic Workers, and the methods of H. Poels, which ensured that the industrialisation of Limburg did not go hand in hand, as in so many countries, with the progressive dechristianisation of the workers, were soon being imitated in places outside Holland. In the cultural domain, by contrast, Dutch Catholics continued to make a poor showing. No bishop that can compare with a Dechamps in Belgium or a Mermillod in Switzerland; the clergy were full of zeal but reared from an early age in seminaries sedulously isolated from the world and conceiving their apostolate in a narrowly clerical perspective. As for laymen, although one thinks of a few – a W. Nuyens and still more an Alberdingk Thijm in the nineteenth century, a G. Brom and the members of the Klarenbeekse Club, founders of the review *Van onzen tijd,* or H. H. Moller, a pioneer of Catholic pre-university education, in the early twentieth – who tried with some success to let in a little air, their efforts were seriously frustrated by the aggressively integrist campaign mounted in the *Maasbode* by the Abbé Thompson, with approval from the bishop of Haarlem. A generation had yet to pass before the Dutch Church, freed in 1908 from its dependence on the Congregation for the Propagation of the Faith, would seem completely adult.

8. SWITZERLAND

In Switzerland, although the defeat of the *Sonderbund* in November 1847 had dealt the seven Catholic cantons a severe blow, the recognition of full freedom of worship under the federal constitution of 1848 improved the legal position of Catholics in cantons where they formed a minority, as witness for example the building of two fine churches, Notre-Dame in Geneva and Saint-Pierre in Berne. But throughout the third quarter of the nineteenth century the freethinking radicals kept up a systematic campaign of hindering the free expansion of the Church. Many surviving monasteries and convents were suppressed and in some cantons confessional schools were abolished. Other cantons, with support from churchmen of Josephinist leanings who had fallen under the sway of Wessenberg, who lived to 1860, claimed the right to control minutely every aspect of diocesan life and this led among other things to the banishment between 1848 and 1856 of the bishop of Lausanne, Mgr Marilley, who had protested against the measures contemplated. After several years of calm, tension again started to build up, becoming even more acute after 1870: taking advantage of the agitation stirred up by the Vatican council in ultra-liberal Catholic circles, long desirous of a reform of the Catholic Church in a democratic and anti-Roman sense,[50] the radicals resumed the offensive, following the example set by the Prussian *Kulturkampf*. In the canton of Geneva and in the Bernese Jura in particular, the majority of churches were handed over by the civil authorities in 1873 to the Old Catholics and for two years Catholic services could only be held in barns or similar places. A fair number of the rightful *curés* were sentenced to banishment, as were two bishops. The revised constitution of 1874 stressed in no uncertain fashion the supremacy of the State over the Church and forbade the foundation of new congregations and even of new convents. The nunciature, based at Lucerne, had to close in 1874 and was not revived until 1920, when the Holy See's delegation representing the Pontifical Commission for the Relief of War Victims was transformed into a nunciature, based from then on in Berne. The conflict, made for a time more bitter by the aggressive reaction of young intransigent Catholics, was to die down during the 1880s, thanks in part to the flexible attitude of Leo XIII and Mgr Ferrata, but sundry measures in harassment of Catholics continued in force for many years to come.

These trials nevertheless had their positive side, which should not be overlooked. They were an incentive to Catholics to re-deploy their resources. While, politically speaking, the Swiss Catholics showed themselves disciples of Montalembert, very popular on account of the support he had shown for their cause in 1847, they borrowed from Catholic Germany the idea of a central and inter-cantonal organisation combining all the voluntary associations under the aegis of the 'Piusverein' (established 1857) and also the idea of pooling their efforts to help Catholics dispersed in

50. On this movement see E. Campana, *Il concilio Vaticano* (Lugano 1926), II, 569–627.

regions of Diaspora (in which over a thousand churches were built in the space of a few decades). The flourishing of Catholic social organisations in the industrialised cantons, where Catholics were in fact in a minority, [51] explains how it was that only a few years later Switzerland became one of the first centres of social Catholicism. Three names stand out from this period: the Capuchin Theodosius Florentini (1808-65), dedicated and inventive initiator of charitable enterprises, founder of countless hospitals and schools for the lower classes; Mother Maria Theresia Scherer (1825-88), the first superior of the Sisters of the Holy Cross of Ingenbohl, an order which under such an outstanding director was to show considerable expansion throughout Central Europe; and in French-speaking Switzerland Gaspard Mermillod (1824-92), *curé* and then vicar-general of Geneva, future bishop of Fribourg and future cardinal, one of the most active agents in the adaptation of Swiss Catholicism to the new conditions, for whom the *Kulturkampf* cost ten years in exile. After 1880 there was a fresh upsurge of Catholic vitality which bore tangible fruit in the first congress of Swiss Catholics, held at Lucerne in 1903, and in the foundation at Fribourg in 1889 of a Catholic international university, thanks to the combined exertions of two zealous laymen, G. Python and P. Decurtins, and of their patron, Mgr A. Egger, bishop of Sankt Gallen from 1882 to 1906, the most outstanding among the Swiss bishops of the late nineteenth century.

9. RUSSIA AND POLAND

Although on balance the period 1848-1914 brought clear benefit to the Catholic minorities in Protestant countries, the same cannot be said of Catholics in Orthodox Russia. The long ordeal of the Uniates is described in a later chapter. [52] The Latin Catholics, most of whom lived in the Polish provinces, had their hopes raised by the agreement of 1847 only to see them dashed when the government showed its determination to keep a tight control on ecclesiastical life in every department and at every level: diocesan administration, the parochial ministry, recruitment to the religious orders. In the circumstances it is not surprising that many priests and religious, in the hope that a more democratic regime would rid the Church of such stifling restrictions, gave increasing support to the opposition from the left, whose main objective was social reform but which was skilful enough to play on

---

51. Though a minority, the Catholics were a growing minority because of the immigration of workers from Catholic cantons. This was what led to the separation of Church and State in the canton of Geneva in 1907 and at Basle in 1911, which in practical terms improved the position of the Catholics. 'This vote, Pastor Picot observed, marks a victory for the ultramontanes and for the out-and-out enemies of religion rather than the triumph of the principles of religious liberty, for it is not Vinet but Voltaire and Mermillod who carry the day' (quoted *Revue d'histoire et de philosophie religieuses*, IV (1924), 550).
52. Cf chapter 17, 462.

the romantic nationalism to which the lower clergy are often susceptible. Although the Holy See and the episcopate held aloof, the activities of these patriotic priests served to identify the Church with revolutionary agitation, reinforcing the suspicions of the Russian authorities and leading to ever more interference. All the same, conditions were lacking for the development of a resistance movement along the lines of the Irish campaign for Catholic emancipation or of the German Catholics' defiance of the *Kulturkampf.* Under the regime of the police State there was no political forum, no newspapers, no medium of any kind through which such a voice could make itself heard, besides which, many sees were either left vacant by the civil authorities for years at a time or had as their occupants men inadequate to the occasion, men whose Josephinist or Febronian-inspired clerical upbringing made them all the more disposed to condone certain breaches in the canon law. In addition, a portion of the higher clergy, representative in particular of the nobly born, believed from motives compounded of social conservatism and hatred of the Germans that collaboration with Russia still represented the lesser evil.

The Polish rebellion of 1863 worsened the situation, for the Russian authorities reacted very harshly in face of the support it had received from a section of the lower clergy and above all from religious, acting often without the knowledge of their ultimate superiors. More than 400 clerics were deported to Siberia and 114 out of the 197 remaining religious houses were closed, with the result that by 1874 the total number of religious stood at 264, compared with 1638 ten years earlier. Apart from this, the processions and pilgrimages which were such a feature of popular piety were increasingly prohibited and there was an intensification of police surveillance, not merely of sermons but in some cases even of confessions. Repeated protests from Pius IX only exacerbated the situation, to the point that the government refused to allow the Polish bishops to attend the Vatican council. The accession of Leo XIII and in Russia of Alexander III brought the beginnings of a *détente.* Following an agreement signed in December 1882, the Polish bishops were granted an amnesty and the seminaries were allowed to reopen. From 1887 there was a gradual resumption of the diplomatic relations severed twenty years previously, for St Petersburg had come to recognise the value of the Vatican as a card against the rising power of Germany. But despite the sympathy with Catholicism awakening in one or two small groups influenced by Soloviev, the procurator of the Holy Synod, O. Pobjedonotsev, pressed on at the local level with the traditional policy of Russifying the Church and the schools, progressively curtailing the religious liberty of Catholics, as also of Protestants, to the benefit of the official Orthodox Church. The Holy See, which regarded good relations with St Petersburg as a lesser evil, dissuaded the Poles even so from any form of agitation, which could only be to the advantage of social disorder. There was to be no real slackening in Russia's intolerant Caesaropapism until the revolution of 1905,[53] and even after that a number of pettifogging restrictions were destined to remain in force until the the collapse of the Tsarist regime, and the government was to make a point of supporting the schismatic sect of the Mariavites.[54]   However disappointing on the constitutional side, the balance sheet was not altogether unfavourable. For instance, although educated circles in Poland long continued under the rationalising influence of the Enlightenment, from about mid-century there were signs that the upper classes, who appreciated the Church's stabilising influence in face of revolutionary aspirations, were changing in a way reminiscent of the development several decades earlier in France. This change of attitude, adopted from motives of self-interest, gave encouragement to a more deeply-seated religious revival which drew on the fresh currents of spirituality springing up in Europe as a whole throughout this period. And if the closing decades of the century saw Western positivism gaining ground among the intellectuals, and the socialists stepping up their denunciation of the clergy as allies of the landlords,[55] the Catholic Church was still so closely bound up in the popular mind with Polish national feeling that religious observance, even in working-class circles, remained at a very high level, and this despite a rise in population with which the supply of priests had not kept pace (in 1910 there was on average only one priest to every 2800 faithful compared with one to every 1400 in 1850). The Catholicism in question was doubtless of a very conventional type, with conformism often taking precedence over personal conviction. But it had its vital side, as witness for example the fruitful endeavours of the Capuchins, great propagators of Marian piety, and above all the remarkable development along modern lines of congregations for women. Whereas in 1864 there had been only one female religious in every 12,000 faithful, by 1900 there was one in every 1070, and in the meantime the population had increased. The bulk of this expansion occurred in the clandestine con-

53. Following Nicholas II's ukase of toleration of 17/30 April 1905, which abolished the penalties prescribed for desertion of the official Church, in Russia itself there were about 200,000 conversions to Catholicism over the next few years.
54. Originally inspired by the visions of a widow, M. Kozlowska, and founded as a religious congregation with the help of the Abbé J. Kowalski, after their condemnation in 1906 on grounds of fanaticism the Mariavites broke with the Church and in the years before the First World War accumulated a membership of some 200,000. In 1909 Kowalski was consecrated bishop by the Old Catholics of Utrecht. See E. Driessen, *De wijding van I. Kowalski*, Utrecht 1911, and P. Feldman, *Die altkatholische Kirche der Mariaviten*, 2nd edn, Plock 1940.
55. The awakening of the Catholic social conscience was much more tardy in the Russian part of Poland than in the parts of Poland annexed to Austria or Prussia. There was nevertheless a small but clandestine Catholic workers' movement even before 1891 and after 1905 a few associations of Christian workers came into existence.

gregations for tertiaries founded by Honorat Kozminski (1829-1916), whose members carried out their teaching or social work duties in lay dress as a means of evading the government's restrictions. By about 1904 there were close on seven thousand women in 'Fr Honorat's movement' [56] and in addition there were two congregations for men; but by 1908 the disquiet of the bishops was such that they decided the movement must be brought within the traditional religious framework, and this promising development was brought to a halt.

56. It is to be hoped that the very interesting work of Mme. E. Jablonska on this subject will be made available to the Western public; in the meantime, as an addition to E. M. de Beaulieu, *Le P. Honorat de Biala,* there is her brief contribution to the collection *Millénaire du catholicisme en Pologne* (Lublin 1969), 136-41.

6

THE VITALITY OF THE
CHRISTIAN FAITH

THE nineteenth century, so often depicted in the Catholic press of the time and in countless pastoral letters as an age of religious decadence and of mounting success for irreligion and immorality, was also, looked at more closely, an age of spiritual ferment. Although some of the forms it took may today appear outdated, they signified none the less a vigorous effort on the part of an élite, far more numerous than is commonly supposed, to lead lives of deeper Christian sincerity and to react with greater effect to the threat presented by the encroachment on all sides of positivism and materialism. Against the falling numbers of Sunday and Easter duties and the dwindling in certain regions of vocations to the priesthood, against the pettifogging or violent attacks by public authorities on the Church and her works, against the great strides made by the 'godless' press, we can set the appreciable improvement in the quality of the diocesan clergy during the period covered by the pontificates of Pius IX, Leo XIII and Pius X (dealt with in the next chapter), the remarkable revival of religious orders and congregations, the many outward signs of individual and collective piety, the beginnings of a revival of devotional literature and the great expansion of charitable and other associations of every description, for which we must assume that a more than ordinary devotion and generosity among the mass of the faithful was at bottom responsible. When all this is taken into account, it is easy to see how Daniel-Rops was able to speak of 'a spiritual *revival* for which it would be hard to find a parallel down the centuries'.

The second quarter of the nineteenth century had brought confirmation that the religious orders and congregations, tried almost beyond endurance by the cumulative storms of the French Revolution, were to maintain the recovery whose first signs were already apparent in 1815. This revival became more marked during the second half of the century, despite fresh measures of secularisation in Italy, Poland and Latin America which bore heavily on the older orders. Indeed, during the pontificate of Pius IX membership of the older orders dropped again by a third. The Franciscans fell in numbers from 22,000 in 1850 to 14,000 by about 1885, the Capuchins from 11,152 in 1847 to 7582 by 1889 (in Italy alone, the period 1866-71 saw the closure of 681 houses which housed between them more than seven thousand religious, although 307 of these houses were recovered during the following decade); the Conventuals, of whom there were still seven thousand in 1850, had shrunk by 1900 to fifteen hundred; the Dominicans fell in number from 4562 in 1850 to 3341 in 1876; the Minims declined further from their mid-century figure of 500 (compared with nine thousand before the Revolution) to less than 200 at the end of the century; Brazil, where in 1827 the Benedictines had seven abbeys and four priories, could muster only a dozen monks when Dom G. Van Caloen arrived in 1894 to retrieve the situation. But to compensate there was a general rise in numbers in Western Europe as a whole and in North America and this, in conjunction with an accompanying and appreciable improvement in quality, caused the religious orders to be a key factor in the growth of voluntary societies, in the spread of the apostolate, especially in mission countries, and in the deepening of spiritual life.

The pace of recovery can best be illustrated from a few statistics. While it is true that the numbers of Canons Regular, despite the gradual reconstruction of the Premonstratensian order, continued to remain stationary and that the Carmelites declined by a further ten per cent, the Benedictines by contrast grew from 1600 in mid-century to close on 6000 in 1900 and the Trappists from 1284 to 3700, despite the enduring prejudice, found even in certain Catholic circles, against the monastic life as a relic of the Middle Ages only the most obscurantist devotee of Romanticism could want to preserve. Towards the end of the century the Franciscans and Capuchins saw their downward trend reversed and after 1908 the latter were once again to exceed the 10,000 mark. By 1914 the numbers of the Dominicans were up to what they had been in 1850; the Redemptorists showed an even more spectacular rise, from 1238 in 1850 to 4069 in 1910, but they were surpassed by the Jesuits, despite fourteen expulsion orders in the pontificate of Pius IX alone. Standing at 4652 in 1852, their numbers had risen by 1886 to 12,070 and by 1914 reached 16,894. This great access of numerical strength enabled the Jesuits not only to foster the influence they had with the upper classes, an influence sustained by the prestige of their schools and by their preaching, their publications, and their numerous personal contacts (not always free of political designs), but also to extend their operations among the masses by organising parochial missions and running voluntary societies; nor should we overlook the very active Jesuit element in the

Roman Congregations, where the secular clergy and the older religious orders had few representatives able to compete, not to mention the semi-official standing with the Holy See of the Jesuit journal, *Civiltà cattolica*. Congregations of Brothers, which before the Revolution accounted for less than one per cent of all religious, started to attract vocations in growing numbers. To refer only to those under pontifical jurisdiction, by 1850 their members accounted for 9000 out of the 83,000 grand total of all religious and in 1900 for 30,000 out of a total of 135,000. The Brothers of Christian Schools in particular nearly doubled their numbers between 1854 and 1874 (rising from 6000 to 11,570) and by 1900 had reached 16,327 (but they were to be dealt a severe blow when the French government's measures against congregations forced the closure between 1904 and 1908 of 12,282 of their houses). The Daughters of Wisdom and the Ursulines made equally remarkable progress though not quite on the scale of the Daughters of Charity (or Sisters of St Vincent de Paul), who reached 20,000 even before the end of Mère Étienne's period as general (1843-74) and whose involvement in missionary and social work of every description continued to grow in the course of the next few decades.

Even more remarkable was the progress made by congregations of more recent foundation, many of which were better adapted to the needs of the modern world. The Oblates of Mary Immaculate, of whom there were 270 in 1850, had increased fifty years later to 1525 and in 1914 stood at 3110; the Marianists grew during the second half of the century from 421 to 1986 and the Marist brothers from 826 to 3105, under Brother Theophano's period as general (1883-1907) gaining a foothold within just a few years in Italy, Spain, Canada, the United States, Colombia and China; the Claretines, a Spanish foundation, advanced from 217 members in 1875 to 1476 in 1900; the Salesians, founded at Turin by Don Bosco in 1875 and numbering 900 by the time of his death in 1888, by 1900 had risen to 3526 and by 1914 were active in thirty-one countries, sixteen of them in Latin America; the White Fathers of Africa, founded in 1868, forty years later already had a membership of 600 priests and 400 brothers and students for the priesthood while the Steyl Missionaries, Missionaries of the Divine Word starting from 4 in 1875, had increased to 805 by 1900 and by 1910 stood at 1370. The congregations for women were also expanding. To quote just a few examples: the Good Shepherd Sisters of Angers, having been reorganised by Euphrasia Pelletier, at the time of her death in 1868 numbered 2067 and by the year 1901 had increased to 7044, distributed in twenty-four separate provinces. The German Franciscan Sisters of Salzkotten, of whom there were only about thirty in 1862, by the year 1918 numbered 2000 and those of St Mauritz (Munster), less than a hundred in 1872, by 1918 had reached 3450. The Little Sisters of the Poor, founded by

J. Jugan in 1840, by 1911 numbered 5400. The two Swiss Congregations of the Third Order of St Francis, Ingenbohl and Menzingen, founded by Fr Fiorentini in 1844, by the start of the twentieth century had a membership running into thousands; the Dutch Franciscan Sisters of Heijthuijsen increased from a few dozen in 1846 to 2700 in the year 1917; and the Franciscan Missionaries of Mary, founded in 1877, had shot up by 1930 to 6500.

The phenomenon was especially striking in France, which by 1877 already had a total of 30,287 men religious (about twenty thousand of them in brotherhoods) and 127,753 women, compared with 25,000 and 37,000 in 1789, since when the population had risen by only thirty per cent.[1] It is to be noted, however, that many French congregations had important outposts in foreign countries – at the time catastrophe struck in 1904 the Brothers of the Christian Schools, for example, had five thousand members outside France – and that others, the Oblates of Mary Immaculate for instance, rapidly became international in character or even transferred their centre of gravity to the New World, as was the case with the Clerks of St Viator, the Priests of St Basil and the Holy Cross Fathers. On the other hand, although more than forty per cent of the congregations for men of pontifical right founded during the second half of the century were based on France or northern Italy, the share of other European countries rose to forty-three per cent, compared with thirty per cent in the period 1800–50, and that of non-European countries (principally the United States and Canada) to fourteen per cent, having been practically nil before 1850. Still more striking was the proliferation of congregations for women: in the brief period 1862-5 the Holy See approved seventy-four such foundations, compared with forty-eight for the whole decade 1850-60.

These figures have a double interest. In the first place, even if we have to allow that in rural areas entry into a teaching order might constitute a rise in the social scale and that the multiplication of 'mission schools' and juvenates may have given a somewhat artificial boost to recruitment, the flourishing state of the orders and congregations, for which there had been no parallel since the twelfth and thirteenth centuries, can surely be taken as evidence of strong religious vitality in a society from which, to judge only by superficial appearances, spiritual values appeared to be in retreat. And although even at Rome interest concentrated on congregations engaged in active work, the success of the contemplative orders (at the start of the twentieth century the

---

1. It must be pointed out, however, that the figures varied greatly with the country. Whereas in 1901 (on the eve of the expulsions) France had 11,300 religious priests, that is to say about one-fifth of the secular clergy and three for every ten thousand faithful, Germany in 1915 had only one religious priest for every ten thousand faithful (compared with 9.6 secular priests). The Netherlands on the other hand had almost as many religious priests as secular.

Poor Clares had about 500 convents and the Carmelites 360, with an average of twenty members to each) proves that in this least mystical of centuries the mystical way of life attracted souls as compellingly as in its greatest days. The second point to notice is that the men religious in their tens of thousands and the women in their hundreds of thousands (by 1939 there were a round million, in all parts of the world), were a substantial support to the apostolic mission of the Church (in preaching retreats, teaching the catechism, organising the publication of religious literature, conducting missions), making it possible for the Church to engage in educational and social work (with the emphasis increasingly progressing beyond the handing out of temporary relief to the point of caring for the poor from the cradle to the grave) in a manner that was often almost as effective, even if the institutional forms were different, as under the *ancien régime*.

What made the influence of the regulars still more potent was the improvement in quality that had accompanied their growth in numbers. One of Pius IX's first actions on becoming pope was to create a new Roman Congregation *super statu regularium* with a view to reforming the relaxed discipline in some of the older orders, brought about by the attitude prevailing in the eighteenth century and by the turmoil of the revolutionary period. As a further counter-measure he encouraged greater centralisation within the orders. For instance, to reduce the individualistic tendencies of the separate houses he approved the setting up in Austria and above all in Italy of Benedictine congregations. Pius IX stressed also the subordination of the regulars to the Roman Congregations and on occasion he showed no hesitation in using his authority to appoint superiors for one or other of the orders (in 1850 for the Benedictine congregation of Subiaco and for the Dominicans, in 1853 for the Redemptorists, in 1856 and again in 1862 for the Franciscans). Although the abbeys, clinging stubbornly to their independence, were often a stumbling-block, in the centralised orders these reforming efforts met with fairly rapid success. It is thus not surprising that Leo XIII took advantage of the Holy See's increased prestige in the Church following the Vatican Council to apply further pressure, even where it went against the grain of the parties concerned, in the interests of a reorganisation which seemed to him salutary as much for the maintenance of discipline as for the advancement of studies. In 1887 he instructed Mgr Dusmet to prepare a plan for the partial centralisation of the Benedictine order and with this aim in mind, to set up the College of St Anselm in Rome. This plan, much argued over in one section of the order, led to the erection in 1893 of a confederation which preserved the autonomy of the abbeys but conferred on an abbot-primate the right of canonical visitation whenever need arose. A plan, mooted as early as 1892, for the unification of the four Trappist congregations was finally approved in 1905. In 1893 the Augustinian Hermits were united under a single general. More significant still, since it related to an order ten times as numerous, was the decision taken in 1897 by the four families of the Franciscan observance – the Observants, Recollects, Riformati and Alcantarins – to unite under a single general. This decision, which included agreement to suppress the differences between their individual customs, was only reached after fifteen years of careful preparation by generals Bernardin de Portogruaro and Louis Canali. In 1900 about a hundred Ursuline communities in Europe and America agreed to new constitutions providing for a degree of centralisation under a prioress general, and over the next few years many other communities came to join this Roman Union. Leo XIII, and in due course Pius X, encouraged as many orders as possible to transfer their mother houses to Rome or at any rate to establish large international study houses in Rome. Control was tightened still further by the creation in 1908, as part of the reorganisation of the curia, of a Congregation specifically devoted to the religious orders to which, for example, superiors were required to furnish triennial reports under ninety-eight headings. Added to all this, at the time of the anti-modernist reaction Rome made a practice of sending out commissioners, to France in particular, who meted out judgments of at times excessive severity, as in the case of Dom Grea (a precursor long misunderstood) in 1908 or of the Brothers of St Vincent de Paul in 1913.

The proliferation throughout the Church of new congregations, in particular of women, was watched with especial sympathy by the Holy See, which had been quick to appreciate the overall importance of their permeation of every branch of the apostolate and the need to adapt the traditional rule for women religious, with its emphasis on strict enclosure, to the totally new social conditions of the nineteenth century. Guided by Mgr Bizzarri, well known for his energy and realism, the Congregation of Bishops and Regulars attempted merely to canalise a movement which, although it might at times have an air of ecclesiastical anarchy, reflected the desire of priests and charitably disposed laymen to cater for the multiplicity of needs they uncovered at the local level. Aware that there was a great diversity of aims and circumstances, Mgr Bizzarri was careful not to impose a uniform type of constitution. This was especially so in the period down to 1860, when he left each congregation free to formulate its own statutes, merely reserving the right to inspect them and to suggest possible modifications. In 1862 he issued a *Methodus* which, while still not having the force of law, attempted to isolate certain common norms. Pressure of circumstances thus led to the gradual working out of a new rule for congregations of simple vows. The First Vatican Council had no time to examine the eighteen decrees drafted for the purpose, but the work of the preparatory commission was not wasted since it formed the basis of the constitution *Conditae a Christo* of 8

December 1900. This was the first to rule on the status of congregations of this type, making official, for example, the distinction between congregations of pontifical and diocesan right. The constitution was complemented by *Normae* issued six months later. These dealt with the internal organisation of the congregations and, although they lacked the force of law, they were rapidly accorded that status in practice. Finally, in July 1906, a *motu proprio* brought the approval of new diocesan congregations under Rome's control, a move deemed necessary to avoid a fragmentariness likely to have particularly damaging effects on the training of novices.

Fruitful though it was in souls and highly beneficial to the Church, the remarkable expansion of religious orders and congregations in the nineteenth century was not without its attendant weaknesses and limitations. The women's congregations in particular showed a general tendency to load their custumaries with minute rules and regulations, a failing that can be traced back to the spirituality of the period which for want of a firm doctrinal foundation often degenerated into prescription, and one which contemporary ideas of feminine education did nothing to discourage. Another weakness is stressed by Fr Hostie. Common to the efforts to restore the older orders was a fierce determination to preserve the ancient heritage unchanged, even down to details that had become quite meaningless, though this did not prevent increasing involvement of monastic orders in the active ministry, a tendency strengthened by the growing indistinctness of the line between monachism and priesthood. The founders of the new institutes were equally uninventive, being usually content to borrow piecemeal from existing formulae and often ending up with an amalgam of heterogeneous or even incompatible elements. The exceptions, those who showed signs of originality, soon encountered a twofold resistance, from the prevailing mentality and from officialdom at Rome, which was all in favour of flexibility so long as it was contained within a traditional framework. The case of Dom Bosco is revealing. His was one of the most revolutionary of the new foundations, both in the atmosphere it exuded and in the ambiance it created, but Bosco had to rewrite his rule several times before it satisfied the authorities, anxious as they were that new initiatives should conform to the approved formulae of a bygone age.

Towards the end of the century, Rome showed signs of becoming slightly more adventurous. In 1889, after considerable difficulty, Honorat of Biala, a Polish Capuchin, secured official approval for congregations whose members followed the religious life while wearing lay dress, an expedient adopted to evade vexatious restrictions imposed by the Russian government. Even so, the decree made clear that the three vows were to be regarded merely as private vows and that the congregation itself could have the status only of a pious association recognised by the ordinary of the locality. The formula was to be revived in France during the early years of the twentieth century as a means of preserving the religious life in face of anti-clerical measures aimed at the destruction of the congregations. On the other hand, although pioneers such as the Abbé Calippe or Fr de Foucauld were starting to entertain modest dreams of religious communities of a proletarian style, it would be decades before any such projects could take shape.

For centuries religious orders had extended their influence among the pious laity by means of tertiary orders, the best known being that of the Franciscans. Much reduced by the Revolution and its aftermath, from 1860 the tertiary orders came to life again, first in France and a decade or so later in Italy, Spain, Germany and England. At much the same time there also appeared in France an example of a new type of institution, midway between the usual tertiary order and the religious congregation properly called, the forerunner of what was to be later known as the secular institute. This was the society of the Daughters of St Francis de Salles, founded in 1872 by Madame Carré de Malberg, which by degrees spread to all parts of France and eventually to other countries. In approving its constitutions in in 1911, Pius X drew particular attention to the inclusion of married women alongside spinsters and widows and to their twofold aim: 'sanctification of each individual member and a continuous apostolate'. The year 1872 also saw the foundation at Jaen of the first Spanish secular institute, that of the Teresians, whose constitutions were to be used a little later as the model for the constitutions of Opus Dei.

While the flourishing of religious orders and congregations is a good barometer of Catholic vitality, it is not the only one. Equally to be taken into account are the intensity and direction of popular piety. Now in devotional habits, as in so much else, a profound and lasting change had taken place during the middle years of the nineteenth century. The austere and undemonstrative piety characteristic of the preceding generations, confined in practice to an élite, gave way to a piety more accessible to the masses and giving greater scope, because of its stress on a multiplicity of exterior devotions and on frequent attendance on the sacraments, to emotional participation. Devotion came to focus increasingly on the suffering Christ, opening his heart so full of love towards men. But it also focused, often with a want of discretion which helped to deepen the gulf between Catholics and Protestants, on the Virgin, mother of mercy, and on certain saints beloved by the people, St Antony or St Joseph. The latter was proclaimed by Pius IX in 1870 patron of the universal Church. His cult, fostered by Leo XIII (who also instituted the feast of the Holy Family) was to become particularly strong in Canada. Pilgrimages, which had all but died out in the eighteenth century, returned to favour. They took as their objectives Mariazell in Austria, and Altötting in Germany, Einsiedeln in Switzerland,

Compostella, Montserrat and Notre Dame del Pilar in Spain, Assisi, Loretto, Monte Gargano and naturally Rome in Italy, Chartres, Vézelay, Sainte-Baume, Rocamadour in France, to which were later added Salette, Ars, Paray-le-Monial, Montmartre and above all Lourdes, from 1900 a centre of increasingly international importance. Nor should we overlook the pilgrimages to the Holy Land, a speciality of the Assumptionists, which started as early as 1882.

The transformation owed something to the conjunction of a number of favourable circumstances, for a start the romantic enthusiasm for everything reminiscent of the Middle Ages. But individuals and communities who exerted a conscious influence should be recognised as having played a considerable part: Roman-educated priests such as the English Oratorian F. W. Faber (1814-63) or Mgr Gaston de Ségur (1820-80) who in their widely-read publications propagated north of the Alps the popular devotions that had delighted them in Italy; popularisers of the spirituality of St Alphonsus Liguori, with its total confidence in God's mercy and heartfelt devotion to the Virgin and the Eucharist; the Jesuits, foes *par excellence* of everything reminiscent of Jansenist rigorism and doubly influential in their increasingly common capacity of retreat directors for priests and religious; the convent boarding schools run by French nuns in all parts of the world which helped to diffuse among Christian families until well into the twentieth century a somewhat sentimental form of piety; and lastly the three popes, Pius IX, who gave his blessing to the return to favour of indulgences, Leo XIII, who devoted several encyclicals to the Blessed Virgin and more specifically to the practice of reciting the rosary and who established the cult of the Sacred Heart on a more official basis, and Pius X, who made a vital contribution to the promotion of eucharistic worship.

This new devotional trend, which has to be seen as related to the advance of Ultramontanism, was not without its unfortunate side. In expression it was often insipid and infantile, as can be judged from its many artless hymns and a body of devotional literature whose good intentions were no protection against mediocrity and bad taste. It drew too much of its inspiration from suspect sources, legends of the saints for instance, whose critics were apt to be taxed with rationalism,[2] or the so-called revelations of Anna Katharina Emmerick.[3] The accent was too often on the observance of a

---

2. It took time for the results of the Bollandists' researches to be assimilated. Even as late as 1900, the Abbé Hemmer's rather scathing report to the congress of Bourges on the vagaries of popular devotion was greeted with cries of protest (cf R. Rémond, *Les Deux Congrès ecclésiastiques* (Paris 1964), 159).

Notice must also be taken of the large-scale resumption of canonisations under Pius IX and Leo XIII (cf. J. Schmidlin, *Papstgeschichte der neuesten Zeit*, II (Munich 1934), 304-6 and 540-3).

3. Published first in 1833 by the poet Clemens Brentano and afterwards by the Redemp-

code, a code more moral than religious and one enjoining an individualist and legalistic type of morality; and the stress on individual devotions narrowed still further the perspective of the many faithful who had already lost contact with the Bible and the liturgy. But for all its maladroit expression, the new trend represented a wholesome reaction of Christian sentiment against the attenuated Christianity, verging closely on deism, that had gained the upper hand in many circles in the course of the preceding century. The stress on regular confession and the exhortation to more frequent communion drew attention to the essentially sacramental character of Catholic life. More important still, the intense concentration, even if carried to excess, on the Infant Jesus in the manger or on the Sacred Heart, focused attention on the reality at the centre of Christianity, Christ the love of God incarnate, inviting all men to love him in return.

The rediscovery of Christ was accompanied, as was only natural, by a renewal of devotion to his mother. The mounting tide of Marian devotion among the mass of Catholics was given further impetus by a series of apparitions of the Virgin, all at places in France but soon to become famed throughout the world: in particular to Catherine Labouré in 1830, the start of what has been called the 'epic of the miracle-working medallion' and most renownedly to Bernadette Soubirous at Lourdes in 1858.[4]

The fact that H. Lasserre's *Notre-Dame de Lourdes* (1889) was one of the nineteenth century's best sellers (close on a million copies, not counting translations into a dozen and more languages) surely speaks for itself. Every country saw a rapid growth of Marian congregations and of societies of Children of Mary, officially re-established by Pius IX in 1847. Observance of the May devotions met with growing favour and by the end of the century had become almost universal, though without detriment to the upsurge of popular piety in many other forms. It is also symptomatic that between 1802 and 1898 not a year passed without the foundation of one or even several religious congregations dedicated to the Virgin, with France well in the lead, followed by Belgium, Italy and Spain.[5] The definition of the dogma

---

torist K. E. Schmöger (1858-60), appearing almost immediately in translation in a variety of languages, these revelations had a very keen reception. The question how far Brentano may have expanded the notes he took at the bedside of the stigmatised by drawing on earlier writings and by giving free rein to his imagination is one on which historians are divided. The most recent are less harsh in their judgment that was W. Hümpfner (cf. *Dictionnaire d'histoire et de géographie ecclésiastiques*, XV, 432-3).

4. See L. Misermont, *La Bienheureuse C. Labouré et la Médaille miraculeuse*, 3rd edn, Paris 1935. As to Lourdes, all earlier publications have to be reconsidered in the light of the massive dossier assembled by R. Laurentin: *Lourdes. Documents authentiques*, 7 vols, Paris 1957-66, and *Lourdes. Histoire authentique des apparitions*, 6 vols, Paris 1961-4.

5. See E. Bergh, *Maria. Études sur la Sainte Vierge*, III (Paris 1954), 463-88. Some were record years, for example 1850 and 1854 with sixteen and fourteen foundations respectively.

of the Immaculate Conception by Pius IX in 1854,[6] itself the climax of a great wave of piety made articulate in the episcopal petitions, was instrumental at once in intensifying the devotion of the faithful and in directing the attention of theologians to an examination of the Marian privileges. Leo XIII, the 'diplomat pope', was deeply devoted to the Virgin and always eager to commend the recitation of the rosary; he was the first pope to develop the theme of Mary's spiritual maternity. Pius X made the fiftieth anniversary of the definition of the Immaculate Conception an occasion of unusual splendour and organised for that year (1904) an international Marian congress at Rome.

The same year saw the publication by a Belgian Redemptorist, Fr Godts, of the first book expressly dealing with Marian meditation, a theme that was to become very popular in the interwar period. Unfortunately, certain manifestations of this Marian revival were tawdry or even infantile in character, requiring in some instances intervention from the Holy Office; and if we except isolated contributions by Passaglia, Malou, Newman and Scheeben, the written effusions were for the most part painful in their mediocrity.

The large place accorded to Marian devotion in Catholicism from the mid-nineteenth century prompted in various minds, especially on the Protestant side, the question whether it had not eclipsed the role of Christ in the eyes of the faithful. In a few instances there was undoubtedly a grain of truth in the criticism, but it has to be remembered that if the nineteenth century was a Marian century it was also, in Mgr d'Hulst's just description, 'the century of the Sacred Heart'. Confined originally to one or two restricted circles, devotion to the Sacred Heart owed its first popularisation to parochial missions preached in France during the Restoration period, but it did not become widespread until the time of Pius IX. He encouraged the movement by his extension of the feast of the Sacred Heart to the universal Church in 1856, at the request of the French bishops,[7] and by the beatification in 1864 of Margaret Mary Alacocque. Among its most ardent supporters were the Jesuits, who helped to publicise the movement in a magazine, *Le Messager du Sacré-Coeur*, which Fr H. Ramière launched in

6. In addition to *Dictionnaire de théologie catholique*, VII, 1189-1218, see *Pareri dell' Episcopato cattolico...sulla definizione dogmatica dell' Immacolato concepimento della B.V. Maria*, 10 vols, Rome 1851-4, and V. Sardi, *La sollenne definizione del dogma dell' Immacolato concepimento di Maria. Atti e documenti*, Rome 1905.

7. One reason for the large place occupied by France in the world-wide diffusion of the cult of the Sacred Heart during the nineteenth century was that the legitimists, who took a prominent part in Catholic affairs, remained mindful of Louis XVI's vow during his imprisonment in the Temple to dedicate France to the Sacred Heart and of the fact that in the La Vendée rising the Catholics had fought with the sacred emblem affixed to their breasts. These memories were to give a particular colouring to the ceremonies, becoming more and more splendid, enacted at Paray-le-Monial and after 1876 at Montmartre.

1861 as the organ of the Apostleship of Prayer, an association which at the beginnings of Leo XIII's pontificate was already established in a dozen countries and by 1914 numbered several million. As a measure of the growing popularity of the devotion we can point to the successful introduction of litanies of the Sacred Heart, the month of special devotion to the Sacred Heart and the observance of the 'first Friday'. The number of religious congregations founded in the name of the Sacred Heart increased and they ceased to be a French speciality. Whereas between 1815 and 1846 seventeen such congregations were founded in France against three in Italy and two in Belgium, between 1846 and 1878 twelve were founded in France, eleven in Italy, three in Spain, three in Belgium, three in the United States and one apiece in Germany, Lebanon and Australia. [8] Another development as the century advanced was the growing emphasis in ultramontane circles on the duty of securing recognition of the Sacred Heart as sovereign in society and it was this goal, viewed in some minds from an undeniably theocratic standpoint, that came increasingly to dominate the movement. Following the consecration of individuals, families, [9] religious congregations and dioceses to the Sacred Heart, the call went out for the official consecration of nations (Belgium led the way in 1869, followed in 1873 by France and by the Ecuador of García Moreno) and even of the entire universe. In 1875 a petition to this effect, signed by 525 bishops, was submitted to the pope by Fr Ramière, the driving force behind the movement. Pius IX thought it better not to precipitate matters and went only so far as to send out through the Congregation of Rites a formula of consecration approved by himself which he urged should be recited publicly on 16 June 1875, the two hundredth anniversary of the great revelation. But a new approach in 1898, made on the initiative of a German nun, Maria of the Sacred Heart Droste zu Vischering, Superior of the Good Shepherd of Porto, was more successful. In the encyclical *Annum Sacrum* of 25 May 1899, the first to be devoted exclusively to the cult of the Sacred Heart, Leo XIII established the cult on theological foundations by stressing its reparative aspect. This was followed by the official act of consecration, pronounced by the pope on 31 December 1899, the night that ushered in the dawn of the new century. [10]

8. Cf E. Bergh, 'La vie religieuse au service du Sacré-Coeur', in *Cor Jesu*, II (Rome 1959), 457-98.

9. Beginning in 1907, and with encouragement from Pius X, the practice of 'enthroning the Heart of Jesus within the family' was advocated with great fervour by Fr Mateo Crawley (1875-1960) of the Congregation of the Picpus, who was to become during the interwar years one of the great world-wide apostles of the devotion to the Sacred Heart.

10. On this ceremony and its backwash see E. Bergh, 'Le cinquantenaire de la consécration du genre humain au Sacré-Coeur', *Nouvelle Revue théologique*, LXXI (1949), 606-20, supplemented (for the role of Mother Droste) by G. Oesterle, in *Benediktinische Monatschrift*, XXV (1949), 177-286.

The erection at Rome in 1903 by Leo XIII of an archconfraternity pledged to offer votive masses in honour of the Heart of Jesus, as also to the communion of the first Friday, underlined the close link that existed throughout this period between devotion to the Sacred Heart and eucharistic worship. The latter at first chiefly took the form of adoration of the Blessed Sacrament but this was increasingly supplemented, despite resistance from latter-day Jansenists, by the practice of frequent communion.

At the accession of Pius IX perpetual adoration of the Blessed Sacrament was almost unknown outside Italy, but before long the practice had become worldwide (it was introduced into Canada by Mgr Bourget and during the decade 1850-60 penetrated the United States). At the same period the Roman practice of nocturnal adoration spread north of the Alps, in the first instance into Germany, introduced there by a convert, Hermann Cohen, and then into France, promoted in the north by the efforts of an industrialist, Philibert Vrau, and from 1870 becoming associated above all with the sanctuary at Montmartre, which rapidly developed into an international centre.

In the adoration of the Blessed Sacrament the accent had long been placed on reparation for the outrages inflicted on Jesus Christ, but in France the idea took on a new colouring: reparation not merely for the offences of individual sinners but above all for the secularisation of society at the hands of public authorities. This was the background to the germination in France around 1875 of the idea of international eucharistic congresses, conceived as impressive spectacles whose aim was to make the eucharistic presence more vivid to the indifferent masses and at the same time to instil into Catholics, intimidated by anti-clerical policies, a sense of their strength and solidarity. The movement owed its beginnings to a devout laywoman, Mlle Tamisier, who received encouragement from Mgr de Ségur – a name that crops up in connection with all the pious initiatives of this period – and from two bishops in neighbouring countries, Mgr Mermillod of Fribourg in Switzerland and Mgr Doutreloux of Liège. The original idea was to exploit the revived interest in pilgrimages by organising pilgrimages of reparation to the principal sanctuaries associated with a eucharistic miracle. But Mlle Tamisier soon had the inspiration of incorporating a study programme, turning the occasions thereby into true congresses with an international appeal. The first met at Lille in 1881 and was a relatively modest affair, but with each passing year the numbers attending grew and Rome's encouragement became more positive. With the accession of Pius X, the pope of the Eucharist, and the appointment as president of the multilingual and exceptionally energetic Mgr Heylen, bishop of Namur, a new phase in the history of the congresses began. In the first place as regards numbers, the congress at Lourdes in 1914 was attended by ten cardinals and two hundred bishops, who were alone equal in number to the entire contingent of outsiders (i.e.

people not from the host diocese of Cambrai) present at the first congress in 1881. Second, there was greater emphasis on the international character of the movement. Out of the first fifteen congresses, nine had met in France, four in Belgium and one in French-speaking Switzerland – territories commonly regarded as French by extension – and it has to be remembered that the one exception, the congress at Jerusalem in 1893,[11] was held at a time when France was very much at home in the Middle East. But to celebrate the twenty-fifth anniversary of the movement, which fell soon after he became pope, Pius X decided that the congress of that year, 1905, should be held in Rome with the pope himself presiding. Then after Tournai in 1906 the pope chose for three years in succession meeting-places in countries with a Protestant majority: in 1907 Metz, at that date part of Germany, in 1908 London, in 1909 Cologne. In 1910 the congress went overseas to Montreal and in the three following years visited Madrid, Vienna and Malta. This widening of the horizons was made all the more natural by the practice that had grown up in recent years of holding national congresses. There was also some change of direction. The original aims, it is true, were not lost sight of and the congresses remained as their initiators had meant them to be, public demonstrations intended to stimulate enthusiasm for all forms of adoration of the Blessed Sacrament, to rid Catholics of their fear of public opinion, and to proclaim the kingship of Christ in society in face of its rejection by the secularisers. From this point of view the congresses of Madrid and still more of Vienna, when the emperor and the archdukes, in full dress uniform, followed the procession amid the vast throng of participants, were models of the genre. But another aspect, present only in muted form under Leo XIII, was allowed to come increasingly to the fore: the desire to encourage through the congresses the habit of frequent or even daily communion. Pius X made deliberate use of the congresses first to prepare the ground for his celebrated eucharistic decrees and then to test out their absorption and application. Having started as a pious initiative, the eucharistic congresses thus became in the hands of the Holy See a highly effective channel for reminding Catholics that the Eucharist was not only an object of worship but also the source of their essential sustenance.

Although it was Pius X who gave the decisive lead, the movement in favour of frequent communion had started before his time as pope, in the middle of the nineteenth century. As far back as 1851 the Congregation of the Council had amended a chapter of the Provincial Council of Rouen which forbade the admission to communion of children below the age of twelve, and in 1860 a papal brief warmly commended a book on *La très*

11. It was Leo XIII himself, in pursuit of his policy of *rapprochement* with the Orthodox Churches, who had desired it should meet in the East. For further details of the congress see chapter 17, 466-7.

sainte communion in which the author, the ubiquitous Mgr Ségur, counselled weekly communion for the great majority and saw no great objection to communion every other day or even daily. Although it raised a storm among the more old-fashioned clergy, the work sold 180,000 copies in France and was translated into German, English, Spanish, Portugese and Dutch. Ségur's was not the only voice raised in France in favour of frequent communion. He had been preceded as far back as 1855 by Mgr Gerbet and by Mgr Dupanloup, on most other points his complete opposite. In Belgium eloquent support for frequent communion came from the Flemish poet priest Guido Gezelle [12] and in Spain, despite the reservations of the hierarchy, from a French Jesuit, Leonard Cros. But the country where reaction against Jansenist severity in the matter set in most strongly was Italy. While the saintly Don Frassinetti was composing his *Il convito del divino amore* (1868), in which he defended frequent communion on the grounds of its Christian antiquity, S. Cottolengo was dispensing the Eucharist daily to any inmates of his hospice who requested it, and Don Bosco declared himself in favour of the communion of young children. Among Don Bosco's admirers was Mgr Sarto, who in his dioceses of Mantua and Venice made the development of eucharistic worship an essential part of his programme. It is not surprising that on becoming pope he set himself to extend this programme to the Church universal.

A decree of the Congregation of the Council of 20 December 1905 settled the controversy of recent years between upholders and opponents of frequent communion by defining two sufficient conditions, the state of grace and right intention, and it urged the faithful to communicate 'very frequently, even every day'. One rapid consequence of the decree was the formation under various designations – in Belgium 'Ligues du Sacré-Coeur', in England 'Knights of the Blessed Sacrament', and so on – of eucharistic guilds intended to make its teaching a reality in the life of the parishes. Subsequent decrees encouraged communicants with indulgences and made communion of the sick more feasible by abolishing the eucharistic fast for those bedridden for more than a month. Moreover, in September 1906 the Congregation of the Council made it clear that the words 'all the faithful' in the decree of 1905 applied equally to children who had made their first communion, and since there was disagreement in the Church over when the 'age of reason' requisite for first communion was reached, another decree, this time of the Congregation of Sacraments (8 April 1910), ruled that it was suf-

---

12. In 1883 Mgr Faict, bishop of Bruges, noted that the number of communicants had 'substantially increased' in his diocese over the past thirty years and that on Sundays communion was dispensed every quarter of an hour (A. Haquin, *Dom Lambert Beauduin et le Renouveau liturgique*, Gembloux 1970, 18. See the same author's 'La pastorale des curés du diocèse de Namur', *Revue diocésaine de Namur*, XX (1966), 455-72.

ficient for the child to be able to distinguish 'the eucharistic from ordinary bread' and hence that it was unnecessary to postpone the age of first communion to ten, twelve or even fourteen, as was often the practice north of the Alps. This measure, which appeared to many more revolutionary than it was in fact, at first met with resistance, especially in France, but that it was very soon accepted as customary is proved by the foundation in France in 1914 of the 'Croisade eucharistique', destined after the war to become world-wide in its influence.

It is to be noted that the eucharistic decrees of Pius X relate to communion as such, independently of its liturgical context. Their standpoint is still that of the nineteenth century, in which eucharistic devotion was concentrated much more on the Host than on the Mass. In other ways, however, Pius X contributed greatly to the rediscovery of liturgical devotion within the Catholic Church. The beginnings of the movement go back to the middle of the nineteenth century and are associated with men such as Graf and Hirscher in Germany and Dom Guéranger in France. But the proposals of the former to introduce the vernacular into the celebration of the Mass ran into strong opposition while the treasures amassed by the Abbot of Solesmes in his *Année liturgique* (1841 onwards) long remained the discovery of the chosen few. Once sown, however, the seed slowly started to germinate. In 1865, in a little book *Choral und Liturgie,* Dom Maur Wolter, resuscitator of Beuron, communicated to German Catholics, in pages glowing with a disciple's enthusiasm, Guéranger's most important ideas regarding the Church as a praying community and the unsurpassable richness of the spiritual sustenance to be found in the Divine Office. Indicative of the reawakening of interest is the fact that in 1875, after a lapse of thirty years, the *Année liturgique* resumed publication in France and was translated into German, English and Italian. Another landmark was the publication in 1882 by a monk of Maredsous, Dom Gérard van Caloen, of a *Missel des fidèles, contenant le texte du missel romain avec traduction française et notices explicatives, liturgiques et historiques* which rapidly sold out (admittedly only three thousand were printed), followed two years later by the publication by Dom A. Schott of its German counterpart. Although liturgical teaching in most of the seminaries continued at the level of initiation into the rubrics, elsewhere the scientific study of the liturgy was starting to revive, first and foremost in England (centred on the Henry Bradshaw Society) but also in Germany (V. Thalhofer, S. Bäumer, A. Baumstarck), in France (L. Duchesne, P. Batiffol, U. Chevalier, the *Dictionnaire d'archéologie chrétienne et de liturgie,* which started publication 1903), and in Italy (G. Mercati). A new spirit also entered into the Church's music, where it was desperately needed, with composers such as A. Bruckner in Austria, F. X. Witte in Germany and C. Franck in France. At the same time the erudite researches of the Solesmes School[13] were preparing the ground for the restoration of plainsong, the virtues of which were made known to a wider public by societies such as the German *Cäcilienverein* (making use, unfortunately, of the very poor Pustet or 'Medicean' edition) and congresses such as the one at Arezzo in 1882, which marked an important turning-point.

But these efforts were after all but the modest prelude to a movement which, from the beginning of the twentieth century, began to swell in volume, to receive official ratification in Pius XII's encyclical *Mediator Dei* and again from the Second Vatican Council. As so often in the Church the movement was twofold, stemming from initiatives taken both at the centre and on the periphery.

One of the first acts of Pius X's pontificate was the *motu proprio Tra le sollecitudini* of 22 November 1903. Its immediate concern was with the restoration of church music in accordance with the ancient traditions of the Roman Church, but its scope was so much broader that it has been called 'the charger of the liturgical movement': for the pope intervened not as an aesthete or an archaeologist but as a pastor concerned to enhance the dignity of God's house, the place where the faithful come together to unite in offering the Church's prayers and in the solemn and public celebration of the liturgical offices. The *motu proprio* put forward the Gregorian chant, 'so happily restored to all its fulness and purity by recent researches' (an allusion to the work of the Solesmes School), as 'the most perfect example of sacred music' but it did not insist on the exclusion of all else, the mistake made by certain executants of the pope's wishes, who deluded themselves that plainsong could be made accessible to the great mass of the faithful. [14] A second *motu proprio* (25 April 1904), drawn up like the first under the guidance of Fr de Santi, S.J., now increasingly recognised as the key figure in the Gregorian reform, announced the setting up of a special commission to prepare an authorised Vatican edition of the Gregorian melodies. The commission was soon faced with a dilemma. Was it necessary, as Dom Mocquereau believed, to insist in a liturgical edition on strict fidelity to the readings of the earliest manuscripts, some of which might be jarring to a

13. On the work of Dom J. Pothier (1835-1923), author of *Mélodies grégoriennes,* published 1880, and of Dom A. Mocquereau (1849-1930), whose *Paléographie musicale* started to appear in 1889 (Vol. VII is of special interest), see P. Combe, *Histoire de la restauration du chant grégorien,* Solesmes 1961, which also describes the difficulties of every kind they had to contend with, in particular the exclusive rights unfortunately granted by the Congregations of Rites in 1871 to the Pustet edition.
14. Cardinal Merry del Val's testimony is of interest: 'Pius X was warm in his welcome for the works of modern composers but he expected them to keep strictly to the rules and to make their compositions so far as possible an echo and extension of the chorale. He did not agree with certain fanatics who wanted all non-Gregorian music banished from our churches, which he thought was going much too far', *Pie X, Impressions et Souvenirs,* (Rome 1950), 81-2.

modern ear; or would it follow the course recommended by Dom Pothier, more eclectic in his outlook than his young disciple, and which was desired by the Germans, namely to accept some of the alleviations introduced at a later date? As a way out, the pope tacitly by-passed the commission and gave to Dom Pothier alone the task of preparing the edition, which came out in separate parts between 1905 and 1912. To set the seal on the reform in 1911 a Higher Pontifical Institute of Sacred Music was established at Rome under the presidency of Fr de Santi.

In the meantime and largely at the instigation of Mgr Piacenza, professor of liturgy at one of the Roman universities, Pius X had embarked on another reform, which had been on the agenda ever since the First Vatican Council. This was the reform of the breviary, undertaken not in order to correct historical errors – a commission for this purpose had in fact been set up by Leo XIII in 1902 – but with the object of restoring Sunday to its place of honour in the liturgical cycle and of reviving the weekly recitation of the psalter. The multiplication of festivals and votive celebrations, each with its special office, had produced a situation in which the Sunday and weekday offices were very rarely offered and in consequence many psalms hardly ever had a hearing. As was his usual practice in such matters, Pius X entrusted the detailed work to a special commission which worked independently of the Congregation of Rites, a body so resistant to change that any serious reform would otherwise have been impossible. The principles of the reform were enunciated in the bull *Divino afflatu* of 1 November 1911. No feast was suppressed, but Sunday was almost always given precedence and on other days, including feast days, the weekday office was to be used, with allowance for the recital where appropriate of certain hymns, lessons and chapters proper to particular feasts. The annual cycle was thus reinstated and at the same time the office was made more varied (and also shorter, particularly on Sundays, which was in keeping with the general desire of the clergy). The commission's next task was to produce a new standard edition of the breviary (it appeared in 1914). The original plan was for a completely new edition, but in view of the prolonged study needed for such an ambitious undertaking it was decided to make do for the time with provisional measures. In the pope's mind this was intended to pave the way for a more fundamental reform, but after the death of Pius X the project was held in abeyance for twenty-five years, which was perhaps just as well, since specialists had been severely critical of the way in which the commission, most of whose members lacked the necessary expertise, had set about its work. It certainly seems, as Mgr Amann remarked,[15] that 'Pius X easily persuaded himself that all problems, even those relating to art and

---

15. *Dictionnaire de théologie catholique*, XII, col. 1736.

scholarship, could be dealt with by means of authority'. He nevertheless had the great merit, as in the matter of church music, of clearing a path through a steadily thickening jungle, a result unlikely to have been achieved through normal administrative channels, and through his reinstatement of the Sunday and weekday offices, especially in Lent, of placing the emphasis once again on the celebration of the mysteries of Christ within the framework of an annual cycle.

While this restoration of Catholic worship was proceeding from above, Belgium was witnessing the beginnings of a pastoral liturgical movement which, after a pause in its progress during the war, continued to develop throughout the pontificates of Pius XI and Pius XII. It naturally had its precursors and parallels, but its chief architect was Dom Lambert Beauduin, a Benedictine of the abbey of Mont-César (Louvain). He drew his inspiration from a sentence in the *motu proprio* of 1903 in which Pius X recommended 'active participation by the faithful in the divine mysteries'; [16] and helped by his previous experience as a diocesan priest and his remarkable talent for organisation he succeeded in awakening parishes to an interest in the liturgical movement, which until now had penetrated only to restricted groups within the orbit of Benedictine abbeys. Having aired the question at the Malines congress of 1909, he organised the distribution in hundreds and thousands of a booklet containing a translation, with commentary, of the Mass for each Sunday. Nor did he neglect the systematic education of the parochial clergy, reaching them through a review, *Les questions liturgiques,* through pamphlets such as *La piété liturgique* (1914), which deserves a special mention as a little masterpiece of the movement, filling to perfection its aim of basing pastoral action on solid doctrinal and historical foundations, and through the annual and increasingly successful 'liturgical weeks', which helped substantially to spread the ideas of Mont César well beyond the frontiers of Belgium.

---

16. The official Latin translation of the Italian original of this passage is not entirely accurate (see *Questions liturgiques et paroissiales,* XXXII, (1952), 161.

7

PASTORAL WORK AND
CATHOLIC ACTION

ALTHOUGH we have as yet very few sociological studies of the ordinary clergy during the nineteenth century,[1] there is enough evidence to show that from the middle years of that century, allowing for obvious differences of national tradition and social environment, the type of pastor with which the modern world is familiar was gradually being formed. For this a number of different elements were responsible.

First and foremost there was the personal influence of the popes. The raising of the moral and spiritual standard of the clergy was one of Pius IX's most constant themes, to which he returned regularly not only in his encyclicals and allocutions but still more frequently in his private correspondence, surely proof that he was not indulging in empty rhetoric. Many of Leo XIII's encyclicals, letters and allocutions testify to his particular interest in the intellectual training of priests and also, especially in the late years of his pontificate, to his concern at a slackening among the younger clergy in a feeling for discipline. Pius X, who in his encyclical *Communium rerum* (1909) also gave us his portrait of the ideal bishop, took a truly personal interest in the common priest, with whom he had come into close contact during his time as bishop: throughout his pontificate he was constant in his appeals to the clergy to commit themselves ever more wholeheartedly to the demands of their vocation,[2] and the Exhortation he composed in August 1908 to mark the fiftieth anniversary of his ordination, a true spiritual document of the priesthood, has long remained a classic.

There were bishops in plenty who echoed these themes. Some did so in

1. An exemplary lead was given by C. Marcilhacy, *Le Diocèse d'Orléans sous l'épiscopat de Mgr Dupanloup* (Paris 1962), esp. 48-191.
2. A. M. Lanz, 'Pio X e la spiritualità del clero diocesano', *Civiltà cattolica*, year 103, Vol. I (1952), 141-50.

print, indeed in books that were to be translated into many different languages and reach a vast public: Manning's *The Eternal Priesthood* (1883); Gibbons's *The Ambassador of Christ;* and striking a new note, prelude to the renewal of spirituality among the diocesan clergy that was to characterise the inter-war period, Mercier's *La Vie intérieure, appel aux âmes sacerdotales* (1918). More usual is to find the bishops issuing practical directives, commending various religious exercises or weekly confession, making arrangements for periodic retreats followed up by monthly recollections. Furthermore, these episcopal prescriptions chimed with the spontaneous aspirations of a growing number of priests who had formed themselves, for the sustenance of their zeal and their spiritual life, into priests' associations: and although as a rule they were limited to the individual diocese, a few of these associations achieved an international standing, for example, the Union apostolique des prêtres séculiers founded at Orleans in 1862 and the Associatio perseverantiae sacerdotalis founded at Vienna in 1868. To all this must be added the growing influence on the clergy of the religious, arising from the greater contact between the two in the everyday work of the ministry and from the fact that the clergy turned to material published by the orders for their staple devotional reading.

The influence of religious helped to reinforce in the secular priest the tendency to keep himself separate from the world, an attitude systematically inculcated in the seminaries and underlined in Latin countries by the general habit of wearing the soutane. He thereby ran the risk of losing contact with the society in which he was required to exercise his ministry. For this reason some have wondered in retrospect whether for all the undeniable benefits, notably in improving the spiritual quality of the clergy and creating greater awareness of the demands of the sacerdotal ministry, there was not a double edge to the policy of promoting to such an extent the Sulpician model of priest, the man of prayer leading a withdrawn and sacrificial life, which was an inheritance from the French school of the seventeenth century.

The disadvantage to the sacerdotal ministry of this isolation from the world shows up in the generally mediocre quality of the preaching, so far as it can be judged from the published sermons of the period. For all the time and effort expended on them the content is disappointing, for the preachers seem for the most part preoccupied with the re-evocation of a still cherished past, having little understanding of the world in which they lived. This ignorant fear of the world, met equally in the pious literature of the time, was reinforced by a notoriously inadequate philosophical and theological training which gave the priest a view of the world based on outdated and distorting categories.

Towards the end of Leo XIII's pontificate more and more voices were raised in criticism of the outmoded character of the teaching given in the seminaries, teaching made all the more precarious by the fact that the majority of the professors were self-taught. Whereas the book in which E. Fani, professor of the seminary at Florence, set down his thoughts on the subject (*L'Educazione del giovane clero nei Seminari e i nuovi tempi,* 1882) was put on the Index, the *Clerical Studies* of John Hogan, a Sulpician who was superior of the seminary at Boston, published fifteen years later (1898, French translation 1901), met with a better reception. It inspired the *Lettres sur les études ecclésiastiques* (1900-1) of Mgr Minot, archbishop of Albi. Mention should also be made of the new regime, a great novelty at the time, instituted by Mercier in the 'Leo XII' seminary he ran from 1892 in conjunction with the university of Louvain, in which a spirit of trust replaced the more or less strictly regimented supervision normally employed and in which the accent fell most heavily on the personal and spiritual formation of the seminarists.[3] But this original experiment long remained virtually unique.

The problem of the seminaries presented itself in particularly acute from in Italy, by reason of the large number of very small dioceses which lacked the material resources to organise a seminary on any serious bias. Pius X, who had once been spiritual director of the Treviso seminary and who as bishop of Mantua and patriarch of Venice had expended much effort on improving the seminaries in his dioceses, made a direct attack on the problem as soon as he became pope. Although the measures he prescribed were aimed specifically at Italy, he also thought them valuable as a model for the Church as a whole, and certain statements, whether emanating from the pope himself or from the Congregation concerned, let this be clearly understood. One of the purposes of the apostolic visitation of all the Italian dioceses decreed in March 1904 was to investigate the state of the seminaries (not omitting the smaller seminaries in which the great majority of priests received their preparation for the priesthood), and at the beginning of 1905 a pontifical commission was set up, to work out plans for reform in the light of the information gathered. The pope's confidential adviser in this matter was Fr Benedetti, M.S.C. After three years of work the commission published a detailed new curriculum for the seminaries (10 May 1907) and laid down standards of moral and spiritual training (1 January 1908). Although the tenor of the programme as a whole was to reinforce the defects of a self-contained educational system, it did contain measures which pointed in the right direction. Even so, the results were somewhat disappointing, mainly because of inadequacies in the teaching staff and because the drastic purge accompanying the anti-modernist reaction made still worse the dearth of men competent to carry out the programme. The undiscriminating character of this reaction had the further consequence, which affected other

3. See the composite work *Le Cardinal Mercier, fondateur de séminaire,* Louvain 1951.

countries even more than Italy, of checking and sometimes wiping out for a whole generation the sporadic efforts being made at the turn of the century to remedy the flagrant deficiencies in most of the seminaries.

While clerical education was slow to adapt to the new conditions both in the Church and the world, among priests in the active ministry the efforts at adaptation increased as the new century advanced. To be sure, a great many priests of this pre-1914 era still bore out the truth of Taine's celebrated characterisation, which is applicable not only to France: 'the faithful sentinel at his post, patiently awaiting orders from above, performing correctly the duties of his lonely and monotonous watch'. Their activity consisted of the bare essentials, the celebration of Mass – to weekday congregations in some countries of two or three women – and preaching on Sundays, teaching the children their catechism, hearing a few confessions, administering the last sacraments to the dying. But let us beware of hasty generalisations. The priests who ministered to the villages of central and southern Italy were usually closely involved, sometimes too much involved, with the daily lives of their parishioners, much more so than their counterparts in France. Again, in England or Ireland the priests of populous parishes often filled the role not only of spiritual father to their flock but also that of 'counsellor' on temporal matters, acting sometimes as spokesman in pressing claims against the civil authorities. On the other hand, even in countries where the clergy's retreat into purely ecclesiastical functions was most pronounced, there are signs of the gradual emergence of a kind of active asceticism which often impelled priests to be more assertive in their ministry. A positive lead in this direction was given as early as the pontificate of Pius IX, by founders of religious congregations, for example Fr d'Alzon and Don Bosco, but the phenomenon was not confined to the religious. Dupanloup urged his parish clergy not to be content with waiting on the faithful in the churches but to go into people's homes to stir up the indifferent. To make them more zealous he resorted to the survey technique. In this he was something of a pioneer, although he was not the only one, as is sometimes believed. Furthermore, although in all essentials the sacerdotal ministry continued to be centred on the parish, alongside the *curé* and the *vicaire* a new type of priest was appearing on the scene, the priest in charge of the voluntary organisation.

The growth of voluntary organisations (*œuvres, Vereine*) was a characteristic of nineteenth-century Catholicism and was one of the reasons for the persistence of the ghetto-like atmosphere which today is often deplored. The purpose they were intended to answer had been clearly defined by Mgr d'Hulst, who was fond of saying that the parish of the future was likely to be a conglomeration of *œuvres*, for in a perspective no longer officially Christian there was need 'to create artificially environments in which the supernatural life could freely develop'.[4] This helps to explain why

Pius X was so emphatic that the strictly confessional character of voluntary organisations be upheld, even in the case of organisations as secular in their objects as trade unions,[5] and that Catholics should refrain from collaborating with religiously neutral organisations, as they were being urged to do by certain progressives, who had a more realistic view of the situation as it appeared at the dawn of the twentieth century. But these were as yet isolated voices, and the second half of the nineteenth century had witnessed a contrary development in the form of a marked proliferation of Catholic voluntary associations. In the later years of Leo XIII's pontificate many of the new organisations were socially orientated, recalling in modernised form the *curés physiocrates* of the eighteenth century and their efforts to educate their people in temporal affairs, for in most of these organisations it was the priest who took the lead and held the authority, leaving to laymen only the role of docile auxiliaries. As the organisations, clubs and societies multiplied it was thought useful to set up co-ordinating bodies, where possible on a national scale, as in the German-speaking countries and later in the United States, or failing that at diocesan level; but in the Latin countries a more anarchical spirit prevailed and the organisations remained much longer an affair of purely local or individual initiative.

Another manifestation of the concern to provide an *ersatz* of Christendom for Catholics living in an increasingly secular world was the great effort devoted to the expansion of Catholic education. The schools question was already felt to be acute during the pontificate of Gregory XVI, and as education became more generally available the clergy became more and more convinced that it was necessary to provide, at whatever sacrifice, a positively Catholic form of education. For although in the German countries a solution had been found that was satisfactory to Catholics and which continued to work well, in the Latin countries the State schools were veering away from a Christian orientation and in Anglo-Saxon countries they were predominantly Protestant. It was in circumstances such as these that the church authorities, with explicit encouragement from the Holy See and with an urgency that varied with the country, came to set up a complete system of Catholic educational establishments alongside the State system and often in direct competition with it. In some countries there were even Catholic universities (in Belgium from as early as 1834, in Ireland from 1851, in France from 1875, in the United States from 1887; new foundations were still being made after the First World War, thus the Catholic universities of Milan, Nijmegen and Lublin).

The conscientious zeal with which so many priests devoted themselves to

4. *Mélanges oratoires*, III (Paris 1900), 112.
5. For the serious disagreement on this subject between Pius X and a section of German Catholics see chapter 5, 93-4 and chapter 8, 163-4.

work in these three fields, the parish, the voluntary organisation and the school, was unfortunately accompanied all too rarely by the pastoral imagination needed to review the classical methods in relation to the sociological and cultural changes taking place all round. Faced with the advance of religious indifference, which in the towns increased with the concentration there of a rootless proletariat and in the countryside with the spread of railways, the deeper penetration of newspapers and the more universal liability to military service, and faced what was more with a phenomenon that could scarcely fail to escape notice, even where the figure for Sunday observance did not fall, as it did in Brie in 1903, to 2.4 per cent, very few of those in authority seemed to recognise that attempts to provide more places for worship and bigger staffs for parishes were of secondary importance compared with the prime task of devising and perfecting new pastoral approaches that could enable contact to be re-established with the masses who had deserted the Church or were creating their own organisations outside it. A typical and telling example is provided by the prelates who preached adaptation to the times in the political sphere and yet in the pastoral sphere continued to defend 'the old tried methods' in face of the more enterprising notions of younger priests. For in spite of everything there were changes in the wind, especially from the time of Leo XIII.

One or two interesting developments, in particular as regards the press, had in fact got under way much earlier. As far back as 1844 it was remarked in the *Revue des deux Mondes*: 'Laymen have turned theologian and theologians journalist. There are members of the clergy for whom the press is nowadays an extension of the pulpit, for they realise that newspaper columns carry more weight than sermons.' The remark was made about France, but it was true of Western Europe as a whole. Probably to begin with it applied more to the reviews than to the first Catholic dailies. The latter usually had a very limited circulation and cut a relatively feeble figure, for want of material and intellectual resources, beside the organs of the free-thinking press. In some cases they were also handicapped by the suspicious attitude of a higher clergy fearful of journalistic meddling in the Church's affairs. But in the later part of the century the situation improved, especially in Germany and in France, where the Assumptionists with their publishing house, Bonne Presse, deserve particular mention. The fact remains, however, that these were Catholic papers published for an almost exclusively Catholic readership. They were not organs designed to provide non-Catholics with accurate information about the Church, nor did they seek to persuade non-Catholics to modify their moral and religious opinions. During the pontificate of Pius X a few enterprising Italian Catholics tried an experiment of this kind with their *stampa di penetrazione,* but they soon incurred the pope's formal disapproval.[6]

In the field of pastoral work proper there were two aspects receiving special attention in Germanic circles in the years before and after 1900, one being the teaching of the catechism.[7] Efforts at reform were greatly stimulated by the foundation of two specialist journals, one at Munich in 1875 and the other at Vienna in 1878, in which a new and more inductive method of teaching was gradually worked out: instead of starting with the abstract text and then expounding it, the new method went the other way about and made the child's experience lead up to the text of the catechism. This Munich method spread to other countries, its diffusion being assisted by conferences held in 1906 and 1912, but a generation was to elapse before attention started to focus on the more fundamental question, to which the psychological and pedagogical problems were subsidiary, that of the content to transmit: 'religious knowledge' conveyed in scholastic terms, or tidings of salvation in the words of Holy Scripture.

Another problem receiving attention at this time, the inadequacy of the parochial provision in large towns, was still more serious and had been long neglected. In working-class suburbs, where the position was especially bad, parishes of thirty to forty thousand souls were not uncommon and in some cases the figure was even higher.[8] Vienna had several parishes with more than sixty thousand inhabitants. In Paris in 1906 the church of Saint-Pierre de Montrouge had ninety thousand, that of Notre-Dame de Clignancourt well over a hundred thousand (121,000). As for Rome, at the accession of Pius X not only did the parishes of San Lorenzo and Sant' Agnese exceed 170,000 faithful, there were in addition some three hundred thousand souls living in the outer periphery for whom there was virtually no parochial provision at all. The publication by a Viennese professor H. Swoboda, in his book *Grosstadtseelsorge* (1909), of the findings from a survey conducted throughout Western and Central Europe was from this point of view an important landmark in the history of the modern pastorate.

It was nevertheless in France that the quest for new approaches was at its most active during the closing years of the nineteenth century. If in reading

6. *A.A.S.*, IV, 1912, 695. On this painful episode, which dashed what had been great hopes and in which the saintly Cardinal Ferrari was so distressingly involved, see in particular: *Giovanni Grosoli*, (Assisi 1960), 81-101; L. Bedeschi, 'Significato e fine del trust Grosoliano', *Rassegna di politica e di storia*, X (1964), 7-24; M. Vaussard, *L'Intelligence catholique dans l'Italie du XXe siècle* (Paris 1921), 63-83; M. Torresin, in *Memorie storiche della diocesi di Milano*, X (1963), 37-304.

7. It should also be mentioned that Pius X, who attached considerable importance to the teaching of the catechism, devoted one of his encyclicals to the subject *Acerbo nimis*, 15 April 1905) and ordered a revised version (very scholastic in treatment) to be drawn up for the ecclesiastical province of Rome, which he hoped to see adopted in all dioceses (*A.A.S.*, IV (1912), 690-2).

8. In addition to Swoboda's volume (Regensburg 1909) cited in the text see J. Dellepoort, N. Greinacher and W. Menges, *Die deutsche Priesterfrage*, Mainz 1960.

the reports and discussions of the ecclesiastical congress organised by Lemire at Reims in 1896, at which some seven hundred priests were present, one is struck by the mixture of antiquated and forward-looking solutions, it could also be said that, although many suggestions put forward were still traditionalist in character, there was a freshness of spirit in the debates. Admittedly, the congress involved only a tiny minority, but four-fifths of those present belonged to the parochial clergy and their influence grew from year to year, thanks to regional congresses – the travelling about of the *curés* being something quite new in France – and still more to the proliferation of pamphlets and magazines, not to mention the reviews, in particular the *Revue du clergé français,* which under the editorship of Abbé Bricout provided a forum for the priests most deeply engaged and was avidly read by the younger clergy. The latter were in fact increasingly aware that the priest had lost contact with the people and that there was a crying need, in the words of Y. Le Querdec (a pseudonym used by G. Fonsegrive) to 'exchange the passivity of the presbytery for the activity of the mission field'. This last expression is one that crops up several times – we find the Abbé Naudet referring to 'France the mission field' as early as 1893 – and many people, in their quest for new approaches freed from the shackles of standard parish routines, advocated 'industrial missionaries', an idea originally propounded in 1886 by Mgr Doutreloux, bishop of Liège, and first put into practice in 1893 in the diocese of Tarbes, and even 'worker priests'. [9] Naturally enough the greatest keenness for this missionary form of pastoral renewal was to be found in Christian democrat circles, but its influence was also felt much further afield. To be convinced of this one has only to compare the *Nouveau manuel du séminariste* produced by G. Letourneau, a Sulpician, in 1906, with the manual that had remained in use down to the end of the nineteenth century. Furthermore there were bishops, Mgr Latty for example, and still more conspicuously Mgr Gibier, who were willing to give their sanction to a movement which not only affirmed by example the primacy of the pastoral mission over administrative functions, but which also advocated a more systematic appeal for laymen for their collaboration.

This last idea, which created quite a stir in France around 1900, was an already well-established practice in Germany. The foundation of active Catholic associations in Germany went back to the middle years of the nineteenth century and they presented an astonishing array, each being designed to meet a specific need: purely religious needs, as in the case of the Marian congregations, the promotion of wholesome reading matter in books

---

9. For a very thorough study of the evolution of the idea of worker priests in the period 1890-1910 and of the reverberations of it in Italy, see É. Poulat's introduction to the new edition of the *'Journal d'un prêtre d'après-demain' (1902-1903) de l'abbé Calippe* (Paris 1961), 100-56.

and newspapers, aid to missions, assistance to emigrants (Raphaelverein) or to Catholics scattered in Protestant regions (Bonifatiusverein), charitable objects, as in the case of the Society of St Vincent de Paul and kindred societies (from 1897 linked at inter-diocesan level by the Deutsche Caritasverband), the needs of special groups, for example Catholic students, Catholic artists, and above all apprentices, peasants and factory workers who were brought together in associations for the protection of their interests as workers as well as for the good of their souls. In many of these *Vereine* the impetus and the direction came from laymen, to whom the chaplains left a large measure of initiative. The same applied to the co-ordinating body, the Katholische Verein Deutschlands, which at its annual conference, the *Katholikentag,* discussed the most burning issues of the day in complete freedom. The first of these Catholic congresses had met at Mainz in October 1848,[10] bringing together the various groups that had sprung up spontaneously in the various regions over the past few months, to prepare them to use to best advantage the freedom the members of the Frankfurt constituent assembly proposed to confer on the Churches.[11] This gathering of Catholics in response to the needs of the moment makes the date appear a major landmark in the history of lay Catholic Action in the nineteenth century.

But there is always the danger of falling into anachronism, and we should be careful not to identify without more ado the German 'Catholic movement' of the nineteenth century with Catholic Action as it was to be conceived under Pius XI. The *Vereine* remained true to the general pastoral perspectives of their time in that their principal if not their unique objective was the protection of Catholics and the defence of the Church rather than evangelisation with a view to reconquests.

In this respect the French youth organisation, the Association catholique de la jeunesse française (A.C.J.F.), seems already to be more modern in its outlook. Founded in 1886 by Albert de Mun with the aim of enabling young people to 'co-operate in the rebuilding of a Christian social order' in the three ways indicated by its motto 'Piety, Study, Action', the A.C.J.F. was launched originally as 'a little vessel in the wake of the Œuvre des Cercles'. Characterised in its early days by the counter-revolutionary ideology implied by the *Syllabus,* it moved gradually towards closer involvement with modern society along the lines suggested by Leo XIII in his encyclicals *Immortale Dei* and *Rerum novarum* and finally came into its own under Henri

10. For its proceedings see *Verhandlungen der I. Versammlung des Katholischen Vereins Deutschlands*, Mainz 1848.
11. In Bavaria, at Cologne and in the grand duchy of Baden, largely as the result of lay initiative; see the first four chapters of J. B. Kissling, *Geschichte der deutschen Katholikentage*, I, Münster 1920.

Bazire (president from 1899 to 1904), who launched the slogan '*Sociaux parce que catholiques*'. For long a mainly student-orientated organisation, the A.C.J.F. now sought to extend its operations to all social classes, emphasising from the time of the congress held at Besançon (1898) the necessity for 'the evangelisation of like by like' and endeavouring, in the words of J. Lerolle, speaking as its president in 1907, 'to win public opinion and to win it by social action', in the hope that the active engagement of an élite of convinced Christians in trade union and co-operative movements would eventually break down the wall of misunderstanding which kept the labouring masses outside the Church. Having chiefly in mind their double responsibility towards the Church and towards society, the leaders of the A.C.J.F. did not start out with any explicitly formulated theory of the Catholic laity and its place in the Church, but their ideas on the subject gradually crystallised, first in virtue of a specific internal momentum and then because need arose to define the position with regard to breakaway groups and with regard to groups from which the A.C.J.F. explicitly wished itself to be distinguished. This was the case in particular regarding the Sillon, a movement originally very similar in character but which was developing in an increasingly divergent direction. [12] The A.C.J.F. wanted to stay 'on ground exclusively Catholic' and to maintain its stress on fostering the spiritual development of its members and the intensity of their Christian life (P. Gerlier, president from 1909 to 1913, was to make this one of his essential aims). Despite the large measure of recognition accorded to lay as against clerical initiative – the chaplains were there as 'ecclesiastical adjutants', an idea Albert de Mun borrowed from the army chaplaincies – the A.C.J.F. had every intention of remaining loyal to the statutes which placed it 'under the tutelage of the Roman Pontiff and of our lords the bishops of France' (art. 2). In a letter of 22 February 1907 Pius X gave wholehearted approval to the direction the movement was taking. While allaying the fears of the scrupulous that the nation-wide character of the A.C.J.F. was incompatible with the Church's diocesan structure, he praised the association for its 'wise rule of providing each group with a pious and well-educated priest, not merely to preside at religious gatherings but to direct your doctrinal studies and discussions' and he stressed that the 'greatest merit' of the A.C.J.F. was 'the unswerving obedience with which you observe the rulings of the Roman pontiff in regard to Catholic and social action, and the care you take, when it comes to putting them into practice, to follow the guidance of your bishops and other pastors.' [13]

This last was a point that greatly exercised Pius X, anxious as he was in

12. See chapter 3, 48-51.
13. Full text in C. Molette, *L'Association catholique de la jeunesse française 1886-1907* (Paris 1968), 735.

general to encourage more collaboration by laymen with the clergy, [14] and he had already had occasion to formulate the principles quoted above. This was in the encyclical *Il fermo proposito* (1905), the purpose of which was to check the growing tendency of a section of the Italian Catholic movement to assert its independence of the hierarchy's authority.

The importance of this encyclical in the elaboration of the doctrine of Catholic Action justifies devoting a little space to charting the vicissitudes of the Movimento cattolico, a movement long neglected by Italian historians but which in recent decades has attracted a surprising degree of attention, from scholars of all shades of opinion. Its origins go back to the later years of Pius IX's pontificate when the great mass of Italian Catholics were sulking in passive expectation the imminent collapse of the kingdom of Italy, as it had emerged from the Revolution. It was initiated by a group of laymen in Bologna whose leader, Casoni, a lawyer by profession, dreamed of setting up a large-scale organisation that should embrace the entire country and aim to re-catholicise society, with the ultimate object of making it possible for Catholics to capture political power. Backed by the founders of the Società della Gioventù cattolica italiana (Count G. Acquaderni, likewise from Bologna, and a young Roman, M. Fani), the idea gradually gained ground and after the occupation of Rome the *Civiltà cattolica* took up the theme, seeking to persuade Italian Catholics that although they had already accomplished much as individuals, only in union would they find strength. The next few months witnessed the birth of organisations such as the Società romana per gli interessi cattolici and at Florence the Società promotrice cattolica delle buone opere (which was to become the nucleus of a federation of Catholic voluntary charitable associations), and this ferment of activity led in turn to the holding at Venice in 1874 of the first Italian Catholic congress, modelled on the German *Katholikentage* and the Malines congresses, but more superficial and more oratorical in style. The active wing of Italian Catholicism had thus turned its back on conciliatory approaches to modern society along the lines of Catholic liberalism and opted for a militant movement based on the principles of the *Syllabus,* which by its anathemas against liberal society had served to galvanise the energies of the *intransigenti.* But it was one thing to set up the Opera dei Congressi e dei comitati cattolici, launched in 1875, as a centralised body to promote Catholic Action, quite another to make it effective. Many obstacles stood in the way:

14. A remark of Pius X's reported by Mgr de Bazelaire has often been quoted. Talking one day with some of the cardinals, Pius X asked them: 'What is most needful today for the lasting good of society?' 'To build more schools', said one. 'To found more churches', said another. 'To recruit more priests', said a third. Having said 'no' to each in turn, the pope finally gave his own answer: 'What we most need today is a group of well-informed and virtuous laymen in each parish, full of determination and true apostles!'

lack of interest in the south, where the local committee often existed only on paper, a very active desire in other places, notably Rome, [15] to preserve local autonomy; reluctance on the part of many of the clergy to see laymen entrusted with positions of influence. It is easy to see why the movement was slow to gather strength. After 1887, however, when Leo XIII had abandoned all hope of conciliation with the new Italy and was hesitant to rely too much on the bishops, many of whom seemed too pro-government for his taste, the pope did all he could to support this effort at mobilising Catholic forces under a leadership which combined intransigence in politics with a readiness to do battle in the social field, in order that the masses should remain in sympathy with the Church's resistance to the liberal ruling class. Although a sizeable section of the intelligentsia and the ruling class, especially in Milan and in the South, stayed outside the movement, objecting to it on the score of its consistent hostility to modern values, it was not long before the great mass of Italian Catholics had been roped into what was in effect a highly centralised organisation. Although the base was provided by the parish committees (there were 3982 of them in 1897), little attention was paid to varying local circumstances and the orders came invariably from a central committee in which nearly all the members, the president, Gianbattista Paganuzzi, included, were originally from the Venetian region, the most traditionalist in all Italy.

The positive aspects of this movement, for many years ignored, are undeniable. For all the superficial character of many of its manifestations, it produced a real deepening of religion and succeeded to some extent in arousing the laity to its responsibilities in the Christian community. It established fruitful contact between priests and militant laymen of the various regions, a useful service in a country which long after its political unification remained heavily compartmented. It contributed to the slow but steady development, in terms of quantity at least, of a local Catholic press, and above all it had a number of solid achievements to its credit in the social domain. [16] But there were weaknesses: a disproportionate reliance at the local level on the clergy, often to the point of sterilising lay initiative, combined in seemingly paradoxical fashion with short-circuiting of the diocesan authorities by the 'bishops in top hats' (Mgr Scalabrini's name for the managing committee), who worked in close alliance with the Vatican; the added encouragement it gave to the Catholic tendency to remain aloof from the rest of the community, an isolation particularly marked in the cultural domain (hence, for example, the general mediocrity of the Catholic press and the absence of any creative

15. For an account of these difficulties and the way in which at the end of the century, thanks to the skill of the young Mgr G. Radini Tedeschi, they were finally surmounted, see M. Casella's article in *Rivista di storia della Chiesa in Italia*, XXXIV (1970), 129-79.
16. On this last point see chapter 8, 159-61.

spirit from its fifth section, devoted to Christian art); above all, the weakness inherent in an organisation which by reason of its origins was by way of being both a Catholic Action movement and a political party, with the result that the doctrinal intransigence necessary on the religious front tended to be transferred to its political positions, and the ecclesiastical authorities could claim to control minutely all its activities, even in the purely secular domain.

Before long these inner contradictions were forced out into the open by a group of young followers of Romolo Murri, the dynamic priest who in 1895 founded the Federazione degli Universitari cattolici italiani (F.U.C.I.). Murri's group took advantage of the crisis arising from the government's savage attack on the Opera dei Congressi in May 1898[17] to persuade the Vatican that the former president, Paganuzzi, who was clearly too set in his ways, should be replaced by Count Grosoli, a native of Ferrara, who was forty-three years old and more responsive to modern ideas. But the Secretariat of State, although in agreement over the need for updating the aims and methods of Catholic Action, intended there should be no relaxation in the subordination of such action to the control of the hierarchy. The new statutes of the Opera accordingly stipulated that the young Christian democrat sections should have a chaplain, appointed by the ordinary of each diocese. This did not suit Murri, who was hoping for an autonomy wide enough to allow him to operate on political territory in a manner that would run counter to the Church's ruling. He protested, first in his new weekly, *Domani d'Italia,* and then in a rousing speech on the theme 'Liberty and Christianity' which he delivered at San Marino on 24 August 1902. Although this was immediately censured by Rome, when Murri appeared at the congress of the Opera held at Bologna in November 1903, at which his supporters were overwhelmingly in the majority, he received a tremendous ovation. But the trend he represented was too much opposed to the ideas of the new pope for the latter to allow such an equivocal situation to continue. On 30 July 1904, seizing the opportunity provided by a blunder of Grosoli's, Pius X declared the Opera dei Congressi dissolved and in the following year, having enunciated in the encyclical *Il fermo proposito* the principles which should regulate Catholic Action, he instructed Toniolo and

---

17. 70 diocesan committees out of 190 were suppressed, as were 2500 parochial committees out of 4036, 600 youth clubs out of 708 and 3000 Catholic associations of all types. Publication of many Catholic newspapers was suspended and the most ardently committed of the editors, Don D. Albertario, was arrested and condemned for 'ideological complicity' with revolutionary movements (for the details see G. Spadolini, *L'opposizione cattolica da Porta Pia al '98,* 4th edition Florence 1961, 463-70, though the author's interpretation of these events should be treated with caution). By the following autumn, however, most of the sections had been reconstituted and there were many places where the government's resort to force proved a spur to fresh endeavour. But the episode in fact had lasting and serious consequences in that it hastened the split between the conservatives and the young Christian democrats (see chapter 5, 86-7).

two men of the younger generation, Count Medolago and Pericoli, president of the Young Catholics, to devise a new framework for its organisation in Italy. The plan approved in 1906 provided for three bodies: the Unione popolare, inspired by the German *Volksverein,* the purpose of which was to bring together Catholics of all classes with a view to preparing them to take part as Catholics in public life, but which in fact had very little influence; the Unione economico-sociale, taking over from the second section of the Opera dei Congressi, which Pius X had allowed to survive because of its many practical undertakings; and the Unione elettorale, the very name of which implied that a relaxation of the *non expedit* ruling was in preparation. This assemblage was eventually completed by the addition of the young men's Catholic association, which had never been engulfed in the Opera dei Congressi, though not for want of trying on the part of the latter, and of the union of Catholic women (founded 1909).[18] The presidents of these five organisations formed a directorate *(Giunta direttiva)* of Catholic Action, which had as its secretary a young Sicilian priest with a future, Don Sturzo.

The encyclical *Il fermo proposito,* the immediate occasion for which was the crisis within the Italian Catholic movement at the start of the twentieth century, has often been regarded as the first official charter of organised Catholic Action, inasmuch as it urged laymen to cultivate, in addition to the individual virtues, the practice of 'pooling their vital energies in an effort to restore Jesus Christ to his place in the family, in the school, in the community'. But if in laying such stress on an organised lay apostolate Pius X seems ahead of his time, his definition of the form it should take reveals him by contrast as conservative: 'Voluntary associations which directly supplement the Church's spiritual and pastoral ministry . . . must be subordinate in every detail to the Church's authority . . . But even associations of the other type, whose purpose is to restore in Christ a truly Christian civilisation and which constitute Catholic Action in the sense given above, can in no way conceive themselves independent of the advice and superior direction of ecclesiastical authority.' The passage is typical of the pope's perspective on the matter: long aware of the indispensable part played by laymen in enabling a leaven of Christian principles to work in secular life, but having still failed to perceive the specific contribution Catholic Action had to make to the polity, Pius X envisaged Catholic Action almost exclusively as an exten-

---

18. The desire to enlist women in the campaign for the spiritual regeneration of society had given rise as early as 1904 to the foundation by Signorina A. Coari of the Federazione femminile milanese, which aimed to be a national movement but was regarded with suspicion by the Church authorities, wary of a feminist organisation with Christian democrat backing. The formula eventually adopted was for an organisation composed exclusively of Catholic women and dedicated to missionary aims, ladies of good society being expected to take an interest in women of the working classes. Cf P. Gaiotti di Biase, *Le origini del movimento cattolico femminile,* Brescia 1963.

sion of the action of the clergy. He therefore prescribed for it, drawing on memories of formulae that had worked well in the Veneto, a more or less uniform type of organisation in which laymen were left with little more than the role of executants, working under the strict control of the bishops. Although in order to be effective laymen were obliged to take joint action, not merely for evangelistic purposes but equally for purposes connected with the defence of their interests as workers, the running of newspapers and even to prepare for political elections, there could be no question of their doing so in other than strictly confessional organisations, which had to be incorporated within the parochial and diocesan framework and deprived of all freedom to act independently of the episcopate, which in turn was narrowly subject to instructions from Rome. The ecclesiology that inspired this highly clerical view of Catholic Action finds clearest expression in the encyclical *Vehementer* of 1906: 'The Church is by its very nature an unequal society: it comprises two categories of person, the pastors and the flocks. The hierarchy alone moves and controls . . . The duty of the multitude is to suffer itself to be governed *(gubernari se pati)* and to carry out in a submissive spirit the orders of those in control.' In this domain, as in many others, Pius X was both a precursor and a traditionalist.

8

THE BEGINNINGS OF SOCIAL CATHOLICISM

BETWEEN 1848, the year when Marx published the *Communist Manifesto,* and 1891, the year when Leo XIII published the encyclical *Rerum novarum,* nearly half a century elapsed. The two dates have often been contrasted to show how belatedly, by comparison with the socialist movement, the Church became aware of the working class question. In reality the picture was one of greater nuances, although it is undeniable that the Church, in this particular field, allowed herself to be outdistanced by socialism. Thus despite the wave of reaction following 1848, Marx succeeded in setting up the First International as early as 1864 and had soon awakened the industrial proletariat to a common hope, whereas the majority of Catholics, and the majority of Catholics in authority, were to remain blind for most of the century to the necessity for 'structural reform' and to continue to regard attempts to improve the lot of the working classes by means of institutional change as perilously close to revolution. This was due, it may be remarked, not so much to lack of generosity or ignorance of the wretched condition of the workers as to sheer incomprehension of the new problems posed by the industrial revolution. But the picture would be grossly oversimplified if we were to overlook the existence alongside the rest of a keener-sighted minority of laymen, priests and bishops who were awakened quite early to a genuine social concern by their realisation that the working class question was a matter not merely of charity but of social justice.

In connection with these efforts which prepared the way for the encyclical *Rerum novarum* we should first mention an aspect that used to be overlooked. Contrary to what might be expected, the socially aware Catholics of the late Pius IX and early Leo XIII period were not to be found in the circles most appreciative of political democracy — the liberal Catholics of France and Belgium, the Italian *transigenti* — but among liberalism's most decided opponents, on the face of it 'reactionary' figures, as from many points of view indeed they were. Although apparently disconcerting, on a closer look the phenomenon becomes easier to explain. In the first place, many of these early pioneers of social Catholicism belonged by birth to the landed aristocracy. Less involved than liberal Catholics in business affairs, they were therefore less sensitive to the famous imperative of the 'iron law' of competition. But above all the socially aware Catholics of the period 1860 to 1890 regarded social action – conceived most of the time in a highly paternalistic perspective – as a means of rallying the mass of the people to their cause, that is to say, to their struggle against the anti-clerical bourgeois oligarchy, which they detested on two counts: first for being anti-clerical, second for presuming to substitute the power of money for the old social sanctions. This at once makes it clear why the projects of socially aware Catholics were so often inspired by a nostalgic vision of returning to the patriarchal and corporative past rather than by a desire for realistic accommodation by the new and irreversible situation created by the industrial revolution.

The link between anti-liberalism and social concern was established very early in the *Civiltà cattolica,* as in assertions such as Fr Taparelli's in 1852 that the guilds, suppressed by the French Revolution, belonged to the natural law, and Pius IX took care in the encyclical *Quanta cura* to denounce not only the delusion of socialism, with its claim to replace Providence by the State, but also the pagan character of economic liberalism, with its exclusion of moral considerations from the relations between capital and labour.

These ideas inspired many of the originators of the 'Italian Catholic Movement', who in a still largely unindustrialised country were concerned above all with the deplorable situation of the peasantry. Under the wing of the Opera dei Congressi, the leaders of which were fanatically hostile to the liberal State, there grew up following the congress at Bergamo in 1877 a whole network of voluntary organisations, concentrated particularly in the north – where the effects of social propaganda were beginning to bite – the purpose of which was to grapple with the social and economic needs of the lower classes. It was likewise within the Opera that a start was made in Italy on working out a 'sociology', as it was termed at the time, in which the stress was more on the demands of morality and religion than on material interests, the chief exponent of which was Professor Giuseppe Toniolo. This Italian social movement taking shape during the first half of Leo XIII's pontificate, and which a galaxy of young historians has rescued from oblivion over the past twenty years, had only limited effect, not only because it was content with a pale imitation of what was being done in neighbouring countries, but also because under the influence of the leading men in the Opera dei Congressi it for so long balked at the idea that political democracy was a necessary condition for obtaining worthwhile social reform.

French social Catholicism, while much more original in its thinking, long suffered from the same limitation. Under the Second Empire the relatively few who engaged in good works and who were troubled by working-class poverty were inspired for the most part by the theories of Le Play, [1] which in combination with their narrow interpretation of the *Syllabus* helped to steer them, with very few exceptions, towards a doctrine of 'counter-revolution', hostile to the rights of man and to egalitarian democracy. After the shocks administered by the Commune there were certainly signs of a change on the way, but there was to be very little alteration in basic attitudes until the very eve of *Rerum novarum*. Almost nowhere did the idea dawn that the workers themselves should be entrusted with responsibility for running the Catholic social organisations created for their benefit. Yet this was precisely the moment when in France, as throughout Europe, the working-class movement was developing an increasing resistance to paternalism. It is thus hardly surprising that the workers were wary in their attitude towards social enterprises launched by Catholics, or that the latter failed to make an impact on the true working-class élite. A case in point is the 'Oeuvre des Cercles catholiques ouvriers', founded at Christmas 1871 by a young army officer, Albert de Mun. The movement's hostility towards the principles of 1789 and its nostalgia for the social order of an earlier age inevitably made it appear reactionary, although in social concern Albert de Mun and his group were in reality far in advance not merely of the Orleanists but also of most the republican leaders of their day. Although apparently a failure, the Oeuvre des Cercles was to exert a lasting influence on the development of the Christian social movement in France, having served to bring before a wider public the concrete achievements of a model Christian employer, Léon Harmel, and the theoretical programme evolved by René de La Tour du Pin in his Conseil des Études.

This latter group, especially active in the 1880s, was composed of sociologists and theologians working together to design a Christian social order on the basis of a return to the corporative or guild principle. Anachronistic some of their theories might be, but as Abbé Talmy has now shown us, on several essential points their thinking was more advanced than that of many pre-1914 Christian democrats. As a result of rediscovering Scholastic teachings, for example, they took up positions on the limitation on the right to private property and on the State's right to intervene in economic affairs which were not far removed from certain socialist

1. On Frédéric Le Play (1806-82), social economist and founder of the Société internationale des Hautes Études d'Économie Sociale, see J. B. Duroselle, *Les Débuts du catholicisme social en France*, 672-84 and D. Herbertson, *Frédéric Le Play*, Ledbury 1952.

opinions. But by no means all French Catholics interested in the working class question subscribed to such daring views. Quite the contrary, there was another school in which these views were vigorously opposed. This was the school alluded to by contemporaries sometimes as 'the school of Angers', on account of Bishop Freppel's vocal patronage of it, and sometimes as 'the Belgian school', on account of the intellectual lead given to it by Charles Périn,[2] brilliant teacher of political economy at the university of Louvain and author of a treatise *De la richesse dans les sociétés chrétiennes* which was translated into most European languages. Now Périn was a doughty fighter against liberalism on the political and ideological fronts, but although he was vigorous in his exposure of the exploitation of the workers by the new bourgeoisie and made no secret of his opinion that in economic matters the moral law ought to prevail, he refused to countenance any intervention by the State, expecting the resolution of social problems to come from private initiatives and the spread of the Christian spirit among employers.

These views found great favour among Belgian Catholics, for their whole defence of their religious rights rested precisely on this principle of freedom and they had no wish to encourage the Statist tendencies of their opponents.[3] In France these views were propagated by the *Revue catholique des institutions et du droit,* the journal of the association of Catholic lawyers, and a number of Catholic factory owners in the north tried to put them into practice. In 1884, on the initiative of C. Féron-Vrau, these employers formed an association. But although prolific in concrete achievement, this association was patently paternalistic in inspiration and dominated by a profound distrust of the State, reading into it all the features of the Jacobin State, notorious oppressor of the Church.

In Germany industrial development was of more recent origin. But it was German Catholics, paradoxically enough, who initiated the more realistic social movement, open to the idea of trade unionism and prepared for the limitation of economic freedom by social legislation, which was to find its first official expression in the encyclical of Leo XIII. This social dimension to German Catholicism, which was not to be fobbed off with works of pure benevolence, as happened all too easily in France, enabled the Church to maintain close links with the masses and to count on their support in the struggle with the radical bourgeoisie at the time of the *Kulturkampf.* It is

2. See the article on him by A. Louant, *Biographie nationale* (of Belgium), XXX, cols 665-71.
3. On this paternalist form of Belgian social Catholicism see R. Rezsohazy, *Origines et formation du catholicisme social en Belgique,* ch. 3. On the highly conservative attitude of the Belgian bishops, who even in the industrial dioceses were to be very slow to grasp the true dimensions of the working class question, regarding it for too long merely as identical with the problem of recovering lost ground, see the two chapters by Mgr A. Simon in *150 Jaar Katholieke Arbeidersbeweging in Belgïe* (Brussels 1963-5), I, 111-42, and II, 187-226.

true that, down to 1870, German Catholics who tried to carry out the 1848 precept of bringing 'the Church to the people and the people to the Church' concerned themselves mostly with the betterment of craft workers and the organisation of the peasantry. But attention gradually came to focus equally on the working class question proper. Organisations sprang up, most of all in the industrial regions of the Rhineland which, in addition to serving the traditional primary objectives, the saving of souls and the relief of poverty, made it their business to provide workers with a solid base from which to press their claims for improved working conditions.

If the working class question appeared increasingly to German Catholics a field demanding institutional reform rather than the mere organisation of relief, the change was due in large measure to the dynamic lead given by Mgr Ketteler, bishop of Mainz. Those who regard Ketteler as a pioneer of Christian democracy have frequently misrepresented his role. When Ketteler, the Westphalian aristocrat, protested at the sufferings inflicted on the poor by the social system of his day, the ideal he had in mind was a return to the corporative social organisation of the medieval German empire. This does not detract from his importance as an influence on the social Catholicism of the nineteenth century, to which he made an especially valuable contribution through his book *Die Arbeiterfrage und das Christentum,* 1864, which was the fruit of fifteen years' reflection. Not content with proposing various concrete reforms, he endeavoured to show that the solution of the working class question could be envisaged only in relation to a general concept of society which eliminated both the individualism of the liberals and the totalitarian claims of the modern centralised State. In this book Ketteler in effect advanced for the first time the theory of the corporatively based social organism which was to be the staple of Catholic social doctrine for the next half-century and more; and on more than one occasion during the last quarter of the nineteenth century it was to conflict more obviously with the individualist ideal of economic liberalism than with the socialist ideal, whatever practical suspicions and theoretical objections there might be of the latter.

This was certainly the case with the Austrian school under its leader Baron K. von Vogelsang. By birth a German aristocrat, Vogelsang was converted to Catholicism by Ketteler and in 1864 removed to Vienna, where he became editor-in-chief of the *Vaterland,* the organ of the federalist Austrian landed aristocracy and very hostile to the newly emerging great banking and industrial concerns, many of which were under Jewish control. In 1879 Vogelsang founded the periodical which was to become the celebrated *Monatschrift für christliche Sozialreform.* He used it to mount an attack, inspired by Ketteler's ideas, on the capitalist regime which had come out of the Revolution, criticising it with such vehemence that he was later to acquire the label 'Christian socialist', and defending the idea of State intervention as the remedy for the disorders stemming from anarchical individualism. Vogelsang converted to his views a group of young Austrian Catholics, among them the Abbé Schindler, who succeeded him as leader of the Austrian school, Karl Lueger, future burgomaster of Vienna and responsible for an ambitious programme of social reform, and Prince Charles von Löwenstein, who was host on his Haid estate between 1883 and 1888 to a series of conferences from which emerged, among other things, the celebrated 'Haid Proposals'.

These proposals strike us today as hardly adequate in scale to the vastness of the change in industrial society, but at the time they came as a great novelty to anyone outside revolutionary circles and were met with strong disapproval from the bishops. They were made known to a wider public through an international review, the *Correspondance de Genève,* which was founded and edited by von Blome, a member of Vogelsang's group and, like Vogelsang, a German convert.

The various groups of Catholics preoccupied with the working class question in Germany, Austria, France, Belgium and Italy had not remained in complete ignorance of one another. They were kept informed of each other's activities by the exchange of literature and also through occasional encounters, of a more or less casual nature. Many of these meetings took place in Rome, at the winter residence of an Austrian ally of Vogelsang's, the Count von Küfstein, whose informal study circle for the investigation of social questions, had the blessing of Leo XIII although the pope had not, as is sometimes said, taken the initiative in setting it up. It soon seemed desirable to make these contacts more regular, and to this end a Catholic union of social studies was formed (the Union catholique d'études sociales) which from 1884 met annually at Fribourg in Switzerland under the presidency of Bishop Mermillod, its aim being to work out a version of the corporatist theory of society adapted to the needs of the modern world. The result of the deliberations was kept secret but regular reports were sent to the pope, whose interest in the subject was becoming keener. Although he had not taken up the suggestion, emanating from France in 1881, of inviting the European governments to Rome to work out an international code of labour – hardly a realistic proposition in the prevailing diplomatic climate – the idea of an encyclical on the social question had for some time been maturing in his mind.

He was finally convinced that the time had come for him to intervene officially by a number of external happenings, of which we should mention in particular: the pilgrimages to Rome organised by Léon Harmel for French workers (the first was in 1885), which had the aim of bringing the labouring masses closer to the pope and of bringing the pope into direct con-

tact with the factory worker; the intervention in 1887-8 of Cardinal Gibbons, archbishop of Baltimore, on behalf of the Knights of Labor,
America's earliest labour organisation, which was threatened with condemnation by the Holy Office, some American bishops having complained that
it smacked too much of a secret society and was likely to be involved with
anarchism; Cardinal Manning's support for the workers in the London
dock strike, the fame of which spread throughout Europe;[4] and lastly a new
flare-up, in 1890, of the controversy between 'interventionist' Catholics and
the Angers School, which was sparked off by a congress organised by Mgr
Doutreloux at Liège.

With so many convergent streams, it was becoming increasingly clear
that the supreme authority must speak. When it did so, through the encyclical *Rerum novarum* (15 May 1891), Leo XIII was to decide the principal points at issue in favour of the Liège school, which was in the direct
line of descent from the social thinking of Ketteler and the Fribourg union.
In this respect, therefore, the encyclical marks the completion of an important stage in the history of social Catholicism.

The encyclical *Rerum novarum,* as we have seen, was the product of
numerous initiatives which had no connection with Rome, and this
demonstrates once again the importance of laymen in the down-to-earth existence of the Catholic Church. That is not to say that the encyclical was not
equally the work of Leo XIII. We are reasonably well informed about how
the text took shape, thanks to the publication of the various preliminary
drafts.[5] We can for example trace through the three successive versions – Fr
Liberatore's initial draft, its revision by Fr Zigliara and the definitive text,
meticulously gone through by the pope – the gradual supersession of the
idea of a corporative regime by that of the trade association, envisaged as
composed ideally but by no means necessarily of both workers and
employers, which left the door officially open to the formula of the future,
the all-labour union. On the other hand, while the initial decision to reject the
excessive liberalism of the Angers school in favour of State intervention in
social and economic affairs survives intact, the many nuances and muted
notes introduced into the later drafts are sufficient indication of the circumspection and hesitation with which the Holy See committed itself to this
path. Besides, to understand some of the hesitations of Leo XIII who, while
he wrote not a single line, imposed his thinking on the text at every turn and
left his mark unmistakably on the whole, we must take equally into account
that for all his desire to react, on the authority of the Scholastic tradition,

4. See E. S. Purcell, *Life of Cardinal Manning* (London 1896), II, 638-71. Manning's contribution in the social field is brought out by V. A. McClelland, *Cardinal Manning, his public
life and influence, 1865-1892*, London 1962.

5. G. Antonazzi, *L'enciclica Rerum novarum, testo autentico e redazioni preparatorie dai
documenti originali*, Rome 1957.

against an individualist conception of society and property, he was very anxious to give no pledges to socialist doctrine under the totalitarian aspects it so often presented in his time.

The encyclical *Rerum novarum,* apt to be extolled in Catholic circles between the wars as 'the workers' charter', was regarded in other quarters as fundamentally anti-socialist, if anything somewhat reactionary and in any case of little real moment in the history of the workers' struggle for emancipation. There is no denying that, as well as being somewhat tardy, the encyclical resorts to abstract argument, and makes no analysis of the actual situation created by the development of capitalism; or that it is much taken up with ethical considerations and remains vague on most of the practical problems of its day. Nor can there be any doubt that the encyclical was partly inspired by fears of seeing Catholic workers increasingly attracted to socialism. But there are more positive aspects. In the first place, there was merit in Leo XIII's disengagement from the utopian dreams of the preceding decades, in which the majority of socially-minded Catholics had been led by their yearnings for the preponderantly rural society of a former age to criticise bourgeois society from a pre-capitalist standpoint and to advocate a return in some more-or-less updated version to the corporatism of the *ancien régime,* which for large-scale industry was certainly a blind alley. Leo XIII had the realism to place himself on ground closer to that of reformist socialism and to seek improvement for the working class within the framework of existing institutions, among them the workers' union, the legitimacy of which was recognised, even if with some reluctance. Next, it was not to be dismissed lightly that the highest spiritual authority had made solemn proclamation of the rights of workers and the injustices of the liberal system taken as a whole. While there is no denying that the workers' movement was under way well before *Rerum novarum* or that the credit for launching it belongs in essence to the socialists, this was the first time it had received a stamp of approval from any of the great forces of order in the world. This was a great advance in helping to remove the revolutionary connotation the movement had held so far in the eyes of the great majority of the bourgeoisie. From the psychological point of view this was certainly not negligible. As for Catholics, while they would continue to many years to feel misgivings, they had to admit that some change was indeed called for; and if there were many who still clung to some form of corporatism as a solution, the more forward-looking were already committing themselves to the path of Christian democracy.

But the path of Christian democracy did not prove easy, and that for two reasons. First, many who accepted that, from now on, institutional changes were necessary in order to improve the lot of the workers were nevertheless determined that changes should be made in conformity with the old maxim 'for the people but not by the people', or at least under the strict supervision of clerical authorities. Such in particular was the view of Pius X. Certainly he wanted to see an improvement in people's living conditions – he had given proof of his concern by establishing a chair of economic and social science in his seminary – and many of his pronouncements testified to his heartfelt wish that Christian charity should lose nothing of its social dimension. But he all along envisaged social action in the strictly paternalistic and clerical perspective he shared with his Venetian contemporaries. Second, it was not entirely clear what was actually meant by Christian democracy. The expression had originated in Belgium and then won gradual acceptance elsewhere. But if its purpose was to distinguish 'Christian' democracy from the 'false' democracy of the radicals and individualists, opinions differed as to the exact bearing of the Christian reference. Were Christian democrats to form themselves into a confessional party with the ultimate aim of re-establishing a Christian State on popular foundations, or was it enough simply to accept from Christian motives part of the liberal heritage, namely the secular State as the means whereby believers and unbelievers could work together to obtain greater social justice? Here again Pius X left no doubt as to his views: there could be no abandonment of the ideal of a return to an integrally Catholic social order, which had been the goal of papal policy since the French Revolution. In these circumstances it is not surprising that many Christian democrat leaders regarded the pontificate of Pius X as their sojourn in the wilderness. But the historian should also take note of a point made by Fr Jarlot: 'If after the First World War Catholic labour organisations, both agricultural and industrial, had reached the point of forming national and international federations, it was because the ground was prepared, in Germany, Holland, Belgium, France, Spain, Italy and other countries, under the pontificate of Pius X. The seed sown by Leo XIII sprouted under Pius X and under Pius XI was to come to full flower.'

It is not possible to follow here the ups and downs of the movement in the different countries, where its characteristics varied greatly according to the local circumstances. In some countries it had the open support of the hierarchy, as in Australia, where Cardinal Moran was quite unabashed in declaring his sympathy with 'Christian socialism',[6] in others the incentive came from enterprising priests working in populous parishes, for example Alfons Ariëns in the Netherlands, who was inspired by German example to

6. Cf. P. Ford, *Cardinal Moran and the A.L.P. A Study in the Encounter between Moran and Socialism, 1890-1907*, Melbourne-London 1966. In England by contrast, Manning's successors, Cardinal Vaughan and more particularly Cardinal Bourne, were very reserved in their attitude towards the working class movement and so far as the majority of Catholics was concerned, the social encyclicals long remained a dead letter, despite the tentative efforts of V. McNabb, O.P. and C. Plater, S.J., founders in 1909 of the Catholic Social Guild on the model of the Fabian Society.

found in 1889 the first Catholic association intended exclusively for the workers and two years later the first Catholic trade union for factory employees.[7] In other countries, by contrast, the movement had to contend with the distrust of a clergy whose sensitivity to social problems had been blunted by too close an involvement with the ruling class, as for example in Spain;[8] or it ran into opposition from neo-corporatists, as in Austria, where L. Kunschak, who in 1892 bravely set up the first Christian trade unions, had great difficulty in bringing the grievances of the working class movement to the notice of the Christlich-soziale Volkspartei, which was geared to the interests of the petty bourgeoisie. All that can be attempted in any detail here is to sketch the situation in four countries where the internal controversies had repercussions well beyond the national boundaries.

First Belgium, where the paternalists had been very much in command and were to remain in control of most of the charity-orientated organisations down to 1914. The creation in February 1891, a few months before the issue of *Rerum novarum,* of the Ligue démocratique belge, marked an important turning-point and the change of emphasis became still more noticeable when A. Verhagen took over the presidency from J. Helleputte in 1895 and succeeded in breaking away from the corporatist perspectives of his predecessor. Operating as a pressure group, the Ligue enabled Christian democracy to make its voice heard in parliament and to secure, in face of furious opposition, the voting of several important reforms for the benefit of labour. Although its direction remained in all essentials the monopoly of the non-working class, the Ligue came out as early as 1892 in favour of the trade-union formula which excluded employers and from 1901, after a slow start, this type of union gradually won acceptance, thanks in particular to the sterling work and qualities of Fr Rutten, O.P. By contrast, the Abbé Daens's attempt at a truly democratic Flemish 'Christian Labour party'

---

7. On the great work done by Ariëns from his parish base at Enschede in Twente see G. Brom, *A. Ariëns,* 2 vols, Amsterdam 1941. Although the Dutch episcopate long continued to be paternalistic in its attitude, Ariëns had support from the archbishop of Utrecht. In the succeeding decade the Catholic working-class movement, having started in the north, spread gradually south. Mention should also be made of J. F. Vlekke, one of the few factory employers of the period to progress beyond a paternalistic relationship between management and workers (cf. F. Van der Ven, *J. F. Vlekke, 1849-1903, ein pionier der sociale ondernemingspolitiek in Noord-Brabant,* Tilburg 1947).

8. Some efforts were made, especially in the rural sector (where syndicates set up by priests with a view to organising agricultural credit came together in 1912 to form the Confederación nacional catolico-agraria) but also in the factory sector. In 1880 one pioneer, the Valencian A. Vicent, S.J. (1837-1912), started to set up workers' circles but the Consejo nacional de las corporaciones catolicas de obreros escaped his influence and developed in a conservative direction. A few of his disciples tried without much success to promote Christian trade unionism proper: Professor S. Aznar, founder in 1910 of the review *Renovación social,* two Dominicans, Gerard and Gafo, above all G. Palau, S.J., founder of Acción social popular at Barcelona, were eventually obliged to emigrate to the Argentine.

(founded 1893) was wrecked after a few years by the intrigues of Charles Woeste's conservative group and by the disquiet the venture aroused in the bishops, who were very anxious to keep the Catholic party united in face of anti-clericalist attacks.[9] A similar fate overtook the Abbé Pottier, between 1886 and 1895 one of the leading representatives of Liège Christian democracy, who was obliged to stay more and more in the background until in the end, after the death of Mgr Doutreloux, he was forced by conservative pressure to leave the country. But the conservatives were soon to change their tune. Pius X surprised them by recognising the autonomy of the Ligue démocratique belge within its own sphere, on condition it did nothing to jeopardise the unity of the ruling Catholic party, and he stated explicitly that the severe admonitions addressed to Murri's Christian democrat group did not apply to them. 'In Belgium', he pointed out, 'you have good democrats; you Belgian Catholics, whether conservative or democrat, are all in harmony with your bishops.' [10] As to the bishops, while some continued very guarded in their attitude towards the Christian democrats, this was not the case with the new archbishop of Malines, Cardinal Mercier, who was roundly to assert: 'When socialism strives for a more just distribution of public wealth, socialism is right'.[11] Mercier showed open support for the Christian democrats on more than one occasion, and it was partly thanks to him that the Fifth Catholic Congress of Malines, held in 1909 despite the tenacious opposition of Woeste, was a triumph for their group. In 1907, moreover, two of their number had become members of the government, which helped to speed up the voting of several measures for the benefit of labour. In short, on the eve of the First World War Belgian Christian democracy already contained in essence the ingredients that would characterise it for the next half-century. It had become a vital factor in the Catholic party, and through the trade unions, the mutual insurance societies, the co-operatives and the various other kinds of association it was acquiring an increasingly important place in the working, economic, cultural and religious life of the country.

In Germany as in Belgium, the start of Leo XIII's pontificate found the socially-minded Catholics divided into two opposing schools. The first, whose most prominent representative was Baron von Hertling, saw a serious danger in the ever-growing power of the State. But the other, the adherents of which tended to be chiefly of the younger generation, was not dismayed

9. In 1898-9 Daens severed his connections with the bishopric of Ghent and drew closer to the socialists. He was to be condemned by Pius X in 1905. On this whole affair, in itself of minor importance but highly sympomatic, see H. J. Elias, *Priester Daens en de Christene Volkspartij*, Aalst 1940; K. Van Isacker, *Het Daensisme*, Antwerp 1959; L. Wils, *Het Daensisme*, Louvain 1969.

10. Letter from Baron d'Erp, quoted in *Rivista di storia della Chiesa in Italia*, XII (1958), 240, n.70.

11. Speech of 5 July 1909, printed in his *Oeuvres pastorales*, II (Brussels 1912), 324-5.

at the prospect of some degree of State socialism and looked in the works of Fr Hitze (1851-1921) its leader, to 'a wide-ranging and thorough-going legislative programme, implemented by the strong arm of the State' as 'the sole means of achieving the re-ordering of society'. [12] Nevertheless, as in Belgium, there was great concern not to jeopardise the political unity of the Catholics, especially while the consequences of the *Kulturkampf* were still making themselves felt, and it is significant that Windthorst, whose views were in sympathy with Hertling's, figured along with Hitze as one of the founders in 1890 of the Volksverein. It was a disciple of Hitze's, A. Pieper, who for the next quarter of a century directed the Volksverein from its headquarters at München-Gladbach. Although the Volksverein had sections for middle class and agricultural workers, its main effort was concentrated on the urban working class. Here it was useful in injecting new life into some of the older clubs and associations which, after a period of great activity in the 1850s and 1860s, had tended during the Bismarck era to fall into abeyance. But its chief contribution was in encouraging the formation of trade unions. And the question of trade unions lay at the heart of an increasingly bitter controversy which rocked the German Catholic world in the last decade before 1914.

After a shaky beginning in 1890, 'Christian' trade unions (that is unions comprising Catholic and Protestant workers) had begun to be developed in the Rhineland and Westphalia, with the encouragement of most Catholic politicians in the west of the country. In 1900 a federation had been formed, the Gesamtband christlichen Gewerkschaften Deutschlands, which in 1909 acquired in Adam Stegerwald an extremely energetic secretary general. Cardinal Fischer, archbishop of Cologne, welcomed the trend and on several occasions defended it to the Holy See. But a section of the clergy and bishops, with Mgr Kopp, archbishop of Breslau, and Mgr Korum, bishop of Trier, at their head, was opposed on principle to the formula of interconfessional unions, especially since the latter showed themselves disposed to collaborate quite closely with the socialists. They favoured instead the setting up of unions for specific trades within the framework of existing Catholic organisations and they tried, it may be said without much success, to implant in the west and south of the country branches of a Catholic working people's organisation, the Verband Katholischer Arbeitervereins Nord und Osterdeutschlands, which had been set up in 1897 with its headquarters in Berlin. The conflict between the two schools, 'of Cologne' and 'of Berlin', broke out in 1904 into a headed pamphlet warfare and gave rise to a number of unpleasant incidents. But in addition to highlighting the interconfessional issue, the conflict presented Catholics with some fundamental choices: the

12. F. Hitze, *Kapital und Arbeit* (Paderborn 1881), 120.

possibility of returning to the corporative type of economic and social regime or the necessity of being content to mitigate the capitalist system by social reform; the legitimacy of strikes as a weapon in the struggle to improve the condition of the working classes; and most fundamental of all, the question how to judge whether Catholic labour organisations were to be placed under the control of the Church or indeed whether, laymen being responsible for their secular activities, the clergy were to restrict themselves to giving advice on the moral aspects. The conflict reached its climax at the end of Pius X's pontificate, exacerbated by the integrist counter-offensive.

In France, socially concerned Catholics of the paternalist type by no means disappeared from the scene following the publication of *Rerum novarum*. With increasing assistance from the clergy, whose part had hitherto been small, the paternalists continued to display their devotion and ingenuity in the creation of a great range of clubs and associations. These were designed principally for peasants and skilled workers, but the ordinary factory worker was not completely overlooked and at the same time efforts continued, though with no real success, to set up industrial unions of the mixed type (comprising workers and employers). The employers banded together as the Patrons du Nord stuck doggedly to their positions. They used all their resources to oppose the formation of Christian unions composed exclusively of workers and they came out strongly against Léon Harmel, who was trying to promote the interventionist view defended by the Liège school and approved by the encyclical. In 1895 they agreed to bow to the decision of Leo XIII but their deep-seated opposition continued. The solemn audience Pius X granted to the Patrons du Nord in 1904 was to appear to contemporaries, with good reason, as a vindication, from which they profited all the more when the abolition of the State's subsidies to the Church in the following year substantially increased the influence of such generous benefactors with the clergy. But it did nothing to improve their impact on the workers. As one of the leaders of the Patrons du Nord remarked in 1913, 'for the past twenty years we have simply been marking time'.

But noticeably gathering strength after 1891 was another stream which M. Montuclard in deference to the abortive effort of 1848, calls the 'second wave' of Christian democracy in France. This movement, incidentally much more complex than appears from Montuclard's thought-provoking but over-schematic sociologist's account, arose out of various largely uncoordinated initiatives whose convergence, achieved in face of the considerable doctrinal confusion prevailing at the outset, was an event of some significance. It was characterised by its acceptance at one and the same time of liberal values, which the pioneers of social Catholicism had spurned, and of the goal of a socially orientated Christian democracy, to which liberal Catholics remained antipathetic. Owing its initial impetus to Léon Harmel's propaganda inside the Oeuvre des Cercles, from which it was soon to cut loose, the movement took firmer shape as the more clearsighted came to recognise the impotence of organisations of the traditional type and the need to adopt the formula of the workers' union. But fired by Belgian example it soon transformed itself into a party committed to political action and in particular to *ralliement* to the Republic. Apart from a sprinkling of militant working-class Catholics and of some enthusiastic laymen with a *petit-bourgeois* background, the main movers were the visionary young priests [13] known as the *abbés démocrates:* Gayraud, Six, Dabry, Naudet and boldest and most eloquent of all Lemire, the figure soon most closely identified with the movement. It occupied the front of the stage for some years, above all in northern and north-eastern France and later also in the Lyons region, [14] receiving open encouragement from the pope and basking briefly in episcopal favour. But from 1898 it was to fall into a rapid decline, so much so that after 1900 only a few isolated survivors remained. The miscarriage of the movement is not to be explained solely by circumstances such as the conservatives' opposition to a programme of social reform which today appears very modest, or the failure of the policy of *ralliement,* or the lack of leaders capable of persuading a number of headstrong individuals to work together, or even the competition of Marc Sangnier's supremely energetic Sillon, [15] the first movement of its kind in France to possess the popular touch. What has also to be borne in mind is that the *abbés démocrates* were very soon seen to be raising a series of important questions, some of them even more fundamental than those at the base of the German controversy over trade unionism: the place of the Christian in a secularised society, [16] recognition of the Christian values implicit in secular activity, even the question of 'democratising' the government of the Church. For to demands for a new social and political order − the exact opposite of the hierarchical ideal

13. Worth noting is the comment of R. Cornilleau, *De Waldeck-Rousseau à Poincaré,* Paris 1926, 43: 'What the Christian democrats lacked was a Jaurès, that is a lay leader to act as the brains and voice of the party. Their movement looked altogether too churchy, not to say clerical.'
14. See for example J.-M. Mayeur, 'Les Congrès nationaux de la "Démocratie chrétienne" à Lyon (1896, 1897, 1898)', *Revue d'histoire moderne et contemporaine,* IX (1962), 171-206.
15. On the origins of the Sillon, see ch. 3, 48-51, and for further details the first two sections of the thesis by J. Caron, *Le Sillon et la Démocratie chrétienne, 1894-1910,* Paris 1967.
16. On this point, however, the Christian democrats were themselves divided. Only a minority resigned themselves to accepting the society born from the Revolution in which the Christian has to be content with acting as a leavening agent through participation in non-confessional institutions. Many dreamed by contrast of a new Christendom, popular but also clerical in character, fruit of an alliance between the Church and the people on the model of medieval society as depicted by the Romantic historians but departing from the model in comprising a network of Christian institutions contained within a democratic framework and based on universal suffrage (or on a variant of it: the family vote, as tried out in Belgium, representation by trades, as suggested in La Tour de Pin's programme).

(but which nevertheless continued to harp on peasant virtues and other equally traditionalist themes) – were added aspirations towards a general religious renewal, covering morals, the spiritual life, the pastoral ministry and ecclesiology,[17] which many of the bishops, for whom Mgr Isoard and Mgr Turinaz acted as spokesmen, found disturbing. The indiscretion of young priests and seminarists in appearing to confuse love of the poor with contempt for the upper classes and in whom the priest seemed too often obscured by the social and political activist, and on top of that the savage attacks of the integrist press, which identified Christian democracy indiscriminately with modernism, in the end made the position of the *abbés démocrates* untenable and a number of them eventually incurred the Church's censure, Naudet and Dabry in 1908, Lemire in 1914.

Between the two extremes, those determined not to abandon paternalism or the corporative ideal, and those determined to reconcile French Catholicism, in spite of itself, to democracy pushed to its ultimate conclusions, there developed slowly and with difficulty, but nevertheless steadily, a centrist stream which followed the cautious line laid down in *Rerum novarum*. To it belonged the parliamentary Catholics of Albert de Mun's group, who were instrumental in working out some of the earliest proposals for social legislation, and likewise the moving spirits in the A.C.J.F. This movement was originally counter-revolutionary in its ethos but, under the presidency of Henri Bazire, had become increasingly involved in social questions, encouraging its members to collaborate in setting up not only workers' reading-rooms, agricultural insurance agencies and workers' savings banks but also trade unions proper (the theme of the A.C.J.F. conference in 1903) and aid for strikers, not hesitating to entertain the idea of co-operation with socialist reformers. Also connected with this moderately progressive stream were newer bodies, founded in the early years of the twentieth century: the Union d'études des catholiques sociaux (1901), in the description of H. Rollet a kind of 'legislation workshop'; the Semaines sociales (1904), a kind of itinerant university which visited a different town each year and offered its 'students' – a fairly mixed bunch – a wealth of fresh insights into the great social questions of the day (omitting, however, to deal with the strictly economic aspects). It was due to the tact of the organisers, two prominent bourgeois from Paris, Henri Lorin and Adéodat Boissard, and a modest clerk from Lyons, Marius Gonin, that despite sundry alarms the Semaines sociales never fell foul of the ecclesiastical authorities, although its enemies were almost the same as those of the

17. Montuclard even claims to detect 'beneath identical professions of orthodoxy and loyalty profound divergences which set Christian democrat thinking in total opposition to that of Catholics at the end of the nineteenth century' ('Une crise de la pensée catholique à la fin du XIXᵉ siècle', *Annales de la Faculté des lettres d'Aix*, XLIV (1968), 33-65).

Sillon.[18] Mention must equally be made of the Jesuits' Action populaire, founded in 1903 by Fr H. Leroy and directed from 1905 by Fr G. Desbuquois, the purpose of which was to 'help others to act', by bringing interested people together and providing them with sound and stimulating advice in the form of lectures, literature and counselling, and by spreading knowledge of all 'genuinely Catholic undertakings', that is undertakings which conformed to the general directives contained in papal documents (no protection, as it turned out, against suspicions and denunciations on the part of the integrists); and of the Secrétariats sociaux, also concerned to disseminate views and stimulate action, founded by Conin in the late nineteenth century but initially confined to the Lyons region, only spreading to France as a whole when the A.C.J.F. started to take a hand in 1910. Finally, although the results were much more modest than in Belgium or Germany, we should note at the level of organised labour the appearance of the first Christian trade unions. The movement goes back to the foundation in Paris in 1887, on the initiative of the Brothers of the Christian Schools, of a clerical workers' union, the Syndicat des employés du commerce et de l'industrie, which became the driving force; having called together the first inter-union Christian congress in 1904, this union took the lead in 1912 in forming the Fédération française des syndicats d'employés, but it did not succeed in taking root in major industry.

The record, in short, shows a number of interesting initiatives, a ripening of Catholic social doctrine (subjected in some of its most delicate areas to bold speculation, when perhaps what was needed was more systematic exploration), a gradual breakthrough, effected in conditions much less favourable than under Leo XIII, but all of it the work of a group which, down to 1914, was to remain very limited in numbers and almost entirely devoid of episcopal support, a picture in contrast with the one found in neighbouring countries.

In Italy, for example the social question had become a major preoccupation of the highly authoritative Opera dei Congressi,[19] the intransigence of which was in no way identified with the social conservatism of the liberal bourgeoisie. On the contrary, liberalism, the ideology of the bourgeois society engendered by the Revolution, was regarded in Opera circles as the root of all the social evils, the emergence of socialism included. The second and by far the most active section of the Opera, which in 1887 had changed its name from the original title 'Charity and Catholic Economy' to 'Christian Social Economy', could count on the co-operation of a substantial number

18. The idea was to be imitated in Spain as early as 1906, in Italy from 1907. There were also 'social weeks' in Germany, but these were of a different type, being limited to a small number of specialists.
19. On this see chapter 7, 139-41.

of the clergy, who tended to be closer to the people than their counterparts in France, and on backing from a section of the Catholic press, with in the van Don Albertario's *Osservatore cattolico,* the paper largely responsible for awakening Catholic opinion in Italy to the social problem, a problem which in a country still so little industrialised revolved chiefly round the condition of the peasantry. The Italian Catholic social movement was also fortunate in having at hand one or two experienced practitioners, for example Don Luigi Cerutti, who between 1893 and 1898 covered first the Veneto and then the whole of northern Italy with a network of agricultural credit banks (there were 893 in 1898) and N. Rezzara, who turned the province of Bergamo into an exceptionally lively centre of Christian social action. It is true that most of the leading men in the Opera dei Congressi long remained pater-nalistic in their outlook and that control of the organisations intended for peasants and workers (the network was now spreading from the north into other regions, notably into Sicily) remained almost invariably in the hands of clergy or lay notables. But during the 1890s things started to change.

In December 1889 Toniolo had helped to found at Padua the Unione cat-tolica per gli studi sociali and had provided it in 1893 with a serious journal, the *Rivista internationale di scienze sociali,* to disseminate its views. The Unione made its presence felt in various ways, by setting up study circles specialising in social questions, soon to be found in most of the principal cities of Italy, by founding chairs of social economy in a number of seminaries, by organising two social congresses, one at Genoa in 1892 and the other at Padua in 1896, and by drawing up in 1894 the 'Programme of Milan', which was an endeavour to translate into practical terms – with an undeniable boldness considering the period – the principles enunciated in *Rerum novarum.*[20] However, the official title of the programme was symptomatic of the defensive mentality which prompted this burst of social activity: 'Catholic programme to counteract socialism'. Moreover, in his pursuit of a chimerical vision of uniting all Catholics round a 'democratic' programme directed in the best neo-Guelf tradition by the pope, a programme which, to avoid argument, had to remain vague and abstract, Toniolo was bound to finish up by emptying Christian democracy of its content.[21] But younger Catholics, fired by foreign example, were reacting in increasing numbers against this attitude, which they saw as hindering the natural ripening of the movement into a force for change and popular eman-

20. The programme called not only for the revival of trade associations and the abolition of usury but also for agricultural workers to have a share in the improvement of large estates, and factory workers in the profits and even in the capital. It was not easily accepted by the Opera dei Congressi.
21. See for example the Christian democrat reaction to Toniolo's famous lecture of 1897 (cf. F. Fonzi, 'L'epistolario di G. Toniolo', *Quaderni di cultura e storia sociale,* III (1954), 22-32).

cipation, acting in the parliamentary sphere along the lines pioneered by French and Belgian Christian democrats. But a development of this nature was not acceptable to the Holy See, which was convinced that the ruling on political absention must be maintained so long as the Roman question remained unsettled; and the leaders of the Opera dei Congressi, whose conservatism had become even more pronounced after the events in Milan in 1898, when the government had suppressed socialism and the Catholic movement at one fell swoop, were twice as anxious as the Holy See to discourage the new tendencies.

The views in question had been nurtured by an avid study of *Rerum novarum*, which in Italy had impressed most deeply by its anti-liberal perspectives. Around 1900 they were in evidence from north to south of the peninsula, but in forms that varied greatly with the local circumstances. Some people, opposed to economic and social liberalism though they might be, remained strongly under the influence of the traditionalist inheritance which had fed the ideology of the intransigents. They therefore exalted the virtues of the land and of local autonomy, continued to expand the network of Catholic friendly societies, rural co-operatives and farmers' credit banks and in some cases still clung to the corporatist ideal. Others, stimulated by the presence of active socialist cells, set about organising unions exclusively for the workers and came forward with demands for labour legislation, a ministry of labour and a system of social insurance. The former, especially when they were northerners, believed with Filippo Meda[22] that it was preferable, in order to have a chance to implement their social programme, to place themselves on constitutional ground; and they did not refuse, when the time came, to collaborate with the conservative democracy of Giolitti. The latter, much more radically inclined, refused to have any dealings with the bourgeois State, although they were just as conscious as the rest of the need to campaign in the political arena. This was the case with Don Sturzo, in Sicily, and still more with Romolo Murri (1870-1944), a priest born in the Marches who attracted a great following among students and seminarists. It was above all round Murri and his review *Cultura sociale,* founded 1898, that the opposition of progressive young Christian democrats inside the Opera dei Congressi polarised for a few years, gathering to itself support from a growing number of the younger clergy. This last development was displeasing to the majority of bishops, who were hostile to the movement not only on political and social grounds, but precisely because they feared to see their authority undermined by a transposition of democratic principles to the internal government of the Church.

22. For the career of this Milanese layman (1869-1939) who, having left militant *intransigentismo* along with Fr Albertario, became the first Italian Catholic to enter the government, see G. De Rosa, *F. Meda e l'età liberale*, Florence 1959.

Leo XIII, who was both conscious of the need for a wider viewpoint than that of the conservatives and very anxious to keep Catholic forces united, sought with his encyclical *Graves de communi* (18 January 1901) to direct the exuberance of the Christian democrats into safer channels.[23] While recognising the legitimacy of the expression 'Christian democracy', which from certain Catholic quarters, notably the *Civiltà cattolica,* was under heavy attack, the pope, adopting the socio-ethical standpoint of Toniolo, defined the term in a very restrictive sense: 'In present circumstances it must be employed only in a completely non-political sense and taken as implying no more than Christian action for the people's good.' While this was a far cry from the *abbé démocrate* slogan 'for the people and by the people', at least it did not close the door to further activity of a moderately reforming type.[24]

Although the prevailing climate of their formative years had left Italian Christian democrats with nostalgic yearnings for a single confessional movement, uniting all Catholics, and with a greater submissiveness to clerical direction in temporal matters than was common among their foreign counterparts, the more progressive among them refused to be subdued by this application of the brake, which some took to be back-pedalling. And the young guard were still not satisfied when in October 1902 Leo XIII met some of their objections by making a change in the leadership of the Opera dei Congressi which gave it a less conservative and elderly tone. Even within the group favouring social reform there was a widening split between the moderates who supported Meda's line and the extremists who had rallied to Murri's banner. The change of pontificate increased the tension, for Pius X was even more hostile than his predecessor to Murri's aspirations to freedom from the hierarchy's control in social and political affairs, even though − perhaps chiefly because − Murri was anxious to see the clergy undertaking to direct Catholics in these secular domains: for his programme remained faithful to its origins in retaining some markedly clerical features. The open rupture came in November 1905, when Murri and his allies, incensed by the obvious drawing together of the official Catholic movement and the moderate liberals, broke away to form their own Lega democratica nazionale. But the latter, repudiated by the Vatican and cold-shouldered by the socialists, failed to make an impact, and by the time Murri was excommunicated in the context of the anti-modernist reaction in 1909, he had long since been deserted by most of those who had helped him launch the movement.

23. *A.S.S.,* XXI (1901), 3-20. French translation in *Actes de Léon XIII,* VI (Paris 1934), 204-27.
24. As regards the last point, it is instructive to compare the first draft by Cardinal Cavagnis with the final text, the tone of which is noticeably less conservative, although it still stresses the difference between the Christian social programme and a socialist programme (cf. G.

The majority of socially concerned Catholics took refuge in the Unione economico-sociale, which replaced the 'second' or social and economic section of the Opera dei Congressi when the latter was dissolved by Pius X. But the atmosphere was not particularly encouraging and, aside from one or two interesting projects, for example the foundation at Bergamo in 1910 of a school for training Catholic social workers,[25] there was little to show in the way of positive achievement. Hence the launching before long of a new challenge from the left, as when Miglioli and Don Cecconcelli protested at the meeting of the congress in Modena in 1910 against the continuing suspicion in which unions composed exclusively of workers were held by those in authority.

This matter of trade unions was about to rear its head again over the next few years, and in a context much wider than that of Italy. The enemies of Christian democracy were spurred on by the encyclical *Pascendi* to denounce it as one of the heads of the modernist hydra, 'social modernism' and 'political modernism' appearing in their eyes a consequence of modernism in religion. The proponents of 'integral Catholicism' claimed that the social question was above all else 'a moral and hence a religious question, which only Catholic teaching strictly in accordance with Rome will resolve'.[26] From 1909 they became increasingly savage in their attacks on socially committed Catholics who, for the sake of greater effectiveness, departed from the model hitherto accepted in Christian civilised countries and organised the defence of the working classes on a neutral 'trades' basis, thus permitting collaboration with non-Catholics, or who, while keeping the confessional label, defined trade unions in terms of their economic and social function, without placing in the forefront their moral and religious goal. The conflict broke out in different parts of Western Europe at much the same time: in Italy, as we have just seen; in France, where the attack concentrated on the Action populaire of the Jesuits;[27] in Belgium, where the inquisitors of the 'Sapinière' more than once took Fr Rutten to task;[28] in Holland, where Fr Poels, brilliantly successful organiser of the workers' movement in Limburg, was denounced by the integrists of the 'Leyden school'.[29] But the epicentre of the storm lay in Germany.

Martina, in *Rivista di storia della Chiesa in Italia*, XVI (1962), 492-507).
25. Founded by Count Medolago Albani with the aim of giving doctrinal training to militants and chaplains engaged in Catholic Action. Cf. B. Malinverni, *La Scuola sociale cattolica di Bergamo*, Rome 1960.
26. Foreword to the first issue (7 December 1912) of the *Correspondance catholique* of Ghent, organ of the Sodalitium Pianum ('Sapinière') in Belgium.
27. Many details, often from unpublished material, are given by P. Droulers, *Politique social et christianisme. Le P. Desbuquois et l'Action populaire. Syndicalisme et intégristes (1903-1918)*, Paris 1969.
28. See among others É. Poulat, *Intégrisme et Catholicisme intégral* (Paris 1969), 284-7.
29. See J. Colsen, *Poels* (Roermond 1955), 514-37.

We have already seen how at the beginning of the twentieth century an ideological cleavage set the 'Berlin' school, loyal to the old tradition of associations exclusively for Catholic workers, at loggerheads with the rapidly expanding 'Cologne' school (with a membership in 1914 of close on one-and-a-half million, against the ten thousand odd of the Berlin school), which worked on the formula of inter-confessionalism and de-clericalisation. Pius X, whose sympathies were clearly with the former but who had to take into account the strength of the latter, and the fact that it had support from the great majority of the episcopate, tried to halt the increasingly bitter controversy by publishing in September 1912 an encyclical on trade unions [30] in which he approved without reserve the Berlin formula, but accepted that others might be tolerated in order to avoid a greater evil. Far from relieving tension, the pope's intervention only made for greater confusion and the controversy was resumed with redoubled vigour, not merely in Germany, where both sides claimed the victory, but equally in France, with a resumption of integrist attacks on Christian democracy, [31] and a little later in Rome, where in February 1914 the *Civiltà cattolica* published what was clearly an inspired article which seemed to be testing the ground for the issue of a new and sterner papal document, intended to warn the Christian trade-union movement against a trend carrying it further and further from the social ideology which so far as Pius X was concerned, though certain historical apologists have since tried to deny it, was the only one truly in keeping with Catholic orthodoxy. People who understood that on this point the pope was prisoner of an outdated 'model' (in the sociological sense) and who were anxious for no further delay in the Church's adaptation to the changes in modern society, were at pains to avert the impending blow, and their task was made easier by the fact that an international federation of Christian trade unions had come into existence a few years earlier. [32] Discreet intervention on the part of Cardinals Maffi and Mercier, the general of the Jesuits (who was a German), Toniolo, Harmel, and others, persuaded the pope to stay his hand. In this 'last great battle of the pontificate' (Poulat), the Christian democrats had at length scored a success over their integrist opponents.

---

30. *Singulari quadam, A.A.S.,* IV (1912), 657-62.
31. A public letter addressed by Cardinal Merry del Val to Albert de Mun, 7 January 1913 (see R. Talmy, *Le Syndicalisme chrétien,* 122-4), constituted an initial victory for the integrists, but the succeeding months brought some relaxation in the tension.
32. The way having been prepared in the late nineteenth century by the drawing together of the Dutch and Belgian federations and later of the Geman textile federation, the International Federation of Christian Trade Unions had been set up at Zurich in 1908. There was also regular contact between the leading newspapers with Christian democrat leanings.

THE GRADUAL REVIVAL OF THE ECCLESIASTICAL DISCIPLINES

DOWN to the end of Pius IX's pontificate the lead in matters of ecclesiastical scholarship remained, as in the first half of the century, with Catholic Germany. But it would be wrong to suppose that outside the German universities nothing of any value was accomplished.

Even in the field of ecclesiastical history, in which the German universities particularly excelled and the showing of the Latin countries was markedly inferior – witness such distressing illustrations as the success enjoyed by the vast but wholly uncritical *Histoire générale de l'Église* produced by the Abbé Darras and the resuscitation of the thesis regarding the apostolic foundation of the Gallic sees – there were worthwhile achievements to record: in France the work of a Ginoulhiac or a Maret; in Belgium the revival of interest in Eastern Christianity at Louvain and the reinstatement of the Bollandists, with the enlargement of their field of operations to include the Slav sources and Celtic hagiography; above all, the advances made in Christian archaeology at Rome under the direction of Fr Marchi and his favourite disciple J. B. De Rossi (1822–94), work to which Mommsen, for all his contempt for Italian and Catholic scholarship, felt obliged to pay tribute.

Equally deserving of mention are some of the theologians active at the Roman College during the third quarter of the century: Fr Passaglia, possibly one of the most gifted of all nineteenth-century theologians, and his successor, the less brilliant but more rigorous Franzelin, an Austrian, who expounded a theology at once positive and speculative, founded on an exceptional acquaintance with the writings of the Greek Fathers and, in intention, an effort at organic synthesis of the facts of the faith as mediated by the images of the Bible rather than a philosophical investigation of revealed truths.

But outside Rome it was apologetics that almost everywhere held the forefront of the scene in terms of quantity at least: for to the revival of sympathy with medieval Catholicism which had characterised the Romantic generation there succeeded the casting in doubt of Christianity at its foundations. The authority of the biblical writings was contested in the name of more rigorous historical criticism, as also in the light of the archaeological discoveries in the Middle East and of the findings of the palaeontologists. Comparative history of religions began to pose the problem of the transcendence of the Judaeo-Christian revelation. The very foundations of theism were called in question by the Hegelian left, while Herbert Spencer, continuing the English empirical tradition, was helping to propagate well beyond the shores of his own country an evolutionary interpretation of the world which was alleged to supersede the idea of creation, while the France of the Second Empire had its own package for export, made up of Comtist positivism blended with English agnosticism and German materialism, which found its way as far afield as South America. Faced with these multiple challenges, the general run of apologists showed a surprising lack of resource, confining themselves to the reiteration with varying degrees of eloquence of the familiar classical arguments, seemingly unaware that the transformation in the intellectual climate was making them less and less effective. One is struck in particular by the paucity of Catholic writings from the last two decades of the century tackling with any competence the important problem of the conciliation of the Christian faith with the new scientific outlook. An exception, however, was the foundation in 1875 by Fr Carbonelle, S.J. of the Société scientifique de Bruxelles, which aimed to unite in discussion Catholic scholars of different nationalities, and the launching two years later of the society's journal, the *Revue des questions scientifiques*.

Some apologists did in fact make an effort to understand the viewpoint of those they sought to convince. Thus in Italy there was G. Bonomelli, in Belgium the Redemptorist V. Dechamps, who evolved his own 'Providential' system and defended it, in a series of articles published between 1857 and 1874, against at times lively criticism. In France there was Fr Félix, who tried to exploit his contemporaries' enthusiasm for progress, and more important Fr Gratry, who in a confused way perceived the line Ollé-Laprune and Blondel were to take in the next generation.

But towering far above the rest in the fecundity of his ideas holding promise for the future was John Henry Newman. With its stress on the historicity of dogmas his *Essay on the Development of Christian Doctrine* (1849) was a truly pioneering work. The ideas he developed in the *Grammar of Assent* (1870) regarding the role of 'a dialectic of conscience' and the need for the subject to be in a state of psychological preparedness for intellectual justification of the act of faith, have a remarkably modern-sounding ring; and in his *Letter to the Duke of Norfolk* (1875) and the revised edition of his *Via Media* (1877) he opened up fresh perspectives on the ecclesiological side. Unfortunately there was almost no one among his contemporaries prepared to follow up the paths he had perceived to be fruitful and the deceptively ephemeral aspect of his writings, which appeared in essay form, made them all the less likely to come to the attention of professional theologians. Nor should we forget the suspicions entertained of his orthodoxy until Leo XIII, immediately on his accession, made him a cardinal, suspicions which illustrate one of the least pleasing aspects of the intellectual climate of the Roman curia under Pius IX.

The German preoccupation with speculative theology that had inspired the work produced by Hermes and Günther during the second quarter of the century was by no means a spent force. Günther's ideas continued to attract enthusiastic attention throughout Germany and Austria and Kuhn's lectures at Tübingen, which continued until 1882, lost none of their popularity. It is none the less true that the historical aspect of the ecclesiastical disciplines assumed from mid-century an increasingly preponderant place. This development, which was characteristic of the intellectual life of the period as a whole, gained added impetus from the growing preoccupation with apologetics sparked off by the calling into question of many traditional positions by radical exegetes and historians of dogma on the Protestant side. Although in the biblical field the contribution from the Catholic side, while not entirely negligible, continued to lag behind, in the field of dogmatic and ecclesiastical history there was a notable flowering. First in the field was Tübingen, where while Hefele was at work on his monumental *Conciliengeschichte* (1855–74) a galaxy of younger scholars, centred on the *Theologische Quartalschrift,* were profiting from the new critical methods to chart the stages in the progress of Christian thought; but the great centre was Munich, thanks to the growing fame of Ignaz Döllinger (1799–1890). Döllinger's influence, of a kind almost inconceivable today, made its impact less through his publications, widely noticed and translated though they were, than through his lectures, whose range of influence was extended by the many students who came to occupy chairs in Germany, Austria and Switzerland, his private audiences with individuals, who were captivated by the richness of his intellectual discourse and the simplicity of its tone, and his correspondence, which embraced the entire scholarly world of Central and Western Europe.

Döllinger and most of his colleagues in the university world aimed above all to rid educated Catholics of their feelings of inferiority in face of a flourishing Protestant and rationalist science. They wanted to show it was possible for Catholics to compete on equal terms and to persuade them of their complete freedom to engage in scientific enquiry except in those cases, relatively few, where dogma was clearly in issue. They hoped in this way to win for the Church in Germany an influence in the world of thought comparable with the influence she was in the process of acquiring, through the medium of political and social activity, in German public life. But there were German churchmen, in particular Ketteler, bishop of Mainz, who saw things differently. They had in view the great mass of Catholics − peasants, artisans, middle classes − whose Christian beliefs, strengthened by the ministrations of a more devout and more zealous clergy, would find outward expression in a powerful array of well-disciplined voluntary associations, transmitters of the instructions of the hierarchy to Catholics in all walks of everyday life. Since for this purpose the need was for good rather than for learned priests, Ketteler and those who thought as he did were strongly opposed to the German system under which young clerics were obliged to follow theology courses in the faculties of State universities and they wanted to replace it by the system of diocesan seminaries operating in France and Italy. In addition, many were anxious to see young laymen removed from a university setting in which the professional body was not only overwhelmingly Protestant but often rationalist in outlook, and they therefore favoured the foundation of a Catholic university. [1]

These schemes, mooted in the reviews and supported by groups who took their cue from Ketteler and his circle, were strongly criticised by all such as Döllinger who feared to see Catholic youth growing up within a closed system, deprived of the scientific resources which in their view only the old universities were fitted to provide. What made them the more fearful of seeing Catholics cut off from contemporary scientific life was that their adversaries, having in general little sense of the urgency of the problems raised by historical criticism and being convinced that, since Kant, all speculative thought in Germany had run into a blind alley, were in favour of a return to Scholasticism.

Among these German neo-Scholastics were individual thinkers of undoubted merit: the Mainz dogmatician J. B. Heinrich, who took the trouble to complement the classical expositions with a thorough study of the Bible and the Fathers; the historian K. Werner, whose writings on medieval philosophy showed that devotion to Scholasticism was quite compatible with sound historical learning; most of all, J. Kleutgen, S.J., whose merit was to present the traditional doctrine in the synthetic perspective of the great modern philosophical systems, showing it to be capable of adaptation to the new problems, and M. J. Scheeben, a young teacher at the Cologne seminary, who managed to combine the Scholastic tradition and the

---

1. The idea was put forward as early as 1848 and from 1861 took definite shape; but a number of difficulties, and after 1870 the *Kulturkampf*, caused it to be abandoned. See G. Richter, *Der Plan zur Errichtung einer Katholischen Universität zu Fulda*, Fulda 1922.

patristic upbringing he had received at the Roman College with all that was most meritorious in the German talent for speculation. Yet it has to be acknowledged that the productions of this neo-Scholastic school were in general mediocre, and that many of those who were hostile to university theology had little awareness that in several fields the progress of historical methods made it necessary to revise the point of view.

More regrettable still, certain neo-Scholastics, chagrined at being held in contempt by the university world, sought to strengthen their position by appealing to Rome. Furthermore these denunciations, obligingly supported by the nunciature in Munich, did not always proceed solely from zeal for the truth but were prompted in some cases by personal jealousy. Now at Rome, where interest in scholarship was at a low ebb and the reaction against liberalism was in full swing, there was all the more readiness to listen to these accusations because of the general reputation of German professors that they refused, in the name of scientific freedom, to bow to any authority save that of their peers. Indeed, it was with the express purpose of reminding German theologians of the importance attaching to the decisions, even if they were not infallible, of the Church's ordinary *magisterium* that H. Denzinger, ex-student of the Gregorian and since appointed, not without some difficulty, professor of dogmatics in the theology faculty at Würzburg, published in 1854 his celebrated *Enchiridion symbolorum, definitionum et declarationum*.

Such was the background to the sudden condemnation in 1857 of the entire body of Günther's work and to the placing over the next few years of a growing number of publications on the Index. Magnified by distance, Rome's suspicions of German scientific scholarship were rapidly enlarging and started to encompass the most illustrious, Döllinger first and foremost.

Added to Döllinger's resentment at the damage to his prestige in the eyes of Catholics and his irritation at hearing doubts cast on his scholarship by people quite incompetent to judge, was his alarm at the sight of the intellectual forces of German Catholicism divided against themselves, at a time when there was greater need than ever to present a united front against the more and more searching attacks of infidel science, for despite his growing hostility to the policies of the curia, Döllinger's devotion to the Church remained unshaken. His suggestion for a conference of Catholic scholars at Munich at the end of September 1863 was made with a view to reconciliation. But his opening address on 'Theology past and present', in which he claimed for theology the right to complete freedom of movement — 'as indispensable to science as air is to the human body' — and for theologians a role parallel to that of the Church's ordinary *magisterium* — 'in the same way that prophecy existed alongside the priestly hierarchy among the Hebrews' — only added fuel to the flames. He made things no better by making it appear, from a passing reference to the complete decadence of theology in the Latin countries, that it was the German professors he saw as the true spiritual directors of the Church. Informed by the nunciature and by Döllinger's enemies of what had passed, Pius IX wrote a letter to the archbishop of Munich.[2] He condemned the attacks on Scholasticism, deplored the fact that a meeting of theologians had taken place without instructions from the hierarchy, although it was for the latter to 'direct and supervise theological activity', and made it clear that the Catholic scholar was not only bound by the official definitions but also had to take into account the ordinary *magisterium*, the decisions of the Roman Congregations and the staple teaching of the theologians.

This disavowal only made the polemical battle rage more fiercely between the two camps: on the one side the 'Deutsche Theologen', led by allies of Döllinger and soon equipped with their own journal, the *Theologisches Literaturblatt,* founded in 1865 by a young Bonn professor, F. Reusch; on the other the 'Roman School',[3] whose main strongholds were the Mainz seminary and the Jesuit theological college (where in 1864 Fr Riess founded the *Stimmen aus Maria Laach,* to furnish commentaries on the teaching of the *Syllabus*), but which also commanded support in the theology faculty at Würzburg, where Denzinger had been joined by two other former Gregorian students, Hergenröther the ecclesiastical historian and Hettinger the apologist, both of them scholars of merit and moderate in tendency. The radicalism and growing lack of Catholic spirit displayed by some of the young Müncheners and the sectarianism and narrow-mindedness of several in the 'Roman' camp conspired to heighten the tension, which during the First Vatican Council reached breaking-point. Following the definition of papal infallibility a number of the German professors broke with the Church, to come together again in the 'Old Catholic' movement. German ecclesiastical scholarship was to take a generation to recover from this serious draining-off of talent, especially since the unjustified attacks by certain scholastics on Kuhn's work had compromised the Tübingen School, which might otherwise have again exerted a fruitful influence: for it had escaped infection by the historicism and rationalism which increasingly vitiated the Munich School during the 1860s, yet on the other hand was able to compensate from its own tradition for the deficiencies in biblicism and sense of mystery found in the neo-Scholastic school. True, the qualities in

2. *Tuas libenter* of 21 December 1863 (in *Acta Pii IX*, III, 638-45).
3. Called 'Roman' because of its loyal observance of directions from Rome but also because a large number of its adherents had received their theological education in Rome. Confusingly, these opponents of the claims of German learning to intellectual hegemony were nicknamed the *Germaniker*. This was because they were former students of the *Collegium germanicum* at Rome.

question were also to be found in Scheeben, whose *Handbuch der katholischen Dogmatik* (1875–87), although it has certain limitations, must be accounted a major work. But Scheeben, a seminary professor with an exclusively Roman education, carried little weight in the university world and his premature death, in 1888, was another reason why he did not achieve in his lifetime the reputation he deserved. Generally speaking, the description 'bulwark of enlightened conservatism' applied by Fr Hecedez to the Jesuit faculty at Innsbruck could well be extended, bearing in mind the atmosphere created by the *Kulturkampf*, to the totality of German and Austrian theological centres during the twenty-five years following Vatican I.

Although the contrast between the pontificates of Pius IX and Leo XIII has often been exaggerated, when it comes to intellectual policy the distinction between them is plain. One of the great weaknesses of Pius IX's pontificate had been its withdrawal behind defensive positions on the plane of ideas. When the supreme authority intervened, it did so almost invariably in order to condemn, to serve notice, as the chance of circumstances dictated, that such-and-such a line of enquiry was regarded as inadmissible. Under Leo XIII care was at last taken to give Catholics positive guidance in these matters, proof of a keen awareness by the pope of the importance of the 'intellectual front' in view of the threat that had been hanging over Catholicism since the middle of the eighteenth century. The tone was set, as he intended it should be, by his first promotions to the cardinalate: all four of them priests whose lives had been dedicated to study, one of them being Newman, for so long under a cloud in Roman circles (the others were Hergenröther, the well-known church historian, and two architects of the Thomist revival, the pope's brother, J. Pecci, and Fr Zigliara, O.P).

It was in the field of philosophy as the necessary basis of ecclesiastical studies that Leo XIII made his most marked intervention, and he is justly regarded as having given the decisive impetus to neo-Thomism. True, the movement had started before his time. The revival of interest in Scholasticism went back to the earlier years of the nineteenth century and was associated in part with the Romantic vogue for the Middle Ages. It also represented a reaction against trends in modern thought that were held responsible for the current social unrest. Even so, the great post-Kantian idealist systems continued to hold sway in much of the German-speaking world, and many devotees of traditionalism and ontologism were still to be found in France and Italy – there were circles in Italy where Rosmini was exalted as 'the national philosopher'. Furthermore, the majority of nineteenth-century neo-Scholastics were eclectic in their philosophy, being strongly influenced by Suaresian or Cartesian tendencies. As time went on, however, more voices were raised in favour of a return to authentic Thomism: in Germany in the circles round J. Clemens, H. Plassmann, C.

von Schäzler, A. Stöckl, and above all Fr J. Kleutgen (*Theologie der Vorzeit*, 1853–70, *Philosophie der Vorzeit*, 1860–3), in Spain around the Dominican Gonzalez, founder in 1853 of the Thomist-orientated journal *La ciencia cristiana*, in France around the Abbé d'Hulst, in Belgium around Lepidi, who was director of studies at the Louvain theological college of the Dominicans, and A. Dupont, professor of dogmatics at the Catholic university. But interest was greatest in Italy. Although the Roman College remained until the accession of Leo XIII a stronghold of Suaresianism, the Jesuits of the *Civiltà cattolica*, Fr Liberatore in particular, were converted at a very early date into ardent propagandists of Thomism. The two main centres were Piacenza,[4] with the Collegio Alberoni, and still more important Naples. For it was in Naples that G. Sanseverino, with backing from his bishop, Mgr Riario Sforza, a friend of Cardinal Pecci's, had been conducting since 1846 a Thomist Academy, and it was from Naples that he launched the review *Scienza e fede* for the propagation of his ideas. After Sanseverino's death in 1865 the torch was kept burning by S. Tolamo. But there were other centres, notably Bologna, where a Jesuit, Cornoldi, was publishing the militantly pro-Thomist *La scienza italiana* and Perugia where, with the help of his Jesuit brother and a few Dominicans, Cardinal Pecci had founded the Accademia San Tommaso, in which he was able to work out at leisure his programme for the reform of ecclesiastical studies.

Even in the very early months of his pontificate, Leo XIII gave clear indication of his interest in the restoration of Thomism, which he characterised as 'the true Italian school'. Next, on 24 August 1879, there appeared the encyclical *Aeterni Patris*,[5] in which Catholics were recommended to draw in future on the teaching of St Thomas, presented as the quintessence of all that was good in the other Scholastic doctors, as their philosophical authority: above all else in the education of young clergy, but also in their private researches and in addition as an antidote to doctrines that were subversive of traditional values, whether in the domestic, the social or the political sphere.

This encyclical, in one way traditionalist, in another, by comparison with previous habits, quite revolutionary (among other things Leo XIII encouraged Thomists to consult St Thomas's own writings,[6] something that

---

4. For the importance of Piacenza as a centre of Italian neo-Thomism since the eighteenth century see G. F. Rossi, *Il movimento neotomista piacentino*, Rome 1974. The question of the exact role played by Buzzetti and the diocesan seminary on the one hand and by the Lazarists of the Collegio Alberoni on the other is still under debate (see M. Batllori in *Archivum historicum Societatis Jesu*, XXIX, 1968, 180-5.

5. *A.A.S.*, XII, 1879, 97-115. See F. Ehrle, *Zur Encyklika 'Aeterni Patris'. Texte und Kommentar*, new edn by F. Pelster, Rome 1954.

6. A few months later, with this end in view, Leo XIII commissioned the Dominicans to undertake a full critical edition of the works of St Thomas. The early stages proved something

had happened all too rarely) had a mixed reception, many being of the opinion that, by reverting in this way to the Middle Ages, the Church was about to cut herself off from the modern world and its problems. But the pope was determined to keep to his course and to wear down the opposition. His first concern was the Roman universities, which had so far remained outside the Thomist movement. The citadel most important to capture was the Gregorian, because of the growing number of foreign seminarists it attracted. Within two or three years the existing staff had been entirely replaced by a new team formed in the mould of Fr Liberatore, and this trend was later reinforced by the appointment of Fr L. Billot as professor of dogmatics (1885).[7] The pope brought Talamo and Cornoldi to Rome to preside over the reorganisation there of the Academy of St Thomas, while at the same time he encouraged the professors of the Collegio Alberoni at Piacenza in a new venture, the launching of the review *Divus Thomas*. Lastly, the pope appointed Fr Zigliara, O.P., the most outstanding of the Thomists at the Dominican School of the Minerva, head of the Congregation of Studies.

The band of Thomists that Leo XIII had thus assembled in Rome were certainly not without their merits, especially when one considers the difficult circumstances in which they had to work. To them belongs the credit for the final disappearance of the traditionalist and ontological systems and of spiritualist eclecticism, the vogue for which had constituted a considerable weakness in Catholic thought, and they gave back to several generations of clerics the taste for a coherent synthesis of the kind to be found in the work of St Thomas. But they had equally undeniable limitations and shortcomings. The philosophy they presented in their lectures and textbooks tended to be worked out too often in terms of theology, which greatly restricted its 'credibility' in the eyes of the non-clerical public. They abused the argument from authority and were too easily content with a verbal dialectic based on *a priori* definitions, their penchant for repeating formulae instead of thinking them out afresh receiving added encouragement from the

---

of a disappointment, since Rome had not appreciated the textual difficulties that had to be overcome (see the article by C. Suermondt, who was the lynchpin of the enterprise, in *Mélanges Mandonnet*, I (Paris 1930), 17-50 and G. F. Rossi, *Il quarto pioniere della Commissione leonina, P. Cl. Suermondt*, Piacenza 1954, and P. de Contenson, 'Documents sur les origines de la Commission léonine', in *St Thomas Aquinas Commemorative Studies,* II (Toronto 1974), 331-88.

7. Billot's work, now made obsolete by its lack of biblical and patristic foundations, at the time represented a real advance, which explains its success during the next half-century or so. Especially to be admired is the way each point is developed from a central idea which determines the logical construction of the whole, and the way in which a more penetrating theological intuition often succeeds in eliminating illusory problems which for centuries past had been causing difficulty.

use of Latin. Lastly, they were too little conversant not only with modern philosophy but also, which was worse, with the mind and methods of modern science. The general impression left by the Thomism which grew up in and around the Roman universities during the twenty-five years following *Aeterni Patris* is that it was inferior in quality to that of the preceding generation, the generation of Liberatore and Sanseverino. Billot apart, none of the names are now remembered, a fair indication of the mediocrity of what was achieved. It was not from Rome but from another centre that neo-Thomism was to capture the attention of the philosophical public and of the cultivated world.

Leo XIII's first and most urgent objective had been the infusion of fresh blood into the Roman seminaries and universities and the reorganisation of the Accademia San Tommaso. This done, he was on the look-out for other bases from which to promote an international Thomist revival and his thoughts turned immediately to Louvain, the seat at that time of the only full-scale Catholic university in the world and one with which, as nuncio in Belgium, he had once had direct contact.

After some hesitation on their part, the Belgian bishops agreed to sponsor at Louvain in October 1882 a lecture course on advanced Thomist philosophy. This course, given by D. Mercier and delivered in French, was an immediate and resounding success, even with the lay students, for in addition to firmness in doctrine and breadth of knowledge the young professor brought to his lectures an acute awareness of the problems and a highly personal touch. Soon Mercier was full of ideas for expanding the original scheme and in 1887 he submitted to Leo XIII, who signified his approval, a plan for establishing an 'Institut supérieur de philosophie' on the fringe of the faculty of 'philosophie et lettres'. He intended the institute to serve both as a 'graduate centre', training students for research in an atmosphere that preserved for philosophy its independence of theology, and also as a research institute, dedicated to the re-examination of Thomist solutions to problems whose concrete data had been modified by advances in philosophical thought or in the experimental sciences (to which Mercier, in the positivist climate of his times, attached what today seems excessive importance, although this helped to establish him as a useful go-between in many circles which held Christian philosophy in nothing but contempt).

In 1894, with the foundation of the *Revue néo-scolastique*, the Louvain school and its conception of an 'open' Thomism acquired a voice of its own, to the further enhancement of its international reputation. But during the next three years the enterprise came close to shipwreck, in consequence of the lively opposition it aroused in Belgium, where people were beginning to think that Mercier was taking too much on himself, and at Rome, where Cardinal Mazzella, the new prefect of the Congregation of Studies, considered that by attaching excessive importance to scientific training and by enlarging the share of independent research at the expense of systematic instruction in the aspects of philosophy important to theology Mercier was departing too drastically from neo-Thomism as taught in Rome. Furthermore, Mazzella could not approve of the use of French in the teaching of philosophy, thinking it must endanger the propriety of the terms and hence, as it seemed to him, the orthodoxy of the doctrine. Mazzella succeeded in communicating his fears to Leo XIII, but opinion veered round again with the replacement of Mazzella by Cardinal Satolli, who had read Mercier's work with interest. With assistance from Fr Lemius, O.M.I., who staunchly upheld the cause of Louvain, by 1898 the position of Mercier and his institute had finally been confirmed.

Although Rome and Louvain were undeniably the two poles of the neo-Thomist movement, we must not oversimplify: there were other centres, some of which made a truly original contribution. Italy apart, among the major countries it was in France that the movement made the most headway and it was from France, thanks to the world-wide prestige of French books and periodicals, that its influence spread far afield. But while the Institut catholique in Paris and the Société St Thomas d'Aquin were almost wholly orientated towards a Thomism less careful of the letter than of the spirit, somewhat on the lines of Mercier's though not necessarily dependent on it, the tendency of most of the theological colleges and seminaries was to rally to the kind of Thomism taught at the Gregorian. Transplanted to French surroundings, this Thomism of Roman origin exhibited in even more acute form many of the defects already mentioned. Its exponents often relied very heavily on the second-hand accounts purveyed in manuals compiled *'ad mentem S. Thomas'* (rather than on St Thomas's own writings), they passed off under cover of Thomist formulae a doctrine that was often philosophical only in appearance, they had no true conception of the thinking of their opponents, yet as self-styled Thomists, claiming the monopoly of orthodoxy, they were quick to indulge, with a simplism that turned quite naturally to absolutism, in bitter polemics against anyone not in step with themselves. In Switzerland, the presence of the Dominicans at the university of Fribourg guaranteed to Thomism some impregnable positions. The Dominicans were likewise highly influential in Spain, but so were the Jesuits, among whom there was still a strong attachment to Suarez.

In Germany and Austria the movement towards Thomism was much less pronounced, especially since after Scheeben's premature death it failed to produce any advocates as brilliant and open-minded as a Mercier or even a d'Hulst. Against this, however, can be set Catholic Germany's valuable contribution to the work on the history of medieval Scholasticism which had already started before the time of Leo XIII and to which his call for a return to the sources gave added stimulus. The pioneer of this branch of study, later pursued with such distinction by Fr Denifle, O.P. and Fr Ehrle, S.J., was C. Bäumker, author of countless monographs and founder in 1891 of the *Beiträge zur Geschichte der Philosophie des Mittelalters*. Ten years later Maurice de Wulf, a pupil whom Mercier had encouraged to take up research in the history of medieval philosophy, followed in Bäumker's footsteps by launching at Louvain the series *Philosophes belges*.

This historical research not only defined the doctrinal and psychological context in which the works of Thomas Aquinas had their origin, by drawing attention for example to the importance of neo-Platonist currents in the Middle Ages, but at the same time revealed the pluralism of medieval Scholasticism, showing it to have been much less uniform than had long been supposed. Furthermore, the publications — umpublished texts and monographs — put out by the Franciscans of Quaracchi were to confirm the justice of this observation and make it increasingly necessary to tone down a certain Thomist exclusiveness for which there was no historical justification.

This exclusiveness, which largely held the stage in Thomist circles down to 1914, spurred certain Franciscans into efforts at proving that the positions of St Bonaventure and even of Duns Scotus were not far removed from those of St Thomas. Others made similar efforts on behalf of St Augustine. But there were also those who thought it necessary to defend the legitimacy of several philosophical tendencies, each possessing its own originality, to co-exist within this general Scholastic framework. While some claimed a place alongside the Christian Aristotelianism of St Thomas for Augustinian mysticism, others, Fr Déodat de Basly for example, tried to re-activate the Scotist tradition, and even the Suaresians refused to admit defeat. Although an attempt to regain a footing in the Gregorian by keeping out Fr Billot ended in their discomfiture, they still had solid bases in Spain to fall back on until a new champion of Suaresian metaphysics arose in France in the person of Fr Descoqs.

The advance of neo-Thomism under the patronage of the Holy See did not prevent the survival and emergence of other trends in religious philosophy, even though circles won over to neo-Thomism were apt to cast somewhat hasty doubts on their orthodoxy. In Italy idealism still had its Catholic adherents, and in the north of the country in particular Rosmini was still a dominant influence, despite the condemnation by the Holy Office in 1887 of forty propositions taken out of context, a move deemed by many, not without justification, to be the result of reactionary intrigue. [8]

In Germany, while an appreciable number of Catholic philosophers, laymen in particular, remained within the neo-Kantian orbit, the persistent coolness of the clerical world towards neo-Scholasticism was underlined by the success which greeted the philosophico-theological synthesis of H. Schell,[9] from 1884 professor of apologetics at Würzburg. Schell was a man of powerful and original mind, steeped in Christian Platonism, who developed theses largely foreign to the theology of his day, for example concerning religious liberty, the role of the Holy Spirit and the place of laymen in the Church. The boldness of his views and certain imprecisions in his terminology exposed him now and then to criticism, but he had the great merit of presenting traditionalist doctrine in personalist categories, thus becoming a precursor of Christian existentialism, and of making it his constant aim to 'baptise' modern philosophy and science. But with the placing of his principal works on the Index in 1898 his influence, in any case confined to Germany, was prevented from spreading.

It was a different story with the intense ferment of ideas developing in France at this same period, stimulated by a revival of interest in Augustinian thought and in Pascal studies and revolving round the problem of knowledge in relation to religion. The nature of the knowledge derived by faith and the methods of apologetics, which by relying rather heavily on extrinsic procedures took too little into account the psychology of the apprehending subject and the essentially religious character of the believer's assent, excited impassioned debate during the twenty years following the publication in 1893 of Maurice Blondel's *L'Action,* a work whose influence, direct or indirect, on many of the creators of modern Catholicism, men of action as well as intellectuals, can scarcely be exaggerated. The implications for Christian thinking of what were intended as strictly philosophical propositions were worked out in the first instance by Blondel himself, in his celebrated *Lettre sur les exigences de la pensée contemporaine en matière d'apologétique* (1896), and subsequently by a band of more or less avowed disciples among whom Fr L. Laberthonnière was the most outstanding. If the Blondelians often carried their contempt for Scholasticism to extremes, if their anxiety to stress that the quest for the truth must engage the total personality led them at times to discount the value of precise concepts and formal argument, it is

---

8. The controversy over Rosmini, not confined incidentally to the philosophical aspects of his work, overlapped to a large extent with the controversy between the *intransigenti* and the *transigenti* during the last thirty years of the nineteenth century. The polemics to which it gave rise embittered the atmosphere for a great many years. Amid a copious literature see in particular: F. Traniello, 'La questionne rosminiana nella storia della cultura cattolica in Italia', *Aevum*, XXXVII (1963), 63-103 and G. Muzio, *Il senso ortodosso e tomistico delle 40 proposizioni rosminiane*, Rome 1963.

9. On Herman Schell (1860-1906), author among other works of value of a *Katholische Dogmatik* (4 vols, 1889-93) and of *Gott und Geist* (2 vols, 1895-6), see H. Hasenfuss, *Herman Schell als existentieller Denker und Theologe*, Würzburg 1956, and P. Wacker, *Glaube und Wissen bei Herman Schell*, Paderborn 1961.

greatly to their credit that they at last moved the problem of faith on to concrete and religious ground, that they demonstrated the importance of the will in the spiritual life and drew attention to certain non-discursive types of thinking, apt to be neglected by the Scholasticism of their day but essential in the realm of religious understanding.

Philosophy was but one of many fields in which at the accession of Leo XIII the Catholics were at a marked disadvantage. Two fields in particular were made highly sensitive by the prevailing intellectual climate, the natural sciences and history.

The former, for example, cast doubt on the reliability of the Genesis narrative of the creation and brought the theologian up against the problem of biological evolution. A serious attempt was made during the last quarter of the nineteenth century to ensure that Catholics had greater representation in scientific circles. A first step was taken in 1875 with the foundation by Fr Carbonelle, a Belgian Jesuit, of the Société scientifique de Bruxelles to act as an international forum for Catholic scientists. Before long, it had its own journal, the *Revue des questions scientifiques* (1877). Some ten years later a few French scientists – Canon Duilhé de Saint-Projet, author of an *Apologie scientifique du christianisme* (1885), without merit considering its date, Mgr d'Hulst, rector of the Institut catholique in Paris, and A. de Lapparent, the well-known geologist – came forward with a more ambitious scheme for holding regular international congresses of Catholics interested in the sciences in their bearing on religion. The plan not only incurred the ridicule of unbelievers, who doubted whether anyone could be both a serious scholar and a good Catholic,[10] but also met with a cool reception from the ultramontane press and in certain ecclesiastical circles, where it was feared that the assembled scholars, most of them laymen, aspired to act the part of a council and to decide questions within the province of the *magisterium*. But Mgr d'Hulst, who was to become the heart and soul of the enterprise, submitted the plan to Rome and brought it back approved by the pope. The first congress was held in Paris in 1888 and was followed by four others over the next decade.[11] These 'International Scientific Congresses for Catholics' had the twofold merit of helping to awaken Catholic interest in the modern sciences and of enabling scholars of different nationalities to test out their views in an atmosphere of bracing competition. The question that,

---

10. A charge not borne out by the facts as can be seen from the account, a shade optimistic it is true, given by Eymieu, *La Part des croyants dans le progrès scientifique au XIX*e *siècle*, 2 vols, Paris 1920-35.

11. Held at Paris in 1891, at Brussels in 1894, at Fribourg (Switzerland) in 1897 and at Munich in 1900. A sixth was to have been held at Rome in 1903, but the ecclesiastical authorities were afraid of an outburst by Loisy's disciples and the congress did not take place. For some of the details see A. Baudrillart, *Vie de Mgr d'Hulst*, I (Paris 1921), 545-61.

from start to finish, proved most delicate to handle was that of evolution, for on this point the attitude in Roman circles continued for many years to be one of extreme reserve. [12]

Change of outlook and real progress were much more in evidence in the application of critical methods to biblical and patristic writings and to ecclesiastical history, even if we have to agree with H. I. Marrou that 'although Catholic scholars of this period deserve credit for tackling a serious difficulty, they cannot be said to have entirely resolved it', since the end of Leo XIII's pontificate coincided with the beginnings of the modernist crisis, which had to be surmounted before theological methodology could properly assimilate Newman's idea of doctrinal development − even as the twentieth century dawned, Billot was still declaring 'dogmas have no history' − and before positive or historical theology gradually emerged in its own right, following the pioneering work of two French Dominicans, Lemonnyer and Gardeil.

The personal contribution of Leo XIII to the developments in this field in the last two decades of the nineteenth century was less decisive than in the case of the Thomist revival, but it was none the less real and constructive. The opening of the Vatican archives in 1880 to historians of every confession testified in concrete fashion, soon after the beginning of the pontificate, to a change in outlook whose scope was made explicit in a brief of 18 August 1883 in which, alongside references to apologetic considerations to-day quite outdated, the pope reminded Catholics of the historian's golden rule: never to risk telling a lie, never to be afraid of telling the whole truth. In 1892 Leo XIII was to say to Mgr d'Hulst: 'The troubled and perplexed would like the Roman Congregations to pronounce on questions still under debate. I am against it and put them off, for scholars must not be prevented from doing their job. They must be allowed time to grope their way and even to err. Religious truth can only be the gainer.' [13] These were not mere words. Leo XIII's chief merit in the matter was that of leaving scholars at last free to pursue their calling seriously in the interests of the truth, and of not yielding on this essential point to pressure from people who feared the outcome. This remained true even after the conservatives, especially numerous in the Society of Jesus, having found a champion in Cardinal Mazzella, prefect of the Congregations of the Index and of Studies, succeeded around 1895 in regaining some of their influence, as witness for example the letter to the Friars Minor of 25 November 1898 and the encyclical addressed to the

---

12. For instance even such moderate works as those of Fr M. D. Leroy, *L'Évolution des espèces organiques*, and of Fr J. A. Zahm, *Evolution and Dogma*, were the object of censure by the Holy Office, although the intervention of Leo XIII saved the latter from formal condemnation.

13. Quoted by A. Baudrillart, *op. cit.*, I, 456.

French clergy on 8 September 1899, warning against hyper-critical tendencies in theology and exegesis.

In the German countries, despite the upheaval caused by the secession of the Old Catholics, work of real importance was silently going forward. To realise what was accomplished we have only to compare J. Janssen's *Geschichte des deutschen Volkes seit dem Ausgang des Mittelalters* (1876–94), in which the dominant preoccupation is still with anti-Protestant apologetic, with the celebrated *Geschichte der Päpste* (since 1886) of Janssen's pupil L. Pastor,[14] a monument of erudition which, for all its manifestly ultramontane tendencies, was eventually accepted as authoritative in a university world in which anti-Catholic prejudice died hard, and with the positive evaluation of Luther in the essays on *Reformationsgeschichtliche Streitfragen* (1904) by S. Merkle,[15] a scholar whose highly independent views incidentally created something of a scandal in the ultramontane circles. Turning to the field of early Christian literature, we should note that in 1901 the Berlin series *Texte und Untersuchungen* acquired its first Catholic collaborator,[16] and that in the following year O. Bardenhewer entered a hitherto exclusively Protestant preserve with the publication of the first volume of his *Geschichte der altkirchliche Literatur*. It was also at this time that Fr Ehrhard started to command attention in the scholarly world. In certain fields Catholics even seem to have blazed a trail. F. X. Kraus,[17] for instance, who compiled a systematic inventory of the archaeological and artistic treasures of Alsace-Lorraine (1876-92) and who launched the *Realenzyklopädie der christlichen Altherthümer* (1880–86) and Fr M. Schmidt, S.V.D., founder of the review *Anthropos* (1906), which became the recognised organ of religious ethnography. Not long afterwards J. Schmidlin inaugurated the first chair of Catholic missiology and founded the *Zeitschrift für Missionswissenschaft* (1911). Equally indicative, so it appears, were various enterprises launched under the auspices of the

14. On the work of the historian Ludwig von Pastor (1854-1928), the day-to-day progress of which can be followed in his *Tagebücher* (ed. W. Wühr, Heidelberg 1950), see *Die Geschichtswissenschaft der Gegenwart in Selbstdarstellungen*, II (Leipzig 1926), 169-98, and F. Fellner, *Church Historians* (New York 1926), 373-415.
15. On Sebastian Merkle (1862-1945), pupil of F. X. Funk and Würzburg colleague of H. Schell, see the obituary contributed by H. Jedin to *Theologische Quartalschrift*, CXXX (1950), 1-20. In 1901, interestingly enough, Hertling had pointed out that since Döllinger's work on the Reformation, which dated from 1846, nothing serious on Luther had appeared from the Catholic side.
16. J. Sickenberger, *Titus von Bosra*.
17. His massive work on Dante (1897) long remained the authority in Germany. For details regarding this outstanding teacher of church history who was much involved in the ecclesiastical politics of his time, being one of the protagonists of 'Reformkatholizismus' at the turn of the century, and those *Tagebücher* have been published by H. Schiel (Cologne 1957), see *Lexicon für Theologie und Kirche*, VI, col. 596.

Görresgesellschaft (founded 1876): two periodicals, the *Historisches Jahrbuch* (1879) and the *Römische Quartalschrift* (1887), the founding of two institutes, in Rome (1888) and in Jerusalem (1908), the inauguration of the *Staatslexicon* (1887–96) and above all the great collected edition of the acts of the Council of Trent, the first volume of which appeared in 1901. Another sign of the revival of Catholic learning in Germany after the crisis years 1870–80 was the foundation by Diekamp in 1902 of the *Theologische Revue,* which numbered among its contributors some hundred and more scholars working in the universities.

Much less satisfactory was the state of affairs in Italy, where the foundation in 1900 of the renowned *Studie e testi* should not be allowed to mislead us. The great names in Rome at this period were all foreigners, Hergenröther, Denifle, Grisar, Pastor, Duchesne, and the Italian contribution to exegesis and positive theology rarely rose above the level of good scientific popularisation,[18] although in fairness to the Catholics it must be said that the record of the public universities was little better (the orientalist I. Guidi, who was one of the few exceptions, happens to have been a Catholic). Nevertheless, the later years of the pontificate of Leo XIII witnessed the beginnings of a revival, with some solid contributions to local history, in particular from Mgr F. Lanzoni,[19] and the foundation of two reviews, *Bessarione* by Mgr Marini in 1896 and *Studi religiosi* by S. Minocchi and G. Semeria in 1901, not to mention the launching in 1902 of the Societa internazionale di studi francescani. But with the onset of the modernist crisis these promising developments were to be stifled.

In France and Belgium, by contrast, the 1880s were a period of great ferment. In addition to the revival of biblical studies, to which we return in a moment, the following deserve special mention: the work of Mgr L. Duchesne,[20] learned editor of the *Liber pontificalis* (1886-92), trouncer of the legends regarding the apostolic origin of the ancient sees of France (the three definitive volumes of the *Fastes épiscopaux,* 1894, 1900, 1915, were the outcome of systematic research started in 1881), illustrious author of the *Histoire ancienne de l'Église* (1906-10), but notable above all as the master of a galaxy of young researchers who became scholars in their own right –

18. See P. Scoppola, *Crisi modernista e rinnovamento cattolico in Italia* (Bologna 1961), 29-48.
19. His major work on the origins of the Italian dioceses belongs, however, to the interwar period (appeared 1923-7). On F. Lanzoni (1862-1929) see the commemorative volume *Nel centenario della nascita di F. Lanzoni,* Faenza 1964.
20. On Louis Duchesne (1843-1922), professor at the Institut Catholique in Paris from 1877 to 1885 and at the École des Hautes Études from 1887 to 1895, director from 1895 until his death of the French School in Rome, see *Dictionnaire d'histoire et de géographie ecclésiastiques,* XIV, cols 965-84 and *Mgr Duchesne et son temps (Actes du Colloque 1973),* Rome 1975.

P. Batiffol for example[21] – and as editor for two decades of the *Bulletin critique,* a journal of capital importance in that it cleared the air in Catholic scientific circles of the time and substituted for flights of oratory or the conventional arguments of a largely unenlightened piety the rigorous demands of historical criticism; the foundation in 1896 by one of Duchesne's former students, A. Loisy, of the *Revue d'histoire et de littérature religieuses* which, in addition to dealing with biblical questions, devoted considerable space to the religious philosophy of the ancient world, the history of Christian origins and to patrology; the reshaping, also in 1896, of the *Revue de l'Orient chrétien* and the launching in the following year, by L. Petit of the Assumptionists, of the *Échos d'Orient,* which after an uncertain start settled down after a few months to become the recognised French journal for Byzantinists; the reassembling of the Bollandist team, under the direction first of Fr C. De Smedt, founder in 1882 of the *Analecta Bollandiana* which immediately won for itself an unchallenged reputation with scholars of every confessional persuasion, and then of Fr H. Delehaye, whose systematic exploration of *Les Légendes hagiographiques* (1905), occasion for scandal in integrist circles, quickly became a classic; the foundation in 1900 of the *Revue d'histoire ecclésiastique* by two Louvain professors, Cauchie and Ladeuze, who with their feeling for history made a profound impression on the work of the theological faculty and whose cautiously progressive school was at pains to seek out whatever was of value in the work of non-Catholic scholars in Germany and England; the inception in 1900 of the *Dictionnaire de théologie catholique,* followed a little later by the *Dictionnaire d'archéologie chrétienne et liturgie* and the *Dictionnaire d'histoire et de géographie ecclésiastiques;* the launching of a number of series, designed in some cases for scholars – the *Bibliothèque de l'enseignement de l'histoire ecclésiastique* (1896), two eastern patrologies, the one edited by Chabot, the other by Graffin and Nau (1903), the *Bibliothèque de théologie historique* (1904) – and in others for a more popular readership, for example *Les Saints* (begun 1897) and *La Pensé chrétienne* (1904). Admittedly, in this riot of publications not all were of equal value and many are by now superseded, but it is to their authors' credit that within a short span of years they initiated Catholic circles in the Latin countries into problems and methods of research of which they had previously had little inkling, although not without exciting the suspicions of those people, still numerous, who regarded the employment of critical methods as a dangerous concession to rationalism and liberalism.

21. On Pierre Batiffol (1861-1929) see *Bulletin de littérature ecclésiastique,* XXX (1929), 7-18, 49-62, 126-41. He experienced some difficulties under Pius X on account of his *Études d'histoire et de théologie positive* (1902) and *L'Eucharistie* (1905), but *L'Église naissante et le Catholicisme* (1909) had the honour, rare at the time, of being translated into German.

This opposition between conservative and progressive tendencies showed itself most strongly in a field particularly delicate for the Christian faith, that of the biblical sciences.

Until quite late into the nineteenth century Catholic exegis remained very traditionalist in its orientation, as may be judged from the *Cursus scripturae sacrae* edited by three German Jesuits, Frs Cornely, Knabenbauer and von Hummelauer, which only started publication in 1886. But towards the end of the 1880s there was a distinct change, brought about by the impact of a growing number of archaeological and historical discoveries and by the increasing difficulty of rejecting *en bloc* the results of the work that had started in Protestant faculties half a century before. The conservatives, although they began to abandon certain untenable positions or even, as did Fr. Hummelauer, to suggest here and these less rigid rules for a solution, continued on the whole to condemn critical exegesis on the ground that it proceeded from rationalist presuppositions – this was still the perspective of Vigouroux's *Dictionnaire de la Bible* (1891-1912), for all its considerable erudition. In contrast, there were others in growing numbers who thought it essential to apply the principles of historical criticism in their full rigour to the sacred books and who were prepared in consequence to revise the traditional front line in the battles between believing and rationalist exegetes, by making a distinction in contemporary biblical criticism between the findings of literary and historical research, many of which were acceptable or at least open to argument, and theories on Israel's history and on Christian origins that systematically excluded the supernatural. It was from this new standpoint that Loisy, Duchesne's pupil, started in 1883 to lecture on the Old Testament at the Institut Catholique in Paris, that A. van Hoonacker instituted at Louvain in 1889 a new course entitled 'Critical history of the Old Testament' and that M. J. Lagrange, O.P., having received a grounding in the Semitic languages at Vienna, founded the École pratique d'études bibliques at Jerusalem in 1890. Two years later Lagrange launched the *Revue biblique* which rapidly became an international forum for discussion of exegetical research that combined a progressive outlook with respect for the theological data; but because of the bold views expressed on the first chapters of Genesis and on the nature of biblical inspiration the review was soon under fairly vigorous attack, in particular from certain Jesuits. In the same year, 1892, Loisy started for a less specialised readership the review *L'Enseignement biblique,* to make the content of his lectures more widely known. This provoked even harsher criticism and Mgr d'Hulst, in an effort to defend his young professor, published in the *Correspondant* of 25 January 1893 a hastily conceived article on 'La question biblique'; but in fact this compromised Loisy still further, with the consequence that the episcopal trustees of the Institut deprived him of his chair.

Leo XIII had been following for some time the debates between Catholic exegetes and he now took advantage of this affair to issue some official directives. Drafted in large part by Fr Cornely, S.J., the encyclical *Providentissimus*[22] of 18 November 1893 was interpreted in many circles, on the right as much as on the left, as a rejection of the new exegesis. There is no denying that it came out clearly against the tendency to limit biblical inspiration, or at least biblical inerrancy, to matters of faith and morals, but the reminder of principle bore none of the marks of a condemnation and the encyclical presented itself as a positive exhortation to scholars to study the Bible in ways more in keeping with modern requirements and to equip themselves with a good grounding in the Semitic languages and in 'the art of criticism' (while remaining on guard against hyper-criticism and its excesses); in addition, the encyclical acknowledged that Catholic exegesis was not bound absolutely by the interpretations handed down by the Fathers, many of which could be traced to opinions current in their own day, and on several points it suggested interesting principles for reaching a solution, for example regarding problems raised by the progress of the natural sciences (the Bible does not claim to provide scientific explanations but describes things 'as they appear'), hinting very obliquely at the possibility that certain historical narratives might be looked at in a similar manner (taking into account the conceptions men had of historical literature as a genre in the ancient Near East). In short, although seventy-five years later the encyclical may appear unadventurous, its merits as a pioneering effort should not be overlooked. We know in any case that it did not deter Catholics from continuing with biblical research, which on the contrary in the succeeding decade proceeded with an even greater momentum. As evidence we can point among other things to the prominence of exegetes in the International Scientific Congresses for Catholics, the foundation in 1895 of the German series *Biblische Studien* and in 1903 of the still more important *Biblische Zeitschrift,* modelled by its founders, J. Göttsberger and J. Sickenberger, on the *Revue biblique,* to the work being published from Louvain by Professor Van Hoonacker, his pupil H. Poels and his junior colleague P. Ladeuze, the last of whom anticipated here and there some of the methodological conclusions of the *Formgeschichte* school, the launching by Lagrange in 1902 of his series *Études bibliques* and the publication of his little book, *La Méthode historique surtout à propos de l'Ancien Testament,* very well received in many Catholic circles, in which he gave a clear account of the principles inspiring the Biblical School in Jerusalem.

This continuing advance is all the more remarkable in view of the sustained hostility of the conservatives towards exegetes who ventured to depart

22. *A.A.S.,* XXVI (1893-4), 269-92.

from the beaten track. Unable to make the distinction between wholesome and necessary progress and the rash speculations of the few (Loisy and his group in particular), the conservatives stepped up their denunciations to Rome, finding that in certain circles, especially in those round Cardinal Mazzella, S.J.,[23] they fell on willing ears. Typical of the mentality still prevailing in certain quarters in Rome was the publication in 1897 of a decree of the Holy Office upholding the authenticity of the *Comma Johanneum,* an example of ecclesiastical authority claiming to decide an issue falling within the province of textual criticism. The death of Mazzella in 1900 was followed by a certain easing of the tension, as can be seen from the setting up of the Biblical Commission in October 1902: 'Everything known of the influence at work on Leo XIII in the setting up of this commission, the choice of Fr David Fleming as its secretary, the inclusion of a fair number of progressives among the forty-one consultors, the original intention of making the *Revue biblique* its official organ, the regulations drawn up for the commission, all this points to a constructive rather than a repressive purpose.'[24] It was not long, however before a conservative counter-offensive brought about an appreciable change in the commission's orientation, and with the outbreak of controversy over Loisy's more than usually explosive publications, coinciding with the replacement of Leo XIII by a pope less concerned with accommodation to modern aspirations, in a matter of months the climate changed very much for the worse, in particular as it affected the field of biblical studies.

23. On the harmful influence of Cardinal Mazzella see *inter alia* A. Baudrillart, *Vie de Mgr d'Hulst*, II, 172; P. Scoppola, *Crisi modernista et rinnovamento cattolica*, 71; *Le P. Lagrange au service de la Bible*, 105.
24. J. Levie, *La Bible, parole humaine et message de Dieu*, 80-1. On the beginnings of the Biblical Commission see M. J. Lagrange, *M. Loisy et le modernisme* (Paris 1932), 119-35 and F. Turvasi, *G. Genocchi e la controversia modernista* (Rome 1974), 217-28.

10

THE MODERNIST CRISIS AND THE 'INTEGRIST' REACTION

WITH the exception of J. Rivière's well-informed but often one-sided account [1] the history of modernism remained for half a century a taboo subject in the Catholic world. But in recent years, with the publication of some sources, in particular correspondence, it has become possible to look at it with a fresh eye. Much still remains obscure, but what is increasingly apparent is that any scholarly investigation of the modernist phenomenon has to proceed from individual studies of the very varied personalities who, under one head or another, were classed in their own day as modernists, [2] and that in any event the description of modernism given in the encyclical *Pascendi* offers the historian a very inadequate guide. In effect, modernism was first and foremost an 'orientation' (P. Sabatier), a 'tendency' (Loisy) rather than a sum of cut-and-dried doctrines, and although the theologian may possibly be content to criticise documents, even formulae, from an absolute standpoint and attempt to reconstitute a more-or-less coherent system from disparate elements from which he tries to elicit certain implicit assumptions, the historian has to make the effort to understand concrete human beings in all

1. *Le Modernisme dans l'Église*, Paris 1929; on this work see the comments of E. Amann in *Revue des sciences religieuses*, X (1930), 676-92, and of É. Poulat in his *Histoire, Dogme, et Critique dans la crise moderniste* (Paris-Tournai 1962), 41, 289-92 and 295.
2. In use since the sixteenth century to characterise the tendency to prefer modern times to antiquity, the term was employed in a religious connotation by certain nineteenth-century Protestants to designate the anti-Christian tendencies of their age and in due course the radicalism of the liberal theologians. When at the turn of the century a movement started in the Catholic Church favouring structural and doctrinal reforms to keep pace with modern times, it was spontaneously characterised by its opponents, in the first instance in Italy around 1904, as 'modernist'. The term was employed by the encyclical *Pascendi* (1907) in a very precise sense to designate a set of clearly distinguished doctrinal errors to which the heterodox tendencies of this diffuse movement pointed. Cf. A. Houtin, *Histoire du modernisme catholique* (Paris 1913), 81-95 and J. Rivière, *op. cit.*, 13-14.

their true complexity, to penetrate to their ultimate concerns. Now, like many other movements which have troubled the Church over the centuries, the movement of intellectual renewal in the Catholic Church at the beginning of the present century, which paralleled the 'liberal Protestant' crisis in the Reformed Churches of half a century earlier and like that crisis was provoked by clashes between the Church's traditional teaching and the new religious sciences growing up independently of ecclesiastical control, presented many different facets. Some manifestations of modernism, although disconcerting to the conventional mind, were perfectly legitimate; others, though made to appear dangerous by the baldness of their expression, were nevertheless sound in principle; and finally there were manifestations which verged on the heretical and which ended in some cases in becoming entirely devoid of Christian content. What lay behind these variously radical statements was a common desire on the part of men anxious to remain in the Roman Church to concede what seemingly had to be conceded to the modern world in order that Catholicism, shorn of its superannuated contingent elements, might keep in step with it.

The situation was made more complicated still by the fact that in parallel with the ferment of ideas at the level of the religious sciences a certain number of Catholics, more far-sighted than the generality of the faithful and their ecclesiastical leaders, saw fit to call in question the traditional conception of the political and social order and to envisage a thorough-going *aggiornamento* of many of the Church's institutions, of the forms of the pastorate and of the life-style of the committed Christian in the modern world. From this general perspective, in which modernism might be defined as 'the real encounter and confrontation between a religious past set long ago in its mould and a present that found its sources of inspiration elsewhere' (É. Poulat), it was possible to denounce as manifestations of modernism certain types of Christian democracy, the Americanist movement in the form it took in France, and the various movements for church reform that were rife in France, Italy and most of all Germany around the year 1900.

We shall be concerned in this chapter chiefly with the crisis as it developed in the religious sciences. It first erupted in France, occasioned by the application of the methods of historical and literary criticism to the study of Holy Scripture and of Christian origins; but it was not long before the problems encountered in this connection gave a new and burning topicality to the problem already raised between 1860 and 1870 by such as Döllinger and Acton, of how to reconcile the Church's legitimate authority with the requirements of scholarship for at least some degree of autonomy.

The calling in question of a certain number of traditional views by German liberal scholarship had made some of the younger French exegetes aware of the need to redress the believers' front line of defence against the rationalists by accepting for their part the literary and historical findings of critical enquiry while rejecting any conception of the history of Israel and of Christian origins which systematically eliminated the supernatural viewpoint. But whereas Fr Lagrange confined himself to writing for a specialist audience and was careful to demonstrate the conformity of his progressive views with the official teaching of the Church — which did not save him from attack by the conservatives and denunciation to Rome — others showed themselves less cautious and, convinced that Catholic apologetic was due for a complete 'retooling', were not afraid, even when writing for popular journals, to overturn a number of received positions. The most notable of these was Alfred Loisy. Endowed as a scholar with gifts beyond the ordinary and as a writer with a remarkable talent for exposition, Loisy made use of his enforced leisure (he had been obliged after the encyclical *Providentissimus* to resign his chair at the Catholic Institute in Paris) to bring his reflections of exegetical method increasingly to bear on the problems posed by the Scriptures as a whole, on the meaning of the divine truth there expressed and on the part played by the Church in preserving it. The publication in 1902 of the French translation of Harnack's lectures on *Das Wesen des Christentums* gave Loisy the incentive to offer a synthesis of the apologetic system he had gradually evolved. This he did in a little book *L'Évangile et l'Église*, which went on sale in November 1902, to be followed a year later by an elucidatory volume, *Autour d'un petit livre,* which added to the gravity of the import. Loisy himself described his work as being 'first, a historical sketch and historical exposition of Christian development, second, a general philosophy of religion and an attempt at the interpretation of dogmatic formulae, official creeds and conciliar definitions with the aim of harmonising them, by the sacrifice of the letter to the spirit, with the historical data and with modern ways of thought'. [3] Starting from the principle that the exegete must set aside all preconceived opinion as to the supernatural origin of the sacred books and interpret them as he would any other historical documents, without regard to the Church's *magisterium,* Loisy not only put forward, inspired by the German eschatological school, a conception of the work of Jesus very different from the received ideas — 'Jesus foretold the Kingdom and it was the Church that came' — but also invited his readers to question the notion of exterior revelation — 'dogmas are not truths fallen from Heaven' — and hence to accept the legitimacy of a radical evolution in the manner of interpreting dogmas, and similarly in the organisation of the Church.

These revolutionary ideas, often insinuated rather than stated, were

3. *Revue d'histoire et de littérature religieuses,* XI (1906), 570.

favourably received in certain intellectual circles, especially by that small section of the younger clergy always eager for new ideas. But very soon the praise came to be mingled with criticism and attack, voiced not only in conservative circles, whose 'vehemence of language often concealed a total *ignoratio elenchi* ',[4] but by men of very open outlook who were at one with Loisy on a number of his critical conclusions and even on the need for farreaching revision of the traditional Catholic apologetic, but who were unwilling to accept his radical position on the complete autonomy of criticism in respect of the Church's *magisterium* or to call in question, as he did, the very notion of orthodoxy. Such in particular was the position of Fr Lagrange and of Mgr Batiffol, supported in the latter's case by a desire to turn over a new leaf, rather too obvious, in the eyes of Rome. It was also the position of Maurice Blondel, whose papers published under the title *Histoire et dogme,*[5] in which the stress is on the true meaning of tradition in the Catholic system, seen even today extraordinarily perspicacious even if their author, sharing the common difficulty of philosophers in understanding the problems of historians, did not always grasp the true dimensions of the difficulties the 'little red books' set out to tackle.

In later life Loisy at various times declared that he had lost his faith in the divinity of Christ, and even in the existence of a personal God, well before the publication of *L'Évangile et l'Église,* but that he had preferred to give the lie to his real thoughts, believing he had a better chance of achieving from the inside a reform of the Church he thought beneficial to mankind. The biography of Loisy written by A. Houtin,[6] who knew his subject very well, seems at first sight to bear out these statements. But as Poulat has shrewdly pointed out, the very existence of this manuscript, composed in a spirit inimical to Loisy, may in part account for *a posteriori* reconstruction of what Loisy, once he had cut loose from all positive faith, wished to make of his religious development. If this is correct, the credibility of Loisy's statements regarding the exact date at which he ceased to believe, which some have been too hasty to accept, is at once reduced. The letter fragments and memoirs published by R. de Boyer de Sainte-Suzanne under the title *A. Loisy entre la foi et l'incroyance* confirm how far Loisy was from being a Reñan, whose scientific rationalism he abhorred, and from being a Houtin,

---

4. J. Rivière, *op. cit.*, 169. We should note, however, the comment by É. Poulat, *op. cit.*, 291: 'scientifically they were doubtless ill-equipped to solve the problems raised but they were competent enough in theology to pinpoint them and to underline the gravity of the divergences of opinion.'

5. In *La Quinzaine,* issues of 16 January, 1 and 16 February 1904; reprinted in *Les Premiers Écrits de M. Blondel* (Paris 1956), 149-228.

6. On Albert Houtin (1867-1926), a priest and historian who became progressively alienated from the Church and the Christian faith, see É. Poulat, *op. cit.*, 332-63.

who was in some respects his evil genius. [7] True it is that Loisy was making a distinction between faith and creeds as early as 1900, but advances in the sociology of religious understanding, as in the theology of faith and hermeneutics, now permit us to take a less simplistic view of the complete psychological make-up of the modernists than was possible at the beginning of the century.

Whatever doubts there may be about Loisy's personal opinions, there can be none that he was the catalyst of a spreading malaise in the Catholic intelligentsia and that the publication of his 'little books' — placed on the Index at the end of 1903 — sparked off a theological battle that was to last, with one round succeeding another, for many years and to extend well beyond the frontiers of France. While Loisy's conservative opponents denounced him as a new Renan, Loisy's champions harked back to the trial of Galileo or hurled charges that a 'clerical Dreyfus affair' was being hatched. Many people, young people in particular, [8] were drawn to his thought-provoking views, which in their feeling for the complexity of historical realities contrasted sharply with the superficiality and infantilism of the lives of Jesus and accounts of the early Church offered to the Catholic public of the day. The ideas of Newman, often very imperfectly understood, on development in Christian doctrine and the relationship between faith and reason were now, thanks to Bremond, reaching the French public. To the new generation they appeared to confer a cardinal's authority on the new line in apologetic opened up by Loisy and on the less notional conception he was forming of revelation. Something was glimpsed, too, of the fruitful possibilities contained in the affirmation that the Gospels were not historical narratives in the ordinary sense but documents of a catechetical nature, embodying the faith of the first generations of Christians while it was in process of formulation. Some of the Christian democrats were also struck by a parallelism between their own aspirations to adapt the Church to modern society and Loisy's efforts at theological renewal, or between Loisy's assertion of the autonomy of the exegete and historian of dogmas in respect of the Church's *magisterium* and their own assertion of the autonomy of laymen and civil society in respect of the 'clerical autocracy'. The weekly journal *Demain,*

---

7. See É. Poulat, *Une oeuvre clandestine d'Henri Bremond* (Rome 1972), 21-2: 'Loisy's modernism in fact fell plumb in the middle of an interplay of forces, the right wing of which was represented by the progressivism of Mgr Battifol, Fr Lagrange, Fr de Grandmaison, etc., which on the left came up against the rationalism of men such as Turmel, Houtin and Sartiaux. The closeness of Houtin and Sartiaux to Loisy and the ill-defined nature of the 'progressives' opposition served to mask the depth and significance of their disagreement, which was not only a matter of temperament.'

8. For the excitement among the young see É. Poulat, *Histoire, Dogme et Critique*, 270-315, which cites the testimony of Mgr E. Amann, *Revue des sciences religieuses*, X (1930), 676-93.

published at Lyons between 1905 and 1907, which had as its editors two young laymen, was symptomatic of this trend.

Nor was it long before questions were raised which went well beyond the field of biblical problems and dogmatic history. The controversies of the late 1890s over Blondel's proposals for revising the apologetic by application of the immanentist method had gradually died down, but they flared up again when one of his disciples, Fr Laberthonnière, widened the scope of the discussion to embrace the whole problem of religious knowledge. While in the *Annales de philosophie chrétienne,* of which he became editor in 1905, Laberthonnière was constantly urging, in opposition to Thomist Scholasticism, the merits of a philosophy of action of personalist inspiration, the debate with the theologians on this new ground was transformed into an uproar following the publication of an article by É. Le Roy, a young Catholic mathematician and disciple of Bergson's, under the title 'Qu'est-ce qu'un dogme',[9] in which he urged philosophers and theologians to ponder what meaning the dogmatic formulae presented to the faithful by the Church as articles of faith could still hold for a modern intelligence with a scientific turn of mind.

Thus in the space of a few years the Tridentine tranquillity of a whole ecclesiastical world had found itself rudely shaken, almost at one and the same time, on a number of fundamental points: the nature of revelation, of biblical inspiration and of religious knowledge, the personality of Christ and his true role in the origins of the Church and of its sacraments, the nature and function of the living tradition in the Catholic system and the limits of dogmatic evolution, the authority of the Church's *magisterium* and the real import of the concept of orthodoxy, the value of the classical apologetic. These were genuine problems and they called for an answer. The solutions proposed by Loisy, Laberthonnière or Le Roy contained valuable elements, and in some instances provided very useful pointers, as the subsequent development of theology and some of the statements emanating from Vatican II were to prove. But these positive elements were still imperfectly distilled and were often presented crudely or in language that was inadequate and in a manner undoubtedly disconcerting to conformist minds, all the more so when, as with Loisy in particular, the statements were often ambiguous, being susceptible either of a heterodox interpretation unacceptable to the believer or contrariwise of an interpretation admittedly innovating but fundamentally orthodox, and offering a genuine way out of difficulties raised by the problem of the religious sciences. Those who defended the innovators did so from the understanding that, whatever their imprudences and im-

9. Published in *La Quinzaine,* LXIII (1905), 495-526 and reprinted with important additions in his book *Dogme et Critique,* 1907, which gives a bibliography (359-63) of the polemics provoked by the article.

precisions, they had opened up a promising path in a region filled with shadows. But those who opposed them interpreted the equivocal formulations in the first, the heterodox sense, suspecting that this more truly represented the thinking of their authors. Denunciation of the innovators from this source increased in fury as the initial disarray turned increasingly to panic following the proliferation of an equivocal body of literature popularising in crude fashion the issues in debate, and following too the havoc wrought by the fever in the ranks of the younger clergy, who were sadly ill-equipped by their superficial seminary education to keep a cool head, and whose ever more numerous 'defections' were noted with smug satisfaction by outside observers.

Although France was undisputably the epicentre of the modernist crisis, it was not long before echoes of it were heard in Italy and Great Britain, countries in which modernism acquired one or two original features there has sometimes been a tendency to minimise.

English modernism, even when the movement was at its height, was always confined to a very small group; yet by reason of the stature of its two chief representatives, Tyrrell and von Hügel, it exercised on the Continent an influence quite out of proportion to its numerical importance. But it differs from continental modernism in having produced no modernist of any prominence who evolved in the direction of agnostic rationalism.

Efforts to create a synthesis between the Catholic faith on the one side and modern culture and scientific freedom on the other had once before, during the 1860s, set up tensions inside English Catholicism. This storm, of which Acton and the *Rambler* group had been the centre, was of short duration, and the elevation of Newman to the cardinalate helped to clear the atmosphere still further. But two decades of calm were succeeded by a revival of religious liberalism which coincided with the last decade of Leo XIII's pontificate. Among the new Catholic progressives the most eminent was undoubtedly Baron Friedrich von Hügel, son of a former Austrian diplomat and a Scottish mother, who from 1871 made his home in London. For a long time Catholic historians dealt harshly with von Hügel because of his manifest sympathy with the fundamental aspirations of modernism in its early stages and because of the loyal support he continued to give over the years to its leading representatives, even the most compromised, which earned him from Paul Sabatier the title 'lay bishop of the modernists'. But a well-merited rehabilitation is now in progress and it is becoming more and more evident that von Hügel was one of the most seminal religious personalities of his time, one who always steered clear of the religious subjectivism of many of his friends and their tendency to reduce religion to an intra-human phenomenon, defining his own ideal in a letter of May 1903: 'We have to live and to create, not a simple thing, sincere science, but a complex thing, costing but consoling . . . sincere science in and with profound and historical religion, in and with a living Catholicism . . .' [10] And he was clear, as he was to declare one day to Maud Petre, that no book was worth the sacrifice of the sacraments of the Church. Combining German profundity with English empiricism, von Hügel was not a specialist in any one field but he had the advantage, possessed by very few at that period, of being genuinely conversant with the three fields of biblical criticism, religious philosophy and the history of mysticism. Furthermore, he had a remarkable gift for quickening and stimulating minds and souls and a still more remarkable flair, in which his perfect command of the major European languages stood him in good stead, for establishing, by means of his vast correspondence and frequent visits abroad, fruitful contacts between exegetes, theologians and philosophers, in France, England, Germany or Italy, who were groping their way forward along similar lines. Many he cherished not merely as stimulating thinkers but as close friends. What made him all the more energetic in their defence was his keen appreciation of the inadequate and often superficial character of much of the criticism levelled at them from the conservative side, and his understanding of what it was in certain authoritarian procedures of the Vatican that could so frequently disturb a man of the twentieth century, and indeed how little these procedures had to do with religion.

It was largely under the influence of von Hügel that George Tyrrell, much in demand as a preacher of retreats and spiritual director, author of devotional works of unusual delicacy and of apologetic essays particularly well adapted to the outlook of his contemporaries, started to take an interest in biblical criticism and in a neo-Kantian philosophy, and having embarked on this road, came to call in question a number of theses essential to basic theology; although we should not neglect as an additional influence on Tyrrell his acquaintance with the writings of nineteenth-century English liberal Protestants. Becoming increasingly aware first of the importance of the mystical element in religion, as also of the frequent confusion between the Christian faith and its medieval expression, and then of the relative character of all human approaches to the truth, he started to publish under various pseudonyms – to avoid the niggling censorship of the Society of Jesus, to which he belonged – writings in which he demonstrated that Christ did not present himself as a teacher of orthodoxy and that, in consequence, Catholic theology was wrong to define faith as an assent of the mind to a theology said to have been revealed and miraculously preserved from error, when dogma was merely an attempt by man to evoke in intellectual terms, always provisional, the divine power he experienced in himself. Expelled

10. *Selected Letters* (London 1927) 123 (original text in French).

from the Society of Jesus at the beginning of 1906, Tyrrell thought to continue as a Catholic priest, and the two books he published in the next few months, *Lex Credendi* and *Through Scylla and Charybdis* (the excessive dogmatism of theologians on the one side, the too human pragmatism of some philosophers on the other) contained nothing unduly subversive, but he could not refrain from protesting in the press against the encyclical *Pascendi* and the inquisitorial procedures it seemed to him to epitomise, and this brought about his excommunication, Having been pilloried by Cardinal Mercier as the arch-representative of the philosophical and theological modernism described in the encyclical, Tyrrell replied with a stinging attack on traditional Catholicism under the title *Medievalism* (1908), but the more serene mood of the book he had just completed at the time of his premature death (15 July 1909), *Christianity at the Cross-Roads*, certainly seems to indicate that in fundamentals he remained closer than is often claimed to the Catholic Church, at least in the perspective of Vatican II. [11]

In Italy, more than elsewhere, the need for a renewal struck the world of Catholic intellectuals as an urgent necessity, in part in order to fill the cultural void created by the *intransigenti* with their timorously negative attitude towards the liberal revolution, in part to satisfy the aspirations towards greater spiritual freedom which had emerged over the past two generations in Catholic circles where the new dispensation had gradually become taken for granted. The first signs of revival appeared during the closing years of Leo XIII's pontificate, being stimulated by various foreign influences: the publications of the French exegetes and the work of Tyrrell, whose influence in Italy was much greater than Loisy's; the influence in person of Duchesne, settled in Rome since 1895, and still more of von Hügel, a frequent visitor to Italy. However, recent studies and the growing body of published sources have brought clearly to light a number of traits peculiar to Italian modernism, which was not the mere 'by-product' Rivière claimed it to be. It had its roots in a long Italian tradition, linked with the Risorgimento, of political liberalism and aspirations to religious reform, which explains for one thing the preoccupation with emancipation from an ecclesiastical tutelage which in Italy was more burdensome than elsewhere, and likewise the stress on the Church as the communion of the faithful, in contrast with the classical conception centred on the hierarchy. Then again, while French

11. Among the handful of other English 'modernists' in the broad sense, along with Maud Petre, Tyrrell's devoted angel during his latter years (on whom see J. A. Walker in *Hibbert Journal*, XLI (1943), 340-3), we should at least mention Edmund Bishop, the eminent liturgist, to whom A. Vidler has drawn attention in his book *A Variety of Catholic Modernists* (Cambridge 1970), 134-53, though it should be noted that Bishop was a reformer rather than a true modernist, and that in respect of the great truths of the faith and of devotion to the sacraments he never ceased to be a sincere Catholic. See, for others, the chapter in the same work entitled 'Lesser lights and fellow-travellers', 153-90.

modernists were concerned above all else to bring religious studies up to date on the academic plane, Italian modernism was characterised by its efforts to reach a very wide public, which in part explains why it had closer connections than other modernist movements with Christian democracy. Another difference: while the French modernists placed the accent on the criteria of rationality imposed by the scientific orientation of modern culture, many Italian modernists were more susceptible to the mysteries of the charismatic Church and to the nostalgic pull of a return to primitive Christianity.

Following P. Scoppola, we may distinguish three main currents in the reform movement which developed in Italy during the early years of the twentieth century.

The first stream, particularly well represented in Central Italy, was made up of young priests and religious anxious to remedy the backwardness of the religious sciences: apologists such as the Barnabite Giovanni Semeria, close friend of Hügel's, more successful than anyone in assimilating the results of current research and presenting them to the public; exegetes of whom the most outstanding were Fr Giovanni Genocchi and Mgr Umberto Fracassini, two fine examples of the Catholic savant, in whom openness of mind went hand in hand with strict loyalty to the Church, and a younger and more audacious priest Salvatore Minocchi, who had the knack of hinting through his reviews of new books at the fragility of many of the traditional positions and whose periodical *Studi religiosi,* founded 1901, had become a rallying-point for the most enlightened among the younger priests; historians of the Church and of dogma, of whom the most brilliant was Ernesto Buonaiuti, later to become the most prominent figure in Italian modernism[12] but whose *Rivista storico-critica delle scienze teologiche,* launched in 1905, attempted initially to steer a middle course between the more pronounced progressivism of the *Studi religiosi* and the conservatism of the *Civiltà cattolica.* One thing that is striking about all these strivers after an intellectual revival in Italian Catholicism, overriding all the differences of their interests and upbringing, was their common sense of mission, which marked them off very distinctly from most of the French scholars with whom they had intellectual affinities, who by comparison appear much more desk-bound. The aim of the Italians was not so much to grapple with Protestant and rationalist science but rather to deepen the religious culture of the average Catholic, conscious as they were of its deficiencies, which were at-

---

12. The most striking but not the most typical according to P. Scoppola, who insists that Buonaiuti's development of radical views soon isolated him from other leading figures in the movement who, although reformers, and in some cases reformers with a very independent turn of mind, had no thought of renouncing their adherence to Catholic dogma.

tributable to the so easily superficial character of the Catholic faith among Italian Catholics.

Similar preoccupations were to be found in the second group, formed from militants trained in the cadres of the intransigent Opera dei Congressi who had found out, along with its practical shortcomings, its ideological limitations and who tried to surmount them by developing the cultural bases for a genuine Christian democracy. The most prominent of these militants was Don Romolo Murri who, while not fully sharing the aspirations of Minocchi, Buonaiuti and their associates, had become convinced that the lack of intellectual maturity in the Italian Catholic world, and first and foremost among the clergy, made Catholics incapable of facing squarely the problems posed by the Christian's involvement in public life. In his famous San Marino speech on the theme 'Liberty and Christianity' (1902), in which he referred to the work of Tyrrell, Ehrhard and Mgr Mignot, as also to the renaissance in biblical and historical studies, Murri had gone on to express the wish to see Catholicism disencumbered of its superannuated elements by 'a return to the Gospel'. This attitude, which became more pronounced in step with Murri's increasing involvement in a programme of social and political action completely outside the hierarchy's control, attracted to him a number of priests who wanted more or less radical reforms in the Church: a reduction in the number of dioceses, revision of the Index procedures, reform of the seminaries and of the traditional methods of evangelism, abolition of sacerdotal celibacy and so on.

The third group, that of the Lombardy reformers, was in origin very different, since it was descended from the liberal Catholicism of the Risorgimento period. Some were men of action, for example the founders of the Opera Bonomelli, a charity for helping Italians working abroad, but the majority were lay intellectuals with a passionate interest in religious questions, a rarity in Italy at that period. The writer who made the greatest impact on the general public was Antonio Fogazzaro, successful man of letters and deeply imbued with a mystical idealism. In a best-selling novel, *Il Santo* (1905), he depicted an apostle pleading for a reform of the Church in a spirit of charity and, following on from the Rosmini of the 'Five wounds of the Church', he denounced the four evil spirits by which the Church had been invaded, in particular the stiffneckedness which had made the rabbis reject the message of Christ (the comparison came from Tyrrell, widely read in this circle). Less spectacular but more profound was the influence exerted by the review *Il Rinnovamento* founded early in 1907 by a group of young Milanese who were anxious, while remaining faithful sons of the Church, to show all possible openness to the aspirations of their own times and to integrate their Catholic inheritance with the values of secular culture. This review, which through one of its founders, Stefano Jacini, was in close touch with the protagonists of the German *Reformkatholizismus*,[13] stressed for example the primacy of conscience over authority acting from outside, freedom in scientific research and the role of the laity in the Church's life. In line with post-Kantian philosophy, it stressed the importance of the subjective view-point, so much neglected in Scholastic thought. Loyal to its liberal antecedents, it likewise advocated a new manner of conceiving the relations between Church and State, in reaction to the 'blurred' relationship of the past few centuries.

In Italy as in France, the ideas discussed within these various groups, which had relatively little contact with one another,[14] met with a sympathetic response from some of the younger clergy. But the governing circles in the Church were even less well equipped there than in France to grapple with the problems that were raised. There was no Italian prelate, for example, to compare with Mgr Mignot,[15] the courageous and level-headed author of *Lettres sur les études ecclésiastiques* (1908) and *L'Église et la critique* (1909). So the panic in Italy was even greater and, as invariably happens in such cases, the reaction soon raged indiscriminately against all who strayed, even by an inch, from the traditional path.

Inasmuch as Leo XIII had refrained to the last from harsh measures which would have seemed to disavow the progressive movement in biblical studies in its entirety, the placing of Loisy's principal works on the Index at the end of 1903 made it immediately clear that the change of pontificate had brought a change of atmosphere. This impression was confirmed by various other measures introduced over the next few years and by the increasingly conservative trend apparent in the Biblical Commission. The wave of reformism sweeping through Italy increased the scope for anxiety and in 1906 a systematic inspection was ordered of the seminaries, as a result of which a number of professors were removed from their chairs without so much as opportunity to speak in their own defence; and the writings of Laberthonnière – works that had been in print for several years – were placed in their turn on the Index.

13. Cf. below, 199.
14. It was with the idea of making the Italian reform movement more homogeneous in character that a meeting, in which Baron von Hügel took part, was arranged at Molveno during 1907, but the results fell short of expectations. On this meeting, for long something of a mystery and often, though mistakenly, regarded as a kind of pan-European modernist council, see P. Scoppola, *Crisi modernista e rinnovamento cattolica* (Bologna 1969²), 235-44 and M. Bedeschi in *Humanitas*, XXIV (1969), 658-77 and XXV (1970), 482-91.
15. On Mgr E. Mignot (1842-1918), 'the Erasmus of modernism' (J. M. Mayeur), see L. de Lacger, *Mgr Mignot*, Paris 1933 and the more moderate account by É. Poulat, *Histoire, Dogme et Critique*, 448-84, with as complement the letters published recently by M. Bécamel in *Bulletin de littérature ecclésiastique*, LXVII (1966), 3-44, 81-114, 170-94, 257-86; LXIX (1968), 241-68; LXXI (1970), 262-73. For the text of his report to the Secretary of State on integrist intrigues, October 1914, see É. Poulat, *Intégrisme et catholicisme intégral* (Tournai-Paris 1969), 515-23.

Since these warnings had not sufficed to stem the crisis, which assumed on the contrary ever wider proportions, in 1907 Pius X became determined to declare his position officially. After coming out strongly, in a widely noticed consistorial allocution delivered in April, against 'neo-reformism' in religion, in June he addressed to Commer, the Austrian theologian, a brief congratulating him on his stand against the errors of H. Schell, regarded as one of the symbols of German *Reformkatholizismus*. Next, in July, the Holy Office in its decree *Lamentabili sane exitu,* which had been in preparation for several years on the basis of propositions extracted from Loisy's writings by two Paris theologians, condemned sixty-five propositions as characteristic of biblical and theological modernism. This decree was followed two months later, on 8 September, by the encyclical *Pascendi.*[16] Being concerned less with the precise representation of the thought of individual writers, than with the reflection it might have in the consciousness of the community, the encyclical started by presenting a highly artificial synthesis[17] which reduced the various condemned positions to agnosticism, that is the denial of the value of rational proofs in religious matters, and to the immanentist philosophy, which locates the origins of religious truths in man's own vital needs. It then went on to reject the modernist conception of biblical criticism and the new trends in apologetics, as also the pretensions of the modernists as reformers, and ended with a series of measures designed to check the spread of the disease, in particular in the seminaries.

The reaction of those who had fallen under the spell of the modernist chorus leaders was less violent than some had anticipated. In the majority of cases loyalty to Catholicism prevailed and it was the very generality of this submission that was later able to give the impression that the modernist crisis was the affair of a few isolated individuals. Certainly, the great mass of the faithful had been virtually untouched by it, but, in France at least, and to a lesser extent in Italy, the portion of the clergy in touch with developments in the religious sciences and a fair number of young Catholic intellectuals

---

16. The text of the various documents will be found in *A.S.S.* XL (1907), 266-9, 392-4, 470-8, 593-650. On the doctrinal significance of *Pascendi* see J. Rivière, *op. cit.,* 364-7. The drafters of the encyclical have now been identified as Fr J. Lemius, O.M.I. for the dogmatic part and Cardinal Vivès y Tuto for the practical part (cf. *Bulletin de littérature ecclésiastique,* XLVII (1946), 143-61 and 242-3).

17. The artificial character was frequently condemned and many agreed with Paul Sabatier that the encyclical presented 'not a portrait but a caricature of modernism'. A. L. Lilley, an Anglican who was a close and sympathetic observer of the modernist movement in the Roman Church, recognised nevertheless that 'since they had a common inspiration and a common purpose, it was neither unnatural nor unfair that the authority which condemned them should unite them in a common designation and in a common censure' (*Encyclopedia of Religion and Ethics,* VIII, 763).

had been undoubtedly affected by the movement. There were nevertheless a number of breaks with the Church — Tyrrell, Loisy, excommunicated in March 1908, Minocchi, excommunicated a little later — and there was also some show of resistance, in particular Buonaiuti's anonymously published *Il programma dei modernisti,* which was at once translated into French, German and English, and his much more radical *Lettere di un prete modernista.*

These reactions, objectively considered very modest, gave fresh impetus to the anti-modernist reaction, whose implacable character may today appear astonishing. It is not to be explained solely by the methods of church government or by the taste of the contemporary press for virulent polemic. Also to be taken into account is the feeling that the Church was being shaken to the core and the fact that sixty years before Vatican II very few of those in authority (rare exceptions apart) had the perspicacity to foresee that in the end this re-opening of fundamental questions, for which a collective change in mentality was responsible, might not necessarily result in the total reduction of the essence of the Christian faith. The Congregation of the Index intensified its activities, as did the Biblical Commission, always in a still more reactionary sense, and the Vigilance committees prescribed by the encyclical started work in certain dioceses, not always evaluating in a sufficiently critical spirit the denunciations that came their way. Next, although modernism was already in full retreat, Pius X, who was disturbed by the continuance of certain clandestine activities, the importance of which was grossly exaggerated, and who remained convinced that the Church was in 'a state of siege', decided on a supplementary measure. On 1 September 1910, in the hope of flushing out the crypto-modernists, he imposed on all members of the clergy a special profession of faith, additional to that of Pius IV, in the form of a solemn ratification of his previous condemnations. Throughout the Catholic Church as a whole only forty priests at most refused to take this anti-modernist oath, with the exception of Germany, where the measure stirred up a great agitation in the cause of scientific freedom, and where in the end the university professors were dispensed from it, at the request of the episcopate.

Yet it would be quite wrong to conclude from this that Germany had been particularly affected by the modernist crisis. In reality, the resistance in Germany represented a resurgence in the universities of the liberal, anti-ultramontane trend that had manifested itself on several occasions during the nineteenth century. Even the more general movement known as *Reformkatholizismus,* to which allusion has already been made, whose movers, apart from Schell, were the historians F. X. Kraus and S. Merkle and the patrologist A. Ehrhard, had at most a superficial connection with contemporary reforming movements in France and Italy, its attention being focused on problems specific to the German Catholic tradition, in particular its situation following the *Kulturkampf.*[18] *A fortiori,* there was never any real question in Germany, save in the case of one or two little-known theologians, of an attempt to modernise the concept of revelation and faith or to update the essential structures of the Church; and although one of the 'reform' journals, *Das Zwanzigste Jahrhundert,* began in 1909 to describe itself in a sub-title as 'the organ of the German modernists', it was soon brought to heel by its young lay editor, Philipp Funk, who was openly to disclaim any link between the review and French modernism, and for good measure with the 'Los-von-Rom' movement in Austria, declaring that the aim must be to keep to 'an argument *inside* the Church'.

The official repression of modernism by the Church authorities was accompanied by a campaign of denunciation which grew in volume as it proceeded and poisoned the whole atmosphere during the last years of Pius X's pontificate. It may seem strange that this campaign developed most strongly at the time when modernism was in full retreat, but one of orthodoxy's most doughty champions, A. Cavallanti, offered the following justification: 'Just as Arianism, Pelagianism and Jansenism, having been condemned by the Church, disappeared from view but left behind them a train of more subtle and less obvious error, known as semi-Arianism, semi-Pelagianism, semi-Jansenism, so it is today with modernism: having slunk from the stage, unmasked and mortally wounded, it leaves behind a host of other errors which spread like germs and destroy, or threaten to destroy, score upon score of good Catholics.'[19] And in 1913, in a rejoinder to people who thought the definition of modernism should be restricted to its most radical forms, Mgr Benigni remarked: 'As if fever is only fever when it reaches a hundred and four!'[20]

Known to history as the 'integrists', these *zelanti* were proud to style themselves 'integral Catholics' in comparison with the tendency of liberal and modernising Catholics (the two were usually bracketed together) to reduce Catholicism to the minimum: 'We are integral Roman Catholics' was the boast of one of their journals. 'That is, we set above all and everyone not only the Church's traditional teaching in the order of absolute truths but also the pope's directions in the order of practical contingencies. For the Church and the pope are one.'[21] The integrists have often and justly been blamed for the use they made of delation and of clandestine procedures, but it is only fair to add that they were just as prepared to fight in the open, through the publication of books, pamphlets, and above all of a range of journals, in-

18. See chapter 5, 94-5.
19. Lecture delivered 16 November 1908, summarised in *La Critique du libéralisme,* I (1908-9), 421-3.
20. Quoted by É. Poulat in *Intégrisme et Catholicisme intégral* (Tournai-Paris 1969), 340.
21. *La Vigie,* 5 December 1912. Nevertheless, as É. Poulat points out (*Intégrisme,* 522), 'the most ardent in their obedience to Pius X had often shown less enthusiasm for Leo XIII'.

cidentally of rather limited circulation, which they more or less directly controlled.

To what extent was all this activity co-ordinated from one centre, and what was the exact role of the Holy See? Given that the integrists worked partly in secret, answers to these questions were for a long time hard to come by, especially since the Roman archives only became accessible after a considerable period had elapsed. A corner of the veil was lifted as early as 1921, but in circumstances unlikely to give full satisfaction to the scrupulous historian. Further glimpses were revealed in 1950 on the occasion of the process for the beatification of Pius X. A major breakthrough was effected with exemplary professionalism by the historian É. Poulat, who succeeded in dismantling the apparatus of the 'secret international anti-modernist network' set up by a prelate attached to the secretariat of State, Mgr Benigni,[22] the Sodalitium Pianum (the Sodality of St Pius V, often referred to by the initials S.P. or under the code name 'Sapinière'). The tendency after the disclosures of 1921 was to present Mgr Benigni as the animator of the whole integrist movement, acting unbeknown to Pius X who was supposedly almost totally unaware of his often doubtful procedures; and by the same token the Sapinière was made out to be a pressure group commanding substantial hidden power within the Church. The truth, so far as we can now tell, appears to be that it was at once more modest and more official than was once thought. Not only did membership of the S.P. never exceed fifty, but the documents published by Poulat shed a very new light on the disagreements, often quite profound, that divided the people summarily classed together as 'integrists'. Benigni, who wanted to avoid all political involvement so as to keep to the purely religious ground, held aloof from the Action française. He was on unmistakably bad terms with Merry del Val, the Secretary of State, who prudently attempted to restrain Benigni's impetuosity, while the latter accused Merry del Val of excessive diplomatic caution;[23] and relations between Benigni and the Society of Jesus were becoming more and more strained, even though a fair number of Jesuits continued down to the end of the pontificate the intransigent defenders of ultra-traditionalist positions. But if one result of Poulat's investigation was to demythologise the famous integrist conspiracy – matters were much less simple than for so

---

22. On Umberto Benigni (1862-1934) see É. Poulat, Intégrisme, 61-70 and *Catholicisme, démocratie et socialisme: Mgr Benigni,* Paris-Tournai 1977; also *Disquisitio circa quasdam objectiones modum agendi Pii X respicientes in modernismi debellatione* (Vatican City 1950), 197-204; G. Spadolini, ed., *Il cardinale Gasparri e la Questione Romana* (Florence 1973), 109-12.

23. É. Poulat, on the basis of documents that have come to light, is categorical: 'We must make up our minds to abandon the legend of Benigni, man of Merry del Val, and of the Secretary of State pressing intransigence on a good and pious pope who had left him a free hand' (*Intégrisme,* 77).

long imagined – and in particular to 'reduce the S.P. to its true dimensions' – the spread of the integrist ideology far exceeded the circle of S.P. sympathisers – it also showed it could no longer be asserted that Mgr Benigni's machinations took shape quite unbeknown to the pope. We know for a fact that Pius X subsidised the Sapinière and that he not only knew of but encouraged the activities of its founder, from whom, through Mgr Bressan, he received daily reports. He thus personally condoned the existence of a kind of ecclesiastical secret police which today we find hard to accept – Meriol Trevor has gone so far as to describe these years as the 'Vatican's Stalinist era' – but which he considered justified in what he regarded as the Church's desperate plight. We can at best suppose that he did not know everything, and that, had he known more, he would perhaps have found reason to object to certain of the procedures.

The peak period of the integrist reaction was the years 1912–13: 1912 was the year when Fr Lagrange found himself obliged to leave Jerusalem and in which the *Revue biblique* was on the point of ceasing publication; 1913 was the year that opened with the placing of the entire fifth series (1905–13) of the *Annales de philosophie chrétienne* on the Index, a blow made all the harsher by an order some weeks later forbidding the editor, Fr Laberthonnière, to publish work of any description and giving him no opportunity to defend himself. But at this juncture the integral Catholics started to divert their main efforts away from the field of the ecclesiastical sciences to concentrate on what they described as 'modernisn in action': for they detected in the activities of Christian democrats of every hue – making little distinction between a Murri, the French *abbés démocrates,* the Sillon group or the trade-union organisation centred on München-Gladbach – a resurgence in a new guise of the liberal Catholicism criticised by Pius IX in the *Syllabus.* It is typical, for example, that this kind of subject figured almost exclusively in Benigni's correspondence. Since many prominent integrists – Benigni in Italy, Maignen in France, Descurtins in Switzerland, to name only a few – had been warmly in favour of the encyclical *Rerum novarum,* their attitude may at first sight seem surprising. But they were in fact remaining true to the original programme of social Catholicism as conceived in the early years of Leo XIII's pontificate, which made an emphatic contrast between the Christian social order derived from the sovereignty of Christ and the 'social atheism' of the bourgeois society engendered by the revolution of 1789, and they accused the new generation of Christian democrats of a growing tendency, in the name of their social concerns and their recognition of the autonomy of secular life, to emancipate themselves from clerical tutelage. It was from this standpoint that the Italian integrists denounced with such vehemence those Catholic newspapers, known collectively as the *Stampa di penetrazione,* which tried to break away from a narrowly confessional outlook in the hope of influencing the governing class, most of whom subscribed to the liberal conception of society. It was his defence of one of these newspapers that caused the unhappy disagreement which in 1911 set the saintly Cardinal Ferrari in opposition to Pius X. [24]

Several of the incidents to which the integrists' attack on 'modernism in practice' gave rise have been referred to in earlier chapters [25] and it was seen for example that at the beginning of 1914 Christian trade unionism stood within a hairsbreadth of condemnation, having been denounced by the *Civiltà cattolica* as 'implying too much in clean contradiction to the true spirit of the Gospel', a condemnation which however was averted, thanks to powerful representations made to the pope.

By this time, moreover, the very excesses of the witch hunt were nearly everywhere starting to provoke a resistance which did not wait, as is often claimed, for the coming of Benedict XV to declare itself more or less openly. [26] This resistance gradually took shape round certain cardinals and bishops, disquieted for some years past by the way things were going, and round certain members of the Society of Jesus who were becoming aware that Pius X's successor could scarcely avoid instituting a change of policy and that it was important to prepare the way. Several of the best-known Jesuit periodicals were bold enough to come out in open protest as early as 1913, [27] and initiates were left in no doubt that Jesuits who took this line had behind them the support of the general of their order and of his two principal assistants. Pius X, whose bitter complaints over his isolation in the struggle to preserve orthodoxy from dilution become more comprehensible in this context, did not conceal his displeasure. Indeed, he seems to have been on the point of intervening to replace Fr Wernz as head of the Society by Fr Matiussi, who was closely identified with integrist circles, when the almost simultaneous deaths of the 'white pope' and the 'black pope' brought this last episode of the anti-modernist repression to a close.

24. On this serious incident, often quoted as an extreme example of anti-modernist repression, see the *Disquisitio circa quasdam obiectiones* . . . and for completeness and nuances M. Torresin's article, which uses the Milan diocesan archives, in *Memorie storiche della diocesi di Milano*, X (1963), 37-304.
25. See particularly chapters 4 and 8.
26. The letters of Mgr Benigni published by É. Poulat provide ample evidence of increasing discomfort among integrists at the way things were going and of more frequently voiced discouragement in face of the developing literary counter-offensive.
27. For example in *Stimmen der Zeit*, LXXXV (1913), 358-62 and LXXXVIII (1914) 249-58 and in *Études*, CXXXVIII (1914), 5-25. See J. Lebreton, *Le P. L. de Grandmaison* (Paris 1932), 187-93.

PART TWO

CATHOLICISM IN THE ANGLO-SAXON WORLD

11

GREAT BRITAIN:
THE REBIRTH OF A CHURCH

IN THE latter half of the nineteenth century, the Roman Catholic community of Great Britain, although, omitting Ireland, it represented probably no more than 5% of the country's population, assumed in the eyes of the Catholic world an importance far beyond its numerical strength. For this there seems to be a twofold explanation. One can point on the one hand to the hopes of England's impending return to the Roman communion engendered by the Oxford Movement (hopes which, although illusory, were periodically reborn), and on the other to the more material consideration of England's commanding position in the world at this heyday of the Victorian era. England was a nation with a powerful export industry, she had a talent for manipulating the European balance of power to her own advantage, and better still, from the missionary point of view, she was the possessor of an expanding colonial empire.

The eighteen forties had witnessed a transformation, affecting both numbers and quality, in the Catholic community of the British Isles, which for a long time past had consisted of the Church in Ireland, and the scattered and few though slowly increasing Catholics in England, Wales and Scotland. As a result of the wave of conversions brought about by the Oxford Movement, a retiring, inward-turning Church, whose vision was fixed and narrow and whose role in national life was merely marginal, found itself augmented, within just a few years, by several hundred talented intellectuals, many of whom were in close contact with the country's governing classes. At much the same time and as a result of the great famine of 1845–8, the flow of Irish immigrants attracted to England and Scotland by the Industrial Revolution had also suddenly increased in volume, thereby accelerating a development which had been proceeding piecemeal since the early years of the century. English Catholicism, which for the past three hundred years had revolved round a few urban centres and widely scattered country houses whose maintenance of a domestic chaplain might owe more to traditional loyalties than to religious conviction, would increasingly stand out as a Church composed largely of the working class. The members of this proletarian Church lived in towns and ports, they succumbed all too easily to drink, and their Celtic exuberance and devotional extravagance had little in common with the catacomb habits ingrained in most of their English co-religionists of the old stock.

To cope with this flood of the faithful as they accumulated in their hundreds of thousands, settling predominantly in Lancashire, but also around London and in the Midlands, the Catholic authorities had to erect new churches and find more priests. They addressed their chief appeal for the latter to religious congregations abroad, a policy which soon produced problems of a psychological order and of canon law.

These pressures brought to the fore the question of the Church's governments and its need of reorganisation. Unlike Ireland, where the episcopal hierarchy had been preserved through the long years of persecution, England had since the Reformation been reduced to the missionary regime. For a country where Catholicism was shaking off the sloth of centuries this system had its evident disadvantages. Some 'Cisalpine' Catholics, and in Cardinal Acton they had a spokesman at the Roman curia, were opposed to the restoration of the hierarchy, but the persistence of the Vicars Apostolic finally overcame the pope's last lingering doubts and on 29 September 1850 Pius IX published the Brief which replaced the eight vicariates apostolic by an archbishopric based on Westminster, with twelve suffragan sees. Wiseman, who had been named as the new archbishop, was created a cardinal the following day. In an exultant pastoral letter dated 7 October he proclaimed his joy: 'Catholic England has been restored to its orbit in the ecclesiastical firmament from which its light had long vanished.' Loyalty to the Reformation having become in England a more or less essential part of the national character, the triumphalist tone of Wiseman's letter triggered off inflammatory denunciations of what was termed 'papal aggression' – a reaction which English Catholics who had opposed the restoration saw as vindication of their fears. Wiseman refused to be disconcerted and in a matter of days had composed, with help from notes supplied by his episcopal colleague in Birmingham, the judicious Ullathorne, an *Appeal to the English People,* which brought public opinion right round.

The next step, and it was beset with difficulties, was to make the Roman decision a reality.

For a start, the new bishops had to be chosen from a clergy barely 800 strong and comprising priests of varying antecedents, who often differed among themselves over what methods should be employed. With due recognition of Wiseman who, for all his undeniable faults, most notably an excessive leaning towards optimism, was a man of exceptional gifts and acutely sensitive to the needs of his time, we can surely agree with Philip Hughes' characterisation of the first generation of bishops: 'None of them a great man and few to reach more than a comfortable professional competence.'[1]

Then there was the business of bringing the various departments of church life under the regime prescribed for them by canon law. The guiding principles were laid down by the First Council of the ecclesiastical province of Westminster, meeting at Oscott in July 1852, which had the benefit of Wiseman's vision and enthusiasm combined with the solid legal and administrative talents of Mgr Grant, the new bishop of Southwark. But as Morgan Sweeney's unvarnished account makes plain,[2] although further provincial councils were held in 1853, 1859 and 1873, it took several decades to complete the transition from the semi-anarchy of the missionary period to the regular form of government under the Church's common law. To take but one example, despite the resentment felt by many priests, there was a long delay over the introduction of the canon law statute regarding parishes, which only came into effect with the code of 1918. In the early days all effort had to be concentrated on providing the everyday necessities. During the first decade, thanks to the generosity of country squires and a few wealthy converts, it was possible to build several hundred churches and chapels and a number, woefully inadequate, of parochial schools. But all the while the influx of Irish into the industrial centres of England and Scotland was steadily mounting. In the Liverpool region alone the number between 1850 and 1853 rose by 300,000. The situation in the most hard-pressed areas was eased somewhat by the arrival of several hundred priests from Ireland, but this these newcomers created fresh problems, since the Catholic aristocracy, still a powerful influence in Catholic society, accused them of interfering in politics in a way damaging to conservative interests.

The transition from the early nineteenth-century regime of domestic chaplains operating in isolation to a coherent system increasingly controlled by the bishops was paralleled by a period of rapid development in the communities of religious. Between 1850 and 1863 the number of houses for men rose from 11 to 55 and for women from 53 to 108; membership, which in 1850 had still been at skeleton strength and often predominantly foreign in composition, showed a corresponding growth, with converts in particular coming to swell the numbers. Conspicuous in this respect were the Redemptorists who owed much of their success to the dynamism of men such as Father Richard Coffin and Father Thomas Bridgett, both of them converts,

1. In G. A. Beck (ed.), *The English Catholics 1850-1950* (London 1950), 78; cf. 70-7
2. 'Diocesan organisation and administration', *ibid.*, 116-50.

and above all the Jesuits, who were opening colleges in the north and whose house in Farm Street became one of the gathering-places for the élite of London's Catholic society.

The increasing part played by converts in English Catholic life was not without its problems. Wiseman appreciated their superior cultural background and dauntless enthusiasm, which stood out in such contrast to the timidity of the 'old Catholics' and he did what he could to encourage their active participation in the work of their new Church. He demonstrated his confidence by appointing W. G. Ward as professor of dogmatics in his seminary, by using Manning as one of his chief assistants in the administration of his diocese, and by urging Newman to take charge of the Catholic university of Dublin, which Wiseman in his customary and self-deluding optimism envisaged becoming a kind of Oxford for English-speaking Catholics.[3] But this systematic patronage of converts – some of it inept, as in the case of Newman, who once was taken up, only to be abandoned in blind alleys where he wasted his years and his strength – gave offence to Catholics of the old stock, from whom most of the bishops were drawn. Hereditary Catholics, steeped in tradition and profoundly distrustful of new ideas or new practices, found fault with many of their new co-religionists as being either too liberal or too Romanising.

The liberal group, it must be said, was only small, but it was highly influential. Its focus was a periodical called the *Rambler,* founded in 1848 by a small band of converts who were keen that the problems raised by the new criticism should be tackled in a way that satisfied scholarly criteria – a *sine qua non,* in their view, if Catholicism was to command the respect of the educated public. But the scope of the *Rambler* progressively widened, and under the direction of Richard Simpson (1820-76), a former Church of England clergyman of brilliant gifts and caustic temper,[4] it set out to bring Catholic attitudes into line with society's current aspirations. Contributors took a stand, for example, on burning issues such as the inferiority of the education given in Catholic colleges. They criticised, with scant respect, the narrow-mindedness of England's 'old Catholics'. They claimed an equal right with the bishops to discuss questions where dogma was not in issue. They pounced on all the Roman conceptions they found outdated. Most of these champions of liberalism were in fact quite reasonable men who in practice would modify idealistic propositions by the application of common sense, but the criticism they attracted from doctrinaires like Ward – in Ullathorne's description, *'vir super omnia dogmaticus'* – drove them to

3. On the vicissitudes of this university see below, 228-9.
4. This striking representative of English liberal Catholicism has been unduly neglected, but now see D. McElrath, *Richard Simpson. A Study in XIXth century English liberal Catholicism,* Louvain 1972.

make taunting rejoinders whose target was in some cases the bishops, already very jealous of their authority. Exasperated by this *enfant terrible* of a journal and its tirades, the bishops called on Newman to act as moderator, and in 1859 he became its editor. But tempers on both sides were running high and after a few months he felt obliged to resign.

Unfortunately, Newman's name remained linked in many minds with that of the *Rambler,* all the more since, although he disliked the tone adopted by the prime movers, he was known to share some of their preoccupations. Ward, for example, who was always quick and sometimes inopportune in declaring his devotion to the Church, began to denounce his former teacher as a liberal of the worst, dissembling, type; while Manning, who found Newman's Ultramontanism too lukewarm, kept up a stream of damaging reports about him to Rome where suspicions became still deeper when it appeared, through carelessness on Wiseman's part, that Newman was refusing the Holy Office the explanation it expected.[5] Newman was an intellectual of the purest breed. To him, the intransigent views preached by certain Catholics as proof of loyalty to the Church on the contrary did the Church great harm. He was bound to excite suspicion in men of inflexible mind who clung for support to a narrow Scholasticism and who looked to authority to impose a constant limit on the areas of enquiry open to the human mind. As a result, the fruitful influence Newman might have exercised on English Catholicism was compromised for a long time to come, even if, as happened within a few years, his reputation with the church authorities gradually improved, particularly after the remarkable success of his *Apologia pro vita sua,* published in 1864. This literary and psychological masterpiece not only demonstrated his flawless orthodoxy but also, by reason of its patent sincerity, helped to dissipate many Anglican prejudices regarding the Roman Church.

Direction of the *Rambler* had meanwhile passed to John Acton (1834-1902), for the next twenty years or so the most perfect embodiment of English liberal Catholicism. He was born a Catholic, but his cosmopolitan origins and upbringing had given him a highly independent cast of mind. Journeys to the United States and Russia, and the influence of his stepfather, Lord Granville, served to reinforce his passion for political liberty, just as the years he spent under Döllinger, whose favourite pupil he was, filled him with admiration for the work of German Catholic scholars in Munich and Tübingen whose aim was to adapt the Church's teaching to the requirements of modern criticism. Working closely with Simpson, Acton brought to the *Rambler* a prodigious store of learning, a shrewd intelligence and a highly

5. On this very unfortunate misunderstanding see C. Butler, *Life and Times of Bishop Ullathorne*, I, 315-21, and L. Cognet. *Newman ou la Recherche de la vérité* (Paris 1967), 137-45.

developed professional conscience. With these assets, the *Rambler* soon achieved a success in England greater than that of any Catholic publication in the past. But it now had as editor a man who was one day to define himself as a man who 'renounced everything in Catholicism which was not compatible with liberty and everything in politics not compatible with Catholicity'. Not surprisingly, the liberal and independent tendencies of the journal became even more pronounced, and this at a time when the traditionalists were less than ever prepared to notice that beneath the immoderation of its language there was work of real worth. In April 1862, following the bishops' public censure of certain articles on the pope's temporal power, the *Rambler* had to cease. In its place Acton was soon bringing out the *Home and Foreign Review,* with almost the same staff and programme, but he had to shut it down after a year, to avoid open conflict with Rome after the papal brief *Tuas libenter,* which was strongly against scientific liberty. The opportunity to provide Catholic England with a journal of high intellectual standing, which appealed to a Protestant as well as a Catholic readership, had been let slip and would not soon recur — for no one could pretend that the gap was filled by Wiseman's old journal, the *Dublin Review,* which Manning and Ward had reorganised early in 1863, to make it a vehicle for the defence of extreme ultramontane views.

If Manning and Ward showed themselves just as antagonistic towards Newman and the *Rambler* progressives as the majority of hereditary Catholics, this still did them no good in the eyes of the latter. For Manning and Ward, along with F. W. Faber, represented the particular type of ultramontanist convert who thought Catholic life should model itself on the practice in countries where Catholicism had not had to dissemble in order to escape persecution, the convert whose ideal was to introduce into England the forms of devotion current in southern climes, not to mention a style of submissiveness to the pope unparalleled even in Rome. The Catholics of the old stock, whose own religious practice was formal and austere, were fearful of any movement that might stir up the Protestants and were opposed to the importation of an 'Italian religion', little suited to the English national temperament. Even the open-minded Ullathorne, who did not share the prejudices of many of his colleagues regarding the new converts and encouraged their integration into the English Catholic community, expressed disquiet at the want of discretion shown by persons 'whose inexperience was as great as their zeal'.

The bias of the old-established clergy against the converts came out into the open in 1865 when a successor had to be found for Wiseman. The Westminster chapter, backed up by several bishops, registered its objection to the late cardinal's policy by proposing as his successor Mgr Errington, Wiseman's former coadjutor, who had never concealed his dislike, on principle, of the converts' enthusiasm for Rome. This show of independence displeased Pius IX who ignored warnings from Cardinal Barnabò against exacerbating an already tense situation and proceeded to appoint as archbishop a convert from Anglicanism, the very man, in fact, whose growing influence over the aging Wiseman had so upset the opponents of Wiseman's clerical policy. The new archbishop was to be Henry Edward Manning (1808-92), whose qualifications as a churchman of pro-Roman sentiments the pope had already had opportunity to test for himself.

Manning came from an Evangelical background, having gone over to the Church of Rome in 1851 as a result of the Gorham Case, in which the Church of England's dependent connection on the State was exposed to the full light of day. His early biographers did him less than justice. Disraeli's portrait, in *Lothair*, is romanticised. Purcell's, in his *Life of Cardinal Manning*, is very one-sided. Lytton Strachey's, in *Eminent Victorians*, is a caricature. There followed half a century of silence, made all the more absolute by the loss, or unavailability of a large number of archives. The truth is that, for all his faults, Manning was a figure of the first importance, who made a sizeable and, all things considered, beneficial contribution to the development of the Catholic Church in England. It must be conceded that he lacked the capacity to sympathise with other people's intellectual difficulties, that he failed to grasp the problem created by the confrontation between modern philosophical and scientific thought and traditional theology, and above all that he could not imagine there might be truth in viewpoints other than his own. To his own convictions he ascribed a value made all the more absolute by his ready belief in the personal suzerainty of the Holy Spirit. It is also fair to remark that this born administrator was something of a despot to his staff, that his wary political sense veered on occasion in the direction of intrigue, and that his zeal for efficiency, since he was persuaded, often correctly, that no one else was as capable of securing the Church's future in England, could take on the air of personal ambition. But even Manning's opponents increasingly had to defer to his exceptional qualities. He had enterprise and energy, his activity ranged over an immensely varied field, his will was of iron, his tenacity unwearying. Here was a great leader and man of action. Here, too, was a selfless ascetic, inspired by a most exalted ideal of the sacerdotal life which he never tired of urging upon his clergy, and a pastor of unflagging zeal, particularly alert to the needs of the most disadvantaged portion of his flock. And if in the intellectual field his vision was often narrow, he should at least be given the credit, as V. A. McClelland has shown, for having grasped so clearly that in the new industrial society of the nineteenth century the Church's major task was not so much to form Christian humanists and gentlemen on the model sketched out in Newman's famous lectures *On the Idea of a University,* as to maintain contact with the middle and working classes. This was why in politics Manning supported the Liberals, fearing that the Tory sympathies of the 'old Catholics' might result in the abandonment of these fields — the fields of the future — to exploitation by non-Christian forces. Hence too his constant efforts to develop Catholic elementary schools, whose strength he succeeded in doubling, [6] and the prominence he gave to science in his projected Catholic university in Kensington, with the intention of equipping the middle class to play its full part in contemporary society; and hence, in part, his great interest in social questions.

Manning's social concern sprang from his acute sensitivity to the miserable condition of the lower classes, of which he had first become aware in the days of his Anglican ministry. The longer he lived, the more convinced he became of the need to support every kind of movement whose aim was to protect the workers against the abuses of the capitalist system, so much so that towards the end of his life he gave unhesitating encouragement to Protestant undertakings such as the Salvation Army and was equally ready, to the astonishment of one party among his clergy, to collaborate with socialist leaders. Paradoxically, the champion of absolutism in the Church possessed the heat and mind of a great social reformer. He was further encouraged to take this line by tactical considerations: 'My belief is that . . . if the Church is to be spread in England, it will be by its large popular sympathies identifying it, not with the governors, but with the governed'. [7]

So conspicuous were his incursions into the social and philanthropic domain that the cardinal (he received his hat in 1875) came to be regarded in official government circles as having a prescriptive right to a seat on any commission appointed to investigate such matters. In this way he had the opportunity to play a leading part in the Royal Commission on Public Education appointed in 1886 and to contribute, in consequence, to the formulation of the Free Education Act of 1891. Equally important, he was given the chance to realise one of his most cherished desires, 'to bring the Catholic Church once more into open relations with the people and public opinion of England'.

But there was one potential ground of contact with the Anglican establishment which Manning, fortified by his innate obduracy and Ward's insistence, was determined should remain barred to Catholics. To the end of his life he adhered, so far as the attendance of Catholics at Oxford and Cambridge was concerned, to the policy of the ghetto. Some people, not renowned for their willingness to take risks lightly, were already prepared to maintain that it was useless, especially after the failure of the Catholic uni-

6. In the spirit of the slogan 'schools before churches' which had been so successful in the United States, he preferred to leave the decision to build the new cathedral of Westminster to his successor.

7. Notes made in 1880, cited E. Purcell, *Life of Manning*, II, 632.

versity in Dublin, to resist a process which was already under way, always provided that adequate steps were taken to safeguard the students' faith. This was what Newman had in mind when he proposed, early in 1864, to settle himself in Oxford. Manning's fear, however, was that through contact with Protestant circles the élite of English Catholicism 'would be like the laity in France, Catholic in name but indifferent, lax, liberalistic'.[8] Thanks in large measure to the help at Rome of his friend Talbot, Manning secured from the Congregation de Propaganda Fide a ruling which prohibited Catholic families from sending their sons to Oxford and Cambridge, save in exceptional cases. He also made every effort, despite the reservations of many of his colleagues and the still greater reservations of the lay community, to set up a Catholic university in the London area. The decision of principle was taken at the Provincial Council of 1873 and a start was made in Kensington in October 1874. But the scheme very soon proved unworkable, not least because of Manning's refusal to call on the help of the Jesuits, with whom he was in dispute over questions of jurisdiction. Shortly after his death, a group of laymen, in which Ward's son Wilfrid was the moving spirit, addressed a petition to the English bishops which argued that the major universities were no more dangerous to faith, and much less dangerous to morals, than the military academies of Woolwich or Sandhurst, and that as preparation for careers in which Catholics could serve their country with distinction there was no institution which could replace them. Herbert Vaughan (1832–1903), who as Manning's delegate had helped him to carry the day on this issue at Rome, had by now succeeded him as archbishop of Westminster. His common sense persuaded him of the force of the petitioners' arguments, which he accepted the more readily since the number of Catholic students at Oxford and Cambridge was in any case rising, swelled by students from Irish families who considered themselves not bound by rulings procured on the initiative of English bishops, and by young Englishmen who had obtained personal dispensations. Vaughan forwarded Wilfrid Ward's petition – which was backed by the influential Duke of Norfolk – to Rome with a recommendation in favour of its acceptance, and in 1895 the ban imposed by Propaganda some thirty years earlier was lifted.

Over the university question it had been proved that despite his innate distrust of innovation Vaughan was capable, when pressed by circumstances, of taking a broad view. It was otherwise over the question of relations between the Church of Rome and the Church of England. Here Vaughan, the scion of an old Catholic family, showed himself as unsympathetic to any movement with an ecumenical connotation as had Manning, the convert. In 1864 a body calling itself the Association for the Promotion of the Union of

8. Notes made in 1887, cited *ibid.*, II, 349.

Christendom, whose aim was to bring Catholics and Anglicans together as a first step towards the corporate reunion of the Anglican Church with Rome, had been condemned at Rome on the grounds that it represented religious liberalism. This was partly Manning's doing,[9] and in his book *England and Catholicism* (1867), he expressed the view that for Rome to embark on negotiations with a non-Roman confession would amount to a denial by the one true Church of its own infallibility. Vaughan shared these principles and was, moreover, convinced that the only road to a Christian union centred on the pope lay through individual conversions; hence his forceful intervention at Rome to frustrate the initiative launched by Lord Halifax and the Abbé Portal.

Charles Lindley Wood, Viscount Halifax (1839-1934), was a prominent Christian who had deliberately thrown away the prospect of a brilliant political career to devote himself to the service of the Church. From 1867 he was President of the English Church Union, founded in 1844 to defend Tractarian (subsequently Anglo-Catholic) principles in the Anglican Church. His ardent and lifelong ambition to further the reconciliation of his Church with the See of Rome was given a definite direction by an encounter at Madeira in 1890 with the French Lazarist, Fernand Portal (1855-1926). Portal was on the lookout for some effective means of setting the ball rolling between the two Churches after their four centuries of separation, and believed that a resumption of the debate on the validity of Anglican orders, conducted on a scholarly level instead of in the past atmosphere of confessional controversy, might serve to bring representatives of the two communions together in a mood conducive to sympathetic understanding.

There was no initial intention of keeping the English Catholics out of the discussion and in 1893 contact was made with Cardinal Vaughan, who while promising to support requests to the Vatican to search the archives, insisted that examination of a specific issue such as that of Anglican orders ought to be preceded by settlement of the fundamental question, that of papal authority. Halifax and Portal, as proponents of the *rapprochement,* were well aware that they were at the start of a long and arduous undertaking whose success demanded a preliminary lightening of the atmosphere and gradual preparation of men's minds. This might be achieved through frequent meetings at which the two sides could begin by educating one another in the inwardness of their respective doctrines. To begin straight off with a frontal assault on the question of Roman primacy was surely to court disaster. Halifax and Portal were both inclined by nature to minimise difficulties. They decided to ignore the cardinal's objections and to proceed, as they had originally intended, to raise the question of the validity of

9. For this affair see E. Purcell, *Life and Letters of A. Phillips de Lisle* (London 1900), I, 346-422, and C. Butler, *Life and Times of Bishop Ullathorne*, I, 334-68.

Anglican orders. Portal made the first move, with an article written under the pseudonym Dalbus which appeared in *Science catholique* at the end of 1893. His aim was not to force an official decision but to create occasions for contact and dialogue on the lines already intimated. In its early stages the affair thus appeared as nothing more than a premature manifestation of the ecumenical spirit, but Portal, and still more Halifax, made the mistake of wanting to bring the authorities of the two Churches too rapidly into the picture. This timing was all the more inopportune in that Halifax was much less representative of the Anglican Church as a whole than people on the Continent imagined. He spoke neither for its large Evangelical nor Low Church wing, which was deeply hostile to the Anglo-Catholic movement and to a large extent still violently anti-papist, nor for the Broad Church or liberal stream, which pressed free enquiry to the point of advocating fundamental revision of the Creed.

During 1894 Halifax made contact with the Anglican authorities. Benson, the archbishop of Canterbury, adopted the very guarded attitude he would maintain throughout the negotiations, but the archbishop of York was comparatively sympathetic. Portal meanwhile succeeded in arousing the interest of the pope, having presented him with a very optimistic picture of developments within the Anglican Church set in train by the Oxford Movement. The new vistas apparently opening up in England likewise impressed Rampolla, the cardinal Secretary of State, and with his encouragement Leo XIII even contemplated addressing a personal letter to the archbishop of Canterbury – in the context of the time a truly revolutionary idea. But as soon as Cardinal Vaughan discovered what was afoot he at once intervened, and by stressing the appreciable difference between the High Church movement and the Church of England as it really was, secured a change of plan. The pope indeed sent a letter, but it was a public one (14 April 1895) addressed to the people of England and inviting them to pray for the union. The text of this much more traditional document was drafted by Vaughan himself with help from Dom Gasquet, an English Benedictine, and his friend Edmund Bishop.[10] The epistle *Ad Anglos* met with a guarded reception in Anglican circles, yet even this was considered encouraging and Halifax, who had been received in audience by the pope in March, launched in England a regular information campaign. Portal was meanwhile busy in France, inaugurating a league of prayer to supplicate for 'the return of the Isle of Saints to her mother' and founding, in December 1895, the *Revue anglo-romaine.* This was a weekly journal aimed at historians and theologians, packed with information presented in non-controversial terms

10. This point has been definitely established by K. Connelly, using the archives at Downside Abbey: see his paper, 'An historical study of the Apostolic Letter of Pope Leo XIII *ad Anglos'* in *Bijdragen*, Nijmegen-Bruges XXXIII (1972), 65-88.

and also carrying learned articles from scholars like Duchesne and Gasparri on the Catholic side and Lacey and Puller on the Protestant. For their part, the majority of English Catholics viewed all this activity at first with impatience and then with open antipathy. Over and above the matter of principle involved, there were fears that it might check the flow of individual conversions,[11] and also no doubt some displeasure at the sight of Frenchmen, some of whom it must be admitted had no clear grasp of the real complexity of the situation, meddling in what was primarily an English concern.

Anxious to sabotage the conversations between Catholic and Anglican experts envisaged by Halifax and Portal – conversations in which French experts would presumably have played a leading part – Vaughan prevailed on Leo XIII to revoke the question to Rome. A commission of enquiry was set up under the ultra-conservative Cardinal Mazzella with instructions to examine the question of Anglican orders under three aspects, historical, theological and legal. On the advice of Cardinal Rampolla the commission was given a balanced composition, with four members in favour of the validity or at least the doubtful validity of Anglican orders and four members against;[12] but at Vaughan's insistence all eight were Catholics, and the most Portal could achieve was permission for one of the members, Mgr Gasparri, to bypass the ban of secrecy and confer in private with two Anglican experts who had come to Rome with the official approval of their superiors but no official mandate. The commission held twelve sessions between 24 March and 7 May 1886 and devoted particular attention to a lengthy submission drawn up by Vaughan's three delegates. This document, whose errors and omissions have been exposed by J. J. Hughes, did not convert the members who favoured validity. The secretary of the commission reported only four votes in favour of nullity, the remaining four being divided equally between validity and doubtful validity.[13] But the status of the commission of experts – which in fact contained no real experts – was merely consultative, and the final decision rested with the Holy Office. Dom Gasquet and Canon Moyes, whose attitude throughout the affair had been polemical rather than scholarly, were preparing the ground for a condemnation, ably abetted by a young prelate of half-English, half-Spanish extraction, R. Merry del Val. Like them, and like Vaughan, Merry del Val was afraid that recognition of Anglican orders as even doubtfully valid (with the implication that Rome would demand at most conditional re-ordination) might serve to strengthen the old spirit of Anglican independence towards

11. These fears were not shared by people such as W. F. Barry, and in the hierarchy the bishop of Clifton, W. R. Brownlow, who was a convert, but they were rare.
12. The English members Vaughan proposed to the pope were Dom Gasquet, Canon Moyes and Fleming, a Franciscan, all three resolute opponents of validity. It was at Leo XIII's express request that they were joined by a fourth Englishman, of more moderate views.
13. Quoted by J. J. Hughes, *Absolutely Null and Utterly Void* (London 1968), 162.

Roman authority. He had by now supplanted Rampolla as the pope's confidential adviser on English affairs and induced him to share one of the fears of English Catholics: namely, that by requiring only conditional re-ordination, the Roman Church would implicitly acknowledge that the centuries-old insistence on the unconditional re-ordination of converted Anglican priests could have been an error. And so it came about that although the pope still showed signs of benevolence towards the Anglicans, a benevolence still strengthened by the tone of a letter from the archbishop of York to Portal written as late as March, he came down on the side of the cardinals of the Holy Office, who declared their decision on July. It was reached after two hours of deliberation at which the pope was present (and from which Rampolla, significantly enough, was absent), and was unanimous. The cardinals held that the question of the validity of Anglican orders had been long since settled in the negative sense and saw no reason to alter the earlier decision. Portal was requested to cease forthwith his meddling in English affairs. A few weeks later came the bull *Apostolicae curae* (13 September 1896), drafted by Merry del Val after consultation with Gasquet. It declared Anglican orders to be 'absolutely null and utterly void' on grounds both historical and theological (defect of form and intention on the part of the consecrators of Parker, from whom the whole succession of English bishops since the sixteenth century depends). The snub was naturally deeply resented in the Church of England, and a flood of justificatory literature from English Catholics only made matters worse. The cause of *rapprochement* between Rome and Canterbury emerged severely shaken from this unhappy initiative, for whose failure the aloofness of Benson and still more the aggressive reaction of Vaughan were largely to blame. Yet it is worth remarking, as a sign of the times, that Rome's decision provoked no popular anti-Catholic outbursts of the kind that would undoubtedly have occurred had the affair taken place some decades earlier.

There is no denying that towards the end of Victoria's reign the situation of the Catholic Church in England was profoundly different, in both the psychological and the material sense, from what it had been at the time the hierarchy was restored some half a century earlier, even if it must be granted that many innocent hopes awakened by that 'second spring' (as Newman termed it in 1852) remained unrealised.

From now on the number of faithful could be reckoned as well over a million, even without counting the swelling ranks of Irish of the second and still more of the third generation who continued to describe themselves as Catholics but had ceased to practise their religion. [14] The increase was

14. On this see J. A. Jackson, *The Irish in Britain* (London 1963), chapter VII, esp. 145 ff. In 1903 London had 93,000 practising Catholics, at a time when its population included at least 200,000 Irish. People were well aware of the phenomenon, the term 'leakage' first making its

admittedly less spectacular than in the middle years of the century, but it nevertheless continued, and after *Apostolicae curae* the flow of conversions, which had fallen off for a few years, resumed at a steady rate (in 1898 a special college, the Beda, was even founded in Rome for converts and other 'late vocations' seeking to enter the priesthood).

From now on, too, Roman Catholicism in England became largely an urban phenomenon, though the few but widely spread rural representatives continued to increase steadily in numbers, and the old enclaves in the north and elsewhere held on to their traditions. Eight out of ten Catholic families were of Irish descent. They lived for the most part around London, Liverpool and Birmingham, where they worked mainly as labourers, artisans and small shopkeepers. Their living conditions in the inner suburbs of large industrial towns were crowded and relatively poor. They looked to their priests, whose devotion made up for their authoritarian bearing, for advice or indeed direct orders, even on secular matters. They mixed very little with the rest of the population who for reasons connected with nationality, class, and religion were in truth often hostile and this made the process of assimilation much slower than in the United States. In many places it was only during the Second World War that Catholics acquired the habit of combining for social and other purposes with their non-Catholic neighbours. Catholic life was and would long remain concentrated on the parochial church, every stone of which had been paid for by savings squeezed from meagre wages. At the other end of the social scale we meet the Catholic gentry whose forefathers had been recusants. As a group they were augmented by an influx of converts who moved in London's aristocratic and social circles. Taken as a whole, these wealthy Catholics were extremely generous to the young Church and provided it with much of the financial help needed to establish its infrastructure. Lastly, between these two groups – proletarian masses and little cluster of rich landed proprietors, neither fully integrated into the national life – there appeared during the last thirty years of the century a third category, hitherto virtually unrepresented: Catholics who served the liberal professions or who belonged to the literary or scientific world. Some were sons of Irishmen risen in the social scale, others were converts attracted by the personal magnetism of Manning, the successors of the clergymen and scholars Newman had led over to Rome at the time of the Oxford Movement. It is almost exclusively among the ranks of these professional men that one finds the smattering of Catholics who were starting to play a role of local or even national consequence.

Providing priests for this ever-growing number of Catholics continued to pose problems, but between 1850 and 1900 clerical manpower was tripled

appearance in Catholic circles in the late nineteenth century.

and the increase did not halt there, since between 1900 and 1911 the number of priests for Great Britain excluding Ireland rose from 2900 to 4000. Even if Irish priests sometimes proved less easy to recruit for England than for the United States, this source of supply remained of capital importance, although drawing on it created problems for the rest of the Catholic population. Thanks to Manning's influence, the last quarter of the nineteenth century saw a fundamental change in the arrangements for the education of intending priests, with seminaries of the Tridentine type gradually replacing the system, inherited from the old regime, under which future clerics and young laymen had been educated side by side.

The growth in the diocesan clergy made it no less necessary to rely heavily on the services of religious. They were indispensable even for the ordinary parochial ministry where, according to a parliamentary report of 1871, religious were serving 121 parishes, comprising about one-third of the Catholic population. In the schools the need for them was greater still, the chief burden at the secondary level being carried by the Jesuits. But reference should also be made to the Benedictine schools of Downside and Ampleforth, schools which soon vied in standard with the ancient public schools, to Clapham College, opened by the Salesians in 1855, to Newman's novel establishment founded in 1859 at Edgbaston, and on the distaff side to the work of the Ladies of the Sacred Heart and the Sisters of the Holy Child, founded by a convert, Cornelia Connelly, in 1846. The contribution of religious to English Catholic life was both considerable and beneficial and the parishes they had in their charge were often among the best conducted. But the concern of many religious, the Jesuits in particular, to preserve the maximum degree of autonomy, clashed increasingly with the desire of the bishops to control their activities. The Fourth Provincial Council of Westminster (1873) having failed to resolve this dispute, it was referred to Rome where the persistence of Manning and Vaughan — the future cardinal, then bishop of Salford — bore fruit in May 1881 in the bull *Romanos pontifices* which decided all the essential points in favour of the bishops.[15] The mere fact that such a conflict was possible is surely a telling indication of the structural development and crystallisation achieved by the Catholic Church in England within a single generation. Another noteworthy sign was the missionary congregation established by Vaughan at Mill Hill to serve the apostolate overseas; not so many decades had passed since Catholic England had been obliged to summon missionaries to herself from the Continent. As a mark of official recognition of this progress, Pius X decided in

15. This bull is of particular importance because its provisions were afterwards made to apply throughout the Anglo-Saxon world. On the dispute see E. Purcell, *Life of Cardinal Manning*, II, 505-13, and J. G. Snead-Cox, *Life of Cardinal Vaughan*, I, chapter XII, and above all chapter XIV.

1908 to remove the English dioceses from their still continuing dependence on the Congregation de Propaganda Fide and to bring them within the ordinary regime of the Church.

There was also a process of psychological transformation at work. The appointment in 1880 of Lord Ripon, a convert, as Viceroy of India, the inclusion of Lord Llandaff in Salisbury's cabinet of 1886, the elevation of a Catholic, Sir William Shee, to the judicial bench, the appointment of Acton as Regius Professor at Cambridge in 1895, Urquhart's election to a fellowship at Balliol in 1896 – all were indications that the ostracism of which Catholics had so long been the victims was loosening its hold. A variety of factors contributed to this result: the general development of British society, following the breach of the Anglican monopoly by the rising tide of Nonconformity, the growing secularity of outlook and the progress of free thought. [16] There were also positive elements: one was undoubtedly the place Manning had won for himself in public life; another was the light, enhanced by his elevation to the candinalate, cast by Newman – the Newman who had helped to dispel so many prejudices, whether through his *Apologia* or through his remarkable answer to Gladstone when he doubted, after the definition of the papal infallibility, whether it was possible to be at once a good Englishman and a good Catholic, blindly submissive to the pope. [17] True, contempt for the Catholic minority, which the archbishop of Canterbury was wont to refer to as 'the Italian mission', was by no means a thing of the past. It was fed by the general antipathy towards the Irish, which intensified as the nationalist agitation mounted, by the spread, particularly marked during the eighteen-nineties, of devotions like those to the Sacred Heart, which were regarded as superstitious, and by the backwardness of Catholics in regard to biblical criticism. But though the Queen might be suspicious of the Romanising tendencies of the High Church party, relations between London and the Vatican started to improve. Leo XIII's dream – which Manning, for one, considered distinctly premature – that he might live to see the restoration of diplomatic relations, could not be realised; but the British government showed its pleasure in welcoming a papal representative to the Queen's jubilee celebrations of 1887, and more than once took the initiative in consulting the Holy See over episcopal appointments for Malta and Ireland. Edward VII showed himself still more favourably disposed. In 1903 he actually visited the pope, and in 1910 he removed a clause offensive to Catholics from the oath taken by the sovereign at the time of his accession. The international Eucharistic Congress held in London in 1908, though it provoked some commotion in

16. See in particular H. G. Wood, *Belief and Unbelief since 1850*, Cambridge 1955.
17. On this controversy (1874-7) see the striking dossier assembled by B.-D. Dupuy in the collection *Textes newmaniens*, vol. VII. Paris-Bruges 1970.

certain Protestant circles, was itself testimony to the change in climate since the days when Cardinal Wiseman was burnt in effigy to cries of 'No Popery'. As further proof one can point to certain developments over the school problem, for so long one of the hierarchy's major preoccupations. There was a distinct threat, after the liberals had won the election of 1906, that they would revoke concessions granted to church schools of all denominations under the Education Act of 1902. The successful campaign to defeat the government's intentions was conducted by the Catholic authorities, led by the new archbishop of Westminster, Francis Bourne (1861-1935), working in close collaboration with Anglican clergy.

The defection in 1900 of the eminent Catholic scientist St George Mivart, and the stir it created, aroused fears in the hierarchy that after twenty years of calm a fresh wave of reformism and religious liberalism was on the way. But Mgr Bourne, though by no means broadminded in intellectual matters, was wise enough to play down the modernist crisis, which after all affected only a tiny segment of English Catholic opinion, [18] and the Roman Church in England settled down to a half-century of tranquillity and progress. This last was achieved in a variety of fields despite the difficulty of persuading English Catholics to organise for collective action over anything not connected with schools.

During the first half of the twentieth century the number of faithful doubled, rising from one-and-a-half to three million. It was in the south that the increase was most striking. Whereas in 1911 the present-day ecclesiastical province of Liverpool contained 58.4 per cent of the Catholic population and Westminster and Southwark only 26.2 per cent, in 1951 the respective proportions were 37.8 per cent and 42 per cent. [19] This steady increase was accounted for by the high Catholic birthrate and the continued, if slackening, flow of immigrants from Ireland, whom the old and more conservative Catholic stock was now finding it easier to absorb. Each year brought in addition several thousand converts (mostly from the Anglican Church), the annual average rising from 7500 for the first two decades of the century to 12,000 - 13,000 for the interwar years.

The converts, moreover, made a contribution to English Catholicism far greater than that of mere numbers, for they brought fresh blood into a community still turned in on itself and set in its ways. To illustrate the quality of that contribution, in the fields of thought, literature, philosophy, art, drama and journalism, it is enough to cite the names of C. C. Martindale, Ronald Knox, R. H. Benson, G. K. Chesterton, Christopher Dawson, Graham Greene, Muriel Spark, Douglas Hyde. That is not to deny the part played by

18. See chapter 10, 192-4.
19. See A. Spencer, 'The demography and sociography of the Catholic community in England and Wales' in *The Committed Church* (ed. L. Bright and S. Clements), London, 1966.

hereditary Catholics, especially in the years before the First World War. Names that come to mind are James Britten, the botanist who founded the Catholic Truth Society (1884), the poet Francis Thompson, and Wilfrid Ward, editor of the *Dublin Review* from 1906 to 1915, who at the turn of the century was making contact with non-Catholics of very varied intellectual background and viewpoint, just as within his own Church he was building bridges between the hierarchy and the world of writers and intellectuals. Here, too, one must mention Baron Friedrich von Hügel who has every claim to be regarded as English rather than Austrian, of whom it has been said that his influence outside his own Church was greater than any thinker's since Newman. On other name stands out, that of the historian, poet and essayist Hilaire Belloc, a vigorous champion of the Catholic cause during the interwar period. The study of church history owes something to English Catholic scholars: to the contributors to the *Downside Review* (founded 1880); to the men who in 1904 founded the Catholic Record Society; and more recently to Dom David Knowles, Regius Professor at Cambridge. Theology presents a contrast: despite Bede Jarrett's foundation of the Dominican centre (Blackfriars) at Oxford in 1920, despite the progressive improvement of the *Clergy Review* since it first appeared in 1930, and despite admirable efforts like those of Mgr Davis at the University of Birmingham, one can think of no English Catholic theologian since the days of Tyrrell and Vonier who has really commanded international attention. It is fair to add that the training many English theologians received in the Roman seminaries of the interwar period or at Valladolid was not conducive to creative thinking, weighted as it was towards the apologetic and polemical aspects of a course of study which long remained impervious to the revival in the biblical, ecclesiological and pastoral fields taking place on the Continent.

Until quite recently, the contribution of English Catholics to social problems was also very tentative. During the half-century following his death Manning had virtually no successors in this field whether in the hierarchy — Cardinal Bourne's attitude during the General Strike of 1926 is indicative — or in the Catholic world at large. In 1912 when the Jesuit Charles Plater launched with Mgr Parkinson the movement which grew into the Catholic Social Guild, with the aim of making Leo XIII's teaching on social questions more widely known, the literature on the subject available in English was found to be so meagre that at first nearly all the material had to be adapted or translated from the French. This movement also launched in 1921 the Catholic Workers' College at Oxford as a training-ground for Catholic trade unionists. Its principal, Fr Leo O'Hea, S.J., had difficulty in persuading his co-religionists to tolerate the social policies of the Labour Party, whose doctrines appeared to many to be incompatible with

Catholicism. The interwar years, it is true, produced a certain reaction to the abuses of the capitalist system in the form of the distributist movement for which the Dominican Vincent McNabb, and Chesterton and Belloc made such ardent propaganda, but this was a system geared more to a rural and patriarchal world than to an industrial society, and it was not until the forties that movements like the Young Christian Workers inspired by the Belgian Jeunesse Ouvrière Chrétienne of Cardijn got under way, to become a vital force throughout the Commonwealth and in the United States. This success was largely due to Patrick Keegan, whose achievement was recognised by his election in 1960 as President of the Mouvement international des ouvriers chrétiens. Of more recent origin still are the efforts of groups such as Slant (1964) to effect a synthesis between Christianity and Marxism.

England was equally belated in awakening to the liturgical movement – strict adherence to post-Tridentine traditions seeming to English Catholics a very effective way of signalising their separateness from the Anglicans – and still more so in welcoming the ecumenical movement, despite the initiatives of early pioneers such as McNabb and the Benedictine Bede Winslow, founder of the periodical *Eastern Churches Quarterly,* and the Sword of the Spirit movement inaugurated by Cardinal Hinsley (archbishop of Westminster 1935-43) in 1940 as an experiment in practical ecumenism at the level of Catholic social action, which was promptly brought to an end by his successor, Mgr Griffin.

This was still a Church which remained locked, as it had been for generations, within its minority complex and its tightly drawn and all-pervasive 'guild' system (confessional schools, periodicals and publishing houses, strict submission of the laity to the clergy, of the priesthood to the hierarchy). Signs of change had already begun in the thirties with lay ownership of the *Tablet* and the *Catholic Herald*, which in the hands of Douglas Woodruff and Michael de la Bedoyère respectively became well known far outside confessional circles. But it is only as we reach Vatican II and its aftermath, which coincided with the rise of a new middle class in consequence of the opportunities for higher education extended to working-class children under Butler's Education Act of 1944 that we see really significant signs of change. Future generations will no doubt perceive phenomena such as the criticism of 'apartheid' in education expressed by the Union of Catholic Students in 1966, the McCabe affair of 1967, and the storm unleashed by the encyclical *Humanae vitae* in 1968, as the first rumblings of a crisis, which if we judge correctly, will radically transform in structure and outlook, a Church which around 1800 was insignificant and today occupies its full and distinctive position among the religious denominations of Great Britain and in European Catholicism.

For reasons easy to understand, attention tends to concentrate on the history of Catholicism in England, but we have to remember that the Roman Church was represented in other parts of the British Isles. About Wales there is little that needs to be said. Until the end of the nineteenth century it counted very few Catholics among its population. The number of Irish immigrants then started to increase and in 1895 the region was detached from the two English dioceses of which it had formed part and reconstituted as an autonomous vicariate apostolic which three years later became the diocese of Menevia. In 1916 Cardiff was raised to an archbishopric with two suffragan sees.

Scotland, which around 1900 was already estimated to have a million Catholics, presents a different picture. There the pattern is similar, granted a certain time lag, to the course of development found in England: the same great influx of Irish immigrants (100,000 during the famine years of the eighteen forties, and another 200,000 between 1850 and 1880), and with the settlement of the newcomers largely in the Glasgow region, the same displacement of the Catholic centre of gravity, from the north-east to the south-west. There is evidence going back before 1830 of discord between Catholics who were of Irish extraction and the small group of the indigenous, from which at that time virtually all the clergy were drawn. The Scottish-born took exception to the aggressively boisterous devotions of the Irish, which were not only offensive to their own conception of religion as austere and wholly inward-looking, but also a cause of frequent head-on clashes with the Presbyterians – their own policy being always to try to escape notice. From mid-century these troubles intensified, thanks to incitement from the *Glasgow Free Press* coupled with the arrival of priests from Ireland who accused the vicar apostolic of the western region of systematically favouring the clergy native to Scotland. Irish priests, it was alleged, were given the job of founding new missions for the immigrants but, once the church was built, were moved on to start their arduous pioneering work all over again, leaving a Scottish priest to reap the fruits of their labours. By 1865 relations were so strained that Cardinal Cullen, archbishop of Dublin, intervened at Rome and procured the appointment of a priest of Irish origin as coadjutor, but the individual in question (J. Lynch) proved so tactless that the atmosphere became still more embittered. As a way out of the impasse, in 1867 the Congregation de Propaganda Fide comissioned Mgr Manning to look into the situation and recommend a solution. One of the things he thought should be done was to proceed at once, as many of the Irish desired, to the re-establishment of the episcopal hierarchy. This proposal was greeted with objections from two sides. The vicars apostolic considered that the time was not yet ripe, while the British government protested still more forcefully, fearing a violent reaction from the still fiercely anti-papist Protestant population. Rome therefore decided not to precipitate matters. To compose the differences between the two camps, an English administrator apostolic was sought for Glasgow. Mgr Errington having declined the office, the choice fell on the able and energetic Charles Eyre, vicar general of Hexham, who succeed in pouring oil on the troubled waters.

The question of restoring the hierarchy was brought up again in 1876, and this time Rome was willing to grant the Catholics of Scotland what they wished. The negotiations were complicated by the difficulty of choosing for the metropolitan see between the competing claims of Glasgow with its two-thirds of the Catholic population and Edinburgh the capital — not to mention St Andrews, which had historical claims and numbered among its supporters the wealthy and liberal-handed Lord Bute, Scotland's nearest equivalent to England's Duke of Norfolk. Eventually, despite Mgr Eyre's advice that two or three dioceses would be enough, Rome issued a bull (4 March 1878) which created an ecclesiastical province of Edinburgh with four suffragan sees and in addition an archbishopric of Glasgow to be directly dependent on the Holy See.[20] For a Church which at that date numbered only 257 priests this provision was manifestly excessive, and three of the new dioceses were barely viable. It must also be admitted that some of the boundaries ran counter to common sense. But taken as a whole the arrangement proved salutary. In setting up the new structure Irish and Scots co-operated as they never had before and in consequence Catholic life took on a new vigour. From now on the great and continuing problem for the authorities was the Catholic schools, for which a solution started to emerge in 1918 with the prospect, under the Scottish Education Act, of some financial aid from local authorities.

In Ireland, naturally enough, the situation looked very different, given the presence, save in Ulster, of an overwhelming majority of Catholics in the population and the uninterrupted continuity of the diocesan organisation, and the difference is made all the more distinctive by the laity's growing preoccupation, as the century advanced, with the country's political and social problem. The appointment of Paul Cullen (1803-78; made cardinal in 1866) as archbishop of Dublin in 1852 marked the beginning of a new era, politically as well as in church affairs. As has been well said of him, for a quarter of a century and more 'he was the Irish hierarchy. He determined the character of that Church, guided its policy, shaped its destiny, moulded its discipline'.[21] Involved as he was in all the major questions of his day, Cullen has attracted criticism from many quarters, but now that his cor-

20. In 1947, following the creation of two new dioceses, Glasgow too became a metropolitan see.
21. P. O'Farrell, *The Catholic Church in Australia* London 1969), 151-2.

respondence has been published (edited by P. Mac Suithae) we can more readily appreciate the finer shades of his work and character. He was a courageous man, consumed with zeal for the spiritual welfare of his flock, yet realist enough to recognise that half a loaf is often better than none. Possessing these qualities, Cullen became a vastly more influential figure than Mgr MacHale, archbishop of Tuam from 1834 to 1881, who was passionately anti-English and bent on avoiding any concessions which might tie the bishops' hands. Cullen was a first-rate administrator, far-sighted and energetic, perhaps a shade dictatorial. Having spent several years as agent of the Irish episcopate in Rome (acquiring considerable influence in curial circles and becoming thoroughly steeped in ultramontane ideas) he was very well-informed about current developments, and was tireless in his efforts – which were indeed necessary – to bring the clergy up to a higher standard. He suggested to Rome ideas for stimulating pastoral zeal among his priests and brother bishops. He urged the latter to reform Maynooth, the central seminary, and to foster the habit of spiritual retreats. He promoted parochial missions, seeing in them the best counterblast to Protestant proselytising activities (nothing short of an obsession with him and many of his colleagues); and being a man with both feet on the ground, he gave his support to the temperance campaign led by a Capuchin, Theobold Matthew. Pius IX trusted Cullen's judgment implicitly and often took his advice over the appointment of bishops, even when it meant choosing from outside the *terna* presented by the clergy, a procedure symptomatic of a move towards methods of more authoritarian church government but which had its beneficial side in that a somewhat colourless episcopate was diversified by the gradual introduction of men of distinct personality and undeniable pastoral gifts. [22]

Cullen was also much preoccupied with the school question, a cause of dissension among the Irish episcopate in the late forties, and through his persistence eventually secured from the government some not unimportant concessions. But on this subject he was sometimes in disagreement with his colleagues, in particular Mgr Moriarty, bishop of Kerry. The latter had sympathies with liberal tendencies in Catholicism, which made for differences on more than this one issue between himself and the lifelong champion of Ultramontanism. Cullen, as Talbot remarked, was 'a thorough Roman in every sense of the word'. After school came university, at which stage many Catholic students went to Trinity College, Dublin, which although Protestant was under no ban corresponding to that imposed by the English bishops on Oxford and Cambridge. Cullen was nevertheless determined to meet the wishes of the Holy See by establishing a Catholic univer-

22. On this development see J. H. Whyte, 'The appointment of catholic bishops in nineteenth-century Ireland', *Catholic Historical Review*, XLVIII (1962-3), 12-32.

sity in Dublin. The success of Louvain, in a country with an even smaller population, seemed an encouraging precedent and in Ireland one could hope – falsely, as it turned out – that the new university would act as a magnet to Catholic students from England. The episcopate had invited Newman to be its first Rector, but his over-ambitious ideas soon spread dismay among the bishops, none of whom were university-educated. Furthermore, they lacked the funds to carry out his plans, and his choice of English converts as professors succeeded in alienating the sympathies of the Irish clergy. Realising that he was not understood, in 1858 Newman withdrew. [23] Although in difficulty, the institution managed to carry on, but had to wait a long time for its charter of legal recognition from the English government. The responsible authorities were in any case divided on the point, the government tending to listen to Protestants who raised the spectre of Ultramontanism, while the bishops, intent on keeping the university under their control, insisted on all or nothing. It is worth noting that there were staunchly Catholic laymen who feared episcopal control of the university, on the grounds that it would only accentuate the clericalism already so prevalent in all departments of life. The government took the first step towards satisfying the Catholics in 1879 with the foundation of the Royal University of Ireland, of which the former Catholic University, now taken over by the Jesuits as University College, became an integral part. Official recognition of the National University of Ireland, with its constituent colleges of Dublin, Cork and Galway, came only in 1908.

When it came to pressing Irish grievances against the English government, Cullen, who had heartily approved O'Connell's agitation, wanted to keep out of the political arena and frequently urged his priests to do the same. But he was soon forced to recognise that the clergy could not stand completely aside. The bishops could not remain passive while landed proprietors inflicted flagrant injustices on their tenant farmers, and neither could the clergy as a whole, since in the absence of an educated and politically responsible middle class (none such could have emerged, so great was the prevailing poverty), they were the only body with any concrete prospect of furthering popular interests, and it was to them that the people naturally turned. There was no hope of action from the upper classes who, when they were not Protestant, were too closely linked with the English establishment to champion the national cause. Given the existing social structure, political intervention by the Irish clergy was inevitable.

23. See E. McGrath, *Newman's University. Idea and Reality*, London 1951, and A. Gwynn, in *Newman Studien* (Nürnberg 1957), III, 95-110. On the subsequent fortunes of the Irish Catholic University see M. Tierney (ed.) *Struggle with Fortune*, collected papers, Dublin, 1954. It will be noted that over this affair Cullen's attitude towards Newman was more correct than has often been allowed.

The manner and degree of intervention varied considerably. Broadly speaking, the lower clergy supported the nationalists' intrigues with much greater enthusiasm than did the bishops. And the bishops themselves varied in attitude, MacHale for example adopting a harsh and peremptory tone towards the English while Cullen tended to be more conciliatory. Amid all his political manoeuvring, he never lost sight of his pastoral objective and was therefore prepared to make concessions to the government in London, if by doing so he could improve the position of the Catholic faith. Accordingly, when the National Association was set up in 1864–5 to act as a pressure group on Parliament, Cullen wanted to give top priority not to the agrarian question, as many of the bishops and most of the laity desired, but to the problem of the schools. He was moreover unmistakably hostile to the radicalism of the Young Irelanders and their Fenian successors who reminded him of the Italian revolutionaries he had seen in action during his years in Rome. By exaggerating their anti-religious tendencies he had them condemned by the Holy See, but even so a number of priests continued to support them.

Cullen was succeeded at Dublin in 1878 by Mgr E. MacCabe, a conservative like himself and equally opposed to radical nationalism, but who operated on a much smaller scale. In consequence, the most prominent figure in the Irish episcopate during these years was Mgr T. Croke, archbishop of Cashel, who lent open support to the campaign for redress of social and political grievances mounted by Parnell [24] and his Land League against the English government. Leo XIII, who was keen to improve relations between London and the Holy See, intervened on several occasions (for example in 1883 and 1888), repudiating the methods used by the Parnellites and desiring the bishops to break off relations with them. [25] His action produced active disquiet among many Irish Catholics, not excluding some clergy, and there were even people ready to deny that the pope had any right to intervene in political affairs. In 1885, however, in response to the almost unanimous insistence of the Irish episcopate supported by Cardinal Manning, [26] and despite urgent representations from the English government, Leo XIII had found himself obliged to agree to the appointment as archbishop of Dublin of Mgr Walsh (1841-1921), president of the

24. Charles Stewart Parnell (1846-91), although Protestant, opposed the exploitation of Irish tenant farmers by the English and was the leader of a lively group of nationalists in the English Parliament. Their programme aimed at agrarian reform and Home Rule (i.e. an autonomous administration for Ireland).
25. In fact the episcopate was divided over Parnell's campaign; some of the Church's property was invested in land.
26. Manning's concern for justice had already led him to intervene on Ireland's behalf with the English government, and in particular with Gladstone. See D. Gwynn, 'Manning and Ireland', in J. Fitzsimons (ed.), *Manning, Anglican and Catholic* (London 1951), 111-35.

Maynooth Central Seminary and well-known for his nationalist sympathies and open advocacy of agrarian reform. It is significant, though, that the pope, despite the precedent provided by Walsh's two predecessors, did not make him a cardinal, preferring to confer the hat on the archbishop of Armagh (1892). Pius X was much less eager to make token gestures to London. He showed no hesitation, despite the government's keen displeasure, in despatching Cardinal Vannutelli to Ireland as his legate.

Mgr Walsh, who had the education problem very much at heart, played an important role in the negotiations leading to the foundation of a national university for Ireland. He also gave his support to the Gaelic League which aimed at reviving Ireland's ancient language. In administration he was methodical, wise and impartial, and it was largely he who was responsible for the new statutes approved by the national synod of Maynooth in 1900. On the political issue, he opposed the plan to divide the country into two sectors, one Protestant and pro-English in complexion, the other Catholic and nationalist. When the schism occurred between the original Irish parliamentary party and the radical Sinn Fein, his sympathies went with the latter and in 1918 he joined the overwhelming majority of Catholic leaders in opposing the introduction of military conscription into Ireland.

In 1918 the hierarchy, which in 1916 had been trenchant in its condemnation of the Easter rising, rallied in its entirety to Sinn Fein, and in the months that followed remained adamant in face of insistent requests from London for condemnation of the insurgents. By contrast, when the Irish Free State had been proclaimed (1922) and Eamonn De Valera and his radical republicans, dissatisfied with what had so far been achieved, launched the civil war, the reaction of the episcopate was to disown them.

The fact that for close on a century Irish Catholics were largely preoccupied with political and social problems should not blind us to other, less spectacular facets of their religious life. Here we must be content with a passing reference to the Legion of Mary, founded in Dublin in 1921 by Frank Duff, a civil servant in the finance department, which was destined to spread not merely to other English-speaking countries but throughout the world, and to Ireland's record, which she maintains to this day, as a cradle of missionaries. In 1960 there were more than 7000 Irish missionaries scattered throughout the world, that is to say one missionary for every 457 of Irish at home. Through them and more generally through the Irish emigration, Irish Catholics had an immense influence on the development of the Church throughout the world.

12

AUSTRALIA:
THE BIRTH OF A CHURCH

ORIGINALLY a colony for convicts, in the early nineteenth century Australia started to attract voluntary immigrants, most of whom settled in the Sydney region. Among both sorts there was a fairly high proportion of Irish and hence of Catholics. In 1828, out of a population of about 35,000 some 11,230 were reckoned to be Roman Catholics. The only priests in the early days were a handful of deportees who ministered more or less in secret, with the result that for much of the time the faithful were reduced to meeting for Sunday prayers in their own homes. In 1820, following Irish agitation in the British press, the London government agreed to send out a few chaplains at the public's expense. An inopportune attempt by Rome to appoint a vicar apostolic having failed, these priests were attached to the circumscription of the vicar apostolic of the island of Mauritius, a territory which included South Africa, Madagascar and the entire Western Pacific.

After the passing of the Catholic Emancipation Act in 1829 the situation improved. In 1834 London agreed to the appointment of a vicar apostolic, on condition that the person appointed was English and not Irish, and in 1836 Governor Bourke granted what amounted to equal recognition of the four main confessions: Anglican, hitherto in possession of a virtual monopoly, Catholic, Methodist and Presbyterian. There was nevertheless a fairly violent Anglican reaction from when in 1842, thus eight years before the corresponding move in England, Rome set up the normal episcopal hierarchy in Australia, creating an archbishopric at Sydney and two suffragan sees, one at Adelaide on the south coast and the other for Tasmania; but thanks to the tact of the new archbishop the storm soon died down.

John Bede Polding (1794-1877), first archbishop of Sydney, was a Benedictine from Downside. In fact since 1818 the English Benedictines had held responsibility for the vast vicariate apostolic of Mauritius and it was one of their number, the young Dom Bernard Ullathorne, who, armed with the title 'Vicar General for Australia', had arrived in February 1833 to start work in a country where the ecclesiastical structures were still virtually non-existent. Ullathorne succeeded in laying solid foundations for an independent vicariate apostolic, which received as its head his former novice master, Dom Henry Gregory. Polding, aided until 1841 by Ullathorne and then for the next twenty years by Gregory, laboured with true missionary zeal, setting up parishes, building churches, promoting charitable undertakings and launching the first Catholic newspapers. In 1843 he founded a Benedictine house in Sydney, wanting the future Australian clergy to be brought up in a monastic environment so that they might impress Anglicans with their feeling for the liturgy and their culture, and impress on the faithful their detachment from worldly goods, an example not always set by priests who had come out from Ireland in the early years of the century. The reluctance of the latter to conform to the directives of their bishop and his monastic entourage was reinforced by their inbred resistance to English-born superiors. But as Australia's Catholic population grew, Mgr Polding's dream of a missionary Church of the monastic type started to melt away.

At the time the archbishopric of Sydney was created in 1842 ninety per cent of Australia's forty thousand Catholics were concentrated in New South Wales; but fresh waves of immigrants, many of them Irish, coming to settle other regions and, following the gold rush of 1851, in the Melbourne region in particular, had the effect within twenty-five years of increasing the Catholic population tenfold, necessitating the creation first of new parishes and then of new dioceses: Perth on the west coast in 1845; Maitland and Melbourne in 1847 (not to mention Port Victoria on the north coast, soon discovered to be unviable); Brisbane in Queensland in 1859; Bathurst in 1865 and Armidale in 1869, both in New South Wales; Ballarat and Bendigo (Sandhurst) in the State of Victoria in 1874, the year in which Melbourne became the metropolitan see of a second ecclesiastical province. Since the manpower to serve these new parishes had come chiefly from Ireland[1] it was only natural that many of the new bishops were chosen from among the Irish, especially since the local clergy's wishes to this effect were backed in Rome by Cardinal Cullen, archbishop of Dublin, whose word carried great weight with the pope and with the Congregation for the

---

1. A handful of Spanish Benedictines, forced to leave Spain by the laws prohibiting religious orders, came to settle in 1845 in the West, and one of their number became bishop of Perth; but they soon found themselves at variance with their Irish-born parishioners. Their monastery of New Norcia, founded in 1847, was erected in 1867 into an abbey *nullius*, nucleus of a future diocese. Cf R. Rios, *Las misiones australianas de los benedictinos españoles*, Barbastro 1930.

Propagation of the Faith. These Irish priests and bishops were fully determined to turn their adopted country into a new Ireland, 'an Irish spiritual empire' in Cardinal Moran's later description, thinking that the transplantation to this new soil of the pastoral techniques and popular devotions which had proved their worth in the mother country would encourage Ireland's age-old religious traditions, very different in the main from the Benedictine ideal, to blossom afresh.

National antagonism, reinforced by differences of pastoral outlook, was thus a cause of tension between the English monks and the growing mass of Irish. But this was not the only difficulty facing the authorities of the young Australian Church. Many priests were not prepared to conform too strictly to discipline, even when imposed by a bishop as Irish as themselves; and a number of laymen, influenced by the prevailing liberal outlook, were loud in their demands for a more democratically organised Church. Large though these troubles loom in the sources, they should not blind us to the apostolic zeal of the clergy as a whole, which bore appreciable fruit in religous observance as the century advanced, or to the dedication of lay people such as Mrs Caroline Chisholm, who between 1838 and 1857 did remarkable work on behalf of immigrants, and Charles O'Neill (1828-1900), founder of the Society of St Vincent de Paul in Australia.

In the last third of the century, during which Catholic numbers continued their steady rise – by 1901 there were 856,000 Catholics in a total population of 3,872,000 – the great problem confronting the Church in Australia, as in many other countries, was that of the schools. Until then, confessional schools had had the benefit of various government subsidies, but in 1866 there was a change of attitude in the Education Council of New South Wales and under the Public Instruction Act of 1880, its example being quickly followed in the other States, and all such aid was abolished. As a result many Protestant schools had to close; but the Catholic bishops, who like their colleagues in Ireland regarded the parochial school as one of the main foundations of their pastoral work, were not easily daunted, especially since they had as their leader the energetic new archbishop of Sydney, Mgr Roger Bede Vaughan (1877-84) who, although a Benedictine, had long since perceived that his predecessor's monastic ambitions were unrealisable and who shared the views of his Irish fellow-bishops on the need to give the masses a firm framework. Having issued a collective pastoral (1879) roundly condemning the secular schools, the episcopate prevailed to good effect on the generosity of the Catholic community and also sent out a general appeal to the teaching congregations, imploring them to supply replacements for the teachers the Church could no longer afford to pay. At first it was necessary to rely heavily on Europe, but as time went on enough local recruits were forthcoming to fill the need. Furthermore, the two decades prior to 1880 had seen the birth of several Australian congregations (the Good Samaritan Sisters in 1857, the St Joseph Sisters in 1866, the Perpetual Adoration Sisters in 1874), which was yet another indication that the Australian Church was approaching adulthood.

Between 1884 and 1911 this now vigorously expanding Church was dominated by a figure held in perhaps too much admiration during his lifetime, Patrick Francis Moran, cardinal archbishop of Sydney. [2] Nephew of Cardinal Cullen, whom he consciously imitated at every point, he further resembled Cullen in that for a quarter of a century he was the national episcopate incarnate, leaving his mark for years to come both on the internal life of the Church and on the Church's relations with the community at large, including the political establishment. Having, like Cullen, spent many years in Rome, he reinforced the Roman mould of the Australian Catholic Church, following in the footsteps of the dozen or so Irish bishops appointed at Cullen's instigation during the pontificate of Pius IX. Appearing on the scene after fifty years of rapid and inevitably somewhat haphazard expansion, Moran insisted on his episcopal authority to promote unity of discipline on the Church. He demanded unconditional obedience from the laity, insisted on the strict application of the canon law according to the norms prescribed by the Roman Congregations and encouraged the trend towards centralisation by measures such as the foundation in 1885 of a national seminary, which was to have no rival until 1920, the holding of plenary councils (1885, 1895, 1905) to ensure that all the bishops of the country and in neighbouring regions, New Zealand for example, [3] acted in concert, and the organisation of national Catholic congresses (1900, 1904, 1909). Another trait Moran shared with Cullen was a ready tendency to identify

2. His elevation to the cardinalate a few months after his appointment to Sydney might be taken as recognition of the fact that the Church in Australia had finally emerged from its missionary period. In truth it was much more in the nature of a personal compensation, Moran having been set aside at the last minute, for political reasons, as candidate for the Dublin see, which had virtually been promised him.

3. In New Zealand the development of the Catholic Church had lagged considerably behind. Although French Marists had settled there in 1836 and by 1848 two dioceses had been created, Catholics of European origin still numbered only a few thousand, and the Maori revolt of 1856 brought all missionary work to a standstill for ten years (cf. L. G. Keys, *Life and Times of Bishop Pompallier*, Christchurch 1957, and *Philip Viard, Bishop of Wellington*, Christchurch 1968). In 1887, on the recommendation of the First Plenary Council of Sydney, the hierarchy was at last reorganised, Wellington becoming an archbishopric with three suffragan dioceses. By this date Catholicism in New Zealand was already strongly Irish in complexion and conducting its affairs in an atmosphere of pronounced confessional antagonisms (cf. H. M. Laracy, 'Bishop Moran: Irish politics and Catholicism in New Zealand', *Journal of Religious History*, VI (Sydney 1970), 62-76). After 1900 much more attention was devoted to problems proper to New Zealand, especially the schools question. Government subsidies to Catholic schools had been withdrawn at much the same time as in Australia, in 1876. In 1964 the 364,000 Catholics represented one-seventh of the population and one-fifth of the Maoris were Catholic converts.

the claims of Ireland with the interests of the Church, but on the strict understanding that the former were subservient to the latter, with the result that both men would have nothing to do with extremist nationalism, because of the prejudice it created against Catholicism in the minds of the civil authorities. Although criticised on this score by the fanatics of the Young Ireland movement, Moran still did much to reinforce the Irish character of the Australian Church; but with his keen sense of what was appropriate, he understood better than most of his colleagues that what was needed was not to transplant the old, Europe-orientated Ireland to the Antipodes but to build there a new, forward-looking Ireland in which the Irish could develop their potentialities both as citizens and Catholics in a setting quite different from the one that had confined them since the Reformation.

Relying on the climate of political liberty and religious toleration characteristic of the late nineteenth century, Moran accordingly made every effort to encourage Catholic integration with Australian society. But the task proved much harder than he had foreseen. In the first place there was the matter of education. It was quite out of the question for Catholics to give up their schools' network and Moran made on the contrary a considerable effort to expand it, tripling the number of schools in his diocese and appreciably raising their standard, at a cost of close on a million pounds. But he renounced the violent polemics against the State in which Catholics had engaged during the 1870s and showed himself willing for co-operation with the public education authorities, for example in the matter of bringing the curriculum of Catholic schools into line with that in the State schools, which he advocated in what proved to be the vain hope of obtaining the restoration of public subsidies.

It was elsewhere, in the social and political field, that Moran was to show himself a pioneer of the pluralist society thanks to his categorical rejection of the principle of confessional political parties and unions. Putting his trust in democratic institutions of the British type and inspired by the social teaching of Leo XIII, he was eager to encourage the trade-union movement so long as it did not fall prey to revolution-orientated anarcho-syndicalism, and he gave the full backing of his prestige to Catholic participation in the founding of a workers' Labour Party – Catholics made up a third of the country's working population – alongside the existing Liberal and Conservative parties. Whether it is true, as P. Ford asserts, that Moran's influence was mainly responsible for Australian Labour's avoidance of extremist and anti-Christian brands of socialism, remains debatable. What is certain is that he did a great deal to set the Church of Australia as a whole on the path of social justice, proposing norms for a family wage and contracts of employment that took increased profits into account, recommending direct State intervention to bring about a better welfare service and going so far as to give his official blessing to the expression 'Christian socialism'.

But Moran had been too quick to assume that the sectarian anti-popery of the nineteenth century was a thing of the past, and the very success of his efforts to bring Catholics out of their ghetto was enough to provoke a reaction. The foundation in 1901, on the initiative of a forceful Presbyterian, Dill Macky, of the Australian Protestant Association, showed which way the wind was blowing, and from then on until the middle 1920s Catholics were once again thrown on to the defensive. In this new climate the polemical warfare between the confessions was more acute than ever, embittered on the one side by the bishops' deep disappointment over the failure of Moran's conciliatory schools' policy and on the other by the equivocal attitude of a large part of the Catholic clergy during the First World War, the result of their greater sympathy for the cause of rebellious Ireland than with England's struggle against Germany, which could not fail to reinforce the impression that the Catholic community was a foreign body in the State. Within a very few years of Cardinal Moran's death Catholics were as far as ever from his ideal of harmonious integration into the nation. Furthermore, the personality of Mgr Daniel Mannix, archbishop of Melbourne from 1912 to 1962, who for decades occupied the dominant place in the Australian Church once held by Moran, was not conducive to a relaxation of the tension. For all his pastoral zeal and undeniable concern for social justice, this ex-president of Maynooth, Ireland's national seminary, was intransigent, narrow-minded and profoundly anti-English, entirely lacking the diplomatic gifts of the departed Moran.

During the interwar period much effort continued to be expended in pressing the claims of Catholic schools although it was only after 1950 that some satisfaction was obtained.[4] In the meantime, round about 1925, a new issue had come to the fore. With the great majority of the population now Australian by birth, some thought it no longer appropriate to seek bishops from Ireland. This desire to reduce Australia's dependency on the Irish was undoubtedly connected with the growing demands of laymen to be given some freedom of initiative.

The appearance on the scene of the Catholic laity was signalled, for example, by the formation during the 1930s of the Campion Society, an association of Catholic graduates, and of the League of St Thomas More, intended for business and professional men. This was the prelude to the foundation in 1938 of the National Secretariat for Catholic Action, a body with a strong sense of social purpose.

After the Second World War the great importance assumed by anti-Communist agitation raised questions about where to draw the line between

---

4. In 1964 there were 1,545 Catholic primary schools and 494 secondary schools, educating between them 471,000 pupils; there were also nine university colleges.

Catholic Action and political activity, an issue which in 1953 had to be referred to the Holy See. By that date, having profited more than other confessional groups from the recent fresh wave of immigration, Catholics once again represented twenty-five per cent of the total population, and it was estimated that sixty-four per cent of all Catholics were practising. There were close on two thousand diocesan priests, a further thousand religious priests, and the number of women religious exceeded ten thousand. To cite just one further indication among many of the vitality of Australian Catholicism: the contribution per head to pontifical missions was the second highest in the world.

13

CANADA

INTRODUCTION AND BACKGROUND

THE dominant fact of life of Canadian history is summed up in the hyphenated word 'French-English'. As in every nation, sections have competed, classes struggled, smaller racial groups risen up. Yet since the days of the first British rule when Governor Murray wrote that the sixty thousand inhabitants of New France could become 'the most faithful and useful set of men in this American empire', no other fact has replaced the French-English as the basic fabric of the Canadian scene. In no area has this theme been more evident than in the story of the Canadian Roman Catholic Church.

There have been other important ways in which the Church in the vast area north of the United States has been shaped by the total national experience. First of all, the Canadian Church has been, profoundly, an American Church. Seen against the European source from which it sprang, it was, like the society in which it grew, a predominantly liberal phenomenon, with its frontier and pioneer dimensions. Even here, however, a paradox was involved. Although the drive to the frontier presumed a decision for change from a given order, one aspect of this experience was a strong element of conservatism. Because of the daily struggle for survival and basic needs, there was a tendency to fall back on certain pillars of human existence in a less examined way than in a more mature society. Thus arose the unmistakable fundamentalist tendency in all frontier churches, including the Roman Catholic. Within the American political experience, moreover, Canada must be regarded largely as a conservative phenomenon. Here, the French bloc with its inevitable stress on *survivance* has been an important element. Still more basic has been the fact that Canada, beginning with the era of the American Revolution and the Loyalists, was born of a series of decisions, French and English, not to join the United States. Geography, sheer size, and economic development have shaped Canada in emphatic ways. But a political-cultural-social decision stood behind the original articulation, and, by and large, succeeding 'Canadian' decisions have been taken in defiance of economics and geography. Not until the opening of her tremendous northern resources did economic Canada become more than a tenuous East-West ribbon.

These anti-American factors were particularly evident in the years immediately preceding Canadian confederation. For the Church, several other background elements must be added to the picture. As. J. A. Raftis suggests, the toleration of French-Canadian Catholicism provided by the Quebec Act was an important factor both in the long road to Catholic emancipation for the whole British Empire, and in producing the kind of social and political context acceptable to new Catholic immigrants to Canada. Secondly, the overflow of the European religious revival which followed the Napoleonic wars combined with the native French-Canadian missionary zeal to produce a climate favourable to Catholic survival and growth. Thirdly, the impact of the frontier dissipated many traditional religious and cultural barriers, and produced many instances of co-operation and mutual support between different denominations which would have been unthinkable in mid-nineteenth-century Europe. Foreshadowed by the impact of the care of war-wounded by the Quebec sisterhoods during the military rule following the British conquest, the 'binding service of charity bridged many religious differences', particularly in times of epidemic and crisis. [1] At the same time, certain feuds which were transplanted to the New World without dilution tended to be more violent than they had been even in their original context, since both the restraining elements and the reason for the original quarrels often disappeared. The worst Orange Order/Irish Catholic clashes of the mid-nineteenth century, and the legendary Donnelly feud and massacre in 1880 in the area north of London, Ontario, were notable examples of this maverick tendency.

The primary problem facing the English-speaking Canadian Church in the 1850s was simply to provide for the basic religious needs of the flood of immigration paralleling that to the United States in the wake of the Irish famine. At first, the need for priests had to be met from two basic sources, French Canada and Europe, with very few coming from the United States. Soon, however, native vocations from English-speaking Canada and the Maritime Provinces began to fill both diocesan and religious ranks. The problem of adequate seminary training long remained a difficult one, but, like the tensions experienced by the Redemptorists in the United States, several Canadian religious orders with European roots went through crises

1. J. A. Raftis, 'Changing Characteristics of the Catholic Church', *The Churches and the Canadian Experience*, ed. J. W. Grant (Toronto 1963), 87.

which culminated in new provinces and sometimes in distinct societies. Again reflecting the United States' experience, Catholic growth in British North America stirred a nativist and anti-Catholic reaction. In some areas, such reaction was strongly anti-'papal aggression', as in Newfoundland in the early 1860s. More often it included an element of anti-French feeling, as in the case of the Gavazzi riots in Montreal in 1853, and in the running battle over Catholic school rights which plagued the United Province of Canada from 1850 until the Scott Act of 1863.

In French Canada, perhaps the most emphatic lesson of the quarter-century experiment known as the United Province of Canada (1841-67) was the emergence of a French Canadian quite different from the 'outlander' he might have become had the nation followed the direction taken by the leader of the previous generation, Louis Joseph Papineau. This new approach of being both co-operative and decisive in the future of Canada was led first by Louis H. Lafontaine and then by George-Étienne Cartier. Both men taught and symbolised a new kind of *survivance* to their compatriots. Cartier in particular, beyond his key political role, was a major figure in the steel and iron backbone of the Canada-to-be, the Grand Trunk Railway. In literature, this was the age of F. X. Garneau, Octave Crémazie and Louis Fréchette, each of whom gave French Canada a new pride in its history and a new *élan* to its culture.

Within the official Church, the dominant figure was Ignace Bourget, bishop of Montreal (1841-76). A remarkable number of sisterhoods vital to the education and charitable works of the Canadian Church had their foundation during his episcopate. As Marcel de Grandpré puts it, for the first time since the conquest, French Canadians saw, through the medium of religion, 'the possibility of dreaming in the dimensions of a continent'. [2] Preceded by Provencher and Dumoulin in Red River and Demers in British Columbia, the Oblate Fathers moved west in 1845. Soon led by Alexandre Taché, consecrated bishop in 1851 at the age of twenty-seven, the Oblates marked out a story of both suffering and vision. Not the least evidence of wisdom was the degree to which such Canadian missionaries contributed to the avoidance of the kind of Indian wars which darkened the American drive westward.

CONFEDERATION

Canadian confederation was part of the general mid-nineteenth century response to industry, transport, territorial expansion and political centralisation. On the one hand, confederation happened within a British world, which, symbolised by the Corn Law repeal of 1846, was withdrawing

2. M. de Grandpré, 'Traditions of the Catholic Church in French Canada', *The Churches and the Canadian Experience*, ed. Grant, 10.

colonial privileges and reducing colonial obligations. It also happened within an American world which, in the cauldron of the Civil War, threw, as Parrington has said, a 'centralising state into the hands of the new industrialism'. The termination in 1866 of the reciprocity of the Union armies, and the ill-concealed sentiments about Manifest Destiny extending the American Union to the North Pole, all converged to force British North America to seek a new and stronger political existence. Just as there was no more sure-fire popular appeal in nineteenth-century America than 'twisting the lion's tail', so the most predictable popular reaction in Canada was against the picture of mob rule that was supposed to follow annexation or too much influence by the United States. For the most part, British North American bishops remained aloof from the controversy which preceded confederation, but when they did speak out, the warning about American danger was clearly present. Archbishop Connolly of Halifax, despite the growing anti-confederation sentiment in Nova Scotia, gave a measured and articulate argument for Church and State alike to seek union as the only alternative to absorption. The French-Canadian bishops, though generally reticent because of the relatively favourable position of the Church within the United Province of Canada, did reveal some voices favouring the proposed confederation precisely as a bulwark against the American threat. Most persuasive of all in the use of the anti-American argument was the Irish Catholic revolutionary of the 1840s who became the 'poet of Confederation' of the 1860s, Thomas D'Arcy McGee.

Quite important to the development of the Church in Canada was the form of government created by the British North America Act and its subsequent amendments. Beyond the provision for a duality of language in the Act, the main direct impact of confederation on the Roman Catholic Church was the educational arrangement. If the guarantees in the Constitution have not always produced the security they were intended to give, they at least created a presumption favouring minority school privileges, Catholic and other. The net result has been that, in practice, Canada has provincial systems with a wide spectrum of arrangements for Catholic education; all but two provinces give some share of school monies to denominational schools.

THE FIRST QUARTER-CENTURY

The dominant feature of Canada's first generation was that of grand dreams unfulfilled, buoyed up, in Frank Underhill's words, by a 'sense of impending greatness'.[3] Even the most ambitious project of all, the Canadian Pacific Railway, was the story of one near-ruin after another. Somehow, however,

3. F. Underhill, Address at Queen's University, 1955.

the railway got through in 1885, and the chief reason for its completion, as for Canada's perdurance, was John A. Macdonald, Prime Minister for nearly twenty of Canada's first twenty-five years. Macdonald's relationship with the Roman Catholic Church reflected his attitude to every factor on his horizon, pragmatic, faintly threatening, but always genial. He watched the Catholic vote with great care, and with the help first of Cartier, later of Adolphe Chapleau and Hector Langevin, he always retained, despite many rude shocks, a strong political base in Quebec. 'Cultivate the priests, but be ready to use them', was his watchword. It is important to note, however, that, in Raftis's phrase, 'if religion had to work through politics ... politics never became simply religion'.[4] In every province, as in the Federal Government, each major party had its share of Catholic adherents and deputies.

At the same time, the odour of venality which surrounded the Macdonald system as well as some of the Liberal attempts to counteract it, led to more than one attempt to form a Catholic Centre party on the European model. Most notable of these projects was *'le Programme Catholique'*, the lay political expression of Ultramontanism, which gained considerable ground in Quebec during the early 1870s. The movement looked for its inspiration first to Bishop Bourget and later to his successor as ultramontane champion, Bishop Louis Laflèche of Trois-Rivières. Laflèche, however, was soon won away from the lure of a simple 'all French-Catholic' party, largely through the fear of a similar counter-movement in English Canada. One of the most notable by-products of the ultramontane versus moderate division within the French-Canadian Church during the late nineteenth century was the flow of petitions and delegations to the Holy See. The devotion of French-Canadian Catholicism to Rome was thus illustrated. But also demonstrated was a less mature aspect of the same religious atmosphere. Weary Vatican officials were quoted as observing that as many submissions and counter-submissions came from Quebec as from the rest of Catholicism combined. The tension within the French-Canadian community of *Castor* (ultramontane), *Bleu* (moderate Conservative) and *Rouge* (Liberal), was illustrated in the dispute surrounding the division of Bishop Laflèche's diocese in 1885. From the fervent but limited point of view of lay ultramontanes such as J. P. Tardivel of *La Vérité*, the greatest sorrow was that the Rome of Leo XIII seemed so ungrateful. Trois-Rivières was divided in seeming punishment of Laflèche; Elzéar Taschereau, archbishop of Quebec and leader of the moderate forces, was named Canada's first cardinal.

Despite this narrower side of the picture, there was much evidence of great Catholic vitality during the period. The steady extension of parishes

4. Raftis, *op. cit.*, 84.

and building of churches went on in both French and English Canada with little interruption. If some of these buildings, particularly in Quebec, reflected what could be called a *folie de grandeur,* [5] they none the less showed the great determination of a population often burdened with depression to maintain and spread their faith. Teaching orders of priests, brothers and sisters recruited progressively larger numbers, and the Western missions showed many examples of ingenuity and heroism. Most notable was the career of Oblate Father Albert Lacombe, who worked in the west from 1849 until his death in 1916. First sent directly to Fort Edmonton with the traders of the Hudson's Bay Company, Lacombe's parish soon became the huge Cree and Blackfoot territory between the Bow and Peace Rivers. All his life he promoted Indian training schools to ease the hard transition brought by the white civilisation. The year 1874 saw his completion of a remarkable Cree dictionary and grammar. On at least two occasions he almost single-handedly prevented what would have been serious trouble between Indian and white, particularly when he persuaded the majority of the tribes not to join the Northwest Rebellion of 1885. The large modern hotel in Edmonton which bears Lacombe's name gives witness to the universal recognition of his work.

In the Maritimes and in Ontario, pragmatic working arrangements set the tone between Church and State. Despite such voices as Bishop Cameron of Antigonish, Nova Scotia and Archbishop Cleary of Kingston, Ontario, who preferred the explicit struggle against Protestant forces, more significant in the long run were the moderate efforts of such men as Archbishops Lynch and Walsh of Toronto. Working with Liberal Premier Oliver Mowat and in the face of several sharp anti-separate school campaigns led by Provincial Conservative William Meredith, Lynch (1860-88) and Walsh (1889-98) achieved a compromise but workable solution for Ontario Catholic Schools. Notable too in the period was the work of Sir John Thompson, Nova Scotian convert from Methodism, brilliant Minister of Justice during Macdonald's later years, and Canada's first Roman Catholic Prime Minister (1892-4).

None the less, the all-too-recurring mood of Canada's first thirty years was one of pessimism. Despite a 'national policy' of protective tariffs, Pacific railway building and western settlement adopted in 1878, Canada as a nation did not blossom on anything like the scale of her giant neighbour to the south. Perhaps most indicative of all were the population statistics. The total of three and one half million in 1871 had increased, despite immigration, to only five and one third million by 1901. The percentage of Roman Catholics dropped from 42.9 to 41.7 during the same period. Particularly

5. M. Wade, *The French Canadians* (Toronto 1956), 288.

worrisome was the migration of French-Canadian Catholics to the textile mill towns of New England. *'Ils n'auront pas même un bedeau pour les entendre'*, one clerical observer gloomily painted the future for priests and politicians alike in Quebec.[6] Not a few Irish and German immigrants followed the same pattern, staying briefly in Ontario, then moving on to the American midwest.

During the period 1885-96, a series of incidents involving a combination of race and religion threatened to unnerve the country even further. The springboard was the hanging in 1885 of Louis Riel, French-Indian leader of the risings of 1869-70 in Manitoba and 1885 in the north-west. Part hero and part religious fanatic, Riel in death became the focus of Canada's latent French-English and Catholic-Protestant hatreds. With economic depression sharpening journalistic tongues and political elbows, the Riel episode was followed by an Ontario Protestant uproar over the settlement of the Jesuit estates in Quebec, particularly because the Premier of Quebec, Honoré Mercier, had invited Pope Leo XIII to arbitrate the case. Most protracted and potentially disruptive of all was the Manitoba schools question, which involved a six year struggle to reverse, by either court or Federal Government action, an 1890 provincial law which had removed Catholic school privileges in Manitoba. The campaign was unsuccessful, but, in the struggle, the Catholic hierarchy was drawn dangerously close to identification with the Federal Conservative Party, which in turn was crumbling after the deaths of Macdonald and Thompson. It should be noted that, during these controversies, English-speaking Canadian Catholics usually sided with their French co-religionists, generally moderating extreme tendencies and at least qualifying the simple identification of race and religion.

THE TWENTIETH CENTURY AND MATURITY

Ironically, the most significant outcome of these late nineteenth-century politico-religious crises, particularly of the schools controversy, was the coming to power, not a little in opposition to the stand taken by the hierarchy, of the brightest ornament of Canada's first century, Wilfrid Laurier. Laurier's Catholic faith was never an unruffled one, and his religious practice was at times irregular enough to leave him vulnerable to attack. Yet several of his statements, particularly when faced with a seeming contradiction between the demands of his Church and those of his country, have had a remarkable durability. In 1877, in the face of the threat posed by ultramontanes, lay and clerical, whose thinking was dominated by the *Syllabus of Errors*, Laurier set the tone for his career in a moderate but clear declaration of his political and economic liberalism as distinct from the

6. Archiepiscopal Archives of St Boniface, Manitoba, Abbé G. Dugas to Archbishop Taché, 21 April 1892.

European anti-religious variety. In 1896, sixty-four years before John F. Kennedy's historic statement to the Houston ministers, Laurier declared in Parliament that, despite the ecclesiastical pressure brought to bear upon him to support a remedial bill in the Manitoba schools controversy, he was obliged to oppose episcopal wishes. As an elected member and particularly as a leader of his party, Laurier declared, he could and would take his stand 'not upon grounds of Roman Catholicism, not upon grounds of Protestantism, but upon grounds which can appeal to the conscience of all men, irrespective of their particular faith, upon grounds which can be occupied by all men who love justice, freedom and toleration.'[7] In the wake of several bitter disappointments which marked his declining years, Laurier was later to insist that 'it was a mistake for a French Roman Catholic to take the leadership'.[8] Yet in his last important speech before his death in 1919, Laurier gave his young audience a theme which would be taken both as his motto and his epitaph: 'Faith is better than doubt and love is better than hate.'[9] It is significant to note that the Canadian political formula has worked best when strong men of the two founding races have formed the nucleus of the government at Ottawa. It may be equally significant that the three public figures most fondly remembered in English Canada have been moderate French Canadians. The careers of Prime Ministers Laurier (1896-1911) and Saint-Laurent (1949-57) and Governor-General Vanier (1959-67) perhaps suggest some inarticulate vision of what Canadians think they, at their best, might be.[10]

Laurier's approach to religion and to Church-State problems was far from acceptable to all Canadians. Some judged that, particularly as his administration went on, Laurier bowed too much to clerical desires. At the other end of the spectrum, many French Canadians felt that Laurier too often bent over backwards to placate English and Protestant feeling. Most influential in this latter group was Henri Bourassa, who began his career as a supporter of Laurier, clashed with his leader over the Boer War crisis, and over the years represented Laurier's most serious threat from within his own province. Fervent Catholic and brilliant orator, Bourassa in 1910 founded *Le Devoir*, Canada's most consistently incisive newspaper. But not far beneath Bourassa's surface, and easily magnified by more extreme and less able disciples, was the identification of race and creed. In the dispute over French language rights in Ontario schools which raged from 1912 until 1917, Bourassa's most publicised opponent was an Irish-Canadian bishop, Michael Francis Fallon of London. Like Bourassa, Fallon filled great halls

7. Wade, *op. cit.*, 436.
8. J. Schull, *Laurier: The First Canadian*, Toronto (New York 1965), 572.
9. Wade, *op. cit.*, 776.
10. D. How, 'The Canadians Who Might Be', Address, 17 June 1963.

with his oratory, but both tended to narrow the controversy and to inflict more wounds than they were able to heal. During the school rights and conscription crisis of the First World War, Bourassa and his followers nearly united French Canada and nearly tore Canada apart. Once again, it was Laurier's prestige and moderation, ably paralleled by the diplomacy of Archbishop Neil McNeil of Toronto, which was the major factor in preventing a more serious explosion.

All disputes notwithstanding, the Laurier era, propelled by a western wheat and settlement boom, initiated a twentieth century which the Liberal Prime Minister was bold enough to predict would be Canada's century. Although once again the dream outran the reality, the twentieth century has witnessed Canada's rapid development from a semi-colony to a full fledged nation, and, with it, many signs of maturity within the Canadian Catholic Church. In 1899, Archbishop Falconio became Canada's first apostolic delegate, and, in 1908, Canada, like the United States, was removed from the jurisdiction of the Congregation for the Propagation of the Faith. In 1909, the first plenary council of Quebec was held, and meetings of archbishops and bishops increased both in frequency and formality during the 1920s and 1930s. In 1943, the Canadian Catholic Conference, the national association of the bishops of Canada, was established in Ottawa. The bilingual character of the country and of the Canadian Church is reflected in the composition of the departments and offices of the C.C.C. At its centenary in 1967, Canada had one hundred and two archbishops and bishops, serving seventeen archdioceses of the Latin Rite plus the Ukrainian archeparchy of Winnipeg, forty-six Latin dioceses, plus three Ukrainian eparchies. Eight Canadians have been raised to the cardinalate, Taschereau, Bégin, Rouleau, Villeneuve and the incumbent Cardinal Roy at the Primatial See of Quebec, McGuigan at Toronto, Léger at Montreal, and Flahiff at Winnipeg. Canada's population statistics continue to be revealing. Although heavy immigration from Britain reduced the proportion of Roman Catholics in Canada to 38.7 per cent of the total in 1921, by 1971 the proportion had risen to 46.2 per cent, plus approximately 1 per cent of Ukrainian Catholics. By the centenary, Canada had over nine million Catholics in her total population of twenty millions, with about three-fifths of the total Catholic population being of French extraction. The rural-urban division of the Catholic population reflected almost precisely the rural-urban division of the total, that is, approximately 30 per cent rural, 70 per cent urban in 1961, 24 per cent rural, 76 per cent urban in 1971. Slightly over half of the native Indian and Eskimo population of 260,000 have declared themselves as Roman Catholics. Beyond the two basic cultures, the most cohesive and identifiable ethnic group in Canada has been the Ukrainian, strongly supported by the religious dimension, both Orthodox and Catholic.

Since the Second World War, large Roman Catholic groups from Italy and Holland in particular have contributed to the diversity of the picture.

Canadian Catholic missionary efforts have continued to grow in the twentieth century. The huge frontier areas of the North-west have remained largely under the care of the Oblate Fathers. The success of Bishop O'Grady of Prince Rupert in persuading a continuing stream of young people to join his 'frontier apostles' in the rugged interior of British Columbia has been a particular achievement. In foreign mission fields, 1967 statistics showed 4,886 priests, brothers, sisters and lay people at work in developing countries. During the 1960s, Canadian-Catholic missionaries in Latin America alone increased by over 900. French Canada has continued to supply the largest number; from English Canada the work of the Scarboro Foreign Mission Society has been particularly varied and inventive, promoting co-operative economic programmes to accompany spiritual aid. Notable too, especially in the healing of domestic divisions during both world wars and in peace time, has been the work of the military vicariate and the Service chaplains. It is not insignificant to note the transition from the Quebec conscription riots of 1918 to the appointment in 1966 of General Jean Allard as the first commander-in-chief of Canada's unified armed forces.

Although subject to constant re-evaluation and criticism, Catholic educational efforts have continued to attract a great share of energy, talent and money. Elementary, secondary and university-level schools have grown in size and number, with at least as much lay as clerical involvement. In higher education a wide variety of approach has been the distinguishing feature. The degree-granting Catholic university or college is no longer the dominant form; a typically Canadian attempt to have the best of two worlds has set the pattern. St Michael's College, along with colleges of other faiths at the University of Toronto, was the prototype of the Catholic college within the large secular university. Interesting variations on the theme of federation and affiliation have sprung up across Canada. Several Canadian universities, formerly under exclusive clerical control, have moved quickly to become, in effect, provincial universities with varying degrees of denominational character. The universities of Windsor, Ottawa and Laurentian in Ontario, and, in different contexts, Montreal, Laval and Sherbrooke in Quebec, Moncton in New Brunswick, St Mary's in Nova Scotia, and Notre Dame in British Columbia, have been examples of this trend. A wide range of teaching orders of men and women, as well as diocesan clergy, have been deeply involved. In English Canada, the early experimental approach of the Basilian Fathers was symbolised by Henry Carr (d. 1963), who, over a long career, left more lasting and varied imprints on the Canadian Catholic world of higher learning than any other individual. Despite a general Catholic gap in intellectual contribution similar to that in the United States, the Basilian context also provided Canada with one contribution of particular excellence, the Pontifical Institute of Medieval Studies in Toronto. Founded in 1929, the quality of the institute's endeavours has been witnessed by the work of Maritain, Gilson, Gerald Phelan, Anton Pegis, and George Flahiff, later superior-general of the Basilians and cardinal archbishop of Winnipeg. Although his teaching career has been centred largely in Rome, Jesuit Father Bernard Lonergan has come closer than any other Canadian Catholic to founding a distinct school of thought.

Possibly the most international contribution of Canadian Catholic higher education has been made by St Francis Xavier University in Antigonish, Nova Scotia. With such watchwords of Fathers J. J. Tompkins and M. M. Coady as 'Ideas have hands and feet ... men can read and think and learn new ways so long as they live', and 'There is no Catholic way to catch fish', the Antigonish idea of combining adult education with co-operative economic efforts developed its roots in the 1920s. The movement's expansion during the deep depression of the 1930s as well as its impact in developing countries, have proved its durability and adaptability.

If the Antigonish movement made a deep impression on an essentially rural or primary production context, the efforts of the Canadian Catholic Church have not been as effective in meeting the challenge of industrialisation and urbanisation. Despite individual efforts, Canada has had nothing approaching the social consciousness of the labour schools in some American Catholic colleges, and, within the Canadian context, has had no one of the stature of J. S. Woodsworth, great Methodist pioneer in Canadian social reform and its political application. Efforts of Catholic charitable organisations to relieve suffering during the depression were remarkable, but official Church reaction to State-sponsored welfare schemes and particularly to the socialisation programmes of the new Co-operative Commonwealth Federation Party, was generally negative. The response of French-Canadian Catholicism to industrialisation exhibited two tendencies, in some ways contradictory. On the one hand, there was the romantic attachment to the somewhat Jansenistic 'soil and religion' tradition idealised by Louis Hémon's *Maria Chapdelaine*. With this went the suspicion of the urbanisation trend and of organised labour, early symbolised by the condemnation of the Knights of Labor by the otherwise liberal Cardinal Taschereau in the 1880s. On the other hand, there was the Quebec church's practical adjustment to economic and social change, clearly documented by W. F. Ryan, [11] and the recognition of economic factors combined with a strong racial appeal characteristic of the dominant school of Abbé Lionel Groulx in the

11. W. F. Ryan, *The Clergy and Economic Growth in Quebec, 1896-1914*, Quebec 1966.

1920s and 30s. The phenomenon of Maurice Duplessis exhibited the most regrettable aspects of the transition. Coming to power in 1936 Duplessis, with the exception of the war years, was Premier of Quebec until his death in 1959. He leaned heavily on a kind of populist nationalism which both encouraged and was supported by the most narrow and paternalistic elements within the French-Canadian Church. The bitterness surrounding the strike against the Johns-Manville Company at Asbestos in 1949 was a by-product of this reactionary alliance. Quite evident in the strong anti-clerical thrust of the Quebec separatist movement of the 1960s and early 1970s was a reaction against elements in the clergy accused of being a new generation of 'les vendus'.

Many forms of Catholic youth organisation had their beginnings in the inter-war years, although later survival often demanded new methods and new names. Despite difficulties of stringent format and the problem of adaptation from European origins, the Jeunesse Ouvrière Chrétienne and its variations for student, family and rural milieux were established in many areas and contributed several outstanding Canadian leaders. In Western Canada, the Confraternity of Christian Doctrine programme has been most consistent in attracting concerned Catholics. Not unexpectedly, pastoral work at the university has seen the greatest range of experiments and changes. The movement under the patronage of Cardinal Newman has rapidly shifted from a somewhat defensive 'safety island' approach to a wide spectrum of flexible associations. As in other countries, the impact of the folk idiom in liturgy for young people has been remarkable. The rapid building up of service-orientated groups such as the non-denominational Canadian University Service Overseas (C.U.S.O.) has reflected a felt student need to reduce church divisions and barriers.

As with the Church throughout the world after the Second Vatican Council, ecumenical efforts of the Canadian Catholic Church have been varied, sometimes exciting. Canadian Protestantism had, as early as 1925, prepared the way for thinking and acting on unity by the uniquely Canadian experiment of joining the majority of Presbyterians, Methodists and Congregationalists into the United Church of Canada. Despite many obstacles, the United Church and Anglican Church of Canada have in the late 1960s and early 1970s pushed forward a plan for unification. Canada's centennial year was the occasion of the markedly ecumenical International Congress of Theology in Toronto, the most important of its kind after Vatican II. The Christian Pavilion at Montreal's Expo 67 was a stark, and for some a disturbing, symbol of abdication both of triumphalism and sectarianism.

A SECOND CENTURY BEGINS

What kind of Catholic Church faces Canada's second century? With all its variety, it retains many of the best elements of the conservatism and liberalism of the Canadian experience. At the same time it is a Canadian Church which has failed, like the remainder of the country, to find a satisfactory solution to the claims of the native Indian and Eskimo population. It is a Church, particularly in French Canada, which has built more striking and costly examples of modern churches than any comparable area in the world, but where the apprehensions of 'Frère Untel' about a religion too ethnic and too dominated by fear, has already seen some of those churches nearly empty.[12] It is a Church whose record remains quite uneven in achieving co-operation and solidarity between French and English clergy and laity. It is a Church which has not yet persuaded the government or itself to give more than one half of one per cent of the gross national product to aid developing nations. It is a Church which, like other areas in the world, faces the phenomenon of a sharp decline in religious vocations. Compared to the United States, there has not been the same degree of economic commitment and generosity. Paradoxically, however, there continues to be a willingness to experiment, perhaps because the Church in English-speaking Canada has been less embroiled in the entrails of ecclesiastical structure, or because, in French Canada, it recognises signs of a revolutionary situation. The absence of a doctrinaire wall between Church and State has contributed to a greater flexibility than in the United States' experience.

In summary, voices from the past can hardly be called dominant in the contemporary Canadian Church. Canadian bishops at Vatican II were, despite pockets of reaction at the outset, notably more flexible than the majority of their American brothers. In the 1970s, the Labour Day statements of the Canadian Catholic Conference have focused directly on questions of social justice. Cardinal Léger's dramatic choice to conclude his years as an African missionary has been a cleansing shock, the culmination of a career which has run the gamut from conservatism to radical openness to change. Other remarkable figures reveal variety and hope. The vast person of Romeo Maione, for three years international president of the J.O.C., lent a strangely gentle toughness as chairman of the lay advisory board to the synod of bishops meeting in Rome, 1967. Sister Maura of the St Joseph Sisters of Toronto was among the first winners of the medal of the Order of Canada, and Sister Catherine Wallace of Mount St Vincent University in Halifax, was the first woman president of the Association of Universities and Colleges of Canada. Bishop F. J. Klein of Saskatoon, first son of the

12. J. P. Desbiens (Frère Pierre Jérome), *Les Insolences du Frère Untel*, Montreal 1960.

Prairie West raised to the episcopate, in 1964 deliberately tithed his some thirty diocesan priests and allowed his chancellor, the rector of his junior seminary and the pastor of one of his chief parishes to go to the Brazil missions. Baroness Catherine de Hueck Doherty, always faintly suspect for a disturbing insistence on taking the gospel at face value, has carried on an important work of intense lay apostolate training and has never failed to pass the test of compassion and charity. Bishop G.E. Carter of London in 1966 convoked Catholic Canada's first post-Vatican II diocesan synod, involving a majority of lay participants. The 1973 nomination of Bishop Remi de Roo of Victoria as chairman of the British Columbia Human Rights Commission was an unprecedented step.The voice of Father Georges Henri Levesque of Laval University, later rector of the University of Rwanda, has had a profound impact on the roots of Quebec's 'Quiet Revolution', particularly in his appeal to French-Canadian Catholics to rise above defensive parochialism and political corruption. Claude Ryan, following the tradition of Bourassa through André Laurendeau at *Le Devoir*, has maintained an insistence on an intensely French but acutely critical approach. Karl Stern, like Baroness de Hueck and theologian Gregory Baum a direct European contribution to the Canadian scene, has added profoundly to the literature of psychiatry and religious quest. Marshall McLuhan has continued to uncover new and unexamined facets of the exploding society. Pierre Trudeau's accession to the Prime Ministership early in 1968 brought to centre stage an intellectual flair and an appeal to youth hitherto often absent from Canadian public life. Adding to the unique contribution to Canadian life given by his parents, Jean Vanier's combination of gentle spirituality and work with the mentally retarded has become a new sign of hope.

Along with the need to redefine itself against its giant American neighbour, Canada's most pressing second-century challenge continues to be its French-English character. The 'October Crisis' of 1970, although precipitated by small extremist groups, revealed and widened racial and political gaps between Quebec and the rest of Canada. The Canadian Roman Catholic Church, lay and clerical, remains, for better or worse, very much at the centre of the tension. It is possible that, whatever the political outcome of the Canada-Quebec question, the Canadian segment of the Universal Church may solve its 'peculiar' problem by insisting that there are more important problems, and that lessons learned in domestic trial may be Canada's particular contribution to the world.

14

THE U.S.A.

OBVIOUSLY, not all of the varied aspects of the American Catholic story since 1850 can be told within the compass of a single essay of this length; but for the reader who wishes to pursue the subject further, the accompanying bibliographical note and the literature cited in the footnotes will offer guidance. To every student of American history the year 1850 suggests above all else the compromise resolutions of Henry Clay introduced into Congress in January and enacted into law in September, by which it was hoped that the deepening crisis over domestic slavery might be indefinitely postponed, if not finally resolved. Every other aspect of national life was subordinate to this central question, and the Catholics were just as divided as their fellow Americans of other and of no religious faith. The same notable differences existed between those Catholics who lived in the South and kept slaves and their coreligionists in the North who reflected the predominant views of their neighbours in rejecting the institution of human slavery. In other words, it was the touchstone by which at the time a man was judged by his peers whether in public or in private life, and that judgment continued to be made with mounting tension and ill feeling as Americans came to realise that the compromise of 1850 had merely granted a brief interval before the dread decision would have to be made as to whether the nation would remain one or surrender its unity amid the growing demand for secession voiced by many southerners as the sole solution to the problem.

The writer wishes to thank certain friends who generously gave of their time for a critical reading of this essay, or assisted by a careful preparation of the manuscript in Xerox copies. To the following he will always be grateful: the Reverends Raymond G. Decker, School of Law, Loyola-Marymount University, Los Angeles, California; Godfrey Diekmann, O.S.B., Saint John's University, Collegeville, Minnesota; John Whitney Evans, College of Saint Scholastica, Duluth, Minnesota; Roland E. Murphy, O. Carm., Divinity School, Duke University, Durham, North Carolina; Mrs James C. Purcell, San Francisco, California; and Mr Walter J. Schoendorf, San Jose, California.

Before tracing the role of the Church in the Civil War, however, it would be well to present an over-all view of the United States in 1850, with special attention to the Catholics. The white population that year was 19,553,068, not counting the Negro slaves who numbered between 3,000,000 and 4,000,000, with the vast majority of Americans earning their livelihood through agriculture. True, the pace of industrial expansion was quickening and tremendous stretches of uninhabited land were being gradually occupied as the network of canals and railroads – in the construction of which thousands of Catholic immigrant families were employed – steadily bound distant regions closer to the centres of population and brought the West into the mainstream of national life. Yet only in the closing decade of the century would the nation's predominantly rural character give way to an urban civilisation as the United States passed from an agricultural country to the world's leading industrial power. In 1850 the Catholic population was estimated at 1,606,000, which represented an increase of nearly 1,000,000 since 1840, with 700,000 of those being immigrants from fourteen European countries as well as from Canada and Mexico.

By the mid-century it was clear, therefore, that the destiny of the Catholic Church lay with the immigrants, not with that little band of about 35,000 native Catholics who, sixty years before, at the time of the episcopal ordination of the first American bishop, John Carroll (1790), had been centred mainly in Maryland, Pennsylvania, and Kentucky. Of the newcomers the Irish were easily in the lead, there being a net Catholic immigration from Ireland between 1820 and 1850 of 710,791, with the German States second in contributing 151,904, and France third with 64,603. The Irish, of course, had an advantage by reason of speaking English and, too, of having early gained a commanding position within the Church by reason of so many of Irish birth or extraction being appointed to the hierarchy, a situation that would provoke an explosion from the German Catholics in the 1890s. For example, of the thirty-two bishops who attended the First Plenary Council of Baltimore in May 1852, the countries of birth were: United States, nine; France, eight; Ireland, eight; Belgium, two; Canada, two; and one each from Austria, Spain, and Switzerland.

Given the United States' thoroughly Protestant inheritance from the English colonies of the seventeenth and eighteenth centuries, it was not surprising that the growth of Catholicism, and that mainly through immigration, should have inspired two organised campaigns against the Church before the Civil War. The historic bias against Catholicism that had been implanted in American minds from the earliest colonial settlements of the English and that remained a latent factor, now rose to the surface. The advent of the first was signalled by the appearance of *The Protestant*, a weekly newspaper that had begun publication in New York in January 1830, with several Protestant ministers as editors, whose avowed policy was to check the advance of 'Romanism' and 'foreignism'. The Nativists, as they came to be called, later organised politically and reached their peak in the 1840s, but they were succeeded early in the next decade by a secret group, the Know-Nothings, who took on a more menacing aspect by their success in politics. Both groups did widespread damage to the Church by poisoning the minds of countless Americans, doing extensive physical damage to Catholic ecclesiastical properties, and even taking the lives of several dozen Catholics in riots provoked in the cities of the East and Middle West. But the distraction of the slave controversy dissipated the intensity of the anti-Catholic movement, and by 1860 a relative quiet had ensued that would not again be broken by formally organised opposition to the Church until the birth in 1887 of the American Protective Association, familiarly known as the A.P.A.

Meanwhile the Church continued to grow and expand in spite of the opposition, a fact that was demonstrated in July 1850, when the Holy See created three new ecclesiastical provinces with their metropolitan sees in Cincinnati, New Orleans, and New York, in addition to Baltimore (1808), Oregon City (1846), and Saint Louis (1847). This increased the provinces to six, embracing a total of twenty-one suffragan dioceses, from the single Province of Baltimore that had covered the entire country up to 1846. Until the mid-century and beyond, most of the canonical legislation governing the Church had been enacted in the seven provincial councils held in Baltimore between 1829 and 1849 and in the three plenary councils that met there between 1852 and 1884. At the time of several of these gatherings the Nativists were engaged in severe provocation of the Catholics, but the bishops showed remarkable restraint. For example, in the pastoral letter that was addressed to the clergy and laity at the close of the First Plenary Council in May 1852, the bishops exhorted them to show their attachment to their country by their prompt compliance with its laws. 'Thus will you refute the idle babbling of foolish men,' they said, 'and will best approve yourselves worthy of the privileges which you enjoy, and overcome, by the sure test of practical patriotism, all the prejudices which a misapprehension of your principles but too often produces.'[1] Only rarely did the hierarchy's formal statements depart from this type of reaction to hostility toward the Church, a procedure that probably netted more gains than would otherwise have been true.

By the time of the First Plenary Council the tensions which divided

---

1. Hugh J. Nolan, ed., *Pastoral Letters of the American Hierarchy, 1792-1970* (Huntington, Indiana: Our Sunday Visitor, Inc. 1971), 140. The most notable exception to this approach was the pastoral letter that closed the Third Provincial Council of Baltimore, dated 22 April 1837, which protested strongly against the anti-Catholic bigotry (*Ibid.*, 60-9).

Americans over slavery were already foreshadowing the civil conflict that would break in 1861. As has been mentioned, Catholics were as divided as any other group of Americans. There was nothing approaching equality of numbers and resources, however, between the Catholic community of the South and that of the North since, with the exception of New Orleans and its environs, the immigrants had for the most part avoided the South in the realisation that the likelihood of their finding jobs there was much less, due to the black slaves. Yet Louisiana, as well as the border States of Maryland and Kentucky, had many Catholic plantation owners whose attitude toward the South's 'peculiar institution' was not discernible from that of their non-Catholic neighbours, just as the attitude of their bishops and priests was for the most part that of the Protestant clergy of the region. The situation was not improved by the failure of those in authority in the Church to go much beyond lamenting slavery's existence, counselling Catholic masters to be kind to their slaves and to see that they received religious instruction, and attempting to establish Catholic schools for freed blacks which had to be closed because of local prejudice. The official position of the American Church was in general that of the leading theologian of the period, Francis Patrick Kenrick, Bishop of Philadelphia, whose *Theologia Moralis* (1841) regretted that persons should be enslaved amid 'the present fulness of liberty in which all glory', and that laws should be passed to prohibit their education and in some instances to restrict their exercise of religion. 'Nevertheless,' said Kenrick, 'since such is the state of things, nothing should be attempted against the laws nor anything be done or said that would make them bear their yoke unwillingly.'[2]

A decade or more before the Civil War several of the leading Protestant churches had split regionally on the slave issue, but the structural unity of the American Catholics was never in jeopardy, even if most northern members of the Church differed basically from their southern brethren on the subject. When, for example, the Ninth Provincial Council of Baltimore assembled in May 1858, with bishops from both North and South, their pastoral letter noted the absence in the ranks of agitation about slavery, and there was a note of pride in their aloofness when the bishops said: 'Our clergy have wisely abstained from all interference with the judgment of the faithful, which should be free on all questions of polity and social order, within the limits of the doctrine and Law of Christ.' [3]And two weeks after the fighting had begun at Fort Sumter in April 1861, the pastoral letter closing the Third Provincial Council of Cincinnati — again with representatives

---

2. Latest edition (Baltimore 1861), I, 166.
3. Quoted in Robert Joseph Murphy, 'The Catholic Church in the United States during the Civil War Period, 1852-1866', *Records of the American Catholic Historical Society of Philadelphia*, XXXIX (December 1928), 296.

from both North and South – declared that while the bishops felt a 'deep and abiding interest' in all that pertained to the country's welfare, 'they do not think it their province to enter into the political arena'. [4]

Individually, however, there were bishops who spoke out strongly, as was true of John Hughes, archbishop of New York, who defended the Lincoln government. On the other hand, Patrick N. Lynch, bishop of Charleston, championed the right of secession and the policies of the Confederacy. Once the war was under way, numerous Catholics were found in both armies with priests serving as chaplains on both sides, and with nearly 800 sisters from more than twenty religious communities performing feats of charity and courage as volunteer nurses to the wounded of the North and South. Since most of the actual fighting took place on southern soil, it was to be expected that the Church's losses in the form of dead, wounded, and ruined buildings would be far heavier in the dioceses of the South than was the case in the North. Inevitably the conflict caused grave tensions within the Catholic community, a fact recorded by Francis Patrick Kenrick, by that time archbishop of Baltimore, when he confided to a friend the predominantly Confederate sympathies of most of his flock and added, 'I do not interfere, although from my heart I wish that secession had never been thought of. . .' [5] Two years later the man destined to succeed Kenrick at Baltimore, Martin J. Spalding, bishop of Louisville, wrote a detailed report on the war for Cardinal Alessandro Barnabò, Prefect of Propaganda, in which he showed his own pronounced Confederate sympathies. He begged the cardinal not to disclose the authorship of the report, for, he said, 'if ever it came to be known here that I had written it it could cause me trouble on the part of the government'. [6] At the end of the war the damages to the Church in the South were enormous, and even seven years after the peace the bishop of Saint Augustine, Augustin Verot, S.S., was not exaggerating when he appealed for help in a circular letter and said: [7]

4. *Ibid.*, 303.
5. Kenrick to Eliza Allen Starr, [Baltimore], 5 August 1861, James J. McGovern, ed, *The Life and Letters of Eliza Allen Starr* (Chicago: Lakeside Press 1905), 148.
6. Spalding to Barnabò, Louisville, 4 August 1863. This document was edited by Thomas [David] Spalding, C.F.X., 'Martin John Spalding's "Dissertation on the American Civil War" ', *Catholic Historical Review*, LII (April 1966), 66-85. On the archbishop's full career, see the same author's *Martin John Spalding, American Churchman* (Washington: The Catholic University of America Press. Consortium Press 1973).
7. *Catholic Mirror* (Baltimore), 25 May 1872, p. 4. In June 1867, Patrick N. Lynch, bishop of Charleston, had reported the well-nigh universal destruction of ecclesiastical properties in his see city and throughout his vast diocese [States of South and North Carolina, 83,700 square miles] where, he said, ruins and suffering were everywhere evident; he added that there were *c.* 750,000 emancipated slaves living within the diocese of whom at most 20,000 were Catholics. Lynch to the Society for the Propagation of the Faith, Charleston, 17 June 1867, *Annales de l'Association de la Propagation de la Foi* (Paris: l'Oèuvre de la Propagation de la Foi 1868), XL, 80-90.

The Diocese of St Augustine ... is very poor, the poorest indeed of all the devastated regions of the South; money cannot be found there even to keep in repair the few churches that exist, much less for the new churches that ought to be built for the accommodation not only of the Catholic whites, but also of the coloured people...

In spite of the deep sectional differences that had divided Catholics over slavery, secession, and the Civil War, their basic spiritual unity was demonstrated in October 1866, when the forty-five bishops of the United States assembled in Baltimore for their Second Plenary Council. The variety of national backgrounds of the prelates was once again reflected in the fourteen who had been born in the United States, eleven in Ireland, ten in France, three in Canada, three in Spain, and one each in Austria, Belgium, Germany, and Switzerland. Martin Spalding, who had succeeded to the premier See of Baltimore in 1864, was named apostolic delegate by Pope Pius IX, and he carefully prepared for the gathering in advance. All of his plans did not carry, however, as, for example, his dream of a university for the American Catholics, about which he consulted a number of his fellow bishops more than a year before the Council, as well as his hope of a vigorous effort to win the emancipated slaves to Catholicism. Regarding the latter he told John McCloskey, archbishop of New York: 'Four millions of these unfortunates are thrown on our Charity, and they silently but eloquently appeal to us for help. It is a golden opportunity for reaping a harvest of souls which neglected may not return.'[8] Although nine decrees relating to the black apostolate were enacted, actually little came of them, and the 'golden opportunity' passed with most of the blacks either establishing their own separate Protestant churches or worshipping with the whites. In all 534 decrees were passed that covered every important aspect of Catholic life, a number being a repetition of the legislation enacted at the plenary council held fourteen years before. In this category were the formalising of ecclesiastical government in diocesan chanceries with the duties of each official delineated, a stronger exhortation to build Catholic schools to obviate the necessity of sending children to the public schools, the customary decrees on seminaries, and a plea for support of the Catholic newspapers at a time when, as the bishops said in their pastoral letter, 'the power of the press is one of the most striking features of modern society...' [9]

For some years after the Civil War the United States still remained a predominantly agricultural nation, but industrialisation was gaining ground rapidly and, as has been mentioned, by the end of the century it was the

8. Archives of the Archdiocese of New York, McCloskey Papers, Spalding to McCloskey, Baltimore, 9 October 1865.
9. Nolan, *op. cit.*, 152-3.

world's leading industrial power. This transformation created grave problems for the Church and constituted one of the key factors that made the last two decades of the nineteenth century the stormiest period in the history of American Catholicism. In this same post-war period the American labour movement took its rise, and the Church inevitably became involved with thousands of Catholic men, both native born and immigrant, finding a living for their families as unskilled labourers in the expanding factories, mines, and related occupations. It was but natural that these men should join the burgeoning labour organisations to protect their rights against the abuses practised by so many factory owners and operators. In the ensuing conflict between capital and labour secret societies of workmen emerged, their contention being that they were forced to operate in secrecy lest the managers destroy their organisations.

It was a situation of this kind that accounted for groups such as the so-called Molly Maguires who appeared in the coal mining regions of north-eastern Pennsylvania in the 1860s. They were unquestionably struggling against real abuses from their employers, but the methods they used could not be condoned. That some had on occasion been guilty of murder and arson there was no doubt, and in the end twenty miners were executed — ten on a single day in June 1877 — and most of these were of Irish Catholic background. With huge numbers of her own members engaged in what a recent historian has called 'these head-on clashes of nineteenth-century Darwinian individualism', a crisis was created for the Church. In the course of it she was criticised for her pragmatism and ambivalence but, as the same historian has remarked, 'the tight rope which had to be walked by the Church makes such judgments oversimplified and one-sided'. [10]

Meanwhile immigration continued to mount with a shift from northern and western Europe to the southern and eastern regions of the continent. That fact was reflected in the countries from which the heaviest immigration came between 1870 and 1900. In the estimated 3,079,000 Catholic immigrants who entered the United States during those thirty years, the following six countries had furnished the largest numbers:

Germany	680,000	Austria-Hungary	412,230
Italy	547,000	Canada	343,500
Ireland	520,000	Poland	294,000

The changing complexion of Catholic immigration was even more striking for the first decade of the twentieth century when the four countries that contributed more than 100,000 immigrants were:

10. Wayne G. Broehl, Jr, *The Molly Maguires* (Cambridge: Harvard University Press 1964), 362.

Italy	802,000
Poland	608,400
Austria-Hungary	553,000
Mexico	120,000

Simultaneously the urban character of Catholicism was being impressed more than ever as the overwhelming majority of the new immigrants flocked into the growing industrial cities where they could normally find quick employment. The ultimate result of this trend was demonstrated in the location of the American Catholics as from 1 January 1872, in three ecclesiastical provinces – one each in the East, the Middle West, and the Far West. The density of Catholic population in the urban areas showed clearly in the figures for the metropolitan sees as contrasted with those of their respective suffragan dioceses. For example, the archdiocese of Boston, confined to five counties of Massachusetts with a total of 2,465 square miles, had 1,893,050 Catholics. This was in contrast to Boston's six suffragan sees which embraced the States of Maine, Massachusetts outside Boston's jurisdiction, New Hampshire, and Vermont, which combined had 57,028 square miles with 1,706,569 Catholics. In the Middle West the archdiocese of Chicago had 2,496,300 Catholics living within 1,411 square miles, while its five suffragan sees of Belleville, Joliet, Peoria, Rockford, and Springfield, all in Illinois and totalling 54,425 square miles, had a combined Catholic population of only 1,070,600. On the Pacific Coast the archdiocese of Los Angeles covered four counties (9,508 square miles) and numbered 1,984,429 Catholics, and the total Catholic population of its three suffragan sees, Fresno, Monterey, and San Diego, was 924,316 spread over 79,593 square miles.

The tremendous numbers and varied national backgrounds of the immigrants, speaking languages strange to American ears, confronted the Church with a baffling array of problems which the bishops tried to resolve in the Third Plenary Council held at Baltimore in November-December 1884. Much of the Church's future development was, indeed, chartered through the council's 320 decrees in such matters as a method for judging secret societies, making parochial schools mandatory for all parishes that were able to have them, laying the foundations for a national university, and establishing detailed regulations to govern religious worship, seminary training, and the lives of the clergy in the ministry. Yet the bishops were not able to anticipate and forestall all the crises induced among their people by the new industrial order. The judgment over the Knights of Labor, the first sizeable American labour organisation, was a case in point, and it divided the hierarchy, with some feeling that the Knights were a secret society that should come under the ban of the Church, while others thought they were a legitimate framework within which the labouring man might seek the vindication of his rights against oppressive employers.

Fortunately, in the end prudence and a sparing use of ecclesiastical authority prevailed, a point that was made by Cardinal James Gibbons at the height of the controversy when he told William Henry Elder, archbishop of Cincinnati, 'A masterly inactivity and a vigilant eye on their proceedings is perhaps the best thing to be done in the present junction.' [11] It was the forceful memorial of Gibbons presented to Cardinal Giovanni Simeoni, Prefect of the Congregation de Propaganda Fide, in February 1887, that prevented the Knights' condemnation in the United States. The cardinal admitted the risks that Catholic working men ran in their association with communists, atheists, and the numerous other types which the mixed character of American society made inevitable. But this did not disturb him unduly for, as he told Simeoni: 'It is one of the trials of faith which our brave American Catholics are accustomed to meet almost daily, and which they know how to disregard with good sense and firmness.' [12]

What did concern Cardinal Gibbons and the friends who helped him in the drawing up of the memorial, bishops John Ireland of Saint Paul and John J. Keane of Richmond, was the threat that a condemnation posed for working-class loyalty to the Church, for it was upon that class that Catholic strength in the United States was principally based. 'To lose the heart of the people', Gibbons had declared, 'would be a misfortune for which the friendship of the few rich and powerful would be no compensation.' [13] That the memorial accomplished its purpose was evident when a historian of the American Federation of Labor, successor to the Knights, spoke of the Church's influence in labour circles a generation after the crisis. He remarked on the presence of the large Catholic membership in the Federation, and he stated that it 'helped to account for the moderate political philosophy and policies of the AF of L for socialism's weakness in the AF of L, and, therefore, for the absence of a labour party in the United States'. [14]

In the same category of social questions that touched the Church in the 1880s was the case of Father Edward McGlynn, pastor of Saint Stephen's Church, New York City, at the time the largest parish in the country. McGlynn, an ardent disciple of Henry George, founder of the single tax

11. Gibbons to Elder, Baltimore, 6 May 1886, John Tracy Ellis, *The Life of James Cardinal Gibbons, Archbishop of Baltimore, 1834-1921* (Milwaukee: Bruce Publishing Company 1952), I, 495.
12. 'The Question of the "Knights of Labor" ', Henry J. Browne, *The Catholic Church and the Knights of Labor* (Washington: the Catholic University of America Press 1949), 370. This is the best critical edition of the memorial carried as an appendix here (365-78).
13. *Ibid.*, 374.
14. Marc Karson, *American Labor Unions and Politics, 1900-1918* (Carbondale, Illinois: Southern Illinois University Press 1958), 284.

movement, became convinced that the evils of industrial society could find a remedy in George's theories about the single tax on land. His superior, Michael A. Corrigan, archbishop of New York, on the other hand, believed that George was endangering the right of private property. From a dispute between the priest and his archbishop the controversy widened to include the principle of ecclesiastical discipline, sides were taken, and there ensued one of the most heated controversies in the American Church, with the lower middle classes in general sympathetic to McGlynn. The archbishop's suspension of the latter from his pastorate was followed by Rome's excommunication in July 1887, when he refused to obey a summons to appear there to explain his teaching on land. Thus the quarrel continued for five years with the widest publicity, and only in December 1892, was a settlement reached when Archbishop Francesco Satolli, who was in the United States at the time as papal ablegate, stated that McGlynn's theories were not contrary to *Rerum novarum*, the encyclical that Pope Leo XIII had published on the condition of the working classes the previous year. In this instance also Cardinal Gibbons had exercised a restraining influence in counselling the Prefect of Propaganda in a lengthy communication of February 1887, not to place the works of Henry George on the Index as Archbishop Corrigan and other conservative churchmen had desired. [15]

While controversies like those over the Knights of Labor and McGlynn's involvement in the single tax movement brought serious division within the Catholic community, the differences over education in these same years were, perhaps, even more widespread and lasting. The principal difficulties pertained to a university for the American Catholics and to parochial or elementary schools, both of which had been the subject of legislation at the plenary council in 1884. As for the university, it owed its life, so to speak, to John Lancaster Spalding, bishop of Peoria. For years he had not only spoken and written repeatedly on the need for such an institution in the American Church, but he had secured the promise from a wealthy friend to give $300,000 toward the beginning of a university. But the bishops in general were not enthusiastic, most of them knowing little about a university and less about its need and how to go about founding one. Moreover, the active role played by John Ireland in the proceedings served to alienate Catholics of German birth or extraction by reason of his rather strident Americanising efforts. The Jesuits were not friendly lest it encroach upon their domain. Likewise sectional rivalries added to the mischief by plaguing the enterprise in its first stages. The result was that the five years between the close of the council and the opening in November 1889 of the Catholic

15. There is no scholarly treatment of the McGlynn case. The popular work of Stephen Bell, *Rebel, Priest and Prophet. A Biography of Dr Edward McGlynn* (New York: Devin-Adair Company 1937) is a journalistic account highly biased in McGlynn's favour.

University of America – a name suggested by Archbishop Ireland – were marked by real differences between the bishops and their respective followers with only token support from many quarters. Through the early years of its existence the institution was hardly more than an advanced seminary with courses exclusively for clerics, and only following the First World War did it take on the proportions of a university, having meanwhile weathered the doctrinal storms of Americanism and modernism, both of which had an impeding effect on its progress as a centre of learning. [16] Like most other American colleges and universities, in the years after the Second World War it witnessed an expansion in buildings and students, the pace of which began to slacken only in the early 1970s. The present enrolment is approximately 6,800 students. During the 1960s several serious infractions of academic freedom received nationwide publicity which injured the university's reputation, for instance the rector's banning as lecturers in February 1963 four distinguished theologians, all *periti* of the Second Vatican Council and the trustees' dismissal in April 1967 of Charles E. Curran, well-known moral theologian, without a hearing, an action which occasioned a strike of faculties and students which brought the university to a standstill for several days and resulted in the trustees' reversal of their previous decision.

In a sense the university may be said to have been a problem without a history for the Catholics of the United States, but that could not be said of their elementary schools. Ever since the heavy Catholic immigration began in the 1830s, with the accompanying hostility of groups like the Nativists who were quick to make an outcry at any suggestion of financial assistance to the Catholic schools from public funds, the Catholics had known a 'school question'. Repeated attempts had been made to reach an understanding with public school authorities but, except for a few places like Poughkeepsie, New York, and Savannah, Georgia, these efforts had not only failed to win financial aid for the parochial schools, but they also frequently failed to prevent the use of the Protestant Bible, hymns, etc. in public schools attended by Catholic children. The result was that the bishops began

16. Among the works on the university, see John Tracy Ellis, *The Formative Years of the Catholic University of America* (Washington: American Catholic Historical Association 1946), Patrick H. Ahern, *The Catholic University of America, 1887-1896. The Rectorship of John J. Keane* (Washington: The Catholic University of America Press 1948), Peter E. Hogan, S.S.J., *The Catholic University of America, 1896-1903, The Rectorship of Thomas J. Conaty* (Washington: The Catholic University of America Press 1949), Colman J. Barry, O.S.B., *The Catholic University of America, 1903-1909. The Rectorship of Denis J. O'Connell* (Washington: The Catholic University of America Press 1950), and Roy J. Deferrari, *Memoirs of the Catholic University of America, 1918-1960* (Boston: Saint Paul Editions 1962). The years 1909-35 which covered the administrations of Thomas J. Shahan and James H. Ryan, were treated in two unpublished doctoral dissertations, both completed in 1972, by Blase Dixon, T.O.R., and H. Warren Willis respectively.

to urge their priests and people more and more strenuously to build their own schools, a policy that became practically mandatory in the legislation of the plenary council of 1884.

Needless to say, this policy imposed a heavy burden on the lower middle classes who composed the majority of the Catholic community, especially when at the same time they were compelled to pay taxes for the support of public schools to which in conscience they felt they could not send their children. With this background in mind, Archbishop Ireland sought to make a fresh start to resolve the difficulty when he addressed the annual convention of the National Education Association in his see city in July 1890. Ireland proposed that the parochial schools should become a part of the public school system of their respective locality by being rented to the latter for $1.00 a year with the understanding that the public school authorities would pay the Catholic teachers' salaries (mostly sisters) and keep the school buildings in repair. In turn, the public school curriculum would be followed in the Catholic schools during the regular school hours and religious instruction would follow thereafter.

Viewed from the distance of over three-quarters of a century the Ireland proposals seem reasonable and justified. But given the archbishop's flamboyant personality which so readily aroused hostility, the ringing phrases of his address in praise of the public school, the suspicions of the American Protective Association, organised only three years before for the express purpose of stopping the advance of the Catholic Church in the tradition of the Nativists and Know-Nothings, and the fact that Ireland had already drawn the enmity of conservative Catholics for his insistence on Americanising the immigrant and for his decidedly progressive views on many public questions, it was inevitable that his address to the N.E.A. should occasion an explosion.

The reaction was not long in coming, and by the autumn of 1890 the archbishop of Saint Paul was being attacked from outside the Church by the A.P.A. and others who charged him with trying to steal the public school by indirection, and from within the Church by Archbishop Corrigan of New York, the bishops of German background, and the Jesuits, all of whom held him guilty of selling the parochial school in defiance of the conciliar decrees of 1884. So bitter did the controversy become that the Holy See made inquiry about it, and although Cardinal Gibbons and others came vigorously to the defence of Ireland, Leo XIII at length took the matter into his own hands, appointed a commission of cardinals to investigate the dispute, and thus the question was removed from the immediate combatants. The decision came in April 1892, when it was made known that the system Ireland had proposed, and which he had instituted in several of the parishes of his archdiocese, was not in contravention of the legislation of the Third

Plenary Council. In other words, *tolerari potest*. In the aftermath a great deal of bitterness continued to be felt and expressed on both sides, but in the practical order the experiment of the parochial schools becoming part of the public-school systems in the two parishes of the archdiocese of Saint Paul was for a variety of reasons abandoned, and by the middle of the 1890s a relative calm had again descended on the embattled forces that had fought so furiously over the question. [17]

Unlike other controverted questions of the late nineteenth century, however, that of the schools received no permanent solution or settlement. The expansion of the Catholic school system continued almost without a break into the 1960s. Around the middle of that decade, however, a marked change appeared. The trend can best be seen in the contrasting figures for the five-year span between 1 January 1967 and 1 January 1972, as shown in the following summary:

	1 January 1967	1 January 1972
Elementary schools	10,927	9,258
Students	4,369,845	3,111,635
High schools	2,341	1,815
Students	1,103,761	961,996
Students under Catholic religious instruction in released time programmes in the public schools	5,044,826	5,579,060
Full-time teachers in Catholic schools:		
Sisters	103,582	70,664
Lay teachers	82,838	104,236

These figures tell their own story about the Church's elementary and high schools in the United States since 1967. The closing of 1,642 elementary schools and 526 high schools in five years with 1,258,210 fewer students in the former and 141,765 fewer students in the latter, a trend that at the present writing shows no notable sign of lessening, is in no way matched by the increase of 534,234 Catholic students who were receiving religious instruction in the public schools' released time programmes. And the loss between 1967 and 1972 of 32,918 full-time teaching sisters obviously increased the financial costs of the Catholic elementary and high schools in view of the 21,398 more full-time lay teachers added during the same period to whom higher salaries had to be paid. As a consequence pastors became more and more inclined to question the necessity of parochial schools. In 1964 a

17. The most informative work on the subject is still Daniel F. Reilly, O.P., *The School Controversy, 1891-1893* (Washington: The Catholic University of America Press 1943).

laywoman, Mary Perkins Ryan, set off a lively debate by her book, *Are Parochial Schools the Answer? Catholic Education in the Light of the Council*,[18] a debate that still greatly preoccupies many Catholics. Professional groups such as the National Catholic Educational Association with a membership of over 15,000 embarked on elaborate studies of all aspects of the schools in an effort to formulate realistic policies to meet the new situation and to chart the course that should be pursued in the years ahead. How successful they will be remains, of course, to be seen.

Through each of these internal conflicts of the American Church a constant factor has been the differing national backgrounds of those who composed the Catholic community. Although the peak year of Irish immigration had been reached as far back as 1851, by virtue of their familiarity with the language of the country and their general adaptability and talents for ruling, the Irish had early gained a commanding position in the Church which they continued to hold. Thus long before the year of highest German Catholic immigration (1882), to say nothing of that of the Italians (1907) and the Poles (1921), the Irish had been in control of the majority of dioceses, and especially of the most populous and prosperous ones. Of the seventy-two bishops in attendance at the Third Plenary Council in 1884, for example forty were of Irish birth or extraction. In contrast, by the turn of the century, the Catholics of German birth or background were represented by only eleven bishops in a hierarchy of ninety or approximately one-eighth of the total.

The Irish had, indeed, far outdistanced all other nationalities in the net Catholic immigration for the half-century between 1820 and 1870 with 1,683,791, during which time the Germans had sent 606,791 Catholic immigrants. But in the years after the Civil War the situation was reversed, there being 520,000 Irish between 1870 and the end of the century, a span of years that brought an estimated 680,000 Catholic Germans with 412,230 from the Austro-Hungarian Empire, as well as 547,000 Italians and 294,000 Poles. Yet in spite of these new elements in the Catholic population the Irish ascendancy was maintained, and by the time the hierarchy reached its sesquicentenary in 1939, of the 462 bishops to date in the American Church ninety-four or nearly twenty per cent had been born in Ireland, while Germany and German-speaking countries like Austria and Switzerland accounted for forty, that is, less than ten per cent of the total number of bishops since 1789.

If emphasis has been given to the national backgrounds of the American bishops it is not due solely to the accurate data that are available at that level where such is lacking for priests, religious, and laity. It is because the

18. New York: Holt, Rinehart and Winston.

situation described above served to put a predominantly Irish stamp upon American Catholicism that has remained to the present time. Tension between the Irish and Germans was discernible at an early date in some parts of the Church as, for example, in the archdiocese of Saint Louis, where the policy of perpetuating succursal churches for the German Catholics during the administration of the Irish-born archbishop Peter Richard Kenrick (1841-93) in neighbourhoods where the recognised local head of the Catholic community was the pastor of the nearby 'Irish' church, was naturally resented. It was a somewhat ironic circumstance in view of the fact that, wherever the Germans had been allowed a free rein, they had acquired a reputation for more complete and better organised parishes than the Irish. This was an observation made by others besides Canon Peter Benoit of the English Saint Joseph's Society for black missions who visited the United States in 1875. During his stay in Baltimore he commented in his diary: [19]

> The Germans have three churches in Baltimore. They have adopted the voluntary system and have flourishing congregations. No one individual gives much. But all give. Their schools are flourishing. Their children are brought up piously... The Archbp [James Roosevelt Bayley, a convert] told us that the Germans surpass the Irish in their steady support in their Catholic establishments.

Inevitably charges of discrimination were sent back to the homeland and in 1883 Peter Paul Cahensly, Secretary of the Saint Raphael Society for the Care of German Catholic Immigrants, decided to investigate at first hand the state of the German immigrants *vis-à-vis* the Church in the United States. The suspicions aroused by Cahensly's tour of the country were confirmed three years later in the eyes of some when it was learned that a document containing charges of Irish domination and of neglect of the German Catholics had been submitted to the Holy See by Father Peter M. Abbelen, who had secured the signature of Michael Heiss, archbishop of Milwaukee. The Abbelen report occasioned several indignant replies, one from the archbishops of Baltimore, Boston, New York, and Philadelphia. Opposing groups of priests were organised, and the dissension within Catholic ranks was thus heightened just at a time when an extreme form of Americanism, lending support to theories of Nordic racial superiority, was on the rise in the United States. The founding in 1887 of the American Protective Association, of course, made the crisis all the more acute, since their ostensible purpose was the elimination of threats to the nation's security posed by

---

19. 'Hasty Notes of a Journey to America...', p. 30. The writer is grateful to Peter E. Hogan, S.S.J., Archivist of the Society of Saint Joseph, Baltimore, for a copy of the Benoît diary.

'foreigners', and especially by a 'foreign' institution like the Catholic Church.

Further provocation came from abroad when a Catholic congress at Liège, Belgium, in September 1890, heard a French Canadian pastor from Albany, New York, declare that indifference toward the immigrants had resulted in twenty million souls being lost to the American Church. Three months later a conference of directors of the European Catholic immigrant aid societies at Lucerne, Switzerland, drew up a document for Pope Leo XIII which maintained that ten millions had been lost to the faith in the United States. With publication of these sensational stories a storm broke on both sides of the Atlantic, and in July 1891 President Benjamin Harrison made anxious inquiries of Cardinal Gibbons at a chance meeting in Cape May, New Jersey.

Fortunately, however, in the end the extremists in neither camp prevailed. The Holy See refused to yield to the request for something akin to national blocs within the American hierarchy, nor on the other hand, did Rome support the policies of a few extreme Americanisers who would give scant respect to the old world languages and social customs among their immigrant coreligionists. Yet the problem was by no means solved, for just as there continued to be periodic friction between Germans and Irish, so from time to time protests were made by other immigrant groups against what they considered abuse or neglect experienced at the hands of bishops, priests, or fellow Catholics of other national strains. The Bohemians in the archdiocese of San Antonio, the French Canadians in the archdiocese of Boston and several of its suffragan sees, the Italians in the archdiocese of New York, the Hungarians in the diocese of Cleveland, and the Poles in the diocese of Scranton and in other dioceses – all were at one time or another disgruntled with their lot in the American Church.

In several cases this dissatisfaction resulted in schism. During the years 1876-8 Henry Sienkiewicz, the famous Polish writer, was in the United States, and he commented on the generally happy circumstances in which he had found the Polish Catholic communities where, he said, 'the main force. . .which maintains some degree of moral unity. . .is the Church and the Polish priests'.[20] But that condition did not always obtain, and by the 1890s there was serious dissension in certain parishes in Scranton, Buffalo, and Chicago between Polish pastors and bishops of Irish birth or background. A case in point was Father Francis Hodur, who differed from bishop William O'Hara of Scranton, was excommunicated in 1898, gradually gathered a following among fellow Poles in Scranton and other cities, and in 1907 had himself consecrated by the Old Catholic archbishop of Utrecht.

20. *Portrait of America. Letters of Henry Sienkiewicz*, tr. and ed. Charles Morley (New York: Columbia University Press 1959), 282.

Thus Bishop Hodur became the founder of the Polish National Catholic Church which in 1960 (most recent statistics available) numbered 282, 411 members served by 151 priests in 162 parishes located in six dioceses.

Another schism was caused by disagreements concerning liturgical rites, as well as ecclesiastical jurisdiction and customs, between a minority of the Ruthenian Rite Catholics and the Latin Rite bishops. From the time that these Ukrainian Catholics began to immigrate to the United States in large numbers in the 1870s there was trouble, nor did the appointment in 1907 of Soter Stephen Ortynsky, O.S.B.M., as their own ordinary and the establishment in May 1913 of an exarchy (diocese) separate from the jurisdiction of the Latin Rite bishops terminate the difficulties. Had there been a more sympathetic attitude towards those of other rites by the Latin hierarchy and clergy, the defections might have been greatly reduced, if not altogether prevented. But directives from the Holy See, while acknowledging their separate status, were influenced by the Latin Rite ordinaries, as was true of the decree *Cum data fuerit* of March 1929, which held to the previous prohibition of married men being ordained and of priests administering the sacrament of confirmation, both of which were allowed to the Ruthenians in Europe. In consequence, a number of Ruthenian priests left the Church in the United States and one of their number, Orestes Chornyack, received episcopal ordination and started the American Carpatho-Russian Orthodox Greek Catholic Church which by 1972 counted 104,600 members with sixty-four ordained clergymen serving in sixty-seven churches.

Yet the ultimate picture among the eastern rite Catholics was by no means entirely a negative one, as the 444,896 Ruthenian Rite Catholics of 1 January 1974, served by eight bishops and 501 priests in 406 parishes, spread through two provinces comprising six ecclesiastical jurisdictions, made evident. Moreover, in January 1966 an independent exarchate was established for both the Maronites and the Melkites, each with its own bishop, the former having 65,541 lay members in forty-three parishes with fifty-eight priests in the exarchate, and the latter having forty-one priests ministering to 21,676 souls in twenty-five parishes and three missions.

Although the American Church remains probably the most varied in its national strains of all the branches of the Universal Church, in leadership it likewise remains in good measure an 'Irish' Church. The fact that in 1974 nine of the eleven American cardinals were of Irish birth or extraction, and that four of the six prelates elected by the National Conference of Catholic bishops as delegates or alternates to the synod of bishops of September 1974, were of the same national background, should make that clear. In the main those of Irish birth and ancestry have ruled well over their coreligionists of other ethnic strains, although those of German descent — and that especially in the Middle West — have in general been in advance of them in progressive movements like the liturgy, the social apostolate, and encouragement of lay participation in the framing and execution of the Church's policies.

In some ways the Irish, however, have left a stamp on the Catholic community that it were better had not been there. For example, the 'clerical' Catholicism noted by many foreign visitors up to a decade ago had sprung principally from a people among whom the word of the bishop and of the priest was law. It was the same source that gave rise to a kind of Jansenistic attitude toward sex, as well as constant demands for money from the pulpit, both subjects of frequent comment by visitors from abroad. And related to this 'clerical' Catholicism in the eyes of many have been the luxurious residences of many of the bishops and priests, with an accompanying life style that has in recent years drawn increasingly sharp criticism from the Catholic laity. It is not meant to suggest that these features of Catholic life have been associated exclusively with those of Irish birth and ancestry; but it is scarcely open to denial that as the Catholics moved in mounting numbers into the so-called affluent society, it was those of Irish heritage who set the pattern and led the way.

As in all major aspects of the Catholic life of any country, however, the picture in this regard has been a mixed one. No American ordinary of Irish birth or descent, for example, ever excelled the Renaissance magnificence of Cardinal George Mundelein, archbishop of Chicago (1915-39), nor, on the other hand, was Cardinal Francis Spellman, a man entirely of Irish background and the subject of adverse comment on a number of counts, ever severely criticised for extravagant living during his twenty-eight years as archbishop of New York. Speaking solely of the region beyond the Rocky Mountains known as the Far West, a good example was set in this matter in Los Angeles, where the pretentious episcopal residence in Fremont Place was given up some years ago and where the present cardinal archbishop resides in the rectory attached to Saint Vibiana's Cathedral in a downtown neighbourhood. The same could be said of the increasing number of bishops in the last decade who have taken modest dwellings such as the archbishop of Hartford and the bishops of Boise, Helena, Juneau, Santa Rosa, and Spokane, to name only a few. In contrast to these bishops living mostly in the Far West, however, the same region witnessed since the Second Vatican Council conspicuous residences acquired by the former archbishop of Portland and the bishops of Monterey and Oakland that have been targets for pointed criticism. The same is true of the older residence of San Francisco's archbishop in one of the city's most fashionable neighbourhoods, and still more so of the hillside mansion purchased and enlarged by the first ordinary of the new (1962) diocese of Santa Rosa.

While the problem of conflicting nationalities was eased by the passage of the immigration act of May 1924, which drastically reduced the numbers admitted from most European lands, it afforded hardly more than a prolonged breathing spell for the Church. In the era of the Second World War immigration from Latin America mounted, especially from Mexico, and simultaneously Puerto Ricans and Filippinos migrated by the thousands from their heavily populated island homes to cities like New York, Chicago, San Francisco, and Los Angeles. True, most of these people from countries once ruled by Spain had been baptised as Catholics, but normally they had little religious instruction and were, therefore, in need of a good deal of time and attention. The presence of so many Mexicans in the south-west and California, and of Puerto Ricans and Filippinos there and elsewhere, meant the Church could not relax, and even as late as the 1960s, with the government's more liberal policy toward immigration from Europe, Catholic churchmen continued to experience some of the anxieties of their predecessors of a century before, even if not in so acute a form. It has been estimated that the Spanish-speaking may constitute as high as one-fourth of the Catholics of the United States. Recognition of this fact was seen in the appointment of several bishops of Spanish background in recent years, the most striking being that of a pastor of Albuquerque, New Mexico, Robert F. Sanchez, who in June 1974 was named tenth archbishop of Santa Fe. All things considered, the 'Church of the immigrant', as she was frequently described, substantially accomplished her mission, and the service rendered the Republic was well expressed by one historian who stated: [21]

> It might, indeed, be maintained that the Catholic Church was, during this period, one of the most effective of all agencies for democracy and Americanisation. Representing as it did a vast cross-section of the American people, it could ignore class, section, and race; peculiarly the Church of the newcomers, of those who all too often were regarded as aliens, it could give them not only spiritual refuge but social security.

The service rendered by the Church in this regard would today be seriously discounted by the proponents of the new vogue of cultural and ethnic pluralism, among whom certain Catholic writers have been the most articulate. Several generations removed from the events described above, their point has validity for the enrichment afforded by the immigrants' varied cultural heritage. But in the period when the immigration movement was at its peak, it is difficult to see how the Church's leaders could have done anything but promote the programme of Americanisation that they espoused.

21. Henry Steele Commager, *The American Mind. An Interpretation of American Thought and Character since the 1880's* (New Haven: Yale University Press 1950), 193.

It was this very process of Americanisation as practised by some Catholic leaders in the United States, however, that brought a new type of trouble as the nineteenth century came to a close. No people can escape from the effects of their environment, any more than they can escape from their past. Granted that the marked hostility of groups like the A.P.A.s, the Ku Klux Klan of the 1920s, and Protestants and Other Americans United for Separation of Church and State (P.O.A.U.) of the years after its founding in 1947, was calculated to keep Catholics locked within their religious and ethnic ghettos where often they had little or no contact with other Americans, none the less, they were surrounded by the national ethos and it left its mark upon them. As Catholics rose in the social order with their notably improved financial status, that mark became all the more conspicuous, for example, in the findings of the federally financed National Fertility Study of 1970 which showed that Catholic married couples had reduced dramatically the number of children they were having and intended to have. In the language of the demographers who directed the study: 'Catholics are becoming more and more like other parents in their use of the pill and other contraceptive devices.' [22]

The same phenomenon was noticeable in many other ways, not the least in the relative lack of speculation and theorising among the Catholics of the United States. Like their fellow citizens of other faiths, their genius lay in the practical order, for example, in their ability to organise and discipline the vast mass of humanity that found its way to American shores in the years after the Civil War, and at a later period, in the Catholics' relief services during and after both World Wars, which made a major contribution through the various agencies sponsored officially or indirectly by the National Catholic Welfare Conference. In this shying away from the theoretical, they were reflecting the pattern of most other Americans who admired practical achievement but who had little time for the arts of speculation. In this sense there was truth in the witticism that 'in the Old World an ordinary mortal on seeing a professor tipped his hat while in America he tapped his head'. [23]

One of the most pervasive elements in the national ethos was that represented by the expression 'the American way of life'. Again like other Americans, most Catholics became enamoured of that philosophy which – aside from its religious overtones – until recent years was not distinguished for the premium that it put on things of the mind. Given the Catholics' impoverished and often illiterate immigrant background, plus their ever-pressing necessity of earning a livelihood, and above all, perhaps, the uncritical system of education in which they had been reared that left little

22. *San Francisco Chronicle*, 30 May 1972, p. 4.
23. Merle Curti, 'Intellectuals and Other People', *American Historical Review*, LX (January 1955), 259.

scope for freedom of thought, it was understandable that they should have arrived at almost the halfway mark of the twentieth century before they began to bestir themselves in a really serious manner and to make some belated impact in the learned and artistic life of their country.

Yet somewhat ironically, in spite of this intellectual sterility and impoverishment, of the failure to produce a proportionate number of scholars and scholarly works, as the nineteenth century closed, the Catholics became the centre of a storm in theological circles that had reverberations in both the old world and the new. The trouble took its rise in the eagerness with which the more progressive American churchmen espoused their national way of life, with sincere conviction to be sure, but also with the hope that they might induce their immigrant flocks to cast off their old world ways, accept the thought and customs of their adopted country, and thus rid their coreligionists of the charge of 'foreignism' so frequently hurled by Americans who suspected and disliked the Church of Rome. The Catholic Church's undeniable progress in the United States naturally attracted attention abroad, and in no single group was it more enthusiastically reflected than among the *ralliès*, the progressive and articulate minority of French Catholics who had espoused Leo XIII's policy of rallying the Catholics of France to their republican government. This was mortally offensive, however, to the majority of Catholic monarchists who were not disposed to be converted to republicanism by those who had visited the United States and returned home believing that it was along American lines that there lay the most promising future for the Church of France. Among the enthusiasts for American ways was Paul Bourget, the novelist and literary critic who, only a week after his arrival in New York in 1893, commented on how well known the liveliness of American Catholicism was in Europe. 'What is the secret of this vitality?' he asked. 'At present I can only grasp the too apparent contrast between our own churches and this one.' [24]

To conservative European Catholics there was more to Catholicism in the United States than its 'vitality'. The informed among them were aware of the steady diluting of Christian dogmas that had taken place in American Protestantism, a trend that, as early as 1854, had caused the Swiss-born Protestant scholar, Philip Schaff, who became the ranking Protestant church historian of the United States, to tell a Berlin audience concerning the American religious tendency: 'It expands more in breadth than in depth ... It wants the substratum of a profound and spiritual theology.' [25] When, therefore, they read the statements of Catholic progressives like

24. *Outre-Mer: Impressions of America* (New York: Charles Scribner 1896), 23.
25. *America. A Sketch of Its Political, Social and Religious Character*. A reprint with an introduction by Perry G. E. Miller (Cambridge: Belknap Press of Harvard University Press 1961), 95.

Archbishop Ireland, Bishop Keane, Father Isaac Hecker, founder of the Paulists *et al.*, these Europeans grew suspicious that the laudable motive of the so-called Americanists to have Catholics adapt themselves to the national way of life in social and political matters, might also contain the germ of a dangerous religious adaptation.

It was into that kind of atmosphere that there came in 1897 the French translation of an uncritical and hastily written biography of Hecker by Walter Elliott, an ardently admiring confrère, with a glowing introduction by Archbishop Ireland. Moreover, the book carried a preface by the Abbé Félix Klein of the Catholic Institute of Paris which one reviewer later said 'out-Heckers Hecker precisely in those points on which it were possible. . . for a critic bent on fault-finding to attach to his words a meaning of doubtful orthodoxy'.[26] The Hecker biography proved to be the herald of a controversy that became so furious that the archbishop of Paris forbade 'Americanism' to be mentioned in the pulpits of his archdiocese, and in the following year the pope appointed a commission of cardinals to investigate the dispute and report to him.

Meanwhile the fury of the debate continued through 1898 with a clear line of cleavage between those who supported what they believed to be the views of the Americanists and those who just as vigorously condemned them, each side having its own periodicals through which its opinions were expressed, to say nothing of the books that were published on the subject. It would be difficult for an impartial student, either then or now, to get a clear and unwavering idea of what constituted Americanism, so many variations were there among the contending forces. A summary of what the opponents of Americanism regarded as the heart of the matter was contained in Leo XIII's apostolic letter, *Testem benevolentiae*, of January 1899, which condemned the alleged teachings, a letter which, incidentally, Gibbons, Ireland and their friends had tried in vain to forestall. At the outset the pope was careful to state that the controversy had broken out over a translation of the life of Hecker. The general motive for the 'new opinions' was based, it was said, on the desire to have the Church adapt herself to modern civilisation so as the more easily to win those outside her fold. To accomplish this end it was opportune in the minds of the Americanists, said Leo, 'to pass over certain heads of doctrines, as if of lesser moment, or to so soften them that they may not have the same meaning which the Church has invariably held'.[27] The false ideas were as follows: (a) a rejection of all external spiritual guidance in the belief that the Holy Spirit supplied greater gifts to men now than in past ages; (b) extolling the natural virtues to the neglect of the super-

26. 'Father Hecker and His Critics', *The Tablet*, LXI (London, 18 March 1899), 403.
27. 'True and False Americanism in Religion', John J. Wynne, S.J., ed., *The Great Encyclical Letters of Pope Leo XIII* (New York: Benziger Brothers 1903), 442.

natural virtues; (c) furthering the active rather than the passive virtues; (d) minimising the value of the vows taken by members of religious congregations; (e) advocating the abandonment of the customary methods used to win converts and introducing new approaches into the apostolate. For reasons which he set forth in detail the pontiff said, 'We cannot approve the opinions which some comprise under the head of Americanism'. In conclusion he stated, however, that if by 'Americanism' there should be designated the laws and customs peculiar to the United States, as is true of every nation, 'there is surely no reason why We should deem that it ought to be discarded'.[28]

As was to be expected, the leaders of the opposing camps showed a marked difference in their reception of the apostolic letter. In the United States the so-called Americanists were indignant at the imputation of doctrinal errancy, as for example, Archbishop Ireland, who told Leo XIII that a wrong had been done to the Catholics of his country in designating 'by the word "Americanism", as certain ones have done, such errors and extravagances as these'.[29] A month later in a private letter to the pontiff Cardinal Gibbons declared that he deliberately called this doctrine 'extravagant and absurd', for it had 'nothing in common with the views, aspirations, doctrine and conduct of Americans'. He did not know a single bishop, priest, or member of the laity in the country who had 'ever uttered such enormities'.[30] The conservative leaders, on the contrary, were elated, and Archbishop Corrigan publicly thanked Leo XIII for saving the American Church from heresy, while the bishops of the Province of Milwaukee – probably with John Ireland in mind – expressed to the pope their 'pain and just indignation' that some had not hesitated to proclaim repeatedly 'in Jansenistic fashion' that there was hardly an American who had held these views and that the Holy See itself, 'deceived by false reports, had beaten the air and chased after a shadow...'[31]

That there was a distinct approach to the apostolate on the part of the progressive churchmen in the United States there was no doubt, and that they sought to have the Church make herself appear as up-to-date and appealing as possible to non-Catholic Americans, was equally true. In pursuance of this objective some of these men on occasion gave expression to views that jarred their conservative colleagues. None of them was a highly trained theologian, and their sometimes naive praise of their country and its institutions, their espousal, in other words, of the 'American way of life' in

28. *Ibid.,* 452.
29. The full text of Ireland's letter of 22 February 1899 to Leo XIII may be read in James H. Moynihan, *The Life of Archbishop John Ireland* (New York: Harper & Brothers 1953), 125-6.
30. Gibbons to Leo XIII (Baltimore 17 March 1899), copy, Ellis, *Gibbons*, II, 71.
31. *The Review* VI (Saint Louis 27 July 1899), 145.

its political and social context, impressed their critics as suggesting an American form of Gallicanism or, what was worse, support for philosophical liberalism. It was the kind of impression that prompted Bishop Bernard J. McQuaid of Rochester, for example to tell Cardinal Miecislaus Ledochowski on one occasion: 'Of late years, a spirit of false liberalism is springing up in our body under such leaders as Mgr Ireland and Mgr Keane, that, if not checked in time, will bring disaster on the Church.'[32] One need not employ much imagination to comprehend the effect of a remark like that on the Roman curia of the 1890s. But that these men ever entertained any idea or suggestion, as was true of the views of certain modernists that came to the surface soon thereafter, that only symbolic values were to be attached to basic dogmas like the Eucharist and Christ's resurrection, was simply not true. On the contrary, they would have heartily agreed with George Santayana in viewing modernism as suicide, as a mortal concession to the spirit of the world. As Santayana said: 'It concedes everything; for it concedes that everything in Christianity, as Christians hold it, is an illusion.'[33] Yet both in Europe and the United States there were those who saw Americanism principally as a prelude to modernism, and a considerable number of writers may still be found who maintain, in the words of Emmanuele Chiettini, O.F.M., writing in 1948, that in Americanism there was present 'in germ many errors which were later condemned by Pius X under the collective name of modernism'.[34]

As for modernism in the Catholic Church of the United States, as was true elsewhere, the spirit engendered by men like Monsignor Humberto Benigni and his *Sodalitium Pianum* in the years after the papal encyclical *Pascendi* of September 1907 was detrimental to scholarly effort in ecclesiastical circles. Thus the most learned journal of the American Church to date, the *New York Review*, was frightened out of existence in June 1908, by the action of the timid archbishop of New York, John Farley. Certain priests with a scholarly bent came under suspicion, for example, James F. Driscoll, rector of Saint Joseph's Seminary, New York, who was one of the editors of the *Review*, and who was suddenly removed from his post as rector in 1909 and appointed a pastor. Delation by a colleague at Saint Bernard's Seminary, Rochester, prevented Edward J. Hanna, professor of dogmatic theology, on two occasions from being appointed coadjutor with the right of succession, to Patrick W. Riordan, archbishop of San Francisco,

32. McQuaid to Ledochowski (Rochester February 1895), Frederick J. Zwierlein, *The Life and Letters of Bishop McQuaid* (Rochester: Art Print Shop 1927), III, 224.
33. *Winds of Doctrine* (New York: Charles Scribner's Sons 1913), 57.
34. 'Americanismo', *Enciclopedia Cattolica* I, col. 1056. In the same category was the statement of H. Daniel-Rops that the Americanism of men like Ireland and Hecker 'constituted a practical preface to modernism', 'Il y a cinquante ans, le modernisme', *Ecclesia, Lectures chrétiennes* No. 77 (Août 1955), 13.

at the latter's request, although five years later he was made auxiliary bishop. Francis E. Gigot, another editor of the *New York Review*, was likewise under some suspicion as a modernist, as was Joseph Bruneau, S.S., of Saint Mary's Seminary, Baltimore, and Cornelius C. Clifford of Immaculate Conception Seminary, South Orange, New Jersey, who was removed in 1909 and nominated to a pastorate. It was the same spirit that deprived Henry A. Poels, associate professor of Old Testament in the Catholic University of America, of his chair in April 1910, because he refused to subscribe to the Pontifical Biblical Commission's directive that Moses was the author of the Pentateuch.

None of these men was a modernist in the true sense, but it was not a time when a man could expect a fair hearing and an opportunity to answer charges made against him, and thus some remained under a cloud until their death. That was not the case with three other priests of the American Church, however, namely, William L. Sullivan, C.S.P., pastor of Saint Austin's Church, Austin, Texas, and chaplain at the University of Texas, John R. Slattery, S.S.J., one time Provincial of the Society of Saint Joseph, and the Irish-born Thomas J. Mulvey of the diocese of Brooklyn. Sullivan, Slattery, and Mulvey all acknowledged that they were modernists, abandoned their priesthood, married, and were never again reconciled to Catholicism.[35]

While movements of this kind were preoccupying those in the Church's intellectual centres, her American membership was mounting until by the opening of the new century it numbered 12,041,000 out of a total white population of 66,809,196. That the tide of Catholic immigration had in no way receded was evident from the fact that of the increase of 7,787,000 between 1900 and 1920 nearly fifty per cent, or 3,518,000, had entered through that channel. By 1908 the frontier which had played so significant a part in the development of the United States had some years previously disappeared, and the Church's fourteen ecclesiastical provinces containing seventy-six suffragan dioceses stretched across the entire continent. It was not surprising, therefore, that in June of that year the American Catholics should have been removed from the jurisdiction of the Congregation de Propaganda Fide and made a part of the Church's regular government.

The Holy See's action of 1908 was only an external sign, however, of the maturing process at work within American Catholicism, and the religious life of the people went on very much as before. The insistence of the bishops on the obligation of attendance at Mass on Sundays and certain holy days was obvious in the decrees of the plenary councils of 1866 and 1884, and in

---

35. There is no history of modernism among American Catholics. In John Ratté, *Three Modernists, Alfred Loisy, George Tyrrell, William L. Sullivan* (New York: Sheed and Ward 1967) one will find a lengthy chapter on Sullivan, the American ex-Paulist (259-336).

this regard the hierarchy achieved a good measure of success in fixing a tradition among the faithful that endured down to the mid-1960s. Since that time there has been a marked falling off in church attendance generally among Americans, and in reporting the results of a Gallup Poll released on 8 January 1972, the New York *Times* stated: [36]

> The decline in attendance in recent years has been most pronounced among Roman Catholics. In 1971, some 57 per cent attended church in a typical week, following a steady decline since 1964, when 71 per cent of Roman Catholics attended church on the average...

Until less than a decade ago, however, Catholics' church attendance in the United States remained remarkably high, and under the same conciliar title, 'De Cultu Divino', that made Mass attendance obligatory on Sundays and certain holy days, official warrant was given for the old world religious practices that the immigrants had brought with them such as the Forty Hours' Devotion. The latter had been introduced into the United States by the German Redemptorists who were familiar with it from their congregation's rule of 1764. As early as 1839 the Forty Hours was conducted at Saint Alphonsus Church, Peru, Ohio, and when Blessed John Neumann, C.SS.R., became bishop of Philadelphia, he was the first ordinary to introduce it on a diocesan scale (1853), a practice that soon spread throughout other dioceses.

Other features of the people's devotional life had similar European origins, for example, that centring around the Sacred Heart, the Rosary – to which the Irish were especially attached – and the week-long parish mission which was the nearest Catholic equivalent to the nineteenth-century revivals among American Protestants. The parish mission was gaining prominence in many lands at the time, as in England where in 1843 Father Luigi Gentili and his Italian confrères of the Institute of Charity had introduced the practice, as well as in Ireland where preachers, notably the famous pulpit orator, Thomas N. Burke, O.P., made the parish mission a memorable occasion. In similar fashion Francis X. Weninger, S.J., reached thousands of Catholics of German background in the approximately 800 missions that he preached in the United States after his arrival from Austria in 1848, and ten years later Father Isaac Hecker and his fellow converts of the newly founded Paulists launched a vigorous mission programme throughout the country with a particular effort directed towards interested non-Catholics.

Such in general were the religious practices of the American Catholics down to the eve of the Second Vatican Council. Of the Latin Mass, the

36. New York *Times* 9 January 1972, p. 59.

novenas, the parish missions, the weekly devotions to favourite patron saints usually closing with Benediction of the Blessed Sacrament, and the vespers on Sundays and solemn feast days, only the last had practically disappeared by the 1960s. The frequent reception of the sacraments which characterised the lives of most Catholics in the United States, supplemented by the external expressions of the people's piety mentioned above, were a far cry, indeed, from the vernacular Mass in which the faithful, led by a lay commentator in the sanctuary, actively participate in most parishes since the liturgical changes associated with the era of the Second Vatican Council. There could be little question about which approach ensured a more intelligent and meaningful assistance at the divine liturgy. Yet their lingered pockets of resistance within the Catholic community, even where the local bishop may have bestirred himself on behalf of the liturgical changes. In these parishes the Latin Mass was still offered on occasion, and many of the laity were seemingly content with not much more of an active role than that of over a century ago when the English convert architect, Augustus Welby Pugin, referred to the church pews in a not altogether inappropriate phrase as 'dozing pens'.

The Church of the United States had less reason, perhaps, than that of most nations for a lack of liturgical sensitivity since a flourishing liturgical movement had been launched at Saint John's Abbey in Collegeville, Minnesota, nearly forty years before the Second Vatican Council, though the American activity of the 1920s was in no sense new to the Universal Church as the movement at Solesmes and other centres would attest. Due to the extraordinary creativity and imaginative efforts of Virgil Michel, O.S.B., who in 1926 founded a monthly journal, *Orate Fratres* (since renamed *Worship*), and the vast literature produced by Saint John's Liturgical Press, to say nothing of the splendid pioneer work of Conception Abbey in Missouri, and of individual priests and laymen like Father Hans A. Reinhold, Monsignor Martin B. Hellriegel of Saint Louise, Godfrey Diekmann, O.S.B., Dom Michel's successor, Father Frederick R. McManus, and Mr John A. Manion, the solid foundations had been laid for a liturgical movement that made the transition to the post-conciliar changes much easier for American Catholics. It was a liturgical life such as the eighteenth-century native-born Catholics of Maryland, accustomed to their rigidity and starkness of the manor house worship, so closely akin to the 'Garden of the Soul' variety of their English coreligionists of the period, would scarcely have recognised.

The purpose of the liturgy, needless to say, whether it be that of pre- or post-Vatican II, is to enable the people of God to draw closer to the source of divine life and to help them remain there during their pilgrimage through this world. The American Church, as has been mentioned, had succeeded reasonably well up to the mid-1960s in retaining the majority of her members, but it would be patently false to pretend that she has not suffered severe losses. For more than a century periodic reports of the extent of the losses have circulated, such as that of John England, bishop of Charleston, who in 1836 informed the Society for the Propagation of the Faith, as well as Pope Gregory XVI, that between 1787 and 1835 there had been a loss of 3,750,000 Catholics in the United States. We have already noted the figures on leakage that came out of Liège and Lucerne in the early 1890s. In all these cases the description given by one student of the problem to England's report as 'a network of hazy and rash assumptions'[37] would apply, for they had no scientific value.

Yet losses there surely have been with certain population studies over the last quarter century, showing them to have been between twenty and forty per cent, depending on such factors as locality, ethnic origins, and social conditions. In 1962 the *Official Catholic Directory* gave a total of 42,876,665 Catholics, an increase of 12,451,650 or approximately forty per cent for the preceding decade, which seemed a satisfactory growth. During those ten years there had been 12,443,865 infant baptisms and 1,354,968 converts, a total of 13,798,833. But since the increase reported for the decade was only 12,451,650 the question arose: where were the other 1,347,183? The combined figure of converts for the years 1952-62 was, indeed, impressive, but any satisfaction that might have been derived from that number was quickly dissipated for those who took the trouble to note that the converts exceeded those lost to the Church by only 7,785. What made the situation more serious was that all Catholic population experts were agreed that the *Official Catholic Directory*'s figures were greatly below the true number of Catholics. For example, the *Directory* for the year 1940 reported 21,403,136 Catholics, but after a careful investigation of the data two sociologists concluded that it was safe to say that 'the 1940 Catholic population in the United States was about 30,000,000'.[38] Since there is no reason to believe that matters have radically changed since that time, the 48,465,438 reported for 1 January 1974 was probably below the actual number of Catholics then in the country, even allowing for the notable decline among practising Catholics in the years after 1966. It meant, therefore, that a great many more people had been involved in the leakage from the Church than the *Directory's* figures indicated.

Efforts to explain the losses sustained by the Church, either in the United States or elsewhere, are notoriously difficult for the historian. Certain ob-

37. Gerald Shaughnessy, S.M., *Has the Immigrant Kept the Faith?* (New York: Macmillan Company 1925), 230-1.
38. George A. Kelly and Thomas Coogan, 'What is Our Real Catholic Population?' *American Ecclesiastical Review* CX (May 1944), 377.

vious causes suggest themselves: mixed marriages, lack of priests and of churches in backward areas, immigrants who by reason of an ignorance of the English language drift away, material advantages to be gained on occasion from dissociating oneself from Catholicism, as with the late James F. Byrnes (d. 1972), Secretary of State in President Truman's cabinet, disputes with priests or bishops, lack of religious instruction – all these and more have played a part. More recently, however, it has been difficult to escape the impression that the defections have often found their root in the allurements of an affluent society where spiritual values are at a very low premium, a society into which hundreds, if not thousands, of Catholic families have moved in the last few decades. There has also been the factor of the Catholics constituting a minority in an overwhelmingly Protestant or agnostic population. In that connection the words of Father George Tavard, A.A., who has lived in the United States since 1952, have relevance. He stated:[39]

> An astonishing plurality of religious confessions exist side by side with a total indifference for everything that is religious. The Catholic American is thus situated at the centre of a multitude of influences more numerous and more antithetical than is found anywhere else in the world. He lives in the midst of a pluralism carried to the supreme degree of atomisation.

Still another factor that has played a part in the crisis of faith that has overtaken thousands of Catholics as well as Christians of other denominations is the revolution that became worldwide during the 1960s. Closely allied to it is the refusal to accept the Church's traditional teaching on any number of questions like birth control and divorce. It is impossible to determine how much the changed attitude of Catholics on these matters is due to a diminishing faith and how much to the fact that many of them have simply taken ultimate solutions into their own hands and decided the questions according to norms that are in agreement with their own conscience and the so-called 'new morality'. What is certain is that a far higher level of education has, in turn, brought a sophistication that makes the laity more critical of the Church and of the clergy, more prone to arrive independently at decisions of a doctrinal and moral character than would ever have been true of their grandparents. Most American Catholics could probably name one or more in the above categories from their personal acquaintance. Yet in the final analysis the cause of a person's loss of religious faith usually remains locked within his or her own conscience and never enters the realm of discernible phenomena with which the historian is ac-

39. *Les Catholiques Américains, Nouvelles Frontières* (Paris: Editions du Centurion 1966), 13.

customed to deal with amplitude and accuracy. Perhaps it was something of this kind that Herbert Butterfield had in mind when he remarked: 'We have only to consider our own internal life to realise how little of the inside of men ever reaches the outside world, and how little the world can make of what it sees.'[40]

To return to the aspects of Catholicism in the United States associated with its maturing process in the second half of the twentieth century, the religious orders and congregations are rightfully viewed as an important part of that story. Here the situation during the late 1960s and early 1970s contained both lights and shadows, with the latter often seeming to prevail. While the contemplative life still occupied an honoured place among Catholics, the unrest that was an accompaniment of the post-conciliar years had found its way into the cloister as well, and the wave of enthusiasm that had swept the land near the close of the Second World War had markedly receded. Thus the twelve Cistercian (Trappist) monasteries that had housed nearly 1,200 monks at the beginning of the decade – more than a fourth of the total number for the entire world – prompting the late Abbot General Gabriel Sortais, O.C.S.O. in April 1961 to speak so warmly of Americans as contemplatives,[41] had given way to a decline that by 1974 had reduced the number of Trappists in the country to 570. It represented a sort of purging process that some monks welcomed as beneficial to the order. Nor had the single house each of Carthusians and Hermits of Camoldoli remained untouched by the same trend. This recession had not been as noticeable among the women contemplatives where, for example, the twenty-four monasteries of Poor Clares of the Primitive Observance with their 468 professed nuns and the sixty-two monasteries of Discalced Carmelites with a total of 867 professed sisters, while less than they had known in the mid-1960s, would seem to have experienced less turmoil than their male counterparts.

In the period after 1850 most of the non-contemplative religious experienced for over a century a steady growth. Only in the late 1960s was this increase checked and a notable decline in numbers set in among virtually all orders and congregations by reason of many professed religious reverting

40. *Man on His Past. The Study of the History of Historical Scholarship* (Boston: Beacon Press 1960), 137.
41. Interview with Vincent T. Mallon, M.M., N.C.W.C. New Service Despatch, Lima, Peru, 8 April 1961. Abbot Gabriel attributed the numerous American vocations to the Trappists in part to the books of Thomas Merton [Father Louis, O.C.S.O.]. But he also stated that in his judgment Americans were basically a simple people in the sense that they were guileless and open, honest with themselves and straightforward with others, all of which provided a natural basis for simplicity in their approach to God; secondly, they were generous and gave without counting the cost, a primary requisite for monastic life. Finally, Americans were intuitive rather than logical in their intellectual processes; they were not as much interested in the mechanics of arriving at truth as in the arrival itself, and this on the spiritual level, thought the abbot, enabled the American to go directly to God.

to lay life and the failure of new vocations to replace them. The trend can be illustrated by the following data for certain representative religious groups, with the 1972 totals given immediately after in parentheses. Thus in 1967 the thirty-seven Benedictine abbeys and priories numbered 2,836 (2,574) monks engaged in every aspect of the apostolate, including preparatory schools for boys, seminaries for their own candidates as well as for those of the diocesan clergy, and likewise eleven colleges and one university. In the same year (1967) nearly one-fourth of the Society of Jesus's world membership of 36,038 were located in the ten American provinces where 8,483 (6,805) Jesuits participated in a highly varied apostolate with the largest number assigned to twenty-eight colleges and universities and fifty-seven (fifty-three) high schools. The favour which the religious had with the laity may to some degree be gauged by the fact that among the 1967 total of 59,892 (57,421) American priests, 23,021 (20,694) were religious. Moreover, twenty-six (twenty-five) different congregations of brothers totalling 12,539 (6,946) members played an important role in both the educational and charitable works of the Church, with the largest of these, the Brothers of the Christian Schools, having 2,434 (2,111) members in eight provinces who conducted eight (seven) colleges and 115 (88) high schools, along with other schools of various types.

One of the most widely publicised aspects of the post-conciliar age in the American Church related to the religious sisterhoods. From the time that the French Ursulines came to New Orleans in 1727 to open the first convent in what would later be the United States, the religious women performed an incalculable service for the American Catholic community. This was as true for the contemplatives, whose pioneer foundation of Discalced Carmelites from the Low Countries at Port Tobacco, Maryland in 1790 preceded by some years the establishment of the country's first native sisterhood for teaching and charitable works by the Blessed Elizabeth Seton, a convert from the Protestant Episcopal Church at Emmitsburg, Maryland, in July 1809. The sisters were responsible for staffing the thousands of elementary and secondary schools as well as for founding and operating hundreds of charitable institutions such as hospitals, orphanages, and homes for the aged and the poor. Occasionally their self-sacrificing labours were highlighted for all to see, as has been mentioned in connection with the nearly 800 sisters who nursed the wounded during the Civil War, a service that remained long in the memory of a grateful nation. Now and then public tribute was paid to the sisters by certain persons outside the Church, as was the case in May 1878, when the secretary of the Michigan Board of Charities told the members of the National Conference of Charities and Corrections at their annual meeting:

In all my observations of public charities, I have seen no such careful nursing, such sisterly, motherly, almost saintly ministrations to all the afflictions of poverty, wounds, insanity, and disease, whether in infancy or all intervening stages of life, to old age, that brings childhood again, as that tendered by the various sisterhoods of the Roman Catholic Church. [42]

The general spirit of change and renewal dating from the pontificate of John XXIII and the Second Vatican Council has had a profound effect on American convent life. In some instances the results have gone quite beyond the modernising of the rule and the altering of traditional garb or habit. A period of deep uncertainty ensued in the minds of thousands of sisters regarding the suitability of their way of life for the Church of the late twentieth century, with the consequence that large numbers sought dispensation from their vows so that they might channel their zeal through one of the newer lay institutes or simply return to lay life. Not all have gone as far as the Immaculate Heart of Mary Sisters whose original American foundation was made at Los Angeles in 1871 from their native Spain, and who have split into two separate groups, the one continuing as a canonical community under a moderately modified rule, the other having become a community embracing lay members.

One of the more recent native sisterhoods also underwent a radical transformation. The Home Mission Sisters of America (Glenmary Sisters), founded in 1952 to work in areas devoid of priests and churches and also in deprived neighbourhoods of urban centres, witnessed the departure in 1967 of fifty of the eighty-eight members to form a lay group called the Federation of Communities in Service, believing, it was said, that 'their goals of dedicated service can no longer be realised in the framework of a Catholic religious order'. [43] Yet even where the religious women's changes have not been as basic as in these congregations, the future is highly uncertain. The fact that in a single year, 1966-7, the American Church sustained a loss of 4,750 sisters with the total for the nation dropping from 181,421 to 176,671, a trend that the figures of 139,963 sisters for 1974 shows no indication of

---

42. Henry W. Lord, 'Dependent and Delinquent Children, with Special Reference to Girls', *Proceedings of the Fifth Annual (National) Conference of Charities (and Corrections), Cincinnati, May 21-23, 1878* (Boston: A. Williams & Company 1878), 171. Earlier that year, in the midst of a controversy over Saint Vincent's Hospital in Cleveland, Ohio, taking charity patients, the editor of the Cleveland *Herald* stated (5 January 1878): 'While it would be difficult to find a more earnest Protestant than the writer, yet we have no hesitation in saying that we believe no more devoted, self-sacrificing faithful women who spend their lives in charity and doing good can be found than the Sisters or nuns of the Catholic Church. . .the sisterhoods have, as a class, deserved and received the honour and respect of mankind. Paul J. Hallinan, 'The Life of Richard Gilmour, Second Bishop of Cleveland, 1824-1891', unpublished doctoral dissertation, Western Reserve University (1963), Chapter IX, 11.
43. *The Monitor* (San Francisco) 10 August 1967, 1.

lessening, would seem to demonstrate that further drastic alterations in the customary patterns of all aspects of Catholic life relating to the sisterhoods are inevitable. Granted that a variety of factors have accounted for the decline of Catholic schools, the closing of 1,721 elementary schools and 526 secondary schools between 1967 and 1972, not to mention the increase of lay teachers in the same five-year span by 21,398 to a total of 104,236, bore striking testimony to the adaptations rendered necessary in the Catholic educational system, in no small measure by reason of the serious loss of vocations among religious women.

Another characteristic commonly associated — at least until very recent years — with a mature Church is the contribution made in personnel, resources, and energy toward the spread of Christ's kingdom, whether that be in the foreign missions or in similar efforts at home. From the landing of the priests who accompanied Ponce de Léon's expedition along the west coast of Florida in 1521, the first known to have touched the soil of the future United States, until well into the present century, large portions of the American Church remained missionary territory. During what was preeminently her missionary period this Church was the beneficiary of countless numbers of missionaries from Europe — All Hallows College, Dublin, a missionary seminary, alone educated fourteen bishops and over 1,100 priests who served in the United States up to 1960 — while the missionary aid societies of Lyons and Paris, Vienna, and Munich contributed $7,970,840 in the century ending in 1922. In fact, were it not for the dedicated lives and generous benefactions that reached the United States from Europe and Latin America, the Catholic story of the nineteenth century would have been a far different one from what it was. Yet up to the last years of that century so little had been done by Americans to return their personal services and monetary resources to less favoured peoples, that the implied rebuke of Herbert Vaughan, bishop of Salford, England, on the occasion of the centenary of the American hierarchy in 1889, was not without warrant. In extending his congratulations to Cardinal Gibbons and his fellow bishops, Vaughan asked several rather pointed questions: [44]

Has not the time come for the American Church to take its share in the great Foreign Missionary work of the Church? Can you expect that the second century of your existence will be as blessed and magnificent in its religious history as your infancy has been, if you do not send forth your heroic missioners to bear the torch of faith into those dark regions which are now possessed by the enemy of man's salvation, and by over twelve hundred millions of pagans and unbelievers?

44. Vaughan to Gibbons, Mill Hill, 28 October 1889, *Catholic Historical Review*, XXX (October 1944), 292.

Generally speaking, Americans have been a generous people, and once the obligation to the foreign missions was systematically presented to them, they responded. The annual collections for the Society for the Propagation of the Faith rose steadily and by 1904 had passed the $100,000 mark. By 1919 they had reached a million dollars or more, and the last year that Bishop Fulton J. Sheen served as the society's national director (1966), the contributions were over sixteen millions.

Missionary personnel, however, were another matter and here the Americans were much slower. The earliest foreign mission undertaken from the United States was in Liberia (1842), but it met with disaster from yellow fever and inability to endure the climate. Forty years later two German-born Franciscan brothers, Fathers Remy and Athanasius Goette, left the United States for China, and in 1888 they were followed by the first American-born priest, Francis X. Engbring, O.F.M. But with the following exceptions, namely the single Marist in Japan, Father Nicholas Walter, Brother Joseph Dutton who in 1887 joined the famous Father Damien Deveuster at Molokai to care for the lepers, and the group of six Franciscan Sisters of Syracuse, New York, who reached Hawaii in November 1883 with the same objective as Dutton, no Americans had entered the foreign mission field at the time of Vaughan's letter of 1889.

The new century, however, witnessed a change. The predominantly German Society of the Divine Word in 1909 opened Saint Mary's Mission House at Techny, Illinois, near Chicago, the first Catholic training centre for the foreign missions in the United States. An even more important step grew out of the meeting the following year of Fathers James A. Walsh and Thomas F. Price which led in June 1911 to the establishment of the Catholic Foreign Mission Society of America, better known as Maryknoll. Approval from the American bishops and the Congregation de Propaganda Fide was readily secured, and after a postponement due to the First World War the first band of four priests headed by Price left for China in September 1918. For the first half-century of its existence this first native American foreign mission society enjoyed marked success, and by 1967 there were 1,025 priests of Maryknoll as well as nearly 1,000 others, including brothers and seminarians, to say nothing of the 1,394 professed Maryknoll Sisters. But like all religious groups, Maryknoll suffered a notable decline in numbers after the mid-1960s. Before the decline of the past decade all the missionary communities, including at one time nearly 300 diocesan priests from seventy-seven dioceses, showed a growth similar to that of Maryknoll, and by June 1967 there was a total of approximately 9,500 Americans in overseas missions, more than double the number (4,123) who had been abroad in 1940. The contribution to Latin America was especially notable with roughly fifty-six per cent of the priests, brothers, and sisters from the United States serving abroad being located in Central and South America, the West Indies, and Mexico.

These were encouraging gains, to be sure, even if the over-all numbers appeared slight in comparison with other countries, for instance, with 17,000 priests, religious, and laity in the foreign missions in 1966, Holland with only two per cent of the world's Catholic population yet furnishing twelve per cent of the missionaries in that same year, and Ireland where sixty-eight per cent of the diocesan clergy and seventy per cent of the religious left their native land to serve the missions throughout the world.

On 1 November 1939, Pope Pius XII saluted the American hierarchy's sesquicentenary in the encyclical *Sertum laetitiae*, in the course of which he said:[45]

> We confess that We feel a special paternal affection, which is certainly inspired by heaven, for the Negro people dwelling among you; for in the field of religion and education We know they need special care and comfort and are very deserving of it.

As most students have recognised, the blacks represented a unique group among the home missions of the American Church. From the white man's advent to North America the native Indians had been the object of both devoted missionary care and of cruel exploitation and neglect. The efforts to convert them went on almost uninterruptedly, none the less, often at a frightful sacrifice, and though the history of these missions recorded numerous failures, by 1974 nigh to one-fifth of the Indian population of the country were Catholics with 152,670 out of a total of about 800,000, who were served by 259 priests in 397 churches.

It was the Negroes, or the blacks as many of them prefer to be called, however, who constituted a far more complicated problem. It can be clarified in part, perhaps, by recalling certain episodes from the history of Maryland where Catholics were more numerous than in any other colony before the Revolution, and where the first bishopric of the Catholic Church had its seat. From the colony's birth in 1634 black slaves had been purchased by the Catholic owners of the tobacco plantations just as they were by others, and among these were the Jesuits and the famous Carroll family from whom there came the first archbishop of Baltimore and the sole Catholic signer of the Declaration of Independence. In the archbishop's last will, signed a month before he died in December 1815, he specified that his 'black servant Charles' was to be manumitted within a year after his death. That Maryland was a relatively attractive location for blacks was obvious

45. 'Pope Pius XII's Encyclical *Sertum laetitiae* on the Sesquicentennial of the American Hierarchy, November 1, 1939', Ellis, *Documents*... II, 632.

from the decrease of slaves from 103,036 to 87,189 between 1790 and 1860, while simultaneously the freed blacks increased from 8,046 to 83,942, a figure which according to one authority was 'greater by twenty-five thousand than that in any other Commonwealth'. [46]

Conditions of this kind rendered the position of the Church in Maryland all the more anomalous. Thus nearly forty years after Carroll's death his fifth successor, Francis Patrick Kenrick, whose *Theologia Moralis*, as we have seen, treated the morality of slavery so unsatisfactorily, sent a black convert boy to study for the priesthood at the Urban College of Propaganda at Rome in 1853. Five years later as the time of his ordination drew closer Kenrick informed Cardinal Allessandro Barnabò, Prefect of Propaganda, that the position of freed blacks 'in this region and in many States', was such that a black priest would hardly be able to exercise his ministry among his own since, he said, 'no one would want to render due honour to his status'. The archbishop found it necessary, therefore, to ask Barnabò to assign the young man to a place where he might work for the good of souls, and he added; 'I sincerely regret that these inveterate prejudices be found among us with nothing able to be done to overcome them'. [47]

It is very easy, of course, to pass judgment from a distance of many years on a delicate situation of this kind; yet it is difficult to escape the conclusion that the facts set forth above from Maryland's history may, indeed, contain the key to unlock the mystery of why after more than three centuries of joint habitation and association on the American scene the Catholic Church should in 1974 number only 838,848 blacks in her membership out of an estimated black population of about 24,000,000 or more Americans. *Mutatis mutandis* the same facts could be assembled on the Church in other States, namely, first and foremost, white Catholic prejudice against the black, especially among those of Irish birth or descent who, it should be recalled, have been the predominant ruling element in the Church of the United States. The admirable concern for the black apostolate of Cardinal Patrick O'Boyle, archbishop of Washington (1948-73), has been in this instance something of an exception. Secondly, the seemingly defeatist attitude of many bishops was repeated again and again during the century following Kenrick's letter of 1858, as was true of a conscientious and dutiful prelate like William Henry Elder who, after having ruled the diocese of Natchez for twenty-two years made the strange confession: [48]

46. Ulrich Bonnell Phillips, *American Negro Slavery* (Baton Rouge: Louisiana State University Press 1966), 122. [Reprint in paperback].

47. Kenrick to Barnabò (Baltimore, 23 November 1858), John P. Marschall, 'Francis Patrick Kenrick: The Baltimore Years, 1851-1863', unpublished doctoral dissertation (The Catholic University of America 1965), 'Slavery and the Civil War', p. 11. The writer wishes to thank his former student for supplying this reference.

48. Archives of the Archdiocese of Baltimore, 74-G-10, Elder to Gibbons (New Orleans 22 January 1879).

It is a double reproach to my conscience that I have done nothing substantial for them in all this time. I have a desire always — but it seems to
have been a *velleitas* instead of a *voluntas* — for it has now no effects.

True, there was the rare exception among the nineteenth-century bishops
in John Ireland, archbishop of Saint Paul, who in January 1891, on the
twenty-eighth anniversary of Lincoln's emancipation of the slaves, declared
that though slavery had been abolished in the United States, 'the trail of the
serpent. . .yet marks the ground', and white Americans had failed to accord
their black brothers 'all the rights and privileges of freedom and of a common humanity'. He then asked and gave his answer to a leading question, an
answer that Catholics of the 1970s would have to agree had not even in their
day found complete fulfilment. 'What do I claim for the black man?' asked
Ireland. [49]

That which I claim for the white man, neither more nor less. I would blot
out the colour line. . . It is not possible to keep up a wall of separation
between whites and blacks, and the attempt to do this is a declaration of
continuous war.

That Ireland practised what he preached was clear from the integration of
the schools of the archdiocese of Saint Paul during his thirty-year tenure, as
well as the presence of black students at the College of Saint Thomas in his
see city, at a time when only one other Catholic institution of higher learning
in the land admitted them.

Certainly at no time since the Church was organised under John Carroll
in 1790 were there lacking devoted men and women who gave all or a portion of their lives to the spiritual and material welfare of the blacks. In this
connection one is reminded of black sisterhoods like the Oblate Sisters of
Providence (1829) and the Sisters of the Holy Family (1842), as well as of
white religious such as the Mill Hill Sisters who came from England in 1883,
and the largest and best known of all, the Sisters of the Blessed Sacrament,
founded in 1891 by the daughter of a multi-millionaire Philadelphia banker
of Austrian background, the famous Mother Katharine Drexel. The same
can be said of the men, for example 245 priests and brothers who in 1972
staffed the eighty-six parishes and twenty-eight missions under the auspices
of the Society of Saint Joseph for the black apostolate.

Substantial benefits for the blacks were likewise received from groups
such as the Catholic Church Extension Society founded in October 1905, to

49. Quoted in William A. Osborne, *The Segregated Covenant. Race Relations and
American Catholics* (New York: Herder and Herder 1967), p. 25. See also Moynihan, *op.
cit.*, 228-9, for Ireland's forceful stand on Negro rights.

aid those working in poor and out-of-the-way areas of the country, and from the Glenmary Missioners who were established in 1939 with a similar objective. One of the most effective media for educating Catholic opinion on the race question was the Catholic Interracial Council begun in New York in 1934 with which the names of Father John LaFarge, S.J., and the lay leader, George K. Hunton, were long and honourably associated. Not infrequently the Church actually anticipated the State in furthering enlightened public opinion on black rights, for example, when Joseph E. Ritter, archbishop of Saint Louis, in September 1947, integrated the schools of his jurisdiction, with the archbishop of Washington beginning the same in 1948, and Vincent S. Waters, bishop of Raleigh, doing so in 1953, all in advance of the Supreme Court's decision of May 1954, calling for integration of the nation's public schools. Furthermore, the American bishops' pastoral letter of November 1958 on the evils of racism left little to be desired by way of a theoretical statement based on sound theology.

What reaction these steps had upon the black population in general is impossible to say, although in acknowledging the difficulty of assessing this reaction due to the scarcity of their number in Catholic ranks, one black Protestant minister remarked in 1964: 'What is clear is that there is an unprecedented movement of Negroes toward Catholicism'. [50] An articulate minority of Catholics also gave eloquent and dramatic witness in the marches in behalf of Negro rights at Selma, Alabama, and in other towns and cities. Yet how the weight of Catholic prejudice held the Church back was startlingly revealed in Cicero and Berwyn, predominantly Catholic suburbs of Chicago, which furnished sombre testimony in the summer of 1966 to the depth of the hatred of some Catholics for the blacks and the lengths to which they were prepared to go to prevent open covenants in their community's housing regulations. The frightful riots and destruction in July 1967 in Detroit, a city which enjoyed on this question a progressive administration in both the civil and ecclesiastical orders, gave further reason for alarm. In the judgment of one sociologist, the American bishops seemed only dimly aware of the theological problem that was gathering 'an explosive momentum' in their dioceses, and with the ghastly evidences of the summer of 1967, it was not difficult to assent to his conclusion that the 'rapid pace of change in the 1960s promises to accelerate this theological issued to [a] painful state much sooner than is commonly expected'. [51]

The relationship of the Catholic Church to the American Negro revealed an internal weakness in what to the eye of an outside observer must have appeared a very imposing structure. The external features of the Church

50. Joseph R. Washington Jr, *Black Religion. The Negro and Christianity* (Boston: Beacon Press 1964), 243.
51. Osborne, *op. cit.*, 246-7.

were, indeed, impressive, namely a body of roughly fifty million adherents exceeded in numbers in the Universal Church only by the Catholics of Brazil and Italy, thirty-two ecclesiastical provinces with 134 suffragan dioceses spread over the continental expanse of the United States and also embracing Alaska and Hawaii, ruled by a hierarchy of over 300 numbering eleven cardinals, thirty-nine archbishops, and over 250 bishops. It was little wonder that the American Church of 1974 should have seemed awesome to some outsiders. For a century or more the American genius for organisation had given added strength to the Catholics, where they were native-born or immigrant, by pointing the way and indicating the techniques by which large masses of people could be made to work constructively for a common purpose. This characteristic, which became a hallmark of the American Catholics, showed itself at an early date. It was at Baltimore in 1855 that those of German birth and ancestry founded the German Roman Catholic Central Union, which proved to be one of the most effective agencies for galvanising action and stimulating advanced thought on social questions that the Church of the United States has ever known. As the years went on, a bewildering variety of groups of all kinds came into being under Catholic auspices, the mere listing of which – exclusive of youth and international organisations – filled over seven closely printed pages of fine print in the *1972 Catholic Almanac.*[52] Through the lead taken by James A. McFaul, bishop of Trenton, many of the groups at the turn of the century sent delegates to Cincinnati in December 1901, where the American Federation of Catholic Societies was founded. This loosely knit organisation served the general purposes of united action until the crisis occasioned by the United States' entry into the First World War in April 1917 called for closer ties for Catholic support of the war effort.

A widely felt need often gives rise to a man whose vision and imagination are equal to the creative task that will implement it. Such a person was John J. Burke, C.S.P., editor of the *Catholic World*, who was the *causa agitans* behind the historic meeting held in August 1917, at the Catholic University of America, which, in turn, gave birth to the National Catholic War Council presided over by Peter J. Muldoon, bishop of Rockford, and three of his fellow bishops who piloted the efforts and contributions of their co-religionists through the remaining period of the war with remarkable success. It was this episcopal committee that gave official sponsorship to one of the most advanced statements of the post-war period on the socio-economic order of American industrial society in the so-called 'Bishops' Programme of Social Reconstruction' of February 1919, a document that had been originally written by John A. Ryan, professor of moral

52. 'Catholic Associations, Movements and Societies in the United States', 654-61. Edited by Felician A. Foy, O.F.M. (Huntington: Our Sunday Visitor, Inc. 1972).

theology in the Catholic University of America, and which proved to be more arresting and influential than the lengthy pastoral letter of the entire hierarchy that was dated the following 26 September.

So successful, in fact, was the National Catholic War Council that at the end of the fighting Father Burke, Bishop Muldoon *et al.* proposed that the organisation be kept alive as a co-ordinating agency of the Church's vast and varied peacetime activities. After a brief initial period of doubt during which a handful of bishops opposed the N.C.W.C. at Rome and won a decree of dissolution in February 1922, from the new Pope Pius XI, the organisation's friends mounted a stout defence of their work at the Roman curia. The ban was lifted in July of that year, and with a substitution the next year of 'conference' for 'council' in its title, the National Catholic Welfare Conference proceeded uninterruptedly on its way for the next forty-three years and won the Holy See's commendation to the point where Rome recommended that representatives of other national hierarchies be sent to Washington to study the operations of its eight departments, bureaux, and numerous episcopal committees. In conformity with the directives of the Second Vatican Council, what was now called the National Conference of Catholic Bishops, at its meeting in November 1966, instituted certain changes in its administrative agency which was henceforth termed the United States Catholic Conference.

What in the meantime had transpired in so far as the position of American Catholics in the public life of their country was concerned? From a tiny and despised minority at the birth of the Republic, their steady growth and expansion had made them the principal target of five organised waves of anti-Catholicism and xenophobia between the Nativists of the 1830s and the P.O.A.U. of the 1940s. Even as late as August 1967, the imperial wizard of the revived Ku Klux Klan publicly cited the Catholics, along with the Jews, Negroes, and Communists, as a major menace to American society. Yet the Catholic community continued to flourish in spite of opposition, and by the mid-point of the twentieth century Catholics had achieved conspicuous success in the realm of business and finance, in professions such as law and medicine, and in social circles where the large fortunes of many Catholic families opened to them the doors of an affluent society.

From the viewpoint of the general American public the most striking gains of the Catholics were probably in the field of politics. At the outset of national independence in 1776 there was not a State in which they could either vote or hold office. The legal barriers began to fall in that same year, however, and in July 1831, one of their number, Roger Brooke Taney, was chosen as a member of the president's cabinet, a body in which a considerable number of Catholics have since served. Moreover, after the Civil War period Catholics, in particular the Irish, rose rapidly in municipal politics in cities like Boston, New York, Philadelphia, Chicago, Kansas City, San Francisco, and Newark where the record of many of their kind, unfortunately, wrote an unlovely page of American political history and reflected adversely on their Church. It was in the 1880s that cities like Boston and New York got their first Catholic mayors and although rarely ever free from opposition on the score of their religion, the Catholics, nevertheless, advanced on city, State, and national levels until the setback suffered in November 1928, in the overwhelming defeat of Governor Alfred E. Smith of New York, the first Catholic presidential candidate of a major political party

Yet even the reverse of 1928, severe as it was, proved to be temporary, and thirty years later it had been sufficiently overcome for another Catholic to emerge as a presidential candidate, namely, Senator John F. Kennedy of Massachusetts. The very fact that Smith and Kennedy had been nominated by the Democratic Party, to which the vast majority of Catholics had traditionally belonged, gave indication of what was another sign of the maturing process at work within both the American body politic and the Catholic community. Kennedy's election in November 1960 by a narrow plurality marked a turning-point in the relationship of the Catholic Church to the American Republic. A serious study of that election by four political scientists noted the marked shifts of voters from their customary voting patterns, the 'major cause' of which was Kennedy's religion. 'We feel confident', they said, 'that we will not find any short-term force which moved as large a fraction of the 1960 electorate as did the issue of a Catholic president.' [53] In other words, the anti-Catholic prejudice of many Americans was still a living thing.

That fact to the contrary notwithstanding, the presidential election of 1960 altered circumstances greatly for American Catholics. It is not easy to convey the profound change that that event wrought in the national psychology. One writer perceived its significance about as well as any when he stated: [54]

John F. Kennedy was a mid-twentieth-century representative of the self-confident Catholic response of encounter with the American environment. He symbolised those forces which John Ireland and Al Smith represented at earlier times in different contexts. He believed with other presidential heroes that religious faith is a personal affair, that ecclesiastical authorities had no special claim over public officials, and that God had placed man on earth to exercise freedom and excellence in

53. Philip E. Converse *et al.*, 'Stability and Change in 1960: A Reinstating Election', *American Political Science Review* LV (June 1961), 280.
54. Lawrence H. Fuchs, *John F. Kennedy and American Catholicism* (New York: Meredith Press 1967), 224.

achievement, and that it was up to individual men and women and the United States of America to fulfil God's purpose. To Kennedy, there was nothing in these beliefs which was incompatible with the sectarian religion of his birth, including its theology and authoritarian form of church government.

Because he was a Catholic, representing the one sectarian religion thought to be at odds with the culture-religion of Americanism, Kennedy, as a culture-hero, helped to broaden the basis of consensus in American life by encouraging the forces of encounter within American Catholicism, and by opening the minds of non-Catholics to new opportunities for human communication, learning and growth in dialogue with Catholics.

While both the Church and the State suffered an irreparable loss in the murder of the young president in November 1963, there was a growing number of his coreligionists who were in a position to carry on in a more limited way the encounter and consensus which Kennedy's career had done so much to advance. Thus besides the Catholic associate justice of the Supreme Court and two members of the president's cabinet, the convening of the eighty-ninth Congress in January 1965 found the Catholics for the first time with the largest religious group in the national legislature, 107, as compared to the Methodists who were second with eighty-eight, a status that the former have since maintained. Moreover, the party affiliation of the 107 Catholics was a faithful reflection of the historical association of the members of their Church with the Democratic Party, twelve of the fourteen senators being Democrats as well as eighty of the ninety-three members of the House of Representatives. [55] It was an affiliation, however, that gave every indication of fading as the years since 1965 saw more and more Catholics in the ranks of the Republican Party.

It may not, indeed, have been without significance that President Kennedy had attended Choate School, one of New England's leading secular preparatory schools for boys, the London School of Economics, and had graduated from Harvard University, the ranking university of the United States. In other words, the credit that was owing to his intellectual training, which was much as it is with every man, could not be claimed by the Catholic educational system. The latter, which was the largest private school system in the world, was more noted for its size and numbers than for the quality of education that it imparted. Only with the 1950s did Denis W. Brogan's oft-quoted statement of 1941 begin to lose its validity when he said: 'In no Western society is the intellectual prestige of Catholicism lower than in the country where, in such respects as wealth, numbers, and strength of organisation, it is so powerful'. [56]

The causes for this situation have frequently been analysed, but they are too numerous and varied to be treated here in detail. Speaking solely of higher education, suffice it to say, the Catholics' lack of a native intellectual tradition, the absence of a true understanding and appreciation of higher learning and scholarship among the Church's leaders, the poverty of the immigrant Catholics, the neglect of any effective planning on a national scale for the best employment of the Church's limited resources in trained personnel and money which, in turn, led to an utterly wasteful and needless proliferation of seminaries, colleges, and universities, the tendency of Catholics until recent years to view their educational establishments as existing for a two-fold purpose, namely, to safeguard the faith of their children and to prepare the latter to earn a living, and, finally the presence of all these factors in the midst of the anti-intellectual atmosphere that has pervaded the United States through much of its history – all help to explain why the Catholics' intellectual life had so little viability about it for more than a century and a half. The sole fact that in 1967 the American Church was attempting to conduct a total of 575 diocesan seminaries and training-houses of religious orders (45,359 students), as well as 303 colleges and universities (431,070 students), in itself offered convincing proof of how far the weakening process of proliferation had carried the entire system in relation to its meagre endowments.

Conditions of this kind, needless to say, were not conducive to the maximum development of human talent, with the consequence that the century and a half between the ordination of the first bishop (1790) and the end of the Second World War witnessed relatively little contribution from Catholics to the nation's intellectual and cultural life. True, there were a few whose work had made a favourable impression beyond Catholic circles, for example, Robert Walsh, Mathew Carey, Orestes Brownson, Isaac Hecker, John Boyle O'Reilly, John Gilmary Shea, and Louise Imogen Guiney. They acquired respected reputations as publicists and editors, as well as high esteem for their writings in specific fields, for example Carey in economics, Brownson in philosophy, O'Reilly and Guiney in poetry, and Shea in history. In architecture Patrick C. Keely designed an astonishing number of churches and was the principal Catholic representative of the Gothic revival of his time, and in the fine arts John LaFarge became a noted painter and worker in stained glass, while the genius of George P.A. Healy was largely confined to portrait painting. Yet of these ten Catholics only four owed their training in whole or in part to Catholic schools. Moreover, the American

56. *U.S.A. An Outline of the Country, Its People and Institutions* (London: Oxford University Press 1941), 65.

Church had its counterpart to that of Ireland in the defection from the faith of some of the most talented Catholic literary figures of Irish ancestry, such as the novelists F. Scott Fitzgerald, James T. Farrell, and John O'Hara. Among the leading playwrights Eugene O'Neill was in the same category, although his contemporary, Philip Barry, did not abandon the Church, nor for that matter, had the novelists and short story writers, Mary Flannery O'Connor, Edwin O'Connor, and J. F. Powers. If, however, persistent self-scrutiny and open and honest criticism of the deficiencies of an educational system can contribute to its improvement, then the American Catholics should have had every reason to anticipate a much brighter future, for in 1955 there was mounted a critical self-appraisal that gained momentum, and by the late 1960s there was probably no aspect of Catholic activity that had undergone more severe analysis by the Catholics themselves than that of the quality and character of education given in the Church's seminaries, colleges, and universities. [57]

Furthermore, the Catholic commitment to higher education on the campuses of secular institutions was in the meantime growing with each passing year, so that a conservative estimate in 1967 of the Catholic students in these colleges and universities fixed their number at 920,000, and the next five years brought the estimate to around 1,500,000. One of the chief reasons for the increase was the lower tuition fees at public institutions and the steadily rising fees at private schools, a competition in which only the most prestigious private institutions could hope to retain a broad patronage. In 1967 there were 1,148 priests, of whom 272 were full time, with 942 drawn from the diocesan clergy and 206 from the various religious orders serving on secular campuses. Nearly 100 sisters assisted them, twenty-six full-time, as members of the staffs, of what were called up to the early 1970s 'Newman Centres', which consisted usually of a combination of chapel, classrooms, library, and social rooms. Catholic participation in campus ministry, the current name for these centres, represented one of the most

57. In the rather vast literature that accumulated on this subject the following were generally viewed as the most seminal and provocative: John Tracy Ellis, *American Catholics and the Intellectual Life* (Chicago: Heritage Foundation, Inc. 1956); Gustave Weigel, S.J., 'American Catholic Intellectualism – A Theologian's Reflections', *Review of Politics* XIX (July 1957), 275-307; Thomas F. O'Dea, *American Catholic Dilemma: An Inquiry into the Intellectual Life* (New York: Sheed and Ward 1958); on the seminaries, James Michael Lee and Louis J. Putz, C.S.C., eds, *Seminary Education in a Time of Change* (Notre Dame: Fides Publishers, Inc. 1965) and John Tracy Ellis, 'The Seminary Today', *The Voice* [Saint Mary's Seminary, Baltimore], XLIV (Winter 1966), 7-11; 89-94. Among the best recent publications on the universities were Edward Manier and John W. Houck, eds, *Academic Freedom and the Catholic University* (Notre Dame: Fides Publishers, Inc. 1967); Robert Hassenger, ed., *The Shape of Catholic Higher Education* (Chicago: University of Chicago Press 1967); Neil G. McCluskey, S.J., ed., *The Catholic University. A Modern Appraisal* (Notre Dame: University of Notre Dame Press 1970); and Edward J. Power *Catholic Higher Education in America. A History.* (New York: Appleton Century-Crofts 1972).

challenging and rapidly expanding aspects of higher education under Catholic auspices. And when one considers that it was only in 1889 that the first part-time chaplain was assigned to a group of Catholic students with Father William J. Fierle put in charge of their spiritual care at the University of Michigan, and that not before 1906 were the first full-time chaplains appointed at the universities of Wisconsin and California, it becomes obvious how much progress has been made, even if the present situation still leaves much to be desired in many secular institutions. [58]

In all instances where the historian must deal with vast numbers of people living over a long period of time in highly varied circumstances, common sense would dictate that he should be wary of unqualified generalisations. The history of the American Catholics since 1850 offered no exception, as was evident from any single aspect of that story. Elementary education which, beginning, in the early 1960s, was characterised by great ferment and uncertainty and where amid radical changes as late as 1965 a little over fifty-two per cent of the eligible Catholic children were still in Catholic schools, furnished a case in point.[59] If the gains in quality were, perhaps, more discernible in higher education, there continued to be severe critics within the Church of these institutions. Yet viewed from the perspective of a quarter-century, the progress in the ecclesiastical sciences — to cite only one area of learning — had been real. True, it had not been substantial enough by 1954 to merit mention in Roger Aubert's survey, *La Théologie catholique au milieu du XXe siècle*,[60] nor in the opinion of George H.Tavard, A.A., had it improved over the following decade to a degree where he felt warranted in saying other than that 'the United States lagged behind', while German, French, and Dutch scholarship were still far in the lead. [61]

When one endeavours to assess the ecclesiastical sciences under Catholic auspices in the United States, he thinks, for example, of the *Catholic Historical Review*, a quarterly journal devoted to the history of the Church which had won a respected place since it was launched in April 1915; of the *Catholic Biblical Quarterly* that had begun in February 1939. Its editorial board by the 1970s read like a *Who's Who* in the remarkable advance made in Catholic biblical scholarship in a brief time: Raymond E. Brown, S.S., Joseph F. Fitzmyer, S.J., John L. McKenzie, Roland E. Murphy, O. Carm.,

58. The writer wishes to thank his friend, Father John Whitney Evans, Director of the National Centre for Campus Ministry, Cambridge, Massachusetts, for furnishing many of the facts on this topic from his doctoral dissertation on the history of the Newman Movement in American secular colleges and universities, which was presented at the University of Minnesota in 1970. See also John Tracy Ellis, 'Religion on the Secular Campus: A Prime Responsibility', *Southern California Quarterly* XLVII (December 1965), 357-77.
59. 'Catholic School Growth', *America* 112 (9 January 1965), 34.
60. Tournai-Paris: Casterman 1954.
61. 'The Theological Setting of Vatican II', *The Pilgrim Church* (New York: Herder and Herder 1967), 16.

Patrick W. Skehan and Bruce Vawter, C.M. There was likewise a quarterly, *Theological Studies*, first published in February 1940, by the combined Jesuit faculties of the United States, which soon won and maintained high esteem among theological scholars of all religious beliefs or none, under an able editorial board headed for some years by the late John Courtney Murray, S.J., the most distinguished theologian to date of the American Church. Several of these publications were the official organs of their respective professional groups, such as the *Catholic Historical Review* for the American Catholic Historical Association, a learned society founded in 1919 by a pioneer group of about fifty historians headed by Peter Guilday, then the leading authority on American Catholicism. While most of these societies showed gains after the Second World War, their membership was nowhere what the Catholic population of the country, or even the number of the Church's seminaries, colleges, and universities, would lead one to expect. The historians' association, had in December 1973 only 1,098 members, which in addition to exchanges and subscribers to its quarterly journal meant that after more than fifty-eight years in the field the *Catholic Historical Review* had a total circulation of less than 3,000 individuals and institutions.

In the case of the historians the general malaise that had overtaken the discipline – partly a reflection of Americans' latest wave of anti-intellectualism – was deepened by innumerable Catholics whose principal goal seemed to be their hope to be 'relevant' to contemporary thought and action. As a consequence, in many seminaries the history of the Church all but disappeared as a consequence of student demands for more courses in the behavioural sciences which, they believed, were more closely attuned to the needs of the so-called 'now generation'. Meanwhile the frenetic pursuit by candidates for the priesthood and the religious life of every ephemeral fad raised serious questions about the depth and solidity of the training of these future priests and religious. In this traumatic experience for the disciples of Clio they probably fared better at Harvard than they did at Notre Dame, for in this, as in so many other ways, many Catholics, only recently arrived within the American mainstream, displayed the insecurity and unease of the *nouveau riche*.

'Such is the unity of all history', said Frederick Pollock and Frederic Maitland nearly three-quarters of a century ago, 'that any one who endeavours to tell a piece of it must feel that his first sentence tears a seamless web.' [62] Something of that kind was uppermost in the present writer's mind as he attempted to begin this story at 1850, and the thought returned as he tried to bring it to a close in 1974. In the process he was pain-

---

62. *The History of English Law before the Time of Edward I*, 2nd ed. (Cambridge University Press 1923), I, 1.

fully aware of the omissions, as he was equally aware of the startling recent changes within the Church of the United States that seemed to call for comment.

One of the unmistakable signs of that era of change was the remarkably improved position of Catholics *vis-à-vis* the public life of their country. In other words, if the Church had not yet attained the place where she could be described as Denis Brogan once described the French *curés* as 'part of the national furniture', she had by the 1970s clearly outlived the time when it could be said, as the same writer a quarter of a century ago then remarked with some plausibility, that the United States was 'a Protestant country' while Catholicism was 'not merely the religion of the minority, but of a self-conscious, poor, and apprehensive minority'. Nor would Brogan be prompted to say in 1974, as he did in 1941, that this same Catholicism was 'a private thing' that 'only rarely and then timidly asserts in public its view of the good life'.[63] Rather, all Catholics could by that time say in regard to their country, its institutions, and customs, what Richard J. Cushing, then archbishop of Boston, reflecting on his humble origins, declared before the Congress of Industrial Organisations' meeting in his see city in 1947: 'I belong here'. The transformation, needless to say, had been due to many factors, but in no small measure it was owed to a single man, John F. Kennedy who, it has rightly been said, 'before his death, and perhaps even prior to his election. . .was to do more to blunt the ancient mutual hatred of Catholics and non-Catholics than any American had ever done'.[64]

If by 1960 most Americans of other or of no religious faith were ready to acknowledge that Catholics 'belonged' in the United States, what position did the latter occupy in the international company that composed the Universal Church? Allowing for individual exceptions, they had been seen and heard hardly at all on the international Catholic scene, save for the generally quiet presence in 1969-70 of their forty-nine prelates at the First Vatican Council. Like other national hierarchies in that gathering, the Americans showed no unanimity on the key issue of defining papal infallibility, nor did they win any particular distinction, although Peter Richard Kenrick, archbishop of Saint Louis, was in the judgment of one of the best conciliar historians 'perhaps the stiffest opponent of the definition',[65] while the numerous, vigorous, and varied interventions of Augustin Verot, S.S., who died as bishop of Saint Augustine, were responsible for his being

---

63. *Op. cit.* (rev. ed. 1947), 54, 65, and 67. This edition differed in a number of particulars from that of 1941, e.g. the statement quoted in Note 56 did not appear in the edition of 1947.
64. Fuchs, *op. cit.*, 31-2.
65. Cuthbert Butler, O.S.B., *The Vatican Council* (London: Longmans, Green and Company 1930), II, 176. On Kenrick see Samuel J. Miller, *Peter Richard Kenrick, Bishop and Archbishop of St Louis, 1806-1896* (Philadelphia: American Catholic Historical Society of Philadelphia 1973).

thought 'by common consent. . .the "enfant terrible" of the Council'. [66]

Through succeeding decades individual American Catholics went abroad and returned home without having exercised notable influence in the counsels of the Universal Church, except for Cardinal Gibbons, Archbishop Ireland, Bishop Keane, and Monsignor O'Connell who played a part in the events leading up to Leo XIII's encyclical of 1891 on the labouring classes, and in the image they created in the minds of some in European theological circles by their furtherance of Americanism. But in 1926 the Catholics of other countries got a quick view of the burgeoning young Church of the United States when the Americans played host to their coreligionists from other lands at the International Eucharistic Congress in Chicago. The Second World War took thousands of Catholics to the battlefronts of Europe and Asia, while a combination of organising genius and generosity on the part of those at home touched millions of human beings in every corner of the globe through the assistance given to those stricken by war, famine, flood, and every kind of disaster. In terms of budget, the hierarchy's Catholic Relief Services became 'the largest of the American voluntary overseas agencies', [67] and for the single year ending 30 September 1964, the world's needy were the beneficiaries of American Catholic aid to the total value of $159,925,508.

It was with the Second Vatican Council, however, that the Americans' relative isolation from the stream of world Catholicism began to fade and gradually to give way to a more significant involvement in the affairs of the Universal Church. By the time the large-scale preparatory work got under way at Rome in 1960, there were enough trained specialists in ecclesiastical matters to warrant the participation of sixty-one from the United States, a striking contrast to the single American theologian, James A. Corcoran, who served on the preparatory commission for the council of 1869-70. The change wrought among Americans by the Second Vatican Council was noted by Robert Bosc, S.J., of the Catholic Institute of Paris who, on the occasion of his first visit to the United States in 1960, stated that he had the impression of 'suddenly having been transported back thirty or forty years'. He found numerous devotions, but participation in the liturgy 'seemed almost nonexistent', and what proved even more painful, he said, 'was the general lack of interest, even at Catholic universities and rectories, in any conversation touching on general problems of the Church and the world'. But even in 1960, before the council had yet opened, this foreign observer found two exceptions: first, the liveliness of the religious women who seemed 'thirty or forty years ahead of their sisters in Europe', and, secondly, the

66. *Ibid.*, I, 136.
67. Merle Curti, *American Philanthropy Abroad: A History* (New Brunswick: Rutgers University Press 1963), 523.

dynamic force and new maturity of a lay minority who had discovered the doctrine of the Mystical Body and the implications it had for their role in the life of the Church.[68]

In the meantime the council's preparations were completed and over 200 bishops from the United States joined in the solemn opening of October 1962, and 246 were present for all or part of the four sessions to the closing in December 1965.[69] As the American Catholic community may be said never again to have been the same after Kennedy's election in 1960, so their Church, from the bishops to the clergy, religious, and laity, was not again the same as before the Second Vatican Council. Pope John's oft-quoted figure of 'opening the windows' to let in fresh new air could have been applied with special relevance to the American bishops. So mute were they during the first session that some began to refer to them as the 'Church of Silence'. But as the months wore on they slowly found themselves as they reacted to the stimulation of close contact with bishops from every part of the world. One measure of the difference in their thinking might be cited from the attitude of some of their number towards the reporting of the council by the press. The bishops found the openness and candour with which the newsmen reported what they managed to learn of the sessions from second-hand accounts as little short of scandalous, and there were those who upon their return to the United States from the first session made scolding speeches about the journalists' distortions and indiscretions. Yet in the end it was the official action of the American bishops in setting up a daily press panel that provided one of the most satisfactory media through which the English-speaking world got its information on developments in the council.

Although there were churchmen from the United States, whether bishops or *periti*, who served on most of the conciliar commissions and committees, the Americans' principal contribution was made in the preliminary discussions, final drafting, and debate on the Declaration on Religious Freedom which Pope Paul VI promulgated on 7 December 1965. To this problem they brought the experience of 175 years of the separation of Church and State with its obvious benefits to religion. The Church's official teaching to the contrary notwithstanding, the Catholics of the United States had continued to hold quietly but with sincere conviction to their own national custom, for they, too, were numbered among those of whom Alexis de Tocqueville spoke when after his historic tour of 1831-3 he observed: 'The Americans combine the notions of Christianity and of liberty so intimately in their minds that it is impossible to make them conceive the one

---

68. 'New Americans in the Kennedy Image', *America* 114 (5 March 1966), 321.
69. On the Second Vatican Council, see chapter 23.

without the other'.[70] It was a unique arrangement which people elsewhere had not previously known, so unique, indeed, that the perceptive Viscount James Bryce said of it in 1894: 'Of all the differences between the Old World and the New this is perhaps the most salient'.[71]

Regardless of its advantages, however, the tradition of the Roman curia and of the majority of European theologians made it difficult at times to win the necessary support to advance the conciliar debate. The chief architect of the original draft was John Courtney Murray, S.J., who ironically had been forbidden for a decade before the Council to write or to speak on his speciality, Church-State relations. Through the personal influence, however, of Cardinal Spellman, who shared his views on this subject, Father Murray was named a *peritus* for the second session of the council and was able thereafter to be present in person for the crucial debates.

The American position was by no means lacking in friends among the representatives of other countries, as the final moves made clear. A last-minute effort of the conservatives on 20 September 1965 to prevent a vote failed through the intervention of Paul VI, and the decisive vote taken the following day showed 1,997 in favour and 224 opposed to the schema on religious freedom. Discerning persons saw at once that the declaration had affirmed, as Father Murray said, 'a principle of wider import – that the dignity of man consists in his responsible use of freedom'. Thus did the Americans make their most striking and significant contribution to the Council, the true dimensions of which will be known only as the post-conciliar period of the Church's history unfolds, for as the principal author of the declaration stated:[72]

> The conciliar affirmation of the principle of freedom was narrowly limited – in the text. But the text itself was flung into a pool whose shores are wide as the universal Church. The ripples will run far.

Sooner, perhaps, than Father Murray himself might have anticipated, the 'ripples' swelled into 'waves' that ran far, indeed, for some in his own Church of the United States. Nor, as late as mid-1974, did the situation give reason for belief that the years immediately ahead would be other than a troubled time for the American Catholics, 'an uncertain, anxious time of hope and fear, of joy and suffering', about which Newman in 'The Second Spring' had sought to warn his fellow Catholics of England in that famous sermon of July 1852.[73] The influence exercised on their coreligionists by this

70. *Democracy in America*, ed. Phillips Bradley (New York: Alfred A. Knopf 1953), I, 306.
71. *The American Commonwealth* 3rd ed. rev. (New York: Macmillan 1895), II, 695.
72. Walter M. Abbott, S.J., and Joseph Gallagher, eds, *Documents of Vatican II* (New York: America Press 1966), 674.
73. Charles Frederick Harrold, ed. *A Newman Treasury. Selections from the Prose Works of John Henry Newman* (New York: Longmans, Green and Company 1943), 220. Doctrinal

minority of Americans – and their number was small – was impossible to gauge with exactness. Yet for certain people among this minority, intellectual positions once prevalent among liberal Protestant thinkers but long since abandoned by the latter seemed to hold a fascination, the kind of fascination that one normally associates with what is ideologically new and original. *Mutatis mutandis*, the stance taken by a few of their number suggested an idea expressed during Newman's early years as a Catholic when he declared:[74]

> In proportion as you put off the yoke of Christ, so does the world by a sort of instinct recognise you, and think well of you accordingly. Its highest compliment is to tell you that you disbelieve.

Apart from this minority, found for the most part in academia and the world of letters, the new freedom proved a heady wine for other Catholics as well. The spiritual balance necessary to hold men and women to an exacting commitment made in an earlier and less complicated time, appeared in the case of some to have been gravely shaken if not lost entirely. Departures from the priesthood became commonplace, hundreds took flight from the religious life, and still larger numbers of young men and women who had initially entertained the idea of a vocation to one or to the other, turned back. For some – although by no means for all, since it was reasonably clear that there were those who in the first instance had not the qualities of a real vocation – it was impossible to disguise the situation as other than a crisis of faith, a fact that the Church's historians were under obligation to record. Yet no historian who answered to the name of Christian would do so unmindful of Saint James's admonition: 'There is only one lawgiver and he is the only judge and has power to acquit or to sentence. Who are you to give a verdict on your neighbour?'

As for the laity, not a few among those who continued to care about their Church were cast into a state of sadness and confusion with an accompanying bewilderment about what they should, as Catholics, believe or disbelieve. Reared in a tradition of docility to their ecclesiastical masters, an attitude inculcated by Catholic schools they had attended, these people found themselves confronted by an utterly unprecedented situation. In some in-

---

confusion was not a unique phenomenon among the Catholics. E.g., Albert C. Outler, chairman of a commission appointed by the United Methodist Church in 1968 to investigate teaching among the American Methodists, reported at the Church's Atlanta conference in the spring of 1972 and stated that the Methodists displayed 'a bewildering spectrum of doctrinal diversity. Somewhere in the United Methodist Church there is somebody urging every kind of theology still alive. And not a few that are dead.' (*Time* 8 May 1972, 67).

74. 'Nature and Grace', Harrold, *op. cit.*, 179.

stances Catholic teachers of doctrine and of morals voiced opinions that left an impression that in virtually every problem of human existence there was no longer such a thing as a lasting position to which Catholics were expected to hold and to believe. On almost every subject from the Real Presence to birth control, post-conciliar reappraisals of traditional teaching found the vast majority altogether unready to make the psychological adjustment and mental adaptation that might have eased the trauma suffered by so many. They had been taught in complete good faith in the days of their Catholic schooling that the Church had answers to every question. When they discovered that this was not true – even if she had more answers than any other living source – there were those who were drawn to the other extreme of believing that she had answers to none of the riddles of life in this world.

Historically speaking, of course, the overwhelming majority of adherents of every religion have possessed relatively little sophistication, and in this regard the late twentieth-century Catholics of the United States were typical. In their perplexity many clung tenaciously to the fallacy that lay behind the simplistic approach of a former time. Only among the most perceptive did there slowly, and at times painfully, emerge a dawning consciousness of the deep truth contained in the oft-quoted remark of Adrian van Kaam, C.S.Sp., that 'Life is a mystery to be lived, not a problem to be solved'. [75] The greater number held on in the hope that a more tranquil time would soon dawn. Numerous others, however, for a wide variety of reasons, ceased to be practising Catholics after the fashion of their parents and grandparents. Reference has already been made to the Gallup Poll's survey of church attendance during 1971 which showed a decline among Americans of every religious persuasion. The Protestants' attendance of thirty-seven per cent and the Jews of nineteen per cent still left the decline among Catholics as the 'most pronounced' with their seventy-one per cent church attendance of 1964 having fallen to fifty-seven per cent for those who attended church on the average in 1971. [76]

The explanation for this rather startling fact cannot be found solely in any analysis, be it ever so searching, of the Catholic community taken by itself. 'No man is an Iland, intire of itselfe; every man is a peece of the Continent, a part of the maine.' [77] If those words of the English poet, John Donne (1573-1631), have a faintly archaic ring in the late twentieth century, they embody, none the less, an ageless truth that is as applicable to the Catholics of the United States in the 1970s as it has been for the entire human family

---

75. *Religion and Personality* (Englewood Cliffs: Prentice-Hall Inc. 1964), 13.
76. See Note 36.
77. 'Devotions upon Emergent Occasions', XVII, 1642, Helen Gardner and Timothy Healy, eds. *John Donne. Selected Prose* (Oxford: Clarendon Press, 1967), 101.

since time began. In other words, the situation in which the Catholics now found themselves could not be divorced from the national ethos of the society of which they formed a part. For most of their American history a state of semi-isolation had been the Catholics' lot, in part induced by the hostile environment that surrounded them on every side, in part because of the deeply ingrained ghetto mentality born of their immigrant heritage, with all its attendant fears and suspicions of outsiders as well as feelings of insecurity and inferiority about themselves. Yet once a notable improvement in their economic status had become a reality, there followed almost inevitably a heightening of their political and social position which, in turn induced in many a change in their outlook on religion, a change prompted by their newly acquired relationship to the suburban civilisation of which in the period after the Second World War they became members in ever increasing numbers; in a word, a change in their outlook on life itself.

The altered position of Catholics *vis-à-vis* the general American public can be illustrated best, perhaps, in the political order. True, politics had been one of the first significant areas of national life where Catholics became discernible and influential, especially on the municipal level. Yet up to the presidential campaign of 1960 a political candidate's Catholicism continued in many regions of the country to be a doubtful qualification, where it was not a positive handicap. With John F. Kennedy's election to the presidency that year, as has been said, there ensued an almost sudden and substantial change of public opinion on that score. Thus by the time of the national convention of the Democratic party at Miami Beach in July 1972, it was made known that Senator George S. McGovern, a Methodist, the leading and ultimately successful candidate for the Democratic nomination for the presidency, definitely desired a Catholic as his running mate for the office of vice-president. That was one of the reasons for his original choice of Thomas F. Eagleton, United States Senator from Missouri, who was a Catholic, as were his wife and two children, as well as that of R. Sargent Shriver, former ambassador to France, who was the ultimate candidate for the vice-presidency on the Democratic ticket.

To say that late twentieth-century humanity found itself everywhere engulfed in a profound revolution, the root causes and true nature of which no one could satisfactorily explain, [78] was to state the obvious. Moreover, to say that amid this revolutionary condition the United States was about as violently shaken in every aspect of its national life as any country in the world, was again to state that of which every informed person was fully

---

78. Walter Lippmann, one of the wisest citizens of the Republic, confessed his inability to comprehend this revolution. 'I know of nobody,' he said, 'and I've heard of nobody, who has come anywhere near to understanding fully and practically this revolutionary condition.' San Francisco *Sunday Examiner and Chronicle* 9 June 1968, 3.

aware. There is here neither the space nor the necessity to attempt an extensive discussion of this phenomenon. For the world at large, the problem was posed, if in a simplistic way, in the title of a recent symposium: *Can We Survive Our Future?*[79] In the narrower framework of the American Republic, the principal factors constituting the nation's predicament were candidly assessed in Ronald Berman's *America in the Sixties, An Intellectual History*, [80] and in the even starker prospect of the more recent work of the young writer, William L. O'Neill, *Coming Apart: An Informal History of America in the 1960s.*[81] In so far as the American Catholics were concerned, that which was 'coming apart' had over twenty years ago been perceptively adumbrated by the distinguished Jewish convert psychiatrist, Karl Stern. Most people were even then, he said, still clinging to many patterns largely because of their Christian heritage, of which, he added: [82]

> we are no longer conscious and not because we actually believe in the Christian doctrine of vicarious suffering, or the Hindu teaching of karma, or simply in man's immortal soul. In fact, most of us do not believe in any of these things. Thus, we cling with one hand to modern pragmatism, and with the other to the Hebrew-Christian philosophy. But the gap is widening all the time, and there will be a moment when one hand will have to let go.

It is difficult to escape the impression that for many American Catholics that moment was reached at some point in the mid 1960s, and that at that point the one hand had been forced to let go. In the spiritual vacuum that ensued for them the advanced secularisation, which by that time had become an all-pervading characteristic of their national life, moved in and ultimately coloured everything that related to the scale of values that governed their thinking and their moral conduct.

The omnipresence of this secularising process – with its inevitable influence on the Catholic community – could be illustrated in numerous ways, but the following examples, it is hoped, will suffice. For Americans the Supreme Court constitutes a sort of civil *magisterium*, the justices being the arbiters of what is, or what is not, allowable in the light of the Constitution. In 1961 the court gave a decision regarding the violation of a Sunday closing statute of the State of Maryland. Acknowledging that the original laws which dealt with Sunday labour had been motivated by religious forces, the

79. A symposium edited and introduced by G. R. Urban in collaboration with Michael Glenny, London: Bodley Head 1972.
80. New York: Free Press 1968.
81. Chicago: Quadrangle Books 1971.
82. *The Pillar of Fire* (New York: Harcourt, Brace 1951), 126.

justices, however, contended that the laws' present purpose and effect were, 'to provide a uniform day of rest for all citizens', and the fact that this happened to be Sunday, a day of 'particular significance for the dominant Christian sects', did not bar the State from achieving what were termed 'its secular goals', to which the court added: 'We believe that the air of the day is one of relaxation rather than one of religion'. In treating this decision a recent writer concluded that while in substance it upheld the Maryland law, at the same time the court had been able 'to replace religious rationales with secularistic ones'. [83]

In the following year (1962) there came an even more decisive ruling by the Supreme Court, this time relating to the so-called regents' prayer introduced into the public schools of the State of New York. The prayer in question read: 'Almighty God, we acknowledge our dependence upon Thee, and we beg Thy blessings upon us, our parents, our teachers and our country'. This prayer was declared in violation of the Constitution's first amendment, and James Madison, the amendment's author, was quoted for the benefit of those who, it was said, might subscribe to the view 'that because the regents' official prayer is so brief and general there can be no danger to religious freedom in its governmental establishment'. [84]

Meanwhile the steadily mounting divorce rate, the relaxation of laws against abortion, the all but extinct legal restrictions on any and every form of sex portrayal in the theatre, the literary media, and the films, to say nothing of the wholesale lying and practice of deceit in government, the press, and business – these and numerous other manifestations in both the public and private lives of Americans, had become matters of common knowledge internationally. And the international aspects of this general flight from traditional moral standards was rendered acute, especially for Africans, Latin Americans, and Asians, by the astronomical profits reaped by American industrialists from the manufacture and sale of armaments, a trade that by the 1970s constituted roughly one-half of the world's supply.

Facts of this kind lent substance to the severe indictment of the United States by the charismatic archbishop of Olinda and Recife, Helder Pessoa Camara, the Brazilian churchman described by Pope Paul VI as 'one of the great voices of our time, one of the greatest apostles of this age'. [85] In a

83. Raymond G. Decker, 'Anglo-American Law in the Throes of Secularisation, 1800-1970', 21, citing *McGowan v. Maryland*, 366 U.S. 420 (1961). The writer wishes to thank Father Decker for permitting him to use this paper, which was read at a session of the International Congress of Learned Societies in the Field of Religion, Los Angeles 2 September 1972, entitled 'Morals and the Law: An Historical Perspective'. This paper has been accepted for publication in a future issue of *Thought*.
84. *Ibid.* 22-3, citing *Engle v. Vitale*, 370 U.S. 420 (1962).
85. *The Tablet* 226 (London 1 July 1972), 618. In introducing Archbishop Camara to his audience, Cardinal John Heenan, Archbishop of Westminster, stated that the pontiff, 'far

lecture on 25 June 1972, before London's Catholic Institute for International Relations, the archbishop was at pains to condemn the crimes against humanity perpetrated by Russia and China, the communist powers, but he then added: [86]

> The USA presents itself as the champion, the hero and martyr of the defence of the Free World. It alleges that there was no other reason for its fighting in Korea, and for sacrificing itself, so terribly, today, in Vietnam. [If] it is maintaining direct control over Latin America; if it is extending throughout the whole world [a] tremendously expensive system of air bases and stockpiles of nuclear weapons; if it continues to mortgage itself so heavily in the arms race and in the space race, it wants everyone to believe that above all it does this in defence of Christian civilisation.

No honest and well-informed American, Catholic or non-Catholic, could maintain that Archbishop Camara's unlovely picture constituted a gravely exaggerated or distorted image of their country, nor could any citizen of the republic who acknowledged a viable moral sense do other than agree with the archbishop when he concluded:

> Christians would offer a great service to the cause of truth – and only the truth can free us – if calmly and firmly, with all the moral force at their disposal, they could put an end to this double exploitation conducted in the name of liberty.

There had been a time when such descriptions of American *mores*, whether favourable or unfavourable, had in good measure passed the Catholics by, so much were they, as Newman remarked of the early Christians of the Roman Empire, 'a *gens lucifuga*, a people who shunned the light of day'. [87] But by the mid-twentieth century the immigrant shyness had largely worn off, and in the years after 1950 Catholics moved in ever mounting numbers and with ever increasing confidence into what has often been called the American mainstream, with all the advantages and disadvantages implied in their newly acquired importance. In fact, so thoroughly did many Catholics adapt themselves to the social customs of the middle and upper classes, that as they came among the latter their identity in the eyes of a

---

from disapproving of Dom Helder's radicalism', had described him in the words quoted above. The nature and spirit of the archbishop's 'radicalism' have to some degree been mirrored in the titles of his books, e.g., *Revolution Through Peace* (New York: Harper and Row 1971), and *Race Against Time* (New York: Dimension Books 1972). For a profile of Helder Camara, see the unsigned article, 'Rebel in a Frayed Cassock', *The Observer* (London 25 June 1972), 5.

86. *The Tablet* 226 (1 July 1972), 629.

87. Harrold, *op. cit.*, 215.

foreign visitor would have been virtually indistinguishable.

In other words, had anyone anticipated that Catholics would remain as solid in their religious faith as their immigrant ancestors, or had they thought that the generally declining moral tone of American society would leave them largely untouched, such a person was destined for a disappointment. Put in another way, in almost every particular relating to traditional religious concepts and practices, most Catholic Americans – always allowing for the exceptions – proved in the balance to be as American, if not not more American, than they were Catholic. In one of the most publicised features of this change, namely, the practice of birth control, as previously stated, Catholics were showing a marked conformity to what had more and more become the national norm. [88]In the support given to relaxation of laws against abortion, Catholics were in the main still in opposition, but instances of divorce after twenty or thirty years of married life among Catholics, if as yet behind the national average, were notably on the increase, while there was little or no distinction between Catholics and non-Catholics in the anxiety experienced by American parents over drug addiction among the teenagers and young adults of their families.

Practically every effort to explain the malaise that beset American Catholicism in the mid 1960s emphasised the lack of episcopal leadership as one of the chief contributing causes. In April 1971 the present writer was asked, in his capacity as chairman of the subcommittee on history of the National Conference of Catholic Bishops' Committee on Priestly Life and Ministry, to report to the hierarchy at their Detroit meeting. After noting the growing sentiment in favour of optional celibacy, he there stated: [89]

> Shrill and sensational as much of the reporting of this question has been by the news media, it will not have escaped your notice that important as a majority of priests deem this matter to be, all three of the recent national studies on the American priesthood have shown that – whether right or wrong is another matter – it has been the priests' dissatisfaction with the Church's leadership that has emerged as the prime reason for their current discontents.

Nothing that has occurred in the interval has changed that impression, unless it was the growing number of Catholics, both clerical and lay, who ceased altogether to pay any heed to their bishops, regardless of what the latter might be saying or doing. Thus in the press accounts of the statistical summaries on the Church's situation on 1 January 1972, published in May

88. See Note 22.
89. 'A report to the National Conference of Catholic Bishops, Detroit, Tuesday, April 27, 1971', 10-11.

of that year in the *Official Catholic Directory*, certain wry comments were made about the number of bishops having reached a total of 304, a figure that ranked the Americans second only to the Italians in the Universal Church. The bishops' increase was contrasted with the decline of laity in some dioceses, as well as with the decrease on the national level of priests, religious, and seminarians. Comment of this kind reflected that disfavour in which the bishops were regarded by many, for at no time in the 184 years since John Carroll, the first of their episcopal body, was ordained in August 1790 had the American episcopate's prestige been so low as it was at the dawn of the 1970s.

How was one to account for the Americans' striking change of attitude toward their bishops in the decade since the opening of the council? No answer that presumed to describe what even now remains a somewhat fluid situation, could be satisfactory to all, for in this, as in almost every other issue touching the Church, her American subjects were deeply divided. Of the fact of the bishops' widespread loss of favour, however, there could be no doubt. Since it is the historian's duty to furnish as accurate an analysis as possible of significant data relating to the topic on which he writes, he must assess as best he can a problem that, by its very nature, must remain a central concern for the future of Catholicism in the United States as it is in all other countries.

First, the norms that governed the choice of bishops throughout most of the Church's American experience had by the 1970s become singularly at odds with what most alert clergy and laity felt were then necessary. The reason was twofold, first, that in all religious circles emphasis had shifted strongly in favour of the charismatic, of the spiritually creative, of the original and imaginative, and away from the practical, the prosaic, and the traditional in ecclesiastical leadership. Secondly, the spirit of the age demanded not only openness and honesty in the ecclesial order's human relationships, but, too − and that with increasing insistence − a broad spectrum of participation in the making of decisions and the shaping of policies for the future of all religious groups. On both of these counts the American bishops were found woefully wanting, according to the reckoning of many of their spiritual charges. Mention has already been made of the Americans' predominantly practical turn of mind, a national characteristic that from the beginning appeared with almost monotonous regularity among those chosen to be bishops. Nearly a century ago an Irish prelate was sent by the Holy See as papal ablegate to Canada and the United States, and in the report that George Conroy, bishop of Ardagh, submitted in 1878 to the Congregation de Propaganda Fide there was striking evidence of the point referred to above when he stated that in the United States priority was given in the selection of bishops to financial abilities, rather than to pastoral... Whenever there is deliberation to choose a candidate for the episcopacy, the Bishops of a province feel constrained to seek, at all costs, a man skilled in financial administration. Indeed, it has too often happened that the most valued gifts in the candidate proposed to the Holy See were properly those of a banker, and not of a Pastor of souls.[90]

Should those who had this matter closely at heart in the post-conciliar American Church have read the remarks of the bishop of Ardagh, they might well have been reminded of the old French axiom, *plus ça change, plus c'est la même chose*! For not only had the general situation remained substantially unchanged since 1878, but by the early 1970s a touch of irony had been added when the financial condition of many American dioceses was found to be in a deplorable state. In several instances bankruptcy for a time seemed imminent, notably in the diocese of Santa Rosa, the first ordinary of which had in 1962 allegedly been chosen because of his presumed business acumen![91]

Closely related to the norm of real or imagined administrative talent was the choice of men who had become the personal favourites of powerful ecclesiastics who were eager, as is true in every walk of life, to multiply their own kind. This was a type of whom Lytton Strachey once asked:[92]

was it he who had been supple and yielding? he who had won by art what he would never have won by force, and who had managed, so to speak, to be one of the leaders of the procession less through merit than through a superior faculty for gliding adroitly to the front rank?

In any case, with a few notable exceptions such as the late archbishop of Atlanta, Paul J. Hallinan, the ultimate choice fell upon priests who were regarded as able administrators, who were thought 'safe' on all that related to

90. Archives of the Congregation de Propaganda Fide, Congressi America Centrale, XXXVI (1882 – incorrectly filed), folio 197. The writer wishes to thank his friend Monsignor James P. Gaffey of the College of Notre Dame, Belmont, California, for supplying him with a copy of the Conroy report. On this subject, see the writer's articles, 'On Selecting American Bishops', *Commonweal* LXXXV (10 March 1967), 643-9, and 'On Selecting Catholic Bishops for the United States', *The Critic* XXVII (June-July 1969), 43-55.
91. On the subject of Catholic Church finances in the United States the best work is that of James Gollin, *Worldly Goods. The Wealth and Power of the American Catholic Church, the Vatican, and the Men Who Control the Money* (New York: Random House 1971).
92. 'Cardinal Manning', *Eminent Victorians* (New York: Capricorn Books 1963), 2; After a somewhat trying meeting with William B. Ullathorne, O.S.B., bishop of Birmingham, Newman confided in a memorandum dated 23 September 1866, 'I think Bishops fancy that, as justice does not exist between the Creator and His creatures, between man and the brute creation, so there is none between themselves and their subjects'. Charles Stephen Dessain, ed, *The Letters and Diaries of John Henry Newman* (London: Nelson 1972), XXII, 293.

ecclesiastical polity, and who, perhaps above all, were believed to be men who would meet the specifications of the one whose final word was often the decisive one, namely, the apostolic delegate. For in the selecting process the latter's hand had, if anything, been strengthened by Pope Paul VI's *motu proprio* of June 1969 on the role of apostolic nuncios and delegates, as it had been kept quite intact by a later document of May 1972 embodying norms for selecting candidates for the episcopacy that were alleged to be new and in keeping with current opinion in the Church. [93] All of this, to be sure, was consonant with the strong ultramontanist tone that since the early 1920s had characterised the attitude of American bishops in their relations to the Holy See, an attitude that Peter Nichols described in discussing the non-Italians associated with the Roman curia. He declared: 'By far the worst are the Americans, who lose character and gain fussiness at an alarming rate in Rome's ecclesiastical circles, becoming far more tiresome to deal with than the Italians'. [94]

93. 'Motu Proprio on Papal Diplomats', *Catholic Mind*, LXVII (September 1969), 51-9, and *L'Osservatore Romano* [Weekly English edition], 25 May 1972, 6-7. Regarding this latter document, many were in agreement with the well-known American sociologist, Andrew M. Greeley, when he stated, 'The present administration of the Vatican has displayed once again its remarkable ability to go through the motions of change without making any changes at all. It has mandated a "consultation" of the clergy and laity in the nomination of bishops that is totally without meaning and will have no impact at all on where power really is in the Church.' (*The Monitor* (San Francisco), 15 June 1972, p. 4). The absence of genuine consultation in the new norms was rendered all the more conspicuous when one recalled the practice of the early Church. For example, in a letter of Pope Leo I to Anastasius, Bishop of Thessalonica, after 4 January 446, the pontiff declared: 'No one, of course, is to be consecrated against the wishes of the people and without their requesting it. Otherwise, the citizens will despise or hate the bishop they do not want and thus become less religious than they should, on the grounds that they were not permitted to have the man of their choice.' [Edmund Hunt, F.S.C., (Trans.), *St. Leo the Great. Letters* (New York: Fathers of the Church, Inc. 1957), 63]. In several instances there was widespread resentment among American clergy and laity in their being allowed no voice in the selection of their bishop, even though the resentment was not as openly expressed as that of certain leading laymen of the diocese of Nottingham over the choice of Monsignor James McGuinness, vicar general, with the right of succession to Bishop Edward Ellis [*The Tablet*, 226 (20 May 1972), 484], or that aroused in the diocese of Roermond where the pope's imposition of Bishop Jan M. Gijsen brought on a state of revolt among a number of clergy and laity (*National Catholic Reporter*, 9 June 1972, p. 6).

94. *The Politics of the Vatican* (London: Pall Mall Press 1968), 188. An episode that took place during the bishops' meeting at Detroit on 27 April 1971, and that was summarised by the present writer in an interview, illustrated the point. The appearance and brief address of Archbishop Luigi Raimondi, Apostolic Delegate to the United States, occasioned, it was said, no less than three standing ovations within twenty minutes. 'Don't you think [that]. . . was going a bit beyond the call of duty?' it was asked, to which was added the comment: 'Needless to say, I would wish that the representative of the Holy See should always and everywhere be treated with the respect due to his office, but the incident at Detroit does, it seems to me, symbolise an excessive docility' [*Catholic Herald* (Sacramento) 23 September 1971, p. 2]. In a statement entitled, 'The State of the Priesthood', Andrew M. Greeley, chairman of the subcommittee on sociology of the bishops' Committee on Priestly Life and Ministry, characterised the problem of authority as the 'most serious problem facing the

More might be said about the lack of leadership in the American Church, but in fairness it should be added that a substantial minority of bishops had given intelligent leadership in their own dioceses by building bridges, so to speak, listening to their priests and people, and endeavouring to implement in a progressive and enlightened spirit the directives of the Second Vatican Council. Moreover, of late, signs had begun to be detected of a growing restiveness among a minority of younger and more alert bishops, men who had grown increasingly unhappy with the static and cautious administration of the National Conference of Catholic Bishops and its Washington secretariat, the United States Catholic Conference. If these indications had not as yet been pronounced, they were, none the less, real enough to warrant the anticipation that a loyal opposition might yet emerge that as time went on would become more articulate and draw to itself additional support from others for a more open and imaginative approach to the Church's problems. Again, a further hopeful note was struck with the appointment of the ninth apostolic delegate to the United States, the Belgian-born Archbishop Jean Jadot, who arrived in July 1973. The latter's open, honest, and realistic approach, unprecedented among his eight predecessors, gave evidence of a quick and acute appraisal of current needs, a fact reflected in a series of appointments of bishops to important dioceses that offered promise of a new and perceptive understanding of what was expected of the Church's leaders in the 1970s.

In spite of all the tumult and confusion that American Catholicism had known since the mid-1960s and, too, the reasonable certainty that the immediate future would continue to be a troubled time, perhaps even 'an uncertain, anxious time of hope and fear, of joy and suffering',[95] for which Newman had once asked the English Catholics to prepare themselves, there were also consoling features in prospect. If some post-conciliar groups like the National Federation of Priests' Councils, and particularly the National Association of Laymen, for a number of causes, seemed to falter and to fall back, other groups gave evidence of genuine viability and a burgeoning strength and support.

Thus throughout the land repeated institutes, congresses, and workshops continued to attract large numbers of dedicated clergy and laity who displayed a keen awareness of the Church's current needs. These added both life and lustre to advanced study in the Scriptures, in theology, and in the liturgy, to creative thinking and lively activity in catechetics, and also to an

---

Catholic priesthood today, beyond all question', and he further declared: 'Honesty compels me to say that I believe the present leadership of the Church [in the United States] to be morally, intellectually, and religiously bankrupt' (*National Catholic Reporter* 18 February 1972, 10 and 7).

95. Harrold, *op. cit.*, 220.

aggiornamento among canon lawyers, once a new and vigorous leadership voted in at their San Francisco meeting of 1964 had converted the Canon Law Society of America into one of the most constructive forces for Catholic renewal. If ecumenism did not make the progress that many had hoped, it was due as much to a slackened pace among Protestants as it was to Catholic deficiencies. In fact Albert C. Outler, distinguished Methodist theologian and church historian, stated that a 'severe slump' had overtaken Protestant ecumenical efforts, a situation that had left the Catholics, in his judgment, as 'the most interested and actively committed of all the Churches in Christendom'.[96] In spite of these checks, however, a number of interdenominational committees and study groups continued to probe for ways and means of reaching a more unified position on doctrinal and disciplinary questions.

In this regard, two of the most hopeful ventures were the Institute for Ecumenical and Cultural Research opened in 1968 at Saint John's University, Collegeville, Minnesota, and the Ecumenical Institute for Advanced Theological Studies, an international undertaking financed through its origin and formative stages by Ignatius A. O'Shaunghnessy (d. 1973), and which received its first residents in 1971 at Tantur between Jerusalem and Bethlehem. And, finally, among the varied aspects of Catholic life mention should be made of the apostolate for social justice, a sphere of action where a half-century or more ago pioneers like the late Monsignor John A. Ryan, Monsignor John P. Monaghan, Agnes G. Regan, and others had forged a lasting tradition. Here an alertness to the need for the Church's presence was personified in a large number of men and women, clerical and lay, in the years since the Second World War, notably, to mention only two, in George G. Higgins, a nationally known priest with nearly thirty years of outstanding service, and in Miss Dorothy Day, the heroic co-founder in the 1930s of the Catholic Worker Movement, whose inspiring achievements were fittingly recognised in 1972 when the University of Notre Dame conferred on her the Laetare Medal, its highest distinction.[97]

Amid all the clamour and contradiction that enveloped the American Catholics as they moved uncertainly into the mid 1970s, there were those observers who were of the mind that the numerous rivulets, so to speak, were slowly converging toward a major stream where the principal emphasis was centred in the desire for a deepening of the human spirit through prayer. In that connection, it should be mentioned that startling

---

96. *The Monitor* (San Francisco), 16 March 1972, 2.
97. The memoirs of this extraordinary convert from communism have been told in: *From Union Square to Rome* (Silver Spring, Maryland : Preservation Press 1939), *The Long Loneliness* (New York: Harper and Brothers 1952), and *Loaves and Fishes* (New York: Harper and Row 1963).

changes have at times taken place in a people's prayer life, a fact recently illustrated in regard to the Irish of the last century. As has been said, they
became the predominant ethnic group among the immigrant Catholics of the
United States, and it was the Irish, more than any other nationality, who set
their stamp on the spiritual development among Catholics by their fidelity to
practices such as the Rosary, the Forty Hours, and devotion to the Sacred
Heart, religious exercises that were practically endemic to the entire
Catholic community up to and through the Second Vatican Council. Yet of
this same immigrant people it has been said: 'Most of the two million Irish
who emigrated between 1847 and 1860 were part of the pre-famine generation of nonpractising Catholics, if indeed they were Catholics at all'.[98]

That sudden shifts in a people's religious moods often occur, then, is a
proven fact. Unquestionably the most dramatic expression of a new trend
was the emergence of a Catholic pentecostal movement which had risen late
in the 1960s at Duquesne University, Pittsburgh, and had thence spread to
other parts of the country. The National Conference of Catholic Bishops appointed a committee of its own members to study the movement, and at
their meeting in November 1969 a cautious approval was recommended.
According to this committee, the pentecostals were theologically sound,
showed a 'strong biblical basis', and gave indication that participation had
led the members to a 'better understanding of the role that a Christian plays
in the Church'. For all these reasons, said the bishops, 'Perhaps our most
prudent way to judge the validity of the claims of the Pentecostal Movement
is to observe the effects on those who participate in the prayer meetings'.[99]

In any case, the movement grew apace, and in May 1972 the sixth international conference of the Catholic Charismatic Renewal brought nearly
12,000 teenagers, young adults, and older participants to the university of
Notre Dame, an event succinctly described in a headline that read, 'Respectability and Numbers Soar. Pentecostal Movement Booming'. The implications of this gathering and others of a similar kind for the future of
Catholicism in the United States, continued to be a topic of widespread discussion and speculation. A definitive judgment was obviously impossible at
so early a date, and about as sensible a reaction as any was that summarised
in the title of an editorial on the Notre Dame meeting called 'Time Will
Tell'.[100] When nearly 25,000 assembled in June 1974 for the eighth inter-

98. Emmet Larkin, 'The Devotional Revolution in Ireland, 1850-75', *American Historical Review* 77 (June 1972), 651.
99. The text of the bishops' statement was carried in Kilian McDonnell, O.S.B., 'Catholic Pentecostalism: Problems of Evaluation', *Dialog*, 9 (Winter 1970), 54. See also James F. Powers, S.J., 'Catholic Pentecostals', *America*, 119 (20 July 1968), 43-4, and for the move-ment in Latin America, Jeffrey L. Klaiber, S.J., 'Pentecostal Breakthrough', *America*, 122 (31 January 1970), 99-102.
100. *National Catholic Reporter* (23 June 1972), 1, 16 and 8.

national conference, with a cardinal, twelve bishops, and about 700 priests concelebrating a Mass, with alleged healings at another service, it was apparent that the Catholic Charismatic Renewal movement was showing no signs of slackening. That something reminiscent of Americans' gigantic revivals of the nineteenth century was again abroad in the land there was no denying when shortly after the 1972 Notre Dame conference over 75,000 predominantly Protestant youths from sixty countries assembled in Dallas, Texas, for 'Explo '72', the International Congress on Evangelism, described by *Time* as 'the Jesus Woodstock'.[101]

There were critics who spoke disparagingly of the Dallas meeting as too heavily weighed towards fundamentalism, and the alleged healings at Notre Dame two years later likewise drew fire. What precisely this mass stirring of youth and young adults portended, however, no one could exactly determine. Regardless of the ultimate outcome, like their peers of other Christian churches, young Catholics, and many of their elders as well, were also on the march, and since of necessity tomorrow's Catholicism would to no small degree be the task of the young to shape, the exciting events of the early 1970s may well have held more in store for the Church than had at first been thought.

A far more subdued post-conciliar arrival on the American scene came in the message of that extraordinary woman, Mother Teresa Bojaxhiu of Calcutta, and her Missionaries of Charity. Admittedly, it is not for the historian to essay the role of prophet. Yet it could hardly be thought unwarranted should he or she wonder, in view of the people of God's countless reversals through the centuries, if the secular currents pervading the Catholic community of the United States might not encounter here a check through instrumentalities such as Harlem's house established in the autumn of 1971 by Mother Teresa for New York's 'poorest of the poor', as well as through the subsequent spread of regional units of the Co-Workers of Mother Teresa in America, a group begun about the same time. As the admirers of Mother Teresa multiplied and expanded across the United States, they might well prove a leaven in the mass, as they took to heart personal convictions such as her declaration that[102]

101. *Time*, XCIX (26 June 1972), 66; see also, 'The Christian Woodstock', *Newsweek*, LXXIX (26 June 1972), 52. A religious phenomenon of a far different kind that suggested a revival of diabolism and that was said to enjoy an increasing vogue in the United States, was described in a cover story, 'The Occult: A Substitute Faith', *Time*, XCIX (19 June 1972), 62-8.
102. Quoted by Louis Cassels, 'Mother Teresa – Love in Action', San Francisco *Chronicle* (30 October 1971), 15. At a time when most of the Catholic world's religious communities of men and women found it exceedingly difficult to attract recruits in any numbers, the extremely difficult apostolate of the Missionaries of Charity, which was daily labour among the 'poorest of the poor', experienced the exact opposite. In Malcom Muggeridge's widely publicised interview with Mother Teresa, he asked her if many of her sisters did not find it too

The Church languishes today, not because it asks too much of modern man but because it asks too little.

It has tried to make its faith plausible and palatable when it should have presented the high, hard way of Christ without compromising his demand for total sacrifice of self.

Experiences of the kind described in this essay were, of course, in no sense unique among the Catholics of the United States, for their co-religionists in every part of the world were feeling them in varying degrees. What most Americans, knowing relatively little of their Church's history, failed for the most part to understand was that they were participants, willy-nilly, in a profound cultural revolution, a revolution that inevitably engulfed the Church herself in a way she had not witnessed in the more than 450 years that had passed since Martin Luther broke from her fold. Revolutions of any kind are nothing if not unsettling, especially for those reared in a conservative tradition and strengthened by only a slight heed to history. Moreover, Americans as a people have never been conspicuous for moderation, and this national characteristic has been as prevalent among those owing spiritual allegiance to the Church of Rome as it has among their fellow countrymen. In their disturbed state of mind, therefore, they were unable to fall back on the resource which General de Gaulle observed in Pope John XXIII in an audience of June 1959. The pope, he said, felt a keen anxiety because of the 'spiritual perturbation ... caused by the gigantic upheavals of the century', but he added, the pontiff's anxiety was 'tempered by his natural serenity'. [103] It was a quality enjoyed by relatively few of John XXIII's American faithful.

In spite of this and other deficiencies, however, the communications revolution had opened more and more vistas from the Universal Church to American Catholic eyes. As the latter's education improved and deepened, they sensed themselves as part of a worldwide religious community, and in that community the singular gifts of figures like Cardinal Suenens, Archbishop Camara, and Mother Teresa of Calcutta — only three of a large company — offered inspiration and models for emulation as well. Thus slowly coming to know and to weigh their own position vis-à-vis that of world Catholicism, the Church's sons and daughters in the United States would be brought to comprehend what the primate of Belgium had in mind in his pastoral letter for Pentecost 1971, when he maintained that the Church's

---

strenuous and in consequence dropped out. 'Very few, very, very few have left', she replied. 'We can count them on our fingers. It's the most extraordinary thing that so many of our Sisters have been so faithful right from the very first.' Malcom Muggeridge, *Something Beautiful For God* (New York: Harper and Row 1971), 97.
103. Charles de Gaulle, *Memoirs of Hope: Renewal and Endeavour.* Translated by Terence Kilmartin (New York: Simon and Schuster 1971), 193.

history had not been written, 'in a straight line'. Rather, said Cardinal Suenens:[104]

It has its points of regression and progress but it is good to know that those times which we call difficult according to our scales of measurement are often, when we look back on them, seen to be times of strength, carriers of grace.

104. 'The Perennial Mystery of Pentecost', *The Tablet* 225 (London 12 June 1971), 585. This was a more Christian perspective than that of the Reverend Battista Mondin of the Pontifical Propaganda University, Rome, who held a doctorate in theology from the Harvard Divinity School gained under the direction of Professor Harvey Cox. In *L'Osservatore della Domenica* of 14 May 1972, Mondin stated that there were those – unnamed – who had already predicted that the wave of secularisation sweeping through the Catholic Church of the United States would not be overcome and 'that within twenty years it will be completely annihilated'. ['The U.S. Church. Final Twenty Years?, *Origins. NC Documentary Service*, II (29 June 1972), 98]. For a critique of Mondin's article, see Andrew M. Greeley, 'Looking For a Source of Trouble' [*The Monitor* (San Francisco), 6 July 1972, 4]. A further sample of defeatist literature – in this instance applied to the Universal Church – was the book of the elderly English convert, John Eppstein, *Has the Catholic Church Gone Mad?* (New Rochelle: Arlington House 1971). A more measured conservative appraisal, with reference largely to the United States, was that of the young professional historian, James F. Hitchcock, *The Decline and Fall of Radical Catholicism* (New York: Herder and Herder 1971).

PART THREE

CATHOLICISM IN LATIN AMERICA

15

CATHOLICISM IN LATIN AMERICA

INTRODUCTION
LATE in the eighteenth century, Peruvian clergyman Vincente Amil y Feijóo summoned up theological arguments in defence of political absolutism, thereby emerging as a new spokesman of one traditional aspect of Hispanic America's multi-faceted Catholicism:[1]

> Whether the prince uses his power well or badly, this power is always conferred by God... Even if his government is so tyrannical that he ceases to be a prince and becomes a demon, even so... we must maintain fidelity, not allowing ourselves any other recourse than calling upon God, the King of Kings, that He may opportunely help us in our tribulations.

A great number of the clergy disagreed with this authoritarian doctrine, convinced that the Church should be used as an instrument to protect citizens against political, social and economic abuses. Churchmen of this persuasion stressed the importance of the natural law and maintained that the true role of religion was not to bolster political authority but to safeguard the God-given rights of all individuals in society. Such a man was Peruvian-born Father Toribio Rodríguez de Mendoza, who in the 1790s surreptitiously reformed the curriculum of one of Lima's leading schools (the Real Convictorio de San Carlos) so that emphasis in instruction might be placed on popular sovereignty and the natural rights of man.[2]

Throughout Spanish America by the dawn of the nineteenth century, additional examples of the conflict between the ideas of Fathers Amil y Feijóo and Rodríguez de Mendoza were clearly in evidence. Indeed, it was difficult

1. Quoted in F. Barreda Laos, *Vida intelectual del virreinato del Perú* (Buenos Aires 1937), 62-3.
2. See F. B. Pike, *The Modern History of Peru* (London, New York 1967), 38-40.

to determine what was the true nature of Hispanic American Catholicism. This was no new situation. In Spanish America, as in the motherland itself, there had always been disputes as to whether Catholicism was to serve as an instrument of repression, stressing narrow interpretations of the divine positive law to the advantage of a privileged élite, or as the means of defending the rights even of the humblest in society in accordance with the teachings of the natural law and the more humanitarian and liberal concepts that had always been associated with the faith. [3]

Weakened at the dawn of the independence period by a serious internal cleavage, the Church had also to operate within a social and political ambient that had become decidedly hostile owing to the prevalence of anticlerical sentiments. The essence of anti-clericalism was an attitude of suspicion and even animosity towards the administrative organisation of the Church and towards clergymen in general.

It has been suggested that an unwitting tendency toward heresy inhered in the Creole mentality. [4] In particular, Creoles (those of Spanish descent born in the New World) have seemed to be attracted by beliefs constituting the heresy of quietism. Thus, they have stressed the importance of the individual's identifying his will with the divine will and have questioned the value of the formal sacramental role of the organised Church and its ministers.

Problems arising from internal divisions and a prevailing spirit of anticlericalism were soon compounded by the appearance of new issues. Even while the independence movement was under way, heated dispute between Church and State officials burst out over the issue of patronage. [5] Churchmen and political leaders also began to argue over taxation. One issue at stake concerned whether the national governments should continue the colonial tradition of collecting tithes for the Church. At the same time separate

3. The best single source on the Catholic Church in colonial times is A. de Egaña, *Historia de la Iglesia en América Española desde el descubrimiento hasta comienzos del siglo XIX*, Madrid 1966.
4. Mexican historian Silvio Zavala is convinced of the Creole's tendency toward heresy. See F. B. Pike, ed., *The Conflict Between Church and State in Latin America* (New York 1964), 8.
5. See P. Leturia, *El ocaso del patronato real en la América Española*, Madrid 1925, and R. F. Schwaller, *The Episcopal Succession in Spanish America, 1800-1850: The Americas*, XXIV (1968), 207-71. Vividly describing the catastrophic consequences produced by the patronage dispute, Schwaller points out that for eighteen years there were no proprietary bishops in Argentina; for sixteen consecutive years the archdiocese of Mexico and the archdiocese of Guatemala were leaderless; and for forty-one years Cuenca, Ecuador, was a vacant see. 'With the bishops gone and the clergy decreasing,' Schwaller concludes, 'new leaders arose to fill the vacuum, and unfortunately for the Church, many of these leaders were the ruthless anti-clericals who sought to destroy the Church or establish a national religion... The practice of the Faith slowly faded, and to this day it has not completely revived.'

church courts, provided for by the ecclesiastical *fuero* of colonial times, came in for attack both from intellectuals and government bureaucrats. Moreover, the vast wealth and land holdings of the Church evoked mounting criticism not only from the laity but also from a small number of clergymen.

The issues of patronage, taxation, separate ecclesiastical courts and church property had already been fought out to a large degree in various European nations, beginning as early as the eleventh century, and by 1800 had been substantially resolved. In Spanish America, and also in Brazil, vexatious problems that had concerned Europeans for centuries appeared for the first time only after 1800 and were resolved in the course of a few violence-ridden decades.

With independence achieved, Latin American statesmen tended to look to Europe for ideological inspiration. Delighted in general by the teachings of nineteenth-century liberalism, they were particularly responsive to the anticlerical features of that ideology. Somewhat later particularly in Mexico, Chile, Brazil, and also to a considerable degree in Argentina, Venezuela and Peru, intellectuals and political leaders were infatuated by the works and popularisations of Auguste Comte, and in the name of positivism they attacked many of the traditional practices and beliefs of Catholicism. [6] Then, as nationalism became more and more important in Latin America, some of its spokesmen who professed the need to defend regalistic traditions of the colonial past denounced the Church as an extra-national institution which, if permitted to survive in the new nation States, must be rendered temporally impotent.

At the outset of the independence period, moreover, the Church was involved in the identity problem that plagued the new republics. Many leading intellectuals and politicians were concerned with progress and material development, and they identified with the values that they thought would be conducive to rapid economic advance. To them, it seemed all-important to instil in the citizens materialistic incentives, competitive instincts, and the capitalist drives associated with the individualistic pursuit of wealth. Others wished to conserve the essentially medieval orientation of cultural values that had been a characteristic of the colonial era. They questioned the importance of material development and sought to mute the incentives of individualistic capitalism by maintaining the primacy of non-material, spiritual rewards for the masses and by preserving the collectivism of the guild

6. One of the best studies of positivism in Latin America, although its findings have been increasingly challenged, is L. Zea, *Dos etapas del pensamiento en hispanoamèrica: del romanticismo al positivismo,* Mexico, D.F. 1949. See also M. Jorrin and J. D. Martz, *Latin-American Political Thought and Ideology,* Chapel Hill 1970, and R. L. Woodward Jr, ed., *Positivism in Latin America, 1850-1900,* Lexington, Mass. 1971.

organisation and rural landholding patterns. To a large extent, although by no means exclusively, churchmen took their place in the second ideological school. Furthermore, the clergy, in many instances, asserted that capitalistic individualism was to be rejected because in the final analysis it was the fruit of the Protestant heresy which exaggerated the importance of the individual conscience in matters of religion.

Throughout most of Latin America, with the striking exception of Colombia and the partial exception of Peru, the Church had by the latter part of the nineteenth century lost most of the battles which it had waged against civilian governments. Its economic and political power as well as its influence in the intellectual and cultural realms had been seriously eroded, and as a temporal institution it was capable of wielding only minimal influence. Dismayed by this situation, the clergy tended to attribute the chronic instability and revolutionary ferment that plagued the new republics to the decline of church power and prestige.

Even by the middle of the nineteenth century many church authorities and their lay partisans had begun to insist that the only unifying tradition upon which Latin Americans could construct an orderly society was the Catholicism of the colonial era. Like Father Amil y Feijóo, they stressed the authoritarian aspect of traditional Catholicism. Hearkening back still further to ideas advanced by sixteenth-century Spanish theologian Ginés de Sepúlveda as he prescribed the proper relationship between Indians and Spaniards, the new prophets of authoritarianism averred that the role of the inferior classes was to serve unquestioningly the superior classes.

The men obsessed with order and the rights of those at the top of the socio-political pyramid were never able to establish a broad consensus that favoured their vision of the true Catholic tradition. They were never able even to suppress altogether those within their own Church who, like Father Rodríguez de Mendoza, associated the Catholic tradition with the defence of the rights of all men, and most especially of those least capable of asserting their own rights. Proponents of this tradition were the spiritual heirs of Bartolomé de Las Casas, the Spanish-born protector of the Indians and critic of Ginés de Sepúlveda, who insisted that all mankind was one, and not divided into inferior and superior classes.

If churchmen who identified the closed, authoritarian, hierarchical aspect of Catholicism with the true national tradition, tended during many periods to prevail over their clerical critics, it was largely because their views reflected those of power-wielding civilians. Even if they were anti-clerical, even if they refused to associate themselves with the Church as a political ally, Latin America's ruling classes generally acted to defend a political order that stressed the authority and rights of the exalted while commanding the resignation and emphasising the duties and obligations of the humble.

Given the rigid class structure that had prevailed for centuries, Latin American leaders were well-nigh incapable of acting in behalf of a different type of order, regardless of how much aesthetic satisfaction and intellectual excitement they might find in libertarian and even levelling ideologies.

Although virtually dormant in some countries for nearly a century, that aspect of Catholicism associated with the Las Casas tradition and concerned primarily with the duties and responsibilities of the upper classes and the rights of the masses was beginning, by the late 1950s, to gain more and more adherents among Latin American church authorities. One reason for this was that civilian leaders, faced with new social and economic demands, had begun to discard the aristocratic values of a previous century and to accept the need for an open and pluralistic society in the quest for stability, modernisation, and political development.

The rivalry between the spokesmen of the two Catholic traditions, and the interaction between these two traditions and the prevailing values of temporal society, have largely determined the course of Latin American Catholicism both in its internal development and in its relationship to the body politic. The fact that ecclesiastical leaders had not, by the early 1970s, succeeded in finding a middle way between the two traditions, interfered seriously with the Church's attempt to take advantage of a political climate that had become increasingly benign.

I. THE CHURCH AND TEMPORAL SOCIETY IN LATIN AMERICA
TO THE END OF THE NINETEENTH CENTURY

BACKGROUND

For approximately twenty years following the attainment of independence in the early 1820s, Latin American liberals tended to concern themselves mainly with political considerations. Opposing monarchical schemes, they urged the extension of political participation and the expansion of suffrage. Generally they backed federalism while attacking the evils of centralised authority and maintained that large standing armies posed serious dangers to individual liberties. Liberals also pictured parliamentary supremacy as a political panacea. Moreover, they sought to eliminate traditional compartments in society by suppressing the old subsidiary, corporative entities or organisms that stood between the government and citizens. Rather than the corporative or organic society, they aspired to the non-organic structuring of the body politic so that citizens might be liberated from unnecessary restraints in their individualistic pursuit of self-development.

The first-generation liberals, including in their ranks a large number and in some countries probably a majority of the native-born clergy who had been converted to Enlightenment ideas during their seminary training, [7]did not totally ignore theological issues. Some of them advanced Jansenist-tinged interpretations of grace and espoused deistic views that left little if any room for providence in the determining of human events. Moreover, many liberals felt their respective countries should emulate United States' models and adopt religious toleration and separation of Church and State. Still, the great majority of early Latin American liberals, whether of the clergy or laity, attached overwhelming importance to political and economic considerations, largely ignoring purely religious issues.

Latin American conservatives at the outset of the independence period were also concerned primarily with political and economic matters. To them conservatism meant essentially authoritarian centralism, rule by a tiny élite backed by a powerful army, executive predominance over the legislature, and preservation of privileged corporate groups. In striving to achieve this type of political-economic structure, conservatives did not necessarily feel that they had any natural affinity with churchmen. Quite the contrary, they were disturbed by the number of ecclesiastical leaders with liberal political views.

In the early years following independence, Latin American conservatives, except in Central America, generally managed to contain the main onslaughts of liberalism, even though political fortunes often changed rapidly. Only in preventing the establishment of monarchical government in the new countries did the liberals score a resounding victory, and in Brazil they failed even in that effort. By the late 1830s, however, a new generation of liberals had appeared and in the years to come they gradually gathered strength. Heartened by the European events of 1848, they profited from a growing conviction among Latin American intellectuals that liberalism was the inevitable tide of the future. By the middle of the century the liberals had their opponents on the defensive – except in Central America where conservatism was generally triumphant after 1840 – and in most republics were about to gain the upper hand. The ten to twenty years following 1848 constitute a watershed between the sway of conservatism and the reign of liberalism.

Already by the mid-1830s the liberal-conservative issue had begun to take on a new complexion in many parts of Latin America. Clergymen were tending to desert the liberal ranks, disillusioned in part by the continuing political chaos which they attributed to an alleged breakdown in morality. [8]

7. See R. Arango Jaramillo, *El clero en la independencia*, Antioquia, Colombia 1946; L. Medina Ascensio, *México y el Vaticano*, vol. I, *La Santa Sede y la emancipación mexicana*, Mexico, D.F. 1965; K. Schmitt, *The Clergy and the Independence of New Spain: Hispanic American Historical Review*, XXXIV (1954), 289-312; L. Toro, *Historia de la iglesia en América Latina*, vol. II, *La iglesia en la crisis de independencia*, Bogotá 1962.
8. It is difficult to ascertain if a breakdown in morality actually occurred in nineteenth-

and hoped to remedy through the authoritarian rule of political leaders willing to accept Church guidance. In addition, beginning in the 1840s, Latin America received one of the first waves of clerical immigrants. [9]Arriving on the scene to offset the shortage of priests, the foreign clerics were in general better trained and also, largely because of their European experiences, more conservative in outlook than their native counterparts. Increasingly, foreign priests were able to win to the conservative cause the formerly liberal native clergymen. [10]

The conservative stance assumed by churchmen in Latin America can be viewed as a reaction against the changes which a new generation of intellectuals was introducing into the liberal movement. These young liberals had begun to regard transformation of the traditional organisation and practices of the Church as the essential prerequisite for the implementation of their entire programme. They appeared to be convinced that democratic usages could never be introduced into the body politic until the powerful and influential Church had undergone the liberalisation of its own structure.

In the name of equality of all citizens, liberals insisted that ecclesiastical privileges and immunities, the hallmark of the traditional corporative structure, be abolished. In the name of freedom of thought they demanded liberation from the teaching authority customarily claimed by churchmen in matters both sacred and mundane. Going further than many Gallican-influenced clergymen of the late eighteenth century, they sought virtually complete State control over the Church. In addition, liberals frequently asserted that the Church's wealth and temporal power were contrary to early Christian ideals. In the spirit of many reformers of the Spanish and Portuguese Enlightenment, the liberals sought to deprive the Church of its wealth so that it could no longer carry out its charitable and social welfare programmes. In the liberal view, charity encouraged idleness, prevented the inculcation of competitive, capitalist values among the masses, and thus retarded economic progress. Finally, in the name of federalism and local autonomy, liberals demanded that the Church be freed from the centralistic control exercised by the Vatican and the curia. If they achieved this last objective, liberals could hope to encourage individualism within the realm of religion, thereby matching the individualism which they sought to introduce into the temporal order.

---

century Latin America. No reliable social history of the period has been written.
9. See A. Tibesar, 'The Shortage of Priests in Latin America: A Historical Evaluation of Werner Promper's "Priesternot in Lateinamerika" ', *The Americas*, XXII (1966), 413-20.
10. The writings of the Spanish philosopher Juan Donoso Cortés also exercised vast influence in winning Latin America's Catholic leadership to the conservative cause. A recent edition of the writings of Donoso Cortés that were best known in Spanish America is G. A. Lousteay Heguy and S. M. Lozada, eds, *El pensamiento político hispanoamericano*, vol. XII, *Juan Donoso Cortés*, Buenos Aires 1965

Conservative clergymen reacted energetically against the new liberalism. Just as liberal intellectuals had strayed from what was their proper field of competence by demanding reforms within the internal structure of the Church, so conservative clergymen now strayed from their proper field of jurisdiction by prescribing for the organisation of the body politic.

Whereas liberals wanted the Church, even in its internal structure, to reflect the politico-economic ideals which they championed, clerical conservatives wanted temporal society to reflect what for them was the ideal organisation of the ecclesiastical institution within which order, authority, and hierarchy were stressed and within which individualism was curbed and the profit motive de-emphasised. As opposed to liberals who felt that their ideal society would be endangered so long as the Catholic Church deviated from the temporal patterns they desired, conservative clergymen now decided that the Church would be in jeopardy until political society became a replica of the hierarchical and non-materialistic ecclesiastical organisation.

Before the end of the 1840s, then, the clergy, by and large, had tended to adopt a position that was pleasing to political conservatives among the laity who had regarded an earlier generation of liberal priests as their enemies. As a result an alliance was forged between conservative civilian political leaders and the Catholic clergy. The conservative civilians took to heart the clerical warning that any attack against the authoritarian, hierarchical structure of the Church necessarily heralded an attempt to initiate a levelling movement within the body politic. Both civilian and clerical Conservatives, moreover, distrusted a newly-emerging and increasingly assertive bourgeoisie.

United by mid-nineteenth century in the conservative cause, clergymen and their civilian allies espoused the social philosophy of paternalism. Their fundamental belief was that the natural social order called for the existence of an immobile lower class permanently entrusted with the meaner occupations. Members of the lower class were not expected to rise within the social order, for any endeavour on their part to do so would threaten the providentially-established hierarchical order. Lower-class status, however, did not imply a stigma of any kind or suggest moral shortcomings. Those in the lower classes had the same end of eternal salvation as members of the aristocracy and therefore possessed human dignity. They should, accordingly, be made reasonably comfortable and protected by various paternalistic devices.

The social goal of first-and second-generation Latin American liberals was to give to the lower classes a chance to rise in social status. As the system which they envisaged began to function, it would no longer be necessary for the upper classes to take special measures to provide comfort and security for the masses. Rather, the masses were expected to solve their own problems by taking advantage of the avenues for advance which, theoretically, liberal administrations would provide through expanding educational facilities, suffrage opportunities, and sources of employment.

The success of many Latin Americans of fairly low origins in finding their way through financial success, friendship, business associations, kinship ties and marriage into the relatively open aristocracy of the nineteenth century, helped convince liberals that adequate opportunities for upward social mobility already existed. Any attempt to provide the lower classes with additional openings would, they felt, result in the economically inadvisable and morally unjustified pampering of unworthy people. This conviction was strengthened as liberalism evolved into positivism. Political leaders from Mexico to Argentina, often professing the racial inferiority of indigenous population elements, set themselves to the repression of allegedly unfit classes who were incapable of self-improvement and of contributing to the material development of their countries.

Latin America has suffered unfortunate consequences not only from the conflict of the two ideologies but from the cross-pollination between the two that began to take place in the late nineteenth century. Liberals, especially as they became converts to one of the schools of positivism that flourished in Latin America, were enticed by the practical conveniences afforded by belief in a permanently and necessarily stratified society. Beginning to deny the perfectibility of the lower classes, they grew increasingly indifferent toward supplying its members with opportunities to advance. Disavowing the paternalism associated with Comtian positivism, they opted instead for the social Darwinism of Herbert Spencer. On the other hand, conservatives, borrowing from the ideology of their adversaries, began to question the feasibility of supplying paternalistic protection to groups that appeared totally to lack economic virtues. By the turn of the century it often appeared that the heirs of the old-time liberal-conservative disputants were separated only by disagreement as to the degree of temporal power which the Catholic Church should be allowed to exercise. As a result of this situation a social problem began to assume dangerous proportions, and early in the twentieth century the ruling classes, whether they considered themselves conservative or liberal, had either to address themselves to its solution or face the inevitability of revolution.

1. MEXICO

Mexico embarked upon its independence under the rule of the native-born Agustín de Iturbide. Proclaimed emperor in 1822 and overthrown the following year, Iturbide was supported by what was probably a minority element of the Mexican clergy, made up of priests who wanted to return to the Habsburg traditions of the colonial past and were suspicious of the Enlightenment ideas associated with the Bourbon reforms. To arch-conservative elements, Iturbide remained for over a century the symbol of all that was best in Catholic colonial traditions. He was pictured as the defender of true Mexican traditions who sought to protect the country against the influence of the Protestant heresy and United States-style materialism and individualism. [11]

Liberal elements in Mexico, successful in overthrowing Iturbide and establishing a republic, found in Valentin Gómez Farías their most energetic and zealous leader. Against the attempts of Gómez Farías during the 1830s to strip it of wealth and privileges and to restrict its ties with Rome, the Church was inconsistently defended by the unreliable Antonio López de Santa Anna. Then in 1854 there erupted a revolutionary movement that soon came to be known as La Reforma. Regarded by some, probably with exaggeration, as no less than attempt to introduce the Reformation into Mexico, [12] La Reforma did seek to replace the corporate, paternalistic features of the colonial past with the spirit of classical, *laissez-faire* liberalism. [13]

A new constitution promulgated in 1857 contained articles aimed at introducing the liberal spirit of the times into the economic and political spheres. It also provided for compensated expropriation of church property and abolished the ecclesiastical *fuero*.[14] Echoing the Vatican's condemnation of the constitution, Mexican Archbishop Lázaro de la Garza attacked not only the instrument's anti-clerical provisions but also denounced those articles which established freedom of assembly, press and expression and proclaimed the principle of popular sovereignty.

In Benito Juárez conservative clerical elements faced a man just as dogmatic and inflexible as the archbishop. [15] Juárez appeared to possess an

11. For examples of appraisals of Iturbide made by conservative Mexican Catholic intellectuals see A. Junco, *Motivos mejicanos*, Madrid 1933, and J. Fuentes Mares, *Poinset, historia de una gran intriga*, Mexico, D.F. 1951.
12. See Paul V. Murray, *The Catholic Church in Mexico: Historical Essays for the General Reader*, Mexico, D.F. 1965. Valuable material on La Reforma, presented in an anti-clerical spirit, is found in G. Garcia Cantú, *El pensamiento de la revolución: historia documental, 1810-1862*, Mexico, D.F. 1966. The much-debated topic of how much wealth the Church actually controlled and how important its economic status was in inciting resentment and envy is authoritatively treated in J. Bazant, *Alienation of Church Wealth in Mexico: Social and Economic Aspects of the Liberal Revolution, 1856-1875*, Cambridge, Eng. 1971, and M. P. Costeloe, *Church Wealth in Mexico: A Study of the 'Juzgado de Capellanias' in the Archbishopric of Mexico 1800-1856*, Cambridge, Eng. 1967.
13. A particularly valuable study of the issues involved in the liberal-conservative struggle in Mexico is C. A. Hale, *Mexican Liberalism in the Age of Mora, 1821-1853*, New Haven 1968.
14. See W. V. Scholes, 'Church and State at the Mexican Constitutional Convention, 1856-57', *The Americas*, IV (1947), 151-74.
15. See W. V. Scholes, *Mexican Politics during the Juárez Regime*, Columbia 1957. Melchor Ocampo, one of Juárez's most important ministers, provides valuable insights into the anti-clerical spirit of the times in his *La religión, la iglesia y el clero*, Mexico, D.F. 1965 edn.

inner-light certitude that liberalism was the source of all virtue and that compromise with the forces of the past was unthinkable. Mexico was plunged into a civil war in which the conservative-clerical elements were soundly defeated, not withstanding their recourse to foreign intervention in the 1862-8 period. Subjected to severe restrictions in the last three decades of the nineteenth century, some of which were of a vindictive nature that interfered with its ability to attend to its spiritual mission, the Church ceased to be a significant temporal force. [16]

The major positive accomplishment of La Reforma was the incorporation of the mestizo into the national life. The most disastrous consequence was the destruction of many Indian communal villages, carried out in accordance with the liberal principle of private ownership of property.

The attempt of liberals to force the Indian masses who had been largely inert in a paternalistic system to compete with others on a basis of liberty and equality only left the indigenous masses standing impotent before those who had learned to take advantage of the opportunities provided by rampant individualism. The 1857 constitution was modelled after those of countries where there was an ethnically homogeneous population and where an industrial revolution and the rise of a bourgeois class had rendered their liberal provisions meaningful. In racially divided, pre-industrial, pre-bourgeois Mexico, even as in other Latin American republics, the constitutional provisions of advanced nation States were a mockery of reality. To some degree churchmen were justified in resisting them, although too often they acted out of selfish motivation.

2. CENTRAL AMERICA

After an initial period of liberal dominance, [17] Guatemala under the rule of Rafael Carrera underwent a powerful conservative reaction. A new constitution proclaimed in 1840 restored ecclesiastical privileges and returned previously seized lands to the religious orders. In 1852 the Guatemalan administration signed the first concordat between a Latin American republic and the Vatican. The document promised the preservation of tithes and granted clerics numerous privileges, including control over education and censorship of books. Long-term dictator Carrera also exercised close surveillance, sometimes backed by military force, over neighbouring republics. His influence was in part responsible for the 1861 signing by Honduras of a concordat similar in terms to the Guatemalan instrument. The following

16. Some restrictions were eased during the long period dominated by Porfirio Díaz (1876-1911). See M. González Navarro, *El porfiriato: vida social*, vol. IV in D. Cosío Villegas, gen. ed., *Historia moderna de México*, Mexico, D.F. 1957, esp. 265-73, 360-7, 455-508, 576-8, 632-9.
17. See M. W. Williams, 'The Ecclesiastical Policy of Francisco Morazán and other Central American Liberals', *Hispanic American Historical Review*, III (1920), 119-43.

year El Salvador signed a nearly identical concordat. Carrera's will also came to prevail in Nicaragua, in spite of liberal recourse to the aid of foreign troops under the command of the colourful United States adventurer William Walker.

Not until 1871 were the liberals able to oust their opponents from political control. In that year the liberals of Honduras and El Salvador combined to overthrow conservative leaders in their own countries. They then defeated the conservative armies of Guatemala and initiated an anti-clerical programme that had repercussions throughout Central America.

The self-styled liberals were essentially the political 'outs' of the past thirty years, reinforced by a few intellectuals under the influence of continental liberalism and beginning to become aware of positivism. To the Catholic Church and its political manipulations they attributed the fact that they had for so long a time been denied opportunities to exercise authority. It followed logically in their minds that the temporal power of the Church had to be destroyed.

Summoned by liberal President Justo Rufino Barrios, a Guatemalan constituent assembly in 1879 formulated a new charter which incorporated most of the anti-clerical measures passed during the preceding several years. By the terms of the constitution the Church was denied juridical personality, could own no property, not even places of worship, and was barred from participating in political discussion. The new instrument also provided for the suppression of monasteries, declared the complete separation of Church and State, and secularised public education.

Protestantism was first legally admitted into Guatemala in 1882 when President Barrios, on a visit to the United States, invited the Presbyterian Board to send missionaries to his country, offering to pay the expenses of the first one to arrive. Eight years later the non-denominational Central American Mission was founded by the Reverend C.I. Scofield, and by the end of the century its missionaries had effected entry into all Central American republics.[18]

Except in Costa Rica, Catholicism in Central America had by the turn of the century been forced to accommodate to a series of rigorously anti-clerical enactments. The Church's temporal might and privileges had been either seriously weakened or else totally suppressed and its teaching power significantly undermined. Even in church-controlled schools, religious instruction courses often could not be offered because of curriculum restrictions imposed by the government.

As was true of the earlier La Reforma in Mexico, Central America's

18. See H. Brown, *Latin America: The Pagans, Papists, Patriots, Protestants and the Present Problem*, New York 1901; K. G. Grubb, *Religion in Central America*, London 1937; and F. Crowe, *The Gospel in Central America*, London 1850.

liberal revolution of the 1870s resulted in few social or economic reforms that had widespread impact. Liberalism in Guatemala, in fact, probably contributed to the worsening of the Indians' plight, as the system of debt peonage operated more harshly once paternalistic restraints had been eliminated.

3. ARGENTINA AND CHILE

In the southern extreme of Latin America the Church by the late nineteenth century had been excluded as definitively from the power structure as in Mexico and Central America. The situation in Argentina and Chile, however, had resulted from a process that was more peaceful and evolutionary than in the far northern republics.

The liberal-conservative issue had appeared in Argentina during the 1820s when Barnardino Rivadavia, governor of Buenos Aires province and would-be president of a united La Plata, sought to abolish separate law courts for clergymen, founded a benevolent society to challenge the Church's customary monopolistic control over charity, and endeavoured to found a State-supported public school system. [19] Rivadavia's efforts were largely unavailing, and in the years between 1829 and 1851 the Church benefited from the consistently favourable attitude of dictator Juan Manuel de Rosas. Argentina's conservative Catholic spokesmen have generally tended to regard Rosas in the same light in which their Mexican counterparts view Iturbide. Thus, Rosas is pictured as continuing a golden age that had existed in the colonial period when society had been structured upon hierarchical models and infused by Catholic principles. [20]

Beginning in the 1860s, approximately ten years after the overthrow of Rosas, liberalism, with decided positivist overtones, gained the ascendancy in Argentina. A public education system which prohibited religious instruction was established. [21] And a common devotion to anti-clericalism was one

19. See H. E. Frizzi de Longoni, *Rivadavia y la reforma eclesiástica*, Buenos Aires 1947, and G. Gallardo, *La política religiosa de Rivadavia*, Buenos Aires 1962. See also A. A. Tonda, *El deán Funes y la reforma de Rivadavia*, Santa Fe, Argentina 1961, which reveals the extent to which regalistic clergymen such as Gregorio Funes supported Rivadavia's efforts to secularise religious orders.
20. Objective accounts are E. T. Glauert, 'Ricardo Rojas and the emergence of Argentine Cultural Nationalism', *Hispanic American Historical Review*, XLIII (1963), esp. 5, and C. Smith, *Juan Manuel de Rosas ante la posteridad*, Buenos Aires 1936. A detailed account of relations between Rosas and the Church, written from an anti-clerical position that reveals positivist and socialist influences, is J. Ingenieros, *Evolución de las ideas argentinas*, vol. XVI in *Obras completas* (Buenos Aires 1937), 99-142.
21. See G. Furlong, *La tradición religiosa en la escuela argentina*, Buenos Aires 1957, attacking the 1884 law which established secular, lay education. Opposing points of view are expressed in M. A. Micheletti, *et. al.*, *La doctrina católica en el desenvolvimiento constitucional argentino*, Buenos Aires, 1957. A work of fundamental importance dealing with this period is J. M. Estrada, *La iglesia y el estado*, Buenos Aires 1929. In this work, first

of the few points on which there was agreement between the aristocratic Partido Autonomista Nacionalista, [22] the dominant political party between 1874 and 1916, and the Unión Cívica Radical, a middle-sector, populist opposition group formed in 1891. [23] Members of both parties were in general agreement that the Church must be denied the power to impede progress by imposing allegedly archaic, medieval values within the temporal order.

The suppression of the Church's temporal power undoubtedly contributed to an intellectual climate which facilitated Argentina's remarkable material development in the 1880s. The nation's positivist-influenced leaders, however, were not concerned with social reforms, partly because of their racially-inspired disdain for the mixed-blood population of the interior provinces. To these leaders, moreover, political liberalism meant 'the resolute elimination of any fair struggle for power, a struggle that could be dangerous for the country, which was in a process of transformation'. [24]

Just as in Argentina, so also in Chile the Catholic Church, which had been a comparatively weak institution in colonial times, underwent further loss of power in the second half of the nineteenth century. The confrontation between Church and State, which was to result in a severe setback to the temporal ambitions of many clergymen, began in 1845 when Rafael Valentin Valdivieso y Zañartu became archbishop of Santiago.

Inflexible in his views, Valdivieso was convinced that there could be no compromise with the new, secular, liberal spirit of the times. [25]By his actions the archbishop often suggested that he wanted a theocratic structure and would settle for nothing less than a bipolar balance of power between Church and State in temporal affairs. In his stance the archbishop would shortly be supported by a new political force, the Conservative Party. Membership in this staunchly Catholic, pro-clerical party, according to one of its stalwarts, brought one closer to God. [26]

In President Manuel Montt (1851-61), the archbishop found an implacably regalistic foe, resolutely determined that in temporal matters the State should be supreme, in no way sharing its prerogatives with the

published as an article in the 1870s, Estrada, who was Argentina's leading Catholic intellectual of the second half of the nineteenth century, argues that the Church should be freed from excessive government restrictions.

22. An excellent study which stresses the influence that liberalism and anti-clericalism exercised on the Partido Autonomista Nacionalista is C. R. Melo, *Los partidos políticos argentinos*, 3rd ed., Córdoba, Argentina 1964.

23. See P. G. Snow, *Argentine Radicalism*, Iowa City 1966.

24. See J. L. Romero, *Las ideas políticas en Argentina*, (Mexico, D. F. 1946), 186.

25. Probably the most balanced study of Valdivieso's role in Chilean history and of the entire Church-State issue during the period is provided by conservatively-inclined historian R. Sotomayor Valdés, *Historia de Chile durante los cuarenta años trascurridos desde 1831 hasta 1871*, 2 vols, Santiago de Chile 1875, 1876.

26. See A. Donoso, *Recuerdos de cincuenta años* (Santiago de Chile 1947), 143.

Church.[27] By his stand against the archbishop, Montt alienated many Chilean traditionalists and at the same time gave indirect encouragement to the idealogues who had established the Liberal Party and hoped, before proceeding to the reform of the body politic, to remove every vestige of the Church's political power and even to alter its internal structure.

By the 1870s Chile's liberals, allied with the still more anti-clerical Radical Party, had reduced the Conservative Party to virtual impotence and gained mastery over the political arena. Despite the clergy's resorting to massive excommunications, most church privileges had been removed. No longer were there separate ecclesiastical courts, no longer did the State collect tithes, and no longer did the Church enjoy monopolistic control over cemeteries, education, and marriage. Churchmen complained bitterly but in vain about the impious and heretical influences which were said to be destroying the only true traditions of the land.

As elsewhere in Latin America, the triumph of secular, anti-clerical values in Chile may have contributed to a climate of opinion that was conducive to economic development. In the process, however, social problems were exacerbated. As thousands of Chile's peasants crowded into the country's leading cities in the course of a late nineteenth-century demographic shift, they were cut off from the paternalistic practices that had sometimes mitigated the rigours of their lives in a rural setting. In the cities they were subjected to the unrestrained exploitation of an emergent capitalism which, given the values of *laissez-faire* liberalism, could not conform to concepts of social responsibility.

4. ECUADOR

Juan José Flores, the Venezuelan-born militarist who dominated Ecuadoran politics from 1830 to 1845, hoped to settle the conservative-liberal, Church-State, clerical-anticlerical issue through compromise. Especially in his second term (1839-45), Flores endeavoured to placate liberals by permitting non-Catholics to practise their religion in private and to content conservatives by preserving a highly centralistic, authoritarian, executive-dominated political system. The Flores attempt to establish a compromise by separating purely political from religiously-tinged issues, by responding to some of the wishes of liberals in regard to the Church while satisfying the aspirations of conservatives in regard to political organisation, was doomed to failure by the intransigence of both camps. Following the 1845 overthrow of Flores, Ecuador suffered a decade and a half of chaos and revolutionary ferment as rival regional, ideological and personality cliques struggled for supremacy. Finally in 1860 the Guayaquil-born Gabriel García Moreno

27. See F. B. Pike, 'Church and State in Peru and Chile Since 1840: A Study in Contrasts', *American Historical Review*, LXXXIII (1967), esp. 37-8.

seized power and introduced fifteen years of heavy-handed rule which at least resulted in political stability and considerable economic progress. [28]

A devout Catholic, García Moreno attributed to foreign-bred liberalism the divisiveness that was tearing his country asunder. A widely-based nationalism that could exercise a cohesive force adequate to bind together disparate geographic, ethnic and social groups could arise only, he was convinced, from Ecuador's Catholic traditions. In the attempt to bolster those traditions against all inimical influences, García Moreno entered into an 1863 Concordat with the Vatican which gave to church officials considerable powers over patronage, permitted unencumbered correspondence between the Holy See and Ecuadoran churchmen, strengthened the prerogatives of ecclesiastical courts, guaranteed the Church's right to acquire property, and pledged State collection of tithes.

The García Moreno experiment was ended by his liberal-inspired assassination in 1875. Following that, Ecuador was plunged into two decades of renewed strife and instability. Finally in 1895 the liberals, under the leadership of Eloy Alfaro and Leonidas Plaza Guzmán, triumphed and within ten years introduced an anti-clerical programme establishing civil marriage and legalising divorce, forbidding the admission of new monastic orders, providing for religious toleration, proclaiming a nominal sort of separation that actually permitted vast State interference in church affairs, placing education under secular control, and forbidding religious instruction in public schools.

Among the positive accomplishments of Ecuadoran liberalism were the strengthening of individual guarantees, even though elections were always rigged to prevent the return to power of the numerically stronger Conservative Party, and the incorporation of the mestizo into national life. Negative aspects included the fact that newly-rising middle classes entered into an alliance with the old rural aristocracy to combat social change. Moreover, the introduction of classically liberal economic concepts weakened traditional paternalistic procedures, worsened the plight of the Indians, and in general intensified social problems. [29]

---

28. A strong, in fact, scurrilous, presentation of the case against García Moreno is B. Carrión, *García Moreno, el santo del patíbulo*, Mexico, D.F., Buenos Aires 1959. For an unobjectively favourable assessment see S. Gomezjurado, *Vida de García Moreno*, 8 vols, Quito 1954-68. The work, written by a Jesuit historian, is largely an updating and expansion of the hero-worshipping approach of such earlier writers as A. Berthe, J. M. Le Gouhir y Rodas, and W. Loor. More objective is the treatment found in vol. I of L. Robalino Dávila, *Los orígenes del Ecuador de hoy*, 8 vols, Quito and Puebla, Mexico 1949-69. A scholarly study showing how García Moreno has meant different things to different generations of conservatives and liberals in Ecuador is P. H. Smith, 'The Image of A Dictator: Gabriel García Moreno', *Hispanic American Historical Review*, XLV (1965), 1-24.

29. This analysis is based on A. Pareja Diezcanseco, 'Democracia o demagogia en el Ecuador', *Combate* (San José, Costa Rica), XV (1961), 18-27. For insights into the

Ecuador's Church-State issue, resolved in favour of the liberals only around the turn of the century, continued to excite partisan passions and to distract politicians from issues that were gradually becoming more pressing and vital. All the while many churchmen, supported not only by the well-born but also by the Indian masses, among whom a particularly zealous if not fanatical devotion to at least the outer trappings of Catholicism had originated in colonial times, dreamed of re-acquiring lost privileges. These churchmen concerned themselves little with the socio-economic problems that early in the twentieth century would begin to produce a more radical group of reformers than ever Ecuador had previously known.

5. COLOMBIA

Throughout Latin America, ideology was only one of the factors involved in the conservative-liberal dispute. The terms 'conservative' and 'liberal' were frequently employed to give the semblance of nobler origin to conflicts that involved little more than personal and regional rivalry. Frequently, moreover, pragmatic considerations led to co-operation between conservatives and liberals. Nowhere was this more apparent than in Colombia where family rivalries, personality antagonisms, regional animosities and economic and social frictions reaching back into the previous century contributed to the great nineteenth-century conflict which in oversimplified terms has been described as the clash between conservatism and liberalism. [30]

Disputes which involved personalities as well as the issues of centralism versus federalism and the proper role of the Church in temporal society were among the many factors that helped to bring on a bloody civil conflict known as the War of the Supremes, 1839-41. From this struggle there emerged in triumph a group composed of numerous large estate owners, a good portion of the higher clergy, and a sprinkling of army leaders. The loose affiliation formed by these men, who referred to themselves as the *Ministeriales*, was the forerunner of the Conservative Party.

Following their military victory the Ministeriales, in the early 1840s, imposed a rigid form of political centralism and established a religiously orthodox educational system. By 1848, however, increasingly disunited in their own ranks, they faced a serious challenge from liberals who were draw-

---

Church-State issue provided by Ecuador's great church leader, long-time archbishop of Quito, and distinguished historian, see Federico González Suarez (1844-1917), *Memorias intimas*, Riobamba 1895, *Nueva miscelánea o colección de opúsculos*, Quito 1910, and *Obras escogidas*, ed. J Jijón y Caamaño, vol. X in *Clásicos Ecuatorianos*, Quito 1944. For an analysis favourable to the Church see also Jijón y Caamaño, *Politica conservadora*, 2 vols, Riobamba and Quito 1929-34.

30. See C. Shaw Jr, 'Church and State in Colombia as Observed by American Diplomats, 1834–1906, *Hispanic American Historical Review*, XXI (1941), 577-613. The origins of the liberal-conservative struggle are authoritatively set forth in D. Bushnell, *The Santander Regime in Gran Colombia*, Newark, N.J. 1945.

ing renewed inspiration from occurrences in France. In 1849 the liberals elected their candidate to the presidency and within four years had enacted legislation providing for separation of Church and State and for civil marriage.

Colombia's urban artisan classes, which had in general supported the liberal cause, were soon frustrated and embittered. Liberal legislation reducing or eliminating tariffs adversely affected the economic interests of the artisans. Furthermore, liberal attempts to abolish communal farming not only wiped out many Indian communities but resulted in food shortages when confiscated lands, purchased cheaply by local magnates, were turned over to pasturage.

Disillusioned by liberal rule, Colombians helped vote the Independent Party, headed by ex-liberal Rafael Núñez, into power in 1880. Supported by many moderate conservatives, Núñez and his independents felt that only a return to a strong, centralised system of political authority could begin the painful process of laying a solid basis – more consistent with Colombian historical tradition – for the governmental stability so desperately needed for economic development.[31]

Although encountering difficulties, Núñez managed to dominate the political scene until his death in 1894.[32]The movement which he led, known as *La Regeneración*, resulted virtually in a conservative restoration to power. A new constitution promulgated by Núñez and his supporters in 1886 reestablished centralism and vastly augmented executive powers. In addition, it restored the Church to a powerful position in Colombian life. Advancing still further in this respect, the Núñez regime in 1887 negotiated a Concordat with the Vatican which provided that church property would either be returned or compensation paid and which established a close clerical control over education. Bishops, for example, could determine the selection of textbooks in public schools and bring about the dismissal of teachers who did not satisfy them. At least in the early stages of La Regeneración, moreover, Colombia's leaders showed some concern with social problems and moved to reestablish protective tariffs.[33]

After the death of Núñez, the Church continued to wield a power and influence in Colombia's national life that were probably greater than in any other Latin American republic. Unfortunately Colombia's conservatives, whether of the clergy or laity, did not, following the death of Núñez, take

31. J. L. Helguera, 'Liberalism vs Conservatism in Nineteenth-Century Colombia', in F. B. Pike, ed., *Latin American History: Select Problems,* (New York 1969), esp. 225-8.
32. A friendly but fairly reliable biography is J. Estrada Monsalve, *Núñez, el político y el hombre,* Bogotá 1946.
33. See D. Bushnell, 'Two stages in Colombian Tariff Policy: The Radical Era and Return to Protection', *Inter-American Economic Affairs,* IX (1956), 3-23, and W. P. McGreevey, *An Economic History of Colombia, 1845-1930,* Cambridge, England 1971.

advantage of their enduring strength to seek solutions to the new manifestations of the social problem.

6. PERU

Peru's Church-State, clerical-anticlerical issue had been resolved mainly in favour of conservative interests during the first twenty-five years following independence.[34] Then in the late 1840s the issue flared anew. A second generation of liberals, roused by the events of 1848 in Europe, locked in debate with the priest Bartolomé Herrera, the ablest spokesman of the conservative position that Peru produced in the nineteenth century,[35] and a group of reactionary Spanish priests who were attempting to impose their views on the Peruvian hierarchy.[36]

Peru's new generation of liberals assumed that the political and economic milieu could be liberalised only if the Catholic Church was also thoroughly liberalised in its internal organisation, stripped of its privileges, purged of its hierarchical divisions which so enormously exalted priests over laymen, and freed from the allegedly dictatorial control of a foreign potentate and his curia. Conservative churchmen, on the other hand, felt that the Church's position as an ecclesiastical institution rooted in authority and discipline could be maintained only by forcing the political structure into a similar mould. In their assumptions both liberals and conservatives were, at least in part, mistaken. President Ramón Castilla (1845-51, 1854-62) demonstrated this when he effected an ingenious and enduring compromise between the forces of liberalism and conservatism.

Castilla began his search for a compromise formula in the mid-1850s. When neither side showed a sufficient degree of conciliatory spirit, he acted in 1860 to impose a new constitution that embodied the compromise which he had in the meantime conceived, aided frequently by the advice of moderates from both the ideological camps. The compromise pleased conservatives by keeping intact a centralised and somewhat authoritarian political structure, by safeguarding the Church's wealth and property, by allowing the Church relative autonomy in its internal organisation and considerable freedom from government control, and finally by preserving the

---

34. See F. M. Stanger, 'Church and State in Peru', *Hispanic American Historical Review*, II (1927), 418-37, and A. Tibesar, 'The Peruvian Church at the Time of Independence in the Light of Vatican II', *The Americas*, XXVI (1970), 349-75.
35. See Herrera, *Escritos y discursos*, 2 vols, Lima 1929, 1930, a careful selection of the conservative clergyman's major writings and public addresses. A major study of the liberal-conservative clash showing some empathy for Herrera and the conservative position is D. Gleason, 'Ideological Cleavages in Early Republican Peru, 1821-1872', unpublished University of Notre Dame doctoral dissertation 1974.
36. See F. B. Pike 'Heresy, Real and Alleged, in Peru: An Aspect of the Conservative-Liberal Struggle, 1830-1875', *Hispanic American Historical Review*, XLVII (1967), 50-74.

power of its leaders to speak out on and even to participate directly in politics. On the other hand, to gratify liberals the 1860 charter suppressed ecclesiastical law courts, ended State collection of tithes, and provided for a system of public education which would end the clergy's monopolistic control over instruction.

Castilla's compromise, resembling in its features the programme that Juan José Flores had vainly tried to implement in Ecuador, was successful largely because in the early days of its formulation the president had been able to deal with a conciliatory clerical leader, Francisco Javier de Luna Pizarro, the archbishop of Lima. Upon the death of Luna Pizarro in 1855, José Sebastián Goyeneche y Barreda succeeded to the office of archbishop. A mild and moderate man, trained as a youth in regalistic doctrines, Goyeneche, like his predecessor, proved willing to accept the Castilla compromise, ignoring Herrera's call for a crusade to win a total victory for the forces of theocracy and Ultramontanism.

Because political conservatism had been preserved essentially intact, and because concessions had been made to liberals in regard to the status of the Church, while at the same time hope had been provided them that eventual suffrage expansion would result from the new emphasis on public education, moderates in both ideological-political groups found it increasingly possible to co-operate with one another. After 1860, with the exception of a few flurries,[37] the conservative-liberal, clerical-anticlerical, Church-State issue was essentially removed from Peruvian politics.

7. VENEZUELA

Colonial Venezuela afforded neither a high Indian civilisation with opportunities for fruitful missionary work to attract the more godly clergymen, nor wealth and gracious urban living conditions to attract the more worldly. Never a powerful institution in the past, the Catholic Church was unable effectively to oppose the measures of José Antonio Páez, hero of the independence movement and dominant political figure from 1830 to 1846, which abolished the ecclesiastical *fuero* and ended State collection of tithes. [38]

37. One flurry was caused by Peru's renowned iconoclast Manuel González Prada (d. 1918), who blamed Catholicism for many of his country's ills and attacked the clergy in outspoken fashion. See his *Páginas libres*, Lima 1894. At a later time the brilliant Marxist intellectual José Carlos Mariátegui placed at least some of the blame for Peru's backwardness upon the Church. See his *Siete ensayos de interpretación de la realidad peruana*, Lima 1928. The outstanding Catholic layman Victor Andrés Belaúnde sought to refute the Mariátegui interpretation in his *La realidad nacional*, published originally in 1929 and 1930 as a series of articles in the Lima periodical *Mercurio Peruano*. The Mariátegui-Belaúnde debate was one of the most significant in Peru's intellectual history, even though it produced few immediate political consequences.
38. A good summary is R. Diaz Sánchez, 'Evolución social del Venezuela', in E. Arcila Farias, *et. al.*, *Venezuela independiente, 1810-1960* (Caracas 1962), esp. 210-17, 230-45. See also G. Moron, *A History of Venezuela*, trans. J. Street, New York 1963.

A more serious threat to the Church appeared during the 1870-88 period when political power was exercised by Antonio Guzmán Blanco, a remarkably vain and also able *caudillo*. The son of Antonio Leocadio Guzmán, an early leader of Venezuela's liberals, Guzmán Blanco was more committed to the teachings of positivism than to classical liberalism. He aided the efforts of Adolfo Ernst, an influential intellectual, in introducing the positivist mystique of progress into Venezuelan higher education. He also encouraged the vast expansion of the public education structure, inviting German and United States missions to aid in the establishment of normal schools. To facilitate the spread of the practical values associated with the 'Protestant ethic', Guzmán Blanco encouraged the coming of Protestant missionaries.

In a still more direct attack against the Church's position, Guzmán Blanco suppressed several convents and confiscated their property, and exiled for a time both the archbishop of Caracas and a papal nuncio. He also introduced civil marriage, partly in the hopes that this would lower the exceedingly high illegitimacy rate by making legalisation of unions possible for those with limited means.

It appeared for a time that a direct confrontation, reminiscent of the situation in Mexico during the 1850s, might be shaping up between the Vatican and the Venezuelan government. In 1876, however, a compromise was reached, with Rome tacitly accepting the supremacy of the State over the Church in patronage and related matters and with Guzmán Blanco calling off a move in congress, which he had previously endorsed, to legalise the marriage of clergymen.

Guzmán Blanco's anti-clericalism, which apparently did not go to the extremes of anti-Catholicism, won the widespread support of his citizens, never a fanatical people, and contributed to the emergence of broadly shared values among the populace and the rise of Venezuelan nationalism. [39] On the other hand the Vatican showed a refreshing spirit of compromise, perhaps chastened by its experiences in Mexico where, by holding out intransigently for total victory against its anti-clerical opposition, it had sustained total defeat. [40]

8. BRAZIL

Given the extraordinary powers which the State exercised over the Church in colonial times, powers that had been expanded by regalistic lawyers in the

39. See J. Nava, 'The Illustrious American': The Development of Nationalism in Venezuela under Antonio Guzmán Blanco', *Hispanic American Historical Review*, XLV (1965), 527-43. Also original and carefully documented with Venezuelan sources is R. L. Gilmore, *Caudillism and Militarism in Venezuela*, Athens, Ohio 1964.
40. Clarification of this matter awaits further research in the Vatican Archives.

late eighteenth century so as to transform the Church into the virtual servant of the secular power, trouble was bound to ensue if ever the hierarchy should seek to enlarge the sphere of papal authority over ecclesiastical affairs.

When Brazil proclaimed its independence from Portugal in 1822 the majority of its clergy, as was often the case in Spanish America, were liberally inclined and ready to accept regalistic patterns in Church-State relations. By the 1870s, however, alarmed by new developments which they considered a serious menace to the Church and encouraged by the ultramontanist tone of the 1864 *Syllabus of Errors* and other papal pronouncements, certain Brazilian prelates decided they could defend Catholicism only by ceasing to be the servants of the State and by directly challenging government policies which they considered injurious.

Church leaders had been alarmed by the encouragement given by the religiously tolerant Emperor Pedro II (1840-89) to the coming of Protestant missionaries. They were further perturbed by the attacks which Brazilian intellectuals, in close touch with like-minded individuals in Germany, began to launch against the doctrine of papal infallibility. Many of these intellectuals maintained close ties with the government and their statements were assumed by suspicious clerical leaders to enjoy royal backing.

The immediate cause of the crisis in Church-State relations was a dispute over Freemasonry. Since the eighteenth century, Brazilian clergymen had tended to look favourably upon Freemasonry. In large numbers they had joined the various lodges established in the country. Various papal condemnations of Freemasonry were not published in Brazil because State officials, often backed by the clergy, did not consider the movement a menace.

By the second half of the nineteenth century, however, there were signs that Brazilian Freemasonry, even as in some of the republics of Spanish America, was assuming a more virulently anti-clerical stance and perhaps advancing to an anti-Catholic position.[41] In 1873 concern over the situation led Bishop Vital Maria Gonçalves de Oliveira of Pernambuco, a young Capuchin friar educated in France and recently consecrated, to denounce the masonic influence in his diocese. In response to a communication to the Vatican on the matter, Bishop Vital received a papal brief authorising, if worst came to worst, 'excommunication of the masonic Order', and suppression of religious brotherhoods (*irmandades*) that were under masonic control.[42] Without seeking imperial sanction of the papal brief, as legal procedures required, Bishop Vital published its contents and as a result was shortly faced, together with one other bishop who had extended support,

41. See M. C. Thornton, *The Church and Freemasonry in Brazil: A Study in Regalism*, Washington, D.C. 1948.
42. See C. H. Haring, *Empire in Brazil: A New World Experiment with Monarchy*, (Cambridge, Mass. 1958), 113-25.

with charges of having violated the constitution and the criminal code.
Eventually a compromise solution was found by officials of Church and
State, but not before the two bishops had been arrested and for a time im-
prisoned. Both sides suffered a severe loss of face with many intellectuals,
more and more under the influence of positivism, deciding that Brazil must
simultaneously rid itself of an archaic ecclesiastical and an outdated
monarchical structure.

Following the overthrow and exile of Emperor Pedro II in 1889, one of
the early actions taken by republican legislators was to proclaim the separation of Church and State. Although the State still retained vast powers of
control over the Church — separation in Latin America as often as not has
meant the end of State subvention, not of interference — the two powers in
general co-operated smoothly following the republican legislation. Far
graver than the threat of an antagonistic government was the problem posed
by the religious attitudes of vast multitudes of the faithful.

In the arid reaches of the north-eastern *sertao* (interior) a religious movement led by Antonio Maciel, known as the Counsellor, was beginning to
assume serious proportions in the early 1890s. Although he seemed to
borrow more from the medicine men or shamans of the Tupí Indians than
from Catholic traditions, the Counsellor had at first been accepted by the
rather lax and poorly trained Brazilian clergy. He may even have been
allowed to preach and hear confession in certain Catholic churches. When,
however, the Counsellor began to preach civil disobedience and to advance
overtly heretical religious doctrines, ecclesiastical officials responded with
excommunication. The gaunt and emaciated Counsellor nevertheless continued to be the main religious leader for countless thousands of *sertanejos*.
Not until 1896 did a government force of some six thousand soldiers snuff
out this religious movement by besieging the Counsellor in his encampment
at Canudos and killing him there, together with untold numbers of his
followers.[43]

The description of Brazilian religious practices made by a perceptive
social anthropologist in 1963 [44] was already largely true at the beginning of
this century. In the Amazonian regions the syncretism of Indian beliefs with
Catholicism was the predominant feature of religion, while along the
north-eastern coast African elements and cults had fused with the Catholic
faith. Although producing some fervent lay leaders, the upper classes were in
general 'relaxed' Catholics. The middle classes, especially the women,

---

43. A brilliant account of the religious movement headed by the Counsellor and one of the
masterpieces of Brazilian literature is Euclydes da Cunha, *Os sertoēs,* Rio de Janeiro, 1902.
On Brazilian folk Catholicism in general, and in particular on Padre Cicero, leader of a
political-religious movement generated by a 'miracle' in 1889, see Ralph della Cava, *Miracle
at Joaseiro,* New York 1969.
44. C. Wagley, *An Introduction to Brazil,* third printing (New York 1965), 250.

followed a traditional form of Catholicism which stressed the outward trappings of religion; but some middle groups, particularly in the southern cities, were turning toward Protestantism. The urban lower classes were influenced by spiritualism and African-origin cults, while the rural peasants followed a folk Catholicism that included many practices and beliefs inherited from the distant past and at odds with twentieth-century Catholic doctrines. [45]

9. RÉSUMÉ: LATIN-AMERICAN CATHOLICISM AT THE END OF THE NINETEENTH CENTURY

Between approximately 1820 and the early years of the twentieth century the temporal strength and intellectual influence of the Catholic Church underwent a remarkable decline. Colombia affords the only striking exception to this pattern. The Church in Peru, owing largely to the Castilla-inspired compromise, had been spared from consequential anti-clerical attacks. Even in Peru, though, the power of the Church was often more apparent than real. This was particularly true in the intellectual field where a rabidly anti-clerical positivism was the main ideological current. Although instruction in the Catholic catechism was still required at the national university of San Marcos in Lima, this course was taught by Mariano Amezaga, a man who had advanced even beyond most positivists and become an atheist. [46]

When independence had been achieved in Latin America, many clergymen had acted on the assumption that there would be a return to Habsburg traditions in which Church and State, in close co-operation, would wield the main influence in temporal society. For a brief moment under Iturbide in Mexico, under García Moreno in Ecuador, and perhaps under Rosas in Argentina, this situation had been at least partially realised. About 1900, however, Latin American clergymen, except in Colombia, could scarcely pretend that their divine institution came even close to constituting, together with the State, one of two poles of temporal power and influence. Many religious, however, had not abandoned hope of the eventual attainment of a bipolar balance of power and were anxiously seeking means to enhance the might of the Church. In the first third of the twentieth century circumstances seemed to favour their ambitions. The Church was about to undergo a resurgence which could be largely attributed to the fact that,

45. Useful studies on Brazilian religion include: T. de Azevedo, 'Catholicism in Brazil', *Thought*, XXVII (1953), 253-74; R. Bastide, 'Religion and the Church in Brazil', in T. L. Smith and A. Marchant, eds, *Brazil, Portrait of Half a Continent* (New York 1951), 334-55, and *Les religions africains au Brasil*, Paris 1960; E. de Kadt, 'Religion, the Church, and Social Change in Brazil', in C. Véliz, ed., *The Politics of Conformity in Latin America*, London, New York 1967; and B. Kloppenburg, 'O espiritismo no Brasil', *Revista Eclesiastica* (Petropolis), XIX (1959), 842-71.
46. See Amezaga, *Los dogmas fundamentales del catolicismo ante la razón*, Valparaiso, Chile 1873.

despite surface appearances indicating otherwise, the spiritual values generally associated with Latin American Catholicism were not so weak as its friends feared and its enemies hoped.

II. THE REVIVAL OF CATHOLIC INFLUENCE IN THE EARLY TWENTIETH CENTURY

Out of the Plenary Council of Latin American Prelates, convoked in Rome by Pope Leo XIII in 1899, came an effort to reinvigorate the Church in Latin America and to improve its channels of communication with the Vatican.[47] The Plenary Council also gave rise to a series of provincial councils within the various Latin American republics, one of the first of which was held in Caracas in 1904. The resurgence of the Catholic Church in Venezuela, dating from this provincial council, continued during the lengthy dictatorship of Juan Vicente Gómez (1908-35).

The Church's gradual acquisition of prestige and influence in Venezuela following a period of rampant anti-clericalism in the late nineteenth century was a sign of a general revival of Catholic influence in most parts of Latin America. In an indirect way the resurgence of Catholicism can be traced to the turn-of-the-century reaction against materialism and mechanistic utilitarianism in which an imposing array of Latin American intellectuals participated.

From the northern republic of Mexico where Antonio Caso led the way,[48] to the southern state of Uruguay where José Enrique Rodó was the principal spokesman,[49] Latin American intellectuals joined in a humanistic, hellenistic reaction against positivist and utilitarian concepts.[50] More and more they began to stress the higher human values, by which they meant cultural,

47. The Concilio Plenario Latinoamericano was attended by thirteen archbishops and forty-one bishops. It has been described as the first continental congress in the Church's history. See P. Correa León, El concilio plenario latinoamericana de 1899: Cathedra (Bogotá, n.d.), 1-24.
48. A typical Caso work is Discursos a la nación mexicana, Mexico, D.F. 1922. See also S. Ramos, El perfil del hombre y cultura en México, Mexico, D.F. 1934.
49. Rodó's best-known work is Ariel, Montevideo. On Arielism and other intellectual currents in Uruguay see A. Ardao, La filosofía en el Uruguay en el siglo XX, Mexico, D.F. 1956; G. A. Lousteay Heguy and S. M. Lozada, eds, El pensamiento político hispanoamericano, vol. VIII; José Enrique Rodó, Juan Zorilla de San Martin, Buenos Aires 1967; S.Ramos, ed., Rodó, Mexico, D.F. 1953; S. Rodriguez Villamil, Las mentalidades dominantes en Montevideo, 1850-1900: La mentalidad criolla tradicional, Montevideo 1968; and A. Zum Felde, Proceso intelectual del Uruguay, Montevideo 1941. For a balanced treatment of the period following Church-State separation (1919-59) see R. H. Fitzgibbon, 'The Political Impact on Religious Development in Uruguay', Church History, XXII (1953), 21-33.
50. A valuable source on the preservation of the traditional values of Hispanic culture, containing abundant citations of the pertinent literature, is W. W. Stokes, 'Cultural Anti-Americanism in Latin America', in G. Anderson, ed., Issues and Conflicts (Lawrence, Kan. 1959), 315-38. On this topic see also F. B. Pike, Hispanismo, 1898-1936: Spanish Conservatives and Liberals and Their Relations with Spanish America, Notre Dame, Ind. 1971.

moral, aesthetic and spiritual values. In many ways this movement was a reflection of foreign influences, with Latin America's new generation of intellectuals falling particularly under the sway of Ernest Renan and Henri Bergson.[51]

The reaction against positivism was begun and at first popularised largely by fallen-away Catholics satisfied that humanism was an adequate foundation upon which to base the higher values they extolled. Then roughly between 1910 and 1930, with the situation differing considerably from country to country, a new pattern became discernible. Increasingly the leaders of the spiritual reaction against the vogue of utilitarian and mechanistic criteria began to return to the Catholic Church, persuaded that the higher human values, if they were to prevail, required a theological and supernatural basis.

Not all countries, of course, shared to an equal degree in this type of change in the cultural scene. In Mexico, where after the Revolution of 1910 intellectuals preferred to flirt with radical anti-clerical and sometimes with atheistic doctrines,[52] and in Uruguay, where the Church had never enjoyed more than a tenuous existence and where agnosticism was a significant intellectual force,[53] the reaction against materialism failed to evolve into a major resurgence of Catholic influence. Even in Mexico, however, by the late 1920s José Vasconcelos and, more clearly still, Alfonso Junco typified a growing number of intellectuals emerging as apologists for Hispanic traditions, including Catholicism. Meanwhile, moreover, the Uruguayan Luis Alberto de Herrera was developing into perhaps the most eloquent spokesman of traditional Catholic values that his country has produced.

In this changing intellectual environment a Catholic University movement began to flourish in certain countries. The year 1917 witnessed the establishment of a Catholic university in Peru while in Chile an older Catholic university, founded in Santiago in 1888, began for the first time to acquire academic respectability in the early twentieth century. Both these universities were primarily concerned with forming an élite that could appreciate, guard, and nourish the most exalted of human values.[54] Practical studies were largely eschewed as beneath the dignity of a privileged intellectual class. By the 1930s, in Peru at least, the new Catholic university could claim greater social prestige than the venerable national institution (San Marcos) which, under the pressure of the university reform movement that began at

51. See P. Romanell, 'Bergson en México: un tributo a José Vasconcelos', *Humanitas* (Nuevo León, Mexico 1960), 266-74.
52. See M. González Navarro, 'La ideologia de la Revolución mexicana', *Historia Mexicana*, 13 (Mexico, D.F. 1961).
53. See J. Alvarez, 'La iglesia en el Uruguay', *Latinoamérica*, 23 (Mexico, D.F. 1950), 493-9, and M. Soler, *La iglesia y la civilización: pastoral*, Montevideo 1905.
54. The purposes for which the Catholic University in Lima was founded are described in the editorial of *Estudios: organo de la Universidad Católica* I (1918), 1-2.

Córdoba, Argentina, in 1918, was beginning to open its doors to students of humble origins. In contrast, the Catholic university reserved its instruction for the members of the aristocracy.

Even in Brazil, at one time almost the continental headquarters of positivism and the traditional stronghold of religious indifference, Catholicism began to acquire a strong intellectual standing. By the end of the 1920s, owing in part to the initiative provided by Jackson de Figueiredo,[55] Thomism had become a major philosophical force in higher education. In the following two decades Alceu Amoroso Lima played a conspicuous role in contributing to the resurgence of Catholic intellectual influence.

Early in the twentieth century, understandably desiring to capitalise on the increasingly favourable circumstances in which they found themselves and at the same time perturbed by heightened social tensions and the dissemination of such radical ideologies as anarchism, socialism, and communism, the Latin American episcopacy began to form the laity into Catholic Action groups. The primary purpose of Catholic Action was to awaken the social conscience of the upper classes and to induce them, under church leadership, to take paternalistic measures aimed at mitigating the material suffering of the masses so that social solidarity might be reestablished. This little-studied development in Latin American Catholicism produced consequential results in easing the social problem and undoubtedly reduced the impact of the advocates of violent revolution.

The appearance of radical revolutionaries urging class warfare not only contributed to the rise of Catholic Action but also produced an important change in the politics of certain republics. For years liberals and conservatives had been approaching accord on many social and economic issues, a situation made possible to some extent by an increasing tendency among liberals to reject egalitarian democracy and even to question the wisdom of spreading among the masses the values of individualistic, competitive capitalism. They had remained separated, however, by traditional disagreement over Church-State questions. Faced with an immediate threat to the established order, liberals began to curb their anti-clericalism and to present a common front with conservatives against the forces of sweeping change. Even during the late nineteenth century Bolivia's liberals and conservatives had managed to arrive at a mutually advantageous *modus vivendi*. Early in the twentieth century this pattern spread to Ecuador, where the 'out' conservatives learned to co-operate with the incumbent liberals and in return

55. See H. Nogueira, *Jackson de Figueiredo, o doutrinário catholico*, Rio de Janeiro 1928. Also useful are J. Cruz Costa, *A History of Ideas in Brazil: The Development of Philosophy in Brazil and the Evolution of National History*, trans. S. Macedo, Berkeley, Calif. 1964, and N. Werneck Sodré, *Orientacoẽs de pensamiento brasileiro*, Rio de Janeiro 1942.

received many important political posts, and to Colombia, where the 'out' liberals found a basis of co-operation with the incumbent conservatives. By the early 1930s the Chilean liberals and conservatives had forgotten their ancient Church-State polemic and joined to form an alliance that would remain one of the most powerful political forces for the next thirty years.

Against this background, leaders of Church and State in many Latin American republics began to collaborate, early in the twentieth century, in the endeavour to dissipate the revolutionary potential that seemed to inhere in newly emerging groups. The urban labour force, rapidly swelling as rates of rural-to-urban migration rose, were pacified through government-controlled and sometimes Church-sponsored labour unions which extended fringe benefits, in the form of bonuses, retirement pensions, unemployment insurance and other services, rather than contending for increases in real wages. Enhanced real wages would have brought actual power to the working classes, whereas the extension of fringe benefits tended to keep them in a position of subservience and dependence upon the paternalistic government and allied church agencies. Essentially, the governments of Latin America, with the assistance of the Church through its Catholic Action programmes and labour-union activity, succeeded in introducing a paternalistic structure into an urban setting, thereby absorbing new groups into the prevailing social system and at the same time preventing the emergence of a genuinely pluralistic society. If Church and State were able to co-operate to some considerable degree in easing the social problem, many liberal statesmen entertained grave reservations about the Church's increasing advocacy of the corporative society. This important issue requires a brief explanation.

Most Catholic observers of turn-of-the-century Spanish America, and a good number of ardent secularists as well, expressed alarm at the degree to which the masses were becoming alienated from a social and political system that permitted them not even a minimal degree of participation. They pointed also with apprehension to a situation in which individuals of the labouring classes no longer enjoyed a secure sanctuary in society but were constrained to compete for their livelihood under conditions that rendered minimal their chances of success. As a corrective to these circumstances, which if ignored might result in revolution, they urged the decentralised and corporative organisation of society. Their programme called for breaking down the monolithic, centralised social-political structure into its natural subdivisions (organisms or corporations) and granting to the masses some voice in governing the subdivisions appropriate to them. The hope was that the masses, content with politicisation at the grass-roots level, would leave direction of the body politic at the highest, national level to an élite class.

From corporative decentralisation Catholics expected not only the amelioration of the social problem and the preservation of a hierarchical structure. They further anticipated an extension of the Church's temporal power. In the ideal society which they envisaged, labour organisations and professional groups would be under strict Church dominance and relatively free from the control of a centralised State bureaucracy, which in the prevailing Catholic view was often tainted by excessive materialism, by masonic errors, and even by Protestant heresies.

Many liberals and anti-clerical secularists concurred with Catholic spokesmen on the desirability of a decentralised State that would alleviate revolutionary pressures by providing for popular political participation at the level of professional or local corporations. Still, however much inclined they may have been as the twentieth century advanced, to co-operate with Catholics in waging a common struggle against basic social change, they were not prepared to accept any form of decentralisation that increased the Catholic Church's temporal influence unnecessarily. This situation led to a split within the ranks of the secularist defenders of the *status quo*. Some continued to urge decentralisation, but a large number decided to work through the existing centralised State structure over which anti-clerical forces had gained control in most republics. To a considerable extent, therefore, partisans of secularism abandoned the corporative cause to Catholics, opting instead for a centralised, nation-wide, State-controlled system of paternalistic government administered by a secular bureaucracy. This approach particularly appealed to the growing middle classes whose members hoped to find opportunities for dignified employment within the ranks of a burgeoning bureaucracy.

Despite tensions and continuing rivalries between the clergy and secularist political leaders, the Church at a point fairly early in the twentieth century was again acquiring a place in the establishment and gaining some influence in the power structure. And the cause for this had to be sought as often as not in the actions and aspirations of civilian politicians rather than in the deeds and hopes of clerical leaders. Facing new challenges and problems, hard-pressed civilian leaders, even as they had been wont to do in the nineteenth century, called the churchmen into the political arena as their indispensable allies. Frequently, then, the 'clericalism' of the early twentieth century was actually 'civil clericalism'. Clerical leaders were slow to recognise that disastrous consequences to their long-term interests often resulted from an over-eager acceptance of civilian overtures. Failure to act with due caution would cost churchmen dearly in many Latin American countries when they rushed into the political cockpit to support right-wing nationalistic groups that were often accused, whether with justification or not, of being closely affiliated with fascism.

III. RIGHT WING CATHOLIC NATIONALISM IN THE FIRST HALF OF THE TWENTIETH CENTURY: ITS RISE, DECLINE, AND AFTERMATH

1. ARGENTINA AND BRAZIL

Early in the twentieth century an Argentine oligarchy, its economic might based largely on ownership of vast landed estates, found its exercise of political power seriously threatened by the rising might of the Radical Party (Unión Cívica Radical), representing middle sector and populist interests. Apprehensive over how long they could continue to keep the majority Radical Party out of office through electoral manipulations and fraud, the traditional wielders of power tended to respond approvingly to the right-wing nationalism that many prominent Catholic leaders, both of the clergy and laity, were beginning to expound.

The real need as seen by Manuel Gálvez, a typical spokesman of early twentieth-century right-wing nationalism, was to spiritualise Argentina, to replace the obsessive concern for material gains with an intense devotion to the values of Catholicism which, allegedly, had been uppermost in the colonial and early independence periods but which had subsequently been repudiated by hordes of undesirable immigrants. [56]

According to the secular priest Julio Meinvielle, who in the early 1930s began to propound the message that he would repeat through the next three decades, the world in general had been deteriorating since the Protestant Reformation. Argentina's demoralisation, according to Meinvielle, had begun only around 1853 with the attempt, partially through encouraging immigration, to introduce into the land the liberal concepts of the bourgeois world, the materialism and individualism originally engendered by the Reformation. [57]

Argentina's native-born Creole aristocrácy, hard-pressed especially after 1916 when the Unión Cívica Radical voted its candidate into the presidency, naturally found much to its liking in right-wing, Catholic nationalism. In this movement the aristocracy, and many middle groups which consciously identified with the élite, could find theological justification for fighting to regain the political and economic power that had temporarily been wrested from its grasp by new interest groups in which immigrants figured prominently.

Right-wing Catholic nationalism was an important factor in bringing about the 1930 military revolution that drove a somewhat demoralised

56. Gálvez, *El solar de la raza*, 5th ed. (Madrid 1920), 11-14, 21.
57. Meinvielle, *Politica argentina* (Buenos Aires 1956), 15. A synthesis of the views that Meinvielle began to advance in the 1930s is found in his *Concepcion católica de la política*, Buenos Aires 1961.

Radical Party out of office. [58] Installed in the presidency by the revolution, General José Félix Uriburu sought to introduce the corporative State, the political structure favoured by right-wing nationalists as the only means of countering the levelling tendencies of inorganic, liberal democracy that permitted citizens to participate in political decision-making directly, rather than through their appropriate functional and local corporations. Owing to a variety of circumstances, Uriburu failed in this endeavour, and right-wing nationalists were forced to seek a new political leader. In the mid-1940s some of them thought they had found their man in Juan Domingo Perón. Shortly after the 1946 election which brought Perón to the presidency, Father Meinvielle saw in the colourful demagogue the leader who was about to liberate the masses from the myths of liberalism, socialism, and communism. [59]

It did not take long for Perón to disappoint Argentina's right-wing nationalists. He placed, from their point of view, too much interest in the material comfort and security of the lower classes and in the process began to pose a threat to the oligarchy's political and economic position. For a time Perón even seemed intent upon replacing a system of hierarchical paternalism with one of social pluralism within which the masses would possess sufficient power to force from the aristocracy what they considered their due. Thus social solidarity was threatened by the spectre of the class struggle.

Equally significant in causing a break between Argentina's reactionary nationalists and the administration was the fact that Perón in seeking a programme that might command widespread support among previously contending and mutually jealous groups decided, by 1951, that Catholicism could not be the virtually exclusive element of Argentine nationalism. The shrewd dictator seemed to sense that Argentina could not be forged into a nation by encouraging the defenders of traditional, Creole values to impose their viewpoints, *in toto*, on the inhabitants of the country. Anti-clericalism, religious indifference, and preoccupation with material gain were characteristics that had been indelibly impressed not only upon the middle classes of immigrant extraction but upon many members of the Creole, land-owning aristocracy as well. The whole set of values associated with late nineteenth and early twentieth century liberalism-positivism and anti-clericalism could not be readily obliterated. Thus Catholicism cast in a

58. An excellent analysis of the 1930 revolution and subsequent events is found in Dardo Cúneo, *El desencuentro argentino, 1930-1955*, Buenos Aires 1965. Perceptive essays dealing with this period as well as an extensive bibliography are found in J. Barager, ed., *Why Perón Came to Power*, New York 1968. Also essential for understanding this period is M. S. Stabb, *In Quest of Identity: Patterns in the Spanish American Essay of Ideas, 1890-1960* (Chapel Hill 1967), 146-81.
59. Meinvielle, *Política argentina*, 37.

conventional, Hispanic mould could not constitute, as many right-wing elements demanded, the sole informing spirit of Argentine nationalism. Seeking a third position between clericalism and anti-clericalism, élitist values and the ideas of the majority indigenous and imported traditions, Perón soon hopelessly alienated the extremist champions of right-wing Catholic nationalism.

Upon Perón's overthrow in 1955, the Church appeared briefly to be on the threshold of acquiring consequential advantages. State officials promptly rewarded churchmen for their aid in mobilising anti-Perón sentiment [60] by removing many of the restrictions passed by anti-clerical regimes of the preceding century. In 1956, for example, the Church was granted the right, denied it throughout the republic's previous history, to establish Catholic universities.

It was shortly apparent, however, that Catholicism would be incapable of exercising a significant influence in the immediate post-Perón era. A fundamental reason for this was that the Church had become involved in the most agonising and meaningful debate waged by the country's intellectuals and statesmen, the debate over national identity. Confronting the question of whether the true Argentina was the country of pre-immigration, Creole values (real or imagined) or the country of post-1853, immigrant values (actual or alleged), the Church had clearly taken sides. [61] Identifying with Creole Argentina, it alienated the post-1853 population elements and all who associated with their values.

An additional problem was presented by a serious internal division within Argentine Catholicism. It was caused by the attempt of reform-minded priests to challenge the conservatism of right-wing nationalism with which highly placed clerical leaders had been all too successful in identifying Catholicism. [62] In this challenge may lie the hope for a future resurgence of Argentine Catholicism. But the Church's inward struggle has defied prompt resolution.

The inter-relationship between religion and politics in Brazil during the first half of the twentieth century affords a striking contrast to the situation in Argentina. Getulio Vargas, who ruled Brazil from 1930 to 1945, was relatively successful in forging an eclectic nationalism and in formulating a

60. See A. P. Whitaker, *Argentine Upheaval: Perón's Fall and the New Regime*, New York 1956.
61. An indication of the extent to which many leading spokesmen seek to identify the Church with right-wing, traditionalist, Creole values is afforded by one of Argentina's best-known Catholic intellectuals, Mario Amadeo, in his book *Ayer, hoy y mañana*, Buenos Aires 1956. On this subject see also S. Baily, *Labor Nationalism and Politics in Argentina*, New Brunswick, N. J. 1967, and M. N. Gerassi, *Los nacionalistas*, Buenos Aires 1968.
62. The Jesuit periodical, *El Criterio*, published in Buenos Aires, became during the early 1960s a leading organ of the reform-minded clergy who proclaimed the need for basic structural changes in Argentine society.

programme that won the support of the lower classes, many middle classes, and even a few members of the traditional élite. To some degree Vargas succeeded in this because he did not have to contend with two unyielding and exclusivist camps locked in dispute as to wherein lay the true national identity and destiny. Brazil had already achieved a considerable fusion of cultural values against a political background that was characteristically more pragmatic than dogmatic. [63]

Given this background, the Church was not drawn into choosing sides in a great national debate. Instead, it was able to lend its accord to a developing national consensus. Many churchmen applauded when Vargas rejected identification with the more extremist fascist elements in his country. On the whole the Catholic Church in Brazil in 1945 was not an impressively strong institution; but, having avoided a clear-cut association with an extremist nationalist position that many intellectuals equated with fascism, it was probably as influential as in 1930, and a good deal more so than in 1900. [64]

The Church's position in its relation to the Brazilian State underwent important changes in 1964 when many clerical leaders supported the armed forces *coup* that overthrew the inept, corrupt and leftist administration of João Goulart.[65] Ensuing military regimes rewarded the Church by removing most of the remaining vestiges of anti-clerical restrictions. Actually, the Church-State *rapprochement* represented only the co-operation of conservative clerical leaders with the Brazilian military. Members of a 'new left' movement among the clergy and laity, whose impressive rise in influence

63. See E. B. Burns, *A History of Brazil*, New York 1970; R. M. Levine, *The Vargas Regime: The Critical Years, 1934-1938*, New York 1970; N. Werneck Sodrè, *Raizes historicas do nacionalismo brasileiro*, Rio de Janeiro 1959; J. D. Wirth, *The Politics of Brazilian Development 1930-1954*, Stanford, Calif. 1970; and J. M. Young, *The Brazilian Revolution of 1930 and the Aftermath*, New Brunswick, N. J. 1967.

64. Much light on the Church's involvement in a movement linked to fascism is provided by M. T. Williams, 'Integralism and the Brazilian Catholic Church', *Hispanic American Historical Review*, LIV (1974), 431-52. Williams maintains that integralism, seen by many as a Brazilian variant of fascism, often acted as a political arm of the Church, so much so that a symbiotic relationship existed between the two forces. She concludes that when integralism disappeared, the Church was left in a position of dependence on the government similar to that which had prevailed before the advent of the First Republic in 1889. On this subject see also E. R. Broxson, 'Plinio Salgado and Brazilian Integralism, 1932-1938', unpublished Catholic University of America doctoral dissertation 1972.

65. The circumstances of the Goulart overthrow are skilfully analysed in J. W. F. Dulles, *Unrest in Brazil: Political-Military Crises 1955-1964*, Austin 1970; R. M. Schneider, *The Political System of Brazil: Emergence of a 'Modernizing' Authoritarian Regime, 1964-1970*, New York 1971; and T. E. Skidmore, *Politics in Brazil, 1930-1964: An Experiment in Democracy*, New York 1967. On subsequent events in Brazil, many of them involving Church-State relations, see R. Roett, ed., *Brazil in the Sixties*, Nashville 1972; H. J. Rosenbaum and W. G. Tyler, eds, *Contemporary Brazil: Issues in Economic and Political Development*, New York 1972; P. C. Schmitter, *Interest Conflict and Political Change in Brazil*, Stanford 1971; and A. C. Stepan, ed., *Authoritarian Brazil: Origins, Policies and Future*, New Haven 1973.

was checked by the armed forces *coup*, denounced conservative Catholics and the military for their complicity in perpetuating social injustice and economic backwardness.[66] Increasingly they were joined in these denunciations by moderate Catholic spokesmen. With only its more cautious and *status quo* oriented leaders basking in government favour, the Church confronted a serious internal crisis.

2. CHILE

Even as in Argentina, Chile's Catholic spokesmen in the early twentieth century expressed grave misgivings about liberalism in all of its manifestations. In many ways, however, their attacks against liberalism were more temperate than those of their Argentine counterparts. Moreover, in condemning liberalism Chilean clerical and right-wing elements in general did not vent their ire primarily against the immigrants in their midst. Thus they did not contribute to the bitter divisiveness that blocked Argentina's progress towards nationhood. In Chile, immigrants were scarcely numerous enough to be charged with primary responsibility for the ills of the land.

By 1920 many Chilean liberals, conceding some validity to the conservative claims that social ills were exacerbated by *laissez-faire* economics, began to advocate a programme of reform that entailed government supervision of capital and protection of the working classes. A basic assumption of Chile's Liberal Alliance at this time was that operation of the system envisaged would be entrusted to the central government's bureaucracy in Santiago, made up primarily of emerging middle classes.

In an altogether different approach to the social problem, Chile's leading Catholic spokesmen favoured a system of private rather than government paternalism. In their view, paternalism should be administered through company unions and various semi-autonomous associations on a relatively decentralised basis. Politically, this structure would rest ultimately on a corporative state in which unions and other semi-autonomous groups would enjoy functional representation.[67] A system such as this, its advocates felt, would not only curb the excesses of majoritarian, liberal democracy, but would offer a better means of safeguarding the masses than that of entrusting them in one body to the mercies of a centralised, middle-class bureaucracy.

66. Activities and attitudes of the 'new left' within the Church are described in M. Cardozo, 'The Brazilian Church and the New Left', *Journal of Inter-American Studies*, VI (1964), 313-22; E. de Kadt, *Catholic Radicals in Brazil*, London, New York 1970; Cándido Mendez, *Memento dos vivos: a esquerda catolica no Brasil*, Rio de Janeiro 1966; Helder Pessoa Camara, *The Church and Colonialism: The Betrayal of the Third World*, New York 1969; and T. G. Sanders, 'Brazil's Catholic Left', *America*, 117 (1967), 598-601.
67. The position of the conservative Catholic élite is brilliantly described in J. O. Morris, *Elites, Intellectuals and Consensus: A Study of the Social Question and the Industrial Relations System in Chile*, Ithaca, N.Y. 1966.

Chile's advocates of the corporative state may well have been justified in doubting the willingness of a middle-class bureaucracy to provide sincere leadership in the quest for better working-class conditions. Emerging middle classes, not yet secure in their position, aspiring to reach upper-class status and not resigned to their present rung on the social ladder, often regarded the lower classes with greater disdain and fear than did the established aristocracy.[68] This may be one reason why the Liberal Alliance approach to the social problem, generally although not exclusively preferred by the Chilean legislature to Catholic, Conservative Party programmes, failed so dismally to achieve its announced objectives in the 1924-64 period.

By no means all prominent Catholic leaders accepted the corporative State as the ideal in socio-politico-economic organisation. A few Catholic intellectuals, both of the clergy and laity, began in the mid-1930s to criticise at least certain aspects of the corporative structure, a structure that many intellectuals were coming to equate with fascism. Jesuits, among them Jorge Fernández Pradel [69] and Alberto Hurtado,[70] as well as Catholic laymen, including Eduardo Frei Montalva [71] and other founders of the National Falange which later developed into the Christian democratic Party, began to question concepts of the stratified, hierarchical social structure. They argued that social justice could be provided only through a relatively open, pluralistic society and through political democracy. The influence of Chile's Catholic opponents of a rigid corporative social structure was sufficiently powerful to prevent the Church from becoming as closely identified as in Argentina with what anti-clericals, often with extreme irresponsibility, chose to call a fascist position.

Beginning even in the 1930s, moreover, leaders of Chile's incipient Christian democratic movement had sought to build upon both the Catholic and the nineteenth-century liberal traditions in fashioning an eclectic nationalism. They did not assert that traditional Hispanic Catholicism was the only important ingredient of nationalism. Indeed, they recognised the valid claims of liberalism for a place in Chilean nationalism. Although they rejected classical economic liberalism, they accepted some of the political facets of liberalism and advocated majoritarian democratic usages. To a certain extent Christian democrats also accepted some of the anti-clerical features of traditional liberalism as an established part of the national scene that could not be eradicated. Christian democratic leaders welcomed, for

68. See F. B. Pike, 'Aspects of Class Relations in Chile, 1850-1960', *Hispanic American Historical Review*, XLIII (1963), 14-33.
69. See Fernández Pradel, *Acción Católica*, Santiago de Chile 1941, and *Un nuevo orden social*, Santiago de Chile 1941.
70. See Hurtado, *El orden social cristiano en los documentos de la jerarquia*, 2 vols, Santiago de Chile 1947.
71. See Frei, *Chile desconocido*, Santiago de Chile 1937.

example, the concept of religious pluralism. They avoided direct ties with the Church; and they sought guidance in Christian humanism rather than in sectarian Catholicism.

The willingness of Chile's ecclesiastical leaders by the beginning of the 1960s to sanction this approach and to allow the new political party to remain free from official ties with the Church contributed significantly to the notable victories scored by Christian Democrats in the presidential election of 1964 and in the congressional contest of the following year. In Chile the traditional anti-clericalism was still strong enough to create serious difficulties for a party that maintained close official bonds with the Church. Chilean clergymen at the very highest level of authority accepted this fact, in dramatic contrast to some of their Argentine counterparts.

3. PERU AND BOLIVIA

The warm approbation which Peruvian clerical leaders began in the 1920s to accord to Hispanic traditions quickly brought about the Church's deep involvement in the already centuries-old debate over national identity. The issue in Peru did not involve Creole vs. immigrant values, but rather centred upon the clash of indigenous and Spanish culture. Enthusiastically embraced by conservative Catholics, *Hispanismo* (glorification of the mother lands's values and especially of its religious exclusivism and non-democratic traditions) in Peru soon came to be associated with racial overtones involving anti-Indian prejudices.

Catholic, Hispanophile nationalism, often associated with local variants of fascism, waxed increasingly vitriolic and fanatical, in part because of the extremism of its foes. Marxian socialism and related movements during the 1920s proclaimed a message of virulent and anti-clericalism if not actual atheism, advocated a levelling social revolution and imposition by force upon coastal, westernised Peru of the allegedly superior Andean or Indian way of life. The Andean, Indian way of life was invariably identified by its proponents with socialism. [72]

The Church's consistent tendency until at least the mid-1940s to identify itself with the ideology of *Hispanismo* did not rebound so seriously to its disadvantage as its involvement in an identity problem in Argentina. The values reviled by Argentina's conservative Catholic nationalists were defended by a large and articulate element in society, an element that was politically sophisticated and able effectively to strike back against its critics. The Peruvian population element that could most logically have been expected to react with anger towards the position assumed by the Church on the issue of identity was the Indian mass of the sierra. But the Indians had

72. See J. N. Plank, 'Peru: A Study in the Problem of Nation Finding', unpublished Harvard University doctoral dissertation 1958, esp. 208-13.

not yet been politicised. Unaware of what was transpiring in society, they were oblivious to the racial-cultural prejudices involved in the association of Catholicism with *Hispanismo*. The participating elements in Peruvian society, by and large, were grateful — although they would not always admit so — to the Church for having stood squarely against the danger posed by Indophile socialists.

By the mid-1940s the extremism of socialist Indianism and *Hispanismo* was subsiding as a majority of reputable intellectuals began to share in a consensus that the true national destiny of Peru lay in *mestizaje*, a biological and cultural blending of the two main ethnic groups and their values. No longer faced with the attempt of its foes to use the Indians to destroy it, the Church resumed its temporarily curtailed concern for the protection of the Indians, hoping to play an important role in achieving their eventual assimilation into national society, or if not that, then their security and dignity within their autochthonous culture.

In Bolivia the clergy involved itself only minimally in protecting western culture by leading a traditionalist crusade against communism — a role which many Peruvian clerics imagined they were playing. One reason for the clergy's lack of political involvement was that its members were confronted by a new generation of reform-minded politicians. These political leaders indentified churchmen with the traditional power structure, which they increasingly reviled because of its alleged responsibility for the country's disastrous defeat at the hands of Paraguay in the Chaco War (1932-5), a defeat which was taken as a sign of the old regime's total corruption and depravity. [73]

The grossly undermanned and poorly trained Bolivian clergy remained a weak and ineffective group, not sought out by a new generation of ideologists and politicians who were loosely united in their desire to topple the discredited power structure. When a significant social revolution erupted in 1951 and for a time produced serious efforts to reform the political system, stimulate economic development, and place land in the hands of the Indians, the clergy were, on the whole, mere observers of what was transpiring. Not until 1964, when the military seized power, did the Church begin to acquire greater stature. Many of the military leaders, especially René

73. Useful background material on this period is found in J. V. Fifer, *Bolivia: Land, Location, and Politics Since 1825*, Cambridge, England 1972; E. Finot, *Nueva historia de Bolivia: ensayo de interpretación sociológica*, 2nd ed., La Paz 1954; G. Frankovich, *El pensamiento boliviano en el siglo XX*, Mexico, D.F. 1956; Augusto Guzmán, *Historia de Bolivia*, La Paz 1973; Guillermo Lora, *Historia del movimiento obrero boliviano*, 3 vols, La Paz 1967-70, a splendid social history despite the author's Trotskyite convictions; and H. S. Klein, *Parties & Political Change in Bolivia, 1880-1952*, Cambridge, England 1969. For an insight into the traditional Catholic position see G. Romero, *Reflexiones para una interpretació de la historia de Bolivia*, Buenos Aires 1960; and H. Siles Salinas, *La aventura y el orden*, Santiago de Chile 1956.

Barrientos, liked to defend their programme on the grounds that it was rooted in Catholic humanism.

4. MEXICO AND CENTRAL AMERICA

Shortly after the inception of Mexico's great social revolution in 1910, a new generation of intellectuals began to advance far beyond the anti-clericalism that had characterised the mid-nineteenth century *Reforma*. Sometimes revising the views of their liberal predecessors in the light of Marxist-inspired analysis, these intellectuals wanted, not just to reduce the temporal power of the Church, cut also to curtail the influence of religion in general. In glorifying Mexico's indigenous past, moreover, many revolutionary leaders saw the need to eliminate all that was associated with the Hispanic, colonial era, including Catholicism. Men of these persuasions, largely middle-sector lawyers and intellectuals, wrote into the Mexican Constitution of 1917 various provisions that were exceedingly hostile to traditional religious influences. [74] When President Plutarco Elías Calles began in the mid-1920s actually to implement some of the anti-clerical and anti-religious articles of the constitution, [75] Catholics in the Guadalajara region responded with the so-called *Cristero* uprising which resulted in considerable bloodshed before being suppressed by government troops. [76]

In formulating the official platform upon which its candidate Lázaro Cárdenas was to run in 1934 for the presidency, the Mexican official party (Partido Nacional Revolucionario) called for the revision of Article 3 of the 1917 Constitution so as to require that primary and secondary education be based on the principles of the 'socialist doctrine that the Mexican Revolution supports'. [77] The Mexican hierarchy had bitterly opposed the original wor-

74. See R. L. Melgarejo and J. Fernández Rozas, eds, *El congreso constituyente de 1916 y 1917*, Mexico, D.F. 1917; and E. V. Niemeyer, Jr, *Revolution at Querétaro: The Mexican Constitutional Convention of 1916-1917*, Austin 1974, a carefully researched and judiciously balanced account. The period is also skilfully handled in R. E. Quirk, *Mexico* (Englewood Cliffs, N.J. 1971), 81-104, a work which is rendered all the more valuable by an extensive and carefully annotated bibliography.
75. See E. K. James, 'Church and State in Mexico', *Foreign Policy Association Reports*, XI (1935), 106-16; J. Pérez Lugo, ed., *La cuestión religiosa en México: Recopilación de leyes, disposiciones legales y documentos para el estudio de este problema político*, México, D.F. 1927.
76. A crucial figure in providing leadership to Catholics carrying on the struggle against President Calles was Archbishop Orozco of Guadalajara. A friendly but penetrating biography is V. Camberas Vizcaino, *Francisco el grande: Mons. Francisco Orozco y Jiménez*, 2 vols, 2nd ed, Mexico, D.F. 1966. Another valuable source on this period is A. Olivera Sedano, *Aspectos del conflicto religioso de 1926 a 1929: sus antecedentes y consequencias*, Mexico, D.F. 1966. Two particularly well researched and scholarly treatments of these events are D. C. Bailey, *Viva Cristo Rey! The Cristero Rebellion and the Church-State Conflict in Mexico*, Austin 1974, and R. E. Quirk, *The Mexican Revolution and the Catholic Church, 1910-1929*, Bloomington, Indiana 1973.
77. See L. C. Brown, 'Mexican Church-State Relations, 1933-1940', *Journal of Church and State*, VI (1964), 202.

ding of Article 3 which provided merely for secular rather than socialist education. It reacted in still more hostile manner to the quickly-approved revised version and anticipated the worst when Cárdenas was overwhelmingly elected president.[78]

Writing from the United States where he had been living in exile since 1927, José de Jesús Manríquez y Zárate, bishop of Huejutla, charged that the Mexican revolution was being guided by a Judaic-masonic plot and he called upon the faithful to reject the 'Bolshevik monster'. Also writing in exile from the United States, Archbishop Leopoldo Ruiz y Flores, the apostolic delegate to Mexico, asserted that the danger of communism was imminent and that the Church could not prevent Mexican Catholics from defending their interests.[79]

In 1937 those Mexican Catholics who for some years had seen in *Hispanismo* the means of saving their country from a communist Judaic-masonic conspiracy, merged their previously established organisations into the Unión Nacional Sinarquista. By 1940 this movement of right-wing, Catholic nationalism could boast a following of more than half a million Mexicans.[80]

Sinarquistas denounced the Mexican revolutionists as servants of Moscow, scathingly criticised the liberal influence that had infected the fatherland since the overthrow of Emperor Iturbide, and called on Mexicans to renounce class warfare and opt instead for a mystical regime resting on humanity, love, the Spanish heritage, and the Catholic Church. However much they attacked the Mexican revolution, Sinarquistas did not refrain from incorporating one of its most important ideological ingredients into their own programme. They stressed the dangers of United States imperialism both to the economy and cultural values of Mexico.

Accepting also the pro-Indian sentiments of the Mexican revolution, notwithstanding their frequent Hispanist proclamations, Sinarquistas specifically sought to attract to their programme the Indian peasants of central Mexico, who had long evidenced a deep attachment to Catholic traditions. Much of the Sinarquista success in winning the following of rural Indian masses stemmed from the resentment of the natives against the government's attempt to eradicate all vestiges of Catholic influence.

Intellectually, Cárdenas was undoubtedly committed to an anti-clerical and even anti-religious programme. Apparently he was genuinely fearful

78. The best discussion of the religious issue in Mexican education at this time is found in J. Bravo Ugarte, *La educación en México,* Mexico, D.F. 1966, expressing a moderately clerical point of view; and I. Castillo, *México y su revolución educative,* 2 vols, Mexico, D.F. 1965, 1966, advancing in restrained terms the case for secular education.
79. Brown, *op.cit.,* 205, 209.
80. See A. Michaels, 'Fascism and Sinarquismo: Popular Nationalism Against the Mexican Revolution', *Journal of Church and State,* VIII (1966), 239.

that religious influences would always constitute an impediment to material progress. Above all else, however, Cárdenas was a Mexican nationalist, pragmatically dedicated to the formulation of a programme that would win widespread support, binding Mexicans of all classes and groups together to produce a unified nation that could then proceed toward modernisation and social justice. Surprised by the strength of the reaction against his anti-religious designs, and amazed to discover Catholicism's continuing hold on the masses despite the apparent weakness of the organised Church, Cárdenas came, however reluctantly, to accept the traditional religion as a permanent part of the national heritage. Once he recognised that his anti-religious goals were producing such deep divisiveness as to jeopardise the success of his social and economic reform projects, Cárdenas began to seek an accommodation with the Church.

After 1936, very few additional convents and other properties used for religious purposes were seized by the government. Early in 1937 many State legislatures, undoubtedly with the approval of Cárdenas, began to ease restrictions on the number of priests permitted within their boundaries, while hundreds of churches, closed for several years, were reopened. In November 1937 the charges against Archbishop Ruiz y Flores and Bishop Manriquez y Zárate were dropped. These two bitter foes of socialist education were now free to return to Mexico. The support which the Catholic Church extended Cárdenas in connection with the 1938 oil expropriation helped confirm the tentative reconciliation between Church and State which the president had initiated.[81]

Presented with unmistakable evidence that their firmness and the un-suspected religious zeal of the masses had been rewarded by revolutionary leaders with an accommodation that left room for Catholicism within the national culture, some Catholic spokesmen called off their bitter attack against the Mexican revolution. Sensing that they might, after all, be allowed to participate to some degree in the process of change under way, a few churchmen, no more than a tiny minority at first, began to praise the socio-economic goals of the revolution. In this they anticipated by some twenty years or more the reform stance that various clergymen elsewhere in Latin America would assume.

If Catholicism has not been a genuinely effective force of social reform in Mexico since 1937, the reason cannot be found in the anti-clerical legislation produced by the revolution. Although still on the statute books, this legisla-tion is largely a dead letter. Rather, the reason for the Church's largely in-

81. On this and related topics see F. C. Turner, 'The Compatibility of Church and State in Mexico', *Journal of Inter-American Studies*, IX (1967), 591-602, and D. J. Mabry, *Mexico's Acción Nacional: A Catholic Alternative to Revolution*, Syracuse 1973, dealing with the Church-influenced Partido de Acción Nacional founded in 1939.

effectual role in Mexico must be sought in the extreme reluctance of most of its leaders to take actions which, in a still dangerously charged emotional setting, can be interpreted as political in nature. More so than in any other Latin American republic, disastrous experiences of the past have led the clergy of Mexico to resolve upon an apolitical role.

Although nearly all other circumstances were considerably different, it was nevertheless a social revolution, originating only in 1944, that goaded the Guatemalan Church into making a more enlightened appraisal of the national scene and beginning to establish closer ties with unassimilated Indian masses. Prior to 1944 right-wing nationalism was perhaps the dominant characteristic of Guatemalan Catholicism. After the inception of the social revolution, right-wing Catholic nationalism, under the leadership of Archbishop Mariano Rossell y Arellano, often directed its principal energies toward a sterile crusade against communism and Protestantism. But Guatemala's churchmen did not consciously align themselves against the interests of the peasantry, as Peruvian clergymen had done in the 1920s when confronting an alleged communist menace.

President Jacobo Arbenz, elected in 1951 to continue the recently-begun social revolution, drifted gradually toward the left and was increasingly condemned by church officials for leading the country into communism. Arbenz was overthrown in 1954 and the conservative aristocracy that re-acquired power decided to reward the Church for the strong anti-communist position it had taken. Within a few years the anti-clerical legislation enacted by nineteenth century liberals had been repealed.

Elsewhere in Central America, recognition of the value of the Church as an ally in combating what it was convenient to describe as a communist menace helped produce constitutional changes removing previous restrictions on ecclesiastical activity, particularly in the field of education. [82] The rest of Central America thus tended to come into line with Costa Rica, where religious instruction had traditionally been given, on an optional basis, in public schools.

Costa Rica, long unique among the Central American republics in many respects, had customarily allowed the Church almost as broad a sphere of temporal influence as it had gained in Colombia after 1880. In general, Costa Rican churchmen, led for many years during the mid-twentieth century by Archbishop Victor Manuel Sanabria y Martinez, had taken advantage of their favourable status to advance an enlightened programme of social justice and accommodation to new intellectual currents.

82. See R. N. Adams, *Crucifixion by Power: Essays on Guatemalan National Social Structure, 1944-1966*, Austin 1970; F. B. Pike, 'The Catholic Church in Central America', *Review of Politics*, XXI (1959), esp. 92-6; R. H. Valle, *Historia de las ideas contemporáneas en Centro-América*, México, D.F. 1960; and G. R. and B. A. Waggoner, *Education in Central America*, Lawrence, Kan. 1971.

IV. CATHOLICISM IN LATIN AMERICA AFTER THE SECOND WORLD WAR

1. THE CHURCH AND THE SOCIAL PROBLEM

One of the most striking aspects of the scene in Latin America after the Second World War has been the increasing attentiveness of the clergy to the plight of the masses and their mounting concern and even obsession with social justice. [83] There were numerous reasons for this development, one of the most obvious being the restlessness and awakening of the masses. If clerical leaders failed to assert themselves in this situation then the lower masses, whose great potential power was each day becoming more apparent, would be taken over by such foes of the Catholic Church as Marxists and traditionally anti-clerical middle-class politicians. This much feared possibility seemed to become the reality in Guatemala during the administration of Jacobo Arbenz, in Argentina during the latter stages of the Juan Domingo Perón regime, and in Cuba following the Fidel Castro seizure of power at the end of 1958.

Latin America's urban lower classes manifested increasing restiveness in the period following the Second World War because the system of expanded paternalism, introduced early in the century in part through renewed Church-State collaboration, was no longer capable of absorbing the vastly expanding marginal classes into the established system. The over-all Latin American population was no longer increasing at the comfortable turn-of-the-century rate of 1.2 per cent per year. Instead, for the area as a whole, the rate had risen to an annual average of approximately 3 per cent, the highest in the world. Given the continuing rural-to-urban demographic shift, population in major cities was increasing more rapidly still, frequently at a rate of between 4 and 5 per cent per year. With industry and technology becoming ever more capital intensive, the combined unemployment and underemployment rates in many cities soared to approximately 40 per cent of the labour force. Social pressures heightened, and the worsening plight of the urban masses demanded immediate attention.

In turning toward the masses, church leaders began to develop a new school of theology. Underlying the position advanced by reform-minded Catholics both of the clergy and laity was the theological conviction that the conflict between matter and spirit, on which nineteenth-century liberals had placed such emphasis in demanding the ousting of the Church from all temporal concerns, had no existence in fact. Instead, man must be recognised as

83. Among the many indications of the concern of Latin American churchmen with social problems are *Carta pastoral del episcopado peruano sobre algunos aspectos de la cuestión social en el Perú*, Lima 1958; P. Munoz Vega, Obispo Coadjutor Sedi Datus de Quito, *Carta pastoral sobre las obligaciones morales de promover el desarrollo dentro de la integración nacionál y latinoamericana*, Quito 1966; and *Los obispos de Chile hablan: el deber social y político de la hora presente*, Santiago de Chile 1962.

an indivisible being. Catholic intellectuals have thus sought to formulate a theology that justifies active Church-State collaboration as the only means of ending the privations of marginal classes and attaining lasting social peace.[84]

In most countries of Latin America, clerical leaders are seriously divided over the proper way to proceed toward social reform. To one group of the clergy, a group that is particularly strong in Argentina, Colombia and Ecuador, social justice means the expansion of charitable work within a society that will continue to be stratified and largely closed. On the other hand, numerous Catholics contend that the old social structure is doomed and that paternalism and charity will never suffice to keep the masses in line. They envisage the emergence of genuine social pluralism, with all classes and functional-interest groups enjoying the power to protect their essential rights and to compete on a basis of relative equality of opportunity for whatever advantages the nation has to offer. Complicating the matter still further is the fact that men of the second persuasion are in fundamental disagreement over whether the reforms they advocate should be brought about by imposition, through revolution if necessary, of a new system from above, or by seeking gradually to transform the individuals who comprise the broad base of society.

Many church leaders in the period after the Second World War have implied that a new system enforced from above, the essential feature of which is the redistribution of wealth, can quickly solve social problems and end the need for continuing privation and sacrifice.[85] These men have consistently failed to stress the need to develop the productive skills and socio-economic responsibilities of the lower classes. They have likewise ignored that aspect of political development which lays emphasis upon imparting to previously marginal masses certain skills and sophistication in decision-making processes, both with the over-all body politic and within various semi-autonomous associations.

In contrast, a large number of the clergy have begun to seek to prepare the way for modernisation by encouraging the natural and economically productive virtues of the faithful. In this respect, churchmen are making significant contributions towards political development. Particularly useful

84. See M. McGrath, 'The Teaching Authority of the Church: The Situation in Latin America', in W. V. D'Antonio and F. B. Pike, eds, *Religion, Revolution and Reform: New Forces for Change in Latin America*, New York (1964), 41-58; and I. Vallier, 'Religious Élites: Differentiations and Developments in Roman Catholicism', in S. M. Lipset and A. Solari, eds, *Élites in Latin America*, (New York 1967), 190-232.

85. See C. A. Astiz, *Pressure Groups and Power Elites in Peruvian Politics*, Ithaca, N.Y. 1969; F. Bourricaud, *Poder y sociedad en el Perú contemporáneo*, trans. R. Bixio, Buenos Aires 1967; and F. B. Pike, 'The Catholic Church and Modernization in Peru and Chile', *Journal of International Affairs*, XX (1966), 272-88.

in training men to protect their own interests and to take a role in decision-making processes has been the formation under clerical leadership of numerous credit, consumer and agricultural co-operatives. [86]

Reform-minded churchmen in Latin America came increasingly in the 1960s to speak of a process they call *concientización (concientiçaciao* in Brazil). By this they mean imparting a sense of awareness and class solidarity to workers, and beyond this an appreciation of the potential power that workers have for shaping their own and their country's destiny. Spokesmen of *concientización* lay heavy stress on material incentives, conceived of not so much in individual terms as in a collective effort to achieve the common good and a better life-style for all of society. The fact that the Church, as in the past, claims the right to define the common good, and that it is priests who insist upon directing the awakening of the masses, has led some observers to see in *concientización* a bid by the Church for augmented temporal power within a society facing the likelihood, if not the certitude, of profound transformation.

The changing social and economic attitudes inherent in the concept of *concientización* seem to originate in a changing emphasis in theology. In the past the Church in Latin America tended to assure the masses of redemption through the paternalistic solicitude and supernatural powers of the priesthood and to attach very little importance to the natural virtue and initiative of the individual layman. Since the Second World War, however, and especially since the Second Vatican Council (1962-5), a number of Latin American theologians have placed greater stress on the role of the individual conscience in attaining salvation. Moreover, reforms in the liturgy and moves aimed at enhancing the status of laymen have been concerned with achieving the more active participation of all members in the life of the Church and minimising the barriers of hierarchical organisation. Here are important fields in which theological change can have a meaningful relationship to social, political and economic transformation.

Despite recognition by many churchmen of the close connection between the spiritual and the political development of the masses, probably a majority of the clergy at the outset of the 1970s considered their task to be almost exclusively the propagation of the faith and the nourishment of supernatural virtue. In the viewpoint of these clergymen, attention to secular matters in any guise was likely to detract from fulfilment of their primary goal. Quite possibly these clerics recalled how the Church in its confrontation with nineteenth-century liberalism was stripped of the means necessary to

86. See S.Ruiz Luján, *Para construir un nuevo orden económico*, St. Louis, Mo. 1949, expressing a Colombian Catholic's view of the co-operative movement's potential, and W. C. Thiesenhusen, *Chile's Experiment in Agrarian Reform*, Madison, Wis. 1966, containing an account of the Church's contributions to the establishment of agricultural co-operatives.

minister just to its spiritual mission. Rendered cautious by a historical experience which has left an indelible impression, Latin America's native clergy are apt to abstain from any intrusion into the temporal order which might antagonise prevailing political powers.

Motivated by considerations of personal security and also sometimes by the hope of ultimately fashioning a more viable social order, many clergymen are concerned not so much with the lower classes as with making the Church a vital force among the upper and middle sectors. In seeking to establish more effective ties with society's participating and directing groups, the Church in many Latin American countries is spending a considerable portion of its meagre income on maintaining and expanding the Catholic university system.[87] The Church, moreover, continues to be a powerful force and to expend large sums in augmenting its influence in secondary education. In Brazil, where by far the majority of elementary schools are State supported (about 87 per cent), most secondary schools (about 67 per cent) are privately controlled, largely by religious orders.[88] In Guatemala the Catholic schools instruct only 7.4 per cent of the primary students but 21.1 per cent of those attending secondary schools.[89]

As higher and secondary instruction in most Latin American countries remain the province of middle and upper classes, it is quite apparent that the Church is not directing its main educational thrust towards the lower classes. Its endeavour to maintain high-tuition educational institutions which perpetuate the sort of humanistic curricula appealing mostly to the well-to-do, restricts the opportunity which the Church might have to encourage modernisation. This fact has led some clergymen to suggest that the Church should curtail its private educational structure and take advantage of the increasingly tolerant attitude of political administrations to find positions for priests and active lay Catholics in public schools, especially in those that stress technical and scientific training.

Through means other than education, Latin American clergymen began in the 1950s and 1960s to make a concerted endeavour to establish a closer relationship with the middle and upper classes. The *cursillo* retreat movement and the expanding work of the secretive Opus Dei, a unique religious order founded in Spain in 1928 and made up both of priests and laymen, have been directed towards this goal. The activities of Opus Dei have been widely criticised by Catholics in Latin America who feel that the main concern of the Church should be with the masses, and also by many Jesuits who

87. See F. Sanhueza, 'Les universités catholiques en Amérique Latine', *Rythmes de Monde*, IX (1961), 200-1.
88. Wagley, *An Introduction to Brazil*, 215-16.
89. IX Congreso Interamericano de Educación Católica, *Informativo No. 7*, mimeo., San Salvador, El Salvador, n.d., tables 1 and 3.

perhaps detect in the new order a rival for influence among the more powerful sectors of society. Probably the most unique aspect of Opus Dei within
the context of traditional Iberian Catholicism is its attempt to associate virtue and even redemptive grace with the development of capitalist skills.
However, the capitalist who is formed in accordance with Opus Dei ideals is
expected to turn his expertise not so much towards individual economic
aggrandisement as towards the realisation of the common good.

The split among Latin American churchmen over the issues of pluralism
versus paternalism, instantaneous reform imposed from above versus the
evolutionary change of the mass base of society, and lower class versus middle and upper-class alliances, has been reflected among the Catholic laity.
These very issues have, for example, seriously weakened the Christian
democratic political movement.

2. THE CHRISTIAN DEMOCRATIC MOVEMENT AND THE NEW CORPORATIVISM

The origins of Christian democracy in some Latin American countries, particularly Peru, Ecuador, Guatemala and Venezuela, can be traced to quite
conservative Catholic groups advocating an approach to social problems
quite similar to the paternalism associated with right-wing advocates of
Hispanismo during the 1920s and 1930s. In the mid-1950s, however, under
the influence of innovating Chilean leaders, Christian democracy tended to
assume a new position considerably in advance of its European counterpart
movements. New groups of Christian democratic leaders demanded immediate and even revolutionary solutions to social problems. Rejecting
paternalism, they urged a pluralistic society which in the initial stages might
involve the lower classes in considerable conflict with the middle and upper
classes. Redistribution rather than increased production of wealth was often
advanced as a panacea, and a vaguely defined communitarian society which
would eliminate capital-labour discord and erode the private property structure was advocated. Christian democrats at this time recommended a third
position between communism and liberal capitalism, attacking both
ideologies with equal intensity.

Within a decade it became apparent that the conservative origins of
Christian democracy in much of Latin America had been only temporarily
submerged rather than eliminated. In the 1960s conservative spokesmen
again asserted themselves with Christian democracy, leading to major splits
in the Bolivian, Ecuadoran, Peruvian and Guatemalan parties.[90]

Chilean Christian democrats in their successful presidential and congressional campaigns of 1964 and 1965 defended a platform that was more
conservative than the ideology announced in the late 1950s. They played

90. A useful summary is E. J. William, *Latin American Christian Democratic Parties*,
Knoxville, Tenn. 1967.

down the importance of the communitarian society, stressed production rather than redistribution of wealth, consciously sought the support of the middle classes and wealth groups, damped their attacks against capitalism, and stressed the Marxist menace. Once in power, moderate Christian democratic leaders under President Eduardo Frei were hard pressed to maintain this approach against the attacks of the party's more impatient, revolutionary, and class conflict-orientated elements.[91] The resultant splintering of the party contributed to the triumph of the Marxian socialist Salvador Allende in the 1970 presidential election.

By the mid-1970s, Christian democracy was in serious decline in those two countries, Chile and Venezuela, where it had previously demonstrated the most strength. In the aftermath of the overthrow of Allende by the military in 1973, many Chileans displayed thorough disillusionment with Christian democracy. Some Chileans blamed the party for having been too advanced in its reform programmes and for having helped prepare the way for the short-lived Marxist triumph under Allende. Others criticised the party for having departed too far from the more radical currents of its ideology and for its failure to mount a vigorous denunciation of the alleged abuses of the conservative military government established after Allende had been ousted. Meanwhile in Venezuela the Christian Democratic movement also entered upon decline.[92] The movement's candidate Rafael Caldera had triumphed in the presidential election of 1969. However, after a rather lacklustre administration he was replaced in office, as a result of the 1974 election, by Carlos Andrés Pérez, the candidate of the more secularist party of moderate reform, Acción Democrática.

The fate of the Catholic Church in Latin America, however, is in no important way linked to the success of the Christian democrats. It is altogether possible that the Church can anticipate just as favourable treat-

91. A good exposition of Chile's left-wing Christian democracy is J. Chonchol, 'Proposiciones para una acción politica en el periodo 1967-1970', initially circulated among the Christian Democratic Party's leaders and subsequently published in *Politica, Economia, Cultura*, 239 (1967), special number. A favourable assessment of Chilean Christian Democracy is found in G. W. Grayson, Jr, 'The Chilean Christian Democratic Party: Genesis and Development', Johns Hopkins University unpublished doctoral dissertation 1967, and M. Zañartu and J. J. Kennedy, *The Overall Development of Chile*, Notre Dame, Ind. 1969. A critical attitude pervades A. Olavaria Bravo, *Chile bajo la Democracia Cristiana*, 3 vols, Santiago de Chile 1966-9, and J. Petras, *Politics and Social Forces in Chilean Development*, Austin 1969. Greater objectivity is found in M. H. Fleet, 'Ideological Tendencies Within Chilean Christian Democracy', unpublished University of California at Los Angeles doctoral dissertation 1971.
92. On Christian democracy, more frequently known as Christian Socialism, in Venezuela, where the party is designated by the letters COPEI, see R. Caldera, *Idea de una sociologia venezolana*, Caracas 1957; J. E. Rivera Oviedo, *Los Social Cristianos en Venezuela: Historia, ideologia*, Caracas 1970; and F. Tugwell, 'The Christian Democrats of Venezuela', *Journal of Inter-American Studies*, VII (1965), 245-68. The first two are highly partisan accounts, while the Tugwell article is an objective assessment.

ment from a number of other political parties and movements. Venezuela's Acción Democrática, for example, once a strongly anti-clerical body, took the lead during the presidency of Rómulo Betancourt (1959-63) in suppressing the *patronato nacional* and in increasing the Church's freedom of action within the country. [93] With the exception of avowedly Marxist parties, and perhaps also with the exception of the Brazilian military rulers of the late 1960s and early 1970s, most Latin American political organisations appear to be as much disposed as the Christian Democrats to allow the Church a relatively unfettered role within the national life. Perhaps this is because politicians after the Second World War, unlike the liberals of the nineteenth century, perceive the social function that religion can play in lessening revolutionary pressures from below.

From the mid-1970s, Christian Democracy could no longer be perceived as the wave of the future in Latin America. By then the best hope of churchmen for a voice in secular politics seemed to lie in reaching an accord with the technocratic planners, military and civilian, who had assumed control of several republics and were seeking to foster development through massive central government planning. Under the military regimes which assumed power in Brazil and Bolivia in 1964, Peru in 1968, Ecuador in 1972 and Chile in 1973, attempts were made to reintroduce some of the traditional corporative features of social organisation — features, incidentally, that had been consistently observable in Mexico since the 1920s and 1930s. [94] Old functional groups were strengthened and new ones were called into being, all of them carefully controlled by the State apparatus which wielded a moderating power, the power to channel the activities of the various semi-autonomous corporations into policies dedicated to the common good. In the newly emerging corporativism, the hope of the directing classes was that the mass of citizens, politicised to the extent of being allowed to participate within their own functional associations, would not demand a voice in national-level decision-making. If church officials can reach an understanding with the top level power wielders, they may be able to share to some degree in the exercise of the moderating power. Developments in Bolivia, Peru and Ecuador indicated that churchmen were enjoying some success in their sought-after entry into the top level power echelons.

In Brazil, however, Church and State remained consistently at

93. In 1961 the one-time anti-clerical Movimiento Nacionalista Revolucionario, then in control in Bolivia, also renounced the *patronato nacional* and allowed the Church a generally freer position within the country.
94. On the Mexican situation, see R. G. Eggleston, 'Legitimacy and Ideology in a Corporatist State: A Case Study of Post-1910 Mexico', unpublished Syracuse University doctoral dissertation 1972. On the re-emergence of corporativism elsewhere in Latin America, see F. B. Pike and T. J. Stritch, eds, *The New Corporatism: Social-Political Structures in the Iberian World*, Notre Dame, Indiana 1973.

loggerheads during most of the decade following the military takeover (1964) and thus the clergy were denied an influential voice in corporative policy-making. Circumstances in Brazil, according to some observers, reflect the conviction of its military rulers that a modern State does not require the legitimation traditionally provided by the Church. If the functional separation of Church and State foreseen by these observers actually comes about in Brazil, then the Church may 'be free to define its influence model in coalition with Rome' and return to a 'prophetic' function, 'as in the Old Testament, of interpreting the word of God in concrete situations and thereby denouncing injustice.' [95]

Christian democracy provided some of the most important advocates in Latin America after the Second World War for a restructuring of society along corporativist lines. Ironically, the movement is in decline just as Latin America has begun most resolutely to turn toward corporativism. Christian democrats thus can be seen as the precursors of new policies of which the implementation was destined to be left to others. They can also be viewed as forming a bridge between the Catholic corporativism of the 1920s and 1930s, often associated with *Hispanismo*, and with the more secular corporativism of the 1970s.

3. THE CONSEJO EPISCOPAL LATINO AMERICANO (CELAM)

In preparing to act within the political climate after the Second World War, a climate generally more favourable than that prevailing at the turn of the century, the Church in Latin America was the beneficiary of some unexpected consequences of a decision reached in the 1950s to wage a concerted struggle against a supposed communist menace.

In the wake of their expulsion from China following the communist takeover, many Catholic missionaries transferred to Latin America. Dismayed by the weakness of the Church and by the apparent strength of the forces arrayed against it, many of these men predicted that Latin America would shortly go the way of China if immediate action was not taken. Rome reacted to the warnings of emergency and crisis with the creation of a Pontifical Commission for Latin American. Seeking a united Catholic front, the commission was instrumental in convoking an international Eucharistic Congress in 1955. Upon the conclusion of the congress, which had assembled in Rio de Janeiro, a General Conference of the Latin

---

95. T. C. Bruneau, 'Power and Influence: Analysis of the Church in Latin America and the Case of Brazil', *Latin American Research Review*, VII (1973), 43. See also C. Antoine, *Church and Power in Brazil*, trans. P. Nelson, New York 1973; and Bruneau, *The Political Transformation of the Brazilian Catholic Church,* Cambridge, England 1973. On the 'prophetic Church' in Latin America in general, see L. R. Einaudi, M. H. Fleet, R. L. Maullin, and A. C. Stepan, 'The Changing Catholic Church', in Einaudi, ed., *Beyond Cuba: Latin America Takes Charge of Its Future* (New York 1974), esp. 88-92.

American Episcopacy was held. From its sessions emerged a plan to create the Consejo Episcopal Latino Americano (CELAM). A regional grouping of the Latin American episcopacy, CELAM was the forerunner of similar councils which would appear in Africa and elsewhere. From the outset, many of its participants viewed CELAM as a symbol of the role that the Church might play in contributing to the integration of Latin America not only on the spiritual level but in all spheres of human activity.

CELAM, constituted by the Latin American bishops, one from each country selected by their brothers in the episcopacy, undertook the study of common problems and the formulation of pastoral plans. It entered into intimate collaboration with the Latin American Conference of Religious and with the various centres of socio-religious investigation established in the continent during the 1960s. Continuing to work closely with the General Council of the Pontifical Commission for Latin America in Rome, CELAM also established contact with the various organs created in Europe and the United States for channelling aid to the Church in Latin America. [96]

Although the original assumption of CELAM seemed to be that its best reaction to the communist threat was the holding of old-style missions so as to rekindle the spiritual zeal that would enable the masses to persevere in adversity, several bishops resolved that the only effective long-range approach would be to align the Church with the forces working toward the mitigation of adversity. If nothing else, these few bishops succeeded in impressing upon their more conservative associates the enormity of Latin America's social problem. This they did in part by sponsoring the preparation of significant sociological-economic studies. Furthermore, CELAM conferences were turned into high-level seminars on social conditions, with recognised international authorities, many of them laymen, presiding over sessions at which bishops assumed the role of students. [97] A typical meeting of this sort was the CELAM conference held at Mar del Plata, Argentina, in 1966.

When the approximately 670 Latin American archbishops and bishops arrived in Rome for the Second Vatican Council, many seemed resigned to playing a passive role. A few of their more purposeful leaders, however, determined that the Latin American bishops should capitalise on the experience they had gained through CELAM by presenting as nearly as possible a united front on some of the major issues discussed at the Council sessions. Predisposed to deal in a fresh and imaginative manner with the

---

96. Within a few years of its founding, CELAM began publication of the trimestrial *Boletin del CELAM*. In 1967 CELAM, with its headquarters in Bogotá, initiated the publication of a *Carta Quincenal* and of various documents reflecting the findings of the bishops, working in collaboration with experts in various fields, on social and pastoral problems.
97. See E. Dussel, *Hipótesis para una historia de la Iglesia en América Latina* (Barcelona 1967), esp. 152-3.

problems of the modern world, because they had come to understand the conditions of that world through their CELAM education, the Latin American episcopacy surprised observers by following the leadership of such reform-minded prelates in their group as Chile's Raúl Silva Henríquez and Manuel Larraín and Brazil's Helder Camara and Eugenio Sales. Time and again they delivered an overwhelmingly liberal vote on crucial issues. Following the conclusion of the Council, the Latin American episcopacy displayed an inclination to assume an increasingly autonomous position, thus taking advantage of the unity originally inspired by Rome to assert, in a spirit of collegiality encouraged by Pope Paul VI, greater independence from Rome.

In many ways the diffidence of the conservatives and the relative aggressiveness and determination of the liberal leaders caused the Latin American episcopacy to present a somewhat deceptive appearance in Rome. Once back within their own countries and dealing with immediate local problems, the prelates tended to drift back to a policy of cautious conservatism. Ecumenism, religious tolerance, a dialogue with Jews, Protestants and even communists, concessions to the laity and greater concern with the masses rather than with the élite might be advisable elsewhere in the world. But within the prelates' own dioceses and archdioceses such policies often appeared to be dangerous.

4. THE SHORTAGE OF PRIESTS

If a leadership whose liberalism is often more apparent than real poses certain difficulties to Latin American Catholicism, a more basic problem is presented in the lower echelons by the glaring lack of priests. In 1912 there was for Latin America as a whole an average of one priest for every 4,480 inhabitants. In 1960 the ratio was 1:5,478. One of the more optimistic projections, compiled in the early 1960s, suggests that by the year 2000 the ratio is likely to be 1:6,800. Moreover, in such major countries as Argentina, Chile and Mexico, the growth in the number of seminarians has been proportionately less than the increase in over-all population. Only in Paraguay, Peru and Colombia has the increase in the number of seminarians exceeded the climb in population after the Second World War. [98]

98. In 1960, of the nearly 37,000 priests in Latin America, approximately 18,000 were members of the regular clergy. One of the best sources for the country-by-country data on the clergy in Latin America is the Center for Intercultural Formation (CIF, Cuernevaca, Mexico), *Study No. 1, Socio-Economic Data: Latin America in Maps, Charts and Tables*, compiled by Y. Labelle and A. Estrada, Mexico, D.F., 1963. Equally valuable is CIF *Study No. 2, Socio-Religious Data (Catholicism): Latin America in Maps, Charts and Tables*, compiled by Labelle and Estrada, Mexico, D.F. 1963. Some of the statistics presented in both studies are based on the research of the Fédération Internationale de Centres de Recherches Sociales et Socio-religieuses (FERES, Brussels). Also useful is W. Promper,

One important factor contributing to the scarcity of priests has its roots in the nineteenth century. As the Church was stripped of its wealth and deprived of its temporal power, prestige and influence by triumphant liberalism, the upper classes ceased to be attracted to the priesthood. Nor could the Church, once it had suffered loss of prestige, offer to lower middle classes an avenue of upward social mobility. [99] Owing, moreover, to high rates of illegitimacy and the general absence of a religiously-orientated family life, the lower classes have not provided a large number of priests.

To ease the shortage of religious, Latin America has turned increasingly to foreign clergymen. In Guatemala, the foreign-born account for nearly 85 per cent of the religious. [100] In Venezuela they account for over 60 per cent. For Latin America as a whole in 1960, foreigners comprised 37 per cent of the entire clergy. Colombia, where the Church since 1880 has continued to be a prestigious institution and the priesthood has remained attractive to the well born, is one of the few countries of Latin America where lack of vocations is not a major impediment to Catholicism and where those of native birth continue to constitute a large majority of the clergy.

The influx of large numbers of foreign clergy to Latin America has not been an unmixed blessing − no more so than in the nineteenth century when immigrant priests helped snuff out a promising liberal movement among the native clergy and led the Church into a staunchly reactionary position. In 1960 Spanish priests constituted 54 per cent of the foreign-born clergy in Latin America. Strongly influenced by experiences undergone during the Spanish Civil War, many of them were impressed with little save the need to wage a crusade against communism. Spanish priests, moreover, have tended to view the local clergy with disdain, manifesting the traditional sense of superiority that peninsular-born Spaniards have felt toward Creoles and mestizos.

By the 1960s Spain was beginning to send a new type of clergymen to Latin America. These Spanish priests, products of the religious renewal and move toward liberalisation which was under way in their native land, [101] avoided a negative approach to communism and assumed a role of leadership in the moves to modernise and reform both the Church and society. This frequently brought them into conflict with their more traditionalist

'Statistiques du clergé en Amérique Latine', *Aux Amis de l'Amérique Latine* (Louvain 1961), 140-1.

99. The issue of prestige and the clergy is examined to some extent in F. Hicks, 'Politics, Power and the Role of the Village Priest in Paraguay', *Journal of Inter-American Studies*, IX (1967), 273-82.

100. Conferencia Nacional de Religiosos y Religiosas de Guatemala, *Boletin Informativo y Tercer Informe General*, Guatemala City 1965.

101. See R. Duocastella, J. A. Marcos-Alonso, J. M. Díaz Mozas and P. Almerich, *Análisis sociológico del catolicismo español*, Barcelona 1967.

countrymen serving in the area. Thus the Spanish clergy came to reflect the split that had long impaired the effectiveness of the Latin American priesthood.

Another problem has been presented by the United States priests, who by the mid-1960s were estimated to represent about 20 per cent of the foreign clergy in Latin America. Some of them are accused of failing to understand or to sympathise with Latin American culture and of trying to introduce not only the religious but also the social, economic and political practices of the United States. With nationalism an increasingly important force among all classes of Latin America, the native clergy incline to be suspicious of the new arrivals, whether they come from Spain, the United States, Germany, Belgium, or the Netherlands.

In the coming generations the needs of Catholicism can scarcely be met by the clergy, whether native or foreign. More effective use will have to be made of the laity, and thus the *cursillo* movement, the utilisation of deacons, and the work of Opus Dei may provide important indications of what the future nature of the Catholic Church in Latin America is likely to be. Some of the area's Catholic leaders are convinced that the clerically-dominated Church is headed for virtual extinction, and that with its demise will arise a new and more vital institution in which the main dynamic force will be provided by the laity.

Whatever the future may hold, it was apparent by the mid-1970s that the influx of foreign priests was dwindling, owing in part to the decline of priestly vocations in the more developed countries. Accompanying the fall in number of foreign clergy was a diminution of theological concern with awakening the individual consciousness of all members of the faithful regardless of social and economic status. Churchmen seemed more and more to be returning to the conviction that the spiritual as well as the economic dependence of the masses could not readily give way to self-determination. Future research must establish if the new theological approaches that were so much a feature of Latin American Catholicism in the 1960s were owing largely to the influence of the foreign clergy and the attempts of its representatives to introduce a society-wide value system of liberal individualism which was hopelessly contrary to the Iberian world's cultural *milieu*.[102]

5. THE CATHOLIC 'NEW LEFT' AND 'NEW CENTRE'

Considerable disagreement has for some time been evident over the role

102. This issue is not explored in what is the best study of the impact of the foreign clergy in a single Latin American republic: M. G. Macaulay, 'The Role of the Radical Clergy in the Attempt to Transform Peruvian Society', unpublished University of Notre Dame doctoral dissertation 1972.

which an institutional Church in any guise can be expected to play in a changing Latin America. A group of Catholic intellectuals, constituting what is often referred to as a 'new left', has, for example, begun to criticise Christian democratic and other movements more directly affiliated with the Church as nostalgic attempts to preserve a Catholic society by holding back an inexorable tide of secularism. Catholics of the 'new left' regard themselves above all else as humanists and are vitally concerned with effecting radical changes in society which will be conducive to the more widespread attainment of human development and dignity. Catholicism, they feel, has contributed through the centuries to the formation of a body of thought that stresses humanism and individual dignity; and it is this contribution that is uniquely, almost exclusively, meaningful in contemporary secular society. Catholics should, then, act within various secular institutions, associations, functional-interest groups and political organisations, including those of Marxist orientation, that are also concerned with achieving human dignity by bringing about fundamental changes in existing socio-economic patterns. No longer, they contend, can an institutional Church act effectively as a separate entity within a thoroughly secularised, pluralistic society. [103]

The willingness of a 'new left' among Catholics to co-operate with Marxists is in some ways a modern manifestation of the traditional animus of Iberian Catholicism towards the materialism and greed assumed to be the inevitable products of capitalism. Like many Marxists, the leftist Catholics maintain it is essential to create an economy that is structured to meet the basic needs of citizens rather than to satisfy the profit lust of individuals. In Latin America, moreover, Marxists have frequently been dedicated humanists, convinced that when government provides the basic needs of citizens, they will take advantage of their liberation from a competitive, money-grubbing existence in order to develop their higher intellectual and spiritual capacities. This conviction, apparent as a motivating factor in many of the actions of Fidel Castro, is shared by representative figures of the Church's 'new left'; and it provides an important link between some Catholics and Marxists.

Spokesmen of the Catholic 'new left' urge the Church to abandon its temporal power within the established order and, further, to divest itself of wealth. They maintain that the Church, by seeking an alliance with the ruling classes and by clinging to its wealth, is limiting its power to act with im-

103. On this subject see Paulo Freire, *La educación como práctica de la libertad*, Santiago de Chile 1969; I. D. Illich, *Celebration of Awareness: A Call for Institutional Revolution*, New York 1970; G. Gerassi, ed., *Revolutionary Priest: The Complete Writings and Messages of Camilo Torres*, New York 1971; and T. G. Sanders, *Catholicism and Development: The Catholic Left in Brazil*, in K. H. Silbert, ed., *Churches and States: The Religious Institutions and Modernization*, New York 1967.

partiality as the social conscience for Latin American élites. Undoubtedly the clergymen of the 'new left' are as interested as their traditionalist predecessors in protecting their corporate interests and also in shaping the sort of conditions in society that will facilitate the accomplishment of their spiritual mission. If it seems that they can best realise these goals by dramatically dissociating themselves from an established ruling class which appears to be doomed and by relinquishing wealth, they will not hesitate to take such action.

While a 'new left' clergy may have performed pioneering efforts to create a break between the Church and the established order, their position in the 1970s was being taken over by a non-revolutionary coalition that can be designated the 'new centre'. The clergy of the 'new centre' desire changes in national leadership in order to prevent basic, structural changes in the social order. Like many essentially non-revolutionary military leaders, so also many non-radical churchmen have acquired new concepts of national security that focus not simply on guerrilla insurgents but on problems of economic development and social backwardness. In both the military and clerical viewpoint, the main challenge to security comes from national leaders, often alleged to be in league with foreign capitalists, who are obstructing modernisation by their selfish pursuit of private gain. The remedy envisaged consists of entrusting national destiny to more enlightened and efficient leaders who possess the skill to bring about the over-all development that in turn can generate sufficient capital to provide security to the burgeoning masses.

Churchmen of the 'new centre' wish to cast off their links with an old order, perceived to be no longer viable, in order to establish ties with new élites who are expected to be more successful in developing national economic potential. The future society, which is counted upon to re-establish internal stability, is seen as one which is neither altogether capitalist nor altogether socialist. The new society will encourage the individualistic, dynamic thrust of enlightened entrepreneurs and technicians, but co-ordinate their efforts more than in the past into cohesive national policies. Meanwhile, the masses below will be organised into collective, functional groups which will diminish the individual egotisms of members and, by accustoming them initially to dependence on the group for security, instil in them a mentality of dependence which will predispose them to accept their ultimate reliance upon a paternalistic State.

If the formulae of internal security are to be successfully applied, it is essential that the masses, at least in the early stages of quickening economic development, be shielded against rising material expectations. This can be accomplished, it is hoped, by expanding the non-material rewards deriving from the traditional religion and also from new forms of nationalism. The goal, therefore, is a new society in which Church and State will collaborate in providing non-material rewards for the masses, while at the same time sanctioning the material incentives of new capitalists and technocrats who are seen as the key to modernisation.

The formula of self-reliant capitalism for the upper classes, however restricted by requirements of the common good, and paternalistically-guaranteed security for the collectivised dependent masses, is nothing new in the Iberian world. It dates back in Latin America to the very beginnings of the colonial period and even finds remote origins in some of the high, pre-conquest Indian civilisations. Thus the 'neither capitalism nor communism' refrain in which many churchmen have begun to join military officers and various civilian intellectuals is not revolutionary.

Quite possibly the model of self-reliant capitalism above and dependent collectivism below is not what some of those church leaders who sought to awaken individual consciousness have in mind. Thus the 'new centre' could encounter difficulty in making its viewpoint the prevalent one in Latin American Catholicism.

6. PROTESTANTISM

If many Catholic intellectuals regard the religious vacuum in Latin America, where an overwhelming majority of the people are Catholic in name only, as an unmistakable sign of the secular society, Protestants have often viewed this vacuum in a different light. They have been encouraged by it to perservere in their missionary activity. Frequently they have incurred the animosity of those Catholic leaders who refuse to concede that much of Latin America must be recognised as a mission area and who react to Protestantism in the same manner in which they have responded to communism. [104] In both instances, these Catholic leaders have ignored the underlying causes of the challenges they find distasteful.

Evidence suggests that the rise both of Protestantism and Marxism in Latin America has been facilitated by the lower classes' sense of alienation from the Catholic Church. Protestantism has been must successful in Brazil, where Protestants constitute nearly 7 per cent of the population, and in Chile, where they represent close to 12 per cent of the inhabitants, and may actually attend weekly religious services in larger numbers than Catholics. [105]

104. See E. Ospina, *The Protestant Denominations in Colombia*, Bogotá 1954, a spirited attack against Protestant missionary activity. The Protestant view is strongly set forth in W. C. Easton *Colombian Conflict*, London 1954. A scholarly examination of the issue in Colombia and elsewhere is M. S. Bates, *Religious Liberty: An Inquiry*, New York 1945.
105. Protestantism has also registered considerable success in Guatemala, where about 4 per cent of the population is Protestant. On Protestantism in Latin America see W. S. Rycroft, *Religion and Faith in Latin America*, Philadelphia 1958, and Rycroft with M. Clemmer, *A Factual Study of Latin America*, New York 1963. On Pentecostalism see C. L. d'Epinay, *El*

Various pentecostal groups have gained the largest number of converts, and their most fruitful field has been the lower-class population. Apparently one reason for these developments in Brazil and Chile is that the lower classes, feeling abandoned by and therefore hostile towards the Catholic Church, seek a religion that is as distinct and far removed as possible from the traditional faith. [106]

7. RELIGIOUS SYNCRETISM

In certain Latin American republics, notably Bolivia, Peru, Ecuador and Guatemala, the religious syncretism of the Indian masses presents a greater challenge to Catholicism than does Protestantism. [107] The Church's continuing inability to establish religious orthodoxy among the Indians stems largely from the failure of society to assimilate the Indians into the type of occidental life in which the Catholicism preached by westernised priests is meaningful. This has led some churchmen to conclude that they can ultimately succeed among the native masses only by pushing for the profound, social, economic and social changes which will facilitate the long-delayed assimilation of the Indians.

Some success in spreading Catholicism among the indigenous population has been achieved by locating and training young leaders in Indian communities and then encouraging them to indoctrinate others in the faith. Once a cadre of *catequistas* is formed in an Indian community, social action orientated priests have sometimes used them for broad educational purposes

---

refugio de las masas, Santiago de Chile, dealing with Chile; E. Willems, *Followers of the New Faith*, Nashville, Tenn. 1967, describing the movement in Brazil and Chile; and W. R. Read, *et al.*, *Latin American Church Growth*, Grand Rapids 1969. On the Church and Society Movement, formed by Protestants who seek to play a role in bringing about basic social change, see *Social Justice and the Latin Churches: Church and Society in Latin America*, trans. by J. Lara-Braud, Richmond, Va. 1969. Under attack both from Pentecostalists and conservative Protestants, the Church and Society Movement, known in Latin America as ISAL, has since 1966 published a journal bearing the title of ISAL. An invaluable reference source is J. H. Sinclair, ed., *Protestantism in Latin America: A Bibliographical Guide*, Austin 1967, containing over two thousand listings and extensive annotations.
106. See E. Willems, 'Religious Mass Movements and Social Change in Brazil', in E. N. Baklanoff, ed., *New Perspectives of Brazil* (Nashville, Tenn. 1966), 205-32.
107. See R. N. Adams, *Encuesta sobre la cultura de los ladinos en Guatemala*, Guatemala City 1956, and *Political Change in Guatemalan Indian Communities: A Symposium*, New Orleans 1957. The latter is one of many excellent anthropological-sociological studies published by the Tulane University Middle America Research Institute. See also W. Bennett and J. B. Bird, *Andean Cultural History*, New York 1949; D. Heath and R. N. Adams, eds, *Contemporary Cultures and Societies of Latin America* New York 1965; J. Monast, *L'Univers religieux des Aymaras de Bolivia*, Cuernevaca, Mexico 1967; R. E. Reina, *The Law of the Saints*, New York 1966; D. E. Thompson, *Maya Paganism and Christianity: A History of the Fusion of Two Religions*, New Orleans 1954; and N. Whetten, *Rural Mexico*, Chicago 1948. Two additional sources of great value are J. Steward, gen. ed., *Handbook of South American Indians*, 7 vols, Washington, D.C. 1946-59, and R. Wauchope, gen. ed., *Handbook of Middle American Indians*, Austin 1965.

and even as a spearhead for introducing modern agricultural methods and organising co-operatives.

By the 1970s there had appeared in the Andean American core, formed by highland Ecuador, Peru and Bolivia, a movement that questioned continuing efforts to acculturate Indians into western life-styles. As an alternative, it was argued that Indians should be protected in their own life-styles and in their own agrarian communities, made secure for them and even extended in size through agrarian reform programmes. Advocates of the new approach urge that Indians be organised into co-operatives so that, to some degree, they can be economically integrated into the nation. Culturally, however, they are to be allowed, and even encouraged, to remain apart and to continue to use their native languages rather than Spanish. If these plans for cultural pluralism come to fruition, [108] the Church may have to learn to stress one set of values and life goals among the Indians, another set among the westernised urban dwellers. In a way, this problem is akin to one imposed by the new corporativism which demands, if it is to function smoothly, one approach to collectivised, dependent urban labourers and another to an urban bourgeoisie. Such are the problems the Church must continue to face in societies that have retained particularisms and steadfastly resisted the universalism that has been pursued by the liberal democracies of the western world.

8. THE POPULATION PROBLEM

In the mid-1960s the demographic problem had begun to pose a threat to Latin American Catholicism. Against a background of spiralling population statistics, the Church appeared to be at a serious disadvantage because of its disinclination to expand the sphere of decisions entrusted to the individual conscience of the believer to include the choice of effective means of family limitation.

Surveys of the mid-1960s conducted in several Latin American countries, including traditionally devout Colombia, revealed that a considerable majority of upper-class and about 40 per cent of middle-class women were already employing effective means, that is means other than the rhythm method, of family limitation. [109] Moreover the percentage of upper- and middle-class women who practised birth control was shown to be as high among those who regularly attended mass and participated in other religious

---

108. A convincing case in favour of cultural pluralism in Peru is made by W. P. Mangin, 'The Indians', in D. A. Sharp, *U. S. Foreign Policy and Peru* (Austin 1972), 206-36.
109. Sources on the population problem include D. Chaplin, ed., *Population Policy and Growth in Latin America*, Lexington, Ky, 1971; W. V. D'Antonio, 'The Problem of Population Growth in Latin America', in F. B. Pike, ed., *Latin American History, Select Problems* (New York 1969), 440-82, and J. M. Stycos and J. Arias, eds, *Population Dilemma in Latin America*, New York 1966.

functions as among those who had withdrawn from active association with the Church.

The official stance of the Church no longer interfered seriously with upper- and middle-class women as they confronted the issue of family limitation. However, in many countries the Church's position continued to be a factor, though often not the principal one, in impeding the inauguration of programmes for the dissemination of birth-control information among the poor. Many critics charged that the Church's official policy was contributing to a situation in which, all other things being equal, the poor would probably become proportionately poorer, the rich richer.

By the mid-1970s the situation appeared to have altered slightly. Although Mexico's government under President Luis Echeverría has launched an extensive family planning programme, with at least the tacit support of most church officials, other Latin American governments, with Argentina in the forefront, were urging the need for larger national populations. In these latter countries the Church-State confrontation over the birth-control issue, once predicted by some observers, was no longer at hand. A part of the explanation for this development must be sought in the political ideology of the new corporativism.

Among proponents of newly-emergent corporativism there is an underlying faith in social engineering, based on the assumption that the masses can be diverted from rising material expectations through the non-material rewards ensuing from nationalism, from participation in local and functional associations, and also from religion. If the masses under the manipulation of social engineers can be counted upon to settle for a 'no-frills' type of subsistence as guaranteed them by paternalistic governments, perhaps allied with church officials, then it will be socially safe to expand the population. This, in turn, will make it possible to seek the fulfilment of old goals of national grandeur and to occupy underpopulated territory that otherwise might be usurped by aggressive neighbours. [110]

CONCLUSIONS

However grave the threats to its authority and influence faced in the 1970s, the Church in Latin America had in the period since 1848 survived other challenges that at the time had seemed equally menacing. In spite of its advocacy in the nineteenth century of many positions that proved ultimately to be untenable and in spite of its stubborn attempts to associate those positions with the dictates of the divine positive and natural laws, the

110. The arguments against birth control have assumed increasing sophistication in many Latin American countries during the 1970s. See M. E. Conroy, 'Recent Research in Economic Demography Related to Latin America: A Critical Survey and an Agenda', *Latin American Research Review*, IX (1974), 3-27.

Church came gradually to alter its stance and accommodate to new conditions. It withdrew its massive excommunications, re-interpreted some of its doctrines, and learned to live within liberally-controlled secular States. Even when greatly reduced in temporal power, and contrary to the dire prognostications of its spokesmen, the Church maintained a spiritual attraction for vast numbers of the populace. Although the great majority of Latin Americans, as many as 80 per cent in some countries, ceased to be practising Catholics and persisted in this position into the mid-twentieth century and beyond, they tended to maintain a predisposing tendency toward Catholicism. From time to time they performed actions, dictated to them by their individual consciences rather than by the clergy, that in their own minds at least re-linked them to the Church. In some ways the practice of Catholicism as it evolved in nineteenth-century Latin America anticipated the spirit of daring innovation displayed by some prelates at the Second Vatican Council.

The survival power of Latin American Catholicism did not rest exclusively on the ability of the Church to adjust to conditions that it had initially condemned unequivocally. As often as not, the caution of clergymen in confronting change and new ideas was vindicated, at least in part, by subsequent developments. Thus by the mid-twentieth century few Latin American intellectuals were unwilling to concede that liberalism and positivism had been largely unsuitable to the region's cultural and economic ambient. It was all too evident that these ideological and political movements had produced many of the abuses and excesses predicted by clerical opponents.

Perhaps in the 1970s it is as it should be if only a minority of church leaders have their minds in a revolutionary future, which cannot be as good as its prophets proclaim, while a majority have their hearts in the past, which cannot be so totally devoid of redeeming qualities as critics are wont to claim. Perhaps it is only from a cautious approach, one that aims at class solidarity rather than conflict, and elimination of privileged status, that there can come a resolution of the historical conflict between two Catholic traditions: one that stresses the duties and responsibilities of the upper classes and the rights of the masses, and another that emphasises the obligations of the lower classes and the prerequisites of the élite.

As it confronts the situation in the 1970s, the Catholic Church in most Latin American countries is no longer handicapped by the liberally-inspired restrictions of a generation or two ago. In many countries, the power and influence of the Church may have been permanently weakened by the long-term effects of those restrictions. But future difficulties which arise to deter the progress of Catholicism may well have to be blamed upon conditions inherent in the Church, rather than upon an unfriendly political climate.

In being deprived of its one-time ability to guide events of the temporal world while at the same time excluding all other religious influences, the Catholic Church in Latin America has acquired greater liberty to follow its own internal policies, free from outside intervention. And, although losing the capability of dominating individuals through an exercise of political power, it has gained expanded opportunities, dramatically enhanced by a communications revolution since the Second World War, to deal with individuals and to influence them through persuasion and example. The future will reveal whether an excessive concern with what has been lost will jeopardise the Church's ability to take advantage of what has been gained.

PART FOUR
FROM MISSIONS TO 'YOUNG CHURCHES'

FROM MISSIONS TO 'YOUNG CHURCHES'

IN THE history of Christian missions, the second half of the nineteenth century was characterised by an exceptional vigour. The late eighteenth century had been a time of stagnation, but the early nineteenth, thanks to the revival of the religious life, the birth of organisations in support of missions, and the influence of Gregory XVI, had helped to prepare the bases for a fresh advance, which was about to attain its full dimensions.

This advance was in part stimulated and undeniably encouraged by circumstances extraneous to the Church. Europe in fact was in the grip of an exploration fever which was gradually rekindling the interest of Europeans in distant lands and opening up to them the almost unknown interior of the African continent. In 1856 Semenov completed a ten-year-long exploration of Central Asia. In 1857 the Schlagintweit brothers returned from Turkestan and the Himalayas. Between 1866 and 1868 Doudart de Lagrée and Garnier explored Indo-China. The book *Souvenirs d'un voyage dans la Tartarie, le Thibet et la Chine,* published in 1851, combined the viewpoint of the explorer with that of the missionary, its author being Huc, a Lazarist Father. In Africa, Richardson, Overweg and Barth spent from 1850 to 1854 exploring the Sudan, penetrating as far as Chad. In 1858 Burton and Speke reached Lake Tanganyika. In 1860 Speke and Grant discovered the sources of the Nile, and Duveyrier traversed the Eastern Sahara. Rholfs conducted between 1862 and 1874 a series of explorations of the Sahara. Nachtigal explored between 1869 and 1871 the Eastern Sudan. In 1864 Baker discovered Lake Albert. In 1870 Schweinfurth explored the Uele. In 1875 Savorgnan de Brazza made his way into the interior of Gabon and the Lower Congo. Finally, the central region of the continent was traversed from end to end, by Cameron in 1874-5 and by Stanley in 1874-7. This list, which mentions only the major explorations of the half-century, is a sufficient indication of the vast scale of the phenomenon.

But what most typically appealed to the public of the period may be judged from the response to the journeys of the Scottish Protestant missionary-explorer David Livingstone (1813-73), whose book *Missionary Travels and Researches in South Africa* was hailed on its appearance in 1857 with wild enthusiasm. In 1856, on completing his first great expedition, he had written to a friend: 'I am not so elated in having performed what has not, to my knowledge, been done before in traversing the continent, because the end of the geographical feat is but the beginning of the missionary enterprise. May God grant me life to do some more good to this poor Africa.' [1] To the Royal Geographical Society, which financed his 1858 expedition, he did not hesitate to declare that his ultimate goal was 'to impart to the people of that country the knowledge and inestimable blessings of Christianity'. [2]

The explorations as a whole had of course no such missionary motive; their aims were originally scientific and soon became economic and political. But the interest in almost unknown regions and peoples which they awoke in Europeans, and the strong feelings that were aroused by the exposure from time to time of evils such as the slave trade or the prevalence of poverty among native populations, were translated in the contemporary Christian conscience into an urgent argument in favour of what were known at the time as 'foreign missions'.

It must also be said that foreign missions benefited from contemporary improvements in overseas transport and the multiplication of shipping lines: thus in England, the Cunard Line (1839), in Germany, the Hamburg-Amerikanische (1847), in France, the Compagnie générale transatlantique (1855). With the completion of the Suez Canal in 1869, the sea route to Asia was made appreciably shorter. So the transport of missionaries was a much easier matter than at previous periods. Under the regime of the Second Empire there was the additional bonus that French missionaries, who at that time made up a substantial proportion of Catholic missionary manpower, were granted free passage.

Furthermore, countries which had long resisted the entry of Christian missionaries, and still more any efforts at evangelisation, from now on opened their frontiers and authorised missionaries to settle and work: thus the kingdom of Siam in 1855-6, the empire of Annam in 1862, Cambodia in 1867. In Imperial China a trial period of religious toleration lasting from 1844 to 1846 was followed by the treaty of Tientsin of 1858, which granted religious freedom and accorded to Christian missions the right of settlement,

1. Letter to Arthur Tidman, 2 March 1856, in *Livingstone's Missionary Correspondence* (London 1961), 303.
2. *Proceedings of the Royal Geographical Society*, II (1858) 125.

extended in 1860 to the right to work. Korea followed suit in 1886. Japan authorised in 1858 the building and maintenance of places of worship for foreigners, but the Japanese were debarred from becoming Christians until 1872, when a decree granted them religious freedom and authorised missionaries to circulate freely in the country. These acts of toleration were not spontaneous. They were obtained, often indeed insisted upon, by the Western powers as part of their wider policy of opening up the countries in question to Western trade and influence. The missionaries of the day, happy to take advantage of the opportunity at last offered them, seem to have been content to turn this favourable situation to good account, without stopping to enquire too closely into the circumstances.

It was a similar story with Europe's strengthening colonial hold on Africa, Oceania, parts of Asia (India, Indo-China, Indonesia), inasmuch as the order and stability, the ease of action and communication which this brought in its train opened up for the missionary movement prospects of development on an unprecedented scale.

But however important, these external circumstances did no more than offer opportunity for a missionary advance whose drive was sustained by developments within the Church during the latter half of the nineteenth century.

Here the most decisive factor was the remarkable growth in the manpower available for missionary work. The revival of the religious life which had been a phenomenon of the early nineteenth century was now bearing fruit. Year by year the orders and congregations were able to assign more and more their members to missionary duties, bringing old fields back into cultivation and exploiting new ones. More significant still, the years following 1850 saw the foundation of a whole series of institutes expressly designated for missionary work. The Paris Foreign Missionary Society (MEP), founded in the seventeenth century, had been the only one of its kind until the formation of Libermann's Congregation of the Holy Ghost (CSSp) in 1841-8. From then on the formula became standard, and the scope of the movement can be indicated by merely listing the principal foundations: the Institute for Foreign Missions of Milan (1850); the Sacred Heart Missionaries (MSC: 1854); the Society of African Missions (SMA) founded at Lyons (1856); the Congregation of the Immaculate Heart of Mary (CICM), commonly known as the Scheut Missionaries (1862); St Joseph's Society for Foreign Missions of Mill Hill, commonly known as the Mill Hill Missionaries (1866); the African Missions of Verona (1867); the Society of Missionaries of Africa, commonly known as the White Fathers (WF: 1868); the Society of the Divine Word (SVD: 1875); the Benedictines of Sankt Ottilien (1884); the Pious Society of St Francis Xavier for Foreign Missions (SX), founded at Parma in 1895; the Society of St Joseph of Baltimore

(1892); the Swiss Foreign Mission Society of Bethlehem (SMB: 1896); the Consolata Missionary Fathers of Turin (1901); the Catholic Foreign Mission Society of America, popularly designated Maryknoll (1911). The movement was thus a general one, embracing the majority of Catholic countries. Its effect was not only to increase missionary manpower but to make it multinational. In the past, Catholic missions had been staffed almost exclusively by Frenchmen, and in 1900 they still accounted for two missionaries out of three; but in 1946 the contribution from other countries had risen to such an extent that French missionaries represented only thirty per cent.

A parallel movement, moreover, was taking place among the Protestant communions. In their case the growth may appear less spectacular, but only because Protestant missionary work had always been channelled through specialised societies, so that by 1850 there were already several in existence. Even so, new societies were being founded: in Scotland (1856), Sweden (1856), Finland (1858), Holland (1858), the United States (1894); in England, the Universities' Mission to Central Africa was set up in 1858, in response to appeals from Livingstone, and in 1865 James Hudson Taylor launched the China Inland Mission. Also to be noted is the foundation at St Petersburg in 1870 of the Orthodox missionary society.

Also being tapped, with very important consequences for the future, were sources of manpower which reinforced Catholic missions not only in quantity but also in quality. Missionary work in the past had been almost exclusively in the hands of priests. But missions were now being joined, in ever increasing numbers, by religious who were not priests, members of institutes of Teaching Brothers, Brothers Hospitallers and the like. More novel still, women religious were making their appearance, enlarging the trail so courageously blazed by the celebrated Mother Javouhey around 1824. Noting that by the end of the nineteenth century some 44,000 nuns of European origin had 'abandoned everything, sacrificed everything, to share in the labours of Christ's apostles, to run our schools, our hospitals, our orphanages, our shelters, our dispensaries. . . ', Fr Louvet heaped on their work praise whose extravagance reflected contemporary ideas about feminine frailty, and concluded: 'Such fine, such heroic work will surely be one of the glories of the nineteenth century and redound to the unique honour of Catholicism'.[3]

That last assertion is only fair if it is understood in a broader sense, for by now women were also playing an active role in Protestant missions. They had in fact long been on the scene but, as Stephen Neill points out, 'most of these women were missionaries' wives rather than missionary wives, a distinction of the greatest importance. It was only in the middle of the

---

3. *Les Missions catholiques au XIXe siècle* (Lille 1898), 412.

nineteenth century that all the missions, Protestant and Roman Catholic alike, began to send out single women ... by the end of our period, women in the missions greatly outnumbered men.' [4]

The missionary drive of the nineteenth century derived its strength from the fact that it involved the whole Christian people. Communities attuned to the challenge of a world awaiting evangelism were apt to produce vocations in plenty. Missionary foundations could multiply, secure in the knowledge that the dedication of the missionaries was supported, spiritually and materially, by the Christian people at large. Charities in aid of missions, the most important of which date back to the early years of the century, set up branches in one Christian country after another and were joined by new ones. B. Arens has counted 252 founded between 1850 and 1924 in European countries and in America.[5] Two deserve particular mention, the Society of St Peter the Apostle for Native Clergy founded in Paris by the Bigards, mother and daughter, in 1889, and the Missionary Union of the Clergy started at Milan by Father Paul Manna in 1916. Rome subsequently raised both to the rank of pontifical mission aid societies, placing them on the same footing as the Society for the Propagation of the Faith and the Association of the Holy Childhood.

The sums these charities collected and placed at the disposal of Catholic missions were considerable (between 1822 and 1929, the Society for the Propagation of the Faith alone raised 564,416,311 *francs-or*); but still more to be stressed is their influence in creating a genuine interest in missions among Christians at large. In this connection the countless magazines and journals put out by the charitable and missionary organisations played at the time an important role. They could be accused, it is true, of tingeing the interest in missions with too great a dash of exoticism and still more of helping to disseminate a pessimistic picture of native peoples and their non-Christian religious beliefs. Yet many of them were still the prime means of widening the horizons of Christian Europe. It was through their agency that adults and children, laymen and priests, the learned and the unlearned, were made aware of their missionary responsibility in respect of that other world with which the West was now making contact. The 'fever for geographical exploration' thus had its Christian counterpart.

A large staff of missionaries, support for missions from the mass of the faithful, an apostolate reaching out into nearly every region of the globe, all imply substantial organisation, a laying down of church structures. The pontificates of Pius IX (1846-78), Leo XIII (1878-1903) and Pius X (1903-14) saw a rapid increase in ecclesiastical territories, mostly vicariates and prefectures apostolic, in some cases dioceses. Over-all numerical com-

4. *A History of Christian Missions* (Harmondsworth 1965), 256.
5. *Manuel des missions catholiques* (Louvain 1925), 289 ff.

parisons are difficult to make, because of the changes over the years in the number of 'missionary countries': Great Britain, the Netherlands and North America ceased to figure on the list after 1908, the Near East after 1917, and so on. But even limiting ourselves to regions which remained dependent into our own day on the Congregation for the Propagation of the Faith, it is still possible to illustrate the way ecclesiastical territories were multiplying. For instance, in 1850 the whole of Africa south of the Sahara was covered by two vicariates apostolic (of 'The Two Guineas' and 'Central Africa'); fifty years later, in 1900, the number of territories was sixty one. In the same space of time, the territorial divisions in China rose from sixteen to thirty-- nine, in the Indian Sub-continent from four to twenty-seven, in Oceania from eleven to twenty-two. These figures are a sufficient sample to demonstrate the progress in the organisation of Catholic missions achieved over the half-century.

In many places the introduction of ecclesiastical structures was followed by noteworthy results, sometimes of a quite spectacular nature. Thus in Uganda the beginnings of the White Fathers' mission witnessed in 1886 the glorious epic of the first African martyrs, followed by a rapid increase in the Christian community. In India the social endeavours of Constantin Lievens, S.J. set up a great wave of conversions at Chota Nagpur around 1885. In Rwanda and Burundi during the early 1930s evangelisation was proceeding at such a pace that observers spoke confidently of the Holy Spirit blowing there 'like a tornado'.[6] Results elsewhere were perhaps less dramatic, but they often followed the same general pattern.

This worldwide expansion of Christianity was greeted in the literature of the day with exultation, as in these triumphal lines penned by the superior general of the Holy Ghost Fathers, Mgr Roy, in 1922:[7]

One hundred years ago the missions lay in ruins. Yet today we see them everywhere restored, everywhere prospering, with new Catholics ranged in their millions round the Vicar of Christ. Journey to the Orient, to the depths of China and Manchuria, to Korea and Tibet, through the Tartary deserts, to the great cities and humble villages of India and Ceylon, to Japan, even to Siberia; cross to America and travel its length from Alaska to the Tierra del Fuego; disembark on all the islands of Oceania; traverse the dark continent, cross it from east to west, from north to south: everywhere along the way, amid vast hordes that are still heathen — as we must never allow ourselves to forget — you will find some human

6. The title of the special number on Rwanda of the journal *Grands Lacs* issued 1 March 1935, in which it is mentioned that 'the two vicariates of Urundi and Rwanda are growing at the rate of one parish of a thousand souls per week'.
7. *Annales de la Propagation de la Foi*, XVI (May 1844), 178-9.

soul to join with you in making the sign of the Cross, to intone with you the immortal creed of our Christian faith.

Catholics were not alone in the conviction that they were witnessing the accomplishment of Christ's mandate to preach the Gospel 'to the ends of the earth'. One remembers the celebrated slogan coined by the American Methodist John Mott (1865-1955), 'Evangelisation of the World in this Generation', which at the end of the nineteenth century became the guiding theme of Protestant mission. Commenting on this key phrase and its implications, Stephen Neill remarks: 'It was not unreasonable to expect that the strength of the Western missionary force might be trebled in thirty years, that the Church in many parts of the world would at least double itself within that period, and that the number of national Christian workers might multiply itself fourfold.' [8]

The zeal brought to bear on the accomplishment of this task was directed at this period simultaneously through the missionary and the colonial channel. At its best, colonialism was a movement which aspired to transmit to all peoples the only civilisation deemed worthy of the name, the civilisation of the West. Now as K.S. Latourette has pointed out, 'these tremendous movements which were reshaping mankind had their rise and most extensive development in Christendom, a region in which Christianity had long been potent, and among peoples and nations which were usually called Christian. In that hopeful age there were Christians who pointed to them as evidence of the beneficent effect of the Gospel.'[9]

This is illustrated in especially striking fashion by the anti-slavery crusade preached by Cardinal Lavigerie, with backing from Leo XIII, in 1888. To put an end to a scourge ravaging black Africa, the Church made appeal to the nations of Europe and their governments. The latter signed an anti-slavery convention at Brussels in 1890 which incorporated Lavigerie's proposals and also recommended the 'gradual introduction of the religious institutions of the civilised nations'. Mission and colonisation buttressed one another: the missionary gave the coloniser a clear conscience and in return received support and protection. Christian missions 'supplied Europe's ambitions as a civiliser with the spiritual component they had hitherto fundamentally lacked'.[10]

For themselves, the states of Europe had rejected the Church's influence. Leo XIII strove to make people recognise that if Church and State were distinct powers, building a harmonious society nevertheless required the

8. *A History...*, 395.
9. *The Christian World Mission in Our Day* (New York 1954), 19-20.
10. A. Rétif, 'La grande expansion des missions', *Histoire Universelles des Missions catholiques*, III (Paris 1958), 91.

co-operation of the Church, as custodian of the Gospel. The colonies providentially offered a kind of testing ground. In the colonies it was easier to make people recognise that without the Church no authentic civilisation was likely to take root. No longer accepted without question in Europe, in the colonies the desired collaboration between Church and State was again taking shape and the results would demonstrate, even to the nations of Europe, the benefits for every human society of the political ideal upheld by Leo XIII in *Inscrutabili* (1878), *Immortale Dei* (1885) and a host of other documents. The initiative of the anti-slavery campaign was there to prove it. Similar examples of understanding between mission and colonialism all had to be seen in the same light.

The second half of the nineteenth century thus presents us with the picture of a missionary movement of unprecedented scope and drive. It can nevertheless be seen as a movement advancing under the sign of a fundamental ambiguity, since it operated within the general context of a global expansion by the Western powers and accepted the links which those circumstances almost inevitably forged between colonialism and mission. It was even a willing acceptance, for reasons connected with the Church's recent history in the West. The missionaries were men of their times and the ambiguity of their situation for the most part escaped them.

By slow degrees, however, the objective fact of mission was to become the subject of deeper reflection, which in turn was to help in correcting the perspective. The probing started with the Protestants, who were obliged by the 'private' character of their missionary enterprises to work out a theological justification for them. Scientific study of mission was already being undertaken in some Protestant universities during the second half of the nineteenth century: in Germany, at Erlangen from 1864 by Karl Graul, at Berlin from 1867 by Karl Plath, above all at Halle from 1897 by Gustav Warneck (1834-1910). In Great Britain, Duff started to lecture at Edinburgh in 1867, and it was this same city which became in 1910 the meeting place for a historic gathering, the first Protestant World Missionary Conference. From this meeting sprang in effect the Ecumenical Movement, the International Missionary Council[11] and the *International Review of Missions*. It was to be followed by a series of similar world congresses which would profoundly influence the future course of Protestant mission.

It was the example of the German Protestants, of Warneck in particular, that stimulated the rise of modern Catholic missiology, with Robert Streit, O.M.I. (1875-1930) and Joseph Schmidlin (1876-1944) as its founding fathers. Thanks to their efforts, the Catholic Congress meeting at Breslau in

11. The establishment of I.M.C. was agreed to at the Edinburgh conference, but it started, properly speaking, only in 1921; in 1961 it was integrated into the World Council of Churches, becoming its Missionary and Evangelisation Division.

1911 resolved on the establishment at Münster university of an International Institut für missionswissenschaftliche Forschungen, whose journal, the *Zeitschrift für Missionswissenschaft,* became the first periodical devoted to Catholic missiology; [12] Streit meanwhile embarked on the monumental task of compiling the *Bibliotheca Missionum.* From Germany the movement spread slowly to other countries, in a variety of forms and with a variety of accents. In Belgium Fr Lallemand, S.J. initiated (1923) the Semaines de Missiologie de Louvain, of which the moving spirit between 1925 and 1953 was Fr Pierre Charles, S.J. (1883-1954). Between the two world wars, Schmidlin at Münster and Charles at Louvain were the two leading, and often opposing, exponents of Catholic missiology. [13]

Under the influence of these schools of missiology and of one or two clearsighted individuals, and, so far as Catholics were concerned, thanks to the activity of a series of great popes, mission was about to define its original contribution and assert its independence.

2. FROM FOREIGN MISSIONS TO LOCAL CHURCHES

The first issue on which there was to be reorientation of mission, beginning in earnest during the pontificate of Benedict XV, was the formation and role of a clergy recruited from the ranks of the people being evangelised. Today we take it for granted that foreign missions should transform themselves as rapidly as possible into local Churches, energised by native priests and governed by bishops drawn from their ranks. This was not at all so obvious to missionaries of the nineteenth and early twentieth century, for reasons easy to understand.

These missionaries came from a Europe whose prevailing mentality, in that era of colonial expansion, encouraged them more often than not to make themselves responsible, no doubt with great self-sacrifice but also from a sense of unquestioning superiority, for the spiritual destiny of non-Christian peoples. They were no doubt tempted given the chronic shortage of manpower, to train local priests, but it seemed to them dangerous to entrust the responsibility of the sacerdotal ministry to men sprung from communities only recently evangelised.

In a memorandum on the China missions, submitted to Rome in 1847, Fr Gabet [14] remarked:

12. Replaced 1938-1941 by *Missionswissenschaft und Religionswissenschaft,* and thereafter in abeyance until 1947; resumed publication in 1948 and since 1950 published under the title *Zeitschrift für Missionswissenschaft und Religionswissenschaft.*
13. The names of many other individuals and centres could be cited: for fuller information, see A. V. Seumois, *Introduction à la missiologie,* or Alphonse Mulders, *Missiologisch Bestek.* Also useful is A. V. Seumois, 'Vers une définition de l'activité missionnaire', *Nouvelle Revue de Science Missionnaire* (1947), 161-78, 254-61, (1948), 1-16.
14. Gabet's memorandum has been studied by G. B. Tragella: see his paper 'Le vicende d'un

On the necessity in the abstract for an indigenous clergy there is fairly general agreement; but when it comes to the point, no one is willing to put the policy into practice, and the reason nearly always given is that the people of this country are so devoid of intelligence and so weak in character that they are incapable of conceiving the grandeur and dignity of the priesthood and of fulfilling its demands.[15]

Fr Gabet spoke with experience of China. Mgr Zaleski, apostolic delegate in the East Indies, wrote in 1899 to the Provincial of the Belgian Jesuits: 'Your reverence has undoubtedly heard mention of the prejudices which, unhappily, still exist in certain parts of India against the native clergy...' [16]The situation was clearly little different in Africa. When Mgr Vogt resolved in 1923 to open a seminary in the Cameroons, 'he encountered serious obstacles: in the first place, the speed at which Cameroon society had developed made it impossible to assess how deeply the Christian religion had taken root in the individual; next and more important, the opposition of his diocesan clergy.' [17]Protestant missions were in the same case: 'for half a century and more, Africans were considered to be insufficiently "mature" for leadership in the Church.' [18]

Another reason, of a very different nature, accounts for the relative short-sightedness of many missionaries at the beginning of the twentieth century over the need to develop a local clergy. The reason is to be found in the theological and spiritual tradition in which the missionaries, like the rest of their generation in the Church, had been reared. With their excessively individualist conception of salvation, with their ideal of spirituality revolving round private devotions, with their neglect of community as a necessary dimension of the Christian life, the missionaries were prevented from seeing the need to build their converts into the fabric of an ecclesial community. They thought the last word had been said as soon as grace was available for everyone through the sacraments, in other words when there were enough priests. In the perspectives they had in common with their age, the 'presence' of the Church among a people was hardly going to go further in its demands. It was therefore natural to look on a local clergy as nothing more than a reinforcement, extremely useful no doubt but not indispensable, not something required by the Church's very nature.

---

opusculo sul clero indigena e del suo autore', in the collection *Der einheimische Klerus in Geschichte und Gegenwart* (Schoneck-Beckenried 1950), 189-202.

15. *op. cit.,* 198.
16. *Missions Belges de la Compagnie de Jésus* (1899), 373.
17. M. Chauleur, quoted in R. Dussercle, *Du Kilima-Ndjaro au Cameroun* (Paris 1954), 141.
18. B. Sundkler, *The Christian Ministry in Africa* (London 1960), 44.

Lastly, the actual organisation of Catholic missions helped in some degree to distort their perspectives. By the end of the nineteenth century it had become customary to carve up missionary countries into well-defined ecclesiastical territories confided in each case to one religious congregation or missionary institute. Authorisation to minister within the territory was restricted to members of that institute, and the vicar or prefect apostolic was necessarily chosen from among its members. This 'commission' system, a juridical arrangement, was inaugurated only as recently as 1827-36. The aim was to secure unity and continuity, and there can be no doubt that the system produced some excellent results. Experience showed, however, that it had one serious disadvantage; all too easily, the mission was felt psychologically to be a permanent responsibility and pride of the missionary institute concerned. As Mgr Costantini, apostolic delegate to China, observed in 1925: 'The missions, because they are conceived as religious colonies belonging to this or that institute, have created in the missionaries a special mentality, let us call it territorial feudalism. The archives of the Congregation of Propaganda are stuffed with documents on the subject.' [19] This mistaken viewpoint was not calculated to encourage the development of a national secular clergy, whose appearance signified the reintroduction of a dualistic regime of workers in the mission field. It would perhaps be unjust to imagine that this situation may have militated against the formation of national clergy, but it certainly contributed to the view that they were a makeweight, second-class clergy, called to no higher role than that of auxiliary to the 'apostolic missionary' sent out from a Christian country. [20] Speaking at the third Semaine de missiologie de Louvain in 1925, the Abbé Corman observed: [21]

Until not so long ago, European primacy over all other peoples, even the civilised peoples of Asia, was one of those axioms which everyone or nearly everyone took for granted, and it was a primacy that was to be translated into fact as the European became everywhere master of the world. In the sanctuary the mastery of the European, which most missionaries as men of their times accepted as beyond dispute, was bound to manifest itself through the maintenance of the indigenous element in permanent tutelage: the indigenous clergy, the necessity for which no one doubted, could be no more than an auxiliary clergy, always ready to efface itself in the presence of the missionary.

---

19. Con I Missionari in Cina, I, 273.
20. For the meaning of the term 'apostolic missionary' see below, 401-2.
21. Les aspirations indigènes et les missions. Report of the third Semaine de Missiologie de Louvain (1925), 171.

Such a conception manifestly ran counter to the very clear directives formulated centuries before by Roman authority and frequently reiterated. Created in 1622, the Congregation de Propaganda Fide had expressed itself plainly on the point in a document dated 28 November 1630. [22] In 1659 it had issued its celebrated 'Instruction for the use of Vicars Apostolic setting out for the Chinese kingdoms of Tonkin and Cochin China'. [23] In Pope Innocent XI's brief *Onerosa Pastoralis* of 1680, as in a letter from Propaganda in 1687 to the vicars apostolic in Tonkin, it had been stressed that missionaries were obliged to proceed rapidly to the formation of a local clergy. Many documents of the eighteenth and nineteenth centuries, the most important being Propaganda's instruction *De clero indigena* of 23 November 1845, [24] had repeated these directives. 'But these instructions encountered obstacles of various kinds and until the middle of the nineteenth century they produced only rather meagre results.' [25]

It is obviously difficult, as far as the mid-nineteenth century is concerned, to quantify those 'rather meagre results'; at that period, moreover, the estimate would have to be confined to the Philippines, China, Annam and India. For the end of the century (1896) we have fairly reliable figures: India and Ceylon head the list with 1600 native priests, followed by South-East Asia with 426, China with 373 and Japan, whose first three priests had been ordained only in 1882, with 26 – in all some 2425 priests of Asian origin. [26]It is interesting to note that at this date local clergy outnumbered foreign clergy both in India plus Ceylon (796 foreigners) and in South-East Asia (408 foreigners). In the latter region the empire of Annam counted 336 native priests in 1898, despite the savage persecution of 1857-62 in which 115 priests, that is one-third of the Annamite clergy, and paid for their loyalty to the Church with their lives. [27]As for black Africa, the missions were too recently established for us to expect more than the first-fruits: two Senegalese had received ordination as priests in France in 1840 and a third in Senegal itself in 1852, the Portugese colony of Angola had five African priests by 1853, and the first priestly ordinations in the French Congo and the Gabon dated from 1895 and 1899.

Thus during the last quarter of the nineteenth century there was a serious effort to recruit and educate priests of native origin. Missionary opinion on

22. *Collectenea S. C. de Propaganda Fide*, I, no. 62, Rome 1907.
23. See the text established from several manuscripts by H. Chappoulie, *Rome et les Missions d'Indochine au XVIIe siècle*, I, (Paris 1943), 392-402.
24. For this see C. Costantini, 'Ricerche d'archivio sull' Istruzione "De clero indigena"', *Miscellanea Pietro Fumasoni-Biondi*, I (Rome 1947), 1-78. On these old texts in general, N. Wenders, 'Innovation ou tradition?', *Église Vivante*, VIII (1956), 353-74.
25. C. Costantini, 'Ricerche...', 3.
26. Louvet, *Les Missions catholiques au XIXe siècle*, passim.
27. Cf. J. B. Piolet, *Les Missions catholiques françaises au XIXe siècle*, II (Paris 1902), 485, 446.

the subject was divided, between those who were hesitant, as shown by some of the evidence quoted earlier, and a bolder element, represented by names such as Javouhey, Libermann, Luquet, Marion-Bresillac, Gabet, Comboni, Lavigerie and others. It was to the latter wing that Rome now gave its renewed and determined support, as Leo XIII and, more particularly, Benedict XV revived the old directives and underlined the importance and urgency of recruiting an indigenous clergy.

In 1893 Leo XIII devoted his apostolic letter *Ad extremas* to the founding of seminaries in India; in it he declared: [28]

> The Catholic faith will have no assured future among the Indians and its progress will remain faltering so long as there is no indigenous clergy properly educated in the sacerdotal functions, clergy capable not merely of assisting the missionaries but of promoting by themselves in fitting manner the interests of the religion in their own communities.

It should be remembered that at the date Leo XIII was writing, the Indian clergy in India outnumbered the foreigners; so it was not quantity that was aimed at in the papal text but the formation of a clergy of quality, called on no longer to act as auxiliaries to the missionaries but 'to promote by themselves in fitting manner the interests of the religion in their own communities'. This was the real stumbling-block; it was precisely over this issue that the two schools of thought already mentioned were to come into at times dramatic conflict during the next quarter of a century.

In a work which attracted considerable attention because of the controversies to which it gave rise, a French writer, Canon Léon Joly, observed in 1907 that missionaries had in modern times 'timidly and not without misgivings opened the ranks of the priesthood to the indigenous element, but the Hindu, Annamite, Chinese or Japanese priest has still remained in total dependence on the priest from Europe'. [29] Although it is possible to challenge Joly's contentions on more than one point, his conclusion can be accepted as an accurate summing up of the state of affairs at the beginning of the twentieth century: 'Nowhere have our modern missionaries established completely indigenous Churches'.

Joly was writing in Paris. At almost the same moment a young Lazarist in Peking was setting down in a letter to a friend his 'personal vision of breaking with the past as quickly as possible and turning our Christians into Chinese Christians, with a *totally* indigenous priesthood.' [30] The writer was Father Vincent Lebbe, who was about to become through his words, deeds,

28. *A.A.S.*, XXV (1892-1893), 719.
29. *Le Christianisme et l'Extrême-Orient*, I (Paris 1907), 289.
30. Letter to Dom Bede, 26 May 1908, printed *Lettres du Père Lebbe* (Tournai 1960), 85.

and sufferings the great advocate of the creation of an autochthonous episcopate in China and in missionary countries in general. His thoughts are most clearly expressed in a remarkable letter written in 1917 to his bishop, Mgr Reynaud, a copy of which was forwarded by a friend, Father Cotta, to the Congregation of Propaganda. Having examined in detail the current arguments for and against the 'establishment of a totally indigenous clergy', he concludes:[31]

> The time has come to found a living, fertile, national Church, to be the leaven in the lump, flesh of the people's flesh, blood of the people's blood sanctified in Christo,the only Church with a hope of survival, the only Church to contain in embryo the promise of the future. Preparations for this Church belong no more to the distant view, they have become immediate, crucial and concrete. If we have the will to found this Church, the means are at hand to do it, discreetly, smoothly, by degrees: all that is needed is to will it.

That Rome willed it there could be no doubt. On 30 November 1919 Benedict XV signed the encyclical *Maximum illud,* the most eloquent and authoritative plea imaginable in favour of creating a fully indigenous clergy, indigenous bishops included. L. Levaux, who has compared Benedict's encyclical with Lebbe's writings, feels justified in concluding that 'the comparison leaves little doubt that a file on Lebbe existed at Rome and that Benedict XV must have had it before him when he composed his encyclical'.[32] However that may be, the identity of aim is unmistakable and Fr Lebbe was right, in his letter to Mgr Reynaud, to denounce the position of 'our missions' as 'anti-Roman'.

But it was dangerous to have been so obviously in the right and to have run counter, even with the backing of Roman directives, to the opinion most commonly prevailing among his colleagues. Fr Lebbe became the subject of controversy, a sign that the missionaries in China were in disagreement.[33] In 1920 he was posted away from China, and he was to return only under the authority of a Chinese bishop in 1926. It was precisely during that intervening period that an important turning-point in the modern history of missions was rounded.

The first step needing to be taken was the provision at long last of a training that would really fit African and Asian clergy to be the equals and not the auxiliaries of the foreign clergy. Benedict XV noted that despite a long period of evangelisation there were peoples, some of them highly civilised,

31. *Lettres.* . . 137-58.
32. L. Levaux, *Le Père Lebbe* (Brussels 1948), 215-22.
33. Also partly on account of his attitude over other matters; see below, 418-19.

who had 'failed, after several centuries of exposure to the beneficent action of the Gospel and the Church, to produce bishops to govern themselves or priests whose learning commanded the respect of their compatriots'. He concluded: 'It has therefore to be acknowledged that in certain areas the methods used up till now in the education of mission clergy have been inadequate and defective'.[34]

To remedy this state of affairs, Benedict XV instructed Propaganda to supervise the setting up and proper conduct of regional seminaries. A full-scale seminary for each diocese or vicariate apostolic would in fact have been a utopian luxury; but by acting in concert the territories concerned could assemble a teaching staff of high quality and guarantee a reasonable number of students. The pope's voice was heeded but the resulting activity still fell so far short of what was needed that in 1926, in his encyclical *Rerum Ecclesiae*, Pius XI repeated his predecessor's injunction and added: 'That which a few have begun, we not merely desire but will and ordain should be done in like manner by all who are placed at the head of missions'. Pius XI was about to bring to bear on the realisation of this idea his own firmness and tenacity of purpose. In addition, to ensure the smooth running of the regional seminaries, the Sacred Congregation de Propaganda Fide retained for itself direct control over their conduct, clearly defined in a set of instructions dated 27 April 1934:[35]

1. The regional seminary pertains to the Holy See, which confides direction of the seminary to a religious order or missionary institute, subject to over-all control by the Congregation de Propaganda Fide. Questions of day-to-day administration and discipline are left in the hands of the institute.
   . . .
3. The institute made responsible for the direction of a regional seminary shall submit to Propaganda for its approval:
   (a) the disciplinary code for the seminary;
   (b) the curriculum, syllabuses, timetable and list of textbooks.
4. (a) Appointment of the rector is reserved to Propaganda, after presentation of the candidate by the superior general of the institute.
   (b) Appointment of other teachers and professors is left to the superior general of the institute, who shall submit the names of the persons appointed to Propaganda.
   (c) The rector of a seminary may not be relieved of his duties or transferred elsewhere without the prior consent of Propaganda; transfer

34. *Maximum illud.*
35. *Sylloge praecipuorum documentorum recentium Summorum Pontificum et S.C. de Propaganda Fide* (Rome 1939), 456-7.

of other teachers and professors shall be notified to Propaganda.
5. In the normal way, all philosophy and theology students from the region will attend the regional seminary. Ordinaries will not be permitted to withdraw their seminarists from the regional seminary to send them elsewhere to study without the express consent of Propaganda.

There can be no denying that these measures were part of a thorough-going effort at centralisation, and one might ask with some dismay what authority a bishop still possessed over his future diocesan priests, especially at a time when episcopal collegiality had virtually ceased to exist. On the other hand, the missionary institutes saw themselves assigned an important role, which fitted neatly into the 'commission' system. At the time it was the best, indeed the only possible, way to proceed. Although the regime of regional seminaries later attracted criticism, it remains true that the measures taken by Rome contributed in large measure to the raising of priestly education in missionary territories to a level which, while it ad-mittedly still fell short of perfection, was at least on a par with that offered in many parts of Europe and America.

Among the establishments responsible for training the clergy of mis-sionary countries Rome accords a place entirely on its own to the Collegium Urbanum of the Congregation de Propaganda Fide. To it come students from all the regions dependent on the Congregation, and while they prepare for the priesthood they spend several years absorbing the Roman at-mosphere. With the growth in numbers of missionary clergy this three-centuries-old institution assumed a new importance. Having outgrown the quarters it shared with the Congregation in the old palace on the Piazza di Spagna, the college was transferred to new buildings on the Janiculum. They were opened officially on 13 April 1931 and only a few days later, on 24 April, received a visit from Pius XI, making his first exit from the Vatican after the conclusion of the Lateran agreements with the Italian government. Opportunities for more specialised study were opened up, not only for Propaganda students but for intending missionaries, with the creation in 1933 of a Scientific Missionary Institute. It is divided into two sections, mis-siology and canon law, and confers degrees up to and including the doc-torate. Lastly, on 29 June 1948, Pius XII inaugurated a new foundation, the College of St Peter, intended for priests of missionary origin coming to pur-sue advanced studies in Rome. So through these actions, as well as through the issue of its clearly formulated directives, the Holy See has ensured to the national clergy of missionary countries the education that enables it 'to shine throughout the world as the manifestation of the one and universal Church'.[36]

36. Pius XII, autograph letter of 28 June 1948 marking the inauguration of St Peter's College, Rome: A.A.S., XL (1948), 374-6.

Although indispensable as the first step, improvement to clerical education was not enough without a change of outlook on the part of certain European missionaries who, for reasons that we have seen, were psychologically incapable of imagining an indigenous clergy as anything but subaltern and auxiliary. Today it strikes us as odd that racial or national origin could be regarded as justification for precedences and privileges as between members of a single priesthood. Canon law, moreover, has never made provision for precedence among clerics other than that conferred by function or seniority. Yet there was legal foundation of a kind for the precedence of foreign missionaries over indigenous priests. Rome had granted to missionaries sent out by Rome a certain number of privileges and the title 'apostolic missionary'. In 1908 the Consistorial Congregation submitted the following question, along with other questions of competence raised by the application of the constitution *Sapienti consilio*, to the judgment of the Holy Father: 'Utrum eadem Congregatio (de Propaganda Fide) adhuc tribuere valeat titulum Missionarii Apostolici ad honorem, addita solita facultatum formula', and received the answer: 'Affirmative quoad sibi subditos'.[37] So in virtue of the title 'apostolic missionaries', conferred as a mark of distinction on priests sent out by Rome, the latter had come to regard themselves as in a category superior to that of the ordinary priest ministering in the country of his birth. Mission was the business of the Holy See and its apostolic missionaries, *assisted* if need be by local auxiliaries, called to a priesthood of purely routine duties. With *Maximum illud* (1919) Benedict XV had already come out against the idea of the permanently subordinate indigenous priest, but it was only in 1924 that a decree from Propaganda put an end to the privilege 'quod respicit praecedentiam eorundem Missionariorum Apostolicorum relate ad eos qui hoc titulo non sunt insigniti'.[38]

Privileges and prejudices die hard. In 1926 Pius XI was still to judge it necessary, in a document as general and public as an encyclical addressed to all missionary bishops, to issue the following reminder of truths which today everyone would find self-evident:[39]

There is another reason why you cannot allow indigenous priests to remain relegated as it were to an inferior rank, and dedicated solely to the humblest forms of ministry. Are they not invested with the same priesthood as yourselves and partakers in the selfsame apostolate? And is it not your duty to look on them as on those who must one day govern the communities and Churches you yourselves have founded in toil and

37. *Sylloge. . .* 22.
38. *A.A.S.*, XVI (1924), 243.
39. *Rerum Ecclesiae*, no. 24.

sweat? Let there be no distinction, therefore, between European and indigenous missionaries, and let no gulf separate them; rather, let them be united by the bonds of mutual respect and mutual charity.

The missionaries of the day were undoubtedly no less zealous than missionaries of today. They sought above all the good of the Church. But there were some who could not suppress the feeling that the pope's insistence was inopportune or premature. An echo of this is to be found in a document addressed to superiors of missionary institutes in China sent out from Propaganda on 23 May 1927 under the signature of Cardinal van Rossum: [40]

This Sacred Congregation is aware that in many Chinese vicariates the apostolic injunctions to promote indigenous clergy to higher responsibilities are being carefully heeded; it is also aware that several Chinese priests have already been entrusted with important ministerial duties and have carried them out in satisfactory and fruitful fashion. All this I report to the Sovereign Pontiff and it always fills him with joy.

But the Holy Father's joy was in large measure turned to sorrow when he was told that some of the foreign missionaries, steeped in the old prejudices, are not wholehearted in their obedience to these dispositions of the Holy See and do not co-operate with all their soul to put them into practice; furthermore, some of these foreign missionaries are not afraid to declare that the apostolic texts dealing with the elevation of indigenous clergy to higher positions applied only to special cases and made very little difference to the reality and truth.

From now on, Rome was resolved to press ahead with energy and perseverance. Whatever the local objections, whatever the forces of inertia so often placed in the way, the very plain directives of the missionary encyclicals were no longer to remain a dead letter. The decisive step was about to be taken with the creation and multiplication of ecclesiastical territories handed over with full responsibility to the national clergy of mission countries.

The main turning-point on the road towards the establishment of a national hierarchy was the consecration of the first six Chinese bishops by Pius XI, on 28 October 1926. Invested with great solemnity, this historic event directed the attention of the Christian world to a new era whose beginnings, however, had already declared themselves a few years earlier.

China had given the missionary Church its first bishop as early as the seventeenth century, in the person of Mgr Gregory Lo Wân-tsao, appointed

40. *Sylloge.* . . 278.

vicar apostolic of Nanking in 1674 and consecrated at Canton on 8 April 1685. This tentative beginning unfortunately had no sequel.

In the twentieth century India was the first to have the honour of seeing one of her sons receiving episcopal office in the Latin Church. This was an Indian Jesuit, Francis T. Roche, who was appointed bishop of Tuticorin when it was erected into a diocese and handed over to the Indian secular clergy on 12 June 1923. The Eastern rite, however, could already boast of several Indian vicars apostolic. That same year, 1923, saw the creation of a regular ecclesiastical province of the Syro-Malabar rite, with Ernakulam as its metropolitan see and three suffragan dioceses.

In China the movement got under way thanks to the vigorous impetus given by the apostolic delegation Rome established in the country on 9 August 1922.[41] The first titular, Mgr Celso Costantini, was a providential choice: he worked hard to make some of the directives of Pius XI a reality in China and gave substance to the aspirations of the Chinese clergy and of the better missionaries. 'The question of the indigenous episcopate', writes Fr D'Elia, 'came to the fore as soon as an apostolic delegate appeared on the scene in 1922. One of the first acts of H.E. Mgr Costantini was to secure the appointment of two Chinese priests as prefects apostolic, 12 December 1923 and 15 April 1924.' [42] Thanks to these appointments, two Chinese figured among the heads of China's ecclesiastical territories when they were summoned by the apostolic delegate to meet in national council at Shanghai in 1924 (15 May – 12 June). Many important questions were discussed at this council, but overriding all others was the impression that 'the day of the Catholic Native Episcopacy in China had dawned'. [43]

Down to the end of 1925 the situation in fact remained unaltered, but in 1926 the pace quickened. On 28 February appeared the encyclical *Rerum Ecclesiae* in which Pius XI reiterated the promise that if the Church's directions regarding the training of the clergy were faithfully observed, 'there will be nothing to prevent priests so educated from taking charge of parishes and

41. The political circumstances which led to the setting up of the Apostolic Delegation are described below, 421-2.
42. Pascal M. D'Elia, S.J., *Les Missions catholiques en Chine* (Shanghai 1934), 61.
43. Pascal M. D'Elia, *Catholic Native Episcopacy in China* (Shanghai 1927), 74. See also N. Wenders, 'Le premier concile chinois', *Bulletin des Missions*, Saint-André-Bruges, X, no. 1, 36-42, from which the following passage is worth quoting: 'In 1880 the first synod of Hongkong categorically laid down that European priests should have precedence over Chinese priests. This synod, like the second synod of Peiping, made reservations which were humiliating and discouraging to the Chinese clergy, all the more so in view of the claims the Sacred Congregation of Propaganda was continually pressing on their behalf. When we come to the plenary council of 1924, we find it makes no distinction between Chinese and missionary clergy and ordains that precedence is governed by the general rules of canon law. The abolition of the right of precedence formerly accorded to 'apostolic missionaries' had already administered the *coup de grâce* to a custom which gave the native clergy an inferior status' (p. 40).

dioceses, when in God's good time they are created'. In the following months Rome promoted six Chinese priests to the headship of vicariates apostolic and Pius XI invited them to come to Rome to receive episcopal consecration at his own hands. The ceremony took place in the basilica of St Peter's on 28 October 1926, feast of the Apostles Simon and Jude. The stir this event created was considerable. The new bishops made a tour of several countries of Europe, which prolonged the echo of the Roman ceremony and impressed on many minds sensitive to the historical dimension an awareness that a new age was indeed dawning.

That this gesture on the part of Pius XI was not intended to be left in isolation was plain. A cape had been rounded and the Church's future course outside the Western world was now finally set: the Church was embarked on the transition from the era of 'foreign missions' to that of 'Young Churches'.

But a considerable maturing had to take place before the transition was fully effected. At the time, in the excitement of seeing the first stages accomplished, it could be imagined in some quarters that the appointment of an indigenous bishop and the transfer of responsibility to the local clergy marked in definitive fashion what the missiologists called the 'implantation' of the Church. In retrospect, we today can see more clearly that although fundamental, this transfer was no more than a precondition of the Church's taking proper root among a people being evangelised. Still, it was important that this indispensable condition was met. If during the first half of the twentieth century missiology tended to define mission in terms of the implantation of the Church, this tendency represented initially a very wholesome and necessary reaction to the individualist conception of salvation and the Christian life we noted earlier. The importance attached to the development of the indigenous episcopate did not imply a confusion between mission and the setting up of ecclesiastical structures, although the aberration could admittedly be found in certain missiologists more expert in law than in theology. But the great missionaries of the period knew intuitively that it was a question of entrusting the Gospel to its most valuable witnesses among a given people, namely Christian evangelists sprung from their own midst; that it was a question, in fact, of returning to the missionary style of earlier centuries. The really radical reform of missions, however, was only to come later. For the present, with the creation of native episcopates in Asia and Africa, we are still only at the beginning.

In 1926, as we have seen, not everyone was happy with the declared intention of Rome, which some people judged ill-founded. Before going further, would it not be prudent, it was asked, to await the outcome of the first experiments with non-Western bishops? Efforts to 'prove' the pope's error resulted in quite a spate of polemical literature of whose existence the historian can hardly fail to be aware but which is better left in the oblivion to which later events rapidly consigned it. For the forward march was not halted by the carping and faint-heartedness of critics.

So in 1926 we find China with six native bishops, India with five. In 1927 Pius XI consecrated the first Japanese bishop, and thereafter each succeeding year saw fresh territories in Asia passing into the hands of native bishops. In 1928 two Indians, in 1929 six Chinese, another Indian in 1930, in 1931 three Chinese, followed by another four in 1932 and yet another in 1933, the year which also saw the consecration of the first Vietnamese bishop.

The year 1930 was also memorable for two events of great importance in the Eastern Church: the appointment of an Ethiopian bishop, the first Catholic bishop of African descent; and in India the accession to the Catholic Church of a Jacobite bishop with a substantial portion of his clergy and faithful, which made possible the creation of an ecclesiastical province of the Syro-Malankar rite.

The pace of advance was slow and cautious, but also confident. In Asian countries the appointment of native bishops was no longer an isolated occurrence but a movement gathering strength. Whereas to begin with, native prelates had been placed in relatively obscure territories, they now found themselves occupying key positions: Nanking in 1936, Tokyo in 1937.

When Pius XI died in February 1939, forty-eight mission territories (including seven of an Eastern rite) were in the charge of native bishops: twenty-six in China, thirteen in India (six of them Eastern), three in Japan, three in Vietnam, one in Ceylon, one in Korea, one in Ethiopia (Eastern). It might be thought that with the death of the pope responsible for *Rerum Ecclesiae* the pace would slacken; on the contrary it quickened, and the movement extended its range.

Pius XII gave immediate notice of his missionary intentions in his encyclical *Summi Pontificatus* (20 October 1939). It contained the following notable declaration: [44]

All who enter the Church, whatever their birth or native tongue, are to know they have an equal right of sonship in the Lord's household, where the law and peace of Christ prevail. In obedience to this law of equality, the Church makes it her constant concern to educate native clergy in a manner commensurate with their task, and to augment by degrees the ranks of the native episcopate. To give outward expression to our intentions, we have appointed the forthcoming feast of Christ the King as the day for raising to the episcopal dignity, over the tomb of the Prince of

44. *A.A.S.*, XXXI (1939), 453.

Apostles, twelve representatives from peoples or groups of peoples of the greatest possible diversity.

The consecration of 1939 outdid even the consecration of 1926 in stressing the catholicity of the Church and the absolute equality of all its members. The movement for a native episcopacy was beginning to reach out beyond countries of ancient Asian civilisation to embrace black Africa, represented by the first bishop of Ugandan origin and the first bishop from Madagascar. But another facet was of even deeper significance: grouped side by side around the Holy Father, nationals of missionary countries and western missionaries were receiving in the selfsame ceremony, the same dignity, the same charge, the same counsels. The appointment of a local priest to an Asian or African see was ceasing to be a nine days' wonder and coming to be accepted quite naturally as a normal event in the life of the universal Church.

In this field, as in many others, the Second World War naturally caused a slowing down, but if the pause was perceptible it was only momentary, and the postwar political development of Africa and Asia was to give the movement added momentum.

The rate of progress may be judged from a few figures. As we have said, at the death of Pius XI in 1939, sixteen years after the first Asian episcopal appointment, forty-eight ecclesiastical territories were in the care of bishops of Asian or African origin. Just after the war, at the end of 1945, the total was still only fifty-one. But in 1951, when the twenty-fifth anniversary of the historic consecration of 1926 was celebrated, the total stood at ninety-one, and by the death of Pius XII in 1958 it had climbed to 139. In December 1961, when the summons to Vatican II went out, 162 of the archbishops and bishops residing in their sees were of either Asian (126) or African (36) origin; by the time the council ended there were 228 (160 Asians, 68 Africans).[45]

The Roman Catholic Church was not alone in effecting the process which led from foreign missions to local Churches. The same pattern of evolution can be traced in other Christian missions. This is not surprising: Anglican and other Protestant missionaries also had their roots in the Western world, if not in the same parts of it as their Catholic colleagues, and were therefore imbued with the same general outlook and the same feeling of superiority towards peoples of non-Western descent. We have already noticed that Catholic missionaries of the early twentieth century lacked a strong sense of the Church, and the deficiency was still more marked among Protestant missionaries of the same period, who were influenced even more strongly by

45. It must be stressed that all the figures given here are for the ecclesiastical *territories* and not for the bishops, whose total number would include coadjutors, auxiliaries, etc.

the individualist idea of salvation. 'The early Protestant missionaries seemed hardly conscious that they were founding a new and living cell of a world church. They were concerned more than anything else with the salvation of souls.'[46] In their case there was some excuse for this erroneous viewpoint. Strongly influenced by the Evangelical and Revivalist movements, the Protestant missions owed their existence to the private initiatives of fervent individuals and they were organised, financed and controlled by missionary societies which at the outset had few if any links with the Churches. 'The Evangelical awakening, whether in America, on the Continent of Europe or in Britain, everywhere led to a new concern for evangelism on a world scale. And because the Churches were, for the most part, deeply suspicious of any form of religious enthusiasm, the new zeal for mission was channelled into voluntary societies.' [47] The missionary society, whose membership was not necessarily restricted to a single denomination, for a long time led what might be described as a separate existence. This is how an Anglican authority describes the situation:[48]

> Separation between Church and mission was carried to the extreme possible limits in Germany, Holland and Switzerland. In most cases the missionary had been trained in a special institution, where the studies were not on the same level of academic excellence as in the universities and the examinations of which were not recognised by the Church. He was then ordained not by the Church but by the missionary society, to the office not of minister of the word and sacraments in the Church but of 'missionary', a theological concept unknown to the New Testament. When on leave, he could not preach in any church, since his ordination did not carry with it any right of ministry in his home country. He was simply the employee of a large concern in Europe, submissive to its directions, dependent on it for financial support, responsible to it and to it alone, without direct dependence on or responsibility to any church body. Naturally 'the mission' filled his thoughts and his horizon, and 'the Church' seemed to be a distant and not very important problem of the future.

While there were undoubtedly important shades of difference, the non-Catholic missions of the late nineteenth and early twentieth century thus had certain characteristics in common: a consciousness of western

46. W. C. Lamott, *Revolution in Missions* (New York 1954), 25.
47. M. A. C. Warren, *The Missionary Movement from Britain in Modern History* (London 1965), 149.
48. S. C. Neill, *A History of Christian Missions* (Harmondsworth 1965), 512.

superiority, a theology and spirituality centred on the individual, the dividing up of the mission field between missionary societies.

Not surprisingly, some identical consequences ensued. 'It is clear that the majority of missionaries in the nineteenth century took it for granted that they would be there for ever... (they) were extraordinarily slow to recognise and trust the gifts of indigenous Christians. Even when ordained to the ministry, they were still regarded as no more than assistants to the missionary.'[49] The Anglican Church, it is true, was relatively early in consecrating Africans and Asians as bishops: an Indian in 1912, a Chinese in 1918, two Japanese in 1922 (not to mention Samuel Adjai Crowther from Nigeria, whose consecration at Canterbury in 1864 was an experiment not followed up). But Stephen Neill, himself an Anglican missionary bishop, remarks that all of them, even the most qualified, were little more than 'vicars episcopal' acting as assistants to European bishops. He concludes: 'There was, in fact, an accession of dignity but little, if any, accession of authority'.[50] And although V.S. Azariah, the first Indian to be appointed to an Anglican bishopric, was outstanding as an individual, we learn from Neill that 'the appointment was bitterly combated both by missionaries and by many Indian Christians'.[51]

But in the Anglican Church, as in the Roman Catholic, we are dealing with communities structured round an episcopal hierarchy. It may be asked whether progress towards a truly responsible local Church did not present itself to other missions in a quite different light. The fact is that we see appearing at quite an early date, and playing an important role both at the regional level and in the great interdenominational missionary conferences, a fair number of Protestants of Asian and a little later of African origin. Even at the first World Congress of Missions, which met at Edinburgh in 1910, 'one per cent of the delegates were nationals from the lands of the younger Churches, and they came not as representatives of the Churches but as part of the quota of the parent missionary societies of the older Churches'.[52] Here, however, it is important to take note of a significant difference between the 'monarchical' type of government obtaining in Churches with an episcopal hierarchy and government of the presbyterian or synodal type, characteristic of most of the Churches which had engendered the missionary societies. This collegial form of government, which depends on the exercise of responsibility by laymen as well as by pastors, appears to lend itself more naturally to the enlistment of local collaborators, leading eventually to local control. Little by little, depending

49. *op. cit.*, 258, 515.
50. *op. cit.*, 525.
51. *op. cit.*, 366.
52. K. S. Latourette, *Tomorrow is here* (London 1948), 47.

on how a local community matured, local leaders took a growing part in the government of a Church, until the day came when the parent missionary society or foreign Church declared the local Church 'autonomous'. These declarations of autonomy, nearly all of which are after the Second World War, in fact merely endorsed a state of adulthood already long established.

When the World Council of Churches was formed in 1948, out of the 147 Churches represented, twenty-five were Asian and ten African. At the time of the third General Assembly (New Delhi 1961) the Council included representatives of thirty-three Asian and twenty-eight African Churches sitting on equal terms with representatives from the older Churches of the West.

3. MISSION AND ITS POLITICAL ASSOCIATIONS

Among the circumstances we saw as favouring the missionary advance of the latter half of the nineteenth century we mentioned two that were political: the pressure brought to bear by Western nations, in process of imposing their hegemony on the world, on countries hitherto closed or as good as closed to missionary activity to open their doors; and the assumption elsewhere by Western powers of direct political control, followed by the installation of a colonial regime in which Christian missions found themselves a place.

There was nothing inherently abnormal in the Church's making use of favourable political circumstances to further the spread of the Gospel. She had done so in the first age of expansion, profiting greatly from the *pax romana*. Nor was it abnormal for political powers to use their influence in the interests of religious freedom. When the nations of Europe met at Berlin (1884-5) for the colonial carve-up of Africa, they signed a document stipulating:

All the powers exercising rights of sovereignty in the specified territories ... shall protect and encourage, without distinction of nationality or creed, all religious, scientific and charitable institutions and undertakings ... Christian missionaries, scientists, explorers, shall all and equally enjoy special protection. Freedom of conscience and religious toleration are expressly guaranteed to natives, nationals and foreigners. The free and public observance of all religions, the right to erect edifices for worship and to organise missions pertaining to all religions, shall be subject to no restriction or impediment.

In drawing up this document the Congress of Berlin was complying with a request of Leo XIII, transmitted by the representative of France.

England had been still more explicit at the time of the dissolution of the East India Company in 1858 and the assumption of direct responsibility for the administration of the Indian subcontinent as a 'colony of the Crown'. In her proclamation accepting this responsibility, Queen Victoria declared: [53]

Firmly relying ourselves on the truth of Christianity and acknowledging with gratitude the solace of religion, We disclaim alike the right and the desire to impose Our convictions on any of Our subjects. We declare it to be Our royal will and pleasure that none be in any wise favoured, none molested or disquieted by reason of their religious faith or observance, but that all alike shall enjoy the equal and impartial protection of the law.

To judge by these official declarations, which could be matched from League of Nations and United Nations documents, there was a vast difference, as regards religion, between the colonialism of the nineteenth and twentieth centuries and that of the preceding era when Spain and Portugal, under the *Padroado* system, had deliberately set out to defend and propagate Christianity in the lands under their protective rule. In principle, political intervention was in future to confine itself to safeguarding religious liberty; the work of colonisation and the work of mission, although not totally unrelated, are kept clearly distinct.

In practice things were often very different. On the one hand the Western powers were tempted, in a number of instances, to make use of Christian missions for their own ends. On the other the Christian missions, in their desire to exploit their position to the best advantage, allowed themselves to become actively or passively linked with the colonial system, often in compromising fashion.

Certain examples show political and missionary interest acting in conjunction right from the start. A great Catholic missionary, Mgr de Guébriant, was the author of these revealing lines published in *Le Correspondant* of 25 January 1931:

The missionary's duty is to deliver the truth about Christianity to the people amongst whom he is sent, just as it is his duty to do all he can to keep them from error. Around the middle of the last century the Protestant proselytiser was advancing from one Pacific island to the next and wherever he gained a foothold the Catholic missionary was either implacably excluded or, as in the Sandwich Islands, subjected to vigorous persecution. Experience showed that if Protestantism had not preceded the

---

53. Quoted by Neill, *A History...*, 323. The author notes that the words in italic, which make the declaration start with a personal profession of the Christian faith, were an addition made to the original text by the queen herself.

British flag, it very soon followed in its wake. Any territory which became a British possession was thus lost to Catholicism. Now, at a time when the islands were the prize of the first ship's captain who happened along, and the islanders were often very willing to be bought, it sometimes happened – unfortunately all too rarely – that French missionaries had opportunity to procure in time, that is before the arrival of the British, on behalf of populations up for sale, the benefits of a Catholic colonisation of the French type; in conscience, could they hesitate?

To this question let a French Protestant voice make reply: [54]

French vessels – at any rate under the Second Empire – brought with them Catholic Fathers who were sometimes forced on the local population under threat of the French guns and who gave themselves out as the accredited representatives not only of the one complete and authentic Christianity but also of the sole national religion of France. In consequence the new colony was often riven by bitter conflicts which led as a rule to the departure or even the expulsion of foreign missionaries.

Oceania was not the only place where the possible incursion of a hostile colonial power provided cause for alarm. In Africa, the English Protestants around Lake Nyasa lived in dread of the extension in their direction of Portuguese rule in Mozambique, because '...their law is to have none but Roman Catholic missionaries'; [55] hence the rejoicing among the Protestant missionaries when Great Britain took possession of Nyasaland. 'This month', wrote one of the missionaries to his Committee, 'there has dawned a new life upon this land. British protection was what we had hardly dared to hope for; the utmost we had been taught to expect was that we would not be driven out of the country by the Portuguese . . . Nothing could exceed the heartiness with which we welcome what has been done.' [56] Speaking of the same region, a historian of Catholic missions has no hesitation in declaring: 'It seems to have been thanks to her missionaries that France proved immediately acceptable to all the peoples of the interior: France's claim was nothing.' [57]

It is typical of the mentality of the period that the monumental work brought out in 1902 by Father Piolet, S.J. 'in collaboration with all the

54. J. Bianquis, 'Les débuts de la mission évangélique au XIXe siècle', in L'Évangile et le Monde (Paris 1931), 64.
55. Letter from Bishop Smythies of U.M.C.A., 16 August 1889, quoted A. J. Hanna, The Beginnings of Nyasaland (Oxford 1956), 131.
56. op. cit.,145.
57. J. B. Piolet, Les Missions catholiques françaises au XIXe siècle (Paris 1902), 482.

Missionary Societies' accepted notions of the kind which figure in its conclusion, contributed by a member of the Academy, Ferdinand Brunetière: [58]

> I shall not claim that the Reverend Father Piolet was literally 'inspired' when he gave to his history of *French Catholic Missions* the more general title *France Overseas,* but merely that in these two words he has summed up the situation in a nutshell. Wherever our missionaries have gone, they have indeed 'planted', as we used to say, love of France alongside the Faith. It was due to them that in the East and the Far East, in China for example, France long held the preponderant and privileged position which could and should be hers still, which could and will be hers again, once our government comprehends that aid and support for Catholic action overseas is a means of extending, expanding and consolidating the influence of France. I need no reminding that the zeal of our missionaries has more than once embroiled us in troubles we might have wished to be spared; but the very act of overcoming these troubles redounds to our credit and the vexations are of no account beside the general advantages that have accrued. In the land of the East our missionaries see to the heart of questions our diplomats grasp only superficially. Our diplomats in those parts rely on the missionaries as their surest source of information and as their most trustworthy agents. Elsewhere, especially in Africa and Oceania, our missionaries are what they have always been, trail blazers of French culture.

The political links between Christian mission and the Western nations took one of two forms: in countries which retained their independence the Western nations gave missionaries diplomatic protection; where a Western nation had established a colony, the mission lived in *de facto* association with the regime.

The former type of attachment grew up in countries of the Far East, starting from the religious toleration clause in the treaties imposed on those countries by the Western powers. In China it went much further, in consequence of the protectorate over Catholic missions secured by France after half a century of diplomatic effort, punctuated by the treaties of Whampoa (1844) and Tientsin (1858), the convention of Pekin (1860) and the Berthémy convention of 1856, which received its final form in the Gérard convention of 1895. De Lagrené, the French diplomat who began the negotiations, was a good Catholic with a personal interest in missions. He had at first however no intention of going beyond the declared wish of his government, which was for a commercial treaty. But the missionaries in China were fac-

---

58. Piolet, *op. cit.,* VI, 498-9.

ing serious difficulties. A number of them appealed to the French minister to intervene on their behalf, which de Lagrené saw as an opportunity to secure for his own government an advantage over the Americans and the British, both of whom had also just concluded a trade agreement with China. The clause he arranged to have inserted into the Franco-Chinese treaty went no further than a still very restricted decree of toleration. But from successive revisions France finally emerged as the 'protector' of all missionaries in China and even of Chinese Catholics in their dealings with the imperial government. The French legation was empowered to issue to any missionary, whatever his nationality, a special passport which described him as 'French', vouched him the possessor of rights superior to those conferred by an ordinary passport, and allowed him, if he found himself in conflict with the Chinese authorities, to call on French diplomatic representatives to intervene. Some missionaries, and these included bishops in China, had been very much in favour of this diplomatic manoeuvre; but the Church as such had no part in what was a purely political agreement negotiated between China and France. It should be said, however, that Rome approved the situation *de facto* and for some time to come encouraged missionaries to avail themselves of the good offices of France's representatives.

In 1885, when the Tonkin war broke out, the 'protectorate' was assumed exercised by the representative of Russia, who was temporarily responsible for French interests in China, and during this period Leo XIII wrote to the emperor of China direct to commend the missions to his protection. The following year China made overtures indicating willingness to treat with the Holy See without intermediaries and even to enter into regular diplomatic regulations. But Leo XIII refused to be drawn, partly in order to avoid embroiling himself with the French government and partly, so it seems, because he feared a nuncio would be a less effective guarantee of protection for the missionaries. 'The French protectorate only endured and remained effective because of the support it received in practice from the Holy See, which recommended the missionaries to avail themselves of it.' This observation of R. Gérard's [59] seems justified, even though the texts on which he relies in fact relate to the Middle East rather than China.

From 1888 the protectorate over the Chinese missions ceased to be a French monopoly; other Western governments started to claim it in respect of their own nationals. But the diversification made no fundamental difference to the close links which the Catholic missions had contracted by this means with Western political activity in China.

To judge the full ambiguity of the situation, it should be added that protection of the missionaries served as occasion or pretext for some serious

59. 'La protection des missions catholiques en Chine et la diplomatie', *Bulletin de l'U.M.C.* Belgium (October 1927), 137-67.

infringements of Chinese sovereignty. For instance, it was the murder of two missionaries which provided Germany in 1897 with the opportunity to insist on the occupation of the territory of Kiao-Tcheou. This was how C. Costantini depicted the situation: [60]

The Chinese have been subjected to a horrifying series of reverses and humiliations, inflicted on them by Christian nations; they see the missions as closely linked with the aggressive policies of foreign powers.

Unhappily, the official papers of foreign legations, which have been published, contain references to assistance given to the legations by individual missionaries.

Foreign diplomats, some of them Jews or atheists, handled the affairs of the missions and defended their interests with a rod of iron. There were times when European governments were sending the religious in their own countries to prison and denying them the rights accorded to other citizens, while at the same time showing themselves very solicitous to protect religious working as missionaries in China.

If a hand was laid on a missionary anywhere in China, the consul was immediately there behind him, and behind the consul the representative of a foreign power in Pekin. If any damage had been caused to mission property, if a missionary had been killed, they made the Chinese government pay.

Chinese judges who had to try a case involving Christians went in dread of missionary intervention. In virtue of treaties imposed on China by force and in virtue above all of the foreigner's exemption from Chinese jurisdiction, the missions ended by constituting a State within a State.

The second form of political attachment was the *de facto* association between mission and colonial regimes. Since the passing of the latter, this association has often been condemned, sometimes in exaggerated and unjust fashion. When political tempers have cooled, the critics will perhaps see the realities of the situation in a more objective light. If the Church had failed to support and co-operate in the efforts of colonial regimes to better the lot of local populations, the omission would rightly have been held against her. But how was the Church to do it, if not by entering into some form of understanding with the colonial power? Was she to refuse the assistance of the latter in developing her own services for the benefit of peoples under colonial rule? An answer in the affirmative would betray a total want of realism. It would be untrue to history to assert that the Church 'enfeoffed' herself to the colonial regimes. Numerous instances of conflict between civil and religious authorities, as for example over France's 'Muslim policy' in Africa, readily

60. *Con i missionari in Cina*, I, 45; French translation *Réforme des missions au XXe siècle*, 58-9.

prove the contrary. But it would be equally untrue to history to deny that the Church accepted, at times with reservations but at others without protest, situations created for her by the colonial powers. For instance, the Church very quickly became accustomed to the dividing up of missionary territories in accordance with the nationality of the missionaries: thus so far as resources in manpower allowed, missions in German colonies were entrusted exclusively to Germans, missions in French colonies to Frenchmen, and so on. When Mussolini's troops overran Ethiopia, even Rome found it quite natural to replace the missionaries of other nationalities by Italians. And it should be added that the entire episode was one of the most flagrant examples of damaging compromise. Many Italian bishops openly supported the venture and the pope did nothing to restrain them. The demeanour of the Vatican suggested on the contrary that there was great rejoicing at the opportunities the Fascist conquest opened up for Catholicism. In general, the colonial power preferred, understandably enough, to see its own nationals in positions of influence over the natives. Conversely, missionaries of the same nationality as the colonists were better placed than foreigners to work in harness with the local administration, or if need be, to oppose it. Out of a very understandable concern for efficiency, the Holy See in general went along with this policy, in some cases entering into a formal agreement with the government concerned.

A good example of the policy – and revealing in more ways than one – is provided by the 'Congo Free State', over which King Leopold II of the Belgians had secured personal sovereignty in central Africa before turning it into a Belgian colony. In a letter written in 1880, one of his collaborators complained : 'Nearly all the missionaries settled in the Congo are foreigners; one lot, Baptists, Evangelicals and so on, are thoroughly English in outlook, while the ones dependent on Cardinal Lavigerie are not generally well disposed towards Belgian influence in the Congo.' [61] It is known that English and American Protestant missionaries played an active part in the agitation against the Congo by exposing certain abuses; and Lavigerie had been the author of a confidential report submitted to Rome in 1870 which denounced the Association Internationale Africaine, the body behind Leopold II, as an organisation of Protestants and free thinkers, which Lavigerie proposed his own missionaries should counteract. In the following year, when Leopold offered to establish and subsidise a mission station on condition that it was served by Belgian members of the Société d'Alger operating under the aegis of the A.I.A., Lavigerie refused: 'The only standard apostles serve under' he declared, 'is the Cross, the only flag a Frenchman can place alongside the

---

61. Orban de Xivry to Lambermont, 21 March 1888, in Archives du Ministère des Affaires étrangères de Bruxelles, *Papiers Lambermont* (1885-8), 854/1.

Cross is the flag of his fatherland.' [62] In these circumstances one can see why Leopold was so anxious to make the Congo missions a Belgian preserve. In 1886 he at length prevailed on Leo XIII to approve a settlement on those lines, provided enough Belgian missionaries could be found. This proviso sent Leopold on the hunt for vocations. Through the archbishop of Malines he put to Propaganda a suggestion for a seminary at Louvain to train secular priests for Africa. He made repeated efforts to attract to the Congo the Scheut Missionaries and the Jesuits, hitherto orientated towards China and India. He persuaded Rome to shift French communities of Holy Ghost Fathers from 'his' territory to the French Congo. He won by degrees the assistance of a number of religious congregations in Belgium, and finally, despite the earlier reservations on both sides, he came to an understanding with Lavigerie and enlisted his co-operation. The Treaty of Berlin, which gave a sweeping guarantee of religious toleration, was in fact twisted through the grant of privileged positions by the State to apply only to 'national missions', which in effect meant Catholic missions. A convention signed in 1906 between the Congo Free State and the Holy See became the basis for a collaboration between the government of the colony and the Catholic mission which lasted until after the Second World War. [63]

In this particular case collaboration was close because the power in the colony was wielded by a government well disposed to the Catholic Church. Elsewhere the collaboration varied strictly according to the degree of cordiality between Church and State in the mother country. In all cases the fact of a link between the missionaries and the colonising power was plain. The two world wars helped to make the connection plainer still. With few exceptions, missionaries 'from enemy countries' were interned and many were expelled. Most telling of all was what happened in Germany's former colonies after 1918, when missionaries of German nationality, whether Catholic or Protestant, were replaced by nationals of the victor nation entrusted with the mandate to administer the territory. It would be hard to find a clearer demonstration that colonialism and mission went hand in hand.

It would be wrong, however, to regard this as a completely general phenomenon. Countries like Switzerland, Ireland and Canada had never possessed colonies and yet made a sizeable contribution to the Catholic missionary force, just as a large number of Protestant missionaries came from regions as little concerned in colonialism as Scandinavia, or again Switzerland. In addition, many nationals of the colonialist countries went as

62. Quoted in Baunard, *Le Cardinal Lavigerie*, II, (Paris 1896), 275.
63. In 1948, under the non-Catholic minister Godding, the 'subsidies to *national* missions' were replaced by 'subsidies to *Christian* missions', without distinction of nationality or confession; in 1954, when Buisseret as minister introduced secular education for Africans he precipitated a serious crisis which marked the end in the Belgian Congo of the close association between Catholic missions and the colony.

missionaries to countries with which they had no colonial ties. In this connection, it is interesting to note that the German Churches, both Catholic and Protestant, continued after the loss of Germany's colonies to despatch missionaries in quite large numbers to other parts of the mission field. It should also be noted that many of the Protestant groups especially active in missionary countries belonged to communities with fairly radical ideas about the separation of Church and State, which made their missionaries keep a tenacious, not to say ferocious, hold on their independence of the colonial government. There was doubtless little in all this to alter the fundamental connection between mission and colonialism, but these are modifications to the picture which have to be taken into account.

In any case, the underlying motives of the missionaries themselves have to be considered if we are to make an objective judgment of mission and its political connections. It is certainly possible to find examples from this period of missionaries who acted on occasion as agents for the imperialistic policies of their mother countries; this form of contamination was in reality quite rare. More common is to find the European missionary sharing the naive enthusiasm and patriotic pride which the achievements of colonialism, real or apparent, inspired. Most common of all is to find a straightforward and more or less explicit acceptance of an existing situation, coupled with appreciation and exploitation, for the proper purposes of mission, of the undeniable practical advantages conferred by Western diplomatic or colonial protection. At a time when hardly anyone seemed to question the West's hegemony, it was quite natural that the missionary should not trouble himself in this regard. K.S. Latourette very well sums up the prevailing attitude when he writes:[64]

> The missionaries through whom the spread of Christianity was largely accomplished to some degree sought to divorce themselves from the political and economic activities of their fellow-countrymen. It is true that most of them were willing to accept and some even sought the protection of their governments... However, missionaries had less support from governments than in any age since, early in the fourth century, Constantine had espoused the Christian cause... Many freely criticised acts of exploitation by their governments and by Westerners engaged in industry, mining and commerce. Usually, indeed, coolness and even antagonism existed between missionaries and their non-missionary fellow-countrymen in business and government. Missionaries sought to take advantage of the access to non-Christians obtained through the commerce

64. *The Christian World Mission in Our Day* (New York 1954), 37-8.

and empire-building of the Occident but they strove to make the impact of the Occident a blessing and not a curse.

But whatever the good intentions of the Christian missionaries, and however much they might at times dissociate themselves from Western diplomacy or colonial governments, it was well-nigh impossible for their presence and activities not to be interpreted by local populations as one of the many facets of Western expansion. In the short term this could seem, as it did to many, an advantage: for there can be no doubt that the desire for initiation into a superior way of life, into the secrets of Western supremacy, contributed to the success of Christian missions, which were a source of secular as well as religious education. But concealed within this short-term advantage was a serious long-term danger: was there not an element of ambiguity in conversions obtained in such circumstances, and a danger that once Western supremacy was called in question, Christianity might find itself also rejected as an alien religion?

Some were far-sighted enough to perceive the danger, but it must be admitted that they were few. Among them was the Protestant founder of the China Inland Mission, J. Hudson Taylor (1832-1905). In 1865, going against the general practice of keeping missionaries to the coastal regions where they remained under Western influence, he launched his evangelists into the interior and instructed them to adopt the Chinese way of life: 'He knew that more than the shape of garments was at stake. Behind the choice of trousers or gown, whiskers or pigtail, fork or chopsticks lay the whole question whether Christianity should spread in China as a universal or a Western religion. And behind the missionary's adoption of the dress must lie a willingness to forswear the company and approval of westerners in order to gain the friendship of the Chinese; the Pauline principle of becoming "all things to all men".' [65] Disapproval was indeed what Taylor encountered in other missionary circles, but he stood his ground. In the Boxer rising of 1900 the China Inland Mission suffered more losses than any other Protestant mission, precisely because its members were scattered over the country's interior; unlike other missionary leaders, however, Taylor refused to accept the compensation the British consulate exacted on his behalf. He used to say of his missionaries: 'They must be prepared to labour without any guaranteed support from man, being satisfied with the promise of Him who has said: "Seek ye first the Kingdom".' [66] Another pioneer of Christian disengagement from Western politics in China was the Catholic missionary Fr Vincent Lebbe, who in 1901 remarked to his bishop in Pekin: 'We are here in actual fact, in spirit and intention, a foreign body, indeed a body

65. J. C. Pollock, *Hudson Taylor and Maria* (London 1962), 176.
66. *op. cit.*, 143.

wielding foreign influence. Our Christian communities are semi-colonies.' The great aim of his life as a missionary was to make the Church in China a Chinese Church. We have seen his battle for the Chinese episcopate, but inevitably this led him also to question the diplomatic protection of missions. In 1912 a dispute with wide repercussions brought him into conflict at Tientsin with the French consul when the latter, alleging the need to protect the mission, took the opportunity offered by an enlargement of the cathedral precinct to have the whole area incorporated into the French concession. Lebbe put up a bold defence of China's rights, in defiance of his bishop's instructions to preserve the Church's 'neutrality' and in defiance too of current missionary opinion. His action earned him exile to a place remote from Tientsin and the enduring distrust of many of his colleagues; but among the Chinese it earned him a deep and lasting respect.

Questioning of the link between mission and colonialism was rarer still, especially among Catholics. A Protestant voice was raised as early as 1884, when Alfred Boegner, an official of the Société des Missions évangéliques de Paris, resisted the French government's demand for the replacement of English-speaking missionaries in Madagascar by French nationals: 'There can be no question of expelling foreign missions, English or otherwise, to replace them by French ones. Foreign missions should be accepted on French soil in the same way that French missions are accepted on foreign soil. Whether Catholic or Protestant, their task is spiritual and therefore supranational.'[67] Franz Michael Zahn, a German working with the Bremen Mission in the German colony of Togoland, wrote in 1888: 'I am completely against colonies, and that is all one has to say today to be marked as an enemy of our Fatherland. But when a missionary becomes involved in politics and furthers the colonial acquisitions of Germany through his influence, then I maintain whatever else his intention may be, that he has made a big mistake, if he has not committed a crime.' [68] This advice to steer clear of politics is not difficult to match in writings of Catholic missionaries like Lavigerie or Libermann, and the same goes for criticism of abuses of the colonial regime. More difficult would be to discover any Catholic prior to the First World War, critical of the colonial regime as a whole. As J. Folliet puts it: 'It is as though the great mass of Catholic writers and thinkers were either standing aside from the movement or fell into step without argument. The missionaries themselves seem to have gone with the tide, and such protests as they voiced – thank God there were some! – were directed at the consequences of colonialism, not at colonialism itself.' [69] There is here a

67. Quoted by Maurice Leenhardt in *Protestantisme français* (Paris 1945), 384.
68. Letter to Spieth, 15 February 1888, quoted by E. Crau in *Christianity in Tropical Africa* (Oxford 1968), 81.
69. 'La pensée catholique et la colonisation', *Rythmes du Monde* (1949 no 1.), 3.

peculiar and striking discontinuity with the theological reflection that the first wave of colonial expansion of the sixteenth and seventeenth centuries had evoked from Francisco de Vitoria, Las Casas and Jean de Solvezano, thinkers whose writings were only to be rediscovered in the interwar period, when colonialism itself started to be called in question.

With the gradual transition from missions to local Churches for which indigenous ministers assumed responsibility, the political attachments of mission, whether diplomatic or colonial, appeared in an ever more compromising light. It is significant that Pius XI addressed himself as follows to China's vicars apostolic in the very year, 1926, which saw the consecration of the first Chinese bishops: [70]

It is well known — and the history of every age bears witness — that the Church adjusts herself to the laws and constitutions of each nation and country; she respects, and teaches others to respect, the dignity attaching to the lawful heads of civil society; she claims no more for her labourers in the mission field or for her faithful than the right to live in freedom and security under the common law.

'Nothing but the common law.' We have seen that the reality was very different, especially in China. The Holy Father acknowledged that in time of trouble and persecution missionaries had been grateful for the protection of the Western powers, but he was careful to define the reasons for its acceptance and to mark out its limits: [71]

If the Holy See has not refused to be defended in this manner, it was with the sole object of shielding the missions from the tyranny and injustice of wicked men; but the Holy See had no intention of encouraging in that way whatever designs may have been entertained by foreign governments, using the opportunity offered by the protection of their nationals as pretext.

Even when totally disinterested, political intervention of this kind had become incompatible with perfectly legitimate national aspirations and with the development of an increasingly 'indigenous' Church; nor in most cases was there any longer any reason for such intervention, which survived merely as part of a tradition in which the 'privileges' had outlived the 'services'.

The most thorny problem was that presented by the Portuguese *padroado* in India. The centuries-old privileges of Portugal having revealed themselves as barren in respect of progress by the Church in India, Gregory XVI had

70. Letter *Ab ipsis* of 15 June 1926 in *A.A.S.*, XVIII (1926), 303-7.
71. *Ibid.*

wanted, as far back as 1838, to suppress this right of patronage; the only result was serious trouble. A proposal for a new concordat, first made to Portugal by Pius IX in 1857 and initially rejected, was eventually accepted when the offer was renewed by Leo XIII in 1886. Under it, Portuguese patronage, properly speaking, was limited to territories actually dependent on Portugal, which in addition had the right to intervene in the appointment to certain episcopal sees in British India. As a result of successive amendments to the concordat in 1928-9 and 1940 and finally of an agreement concluded on 20 July 1950, the Church was able to recover full freedom of action, with Portugal renouncing all her former privileges except in territories still under her political rule.

Elsewhere it was easier to make adjustments to a situation for which there was no proper legal foundation, there being no written agreements between the European powers and the Holy See. All that was necessary to make the protection exercised by Western diplomats automatically lapse was for the Holy See to establish direct diplomatic relations with the Asian government concerned.

France had been well aware of this when discussions started in 1886 between Leo XIII and the imperial court of China and did not hesitate to send the pope a virtual ultimatum to make him abandon the project. A similar objection had produced the identical result on the occasion of a fresh attempt by Benedict XV in 1918. Mgr Petrelli had already been appointed nuncio in China, but the French minister in Pekin succeeded in having the plan quashed. The yearbook of the Missions catholiques de Chine et du Japon for 1919 included a summary of Fr Planchet of the French case, in particular the claim that 'the protectorate over the Catholics depended not on the pope but on a clause in the treaty of 1858'. These experiences persuaded Rome to exercise great caution at the next attempt, made by Pius XI in 1922. This time the pope sent to China not a nuncio, whose diplomatic character would have required negotiations and reciprocity with the Chinese government, but an apostolic delegate, that is a representative of himself to the bishops, which the Western diplomats had no power to prevent. In addition, the news of the establishment of an apostolic delegation was only announced to the heads of Catholic missions in China after the delegate, Mgr Costantini, had actually arrived. These were necessary precautions. The Rome correspondent of a Paris newspaper in fact remarked: 'It would be wise for the French government to pay close attention to the visit of the envoy of Pius XI to China, and to take serious steps to ensure that Mgr Costantini has no direct contact with the Pekin government.'[72] His advice was heeded. Western diplomats were very ready with their welcomes for the

72. Charles Carry, 'La France, la Chine et le Saint-Siège', *L'Écho de Paris* of 23 August 1922.

delegate and hastened to offer him their services, but Mgr Costantini was wise enough to keep his distance: [73]

Especially in front of the Chinese, I thought it advisable to do nothing that would give substance to the suspicion that the Catholic religion is in tutelage to the European nations or worse still their political tool. I was determined by my very first gestures to vindicate my freedom of action in religious affairs, and when calling on local officials I refused to be accompanied by representatives of foreign powers. Otherwise I might have been taken for their subordinate.

Mgr Costantini was in fact determined to 'replace as quickly as possible the protection of missions by foreign diplomats by guarantees under Chinese law'. In 1929 an agreement between the Holy See and China was on the point of being signed, but, writes Costantini, 'my visit to the Nanking government and the fear of a possible agreement between China and the Holy See excited alarm and ill-will in the French legation, as also in the French press and in certain French missionary circles', [74] and the project had once again to be abandoned. In fact, direct and reciprocal diplomatic relations between the Vatican and China were not achieved until 1947. In order to disentangle herself at last from a partisan tutelage, [75] which changes in the general political situation had rendered obsolete, the Church had to show great patience and perseverance in face of a determination to continue using missionary activity for the furtherance of political ends.

Mgr Costantini showed the same perseverance in his campaign against the custom of demanding compensation through foreign consulates for damage suffered by missions during times of disturbance. Following a Protestant example, [76] he created a precedent by donating a sum paid in reparation for the murder of a missionary towards the building of a Chinese hospital. Shortly afterwards, the Secretariat of State issued at his request very precise directives on the matter. They stipulated that 'compensation should not be demanded for the murder of a missionary, it being contrary to

---

73. *Con i missionari in Cina*, I, 32.
74. *op. cit.*, II, 87.
75. Anyone inclined to dispute the adjective would do well to read the revealing texts cited by L. Wei, of which the following extract from a despatch of 1880 from the French foreign minister to his legation in Peking may be taken as a sample: 'Let there be no misunderstanding about the nature of the protection we afford to missionaries. . .our sole object is to make use, for the good of France, of the close relations the missionaries have established with Chinese communities and of their unceasing progress . . .' (Archives des Affaires étrangères de Paris, Chine, Mémoires et documents, *M.D.*, XII fol. 404).
76. 'I knew that in 1901 the Shansi Protestants had refused to accept compensation for their dead missionaries and had arranged for the total amount to be allocated to the foundation of a university': *op. cit.*, I, 146.

the mind of the Church to demand monetary compensation for the blood of her martyrs'. As to material damage, any discussion about possible compensation should in future take place between missionary and Chinese authorities, without the intervention of foreign governments. [77]

Slowly but surely the Church was thus freeing herself in China from the political shackles inherited from the past, reverting to a position more in keeping with her spiritual nature. As Pius XI had put it, she asked for no protection 'other than that of the common law' and she asked it from China direct.

By its very complexity, the case of China shows clearly the policy the Holy See intended to pursue: direct negotiation with local authorities on matters affecting mission. This was undoubtedly one of the reasons for the multiplication of apostolic delegations, which were converted into internunciatures when the country in question regained its political independence, and since 1966 into nunciatures. If at the present time it may be possible to criticise certain interferences by Vatican diplomacy in the affairs of local Churches, it must not be forgotten that at a critical moment in history that was the most effective way of rescuing the Church from some regrettably compromising positions.

In parallel with this change in the 'political' status of mission, efforts were also made to rid missionary thought and work of certain attitudes which, although legitimate in themselves, were rather too human. There was little point in eliminating political interference on the diplomatic plane if the minds of the missionaries themselves continued to be susceptible to political influence. Sons of an earthly fatherland which their Christianity exhorts them to love and serve, missionaries nevertheless have to understand that the mission entrusted to them forbids them, by its very nature, to be anything other than ambassadors of the universal Church. In his encyclical *Maximum illud* Benedict XV reminded them of the fact, in words to which most of the subsequent texts hark back. The pope there condemned as 'a hideous blemish' on the missionaries' apostolate 'any indiscreet zeal for the aggrandisement of their fatherland'. He demonstrated that the whole enterprise of mission was rendered suspect if the missionary 'shows he is also concerned with serving the interests of his fatherland'; his duty, on the contrary, was to remind himself without ceasing 'that he represents the interests not of his fatherland but of Christ', so that all who meet him may recognise him 'without doubt as an apostle of that religion which...knows no foreigners'.

Following Benedict XV, Pius XI was several times to insist on the same point. [78] The Holy See's thinking on the subject was made very plain. No missionary worthy the name had the right to promote the material interests of his country of origin or even to propagate its cultural influence. He totally renounced any such right when he agreed to be sent by the Church, and by the Church alone, as her representative to a missionary country. He had to look on that country thereafter as his fatherland and serve it with all his strength. As Pius XII put it: 'He has in effect to regard the country to which he goes bearing the light of the Gospel as his second fatherland, and give it the love which is its due; thenceforth he will seek no earthly benefits, whether for his country or for his religious institute, but only what is needful for the salvation of souls.' [79]

Indirectly, such exhortations very fortunately prepared the way for the political disengagement mission was shortly required to make from the political attachments of the second type, the ties linking mission with colonialism. During the twenty years following the Second World War, the vast empire the West had acquired throughout the world was called in question and subjected to a rapid process of 'decolonisation'. It originated in Asia back in 1945 with the independence of the Philippines, Indonesia and India, and started in Africa, with the independence of Ghana, in 1957, proceeding thereafter at such a pace that 1960 can be called 'African year', because of the many new States that in that year achieved international sovereign status.

In face of this general recasting of the political framework, what was the Church's attitude? She had in fact already obliquely defined it by hastening on the development of missions towards the regime of local Churches. Not only did she thus anticipate – and this also goes for the Protestant Churches – what might by analogy be called her own decolonisation, but in documents such as *Rerum Ecclesiae* she explicitly foresaw, and used as an argument for bringing the local Church to maturity, the day when 'a native population, arrived at a somewhat higher degree of civilisation and political-ly come of age, desires its independence, demands the departure of the civil servants, soldiers and missionaries of the colonial power, and can obtain it only by employing force'. It is remarkable that this hypothesis was en-visaged, as early as 1926, as an eventuality that the text considers in fact fairly remote, but which it mentions without reprobation. It would be tendentious, however, to conclude that the Church was prepared for political decolonisation. It was merely that having adopted, in circumstances we have described and for reasons of her own, the policy of promoting the transfer of

78. In his letters *Unigenitus* of 19.3.1924 (*A.A.S.*, XVI (1924), 133-48 and *Ab ipsis* of 15.6.1926 (*A.A.S.*, XVIII (1926), 303-7), and the Instructions issued by the Congregation of Propaganda 8.12.1929 (*A.A.S.*, XXII (1930), 111-5.
79. Encyclical *Evangelii praecones*, *A.A.S.*, XXXIII (1951), 506.

responsibility to Africans and Asians, the Church was somewhat in advance of political developments. But that is not to say she was consciously prepared for them. In any case, it would not be difficult to point to numerous exceptions, attributable to widely varying local conditions, sometimes in the colonies, sometimes in the mother country.

On the global plane, the (Protestant) Churches' Commission for International Affairs pledged itself in its foundation charter of 1946 to promote to the utmost the wellbeing of dependent peoples including their advance toward self-government and the development of their political institutions. The Commission actively pursued this policy in the years that followed and in 1954 the Report of Section IV of the World Council of Churches Assembly, meeting at Evanston, had stated that the legitimate right of people to self-determination must be recognised. For the Catholic Church, Pius XII expounded in 1945 his doctrine of the supra-national Church and he made frequent reference, as we shall see, to the Church as a respecter of cultural diversity, but we have to wait for his Christmas messages of 1954 and 1955, specifically the latter, to hear him wish for 'a just and increasing measure of political liberty not to be withheld from these peoples (of colonies aspiring to independence) and for no obstacle to be placed in the way'; and these documents as a whole in any case give the impression that the pope was more preoccupied with the violence that might result from a clash of competing nationalisms than with the right to independence as such. In 1960 we at last find John XXIII expressing unreservedly in his message to the faithful of Africa his 'great satisfaction at witnessing one after another so many accessions to full nationhood: the Church rejoices at it and has faith in the desire of these young States to take their place in the concert of nations'.

At the local level, the level at which the Churches found themselves directly affected by political developments, declarations of attitude were forthcoming much earlier and often showed more positive commitment. The multiplicity and diversity of the events makes their analysis here impossible to attempt; we shall therefore confine ourselves to citing this conclusion to a specialised study of the subject: [80]

Confronted with the crisis of the colonial system, the Churches on the whole were in agreement with the transfer of political power to representatives of native populations. There were even examples of open support of nationalist claims against the authority of the mother country (as in Madagascar in 1953). In other circumstances it was a case of the Churches resigning themselves to independence, efforts to obtain a for-

80. M. Merle, 'Conclusion' to the collection he edited under the title, Les Églises chrétiennes et la décolonisation (Paris 1967), 506.

mula for communal co-existence (as recommended for Algeria) having failed. For the most part the Churches fell into line with the movement and gave it discreet encouragement. Nowhere, save in the case of Portugal, did they yield to the temptation of coming to terms with European governments when the latter attempted to preserve their sovereignty by force. Although there were instances on the Protestant side and in some left-wing Catholic circles of colonialism being regarded as an unmitigated evil, the attitude of the Churches as a whole cannot be summed up as representing an anti-colonialist position. The timing and manner of the transfer of power were regarded as secondary beside the fundamental requirement of a 'benign evolution'. The break in continuity was not deliberately sought after, quite the contrary; but it was accepted unequivocally when the circumstances left no other peaceful means for resolving the crisis. It was in this sense and with these qualifications that the Churches can be said to have been in favour of decolonisation.

In reality, as is proved by the sequence of events, the Church showed throughout the process of decolonisation her concern for the maintenance and strengthening, irrespective of these inevitable and necessary political developments, of solidarity between the rich and deprived nations. Political independence did not appear to her an absolute good. She wanted to be sure that the acquisition of political independence did not impair the collaboration between nations on which the development of all peoples depended. This preoccupation was given clear expression in the encyclical *Mater et Magistra* published by John XXIII on 15 May 1961 and in the encyclical which his successor, Paul VI, devoted exclusively to the developing countries, *Popularum progressio,* 26 March 1967. But it was important that, before formulating in this way her teaching on the solidarity of nations, the Church was able to demonstrate by her actions that she was not tied to the politics of the West.

4. MISSION AND CULTURES

Here was however another and much deeper bond than the political that hampered missionary endeavours, namely the Church's cultural link with the West. In itself this link was the perfectly natural outcome of centuries of symbiosis. It only became questionable when it was regarded as binding Christianity to one particular form of civilisation, making the one virtually impossible to adopt without the other. Now it was precisely this view which coloured the outlook of the nineteenth-century missionary, Catholic and Protestant alike. As a Protestant writer has pointed out, both groups were under the impression 'that not only the message of the Gospel but the practical forms Christianity had taken in the West should be reproduced in the non-Christian world; and most supporters felt that the end result would be the creation of a kind of Christianity similar to ours in an environment not much different from that in which we live'. [81] In the euphoria of a West in the full tide of expansion this notion was not to be wondered at. Everything appeared to confirm it: the astonishing spread of a civilisation that undeniably carried with it values of Christian origin, the desire for Westernisation manifested in at least certain strata of the populations being evangelised, the opportunities this circumstance seemed to afford for missionary work... So the identification of 'Christian civilisation' with 'Western civilisation' seemed something one could take for granted. Besides, the average European of around 1900 was so dazzled by his own achievements that he could not imagine any civilisation other than his own. This century 'which was the age of Europe's expansion' writes Fr de Lubac 'was also all too often an age of blind barbarism... So greatly did the pride we took in our machines and our weapons make us unjust towards other peoples, so frequently did the narrowness of an education which claimed to instil in us the one and only human culture close our minds to the glories of human creation under other skies than ours.' [82] Missionaries were infected by this attitude and took it for granted that they went overseas to spread 'civilisation' along with the Christian faith.

Once again the attraction of a short-term advantage was allowed to mask the reality of a serious threat, which was less remote than it seemed. For one thing, the 'Christian' character of Western civilisation was about to expose itself to harsh criticism in the light of two world wars for which that civilisation was held entirely responsible and of Europe's record of progressive internal dechristianisation, and above all in consequence of the calling in question of colonialism. For another, the peoples the West had subjugated were about to reaffirm, with new-found pride, their own cultural patrimony and to reproach the West for its attempts to alienate them from it by a cultural imperialism even more aggressive than the political. The superficial and transient attraction that Christianity possessed by reason of its cultural association with the West was thus in danger of becoming transformed into a cause of antagonism, leading to the categorical rejection of Christianity as a typically alien religion.

By great good fortune, the revulsion of feeling which set in between the wars, and which after the Second World War became irreversible, was not to be carried to this extreme. What happened in effect was that the Church, still no doubt without effecting a universal change of outlook, reverted to her authentic missionary traditions.

This was manifested initially in a series of practical steps taken under Pius

81. Lamott, *Revolution in Missions*, 12.
82. *Catholicisme* (Paris 1938), 225.

XI's pontificate to liberate non-Western Christians from old ecclesiastical constraints which prevented them from demonstrating their loyalty to their country and its customs.

In China, for example, as a result of the famous quarrel over rites in the eighteenth century, Catholics found themselves debarred from taking part in ceremonies in honour of Confucius, which were nevertheless also the expression of fidelity to the ancestral tradition and of loyalty to the fatherland. Since that time the situation had in many ways changed and the civil character of the Confucian ceremonies had become much more evident. The time had come to take a fresh look at the problem: what was to be gained by preserving for obsolete reasons a regulation which excluded Catholics from certain manifestations of their national life? The question became acute when the government of the State created by the Japanese in North-Eastern China under the name Manchukuo reintroduced the official cult of Confucius and made it compulsory. The heads of missions consulted the Congregation of Propaganda and were instructed to begin by studying the problem for themselves. They therefore enquired of the government what the ceremonies signified and examined the various concrete instance of participation that might arise. In May 1935 the heads of mission met at Sinkiang and laid down rules of conduct governing honours paid to the image of Confucius in schools, participation in official ceremonies taking place in pagodas and financial contributions to the building or repair of pagodas. Relying on the government's assurance that the ceremonies had no religious connotation, they thought it legitimate to authorise Catholics to take part, subject to certain reservations over points which might too easily lead to misunderstandings. [83] So the previous code was revised and the new regulations were approved by Rome.

There was a similar problem in Japan and perhaps an even more delicate one, since Japanese patriotic observances included rites known to have their origin in non-Christian religions. This time Propaganda decided the matter for itself and on 26 May 1936 addressed to the apostolic delegate in Tokyo a directive of the first importance. Fearlessly linking the missions of the present with those of the era before the condemnation of the Chinese rites, the document reiterated the principles enunciated in an instruction of 1659: 'Never seek in any way to persuade these peoples to change their rites, their customs or their manners, provided these do not openly conflict with faith and morals...' The Sacred Congregation of Propaganda applied this quotation directly to the immediate case of Japan and laid down precise rules, ratified in full by Pius XI, permitting Japanese Catholics to take part in patriotic ceremonies and to 'conduct themselves on those occasions in the

83. *Sylloge...*, 479-82.

manner customary for citizens, declaring this to be their intention if such declaration seems necessary to avoid misinterpretation of their actions'. [84]

These two decisions signalised a very clear reversion towards a policy from which the Church in recent decades had regrettably diverged, but which was in line with her true missionary tradition. Pius XII gave unmistakable notice, in *Summi Pontificatus,* of his intention to follow the same road; shortly afterwards a fresh directive from Propaganda extended the Manchukuo decisions of 1936 to the whole of China and widened them to include 'rites' in honour of the departed. [85] Rome's instructions being clear and the former controversies long extinct, the oath required from native and foreign priests serving 'in the Chinese empire and the bordering or adjacent kingdoms and provinces' had no further *raison d'être.* So it was claimed in the document abolishing the obligation, which at the same time prudently maintained the ban on any revival of the controversy. So a painful past was blotted out, and it once again became possible for a Chinese to be a full Catholic while remaining loyal to his national traditions.

On 9 April 1940 the missionaries in India were dispensed in their turn from the oath regarding the Malabar rites. The new policy was thus becoming general, but in all the cases so far we have been dealing with peoples of an ancient civilisation, in which the distinction between the religious and the profane was by now easy to establish. Could this understanding policy be extended to other peoples? In 1938 the apostolic delegate in the Belgian Congo, Mgr Delle Piane, submitted to Propaganda a 'proposal to expurgate superstitions found in the funeral ceremony known as "matanga" in the Lower Congo'. Rome's reply left it to the local Church authorities to decide, merely reminding them of the principles enunciated in 1659 and applied recently to cases arising in Asia. There could be no clearer indication that the exactly parallel policy was to be pursued, in Africa or anywhere else. So in general the way was clear for the local Churches to adapt themselves to local customs. It was up to the bishops themselves to judge particular cases, in a spirit now clearly defined in Roman directives. It is none the less astonishing to note the timidity with which, until the Second Vatican Council, missionary bishops made use of the opportunities offered to them in this way.

By contrast, as regards general principles, the position of the Church was becoming firmer and more precise, thanks to the teaching of Pius XII. In his inaugural encyclical *Summi Pontificatus* he not only affirmed his adhesion to the practical measures enacted under Pius XI but made explicit their underlying doctrine: the fundamental unity of the human race was not weakened but on the contrary enriched by the diversity of its cultural achievements:

84. *Sylloge...,* 537-8.
85. Instruction of 8.12.1939 in *A.A.S.,* XXXII (1940), 24.

It is impossible for the Church of Christ, as faithful repository of the divine wisdom her teacher, to attack or underrate the individual characteristics which every people, with jealous piety and comprehensible pride, preserves as its precious patrimony, and she does not think to do so. The goal of the Church is supernatural unity in the experience and practice of universal love; she seeks no exclusively outward uniformity, superficial and therefore weakening. All the particular attitudes, concerns, leanings which have their roots in the inmost fibre of each branch of the human race, provided they do not conflict with the duties resting on mankind by reason of his singular origin and his common destiny, the Church greets with joy and bestows on them her maternal blessing. She has shown many times over, in her missionary work, that this rule is the guiding star of her universal apostolate.

Throughout his pontificate Pius XII constantly returned to this theme, refining it and applying it specifically to missionary activity. 'The missionary is the apostle of Jesus Christ. His mission is not to transplant European civilisation to missionary countries but rather to persuade their populations, some of whom enjoy the benefits of an age-old culture, to accept and assimilate the elements of Christian life and conduct, which should harmonise quite naturally and harmoniously with any healthy civilization...' [86] We have come a long way from the prevailing outlook of the early years of the century. There was no reason, for example, why a Chinese or Indian on becoming a Christian should abandon the style of civilisation proper to his nation. On the contrary, it was his duty to remain true to it in order to quicken that civilisation from within, through the spirit of Christ. The missionary for his part was to strive as far as possible to shed the foreignness that might 'mask' the message of the Gospel, in order in his own person to prefigure in some sense the native Christian of the future. Such in particular was the spirit of Jean de Britto, missionary in India during the second half of the seventeenth century. By canonising him on 22 June 1947 Pius XII underlined, by reference to a lived example, the Church's teaching on missions.

To see this teaching bearing fruit and wholeheartedly adopted by Catholic missions in general, we have to await the era of the Second Vatican Council. But there were already pioneers at work, attracting varying degrees of support, attracting varying degrees of criticism: a Vincent Lebbe in China, a Candau in Japan, a Johann, a Dandoy, a Monchanin in India, an Aupiais or a Tempels in Africa, a Charles or an Ohm in the field of general missiology, to name only the most outstanding.

Protestant missions, having started out linked in a similar way with

86. Address to the directors of the O.P.M., 24 June 1944 in *A.A.S.*, XXXVI (1944), 210.

Western civilisation, advanced, albeit by different paths, to a similar attitude of openness in respect of human cultures and their diversity. Here again there were just a few pioneers who took this line from the start, at a time when the vast majority took it for granted that evangelisation and westernisation went hand in hand. In China for example a Hudson Taylor, who has already been mentioned; in Africa an Arbousset, remarking in 1861: 'The most successful missionaries have identified themselves with the peoples they taught. They respected the language and whatever seemed healthy or comparatively sound in the country's laws and traditions.' [87] However, such was not the general attitude, since as recently as 1957 Philippe Maury observed: 'Even now the young Churches bear the marks of this cultural transposition of Western forms, methods and values'. [88] Nevertheless, it was the development of local Churches in Asia and Africa from seeds they had themselves sown that stimulated Protestant missions, especially after the Edinburgh conference of 1937, to re-examine the 'indigenisation' of the Church. 'A distinction had to be drawn', writes Newbigin, 'between the Gospel and Western culture, and this in turn meant that the Church, as the body which – in whatever cultural environment – lives by the Gospel alone, had to be distinguished from the society in which it was set.' [89] In fact, the birth and development of young Churches in Asia and Africa prompted the non-Catholic Churches to re-examine a whole range of fundamental questions over and above the point just mentioned: confessionalism, like mission, closely bound up with the history of the Christian West, the nature of the Church, church structures, the requirements of ecumenism and so on. [90] For various reasons it would take too long to examine here, the confrontation with non-western cultural traditions made a deeper impression on the Protestant Churches than on the Catholic Church, at any rate down to the Second Vatican Council. But as the final outcome of the developments just described, Christian mission as a whole, Catholic and Protestant, is now in agreement with the conclusion reached by a Protestant theologian in a report on 'Unity and Cultural Pluralism' prepared for the 1966 conference of the World Council of Churches, which took the topic 'Church and Society' as its theme: 'The Church, as the body of the crucified and risen Lord of the whole world, has no need for the support of a "Christian" culture, nation or empire. From the depths of a non-Christian world the Church proclaims the good news of the kingdom whose coming

87. H. Clavier, *Thomas Arbousset. Étude historique* (Paris 1966), 105.
88. Writing as a contributor to the collective work *Évangélisation et Politique* (Geneva 1957), 20.
89. L. Newbigin, *The Household of God* (New York 1954), 2.
90. On this topic see the excellent study by M. J. Le Guillou, *Mission et Unité*, Paris 1960.

will restore the unity-in-plurality which the Lord has been preparing throughout the course of history.'[91]

5. NEW CRISES, NEW PERSPECTIVES

The transformation of foreign missions into 'national' Churches, mission's disentanglement from its political attachments, the acknowledgment of cultural pluralism: all these trends seemed to denote a Church well abreast of the worldwide upheaval which followed the Second World War. In the long run this optimistic picture may well prove correct. As regards the present, however, it must be said that the past quarter-century has seen missionaries in a certain state of disarray.

That there could be a gap between the publication of an episcopal pronouncement on independence and the attitudes actually displayed by missionaries in their day-to-day work is obvious enough. And it was the missionaries' own attitude, far more than the written declarations, which affected the mass of the people concerned. Furthermore, missionaries were apt to dwell more on respect for the established order and the rejection of violence than on the legitimacy of movements in support of independence. They knew little of the forces which impel such movements and too often gave the impression of viewing with apprehension – for which there was some justification – the inevitable transition from the security of colonialism to the probable insecurity of a regime still with its way to make. The ties previously formed with colonialist empires were in part responsible for this attitude, not necessarily because missionaries wanted them preserved but simply because the new situation called for psychological readjustments that were difficult to make.

Certain events only served to confirm these fears of an uncertain future. The most serious was the catastrophe which overtook the Church in China. After the Second World War relations between the Nationalist government of China and the Christian Churches had become extremely cordial. The Churches were making an active contribution to national reconstruction. The Chinese Church was taking shape as an organised entity and gave signs of promising vigour. Catholic statistics showed three and a half million baptised, 140 ecclesiastical territories, twenty of which were archbishoprics, 2600 Chinese priests and more than 3000 priests of other nationalities. China was the first missionary country to see a native raised to the cardinalate in the person of H.E. Thomas Tien, named by Pius XII in 1946. But in 1949 the communist armies of Mao Tse-tung, confined hitherto to the North, took possession of the whole country and the Nationalist government fled to Formosa. The following year already saw the beginning of the

---

91. A. T. van Leeuwen, 'L'individu et le groupe', *Église et Société*, IV (Geneva 1966), 182.

Church's ordeal. Foreign missionaries were expelled, some of them after imprisonment, many Chinese priests were arrested and a number of them executed, missionary activity was obstructed and the government brought very strong pressure to bear, notably through the Triple Autonomy Movement, in an effort to subjugate the churches to the political regime. Since 1955 the Church in China has been a Church of silence. The habit of seeing mission as a conquering progress had been dealt a severe blow, felt all the more keenly when it was implied, as in many commentaries, that with the departure of the missionaries there was nothing left, whereas a Chinese Church with its bishops and priests continued to bear witness to the Gospel, though no doubt under disguised forms and in progressive danger of extinction. Nor was the case of China unique. In 1950 North Korea took perhaps even more drastic steps to eliminate Christianity, and in Vietnam in 1954 there was a great exodus of Catholics from the North, fleeing from the newly-installed regime of Ho Chi Minh. Everything mentioned so far could be laid at the door of communism and, rightly or wrongly, people were apt to suspect communist influence when missionaries in other parts of the world were the subjects of hostile measures.

Yet it would be impossible to account in this way for all the fresh obstacles missionaries encountered: growing difficulties in obtaining entry visas, even after a spell on leave, from States as tolerant both by tradition and by reason of her secular constitution as the Republic of India; public accusations of 'proselytism' and restrictions on the work of foreign missionaries; the transformation of countries with Muslim majorities into Islamic states in which Christians often appeared condemned to rank as second-class citizens; the individual or even wholesale expulsion of missionaries, as from the Sudan (1964), Burma (1966) and Guinea (1967); a very distinct tendency to single out for nationalisation the schools, hospitals and other institutions which had played an important part in the development of missions; serious disturbances entailing material damage and sometimes large-scale loss of life, as in the Congo from 1960 to 1965; the revival of old religions which claimed to be national in character as compared with an 'imported' religion like Christianity.

To these external causes of disarray were soon added others internal to the Church. Some critics, perhaps too facilely, wanted to attribute the troubles of mission to the mistakes and shortcomings of the missionaries themselves. Doubts were raised about methods which had been in use for the past hundred years: the *raison d'être* for specifically Christian schools, hospitals and welfare organisations was questioned, in the old Christian countries as much as in those with young Churches; African and Asian clergy became attuned to the nationalist movement and less willing to accept direction from foreigners, which gave rise at times to serious friction. In addition a train of thought was developing which led to a new missiology, an early manifestation of which was the publication in 1944 of a little book entitled *France, pays de mission?*: 'foreign missions' found their exclusive right to the terms 'mission' and 'missionary' increasingly challenged by those who regarded them as equally appropriate to work among certain non-Christian sectors of Western society.[92] This new way of viewing mission led to questioning of the 'missionary' character of certain situations in which the ministers of young Churches were in effect employed on tasks identical with those undertaken by the pastors of old-established Christian communities. There was, in short, a tendency to situate mission and missionaries in a perspective very different from that of the great missionary upsurge of the nineteenth century.

Another change with important consequences took place in 1957, following the encyclical *Fidei donum*. Recognising that because of the diversification of tasks and the rapid pace of change, especially in Africa, the missionary institutes were no longer sufficient, Pius XII appealed to bishops in the Christian countries to place a certain number of their diocesan priests at the missions' disposal. Apart from a not negligible increase in manpower, this appeal had a twofold consequence. In Europe and America, bishops rediscovered their vocation to evangelise the world as well as their own dioceses; and in the young Churches the presence of these diocesan priests posed in new and more precise form the question of the role of the bishop, until now obscured in a missionary structure in which the religious institute took first place.[93] There thus set in, in respect of missions, a trend whose full significance was to disclose itself at the Second Vatican Council.

After the Second World War another type of missionary appeared on the scene, or rather appeared in greater numbers and in a more clearly defined role: the lay missionary. To begin with, he was little more than an auxiliary, another pair of hands. But little by little, due in part to increasing specialisation but still more to deeper reflection on the responsibilities proper to Christian laymen, this 'missionary laity' — which could take many different forms — emerged as a positive entity which added its own touch to the changing face of mission. One consequence, for example, was that a priority was now given to all questions coming under the general heading of 'development'.

To complete the picture, it should be added that the problems posed by mission ceased to be debated solely within the closed circle of expert missiologists. Having held aloof all too long, the theologians at last recognised that such questions should be integrated into their thinking about the Church. This was certainly a step forward, but their aspect of remoteness

---

92. Cf. the journal *Parole et Mission* (published in Paris) and A. M. Henry, *Esquisse d'une théologie de la mission*, Paris 1959.
93. Cf. J. Bruls, *Propos sur le clergé missionaire*, Louvain 1963.

from the encounters and concerns of everyday life rendered their theories suspect to a number of the men of action who, among missionaries, make up the majority. This was especially the case with efforts at the reappraisal of the great world religions, as under way for example in Germany.

All these circumstances, indicative of the general turmoil in which the world and the Church found themselves engulfed, account for the disquiet, uncertainty and disarray evident in many missionary circles just before the Second Vatican Council.

In Asia and Africa perhaps even more than elsewhere the announcement of the council came as a surprise. Many bishops arrived with no very clear idea of what to expect, apart perhaps from one or two practical directives. As to the missionary institutes, their chief anxiety appears to have been to have their specific vocation re-endorsed. as in many other domains, the council was about to broaden these perspectives immeasurably.

The African and Asian episcopates were soon made aware that numerically speaking they were an appreciable force, whose support was actively canvassed by the major bodies of opinion. More important, as time went on, the conciliar debates, and still more the running dialogue that developed between bishops, experts, theologians and even representatives of public opinion, made the bishops of Africa and Asia increasingly aware of the qualitative contribution that the assembled Church expected them to make, of the fact that on most of the great questions debated at the council they could and should shed a more penetrating light, because of the problems and situations they were familiar with at first hand. This was brought out by the debate on the liturgy, which providentially opened the proceedings. Its effect was to make clear that the time for imposing uniformity by regulation was past, and that the Church was moving towards a healthy pluralism in which the problems cropping up in mission could no longer be regarded as peripheral and to be dealt with by dispensation, but were central to determining what should be the general rule. The Melchite patriarch Maximos IV, speaking for 'another' but no less ancient tradition than that of the West, struck a similar note with his trenchant reminders that the Church's most authentic tradition called not for uniformity but for diversity in unity. Many people found these early debates of the council a great eye-opener.

To appreciate the importance to mission of the Second Vatican Council it is not enough to refer simply to *Ad Gentes*, the decree explicitly devoted to missions. Although *Ad Gentes* received its final form only at the very end of the council and could therefore have taken advantage of the other documents, it remained equivocal, valuable chiefly as witness to a period of transition between the mission of the nineteenth century, relying on the Christian West and its specialised missionary institutes, and post-conciliar mission, in which responsibility is shared by all the 'particular' Churches, including those of former 'missionary countries'. To be valid, a summing up of the council in its bearing on mission ought to take into account the texts and proceedings of the council as a whole. In any case, the future alone will show the full effect of this council on the Church's development in the countries that concern us here.

In the meantime, however, it is possible to make three observations which showed in which direction the current was moving.

First, the council appears to mark the term of an evolution whose course we have just traced: from foreign missions to local Churches, from missions with political strings attached to missions with freedom of action, from westernising uniformity to cultural pluralism; these historical strands are to be found running through the documents produced at the council.

Second, the council shows a very clear awareness of mission as an essential characteristic of the Church as a whole, and a clear understanding that the latter was not to be identified with the Church of the West. It was the first council to include among the Fathers a contingent of Asians and Africans, whose numbers grew in proportion from one session to the next. The council doubtless came too soon for them to make their full contribution to a truly universal, truly diversified Church; in the conciliar documents the imprint of Western thinking is still very marked, but this was now seen as a limitation which must as soon as possible be overcome. The Second Vatican Council thus represents a landmark in the Church's expression of her Catholicity. To be convinced, one has only to note the members elected to serve on the post-conciliar commissions or in the different organs of the curia, not to mention the synod of bishops. This was still no more than a laying of foundations, but it pointed to a future which could not fail to be different.

In this same ecclesial perspective, we should note the remarkable change in the relations between Catholic and Protestant missionaries. When the council was announced, the Anglican missionary bishop, Stephen Neill, wrote: 'Let us be frank and admit that almost everywhere relations are as bad as they could be. A few happy exceptions apart, this seems to be the general rule.' [94] Examples quoted earlier in this chapter appear to confirm this diagnosis, and many others could be found. Among Protestants, as we saw, mission was a spur to ecumenism. Catholics who realised that mission demanded a positive striving for Christian unity remained all too few. [95] At the council, Protestants were present as observers and received a fraternal

94. In 'Voeux pour le concile', *Esprit*, 12 (1961), 815-6.
95. See M. Villain, 'Esprit œcuménique et esprit missionaire', *Église Vivante* (1949), 114-20, and the special issue of the same journal no. 6 (1959) devoted to 'Les missionnaires et l'œcuménisme'.

welcome from John XXIII and Paul VI. The things they said themselves, the things said of them in the council, combined to make it plain that the old mistrust was mistaken and that the way forward was the one way taken in the past by the 'happy exceptions'. A new climate was created, which has given rise to many practical initiatives of co-operation and *rapprochement*.

Finally, the council's pronouncements on topics such as the Church as the people of God, the proper role of the laity, the relationship between the Church and the world, religious liberty and non-Christian religions, all point towards a radical re-orientation of mission and its methods, and amongst other things to 'indigenisation' and 'declericalisation'.

The fruits of the council have still to ripen, but it seems certain that the council brought one epoch in missionary history to an end and opened up new vistas in which the Churches of Asia and Africa figure no longer merely as beneficiaries of the Western Church but as its sister-Churches in full fellowship.

PART FIVE
THE EASTERN CHURCHES

17

1848-1914: FROM THE CRIMEAN WAR TO THE FIRST WORLD WAR

1. THE POLITICAL AND ECCLESIASTICAL FRAMEWORK

THE Crimean War and the subsequent Congress of Paris (1856) marked a decisive turning-point in the fortunes of Christianity in the East. It was indeed the reactivation of the question of the Holy Places that had provided occasion for the war. The question of the ownership of the Christian sanctuaries in Jerusalem had been raised and forced on the attention of the French political authorities as far back as 1848, by three individuals from widely separated spheres: the Lazarist E. Boré, the new Latin patriarch of Jerusalem, Mgr Valerga, and the young archaeologist who acted as French consul, P.E. Botta. Between them they had confected at Jerusalem an audacious plan to recover, if possible by diplomatic means but if necessary by resorting, as in the days of the medieval crusade, to a holy war, the rights they believed illegitimately usurped.

After a period of shilly-shallying on the part of the ministers of the Second Republic, Napoleon III came out in support of Botta's bellicose plans. At the end of 1852 the crisis which had been building up since 1848 was temporarily resolved in favour of France and the Latin Catholics. But there was soon a reaction from the Tsar, who had long been ambitious to see Russian diplomats playing at the sultan's court in Constantinople the same official role that was accorded under the capitulation regime to the French embassy in respect of Roman Catholics. The aims of the Russian government were made plain by Prince Menshikov's mission to the Ottoman Capital of February to July 1853. They amounted in practice to a demand on behalf of the Tsar for a protectorate in due and proper form over all the Orthodox subjects of the Ottoman empire, which would have given Russia continual pretexts for intervening in Turkey's internal affairs. The sultan refused to agree to a policy he correctly judged to be suicidal. As a means of bringing pressure to bear, the Russians occupied the Danubian principalities of Moldavia and Wallachia. The reaction from France and England was immediate, and with one provocation following on another, the 'Holy war' finally broke out. In the proclamations of Tsar Nicholas, as in the proclamations of the French generals and in the pastoral letter of the archbishop of Paris, it was stressed that this was military action for the sake of sacred ends.

Russia's defeat in the Crimea reinforced the preponderance of the 'Western' allies, namely the French and English, in the Ottoman empire. To rob Russia of any future excuse for claiming a protectorate over Orthodox communities, the allies obtained from the sultan important reforms on behalf of his Christian subjects. For the first time Christians and Christian institutions had the benefit of legal rights and even international guarantees. The legislation granting the reforms (Tanzimat), promulgated in the famous Hatti-Humayyoun of 18 February 1856, which the Ottoman plenipotentiaries represented as 'emanating spontaneously from the sovereign will of the sultan', had in fact been prepared well beforehand by the western legations in Constantinople and was confirmed by the congress of Paris. If the Ottoman empire was admitted henceforward to 'participate in the advantages of public law and of the European concern of nations' and had its independence and the integrity of its territory guaranteed, the sultan for his part guaranteed to all his subjects, without distinction of race or religion, all the benefits under common law enjoyed by the citizens of liberal Europe.

The publication of this Hatti-Humayyoun and its international endorsement marked the beginnings of the regeneration of Eastern Christianity in modern times, and not just for the Orthodox and the Catholics: for its significance was immediately appreciated by leaders of Protestant missions in the Ottoman empire, so much so that on 4 March they addressed a letter to the English ambassador at Constantinople, Lord Stratford de Redcliffe, expressing their heartfelt gratitude.

In political terms, however, the Congress of Paris marked the beginning of the internal breakup of the Ottoman empire, for it was about to lose one by one the foundations of its economic, political and military independence. Conversely, under the auspices of the various foreign mortgages, local Christianity was able to expand.

Hardly had the protocols of the congress been signed before ambitious plans of investment and penetration were being drawn up, aiming to integrate the various provinces of the Ottoman empire into 'the civilised world' but subjecting them in fact to the more and more direct control of the foreign banking community. The example of the Suez Canal is the best known, but European competition was equally keen in the Eastern Mediterranean and in the Persian Gulf (establishment of the foreign-controlled Ottoman Bank, the German concession for the Baghdad Railway, and so on). Meanwhile the European chanceries were kept busy in 1857-8 deciding the political status of Moldavia and Wallachia, in 1858-9 Serbia and Montenegro attempted to wrest their independence by armed revolt, and already in 1857 a section of the French press had begun to urge the creation of an Arab secessionist kingdom in Syria for the benefit of Emir Abdel-Kader, the former foe of French colonialism in Algeria, who had finally opted for Damascus as the place of his 'gilded exile'. Next, it was the turn of Mount Lebanon, where social and confessional disturbances provided a pretext for European military intervention under the *Règlement organique* conceded by Turkey in 1862 the district was granted a considerable measure of independence under the superior protectorate of the French and guaranteed by the great powers.

The Franco-Prussian War of 1870 gave Russia the chance to dissociate herself from the undertakings given by the powers at the Congress of Paris, especially as regards the passage of the Dardanelles (Treaty of London, 13 March 1871), and plans reappeared for the dismemberment of the Ottoman empire, encouraged this time by England and opposed by Bismarck and the French (1873-4). The political crisis in Turkey came to a head in 1876 with the deposition of Sultan Abdul Aziz (30 May 1876) and the return to the Muslim caliphate under the suspicious rule of Abdul Hamid, whose long reign (1876-1909) prepared the downfall of the Ottoman empire.

It was during this Turkish constitutional crisis that the agitation in the Balkans reached its height, with war in Serbia (July 1876), the Bulgarian massacres (9 August 1876) and the Russo-Turkish war which broke out in April 1877. The Congress of Berlin (June 1878) in effect set the seal on the long-term policy of dividing the defeated empire into zones of influence, as a preliminary to eventual dismemberment. Austria-Hungary entered into immediate occupation of Bosnia and Herzegovina (July 1878); France secured recognition of the rights she had acquired in Syria and Palestine and of the *status quo* in respect of the Holy Places; while England, at an opportune moment, was encouraged by Bismarck to occupy Egypt. This new turn of the wheel, which gave a fresh impetus to European expansion, heralded the break-up of the old order throughout the Middle East

For a start, as a result of various manoeuvres, the chief protagonists of reform in the empire were removed from the scene: Midhat Pasha, the father of the Ottoman constitution; his successor, the Tunisian Klaireddin; and lastly Ismail, the khedive of Egypt. Paradoxically, this crisis of authority was the prelude to a resurgence of pan-Islamism, but this outburst of national and religious feeling in a new form did nothing to stop the empire's progressive loss of independent control of its internal affairs: in 1879 Egypt had to accept mixed tribunals for cases involving foreigners and on 20

December 1881 the Ottoman Porte acknowledged through the issue of the Moharram decree that it was no longer financially independent. And there were threats at the same time to the integrity of the empire from local insurrections. In 1880-1 there was talk of plans by Midhat Pasha to carve out for himself a principality in Syria under the protectorate of England. Palestine became attractive as a place for settlement to German Protestants from Württemberg and still more so to Jewish organisations in Central Europe and Russia. An official petition requesting the establishment of a 'Jewish state in Palestine' had been presented to the Congress of Berlin (16 June 1878), thus antedating by several years Theodor Herzl's foundation of the Zionist movement. The anti-Semitic outrages in Germany, Austria and Russia caused influential Jewish financiers such as Hirsch, Oléphant and Rothschild and the increasingly numerous and active Jewish associations to purchase land in Galilee and Judea and as far as the Syrian Golan Heights on which to settle agricultural 'colonies' (1880-2), even while Léon Pinsker was publishing in 1882 his manifesto *L'auto-émancipation,* which proclaimed the need for the foundation of a Jewish national home.

France's occupation of Tunisia (May-June 1881) started up a great wave of unrest throughout the Muslim east. At this point the sultan turned for aid to Bismarck's Germany and secured the despatch of a military mission (2 November 1880), prelude to the assertion of a German influence that seemed destined to prolong the life of the Ottoman empire. The failure shortly afterwards of Egypt's effort at national revival put an end for several decades to all hopes of independence in the Ottoman Near East. The way was now clear for the massive and uncontrolled penetration of the Near East by the economic, cultural, social and religious forces of the West.

It is not possible to describe here the many practical forms of tutelage to which the sultan's government had to submit. All that needs to be noted is the growing influence of Germany, a new contender in the area by comparison with France's long-established rights. German ambitions were made manifest during the second Middle Eastern tour of Kaiser Wilhelm II, in course of which he visited Constantinople, Jerusalem and Damascus (October – November 1898).

The twentieth century opened with the European nations still set on a course of universal and unlimited expansion. There were new objects of contention, Kuwait, the Yemen, the oilfields of Northern Syria and Mesopotamia, the linking of the Baghdad railway with the Persian network; and just when Germany believed that the pan-Slav thrust in the Balkans and Asia Minor had been arrested, the Moroccan crisis (1904-7) broke out to demonstrate the acuteness of European rivalry in the Muslim sector of the Mediterranean. Sultan Abdul Hamid allowed all these competing initiatives free rein, endeavouring to reap from them the greatest short-term benefit.

But this attitude, which meant that the arbitrariness of the sultan's internal rule was combined with a humiliating abjectness in international relations, at last made it possible for the Young Turks, after decades of marking time, to bring off their revolution (July 1910). But the institutions of the Ottoman empire were so far gone in decay that the new ministry found they had no choice but to endorse Bulgaria's unilateral declaration of independence and Austria-Hungary's final annexation of Bosnia and Herzegovina.

Already faced, because of the ill-will of the Great Powers towards the regime, with insuperable financial difficulties, the New Turkey also had to face over the next few years an uninterrupted sequence of revolts and wars at all the most sensitive points of the vast empire. The revolt in the Yemen (November 1910) had its counterpart in the revolt in Albania (May 1911). The war between Italy and Turkey over the possession of Tripolitania (September 1911) brought up once again the question of the Dardanelles, and the enmity between Germany and Russia made it possible for Italy to satisfy her ambitions in the Mediterranean. Scarcely had peace been concluded between Italy and Turkey than the Balkan War (October – December 1912) broke out to demonstrate beyond any shadow of doubt the military weaknesses, despite the re-structuring carried out by German experts, of the Ottoman empire.

So a round of secret negotiations began with a view to the partitioning of the 'sick man' or the ratification of the various zones of political, economic and cultural influence. By July 1913 a new map of the Ottoman empire had been drawn up (at the Kiel conversations). And in the spring of 1914 France, England and Germany, the powers directly interested in the Arab sector of the Near East, proceeded with unwonted haste to settle, at the expense of some substantial compromises, all outstanding questions regarding the fate of the Ottoman empire. But the chain reaction of political and military alliances set irreversibly in motion by the assassination at Sarajevo had the effect ultimately of dragging Turkey down with the collapse of the central powers. For Turkey this marked the end of a centuries' long domination of the Balkans on the one side and of the Arab world on the other, and for those regions the end of a particular cultural and religious way of life.

The Eastern Churches had as the immediate background to their lives the situations we have just described in broad outline: in the Near East a slow but deadly process of human and political degradation, in the Balkans a rising tide of nationalism. The destinies of the Churches in communion with Rome (Uniate) depended first and foremost on higher Vatican policy, which in turn depended for backing or inspiration on the diplomacy of the Catholic powers, France in particular. The situation was otherwise with Orthodoxy, which easily had the preponderance, for Orthodoxy revolved round two differently constituted poles: the ecumenical patriarchate of Constantinople, centred on the Phanar and animated by a newlyborn and ambitious hellenism; and the Holy Synod of the Imperial Russian Church which, down to the First World War continued to increase its moral pressure, notwithstanding the Tsars' failure to secure an official protectorate over the Orthodox subjects of the Ottoman empire.

The sultans had for centuries accorded the Greek hierarchy a preponderance, amounting at times to a monopoly, among the various nations professing Christianity within the Ottoman empire, whose incorporation into the empire's own political and religious system of ecclesiastical centralisation had been effected in a way that favoured the Phanar. The nineteenth century saw the growth, along with aspirations to political autonomy, of the desire for autocephalous national Churches, and this phenomenon, typical of contemporary Orthodoxy, manifested itself at a time when the Catholic Church was engaged in the contrary process of reinforcing the monarchical and centralising aspects of its regime. While acknowledging the ecumenical patriarchate in its incontestable historical role of premier see and of sister and in some cases mother Church, although not that its jurisdiction was pre-eminent over the rest, the religious and political leaders of the new nations claimed the right to an autonomous juridical status and to a nationally constituted Church, based on a local clergy and having its own particular institutions. This claim for autocephalous Churches was not indicative of any schismatic or divisive intention; the autocephalous Church was regarded merely as setting the religious seal on political independence and its natural culmination. Without wishing to cut themselves off from universal Orthodoxy or to sever their special, though purely moral, ties with the ecumenical patriarchate, the local Churches were determined to integrate themselves on the temporal, social and political plane with their 'native environment'. The existence and extension of self-governing Churches certainly did not conflict with the historical status of Byzantine Orthodoxy or with the fundamentals of the patriarchal regime, for in their church government all the autocephalous Churches adhered to the uniformity of discipline that was common to the Orthodox tradition. Nevertheless, the setting up of new autocephalies in the States issuing from the break-up of the Ottoman empire did not proceed without serious tension and conflicts, and even brief periods of severed communion between the Phanar and the new national Churches, due to the intervention of factors of a political order.

The first to set the example of 'emancipation' from the ecumenical patriarchate was the Church of Greece. Taking the initiative, the newly constituted kingdom proclaimed its religious independence in 1833 by constitutional decree. Without withdrawing from communion, the patriarch of Constantinople simply ignored this unilateral act. In 1850 the Greek government took steps to effect a reconciliation, by appealing to the ecumenical patriarch and his synod to approve the autocephaly and recognise the Church of Greece as a 'sister-Church', while at the same time, out of deference to the primacy of Constantinople, the Hellenic hierarchy applied to the Phanar for canonical recognition of the patriarchates of Alexandria, Antioch and Jerusalem. A synodal *Tomos* of the following 29 June admitted the Church of Greece to the bosom of Orthodoxy, one and multiform, as a new autocephaly, whereupon the Church of the Kingdom of Greece provided itself, on 9 July 1852, with a proper constitution. Possession of this canonical framework ensured that in future the Church would dispose of her local religious destinies in a way that conformed with the disciplinary tradition common to all Orthodoxy, and one of the first acts of the Hellenic hierarchy was to commission Professor Ralli and Professor Potli to prepare a full edition of the ecclesiastical canons and their most authoritative commentaries. The resulting volumes, published between 1852 and 1859, remain of fundamental importance in the systematic study of Byzantine legislation in the realm of canon law.

The trend towards the internal reconstruction of Greek Orthodoxy affected in the first instance the ecumenical patriarchate itself. In response to the liberal provisions of the Hatti-Humayyoun and at the express suggestion of the Ottoman cabinet (April 1857), the Phanar appointed in August 1858 a 'provisional national council' of the patriarchate, which was responsible for various measures for the regulation of the synodal regime and of the mixed commissions.

The crisis in the Bulgarian Church broke out in 1859 and dragged on for many years, in part because of the conflicting political and religious influences at work. Although to begin with, the Lazarists and early Assumptionists may have succeeded in setting up a somewhat contrived union with Rome, Orthodox Russia was all the while keeping a check on the Slavophil leanings of this neighbouring people. For the Phanar, however, this two-pronged movement spelled nothing but harm for the predominance of its influence in the Balkans.

Underlying the crisis was the desire of numerous Bulgars to resist the systematic policy of hellenisation pursued by the Orthodox hierarchy of Constantinople. One party judged that the best way of securing emancipation from the Phanar was to lean to the side of Rome, provided the continuance of Bulgar religious customs and in particular of the Slavonic liturgy could be guaranteed. Pius IX signified his agreement and in April 1861 the pope performed in person − a sensational and unheard-of event at the time − the consecration in the Sistine chapel of J. Sokolski, the leader of the unionist movement, who had been brought in somewhat provocative manner to Rome by Eugiene Boré. But only a month or so later, on 18 June, the newly consecrated bishop left with a Russian agent for Odessa, bound for an unknown destination. In a matter of months the ten-thousand-and-more-strong company of would-be Catholics melted away as though by magic and the great unionist movement, of which there had been so many hopes, was soon reduced to a few isolated and ineffectual groups.

But this did not mean an end to the movement for religious emancipation from the Phanar, which on the contrary continued to gain ground. Already in April 1860 feelings had reached such a pitch that the Orthodox clergy had erased the name of the ecumenical patriarch from the liturgical dyptichs, and soon afterwards the Greek hierarchy was expelled from the episcopal sees. The Ottoman government agreed on 12 March 1870 to the erection of a 'national Church' under the auspices of a Bulgar exarch supported by a new native hierarchy. The next step was the appointment of the first titular of the autocephalous Church, chosen by the national assembly on 23 February 1872. In reply, the ecumenical patriarch excommunicated the national hierarchy and so the 'Bulgar schism' was born, to divide opinion throughout the Orthodox world for many years to come.[1]

By contrast, the Serbian Church, declared autocephalous by a synodal *Tomos* of the patriarch of Constantinople of 20 October to 1 November 1879, achieved its independence through canonical forms and as the outcome of properly conducted negotiations, once the Congress of Berlin had made Serbia politically autonomous in 1878. The territory of the young Church was to enlarge little by little as more and more provinces became attached to the Serbian kingdom.[2]

The Rumanian Church was recognised canonically as autocephalous by the ecumenical patriarchate only in 1885, although its independence went back in practice to a unilateral declaration by Prince Cuza in January 1865. But the discord on this score between the Phanar and its sister Church did not develop into a legal battle, because at the time the young kingdom was still without natural boundaries and had yet to be recognised by the Great Powers. Once the Congress of Berlin had officially acknowledged the existence of the new kingdom, the national Church could lay claim to autocephaly, and the negotiations between King Carol and Patriarch Joachim resulted in a satisfactory arrangement. It was to be a long time,

1. The successive crises in the Balkan and Danubian regions and the instability of regimes and frontiers delayed the reconciliation of the 'sister-Churches' until the end of the Second World War. On 25 February 1945, with the raising of the ban of excommunication, the autocephalous Church of Bulgaria was officially restored to the bosom of Orthodoxy. When the metropolitan of Sofia subsequently ranked himself among the patriarchs (10 May 1953), this unilateral act of ecclesiastical promotion was not in practice contested.
2. The existing autocephalous Church of Yugoslavia is heir historically to the former autocephalous Church of Serbia, increased in size by the confederation of the six provinces which make up the present republic. The patriarchal title conferred on its head commemorates the former national primacy of Ipek (Petch).

however, before the primate of Bucharest was raised to the dignity of patriarch. The act was finally approved by the Rumanian Holy Synod, passed by the royal parliament, and recognised in accordance with the canons by the ecumenical patriarch in 1925.

In the old patriarchates of the Near East emancipation took a different form, on account of the variety of ethnic and political factors involved.

From the middle of the nineteenth century the patriarchate of Alexandria was an important centre in the diffusion of Greek culture and Greek commercial expertise, thanks to the presence of a particularly enterprising community of expatriates, whose influence extended from Egypt to the Sudan and into the heart of Equatorial Africa. By comparison with the generally conservative tenor of Mediterranean Orthodoxy, the Greek titulars of this see were normally conspicuous for their actively progressive tendencies. Patriarch Photius (1899-1925) was by character the typical open-minded and able prelate, with a strong bent for organisation and efficiency. Working in an environment both cosmopolitan and heavily impregnated with Western culture, he made strategic dispositions of men and resources and founded cultural and benevolent institutions capable of assimilating the densely clustered Arab minorities and of preserving the faithful from 'latinising contamination'.

In Jerusalem, the question of the Holy Places and its manifold political and religious implications gave hellenism and the monopolistic Confraternity of the Holy Sepulchre serious motives for keeping a firm hold on the patriarchate and the other episcopal sees. But with the permanent installation in 1858 of a Russian Orthodox mission intended to stiffen the resistance of the Orthodox Arab communities to Latin and Protestant proselytising, hellenism had to fight doggedly to maintain its influence in face of Slavophil competition. However, as far as the local Orthodox Arab communities were concerned the new situation was not without its advantages, both cultural and religious. After all, the Imperial Orthodox Society for Palestine, founded in 1882 and sponsored by the cream of St Petersburg society, proved its worth by encouraging a sustained growth of cultural and benevolent institutions, some of which even spread to the domain of the patriarchate of Antioch in Syria and into the Lebanon. The next step was for the native Arab element to formulate claims for a fair share in the church government, the episcopate included, and the long patriarchate of Damianos (1908-31) was to be passed in open conflict with the supporters of Arab religious emancipation. But until well on into the twentieth century the autocephaly so fiercely desired was rendered hypothetical by the fluctuating and tragic conditions in which Palestine was forced to work out its political and religious destiny.

In the patriarchate of Antioch, by contrast, the predominantly Arab hierarchy did not wait for political independence before asserting its religious emancipation. On 31 January 1898 the mixed synod elected as patriarch the metropolitan of Laodicea, Meletios. After that, the elimination of the Greek minority from the hierarchy proceeded without a hitch. The patriarchate was once again truly autocephalous, as it had normally been in the centuries before the schism which had divided the Melkite Church and led to the setting up of the united patriarchate in 1724.

The so-called 'philetist' or nationalist movement, culminating in national autocephalies, could have undermined the unitary foundations of Orthodoxy, but the crisis inherent in this centrifugal tendency did not end by splitting Orthodoxy apart. No mass migrations to other churches or confessions ensued. The crisis remained, throughout, a matter of internal fermentation, a decanting into new bottles, which enabled Orthodoxy, one and multiform, to resume its traditional aspect and at the end of the day to surmount the severe ordeal of a nationalist challenge that could have been fatal.

2. PIUS IX AND HIS POLICY OF ASSIMILATION (1847-78)

The opening moves of Pius XI's pontificate included a number of sensational decisions regarding relations with the Christian East. In his encyclical *In suprema Petri* of 6 January 1848 he announced his intention of resuming the dialogue with Orthodoxy and of setting out again on the quest for reunion which had been left in abeyance since the time of Benedict XIV. The restoration of the Latin patriarchate of Jerusalem, with its echoes of the crusading experiment in the Holy City, manifested a spirit of expansion impelling Roman Catholicism to the heart of the Christian East. Lastly, though it was scarely realistic, his plan for a pontifical diplomatic and consular representation in the Ottoman empire was evidence of a desire to become independent of the French religious protectorate.

These initial and not altogether opportune measures were items from a programme which as yet lacked cohesion; but they were the prelude to a campaign of centralisation and Latinisation which was about to unfold in progressive stages and which would culminate at the Vatican council. It is of course always difficult to ascertain the personal opinions of a pope and to distinguish them from the official documents and acts of the pontificate. Significant testimony to the personal thinking of Pius IX is provided by a despatch dated 20 June 1854 and written therefore at the height of the Eastern crisis, from the French ambassador, de Rayneval, reporting a private audience with the pope. While not cherishing illusory hopes, the Holy Father thought the differences separating the Latin from the Greek Church were 'so small that nothing that had been done by either side since the agreement reached at the Council of Florence had invalidated the decisions of that Council'. The cause of the schism, in his opinion, lay in the differences of custom and of ethnic and national traditions, matters of secondary importance in comparison with dogma. He therefore believed that, with greater mutual understanding, more weight would come to be attached to the spirit of unity than to particular traditions.

This personal view seems nowhere near as radical as the measures soon to be taken by the Congregation for the Propagation of the Faith, at that date the body responsible for relations with Eastern Christendom. But we have to bear in mind that the diplomatic and personal factors influencing the eastern policy of the papacy were many and various. For the moment it will be enough to mention two societies which, during the middle years of the century, the period most crucial in the development of the eastern crisis, to a large extent had the ear of the authorities at Rome. One of them, the Société orientale pour l'union de tous les chrétiens d'Orient, had been founded during the first months of Pius IX's pontificate. Personages connected with the society, its promoter the Abbé Terlechki and Russian noblewomen such as Princess Zenaida Grigorievna Volkonskoja and Madame Swetchine, had been behind the encyclical *In suprema Petri;* and Cardinal Franzoni, Prefect of Propaganda, had presided at the society's first annual general meeting, held on 1 July 1847. The society entertained high ambitions of promoting the spread of Uniatism in the Slav world and in the Near East. The other society was the Société chrétienne orientale, founded on 12 October 1853 and like the other, Roman-based. It created more stir at the time because of the personality of its founder, J.G. Pitzipios, an adventurer converted to Roman Catholicism from Greek Orthodoxy. For a short time he had the willing ear of the pope and his book, or rather manifesto, *L'Église orientale* was published in 1855 under the pope's patronage and with Propaganda defraying the costs. Although its author was shortly to be led by the extravagances of his nature and by his changes of political and religious front to serve under new masters, the book was long to remain in certain unionist circles an essential source of information and ideas.

In 1862 the pope decided to separate the affairs of the Eastern Churches from those of missions to the heathen or to Protestant heretics. The apostolic constitution *Romani Pontifices* of 6 January set up a cardinalatial commission, still within the framework of the Congregation for the Propagation of the Faith, specifically to deal with 'matters pertaining to the Eastern Rite' *(Pro negotiis ritus orientalis).* This partial reconstruction of the Congregation preceded by several days the announcement of the re-establishment of diplomatic relations with Orthodox Russia (14 January), but the pope only made his decision public on 8 April, in the encyclical *Amantissimus humani generis Redemptor.* In giving notice of this favour extended to the Eastern hierarchy, Pius IX took opportunity to define the unity of the Church in a rigid sense and to recall the Roman Church's well-intentioned measures to promote the development of Eastern Catholicism. And he did not disguise his astonishment, indeed his bitter disappointment, that certain 'thoughtless and calumnious persons' should have dared to assert that the popes were doing all in their power to latinise the Eastern Christians. Nevertheless, on 30 April, this cardinalatial commission started its work by settling the right of reception of the sacraments of the Eastern Catholics in Latin churches. The principle of the freedom of worshippers was limited only by the right of priority accorded to Eastern rites.

The increasing frequency of interventions by Propaganda in the internal affairs of the Uniate communities occurred at the very time when the latter were beginning to enjoy the benefits of the Ottoman government's liberal reforms. Occasions such as patriarchal elections, the holding of national synods for legislative or disciplinary purposes, and the introduction of structural reforms, were exploited by Rome to impose progressively tighter control and to carry out a policy of alignment which consisted in applying the broad principles of the Tridentine counter-Reformation in order to bring Uniate institutions nearer to the Latin base. The men responsible both for the promotion and for the implementation of this progressive and deliberate policy of assimilation were the Cardinal Prefects Franzoni and Barnabò, along with the apostolic delegates in the East and the Latin patriarch of Jerusalem, Mgr Valerga.

The national Melkite council which was held at Jerusalem in 1849 gave rise to a dispute of some gravity. The causes were twofold: the suspicions entertained of Patriarch Maximos III Mazloum, who was considered to be a 'secret Photian', and certain sacramental practices that were judged contrary to the prescriptions of Trent. The report on the canonical aspects, drawn up in a scarcely irenical or impartial spirit by C. Van Everbroeck, S.J. and Patriarch Valerga, strove hard in the absence of any solid evidence to unmask the presence of an unsubstantial but insidious Gallicanism. The Melkite patriarch, depicted in nearly all the official reports sent in by the French consuls and the agents of Propaganda as filled with an inveterate desire for schism or rebellion, was indomitable in his resistance, which had the effect of hardening the attitude of the Roman authorities to all other Uniate Churches.

Another crisis blew up to reinforce Rome's distrust of Eastern Catholics: this was in the Armenian Church where the patriarch, Hassoun, who was Pius IX's trusted agent, was for years in conflict with the majority of his flock and indeed of his episcopate. Internal quarrels regarding episcopal elections and the role of the laity obliged the pope to intervene as early as 1849-50, and he regarded the Armenian crisis as a more serious threat to the Church's future than the question of the Holy Places.

The holding of national councils gave apostolic delegates the opportunity to verify the fidelity of the Eastern tradition and to measure it against the Tridentine counter-reform, whose social and political context and doctrinal and disciplinary objectives corresponded not at all to the circumstances, historical and otherwise, of Eastern Christendom. Benoît Planchet, S.J., appointed on 18 January 1851 apostolic delegate for Mesopotamia, was to act as the main agent in forcing the old Jacobites and Nestorians united to Rome to latinise their institutions (at the synods of Charfeh, December 1853 – January 1854, and of Rabbah-Hormizd, June 1853). The apostolic delegate for Syria and the Lebanon was Mgr Brunoni, a native of the Levant. He tried to persuade the Maronites to invite Latin missionaries to be present at their synod at B'kerkeh (11-13 April), and although in face of the polite but firm refusal of Patriarch Mass'ad the project had to be abandoned, the Maronite bishops still found themselves obliged to endorse the strongly latinising prescriptions of the synod of Mount Lebanon of 1736, which had become a dead letter. As to the Melkites, Propaganda bided its time until the death of Patriarch Mazloum (1855) and then persuaded his successor, Clement Bahouth, to convene a new synod. This time the apostolic delegate presided and its decrees, carrying this guarantee of authenticity, were approved without difficulty.

The subsequent moulding of church life and institutions proceeded to the accompaniment of crises grave enough to threaten the future of Catholicism among the Melkites, Armenians and Chaldeans. In our brief account of them we shall touch on some of the essential problems of Uniatism.

The dispute with the Melkites over the adoption of the Gregorian calendar made an issue of one of the characteristic features of Byzantine Uniatism. In the past the Uniate Melkite hierarchy had consistently rejected the frequently proffered advice of the Propaganda authorities to adopt the Western calendar, being anxious to retain in this matter of discipline a filial bond with Orthodoxy. At a pre-synodal meeting held before his elevation (on 1 April 1856) to the patriarchate, Clement Bahouth had promised to consider the question of the calendar only with the consent of the body of bishops. No sooner was he elected than he hastened to follow the advice of Mgr Brunoni, the apostolic delegate, and without prior consultation or warning imposed the Gregorian reckoning. The result was an immediate wave of protest, uniting a considerable part of the episcopate and the faithful. Misplaced interference on the spot by the French consuls and the support he counted on receiving from Constantinople had in any case led the patriarch to underestimate the strength and profundity of Melkite national feeling. The opposition party, which formed the majority of the nation, declared its desire to remain Catholic, while totally rejecting 'westernisation'. In accordance with this intention, they gave themselves the name 'Eastern Melkites'.

Unnerved by the extent and solidarity of the reaction, on 4 August 1858 the patriarch suddenly resigned; but Pius IX refused to confirm this abdication, and as a counter move the opposition bishops applied to the Ottoman government for the appointment of a new civil head of the Melkite 'nation'. In the meantime, urgent representations were made to Napoleon III to act in person to restore order, while Pius IX continued to take the part of the unfortunate patriarch against his principal adversary, the metropolitan of Beirut, Mgr Riachi.[3]

Inauspicious diplomatic moves served to heighten the tension and to harden the opposition. Two of the priests most actively engaged, followed by many families in Syria, the Lebanon and Egypt, entered into official negotiations with the ecumenical patriarchate and on 6 December 1860 made their profession of Orthodox faith at Constantinople. One of the priests was consecrated bishop and placed in charge of the new 'Eastern Melkite' Church, which received legal recognition from the Ottoman government as under Orthodox patronage. Alarmed at the prospect that the movement might spread to embrace all who refused to accept the Western calendar, in 1864 Patriarch Bahouth once again submitted his resignation. His successor, Gregory Youssef, was to leave the bishops free to choose between the two calendars. This would enable him to re-establish order in diversity and to attract one of the dissident parties back to his jurisdiction. The calendar schism did not in the end lead to the formation of a new schismatic Eastern community in communion with Rome but to the return of the really intransigent to the bosom of Greek Orthodoxy.

The crisis in the Armenian Church, of which there had been rumblings since the early years of Pius IX's pontificate, rebounded after fifteen years, centred as before on the personality of Patriarch Hassoun and the principles he represented. Antoun Hassoun occupied down to 1866 the see of Constantinople, having in addition the title of primate archbishop responsible for the civil interests of Catholic Armenians. But out of a desire to combine in his own person all spiritual and temporal jurisdiction over the Armenians in communion with Rome, he also aspired to the title of patriarch of Cilicia, an office which had its seat at the Bzommar monastery in the Lebanon. The death of the incumbent gave him his excuse. His ambitions, since they aimed at a united jurisdiction, naturally had the support of Propaganda and of the head of the apostolic delegation in Syria, Patriarch Valerga.

When the electoral synod met in the Lebanon on 4 September 1866, under the presidency of Valerga, it instituted Hassoun, under the name Peter

3. 'Si opus esset, civilis potestatis seu brachii saecularis auxilium implorares quod tibi minime defuturum esse confidebamus', Pius IX wrote to the patriarch on 28 November 1859.

IX, patriarch of Cilicia. At the same time the synod abolished the title and metropolitan see of Constantinople, attaching it to the Cilician see but transferring the seat of the unified patriarchate to the Ottoman capital. The assent of the bishops, whose hand was being forced, was hard to obtain, and they left to the papal delegate the task of drawing up the 'official' report of the synod's work.

The publication the following year, during the ceremonies to mark the anniversary of the martyrdom of SS Peter and Paul, of the bull *Reversurus* (12 July 1867) showed plainly what was really at stake and revealed the full gravity of the crisis. The bull concerned specifically the Armenians, but it was intended it should be applied, in the longer or shorter term, to all the other Uniate communities in order to secure closer control from the centre.[4] The tone of the document was eloquent of the tense atmosphere in which the situation was developing. Pius IX spoke bitterly of the prevalence of the schismatic spirit in the life of the Eastern Church, pointing out that in the past schism had invariably been followed by the spread of ignorance, the sclerosis of institutions, the decay of morals and the relaxation of discipline. It was to avert the agony of Churches born in schism that the papacy was devoting so much anxious care to the regeneration of eastern Catholicism The regulation of patriarchal and episcopal elections had to be seen as part of this reforming process. In future the patriarch was to be elected by the synod of bishops alone, with no participation by the lower clergy or the laity. The election of bishops was also to be a matter reserved exclusively to the synod of bishops, under the presidency of the patriarch; or in the last resort, a matter for the pope, who would choose the most deserving candidate from a list of three. Any direct or indirect participation by ordinary laymen or notables was expressly forbidden. Lastly, the pope signified his intention of extending these rulings in the near future to the other Eastern patriarchates, an intention he had communicated to the Maronite and Melkite patriarchs, Paul Mass'ad and Gregory Youssef, during their present sojourn in Rome.

The two patriarchs in question made plain their strong objections to the rulings and, so far as their communities were concerned, the matter was deferred to a more opportune moment. Hassoun, however, accepted the pope's rulings in their entirety. This was met almost immediately by a show of national resistance, headed by a section of the Armenian episcopate and by religious of the Mechitarist and Antonian Orders and joined by the great mass of notables and faithful. While the Vatican council was sitting, the opposition developed on a scale and gravity which apparently failed to make

4. It is to be noted that in the collections of papal documents the text is given in full or in part, depending on whether it applies to the Armenians or to the oriental patriarchates as a whole.

any impression on the Roman authorities, despite the repeated warnings of French diplomats and of the Ottoman government. Before long the party of opposition had hardened into an outright schism taking its orders from Mgr Kupelian, whose community was recognised for several years by the Ottoman government (1870-9). Hassoun, promoted to the cardinalate, eventually made way for a patriarchal administrator, Mgr Azarian, who in 1879 succeeded him in the patriarchate. It was left to Leo XIII to put an end to the schism, which gradually subsided once it was deprived of the support of the Ottoman government.

The crisis in the Chaldean patriarchate, linked with the name of J. Audo, seems at first sight to concern nothing more serious than a petty quarrel regarding the patriarch's personal jurisdiction over the ecclesiastical territory of Malabar. Elected patriarch in 1847, Audo had the reputation of being at once very loyal to the tradition of his Church and very devoted to the cause of Catholicism: and Valerga, at that time attached to the Kurdistan mission, had in 1843 given him a favourable testimonial to Propaganda as the most obvious candidate for the patriarchate.

At the synod of Rabban Hormuzd in 1853 the patriarch fell in readily with the latinising reforms advocated by Mgr Planchet, refusing only to relinquish the right to direct his patriarchal seminary to the Dominicans of Mosul. In 1856 he was approached by priests and laymen belonging to the Syro-Malabar Christians, who since 1599 had been under the jurisdiction of Latin vicars apostolic, with a request for a bishop of their own rite. In all good faith he notified Propaganda of this request and proposed the appointment of four Visitors, two to be nominated by the pope and two by himself: for he had certainly not forgotten that Julius III, at the time the union of the Nestorians with Rome was first mooted in 1555, had recognised and confirmed the jurisdiction of Patriarch Sulaqua over Malabar. In their reply however, the authorities of Propaganda rejected this conciliatory proposal and denied that the patriarch possessed any spiritual authority over the Syro-Malabar Christians. To dissension over the canonical issue was soon added acute personal antagonism between the patriarch and the new apostolic delegate, the French Dominican Mgr Amanton. Sure of his rights and undeterred by the disciplinary measures, arbitrary to say the least, applied by the apostolic delegate, Audo resorted to the tactic of the *fait accompli*. Matters came to a head for the first time with his appointment of a patriarchal vicar for Malabar (23 September 1860), Thomas Rokos. The immediate crisis was solved by Rome's withdrawal of the apostolic delegate and the recall of the patriarchal vicar, but this was no more than a truce.

Despite diplomatic representations and warnings from Propaganda, the patriarch acceded once again to requests from Malabar and on 5 June 1864 consecrated as bishop Elias Mellous who, in the years that followed, devoted much skill and pertinacity to cementing the attachment of Malabaŕ to the Chaldean patriarchate. The crisis was to flare up again and again, in particular on the occasion of the centennial celebrations of the martyrdom of SS Peter and Paul (July 1867), during the Vatican council (end of January 1870) and in a last great outburst between 1874 and 1877. The direct and repeated clashes between Pius IX and Patriarch Audo were happenings quite without precedent in the annals of contemporary Catholicism, even where Eastern Catholics were concerned. We cannot enter into the details of this crisis, which registered with some accuracy the generally troubled context of the age. But it is important to mention that Audo brought courage and a clear head to the defence of his attitude and that he refuted the unfounded complaints circulating of his conduct by summarising the facts of the case in a letter addressed on 20 February 1875 to the Prefect of Propaganda. This letter was unfortunately overlooked by the historians of the affair, although it had already appeared in print in a semi-official collection. But coming as it did at the close of a pontificate so centralising, so filled with bitterness, so authoritarian, the defence entered by the patriarch was in the wrong key. Audo was suspended from his office to the accompaniment, throughout the Catholic East, of troubled speculation about the outcome of this trial of strength: the Chaldean crisis was taking over from the Armenian. Happily, a compromise solution carried the day. As well as dealing tactfully with the personalities involved, it reconciled in honourable fashion the various principles at stake and in the long run was to prove quite effective.

The three major crises in Eastern Catholicism just surveyed illustrate in their true dimensions − ecclesiastical, psychological and even social − the problems of adapting the Uniatism of the day to the traditional Latin framework. These were all problems arising from concrete situations. About to be aired in the Vatican council, both by the commissions of 'experts' charged with the preparatory work and in the actual debates, were questions of principle regarding the existence of Roman Uniate Churches in the East, their position in respect of papal authority and their relations with officials or agents of the Latin Church.

The Congregation for the Propagation of the Faith had naturally consulted beforehand the leaders of the Catholic hierarchies in the East, without however thinking it appropriate to invite them or their delegates to be present at the deliberations of the commissions. And the masterful part played in the commissions by the ultra-latinising Mgr Valerga was only inadequately counterbalanced by the wisdom and erudition of the two 'archivists' of Propaganda, Serafino Cretoni and Francesco Rossi. Starting on 21 September 1867, the deliberations continued until 9 May 1870. During that time many delicate questions were discussed: the powers of patriarchs, the comparative merits of uniformity and dualism in legislation and discipline, the increasing activity of the missionaries and the latinisation of attitudes and institutions, the future institutionally speaking of the privileged centre for latinising operations conducted by Patriarch Valerga at Jerusalem, and lastly the reform of Eastern monachism. Certain secret plans for the latinisation and assimilation of Eastern Uniatism seemed so sweeping that there was discussion, during the session of 17 September 1869, of ways to lull the fears of the hierarchies concerned and to prevent their possible coalition. [5]

In August 1868, during the time these deliberations concerning the status and destiny of Eastern Uniatism were in progress at Rome, the Rumanian Catholics met at Blaj in legislative synod. Visibly concerned, with the instances of the Melkite and Chaldean patriarchs before their eyes, at the moment in favour of assimilation that was asserting itself in governing circles at Rome, the members of the synod were determined to affirm the constitutional bases of their 'Graeco-Catholic' Church. A draft consisting of ten articles was passed by the synod, but this unequivocal statement of the principles of Eastern Catholicism touched off an immediate reaction and was denounced by the nunciature and by the imperial authorities in Vienna as tainted with schism. The first point made by the declaration was the need to 'restore the constitutional autonomy of the Rumanian Church of Transylvania', with the object of differentiating it from the Latin Church that was dominant in the Austro-Hungarian empire, for the union was 'of a dogmatic order and summed up in the four points established at Florence'. On this same view, 'the dependence of the Rumanian hierarchy on the Holy See' was 'solely of the nature envisaged at Florence'. All intermediaries were therefore excluded: 'No one, whether clerical or lay, can appeal from a decision of the united Rumanian Church to the Latin hierarchy of the country'. These fundamental principles having been stated, the document went on to recognise the right of laymen to join with clerics in choosing candidates for the episcopate. As to the administration of church property and of religious institutes, the laity were to have an active voice in all decisions proceeding from mixed councils, composed of clergy and laity in equal numbers, although decisions of a dogmatic order or relating solely to the hierarchy were of course excluded from their competence. With this division of authority firmly established, it was made the duty of the bishop to summon annually the diocesan synod, which in composition and functions was not exclusively clerical. [6]

5. The minutes of the commission charged to deal with the Eastern Churches are printed in Mansi, XLIX, cols 985-1162. For the session of 17 September 1869 see cols 1100-2
6. The Italian translation of the ten articles adopted at the synod of Blaj in 1868 will be found in Mansi, XLII, cols 802-5. The nuncio in Vienna extracted from the new metropolitan, Ioan Vancea, who had been educated in Rome, a promise to ignore the articles. A provincial council met at Blaj in May 1872 (*ibid.*, cols 463-710). Its decrees form a consis-

Here, then, was the synod of a developed European Church, part Slav and part Austrian, adopting a position which contradicted at every point the officially recommended policy of assimilation. The synod's stand represented beyond any shadow of doubt that Church's frank and forceful response to the policies of Propaganda and to the legislative deliberations of the preconciliar commission on the Eastern Churches.

The Eastern Catholic episcopate of the Austro-Hungarian and Ottoman empires was well represented at the Vatican council, but the diversities of liturgy and discipline, added to the more profound differences of clerical up-bringing and social background, militated against the formation of a common front in face of the large Latin majority of bishops from all parts of the world. No working parties of Eastern prelates were formed, still less was there any general or implicit agreement on a platform of minimal conditions that would ensure the survival of their specific sacramental and disciplinary tradition. Indeed, it was possible to hear Armenian, Syriac or Maronite bishops upholding Latinising disciplinary positions and incurring thereby the scorn of the authentic spokesmen for the Catholic East, upheld in their turn by the reforming wing of the Latin episcopate.

Over the question of the pope's primacy and infallibility there was the same noticeable diversity of opinion among the Eastern prelates. It was not that any of them rejected the belief as such, for it represented the essential dogmatic base of Uniatism; the disagreement was solely over the oppor-tuneness of its definition as a dogma. More of a surprise for the Latins was the plain hostility of some of the Eastern Catholics to the patriarchal positions and to the revaluation of the Eastern tradition. Nevertheless, properly accredited representatives of the principal Eastern Catholic Churches, each according to his own experience and theological insight, made a contribution of positive value for the destinies of Eastern Catholicism.

Although the main speeches of the Eastern prelates cannot be sum-marised here in detail, it would be wrong not to mention some of the most fundamental statements of their position.

The Chaldean patriarch, Audo, weighed in early, on 25 January 1870, with a speech stressing that the specific tradition of Eastern Christendom as regards organisation, in particular its synodal and patriarchal constitution,

---

tent whole but appear manifestly watered down by comparison with the decrees of 1868. Even so, they were still judged to deviate too widely from Roman norms, and it was not until 1881 that Propaganda approved the amended text having demanded, for example, the exci-sion of all references to the nomocanons and to Byzantine canonists. A second provincial council was held at Blaj in 1882 to complete the work of the first in regard to certain points the Holy See would have liked to see examined or which it considered had been inadequately dealt with in 1872 (cf. C. de Clercq, *Conciles des Orientaux catholiques*, II (Paris 1952), 655-66).

had to be preserved. He vigorously condemned the new programme of assimilation, declaring it to be contrary to repeated undertakings given by the popes since the time of the Council of Florence. In any case, the East had its own traditional instruments of reform. Its spiritual regeneration was a task for the Eastern episcopate, working from inside the 'national synods'. [7]

A speech two days later by the Rumanian bishop J. Papp-Szilagji, supplied scholarly arguments in support of the Chaldean patriarch's seemingly gratuitous statements. Expressly inviting the council to recognise the duality of discipline in the Church, he rejected all the reforms that had been imposed on the East, as it appeared in keeping with the spirit and practice of the Decretals of Gregory IX. [8]

Also on the agenda was the question of clerical celibacy, and in his speech of 8 February 1870[9] the Armenian Melchior Nazarin supplied the champions of celibacy with unexpected arguments in support. Having remarked with pride that his diocese of Mardin was served by an exclusively celibate clergy, he went on to list the disadvantages of married priests: they gave more attention to the affairs of their family than of their church, they adorned their wives rather than the altar, they cared more for their children than for their flock.

Two widely noticed and truly ecumenical speeches by Youssef, the Melkite patriarch, raised the discussion to its proper level. On 19 May, having declared his belief in the Petrine primacy, he reminded the Latin majority that they could neither set aside nor ignore Eastern Orthodoxy, recognised as apostolic and catholic by the Council of Florence, as indeed by the Council of Trent, which, out of respect for the 'Greeks' had refused to condemn the dissolubility of marriage on grounds of adultery. While proclaiming the primacy of Rome, the Council of Florence had confirmed with equal solemnity the rights and privileges of the apostolic patriarchs. The Fathers of the Vatican Council had likewise the duty to preserve, not to destroy, the patriarchal constitution. To go back on the work of the Council of Florence, which had set the seal on a *modus vivendi* applicable to the Church universal, would signify the intention to bar the Orthodox Church for ever from the path of unity. [10]

Pius IX lost no time in administering the patriarch a stern rebuke. Next, Mgr Valerga tried to pick holes in the Melkite case by accusing it of Gallicanism,[11] while other Eastern prelates, Hassoun of Armenia and Benni

7. Mansi, L., cols 513-16. See J. Hajjar, *Revue d'histoire ecclésiastique*, LXV (1970), 451-4.
8. Mansi, L, cols 543-6.
9. *Ibid.*, L, cols 683-4.
10. *Ibid.*, LII, cols 133-7.
11. *Ibid.*, LII, cols 353-64, 192-202 and 551-61.

of Syria, denounced Youssef's speech as a piece of demagoguery and tried to play down the patriarchal constitution. Not even the speeches of Strossmayer, impassioned and scintillating, and of Archbishop Purcell of Cincinnati, full of friendly feeling and good sense, could dissipate the unease of an assembly swollen with prejudice against 'schismatic Orthodoxy'.

The Melkite patriarch took the floor again on 14 June, [12] in the hope of widening the council's perspective and persuading the Fathers to take seriously their responsibilities towards the Christian East. For he came to defend not his own cause or that of any particular see but to plead, without false modesty and moved solely by a desire for the universal good, on behalf of an absent portion of the Church, while desiring most sincerely its union with the portion present at the council. Taking to task his opponents in the debate, he addressed to them a challenge that was indeed to remain prophetic: 'If in this assembly anyone was thinking to attack me personally for having assumed this charge (the defence of absent Orthodoxy), for myself I shall make no answer; but when the time comes, they will be judged by those that are absent'. And so he begged the assembly to avoid passing any measures which would undermine the constitutional status of the Eastern Church. His grave words were unfortunately to go unheeded. The Vatican Council thus lost the opportunity to raise itself to an ecumenical level.

The major question of the pope's primacy and infallibility had all but swept aside the question of the 'missionaries' and their latinising activities. Nothing much came out of the debate of the scheme on Apostolic Missions, although in course of it the Maronite archbishop of Beirut, Mgr Tobie 'Aoun, who was well placed to judge of the errors, the presumptions and the shortcomings of Latin congregations operating abroad, delivered a forceful speech on the whole phenomenon of latinisation. [13]

The vote on the dogmatic constitution *Pastor aeternus*, taken on 18 July 1870, had found the Eastern hierarchy very hesitant. Three patriarchs, the Melkite, the Syriac and the Chaldean, signified their opinion by leaving Rome, followed by several of their suffragans. They returned to the East convinced that the process of latinisation and assimilation was about to be extended and reinforced. As far as the Eastern Church was concerned, the Vatican Council suspended its work at a point of open failure. The resulting mistrust, born of a deep sense of frustration and humiliation combined with powerlessness in face of Latin competition, was now slow to come to the surface: in the Armenian schism, in the Chaldean crisis, in the ill-concealed disaffection of the Syrian patriarch as much as in the barely disguised bitterness of the Melkite patriarch, Gregory Youssef. In short, at the death

12. *Ibid.*, LII, cols 671-6.
13. *Ibid.* LIII, cols 142-93.

of Pius IX, not only did the principal problems remain unsolved, but Eastern Catholicism was in distinct danger of losing confidence in its *raison d'être* and its future.

To make the situation still more depressing, it was precisely at this period that the Uniates of the Ukraine, already hard hit by the measures of Tsar Nicholas I in the time of Gregory XVI, had to undergo a new trial in the shape of the reunion with the Russian Church of the Chelm diocese, the sole surviving Uniate diocese in Russian Poland. The process had been set in motion in 1865, by a group of Ukrainian priests, headed by Michael Popiel, who were dazzled by the prestige of Russian Orthodoxy and filled with gnawing resentment against the Poles. Their initiative, in itself quite legitimate, appeared in the circumstances a blatant manoeuvre, for what they proposed was to purge the Ruthenian rite of the many Latinisms which had been introduced since the council of Zamosc in 1720, with the idea that once everything which gave the Uniates their special character had been suppressed, their passage to Orthodoxy might be eased. The campaign went ahead without regard to Roman vetoes and reached the point when Popiel, who had been placed by the government in charge of the Chelm diocese, was able to call without hesitation on the imperial police to impose his plans over the heads of a number of Catholics who remained loyal to Rome. Finally, having collected signatures to petitions from two-thirds of the clergy, at the beginning of 1875 he asked for 'the reunion of the united Greeks with the holy Orthodox Eastern Church, which was the Church of our fathers'. Thereafter, of the major Ruthenian Catholic group there survived only the dioceses which lay in the Austro-Hungarian empire, centred on the metropolitan see of Lemberg(Lwow) in Galicia. Here, too, Russian propaganda tried to stir up national feeling against the Poles because of the humiliating condition to which they had for centuries reduced the Ukrainian people, and a section of the younger clergy acquired the habit of looking on Orthodox Russia as the Slavs' natural protector.

3. LEO XIII, THE RENOVATING OPTIMIST (1878-1903)

Raised to the supreme pontificate at a time of crisis in the East (during the Russo-Turkish war), the new pope immediately inaugurated a policy of seeking understanding with all nations, a policy of moderation, presence and openness, as illustrated by the letters that went out from the Vatican on the very evening of his election, letters addressed not only to the powers which maintained regular diplomatic relations with the Holy See but also to the emperor of Germany, the president of the Swiss Confederation and even to Tsar Alexander II of Russia, whose ecclesiastical policies in Poland only a few months before had brought a vehement protest from the Vatican.

With his keen intelligence and sense of realism Leo XIII recognised in the conflict rocking the two eastern empires on their foundations a sign of the times. The treaty of San Stefano (3 March 1878) and the Congress of Berlin (13 July) made plain the fragility of the whole situation in the East and foreshadowed the preponderant role the 'Western Powers' played from now on in its destinies. Although no longer a temporal power, the Holy See intended to play a part in the grand diplomacy of the age, seeking in so doing to reap the greatest possible benefit in terms of the consolidation and enhancement of its influence.

On 27 August 1878 Leo XIII addressed to his Secretary of State, Cardinal L. Nina, a letter setting out his programme as regards 'the illustrious Eastern Churches', expressing his sincere desire that they might at last again lead a fruitful life and start to 'shine with their ancient splendour'. The end of that same year saw the publication of the encyclical *Quod apostolici muneris* in which Leo XIII condemned 'the unruly factions of socialists, communists and nihilists', already widespread and threatening to undermine the entire fabric of civil society. As a result of this statement the Russian government formed a favourable impression of the new pope and before long – an unprecedented and promising phenomenon – the encyclical was being read aloud, with commentaries, in many of the vast empire's Orthodox churches.

Fr d'Alzon, founder of the Augustinian Assumptionists, saw this as encouragement to proceed with the great Eastern mission that was to supplant 'the false cross'. From his jumping-off ground in Sofia, where the Assumptionist mission was in competition with other more firmly entrenched missionary forces (the Austrian and Polish Resurrectionists) Fr d'Alzon hoped to reach Odessa. In Sofia he busied himself with the training of 'pupils' with a special aptitude for this 'Catholic Crusade'. For he was already dubious about the social and political destinies of the seemingly mighty Russia which had just broken the power of the Ottoman empire. On 2 May 1879 he confidently asserted: 'The present state of Russia cannot last. The Russian colossus seems ripe for political upheaval once the day of Turkish power in Europe is ended, which cannot be far off. That is the moment for which we must be prepared. The nihilists will have done their worst and on this ground swept bare by the tempests of revolution we shall come to plant the true cross...'[14]

Leo XIII took a more realistic view of the course of history and the good of the nations. He worked patiently to restore normal diplomatic relations between the Vatican and the Russian government. A preliminary understanding was reached between Cardinal Jacobini and the Russian ambassador, P. D'Oubril, 19-31 October 1880 and the final agreement was signed two

14. S. Vailhé, *Vie du P. E. d'Alzon*, II (Paris 1934), 670 ff.

years later, 12-24 December 1882. Although no satisfactory solution was found to the delicate questions regarding the Polish and Uniate clergy, the dialogue had nevertheless been officially resumed and, given continuing good will on both sides, the agreement of principle seemed promising.

Meanwhile, after the assassination of the Tsar (13 March 1881) the pope had sent to his successor, Alexander III, his personal condolences and had made an obvious allusion to the murder in his encyclical *Diuturnam illud* (29 June 1881), in which nihilist and revolutionary movements were once again condemned.

Leo XIII made at the same time a number of significant moves in regard to properly religious matters. On 12 April 1881, with his decree *Orientalium Ecclesiarum ritus,* he re-established at the Roman monastery of Grottaferrata a purely Byzantine rite. And to see that the reforms he desired were carried out, he instituted at the head of the Graeco-Italian Basilian community especially vigorous personalities, for example J. Cozza-Luzi and his successor A. Pellegrini. Finally, on 10 June 1882, by his apostolic letter *In supremo* the pope abolished the practice of appointing bishops in an honorary capacity to the titles of sees *in partibus infidelium* in cases where the see in question was actually on Christian, although not Catholic, territory.

These public gestures were the outward signs of an underlying concern with the problems of Christian unity. Trusted advisers were asked to study the situation and assess the prospects for a true dialogue. Two confidential reports, one from the future Cardinal Vannutelli, at that time apostolic delegate in Constantinople, and the other from Carlo Gallien, Turkey's consul general in Rome, were submitted to the pope in 1883. They examined in honest and realistic fashion the causes for the lack of success of the Latin missions in the East.

At this same period the First Secretary of the French embassy to the Holy See, Alfred Lacazes, was drawing up for his government a series of well-documented papers on the new pro-Eastern trend in Vatican policy. In a first report, dated 25 May 1883, he noted the many ways in which the papacy was showing its benevolence towards the Christian East. If the previous policy was an obvious failure, it was because 'insufficient account had been taken of the jealous and suspicious attachment of the various Christendoms to their particular rites'. The legislation imposed by Pius IX on the Eastern Catholics, in particular the prescriptions of the bull *Reversurus,* had reinforced the distrust of centuries, and recent polemical articles in the *Journal de St-Pétersbourg* had persisted in accusing the Holy See of 'desiring the ruin of all the Eastern Churches', notwithstanding the vigorous denials of the *Moniteur de Rome.* But, continued the French observer, the new school of thought now prevailing in Propaganda aimed at the regeneration of the East by itself. The apostolic delegate in Constantinople, Mgr Vannutelli, supported this policy, whose line was to respect the susceptibilities of the Eastern Catholics, to preserve their rites and to interest them in their own destiny. Results of the policy were already visible: in the recall of Hassoun to Rome and his elevation to the cardinalate, and in the foundation of an Armenian seminary in Rome (1 March 1883) and of a Melkite seminary in Jerusalem (January 1882). This policy of encouraging the East had the support of Cardinal Lavigerie. It naturally did not appeal to the latinising old guard whose leader, Mgr Piavi, retained his post of apostolic delegate in Syria and still had support in the Roman curia, but who was viewed with increasing impatience by the 'Christians of indigenous rite placed under his jurisdiction'.

The historian can be sure that in recapitulating the main points of this confidential report he is basing himself on sound information derived from a reliable source. There could be no better description of the general situation just prior to the great advances in Eastern policy made under Leo XIII's pontificate.

Having settled so far as he was able the matters in dispute with Russia, the pope's next objective was resumption of the dialogue with Constantinople. The ecumenical patriarch happened to be engaged at the time in a bitter dispute with the Ottoman government in defence of traditional civil rights bound up with his personal status. Leo XIII used this as an opportunity for instructing the new apostolic delegate, Mgr L. Rotelli, to give the Orthodox patriarch, Joachim IV, his moral support. The patriarch was duly grateful and on 14 July 1884 instructed the grand logothete, Stavraki Aristarki Bey, to convey his gratitude to the delegate, who seized the opportunity to introduce himself in person to the Phanar. The patriarch was gracious enough to return his visit and so through a series of polite interviews contact was resumed between two figures that centuries of antagonism had kept apart. But in inaugurating a policy of *rapprochement* between the two major sees of Christendom, was there not a danger of alienating Hellenic Orthodoxy, always inclined to be combative and suspicious, and Russian Orthodoxy, so eager to supplant the ecumenical patriarchate in the East?

A second confidential report from Lacazes, written at the time of this new papal initiative, analysed the prospects of a reconciliation between the patriarchate of Constantinople and the Roman Church. In his report, dated 29 May 1884, he noted that although the pope had 'as yet confined himself to putting out feelers', his approach had straightaway yielded 'unexpected results'. And the diplomat went on to summarise the main points of the pope's future programme: 'To clear away misunderstandings, to increase the scope of the Uniate Churches, to encourage the training of indigenous clergy, to establish more numerous and more potent centres of gravity: such for the moment are the methods the papacy intends to employ'.

By 1 March 1885 the cardinalatial commission of Propaganda had before it a long *Ponenza* on 'The best ways of promoting the return of the schismatic Greeks to the Catholic Church'. And on 1 June of that year, following lengthy consultations, Propaganda granted Latin religious congregations the right to set up eastern branches in the interests of fostering indigenous vocations. This was also the moment Dom Emmanuel André chose to launch his pioneering *Revue de l'Église grecque-unie* which in 1890 was to become *La Revue de l'Église d'Orient,* before disappearing altogether in 1893 in face of more substantial journals.

Leo XIII's pronouncements in favour of union found a sympathetic echo in the East. The eloquent and far-sighted Strossmayer had not let drop the ideas he had expressed at the Vatican Council and he launched along the same path the philosopher Vladimir Soloviev, who had been called, with some exaggeration, 'the Russian Newman'. It was while he was in close contact with the great patriot bishop that Soloviev set down his *Quelques considérations sur l'union des Églises* (1886), copies of which he despatched to the pope and to the cardinal Secretary of State, which formed the prelude to his major work, *La Russie et l'Église universelle* (1889). Written under the influence of Strossmayer, who contributed the preface, this book marked a turning-point in unionist thought. But the time still seemed unripe for spectacular measures. The pope contented himself with inviting the Benedictines and Catholic opinion at large to take a real interest in the question, while leaving to the authorities of Propaganda the task of developing suitable machinery. Two Uniate synods, of the Jacobites at Charfeh in 1888, and of the Ruthenians at Leopol in 1891, were prepared for with great care at Rome and at each the apostolic delegate presided. In tone they resembled the earlier synods held under the banner of the Tridentine legislation. Thus despite the pope's good intentions, latinisation retained its ambiguous character. Helping to sustain it was the ever-increasing influence in the seminaries of teachers with a Latin upbringing. The international Eucharistic Congress held at Jerusalem in 1893 (13-21 May) provided Leo XIII with occasion to abandon his reserve, and it was to lead to the launching of his major Eastern policies. He appointed as papal legate Langénieux, a French cardinal, who was instructed, along with other less official personages, to make detailed enquiries among the Eastern hierarchy. This congress which, despite certain objections voiced in Jerusalem and Constantinople and even in the Roman curia, Leo XIII had desired should take place, was in fact to reveal the profound antagonism which existed in the Near East between triumphant Latinism and the local hierarchies. Several incidents, and in particular the speech delivered by the Latin patriarch, Mgr Piavi, at the closing session, testified to a direct clash of views between the representatives of systematic latinisation and the champions of an East missionised by itself. Nevertheless, there was one fundamental and permanent achievement: in addition to revealing in all its richness the liturgical plurality of the Christian East, the congress had posed in official and inescapable fashion the problem of latinisation. Those who condemned it, Latins as well as Eastern Catholics, had found support for their case in teachings of the popes; while its defenders appealed in justification to the good intentions inspiring the work of Propaganda and its accredited representatives.

Cardinal Langénieux returned to Europe a convinced supporter of the 'Easternising' view. His report to Leo XIII, dated 2 July 1893, is a model of sagacity, doing honour to the high-mindedness, objectivity and Catholic sense of an impartial observer. He offered a clear-cut analysis of the fears entertained by the schismatics in regard to the presence and activities of the Latins, he described the powerlessness of the Eastern Catholics and then presented his conclusions. What was needed was to inspire confidence in the 'dissidents', fortify the 'Uniates' and moderate the triumphalism of the Latins. Leo XIII found here confirmation for the views long maturing in his mind.

In 1894 the pope celebrated the jubilee of his episcopal consecration. He made this the opportunity to address on 20 June 'to the princes and peoples of the world' a message pleading for unity. Published just after the re-establishment of formal diplomatic relations between the Holy See and the Court at St Petersburg (18 June), the encyclical *Praeclara gratulationis* affirmed the legitimacy of a plurality of Churches within the bond of one faith and one supreme government. Its recognition of patriarchal regimes, in keeping with the line laid down by the Council of Florence, opened up new perspectives in the history of relations between the Churches. Christian unity was ceasing to be a goal attainable only through a change of heart of a 'return of the straying sheep to the fold' and beginning to take on the aspect of a reconciliation of 'separated brethren', the fruit of a growing together of local Churches under the benevolent auspices of a pope who was as willing to make himself a beggar for unity as the Bessarion whose challenging question he reiterated: 'What shall we reply to God on the day He calls us to account for this severance from our brothers?'

Putting his teaching into practice, Leo XIII forthwith invited the patriarchs of the Catholic East to a 'summit conference' at the Vatican. These 'patriarchal conferences', a kind of private synod, were joined by five cardinals, whose views were in general sympathy with those of the Roman pontiff. The conferences consisted of eight widely spaced-out sessions (running from 24 October to 8 November 1894), at most of which the pope himself presided. The discussions were devoted to ways of hastening on the greatly desired *rapprochement* between the Churches. In course of them various suggestions were made and one or two decisions arrived at.

For instance, the Melkite patriarch, Gregory Youssef, called for the creation of a Congregation specifically for the Christian East, totally separate from Propaganda, in which the Eastern patriarchs would be represented by permanent procurators and hence have a deliberative voice. He also considered that the authority of a patriarch should extend to the faithful of his rite scattered throughout the world, in keeping within the principle of personality of law which obtained among Eastern Catholics. He thought it necessary to limit still further the authority of the apostolic delegates, whose operations in the East tended to be arbitrary and uncontrolled. He pleaded lastly for juridical equality between Eastern and Latin Catholics before the universal law, which would put an end to a system of discrimination with the Church.

Leo XIII had his eyes fixed on still wider horizons. Refusing to be discouraged by the political encumbrances represented by the protectorates and zones of influence staked out by the European powers, he announced his intention of setting up a permanent cardinalatial commission to work for the reconciliation of all the 'dissidents' (formally constituted in the apostolic letter *Optatissimae* of 19 March 1895).

The cardinal Secretary of State, Rampolla, took a particular interest in the affairs of Hellenic Orthodoxy and contemplated the foundation at Constantinople of an Institut de haute littérature grecque. After many delays this plan was fundamentally revised for the benefit of the Assumptionists. The latter lost little time in establishing the seminary of St Leo at Kadi-Keui, intending to make the house the focal point of all their existing activities in Asiatic Turkey and subsequently installing in it their Centre for Byzantine Studies, together with their review, the *Échos d'Orient*.

But the most spectacular fruit of the Vatican patriarchal conferences was the publication of the encyclical *Orientalium dignitas* (30 November 1894), to act in future as the organic article defining the relations between the Uniate communities and the Latin missions.

The summit meeting and the decisions that flowed from it caused considerable disquiet in diplomatic circles and ill-concealed dismay among the many devotees of 'Latinism'. Even more marked was the passive resistance to these liberating measures on the part of the apostolic delegates in the East and the principal heads of hierarchy in Latin communities. The *motu proprio Auspicia rerum* of 19 March 1895, which brought the authority of the apostolic delegates into line with the patriarchal jurisdiction, was simply ignored both at Constantinople and throughout the Middle East.

With the Latins in the East taking this attitude, for which they obviously had the tacit support of the authorities of Propaganda, is it surprising to find the Hellenic Orthodox hierarchy showing fresh signs of mistrust? The same question could be asked regarding the somewhat insidious if justified campaign of ridicule, which poked fun at the flagrant contradiction between Roman doctrine and Roman practice.

In his approaches to Slav Orthodoxy, however, Leo XIII seemed to be more successful. The new Tsar, Nicholas II, sent the pope official notification of his accession (November 1894) and the pope replied by conferring on him the Grand Cross of the Order of Christ, a decoration very rarely bestowed on non-Catholic sovereigns. Negotiations were started with a view to settling ecclesiastical matters in dispute, in course of which the imperial government made some significant concessions to papal demands. Thus the administrative restrictions impeding the free functioning of the Uniate communities were to some extent relaxed, and the ukase of Catherine II prohibiting visits of Catholic bishops *ad limina* was actually rescinded. Fresh hopes, which in the event proved premature, were raised when on 16 February 1896 the philosopher Vladimir Soloviev sent to Leo XIII his profession of 'Orthodox-Catholic' faith, accepting the Roman primacy in the sense in which St Basil and St John Chrysostom would have recognised it.

The Armenian question was again in the forefront at this period, in consequence of the massacres perpetrated by the Turks. While taking care not to offend Ottoman susceptibilities, Leo XIII broached the subject in a letter written in his own hand to the sultan on 21 June 1895 and on 29 November of that same year made it the subject of a public allocution. From there it was a short step to rumours of a return in large numbers of Gregorian Armenians to Catholicism, to the eventual great discomfiture of people who fed the public with such illusions.

The moment seemed ripe for the constitution of a hierarchy for the Uniate Coptic Church, a matter in which Leo XIII showed a particular interest. The Vatican patriarchal conferences devoted the session of 8 November to the topic and the cardinalatial commission charged with the reconciliation of the 'dissidents' took the matter in hand. But it was realised that this was no easy undertaking, since a complete hierarchy (patriarch and suffragans) had to be created from scratch and a 'campaign for conversions' launched among a very impoverished population. With help from Austrian diplomacy, in particular from Baron de Sonnleithner on the spot, and by drawing on the considerable resources in manpower of the Latin missions in Egypt, Rome was quite soon successful in forming a Coptic Catholic patriarchate. Cyril Makarios, a young priest duly instructed by the Jesuits, was consecrated vicar apostolic and shortly afterwards given the title patriarchal vicar (6 March 1896). The 'national synod' he was instructed to hold was presided over by the apostolic delegate, Mgr G. Bonfigli, and attended by a large number of Latin consultors (January – June 1898). The Coptic Catholic patriarchate was inaugurated on 19 June 1898, with Cyril Makarios as its head. But the latter soon tired of the latinising tutelage of the missionaries and even lost faith in the papal administration. Summoned to Rome in 1908, he almost immediately resigned his office and in July 1910 reverted for a time to his original Orthodoxy. He became reconciled with the Catholic Church in 1912, but even so a manifestly anti-Roman treatise was subsequently published under his signature, *La Constitution divine de l'Église* (Geneva 1913).

The Malabar question at last found a happy solution as a result of the Vatican patriarchal conferences. Although Propaganda had erected two vicariates apostolic, Trichur and Kottayam, as far back as 1887, the titulars appointed were Latins. On 26 July 1896 the Syro-Malabar Christians at length had the satisfaction of receiving their own hierarchy for the three vicariates apostolic of Trichur, Ernakulam and Kottayam. In 1911 Pius X completed the organisation of this ecclesiastical province, in which Catholicism was destined to enjoy a remarkable revival.

To sum up, Leo XIII's actions in respect of the Christian East, hotly contested though they were, showed positive results. The mature fruit of long reflection and of constant and many-sided consultation, his 'easternising' policy inaugurated a new era in the history of relations between the Eastern and Western Churches. Given the impossibility of addressing himself directly to 'dissident' Orthodoxy, he put his faith, as did the best theological minds of his day, in the efficacy of what was called the 'unionist apostolate'. By fostering the ecclesial, intellectual and material development of Uniate Catholicism, it was hoped to create an ideal model of what the status of Orthodoxy would be in a united Church of the future.

It was a conception that was to have a profound effect on the general destinies of Eastern Catholicism. But matched as it was to a particular set of circumstances, it represented only one stage, albeit a fruitful one, along the road to Christian unity. As with all historical achievements of any originality, there was the risk that it would be followed by a reaction, which duly came about when the great pope died. The pontificate of Pius X was to bring the 'easternising' movement to a temporary halt. The history of the papacy offers many contrasts of this kind between two successive pontificates.

4. THE NON-COMMITTAL POLICY OF PIUS X (1903-14).

Nothing in their previous experience had equipped the patriarch of Venice and his new team of close collaborators with a true understanding of Eastern Orthodoxy and of the new status of Eastern Catholicism; besides which, the energies of the papacy were about to become increasingly engaged with the great theological and philosophical ferment that was rocking the world of Latin Christianity. Pius X adopted towards the Christian East a suspicious wait-and-see attitude, closer to the outlook and dour demeanour of Pius IX than to the buoyant and encouraging optimism of Leo XIII.

Yet the more liberal atmosphere in the Russian empire brought about by Nicholas II's edict of toleration (17–30 April 1905) and the democratic revolution effected by Young Turkey (July 1908) offered inducement to the Eastern Churches to expand from the basis of their traditional institutions.

In Russia seeds of legitimate hope started to germinate in the minority Christian confessions – Old Believers, Latins, Uniates – which until now had been the victims of insidious persecution. [15] The 'easternising' school conceived the idea of marking the fifteenth centenary of the death of St John Chrysostom (1907) by the resumption of initiatives dear to Leo XIII, but all that came of it were a few swiftly forgotten religious ceremonies. [16] An effort was nevertheless made by the Ukrainian metropolitan of Lemberg in Galicia, Mgr Andrew Szeptickij, to re-activate among the Russians the substance and spirit of the Union of Brest-Litovsk. Pius X granted him the right, on 17 February 1908, to implement throughout the vast territories lying open to the unionist apostolate the measures decreed by Leo XIII in the encyclical *Orientalium dignitas*, but this personal indult from the pope was kept secret. Soon afterwards Mgr Szeptyskij opened a Uniate chapel at St Petersburg, to have it closed in 1911 by the imperial police. In 1913-14 he bravely launched a monthly review entitled *Slovo Istini* ('Word of Truth') to act as the mouthpiece for Catholicising circles. The outbreak of the First World War brought this venture to an end; and its promoter was implicated in an anti-Russian political-religious plot. In the Ottoman empire, in parallel with the strictly Latin and latinising missionary expansion there was opportunity for the Eastern patriarchates to develop their institutions, especially in the Asiatic provinces and in Egypt. It was difficult, however, for the less prejudiced eye to discern the properly religious aspects of this activity, obscured as they were by the rivalry on the Orthodox side between the Greeks and the Slavs and by the strivings for political influence in the Latin congregations.

The Melkites and Armenians hoped to revise their laws through the instrumentality of national synods. But to the old obstacles were now added new ones created by a laity able to make its influence felt with the Ottoman government. Patriarch Gregory Youssef continued to be convinced of the legitimacy of the council of Jerusalem convoked by Maximos III Mazloum in 1849, but refused recognition by Propaganda on account of its alleged

15. For instance, during the five years following the edict of toleration of 1905 more than 230,000 faithful, past victims of forcible 'conversion', returned to the Roman Church.
16. The commemorative volume *Le XVe centenaire de S. Jean Chrysostome et ses conséquences pour l'Action catholique dans l'Orient gréco-slave* retains its value as a witness to good intentions rather than as marking a point of departure in the history of Eastern Catholicism.

Gallican tendencies. When he died (13 July 1897), his successor Peter Garaijiri was urged by the Roman authorities to summon the council they so keenly desired. A mixed Latin-Melkite commission sitting in Rome drafted the principal decrees, and two observers from the Holy See were appointed to assist the labours of the hierarchy in the Lebanon, but the Ottoman government imposed its veto on their presence, on the ground that they were foreigners (1901). After the Young Turk revolution, Patriarch Cyril VIII Geha at last gathered his bishops together in synod at Ain-Traz (30 May-8 July 1909), presiding over it himself without the assistance or presence of any apostolic delegate; but on the advice of the Roman canonists, Pius X refrained from confirming the synod's decision.

In the case of the Armenians, Pius X brought pressure to bear on the episcopate to hold the national synod in Rome. Finding that this proposal met with fairly general resistance, he appointed at a single stroke nine new bishops who, together with Patriarch Terzian and one other supporter, were counted on to provide the necessary majority. Summoned under papal auspices, this synod had difficulty in completing its business (it lasted from 14 October to 11 December 1911), for so great was the apathy of the participants that only six bishops stuck it out to the end. Shortly after his return to Constantinople on 5 January 1912 the patriarch found himself relieved of his duties as 'civil head' of his nation by orders of the Ottoman government, acting under pressure from lay notables (31 March 1912). Mgr Terzian was nevertheless still determined to implement the synodal decisions to the letter and to obey the pope's instructions. His imposition of the Gregorian calendar (8 December 1913) finally turned his community completely against him. The old anti-Roman faction revived and the already sorely tried Armenian Church was the victim of increasing internal strife. And on top of this troubled situation Armenia was soon to suffer the disasters of the war and the massacres.

So on the eve of the First World War there was real crisis in the ranks of the Armenians and the Melkites, not forgetting the already mentioned troubles of the Copts.[17] The root cause has to be sought in the strong resentment of any influence held to be alien, in particular that of the Christian West in the full tide of its political and religious expansion. The pontifical decree *Tradita ab antiquis* of 14 September 1912 set the seal in intention and in practice on the recession of the 'easternising' trend which had asserted itself during the pontificate of Leo XIII, for it permitted the many Eastern Catholics who attended cultural establishments run by Latin congregations to follow the religious services and communicate according to the Roman rite, with the one exception of the Easter duties. The exultation of

17. See 469-70.

the latinisers showed how much importance was attached to a measure of this kind, by which it was hoped finally to accomplish the westernisation of the East's intellectual élite.

The war and the death of the Sarto pope put an end to a time of transition. The election of Giacomo della Chiesa on 3 September 1914 revived hopes in the admirers of Leo XIII that Benedict XV was not to disappoint. For the new pope was to launch the work of reunion on a much larger scale and provide it with institutions properly founded in the very heart of the Roman curia.

But before passing on to trace the broad outlines of this new era in the East's life and institutions, we must go back a little in order to describe the form taken by the movement for Christian unity since the middle of the nineteenth century.

5. THE PROBLEM OF CHRISTIAN UNITY

We have so far been speaking of ecclesiastical relations within the over-all framework of Roman catholicity at the intra-ecclesial level. It is now time to take a rapid look at the movement in theological ideas and at the reaction to these problems on the part of theologians and publicists. The historian is here treading on territory still largely unexplored, but it is already possible to indicate the major landmarks and to trace out the changes in attitude and in lines of enquiry.[18]

Pius IX's initiative in defining in the encyclical *In suprema Petri* (6 January 1848) the conditions for a return of the Orthodox, the so-called schismatics, to the Roman communion, drew a 'Synodal reply from the Patriarchs of the East' (6 May 1848) which achieved a wide circulation, even among Catholic circles in the West. In making this reply the Orthodox hierarchy posed the problem at a theological and universal level, their main themes being those that more than a century later were to form the fundamental ecclesiological preoccupations of the Second Vatican Council; in particular, the question of episcopal collegiality and the connections between the Roman primacy and the Petrine succession.

Dominating the whole theological and constitutional debate was a conviction of the integral character of evangelical and apostolic truth. The Roman Catholic Church claimed to be the sole depository of that truth. The 'Reply', which brushed aside the papacy's invitation, made the contrary assertion that Orthodoxy was the champion of the true faith.

The Eastern crisis of 1848-56 gave impetus to an increasing interest in the political-religious problems posed by the Holy Places and the destinies of the

18. For more details see the present author's *Le Christianisme en Orient. Études d'histoire contemporaine 1684-1968* (Beirut 1971), 161-85.

Christian communities in the Ottoman empire. Out of a great mass of literature, enormous for its period, we shall select one or two publications which made a particular stir and cast an especially clear light on the fundamental aspects of the problems raised.

At the beginning of 1850 a Russian diplomat and Slavophil by the name of Tuteff published a study entitled *La Papauté et la Question romaine*. In it he observed that the Roman Church, having asserted herself as the mistress and mainstay of the Christian West, had made it possible, in consequence of her existential breach with the Orthodox and apostolic tradition, for the West to breed the germs of Protestantism and revolution. Nevertheless, he went on, Orthodoxy still hoped to see 'the West recovering from this sickness', which would be to the great benefit of Christendom as a whole.

In 1853 the Abbé J. H. Michon published the narrative of a *Voyage religieux en Orient* which he had undertaken in company with the celebrated orientalist F. de Saulcy in 1850-1. The purpose of his journey was to acquaint himself with the religious arrangements of the Eastern Churches separated from Catholic unity and to investigate ways of bringing them closer to Rome, pending 'the summoning of a general council to resume that work of reunion whose foundations were laid by Bossuet and Leibniz'. The views Michon expounded were faithful reflections of opinion he had gathered on the spot. Many of his pages reflect an up-to-the-minute judgment of the situation in the East and above all in Palestine. He commented on the re-establishment of the Latin patriarchate of Jerusalem that it was 'one of the most providential and fruitful deeds of modern times', always provided that the patriarchate set itself to serve the needs of the local Church, Arab and Melkite, and that it 'abandoned Latinism, for which the Eastern Christians feel an invincible repugnance'; having said which, he remarked in his ingenuous way that it was hard 'to account for a Latin bishop in a place where there are not Latins'. But it was not only concerning the local problem in Palestine that he noted down the reasonable views of people worried about the future of relations between Rome and the Christian East. The problem of reconciling Christians raised in turn the problem of summoning a truly ecumenical council and also of the willingness of the papacy to cease 'absorbing into itself all the powers of the Church'. The most penetrating remarks on this subject Michon gleaned from an unassuming scholar in Brusa, John Tcharmoudjan.

At the end of 1853 an important article entitled 'L'Église d'Orient considérée dans la conjoncture de la crise d'Orient' appeared in the *Revue des deux Mondes*; its author was H. Desprez, a well-informed observer of affairs in the East, both diplomatic and ecclesiastical. After pointing out the many divergences between East and West in ecclesiastical matters, which had resulted in a long-enduring antagonism between these two religious blocs, separated from one another by a profound cultural and social divide, he went on to observe that the dynamism so unfailingly displayed by Roman Christianity confronted in the Christian East a force of inertia which made the latter inexpugnable:

> Let us admit, while deploring the fact, that the Greek Christians undoubtedly nurture lively and long-standing suspicions of the Roman Church. Although since her separation from the Holy See the Church of the East has not a single serious conquest by preaching and proselytisation to her credit, of her defensive capacities there can be no doubt. In all the battles, mounted sometimes with skill and always with energy by the Catholic missionaries, she has conceded not an inch of ground. Against these attacks she has presented a firmly impassive face, a systematic inertia and immobility against which the learning and authority of the Roman Church have until now hurled themselves in vain.

And referring to Rome's efforts over the centuries to detach national minorities from Orthodoxy in order to set them up as rivals and competitors of the Eastern Church he added:

> Not one of those Eastern peoples was willing for schism when the Latin Church made plain her intentions of encroaching on the privileges she granted them, so greatly did national sentiment outweigh all other considerations.

At this period of preoccupation with the problems of the East the chief spokesman, for more than a decade, of the 'Uniatising' school in the Catholic Church was a Russian convert from Orthodoxy, Fr Gagarin, S. J., well known for his part in the beginnings of the review *Les Études*. His influence on the mental climate was considerable and the ideology he worked out long remained classic in missionary circles in the Christian East. In 1853, at a critical point in the Eastern crisis, there had appeared at Paris a French translation of a pamphlet by Mouravieff entitled *Questions religieuses d'Orient et d'Occident. Parole de l'orthodoxie catholique au catholicisme romain*. To this Gagarin made aggressive reply, blaming the bad faith of the Orthodox hierarchy for the failure of the papacy's efforts to 'extinguish the Eastern schism' and condemning in the Eastern Church both the anarchical character of its conciliar system and the immobilism of its repeated appeals to tradition: 'The prudence of the blind, standing still when they do not know the way'. As to the Holy Places, he considered that, since the Crusades, the right to control them belonged exclusively to Catholicism even if, 'in a spirit of tolerance and charity', Catholicism allowed schismatics and heretics access to them for purposes of prayer.

Beside diatribes so prejudicial to the real quest for concordant truth and Christian reconciliation, the publications of Alexis Stepanovich Khomiakov showed a refreshingly irenical and scientific approach.

On reading some of his illuminating pages and comparing them with discourses of Paul VI at the recent Second Vatican Council one cannot fail to be struck by a theological affinity and indeed in some passages by an identity of viewpoint, which is surely proof that this pioneer of modern ecclesiology had an ecumenical message relevant to modern needs. Khomiakov's reflection on the situation in the East as a whole and its religious implications led him to make a masterly contribution to the great debate, in the book published in French in 1855 with the suggestive title *L'Église latine et le Protestantisme au point de vue de l'Église d'Orient*. His strong feelings in regard to protagonists of Uniatism, Gagarin in particular, found vent in some scathing comment; and while he acknowledged that Orthodox religious rites, although existentially important to Orthodoxy as its form of religious self-expression, were not of its essence, he was caustic about people who tried 'to pass the popes off as passionate admirers of the Greek cult' and claimed it took 'enormous effrontery to back-date this tolerance to previous centuries'. But Khomiakov's contribution went beyond the merely polemical and raised the debate to the higher level of obedience to the teaching of the Gospel. In that ecumenical perspective, all the Churches ought to confess their sins and not puff themselves up with false claims to doctrinal invulnerability or the monopoly of holiness. Khomiakov here set his finger on the root evil of the division in the Church.

The seed thus sown was to bear fruit. Gagarin replied to Khomiakov indirectly in a pamphlet with the bold-sounding title *La Russie sera-t-elle catholique?*, written in the flush of victory in the Crimea. Its tone and content were throughout evocative of the political situation of the moment. The diplomatic peace just signed at Paris is seen as prelude to the conclusion of a peace between the Russian and the Latin Church, a peace conceived in terms no longer 'of the absorption of the Russian by the Latin Church, but of reconciliation', which would leave Holy Russia with her institutions intact but emancipated from 'Byzantinist' State control:

For centuries the Russian Church has been in a state of war with the Holy See; the time has come to sign a peace, but it must be honourable and to everyone's advantage. The Russian Church can enter the concert of the universal Church and still preserve her venerable rites, her ancient discipline, her national liturgy and her particular character; she can reknit the ties which once united East and West. The task of reconciliation is not easy; many prejudices stand in the way; but it is not impossible, for it threatens no interest deserving to be taken seriously. All that is needed is the concurrence of three wills. Once the pope, the emperor of Russia and the Russian Church, represented by the bishops or by the synod, have agreed to reconciliation, who is there that can prevent it?

This reconciliation would strengthen the Church against internal enemies in Russia, the country menaced by revolution, but it would also benefit the universal Church in another way. In effect, a glorious destiny could be in store for a Catholic Russia if she harnessed her vital energies to the work of the apostolic mission in Asia. By penetrating that vast continent from the north, she could link up with the Latin missionaries and, in accordance with the old strategy of the Crusades, 'while Islam was being attacked on the shores of the Mediterranean it would also be taken from the rear'.

During that same summer of 1856 the Abbé Michon published a pamphlet with the sensational title *La Papauté à Jérusalem*, intended as a contribution to the solution both of the Roman question and of the problem of Christian unity. Michon's idea was that the pope, threatened with expulsion from the Papal State, should choose in future to reside at Jerusalem. This transfer of the papacy to the Holy City would be of inestimable benefit to Christianity, since without losing his influence over the West the pope would in this way be able to concern himself 'more fully and more competently with the East'. Michon envisaged the pope working in Jerusalem towards a union of Churches 'based on identity of dogmas and on the undeniable historical fact that the last decree of union, proclaimed at Florence, has never since been rescinded'. The body proclaiming this union would be an ecumenical council at which the patriarchs and bishops of the Eastern Church would share in the deliberations on an equal footing with their Western colleagues. Taking a still wider view, Michon believed there could be a fruitful dialogue between the papacy and the Muslim world. The time had passed, he considered, when it was allowable to call 'the great legislator of the Arab tribes the elder son of Satan', Islam being in essence none other than the 'primitive religion of the age of the patriarchs...the religion of Abraham'.

But once the crisis in the East and the excitement over Russian Christianity had subsided, the Christian public became more realistic in its interests and the publicists reverted to more traditional themes. With hopes of a comprehensive reconciliation between the Christian East and the Christian West once again receding, efforts were concentrated instead on fashioning the Uniate communities into tools for the gradual whittling away of the Orthodox bloc.

Pius X believed he was making a useful contribution to that end with the setting up in 1862 of a cardinalatial commission, within the Congregation for the Propagation of the Faith, specifically to deal with Eastern affairs. Fr

Gagarin published in the form of a commentary a revealing study on *L'Avenir de l'Église grecque unie*. In it he analysed the prospects for a re-launching of the Uniate Churches, which he saw as constantly subject to a dangerous gravitational law pulling them now in the direction of absorption by the Latin Church, now in the direction of detachment from Catholicism. Besides which, the troubles currently afflicting several of the Uniate Churches provided matter for serious thought, and this situation forced on Gagarin's attention an empirical fact which had so far escaped his notice: the constitution of the Uniate Churches was of a truly hybrid character, as illustrated by the Melkites, whose 'rite' consisted in 'a medley of Latin and Eastern practices equally remote from the usage of both Churches'. Taking his cue from an earlier theoretical exponent of unionism, the 'venerable' Discalced Carmelite Thomas à Jesu, who in his *De unione orientalium procuranda* had recommended the intellectual, religious and cultural promotion of the Eastern Catholics, Gagarin wanted to see the latter built up as a magnet to draw in the whole of Orthodoxy. For the status of the Uniate Church was not so much provisional as transitional. 'The final state to be aimed at is not absorption of that Church by the Latin Church but absorption by the Greek Uniate Church of the Greek Church in its entirety.' The foundation of Eastern Catholic seminaries of a respectable intellectual standard, with a central seminary at Constantinople or Rome, and the establishment in the East of subsidiaries of the great Latin orders were probably just the measures required to jolt the Greek Uniate Church out of the langour and despondency in which it was plunged.

To make answer to these advocates of proselytisation by means of institutions there were champions of Orthodoxy for whom Catholicism had turned sour. Not only were they well qualified to make reply, they also possessed information derived from impeccable sources. Pitzipios, for example, having reverted to the Orthodox faith, made the political-religious methods of the Roman Church the butt of a lampoon, at once crude and incoherent, which he published at Paris in 1860 under the title *Le Romanisme,* and in 1862 he rounded on his erstwhile papal protector, decrying his 'Eastern' reform of Propaganda and, in his *Réponse à la dernière bulle de Sa Sainteté le pape sur l'union des Églises orientales à celle de Rome,* taking the opposite side to Gagarin. Another defector from Roman Catholicism was the French priest W. Guettée, who was appointed to a confidential position in the chapel of the Russian embassy in Paris. He was the author of a great many works aiming to demonstrate the error of Roman Catholicism, which he accused of schism and heresy in departing from the common tradition of the first Christian millennium, one of the most notable being *La Papauté schismatique ou Rome dans ses rapports avec l'Église* (1863, reissued 1874), based on patristic texts students of the East had overlooked or imperfectly understood, and through his review *L'Union chrétienne* he helped to create a pro-Orthodox climate in many Western circles thrown into disarray by the vicissitudes of the First Vatican Council.

There were also two young German priest-scholars who at this period broke with the Catholic Church to enlist under the intellectual and spiritual banner of Orthodoxy. One was A. Pichler, Privatdozent of the university of Munich, who went to St Petersburg as librarian and who was the author of a strongly committed history of the separation of East and West. [19] Although the hopes entertained of Pichler's scholarship were disappointed, the ecumenical contribution of the other German priest, J. Overbeck, of the university of Bonn, was much wider in scope. Settling in England after his rupture with Rome, he laboured incessantly, through numerous publications and in other ways, to promote a return to Orthodoxy, which he wanted to see spreading to the West and harmonised with the genius and traditions of Latin Europe. He tried hard through his *Revue de l'Orthodoxie catholique* to instil the idea of an Orthodox Catholicism, combining the creed and canons of Graeco-Slav Orthodoxy with the usages and even the liturgies of the prevailing Western cultures.

But these essays in a 'neo-Catholicism' renewed by Orthodoxy amounted to no more than tiny patches on the vast canvas of established Christianity. The Orthodox world remained impermeably within its traditional mould, while new religious forces arising within Catholicism still entertained ambitions of liquidating the Eastern schism. Unquestionably one of the most typical pioneers of this anti-schism offensive of the second half of the nineteenth century was Fr Emmanuel d'Alzon, founder of the Augustinians of the Assumption. In July 1862 he was already trying to persuade the authorities of Propaganda and Mgr Brunoni, apostolic delegate at Constantinople, to co-operate with him in an audacious plan which he thought the political situation of the Ottoman empire must inevitably favour:

> Of all the enemies of the Turkish empire, [he wrote] the most formidable is undoubtedly Russia, whose claims to continual encroachments at the expense of Constantinople are made in the name of the Orthodox Church. Now if we could establish between Constantinople and Russia a zone inhabited by Catholic populations, all pretexts for usurpation would in the long run at least surely disappear; the Ottoman empire might then hope to prolong its existence.
>
> From these simple observations it should be clear how much it is in the interest of Turkish statesmen, whatever their personal convictions, to foster the development of Catholicism in their empire.

19. *Geschichte der Kirchlichen Trennung zwischen dem Orient und Occident von der ersten Anfängen bis zum jüngsten Gegenwart*, Munich 1864. The difficulties the author ran into with the Church's censorship were the causes of his defection.

Such hopes belonged to the realm of fantasy. Yet they apparently inspired a great missionary enterprise, to which Fr d'Alzon was prepared to devote large sums of money and a band of men especially chosen for their dedication and learning. At the end of April 1863 he submitted to Pius IX and the Propaganda authorities a confidential memorandum, drawn up after much consultation with missionary leaders and with E. Boré, superior of the Lazarists, in particular. But his plans found no favour with the Roman authorities. Eminently practical, Pius IX preferred to see the establishment of a seminary which would turn out a 'sound' Eastern clergy. He refused above all to endorse an underground policy aiming at the gradual and imperceptible absorption of Eastern rites, declaring roundly that he had pledged himself to respect them, whereas the founder of the Assumptionists and his allies were convinced that before the 'onward march of European ideas' they must inevitably disappear. The cardinals of Propaganda had objections to the memorandum as a whole, for at a time when the often mooted scheme for re-establishing a Latin patriarchate based on Constantinople had finally been abandoned, Fr d'Alzon continued to press it, envisaging in addition Latin patriarchal institutions for the Bulgar and even, it might be, for the Greek Uniate community.

Another contributor to the debate, less ambitious than Fr d'Alzon, was the Abbé P. Martin, a chaplain of the church of S. Luigi dei Francesi in Rome, who published in Rome in 1867 an undisguisedly biased work entitled *La Chaldée. Esquisse historique, suivie de quelques réflexions sur l'Orient*. The reasons he gave for the religious decline of the Nestorians and of the schismatics in general were the ones commonly produced at that period, but more interesting are his reflections on 'the methods most likely to promote the return of the East, and of Western Asia in particular, to the Catholic faith and hence to the prosperity the East once enjoyed'. He gives a reasoned account of the Catholic West's failure in its 'Eastern missionary work'. If 'the army of bishops and missionaries' sent out to install the Latin hierarchy in Asia and to 'graft it to the Eastern stock so that the all but exhausted life blood of the Mother-Church might once again flow there freely' had been a failure, the reason, he thought, did not lie wholly in failings of the Eastern Christians, for example their venality, their deceit, their distrust; age-old prejudices, reciprocal antipathies, the constant and inopportune meddlings of the missionaries had all played as great a part. The Christians East must therefore be restored 'not solely but principally by the East itself'. By according the Christian East this limited degree of responsibility, the influence of the Latin missionaries could be made more effective, exercised through the intermediary of seminaries over which they would have the supreme intellectual and spiritual control. Among the benefits would be the abolition of the institution of a married lower clergy, the introduction of the

Latin language and outlook into the teaching of theology, and the concentration in Latin hands of the financial aid destined for the Eastern hierarchy which would hence be dependent on the Latins as benefactors. Lastly, to complete the network of supervision and control in the hands of Latin authorities, the Latin religious congregations should disregard the suspicions of them entertained by Eastern Catholics and set up subsidiary branches in the East.

The preparatory commission of the Vatican Council would draw on all these ideas, blending them into a general plan which was probably responsible for a number of Roman initiatives over the following decades. Even the enlightened and audacious policy of Leo XIII seems to have elicited nothing but publications in the traditional way. To hear a new note struck we have to wait, paradoxically enough, for the non-committal pontificate of Pius X during which there appeared, to be received at the time very coolly in Rome, the writings of Prince Max of Saxony: writings which after the accession of Benedict XV inspired many of the pronouncements coming from Rome.

Theologian, historian and liturgist, this prince in Holy Orders brought to the ecumenical dialogue the benefits of seasoned scholarship, lucidity and boldness. As early as 1907, his *Vorlesungen über die orientalishe Kirchenfrage* attracted attention because of the manner in which he handled certain delicate questions in the history of relations between the Churches. The fundamental realism, honesty and unconventionality of his views commended him to the founders of the new journal being launched in Rome in 1910-11 under the title *Roma e l'Oriente*. Invited by them to expound his ideas in the introductory and so to say programmatic article, he composed a short paper, as condensed as it was (for the time) revolutionary, to which he gave the modest title *Pensées sur la question de l'union des Églises*.

If the efforts by the Roman Church down the centuries to achieve reunion with the Eastern Churches had always failed, he wrote, the cause did not lie primarily in the obstinacy or bad faith of the 'Greeks'. In reality, the Latin Church, 'always a little accustomed to command', wanted to impose her own conception of union and ways to effect it on her Eastern sister. Now Rome's conception implied the total or unconditional surrender of the Eastern Church, looked on as a rebel, and repeated efforts to bring this about only served, therefore, to alienate Eastern Christians still further from Rome. For Eastern Christians saw the question from a different angle and although they agreed on occasion to enter into negotiation, as at the time of the councils of Lyons or Florence, they did so under pressure of political necessity and because of the 'Turkish danger'.

There must therefore be agreement on the real meaning of union. In the past as in the present the Roman Church conceded to the Uniate Churches of the East only their particular liturgies and certain points of discipline, and did so only by way of a 'gracious favour'. But the Eastern Church was in existence well before the Churches of the West and had its own legal code, much older than that of the Romans. Submission to the bishop of Rome, in the capacity of primate of the universal Church, could only signify 'abasement before the Church of the West'.

The fundamental error was to have misconceived the historical development of the papacy and the role it played during the first Christian millennium in the West as in the East, in such a way that the papacy appeared to Eastern Christians of today 'in the guise of a Latin institution, but not a catholic and universal one'. As patriarch of the West, the bishop of Rome had wielded only a mediate influence in the East, and then solely when he was engaged in matters relating to the Church universal. But the bishop of Rome wanted to impose on the Eastern Church the new conception prevailing in the West since the Middle Ages. Look, for example, at what happened when Uniate minority Churches were constituted:

> Made completely subject to the jurisdiction of the pope and indeed of a Roman congregation, they have to obey many laws peculiar to the Latins and accept the corpus of Latin theology in all its particulars. They are in fact nothing but Latins in Eastern dress (sometimes not even that), offering up Eastern prayers but no longer authentic representatives of the true Eastern Church. The Uniates are a living contradiction of everything in the early history of the Church and of the East. Far from advancing the cause of unionism in general, the existence of these Uniate Churches does more to retard it ...'

Should one then abolish the Uniate minority Churches? No, but the system so far in operation must be changed. 'It is the duty of the Eastern Church to remain as she is; she has no reason to change her character.' For the Eastern Church was in no sense a fragment, 'a province that had become detached from the Roman Church', as was the case with the Protestants. The Church of the East had the right to her traditional autonomy, co-existential with her origins. If that condition were met, union would be possible; but 'so long as efforts continue to subjugate Eastern Christians to the existing ecclesiastical system, any attempt at union would be in vain'.

Once that primordial difficulty had been resolved, it would indeed be necessary to examine and compose the dogmatic differences that had cropped up over the centuries. For unity of the Church implies unity of the faith.

For centuries, despite differences in discipline and constitution, unity of dogma was a reality. The Eastern Church could not be expected to endorse amplifications of dogma by the Latin Church without being given opportunity to share in a joint review of recent dogmatic definitions. Even the dogmas defined at the Council of Florence ought to be redefined in this same co-operative spirit, for the Eastern Church had subscribed to them at the time only 'with reluctance' and 'from force of circumstances'. In any case, the divergences in dogma between the two Churches derived not from things essential to the faith but from theological systems, which could not be imposed on the Church universal as binding. Nothing short of an ecumenical council, truly free of constraints and moral pressures, could bring about dogmatic unity.

To create unity there must be truth and charity. It was not enough to know the East as scholars knew it. The West had to penetrate beyond their standard formulations and bookish doctrines to the soul of the East, and become convinced of the good faith of the Eastern line of argument. For the effort in the past had all been on the side of piling up the causes of failure at the door of the East, with no corresponding effort to see 'the long chain of errors and faults committed by the West'.

Prince Max showed courage in pronouncing such severe judgments, which he supported with historical examples. He added that such an effort of constructive, honest and well-intentioned self-criticism ought to commend itself equally to the Eastern Christians, for the same passion for truth and the same candour would help to pierce the skin of their complacency and bring recognition of the legitimacy of the Latin positions.

What was wrong, in short, was that East and West were in a state of mutual ignorance and that their lack of concern to discover the truth was allied with a notable deficiency in the spirit of charity. While mutual respect was wanting, there could be no true reciprocal love. The East, it was true, had been plagued for centuries with misfortunes; but the West be held largely responsible for its sufferings, for the East had been left abandoned to its enemies and when the West made plans for liberation, it was with thoughts of reducing the East to a new state of subjection.

Expressions of opinion so deeply felt and sustained by so clear an understanding of Christian history were rare indeed. In these pages, written at the close of an epoch filled to an unusual degree with ecclesiastical crises, Prince Max was in effect summing up the situation of a past age and pointing the way forward to a fruitful dialogue, to the beginnings of a lasting *rapprochement* between the Churches.

18

1917-39: EASTERN CATHOLICISM
BETWEEN THE WARS

1. THE POLITICAL AND ECCLESIASTICAL FRAMEWORK

THE First World War and its immediate aftermath had disastrous consequences for Eastern Christianity. Never since the capture of Constantinople (1453) and the disappearance of the Byzantine empire had Orthodoxy suffered such damage to itself and its institutions. On the surface, nothing appeared to survive of the socio-political framework which, in the two opposing Eastern empires, once sustained a Christianity closely bound up with the very varying structures of the two States.

In Russia, the violent severance of the age-old and indissoluble links between Church and State following the socialist and Bolshevik revolution created a structural void to which was soon added an ideological opposition to the Church whose consequences were incalculable. True, the pan-Russian reforming synod of Moscow (August-October 1917) revived the institution regarded as the symbol and instrument of the Church's independence, namely the patriarchate. But the civil war and the triumph of Bolshevism undermined the unity of the Church, straining its sense of civic responsibility to the limit, and by slow degrees, often through the application of violence, detached from the Church millions of the faithful. Down to the outbreak of the second world-wide conflagration the Russian Church was destined, within Russia itself, to lead a highly precarious existence in conditions scarcely favourable to its survival, remaining a mere shadow of its former self while many of its hierarchs, theologians and thinkers, not forgetting ordinary faithful, were treading the path of exile. By contrast, the numerous communities of the Diaspora as they gradually took shape in all parts of the world, were about to reveal themselves as a source of spiritual life and to open up to many Westerners the religious treasures and positive values specific to the Christian East.

In the former Ottoman empire, Greek-Arab Orthodoxy had to submit to another form of disintegration. The various Christian communities emerged from the war weakened by long periods of famine and by repeated massacres, in Anatolia, in Armenia and Cilicia, in Northern Mesopotamia and in Northern Syria. The dissolution of the empire which followed the armistice of Mudros (30 October 1919) and the Allied occupation of Constantinople (1919-23), and after that the institution of the mandate regime, which gave England and France a privileged position in the Arab provinces in the Middle East, had important consequences for the Christian communities. Instead of dealing as in the past with a single Muslim authority, basically liberal and respectful of their personal and specific status, the various Christian communities had from now on to defend themselves against the lure of several competing forms of alien Christianity, rich in material goods, bent on expansion, and enjoying the support of the ruling powers. In addition, the Arab nationalist-inspired independence movements which soon developed in face of this scarcely veiled form of European colonial imperialism confronted Christians, whether Coptic, Melkite, Nestorian, Syriac or Maronite, with new religious-political choices which split their confessional entity asunder between competing loyalties. It goes without saying that not all levels of the ecclesiastical hierarchy made the same choice.

Following on Young Turkey's entry into the war on the side of the Central Powers, England had hastened to enforce her protectorate over Egypt (18 December 1914). So this African province of the Ottoman empire was withdrawn as an immediate prize for competition between the European powers. In the other provinces, the stake represented by Christian missions appeared to enter into consideration as an important, if not a vital, factor. In the flush of their first victories the Germans were making ready as early as 1915 to claim the missionary and cultural heritage of the French in the Levant. But French Catholicism was swift to enter a counter-claim. In the summer of 1915, French missionary circles claimed that in virtue of the French religious protectorate in Syria their country had a right to the sovereignty exercised by the sultan in Levantine territories extending from the Adana region to Arabia Petraea and from the Eastern Mediterranean to the Syro-Mesopotamian desert. In this political-religious tug of war over the fate of the Ottoman Near East there was a conviction on everyone's part that their nation's ambitions coincided with the wishes of Divine Providence and with the interests of the Church. The Holy See itself was not without its anxieties regarding the future fate of Constantinople. At the time of the discussions in the spring of 1915 between France, England and Russia regarding the possible partitioning of the Ottoman Empire, the young Mgr Pacelli gave to Kelidov, the Russian envoy extraordinary to the Vatican, a message from the Secretary of State expressing the concern of Vatican diplomacy over the future status of Santa Sophia. The possible attraction of Constantinople into the orbit of Russian Orthodoxy appeared to the Secretary of State to constitute 'a catastrophe greater than the Reformation'.

But the political and colonial ambitions of the Allies extended well beyond these religious perspectives, although the latter were not neglected. As the result of successive negotiations culminating at intervals in international treaties, the allies gradually installed themselves in all the Ottoman empire's former provinces in Asia, not without encountering some violent Arab nationalist opposition. Between the end of 1918 and the summer of 1923 the African and Asian Middle East experienced a prolonged period of political tension, punctuated by a number of dramatic events: the clash between England and Egypt culminating in the assertion of independence by the Wafd movement headed by Zaghloul Pasha (November-December 1918); the landing of the French army on the coast of Syria (October-December 1918); that same army's occupation of Thrace and the Allies' occupation of Constantinople (1918-23); the Congress of Marseilles (3-4 January 1919), which affirmed the historical and economic bases of the French presence in the Levant; the arrest and deportation of the Egyptian nationalist leader, Zaghloul Pasha (8 March 1919); the landing of Greek armies in Asia Minor and their campaign against the Turkey of Kemal Pasha (15 March 1919); the diplomatic and religious mission to Syria and Palestine led by Cardinal Dubois, archbishop of Paris (September 1919-January 1920); the journey of the Maronite patriarch to Paris at the head of a Lebanese delegation to put the case for the creation of Greater Lebanon (October-November 1919); the San Remo conference, which adopted the principle of French and English mandates in the Near East (April 1920); the rapid rise and fall of the kingdom of Greater Syria set up by the Hashemite king Faisal and swept away by the French military intervention which culminated in the capture of Damascus (March-July 1920); the creation of Greater Lebanon (1 September 1920); the Franco-English agreements on the territorial delimitation of their respective mandates (23 December 1920); the creation under British auspices of a kingdom of Iraq for the Hashemite king Faisal (23 August 1921), after the latter's brother, Emir Abdullah, had taken command in Transjordan (27 March 1921); England's unilateral declaration of the end of her protectorate over Egypt (28 February 1922); the ratification by the League of Nations of the French mandate over Syria and the English mandate over Palestine (24 July 1922); and lastly the recognition of the Turkey of Ataturk by the Treaty of Lausanne (24 July 1923).

This last event set the seal on the Greeks' defeat in Asia Minor, which represented a fresh defeat for Orthodoxy. The Greeks had embarked on a venture which assumed at times the character of a religious and cultural epic, with the aim of re-installing Greek Christianity at Santa Sophia and of realising the dream of Magna Graecia in the Eastern Mediterranean, but their failure not only dissipated for ever the vision of restoring Byzantine Christianity at Constantinople but also dispersed the millions of Orthodox inhabitants of Asia Minor to the four corners of the earth, just as had happened so recently in the case of the Russian diaspora.

This troubled period during which the modern map of the Near East began to take shape was followed in the countries of the Levant by disturbances set up by new and more bitter nationalist currents, whipped up by the threat of integration with Europe and driven to take a fresh look at the fundamental values on which the civilisation and unity of the Arab world were founded. Ataturk's abolition of the caliphate and the expulsion of the last sultan (1 March 1924) posed the problem in relation to the traditional organisation of the Muslim community. The creation of the Arab kingdom of the Hijaz for the Wahhabi Abdul Aziz ibn Saud (8 January 1926) put an end to Hashemite ambitions to succeed to the caliphate, and in the meantime thinkers were directing their attention, on the strictly theological and juridical plane, to devising new forms for the Arab-Muslim community of the future; one such was Sanhoury, who in 1926 published a work on *Le Califat, son évolution vers une Société des nations orientales* in which he advocated Islamic-Christian understanding as the basis for the political-religious development of the Near East.

In the course of the years that followed, the Arab Near East gradually reconstituted the principles of Arab unity in all domains, notwithstanding efforts by separatist forces to hold it back. The Congress of Syrian Unity held at Damascus in June 1928 was evidence of a deep longing for unity in the territories subjected to the mandate system, and it was in that same year that Hassan-al-Banna started to form in Egypt the first cells of the Muslim Brotherhood. Next, on 18 September 1932, came the proclamation of the kingdom of Saudi Arabia followed, a month later, by recognition of Iraq as an independent state. These international acts of recognition hastened on the political and social development of the other countries. A treaty of August 1936 conceded to Egyptian nationalism the independence in principle it had so long demanded, and the accession of the Popular Front to power in France resulted in September of that year in the recognition in principle of the independence of Syria, and in November of the Lebanon. Some months later the Montreux Convention (May 1937) finally abolished the centuries-old system of Capitulations under which foreigners had enjoyed commercial privileges. A wind of change was blowing through these countries, and they were starting to envisage their future in a new light, that of integral sovereignty. But at this juncture the Second World War intervened to arrest for several years the natural course of development.

The First World War was disruptive of everything that down the centuries had kept Orthodoxy essentially united. In the years that followed, in part because of the divergent and often conflicting policies of the various political and social regimes, but also because of upheavals within the Churches themselves, the fact that the autocephalous Churches formed one communion was not immediately apparent, even to the most sympathetic observer. Nevertheless, the profound conviction of a unity greater than the apparent division into national autocephalous Churches had once again been affirmed, even at the height of the war, by a theologian on the staff of the Petrograd Academy, who at the same time paid homage to the moral primacy of the see of Constantinople. These affirmations, published in a New York theological journal, illuminate for us certain fundamental aspects of the confused and tormented history of Orthodoxy between the wars. J. Sokoloff gave his article the title 'Byzantium, the preserver of Orthodoxy', and he sought in it to establish the common factor linking the autocephalous Orthodox Churches with the patriarchate of Constantinople:[1]

We must be careful not to assess Orthodoxy and its affairs in terms of the categories with which we are familiar. Orthodoxy exists as a unity under common authority of its ancient dogmas and ancient canons. The various autocephalous Churches are not so many schisms, but legitimate national groups, within a unity of faith which all are happy to understand as a mystical unity ... Basing itself on the ecumenical dogmas and canons, the Church of Constantinople, in spite of all its advantages, has never tried to extend its authority over the other Churches of the east even though history has provided many opportunities for this. *Orthodoxy is the principle which joins them all together, and that signifies submission to the ancient dogmas and canons.* At the same time each Church retains its autocephalous dignity, and remains in fraternal charity with the others, each being careful not to diminish each other's independence.'

It is from this standpoint and in this spirit that the historian should address himself to the history of the main autocephalous Churches at this period.

The history of the Russian Church was especially tragic. A pan-Russian council had assembled in Moscow in August 1917 and had proceeded on 28 October to the election and the archbishop of Vilna, Mgr Tikhon, as patriarch of Moscow and of all Russia, re-establishing in this way an institution essential to the autocephaly which had been suppressed in 1720 by

---

1. *Échos d'Orient*, MXVIII (1916-19), 93-4.

Peter the Great. But in the course of 1918-19 the national Church was rapidly shorn of all its privileges and of the bulk of its property and several hundred monasteries were closed. The patriarch's determined opposition to the new regime resulted in the spring of 1922 in his arrest. His removal from the scene encouraged the more rapid growth of a breakaway movement known as the Living or Synodal Church, which in May 1923 held a schismatic *synedrion* at which various progressive measures were adopted: abolition of episcopal celibacy, permission for married priests to contract second marriages, the setting up of a new synodal constitutions for the Church. Patriarch Tikhon thereupon changed his tune: he agreed to recognise the Soviet regime and to promise loyalty to its new constitution (28 June 1923), in return for which he was able to resume his functions and campaign against the breakaway movement. Variously, and often incorrectly interpreted, as much in Russia as elsewhere, the patriarch's new position was founded on a classical doctrine of the separation of the temporal or political domain from the spiritual or ecclesiastical, according to which it was the duty of the Church to keep to her own sphere. [2]

When Tikhon died, on 12 April 1925, the confused state of the Church made it impossible to hold the electoral synod. In order to spike the guns of the breakaway Church the patriarchal vicar, Metropolitan Sergius of Novgorod, entered on negotiations with the Soviet authorities. At the same time a representative of the Roman interest, Mgr d'Herbigny, engaged in a vain attempt to set up a Catholic hierarchy for the whole of Russian territory. The negotiations between Mgr Sergius and the Soviets resulted in the conclusion on 10 May 1927 of a kind of concordat. The government accorded official recognition to the patriarchal Church in the Soviet Republics and recognised Metropolitan Sergius as *locum tenens* in the patriarchal see and its synod. As his side of the bargain, the metropolitan published on 16-29 July 1927 a letter recognising the authority of the Soviets as lawful and urging all members of the Russian Church, including those of the diaspora, to desist from any form of opposition to the regime, on pain of expulsion from the lists of the faithful.

This renewed declaration of loyalty sparked off further disturbances in the Church. Within the U.S.S.R. itself, several metropolitans broke away from the official Church and with their supporters formed a kind of church of the catacombs. Among the Russians of the diaspora, already divided into three sharply differentiated principal blocks, in North America, Western

2. K. C. Felmy, 'Patriarch Tichon im Urteil der Russisch-Orthodoxen Kirche der Gegenwart', in *Kirche im Osten*, VIII (1965), 25-54. See also J. Chrysostome, *Kirchengeschichte Russlands der neuesten Zeit*, I, *Patriarch Tichon, 1917-1925*, Munich 1965; W. C. Fletcher, *A Study in Survival. The Church in Russia 1927-1943*, London 1965; A. M. Amman, *Abriss der ostslavischen Kirchengeschichte* (Vienna 1950), 594-631; M. Mourin, *Le Vatican et l'URSS* (Paris 1965), 60 ff.

Europe and Central Europe (based on the Synod of Carlovtsi), opposition to Metropolitan Sergius was so strong that a number of rival jurisdictions were set up, some of which attached themselves officially to the ecumenical patriarchate of Constantinople while others claimed the right to an autonomous existence within the frame of other autocephalous Orthodox Churches.

The metropolitan's gesture of reconciliation had not, however, earned the Church any diminution of the administrative constraint imposed by the Soviet Republics, which from time to time developed into real persecution (at one point there were 150 bishops interned in a concentration camp on the White Sea), and at the same time the League of Militant Godless were systematically campaigning against religion in any form. Although there was some let-up in 1931 and again in 1936, the bloody purges of the next few years once again bore heavily on the Church whose activity, already much reduced, was pared down to the absolute minimum. Nevertheless, an appreciable part of the population, and of the rural population in particular, stood firm against the anti-religious propaganda, with the result that when the Second World War brought a complete reversal of the situation the Russian Church was seen to have survived to a remarkable degree some twenty years of almost uninterrupted persecution.

The fortunes of the patriarchate of Constantinople followed paths which if less spectacular were at least as precarious. The two encumbrances weighing most heavily on the ecumenical see were, first, the legacy of pan-Hellenism, and second the threat from a secularised and anti-Hellene Turkey.

To assist him in the realisation of his dreams of a Greater Greece rising from the ruins of the Ottoman empire, the Greek minister Venizelos invoked the aid of the bishop of Kition in Cyprus, Meletios Metaxakis, whom he installed in the metropolitan see of Athens, the plan being that he would advance from there to the see of Constantinople. And so it turned out, for when the ecumenical patriarch was deposed (24 October 1918) in response to popular outcry and in deference to the wishes of the occupying powers, 'because of his indulgence towards the Young Turks', it was Metaxakis who, after a vacancy lasting nearly three years, succeeded him on 8 December 1921.

It was during this vacancy in the patriarchal see that the 'ecumenical synod', in response to the appeal from Robert H. Gardiner's World Conference of Union, published in January 1920 its 'Encyclical to all the Churches of the World'. The World Conference had approached Pope Benedict XV as far back as 2 November 1914, reminding him of Leo XIII's labours on behalf of union and soliciting the co-operation of the Roman Church, 'always in the past the champion of Christian unity', but the only outcome of the discussions with the Vatican had been the launching of a 'prayer for unity' (February to April 1916). In the spring of 1919 representatives of the World Conference made an extended tour of Europe and the Near East. They were received in audience by the pope, but the note delivered to them contained only a vague commitment as regards the future. In contrast, the Orthodox leaders in both Athens and Constantinople gave them a warm welcome. On their return to America the delegates of the World Conference published a report surveying the prospects for ecumenical dialogue in which they stressed the advantages to be expected from an ecumenical commitment on the part of Orthodoxy.

It affirmed that[3] the Eastern Orthodox Churches would have an important place in a world conference. It insisted both on the right and the ability that these Churches had to witness to the 'primitive essence' of Christianity. This was due to their long history, their loyalty to the ecumenical councils, their constant witness to catholic faith through the ages of persecution, their special genius which had produced both theologians and martyrs. The presence of representatives of the Eastern Churches was necessary if the Conference was to attain its purpose. The West so often thought in terms merely of the papacy and Protestantism. It tended to forget all about the millions of Christians who were neither Roman Catholic nor Protestant, Christians who were closer to primitive Christianity and might be able to give useful lessons to both the other traditions.

It was this appeal for their collaboration that led the authorities of the ecumenical patriarchate to compose the encyclical addressed without distinction to all the Churches of the world. Writing on behalf of the synod, the member bishops linked their initiative on the one hand with the desire of the Churches to work for Christian unity and on the other with the recent creation of the League of Nations. They set out the goals to be aimed at and the means of achieving them, suggesting a full programme of dialogue and action, which since the Second Vatican Council has begun to be put into effect in the ecumenical sphere.[4] It was the fate of this encyclical to gather dust for many years as a mere historical document produced in a set of circumstances soon overtaken by events or forgotten. Its spirit was destined nevertheless to remain alive, inspiring the Orthodox hierarchy to participate in the various ecumenical conferences of the interwar period and informing their contribution to the Anglican Lambeth Conferences at which Orthodox representatives were present.

3. G. Rientort, 'La World Conference d'Union et les Églises d'Orient', *Échos d'Orient*, XXII (1923), 211-26, esp. 213 ff; see also G. Goyau, 'Sur l'horizon du Vatican', *Revue des Deux Mondes* (15 February and 1 March 1922), 755-81 and 79-113, and more recently, O. Rousseau, 'Sur quelques lettres de R. H. Gardiner, pour l'histoire du mouvement œcuménique', *Irénikon*, LI (1968), 26-32.
4. Text in *Échos d'Orient*, XX (1921), 161-464.

In the meantime, however, the ecumenical patriarchate was obliged to concentrate its energies on the more immediate and pressing tasks of finding ways of adapting the canonical and liturgical institutions of the patriarchate to the new social and religious structures of the postwar period.

One of the first problems to be faced was the plan put forward by Turkey's new master, Mustapha Kemal, for the establishment of a Turkish-Orthodox patriarchate of Anatolia. Debated by the national assembly at Ankara as early as May 1921, this project seemed on the verge of fulfilment through the revolt insidiously encouraged by the *papas* Euthymios, who succeeded in rallying round him a few malcontents and who for a time extended the agitation even to the Phanar, only to retreat before long to frankly chauvinist positions and to the leadership of a small breakaway community, remnants of which still survive.

Meletios VI Metaxakis marked his brief occupancy of the ecumenical see (8 December 1921-10 July 1923) by a burst of intense reforming activity. In the first place, credit is due to him for the constitution of the Greek-Orthodox see of America, to which he gave an ecclesiastical status bordering on that of an autocephaly but preserving a jurisdictional link with Constantinople (from 1931 this important see was to have as its metropolitan the future patriarch Athenagoras). Metaxakis also set up a number of metropolitan sees in Europe, for example in Esthonia, Latvia and Finland. In Albania there was a unilateral declaration of autocephaly in 1922, not formally recognised until 12 April 1937. Patriarch Metaxakis devoted much effort to plans for a pan-Orthodox congress, intended to prepare the way for a pan-Orthodox council to be held in 1925 to commemorate the sixteenth centenary of the first ecumenical council of Nicaea, which would have had before it various measures of reform and adaptation aimed at an Orthodox *aggiornamento*; but with the resignation of Metaxakis in July 1923 this grand design had to be abandoned.

The reversals of fortune experienced by the successors of this dynamic patriarch were so dramatic that pessimistic observers began as early as 1925 to voice doubts concerning the future of the ecumenical patriarchate itself. Deprived of all support from the civil power, it appeared to them on the brink of collapse. The patriarchs continued nevertheless to direct their policies towards the summoning of a general synod. The attempt by Basil III to convoke a council for Pentecost 1925 proved vain. The following year he turned hopefully towards the Vatican and stressed repeatedly to a series of important visitors, among them Mgr Roncalli, the future John XXIII, his conviction of the pressing need for ecclesiastical union and his willingness, despite his advanced age, to go in person to Rome to put to the pope the case for summoning a synod of bishops to study this vital matter.

For the moment, however, realisation of this happy inspiration was made impossible by circumstances connected with the ecumenical movement. Following the Faith and Order Conference at Lausanne (August 1927) Pius XI published the encyclical *Mortalium animos* (6 January 1928), in which he described the Orthodox as 'adherents of the errors of Photius'. The Orthodox in general reacted with indignation and certain prominent bishops, workers in the ecumenical cause, used the occasion to criticise the 'pride of Babel' and to cast doubt on the sincerity of papal appeals for Christian unity. They pointed to Uniatism as proof of Rome's methods of proselytisation and assimilation in her dealings with the Christian East. Even the eirenical Alivisatos openly deplored this refusal of collaboration and dialogue, and in nearly all the autocephalous Churches voices were raised in condemnation of a papal phraseology deemed to be reprehensible. A serious feeling of disquiet again started to build up, estranging official Orthodox circles from Catholic and encouraging Orthodoxy to draw nearer, even in the matter of theological collaboration, to Protestantism in general and Anglicanism in particular. The election of Photius II (7 February 1929) as Basil III's successor in the ecumenical patriarchate demonstrated the willingness of the synod of Constantinople to entrust the moral destiny of Orthodoxy to a man known to have a sympathetic interest in Protestant theology and to be eager to press ahead with the implementation of reforms: the patriarch-elect had pursued his advanced studies in Munich and Lausanne.

Catholics working for unity were well aware of the setback this affair represented to the hopes of *rapprochement* between Rome and Orthodoxy. Dom Lambert Beauduin at once drew attention to it by publishing in 1929 a forthright essay on 'Roman centralisation' in which he trenchantly summed up the Orthodox objections: [5]

Rome [he imagined them saying] personifies in our eyes an ecclesiastical system by nature imperialistic and absorptive, in which an absolute and unconstrainable power tends to concentrate and to monopolise the work of the entire Christian body, just as it tends to standardise and codify, the better to control them, all manifestations of the religious life. Separation, for all the evils it has brought us, has freed us from those constraints, under which we would have lost all our characteristic features, all our traditions, all our laws, all our privileges: we would have ceased to be ourselves.

To round off his remarks, the monk of union added: 'Atrophy at the periphery, hypertrophy at the centre: such is the inevitable outcome of Roman centralisation'.

5. L. Beauduin, *Irénicon*, VI (1929), 145-53.

So began a fairly long period during which the Orthodox Churches led their lives divorced from all contact with Roman Catholicism, all the while strengthening by contrast their relations with the world of the Reformed Churches. In July 1930 a number of Orthodox prelates, among them Meletios Metaxakis, since become patriarch of Alexandria, took part officially in the sixth Anglican Lambeth Conference, which had on its agenda a number of items with inter-confessional implications, for example the question of Anglican ordinations and a limited measure of intercommunion. In November of that same year a conference of Orthodox clergy and teachers was held at Salonika under the auspices of the ecumenical Life and Work movement. Some of the greatest academic names in Orthodoxy took part, for example the Greek Alivisatos and the Russian Zander.

The opportune ending of the Bulgar schism in the spring of 1934 permitted the inter-Orthodox dialogue to be resumed on a wider footing. In the euphoria of this official return to unity, Patriarch Myron of Rumania submitted to the ecumenical patriarch, Photius II, a bold plan, which had been under discussion in non-Greek Orthodox circles for some years, for setting up a permanent Orthodox Synod at Constantinople (December 1935). Presided over by the ecumenical patriarch, this synod would be composed of delegates representing all the autocephalous Churches; its function would be to settle questions of common interest to all Orthodox Churches. But the ecumenical patriarch rejected the scheme on the grounds that it would lead to the supplanting of the patriarchal synod, which in practice decided on inter-Orthodox questions submitted to its consideration.

Nevertheless, the irresistible tendency of the Orthodox Churches to join forces continued to make headway. At the end of November 1936 the first Congress of Orthodox Theology met in Athens, its labours having been mapped out by a preparatory commission sitting in Bucharest. It was to owe much to the contribution of H. Alivisatos as its driving force. The congress reviewed a fully-worked out programme for the re-launching of teaching and research on an inter-university basis and there was evidence of a desire to collaborate in the work of the ecumenical movement and to show the congress's feelings of solidarity with the martyr Church of Russia 'as with all churches suffering for the faith', which made plain that this theological congress was in the true Orthodox tradition.

Seen in that perspective, the presence of Orthodox delegates at the two ecumenical conferences held in Oxford (Life and Work, 12-26 July 1937) and in Edinburgh (Faith and Order, 3-17 August 1937) was fully justified. But it has to be admitted that the slotting of Orthodoxy into a movement still strongly coloured by its original confessional and sociological allegiances was not entirely easy, as witness this humorously rueful comment: 'We Orthodox are simply flowers on the table of the American

Protestant banquet'.

Nor should it be overlooked that alongside the desire for ecumenical commitment and for association with the main stream of non-Roman Christian activity there was an appreciable deepening of Orthodox spiritual life, which led to the proliferation of Orthodox cultural organisations and of more specifically religious and mission-orientated institutes, both among the Russians of the diaspora and in countries such as Rumania, Bulgaria and Greece which had long possessed an Orthodox framework. At the same time an effort at true religious education got under way, which sought to find in the traditions of Eastern Orthodoxy an answer to the problems posed by its altered social and political situation: based often on the monastic ideal transposed to the fully secular life, this truly renovating movement addressed itself to the modernisation and extension of preaching, the promotion of 'Sunday schools' and the organisation of regular study circles whose object was the cultivation and deepening of the spiritual life and of the modes of 'Orthodox action'. It proved in the early days uphill work, but these movements were full of promise for the future and after the trials and manifold tribulations undergone by Orthodoxy during the Second World War they finally came into their own.

2. PALESTINE AND THE QUESTION OF THE HOLY PLACES

The capture of Jerusalem by the Allies (8 December 1917) signified in the eyes of many the rebirth of the crusading era. But Catholicism was no longer the sole contender for this disputed heritage: in the context of this colonialist reconquest, Protestantism and indeed Judaism presented claims they considered equally valid.

In the eyes of the Turkish administration and of the local Arab population, Palestine did not form a distinct geographical or political entity. Palestine was of a piece with Southern Syria, certain districts of which depended administratively speaking, on differing authorities, for example Damascus and Beirut. Under the agreements concluded between France, Russia and England in the spring of 1916, Palestine, generically denominated, was to be withdrawn from the area of plitical contention and placed under international control. But when Soviet Russia called off her agreements, the British Government undertook on 27 November 1917, in the words of the Balfour Declaration, 'to view with favour the establishment in Palestine of a national home for the Jewish people' and to use its 'best endeavours to facilitate the achievement of this object'. This undertaking on Great Britain's part was in flagrant contradiction to her promise to the Hashemite Sharif of Mecca, Husain, to assist him in the founding of an

'Arab kingdom' within the boundaries of the Arab provinces of the Ottoman empire.

After the armistice of 1918, Clemenceau yielded to Lloyd George's insistence that the exercise of higher authority in Palestine should be reserved to the British empire, 'although he would have preferred to see the region under international control'. The Zionist Movement for its part submitted a memorandum to the Peace Conference pressing its own claims to establishment in Palestine, whose frontiers it fixed in advance as embracing former Southern Syria from Sidon to the western slope of Mount Hermon and extending in the east from the Jordan valley to the Hijaz railway. These demands followed the course of a line already projected by England as far back as 1840, at the time of the first Turko-Egyptian clash in the east, as the boundary of a province to be set up under European supervision as a buffer between Syria and Egypt. In the event the boundaries of Palestine under the British mandate were fixed by the Franco-British treaty of 23 December 1920, ratified by the League of Nations on 24 July 1922.

Efforts to alert Catholic opinion, especially in France, to the grave threat to the religious protectorate in Palestine had not been wanting. As far back as the autumn of 1916 Mgr Charmetant, director of the Oeuvre d'Orient, who had long-standing connections with French diplomatic circles and with diplomats representing the Central Powers, had published what amounted to a manifesto protesting against plans 'to sell Palestine to the Jews'. Based on a thorough and first-hand acquaintance with the international and American Jewish press, the 'manifesto' sounded a note of warning against Zionist agitation in Constantinople and the European capitals for the creation of 'a sanctuary . . . an island of refuge for the victims of constant persecution'. It condemned the spirit of conquest which animated these endeavours and analysed the problem under its human aspect, as it affected the Palestinian populations, and under its religious aspect, as it affected Catholics and Orthodox. Nor, in conclusion, did the document omit to refer to France's long-standing political and commercial interests in Palestine. In May-June 1917 Mgr Charmetant returned to the charge with further denunciations of the 'German machinations of Zionism'.

After the war the Palestine question directly engaged the attention of the Holy See, which was able, via the Catholic hierarchy, to exert a discreet influence while also issuing from time to time fervent appeals 'on behalf of Catholic missions in the Holy Land'. On 10 March 1919, for example, Benedict XV delivered an address in consistory in which he sought to stir up Catholic opinion on behalf of the Christian East. He made no secret of his anxieties with regard to the fate of the Holy Places in Palestine: 'The fate the Peace Conference has in store for the Holy Places cannot fail to concern us, for there is no doubting that our grief, as indeed the grief of all Christians, would be great if infidels were given a privileged position in Palestine, and still greater if those august monuments were to be entrusted to the keeping of non-Christians.'

In response to this appeal, an Association of Friends of the Holy Land (Association des amis de la Terra sainte) was formed under the working chairmanship of J. Reinach, with Cardinal Mercier as honorary president. Its aim was to 'campaign vigorously against the formation of any confessional (Jewish) state in Palestine' and it wanted to see the region granted 'at the very least a charter of autonomy under the supervision of a power free of any commitment to Zionism'. Local administration would be in hands of the native populations without distinction of race or religion, and all religious denominations would be allowed unrestricted access to the Holy Places and freedom to develop, the only privileged position being that to be accorded to the Holy See.

It is not possible in this brief space to follow in detail all the twists and turns of this Catholic movement for the defence of Palestine and the Holy Places, which were in any case of no political consequence; but one or two of the more important initiatives deserve to be recalled. At the end of 1919, following in the footsteps of Cardinal Bourne, archbishop of Westminster, the cardinal archbishop of Paris, Dubois, went on a political and religious mission to Syria-Palestine. In the following year an International Catholic Congress on Palestine met at Einsiedeln in Switzerland (12-16 July 1920), but the San Remo agreements on the mandate formula made its resolutions on the subject of the Holy Places of no effect. After the designation of Greater Lebanon as a 'Christian home' in the Near East and the signing of the international treaties, there seemed to be no future in further agitation. It was therefore left to the Latin patriarch, Mgr Barlassina, assisted by the religious congregations, principally the Franciscans, to protect the rights Catholicism had already acquired over the Holy Places. In practice, the Holy Land continued to be the target of attempts at Latin proselytisation, as witness the comings and goings of cardinals of various nationalities between 1923 and 1925 and the formation in different countries of national committees in support of 'Catholic voluntary organisations', but this was a far cry from the original objectives. Moreover, the rigid attitude of the Latin patriarch made him the victim for years on end of insidious attack from the pro-Zionist press and from non-Catholic organisations, which tried in vain to have him recalled to Rome. The Vatican's answer was the suppression through the Holy Office of the Association des amis d'Israël (28 March 1928) and the issue of advice to Catholics to support instead the Archconfraternity of Prayer for the Conversion of Israel, founded in Jerusalem in 1926.

3. THE PAPACY AND THE CATHOLIC EAST

The two great popes who in succession occupied the Holy See between 1914 and 1939 initiated policies which left a profound imprint on the Catholic East, still discernible even after the Second Vatican Council.

To Benedict XV goes the credit for having continued the enlightened policy of Leo XIII. Thanks to him, the Catholic East found an official place within the constitutional framework of Roman Catholicism. The creation of the Sacred Congregation of the Eastern Church by the *motu proprio Dei Providentis* (1 May 1917) brought into being, even before the end of the First World War, an organ of fundamental importance in the re-launching of the drive for unity. Its centralising influence, analogous to that exercised in the Latin West by the other Roman Congregations, was intended to extend to all affairs involving Eastern Catholics, even those of mixed jurisdiction, and to be a means of promoting unionism in two sectors in particular, that of Slav Orthodoxy, on the point of losing the support of Tsarism, and that of Greek-Arab Orthodoxy, whose future destinies appeared to depend on the good will of the Allied Powers. The reports of the consultors which formed the basis of the new pontifical institution were unanimous in stressing the importance of breaking away from the latinising methods and spirit of the past and of presenting the papacy in its truly 'Catholic' character. Benedict XV incorporated this viewpoint, which in the event was unfortunately not destined to prevail, into the wording of the charter setting up the Congregation: ' . . . This present act will make it still more clearly manifest that the Church of Jesus Christ, which is neither Latin nor Greek nor Slav but Catholic, makes no distinction between her sons, and that the latter, whether Greek, Latin, Slav or of other national character, are all of the same degree in the eyes of this apostolic see.' The foundation at Rome of the Pontifical Institute for Eastern Studies (by the *motu proprio Orientis catholici* of 15 October 1917) was intended originally to reflect the 'Catholic' dimension of the Christian Orthodox East, a term employed for the first time without pejorative reservations and without inverted commas.

However, the generally catastrophic plight of Orthodoxy following the political downfall of the Russian and Turkish empires obliged the authorities to adopt a realistic policy, geared to what was immediately feasible in a totally changed set of circumstances. The fact is that, immediately after the fall of the monarchy, the provisional government in Russia had declared an amnesty for all offences of a political and religious nature, and the Russian Catholic community in Petrograd had even managed to secure official recognition, thanks to the representations and influence of the Ruthenian metropolitan of Lvov, Mgr Andrew Szeptycki, and of the exarch, Leonid Fedorov. These ardent promoters of Slav Uniatism lost no time in summoning a synod to Petrograd (29-31 May 1917) with the intention of promulgating statutes for the new Uniate community, over which Federov was to preside as exarch. This premature move was doomed to failure, not only by the revolutionary developments in Russia but also because of the wisely cautious attitude of the Roman authorities.

At Constantinople, the political situation was taking a disquieting turn in the direction of Turkish nationalism. In Georgia, in Anatolia, in Kurdistan, whole Christian communities appeared to be looking to the Roman see. With his address of 10 March 1919, Benedict XV had been at pains to stress the interest Roman Catholicism had in the East. He also had studies made of the conditions for union which ought to operate 'if a dissident Church in its entirety sought to return to Catholic unity'. At the time, as can be seen from confidential memoranda which have come to light, the prospect appeared imminent. In the end, however, the extremely volatile political situation of the times did not permit the adoption of a conclusive attitude on the question.

In any case, the promoters of 'Uniate penetration' in Soviet Russia and in the Greek-Arab Near East were by no means all of one opinion regarding the best course to pursue. Fired by the examples of Mgr E. Ropp, formerly bishop of Tiraspol near Vilna and now archbishop of Mohilev and metropolitan of all the Latin Churches of the former Russian empire, of Mgr Barlassina in Jerusalem, of Mgr Petit and his Assumptionist colleagues in Constantinople and Athens, many authorities on the spot were in favour of allowing responsibility for the 'unionist apostolate' to rest on priests of Western and Latin origin, setting little store on the effectiveness of local representatives of Eastern Catholicism. But authentic spokesmen for Slav and Arab Uniatism insisted on the contrary that, from now on, the main burden had to be borne by Eastern Catholics themselves, though not to the extent of refusing the subsidiary support to which they were entitled from Western missions and religious congregations. Such was the firmly and clearly expressed view of the Uniate Melkite patriarch, Dimitri I Cadi, set down in an analysis of first principles he made for the benefit of Benedict XV (dated 29 June 1920). Not long afterwards, on 18 February 1921, the metropolitan of the Ruthenians, Mgr Andrew Szeptickij, was in Rome addressing an audience of Western religious interested in the new trend in relations between the papacy and the Orthodox East and explaining to them, from the Eastern viewpoint, the role he thought Western monachism should play in the unionist movement.

The premature death of Benedict XV was not allowed to interfere with the putting into effect of his unionist programme. Writing at the time of the pope's death, M. Pernot, one of the best-informed observers of the pontificate, aptly summed up his thinking as follows: 'Benedict XV looked on the Uniate communities as the outposts of Catholicism. White Russia and the Ukraine were to him marches from which the Roman Church would launch its campaign for the conquest of the schismatic portion of the Slav world. He sent to Poland, and intended to send to the Ukraine, the best diplomats the Vatican could command.' [6]

It was precisely one of these diplomats with recent experience of Eastern affairs, Archille Ratti, become in the meantime cardinal archbishop of Milan, who was elected Benedict XV's successor and who, as Pius XI, was to give still more positive impetus to the re-launching of the pro-Eastern policy. In his injunctions, delivered in circumstances of great solemnity, urging Catholics to deepen their knowledge and understanding of the riches stored up in the Catholic patrimony, as also in his enlightened measures aimed at a re-ordering of the affairs of the Christian East and its genuine promotion, he surpassed, in breadth and depth of vision, even the benign intentions of Leo XIII and Benedict XV.

It would take too long to attempt, even in simplified form, a balanced evaluation of Pius XI's work on behalf of the East. But a rapid survey of the progressive enlargement of his unionist vision and of his main measures in respect of Slav and Greek-Arab Orthodoxy should suffice to demonstrate the scope of his intentions and the essential objectives of his vast programme. He showed himself, in this particular domain, at once a farsighted thinker and a forthright man of action.

In his very first encyclical, *Ubi arcano* (23 December 1922), there was discreet allusion to a possible resumption of the Vatican Council, and we know now that preliminary consultations reached a fairly advanced stage. Among the subjects to be discussed was the future of the Eastern Churches, and there was already a proposal that observers from non-Catholic Churches and confessions be invited to attend. [7]

Moreover, Pius XI found he could turn for help in propagating his views to some men already committed to the cause of union. Although the majority still kept to the paths well trodden by previous generations, a few were on the lookout for effective ways of breaking out of what had become a narrow and sterile rut. The launching of the review *L'Union des Églises* (1922) was already evidence of a desire for a more open approach, but what did most to sensitise religious opinion to the problem of Christian unity was the publication of a series of monographs which at the time aroused great excitement. The publication of J. Calvet's *Le Problème catholique de l'union des Églises*

6. For more detail see the same author's *Le Saint-Siège, l'Église catholique et la Politique mondiale* (Paris 1924), 174-5.

7. P. Caprile, 'Pio XI et la ripresa del concilio vaticano', *Civiltà cattolica*, (1966), Vol. III 27-39; 'Pio XII e un nuovo progretto di concilio oecumenico', *Ibid.*, 209-27; commentary in *Irénikon*, XXXIX (1966), 407-10.

(1921) occurred just at the time when C. Loiseau, writing in the *Revue des Deux Mondes*,[8] was bringing the subject to the attention of the wider public and not long afterwards M. Pernot, in his book on *La Question turque* (1922), aired the question of 'Latin triumphalism' in the Greek-Arab Near East. The Assumptionist R. Janin's full-length study, very exhaustive for its period, of the Eastern Churches and Eastern rites (*Églises orientales et rites orientaux*, 1922) achieved wide circulation as a standard account. But the writer who came closest to the views being elaborated by the pope and his advisers was the French priest Pierre Charon, who wrote under the name C. Korolevskij.

The launching of his review *Stoudion* and of his book on *Le Clergé occidental et l'Apostolat dans l'Orient asiatique et gréco-slave* aptly coincided with the publication, on the occasion of the third centenary of St Josaphat, Ukrainian martyr in the cause of union, of the first Eastern encyclical of the pontificate, *Ecclesiam Dei* (12 November 1923). In this encyclical the pope urged the Catholic world 'to make itself more fully and less superficially acquainted with the affairs and customs of the East' since such knowledge was becoming indispensable to a just appreciation of the problem of Christian unity. He reserved in this connection a special role for the Eastern Uniate Churches.

Not long afterwards Pius XI made his views concrete in the letter *Equidem Verba* (21 March 1924) that he addressed to the Benedictines, urging them to apply themselves to the 'work of rebuilding unity'. The idea of the letter, and probably even the text, had been suggested by a Belgian Benedictine, Dom Lambert Beauduin, who had close connections with Mgr d'Herbigny, at that time all-powerful in the Eastern Congregation. The next year saw the foundation, as a direct result of *Equidem Verba*, of the priory of Amay-sur-Meuse (transferred in 1939 to Chevetogne). The pamphlet in which Dom Lambert commended to the public this 'monastic endeavour to promote the union of the Churches' was in the nature of a manifesto, testifying to the apostle's boldness of vision and 'dangerous' enthusiasm for his cause, while the review *Irénikon*, which he launched in April 1926, acted as a sounding-board, down to our own day, for the fertile thoughts and intuitions of a galaxy of talent wholly dedicated to the quest for Christian unity. By contrast with Rome, at that date almost totally preoccupied with Russia, Dom Lambert was very quick to extend the quest to include the whole of non-Roman Christianity, the Reformed Churches included, paying scant heed to the additional difficulties, over and above those inherent in any

---

8. C. Loiseau, 'La politique des rites', *Revue des deux Mondes* (15 November 1921), 380-403; the same, 'Le Saint-Siège, la Pologne et la Russie', *Revue universelle*, X (1922), 172-88.

pilot venture, that the adoption of this broadly 'ecumenical' outlook must inevitably bring down on his head.

Meanwhile, Pius XI was looking more closely into possible ways of re-establishing Rome's broken links with the Christian East. His address on 10 January 1927 to the Italian Catholic University Federation added a new dimension to his programme, for he made reference in it to 'reciprocal prejudices' and to unbelievable 'mistakes and misunderstandings', and reproached Catholics for their 'lack of a just appreciation of their duty of fraternal understanding and sympathy'. Lastly, he paid homage to a 'holiness' conserved by the venerable Christendoms of the East, making use in so doing of terms quite foreign to the usual Roman style and unprecedented in papal pronouncements.

This sincere declaration encouraged the 'unionists' to go deeper into the problem of diversity within Catholic unity. In 1926 Dom Lambert Beauduin had already remarked, apropos of patriarchs, that 'the liturgy was not the only, or indeed the principal domain in which the Latin differed from the Eastern Church' [9] and in 1927 C. Korolevskij published a provocative essay on *L'Uniatisme* and its misdeeds, while in the following year Mgr Bruno de Solages propounded in his *L'Église et l'Occident* views on the interrelationship between Western civilisation and Catholicism which have since become commonplace but which were new at the time. Pursuing the same path, but taking a more lofty view of history and of the existing situation between the Churches, the German F. Heiler took occasion in a paper entitled 'Religious movements in present-day Roman Catholicism' (August 1928) to sum up the first conclusions to be drawn from a movement which already looked promising. He noted within the Roman Church an awareness in *avant-garde* unionist circles that the Church's catholicity postulated recognition of 'charismas specific to the Eastern and the Protestant Churches', whose convergence with the charismas of the Roman Church was salutary to the well-being of the Church universal. It therefore followed, he thought, that efforts for union ought to concentrate on bringing formally constituted ecclesiastical bodies closer together and not, by and large, on the proselytisation of the individual; and he added that one obstacle standing in the way was the work of dogmatic definition accomplished at the First Vatican Council, which needed to be submitted for re-examination and improvement to a new council, with the object of restoring 'the balance between episcopal and papal powers, upset by the unilateral definition of the universal power of the pope'.

There was no prospect at that time of these views being adopted as a complete synthesis. Moreover, they already went beyond the limited objec-

9. L. Beauduin, *Irénikon*, I (1926), 239-44, 267-74.

tives of the unionist movement and were starting to verge on ecumenical territory proper. Now the goals of the ecumenical movement had just been roundly condemned by Pius XI in the encyclical *Mortalium animos* (6 January 1928), and it was not long before Dom Lambert Beauduin, originator of the Monks of Union, found himself disavowed. The new policy, launched by the pope from such excellent premisses, for the moment could make no further headway. The pope was nevertheless prepared to implement some of the proposals already put forward, and these would safeguard the basic principles of the papal commitment to the Christian East.

For a start, on 8 September 1928 he published the encyclical *Rerum orientalium*, which stressed the need for the study of 'Eastern affairs', especially in the major seminaries (but the idea of setting aside one day a week for the teaching of Eastern theology soon boiled down in practice to an 'Eastern Day' once a year, which gradually became an accepted part of clerical education).

A subsequent and more striking move confirmed the genuineness of the papal commitment to honour the Eastern patrimony. Building on a principle already enunciated in the first canon of the codified canon law of the Latin Church, Pius XI decided in January 1929 on the promulgation of a special code of Eastern canon law. By so doing he publicly reaffirmed the principle of 'disciplinary dualism', attacked at the Vatican Council, as became all the more evident when his immediate collaborators were pleased to announce that the codification would deal 'not only with the form . . . but also with the substance'. The preparatory work, begun in 1929, in fact moved very slowly and it took twenty years for the first results of it to emerge.

In any case, while continuing to support the activities of his carefully chosen collaborators, from 1930 Pius XI apparently ceased to concern himself directly with their labours, the Christian East having by now acquired an institutional niche in the very heart of the supreme government of the Roman Church.

Papal policy in regard to Slav Christianity had to reckon both with the Bolshevik regime in the Soviet Socialist Republics and with the newly resurrected Polish state, which numbered three and a half million Uniate Ruthenians among its inhabitants, but whose leaders were markedly hostile to all things Eastern.

The Genoa Conference (April-May 1922) had aroused hopes of an informal understanding between the diplomacy of the new pope and that of the Soviets. Pius XI appointed to act for him on the spot an experienced diplomat, Mgr Sincerot, subsequently secretary of the Congregation of the Eastern Church, and he hoped much from the success of this first dialogue between the old western Europe and the new Bolshevik Russia, but traditional diplomacy, supported turn and turn about by the rigidity of

Catholic public opinion and the root and branch opposition of the Russian diaspora, made the prospect of an effective Catholic presence in Russian territories very remote.

In the circumstances, only one way remained open to the Roman Church to profit in terms of revived Catholic influence in Russia from the disintegration of the Tsarist Church: the sending of a mission for famine relief. On terms negotiated by a young diplomat, Mgr Pizzardo, a pontifical mission composed of religious of varying nationalities left for Russia in the summer of 1922. However, when to its humanitarian endeavours the mission insisted on adding advocacy of unionism or even merely of religion, it was forced to withdraw. The net result of the missions conducted by Mgr d'Herbigny in 1925-6 was little different and, to make matters worse, the whole approach of this 'expert' in Russian religious affairs was already starting to alienate people who were less sophisticated than he but more concerned for the dignity and survival of Orthodox Catholicism in Russia. The enterprises launched by d'Herbigny as head of the pontifical commission *Pro Russia,* an office he held from 6 April 1930, did not survive his fall from favour in 1935; the one exception was the Roman *Russicum* or Russian College, which still exists in token of the papacy's apostolic concern for the Slav Orthodox world.

These Jesuit-run enterprises were complemented by an institution whose conduct Pius XI entrusted to the French Dominicans. It took the form initially of the Russian Seminary of St Basil, set up at Lille in 1925, but this was soon superseded by the Roman *Russicum,* with the result that what had been originally intended as a contribution to clerical education gradually transformed itself into a centre for research and study. Known as the Istina, its scholarly activities, at first modest in scope, in time started to attract the attention and respect of the ecumenists. In 1934 the centre started publishing a review, *Russie et Chrétienté,* which, after the centre's transfer to Paris, changed its name to *Istina* and acquired as companion a monthly bulletin, *Vers l'unité chrétienne.* The historian cannot fail to be struck by the decisive part that these journals, discreetly edited by Fr Pierre Dumont, played alongside *Irénikon* in promoting a better understanding by the West of the Christian East.

But not content with these generalised measures, Pius XI showed particular concern for the plight and future destinies of the local Uniate communities. Metropolitan Andrew Szeptickij, in the opinion of C. Korolevskij 'the hierarch who wielded the greatest influence in the Eastern Church during the first half of the twentieth century', gave him valuable support with his plans for the reorganisation of the Ukrainian dioceses in Poland and the reform of the Basilian monks. It was hoped through the Roman Ukrainian College to link the higher clergy and the clergy of the future more closely with the apostolic see. The metropolitan realised from his own experience as a former monk that the Ruthenian Congregation of the monks of St Basil, governed by the Western code, did not fully correspond to the Eastern idea of monachism, and even before the First World War he had already devised plans for a new foundation, inspired by the Byzantine *Stoudion* but adapted to the social and religious structures of the country. This was the origin of the Studite congregation for which, overriding the objections of some of his openly latinising suffragans, he obtained Rome's approval in 1923. The same latinisers also checked his attempts at liturgical reforms, desired in fact by Rome, designed to eliminate a number of clumsy imitations of Latin usages.

Bulgarian Uniatism, although taken in hand by the Assumptionists, had been marking time since the end of the nineteenth century. The appointment of Mgr Roncalli as apostolic delegate to Sofia and as vicar apostolic to Bulgar Catholics was helpful in removing certain old encumbrances but without effecting any substantial alteration in the general situation of the Catholic minorities, Latin and Uniate. Mention should be made of the establishment at Sofia in 1935, with the pope's personal encouragement, of a 'Byzantine Carmel' which combined observance of the Latin rule with the practice of an exclusively Byzantine liturgy, a novel formula which it was hoped would serve to revive the contemplative life of Eastern enclosed nuns.

We turn lastly to Rumania, which in 1927 entered into a concordat with the Holy See and which could boast of a number of compact and keenly committed Uniate communities whose prevailing mood, thanks to a spirit of emulation with the Orthodox majority, was one of renovation. A large establishment in Rome, situated close to the Ukrainian College, trained up the Rumanian clerical élite along the unionist lines advocated by the Assumptionists. The 'Carmel of the Annonciades', founded in 1938 on the model of the Sofia Carmel, was to prove to Orthodox monachism the vitality of the contemplative rule among the Uniates.

The initiatives and pronouncements of Pius XI in respect of the Greek-Arab Near East were many, their object being to re-order or re-activate the religious, social and cultural life of communities which had either totally disintegrated or had fallen into deep disarray following the downfall of the Ottoman empire and the failure of the Greek offensive in Asia Minor.

The most recent and most grievous ordeals suffered by the Armenians had been those in Anatolia and Cilicia, where thirteen ecclesiastical circumscriptions, along with their titulars and congregations, had disappeared in the turmoil. Having previously been installed by Hassoun at Constantinople, the Armenian patriarchate was transferred back in 1928 to Beirut and at much the same date the Syrian Catholic patriarch removed himself from Mardinn, now part of Ataturk's Turkey, to take up residence likewise in

Beirut. The Nestorian Christians of Northern Mesopotamia had to suffer until 1936 the consequences of the political instability of the region, tossed to and fro between the local nationalist movement and the sham of European protection. Three Chaldean dioceses no longer had any faithful. Refugees fleeing from Turkish territories poured for years on end into Northern Syria, seeking a resting-place in the urban centres or desert plains.

In the lands subjected to European mandates the development of the many communities of Eastern rite was marked by paradox: for an improvement in patriarchal structures and personal status and a distinct rise in the social and cultural level went hand in hand with an increasing attachment to the spiritual and ecclesiastical structures of a type of Catholicism heavily imprinted with colonialism. In his book *Une enquête aux pays du Levant* (1923), Maurice Barrès analysed with great acuteness this transformational phenomenon, which seemed to be linking the destinies of the venerable, and until now profoundly traditional, Christianity of the Near East with those of an Anglo-French form of civilisation. So greatly were the élite, clerical and lay, affected by this characteristic manifestation of cultural and religious osmosis, whose beginnings went back to the end of the nineteenth century, that they seemed quite prepared to dissociate themselves from their origins and to sever their links with the surrounding culture, at the risk in the long run of cutting themselves off from the bulk of the Christian population, still deeply embedded in the traditional ways.

The vogue for educational establishments run by foreign Latin congregations, the Latins' monopoly of clerical education, the canonical reforms put in hand for Eastern monastic institutions, the actual considerations governing appointment to certain episcopal sees, the methods adopted for moulding the Christian cadres of the future, all inevitably contributed to the linking of the Christian élite, and the Catholic élite in particular, to a way of life and thought imported ready-made. The success in the cultural field of French-Arab bilingualism, not merely in the Lebanon but also in Egypt, Syria and even in Palestine, aroused hopes of its possible extension to other domains of religious and social life. It was estimated that two generations would suffice, in a society already so sharply differentiated, to bring about a radical discontinuity between Eastern Christians of the old style and the new. It is worth noting that this social and religious grooming of a new élite was in progress at a time when, throughout the Arab world, the masses were starting to assert with increasing vehemence their ardent desire for the recovery of independence and unity.

The ultimate objective of this gradual exertion of a stranglehold on the primitive and age-old values of an authentic Christianity had emerged quite clearly from the labours of the commissions preparing for the First Vatican Council. At the period we are speaking of, circumstantial articles appearing in local journals, in particular those published by the Catholic printing house in Beirut, and in the foreign reviews *(Échos d'Orient, L'Union des Églises, L'Unité de l'Église)*, dealing with topics such as the moulding of popular piety, clerical education, Eastern religious institutes, the transfer of certain episcopal titulars and the role played by the provincial superiors of the Latin congregations, were open testimony to the spirit it was intended to impress on the future development of Christianity in the African and Asian countries of the Near East. This way of operating was confirmed in highly significant fashion by the elevation, in December 1935, of the Syrian Catholic Patriarch, Ignatius Tappouni, to the cardinalate. [10]

In Palestine, a similar pattern of development added to the bewilderment at the seeming inconsistency of papal policy in respect of local Christianity. It appears that in the early days of his pontificate Pius XI thought seriously of bringing to an end the latinising operation embodied in the patriarchate of Jerusalem. Put in the picture by the precise and detailed reports he received from well-informed observers such as Dom G. Fournier, a Benedictine of Maredsous and former prior of the German monastery of the Dormition in Jerusalem, Pius XI was almost persuaded to abolish the patriarchate and leave the field free for the Franciscan Custody and the Catholic Greek-Melkite patriarchate, but as a result of forceful political intervention provoked by the partisan and personal character of Zionist attacks on Mgr Barlassina, who had support both in the curia and among influential members of the French hierarchy, the pope eventually abandoned the idea. The appointment in 1927 of Mgr Pascal Robinson as visitor apostolic to the patriarchate, with which he had a close acquaintance going back to 1919, made it look as though structural changes of the kind desired by indigenous members of the Latin patriarchal clergy were in preparation. In the end, the Vatican shied away from drastic measures and contented itself with the creation of a Uniate Melkite bishopric in Transjordan (1932), hoping thereby to set a limit to the spread of latinism among the numerous Arab and Orthodox communities of the new emirate. This watered-down solution amounted in fact to success for the would-be latinisers of Eastern Christianity in Palestine. And as proof of the persistence of their triumphalist mentality, we can point to the distinctly fanciful work published by a member of the staff of the patriarchate, F. Talvacchia, under the title *Rito romano e riti orientali* (1947).

In this context, the regional Eucharistic Congress held at Beirut in June 1939, the setting up of Eastern branches of the major religious congregations and the stepping up of recruitment of Eastern Christians to those orders, and the encouragement of Eastern 'missionary' institutes prepared to

10. *La Croix* of Paris, 8 December 1935.

take the rules and spirit of the Latin canons as their guide, can all be seen as evidence of an equivocal desire to create a kind of bi-ritualist mentality, to match the bi-ritualism of the liturgy. And so the Uniate communities seemed to be launched on a road which offered the prospects of material prosperity and intellectual advancement but which was leading them towards a loss of religious identity.

The publication by a former missionary in Egypt of a *Manuel du catéchiste en Orient* (1939), sponsored by the local Latin hierarchy and therefore assured of a wide circulation, was a manifestation of the folly of resorting to a method which relied on systematic denigration of the record and ethos of the Eastern Churches. It had, however, the effect in certain Eastern circles of provoking a healthy reaction, marking the beginning of the revival that was to take place following the upheavals of the Second World War.

The subjection of Eastern communities in union with the Holy See to a flood of latinising influences naturally enough confirmed Orthodoxy in its radical opposition to everything represented by the form of 'Eastern Catholicism' which went by the name of 'Uniatism'.

The campaign against Uniatism was taken most seriously in Greece, where it was given official doctrinal and legal backing and launched on a national scale. Greek Uniatism was a comparatively recent and very limited phenomenon, having first appeared at Constantinople towards the end of the nineteenth century and then removed itself, after the Greek débâcle in Asia Minor, to Athens. Within a relatively short time, to be precise on 7 April 1925, a circular violently attacking Uniatism was being read aloud, on the instructions of the primate of Greece, Mgr Papadopoulos, in all the churches of the kingdom. This launching of the offensive started up a fierce argument with the head of the tiny Uniate community, Mgr Calavassy, and the debate subsequently grew to such proportions that the courts and the Council of State were obliged to intervene. But the argument at the national level, which did not remain confined to Greece and which was taken up by the major representatives of the religious press, was a means of making unionists and church leaders aware of the problem of 'Uniatism' in its theological and historical essentials.

As far as Greek Orthodoxy was concerned, however, the quarrel over Uniatism from 1925 to 1933 was little short of an obsession, in which political and emotional factors played a damaging and confusing role. In the eyes of the Greek hierarchy, Uniatism represented a method of proselytism cunningly confected in the sixteenth century by the Jesuits, for use in particular in the Polish context, and the preservation of the 'Greek' rite was merely a cover for Rome's objectives of progressive absorption and latinisation. 'Of all Latin propagandists', wrote Mgr Papadopoulos, 'the Uniates are the most dangerous' and he went on to say: 'Believe me, Uniatism is still regarded with horror by the Orthodox, because it represents deceit and imposture in matters of religion. We respect the sincere preaching of a Latin priest but we abhor, let me tell you, the preaching of an advocate of Uniatism. . . .' [11]

So on the eve of the Second World War there was still a fundamental ambiguity of attitude towards the content, destinies and specific role of Uniatism, as marked on the side of recalcitrant Orthodoxy as on that of Roman Catholicism. The situation was about to be substantially modified, as a result of the upheavals of the war and of the global redivision of political power that followed it, not to mention the nationalist struggles for independence in the Near East.

11. V. Grégoire, 'Les catholiques de rite byzantin en Grèce, leur situation juridique', *Échos d'Orient*, XXXII (1933), 234-45.

19

1940-68: FROM PIUS XII TO THE SECOND VATICAN COUNCIL

IN DEALING with this recent period, the historian has for the most part to be content with blocking in the main outlines of the course of events, making an effort to understand their significance and bearing, but not forgetting that he is acting as little more than a chronicler. The reason is not only that many of the primary sources of this 'history' are still inaccessible, but also that the underlying intentions of the principal actors are not apparent from the documents or from their actions, and that the length of the shadow cast by many of the events will not become plain until some time in the more-or-less distant future. This applies as much to the social and political transformations taking place in the vast dominions in which Eastern Christianity had taken root, in the Old World as in the New, as it does to the religious and cultural upheavals taking place inside the great Christian confessions with which we are here concerned: on the one hand the papacy, in its progress towards open commitment to ecumenism.

On the political and social plane, the salient features of these decades were the atmosphere of 'cold war' between the two major blocs, the phenomenon of decolonisation, the mounting aspirations of Eastern nations in search of a renewed cultural identity, and lastly the emergence with some difficulty of a 'Third World' neutralist force, which sought to progress beyond the confrontations of the Great Powers and of the competing ideologies which acted as such powerful constraints on the destinies of the modern world.

On the cultural and religious plane, the period saw a radical upsetting of many traditional positions. Although the pontificate of Pius XII appeared to embody in their ultimate form the principles of religious monarchy affirmed by the First Vatican Council, his successors have been more disposed to adopt a policy inspired by conciliarism, in which episcopal collegiality provides a framework for the exercise and extension of papal action. There was an equally remarkable change of front at the two main poles of Orthodoxy, Constantinople and Moscow. Both can be said in general to have exchanged an attitude of defensiveness and isolationism for one of willingness to enter the path of interconfessional conversations and of ecumenical dialogue both with Roman Catholics and with the World Council of Churches. The latter, born in a climate of indifference or even of suspicion, at last established itself during this period as a rallying point, or to be more exact, as an open forum for interconfessional meetings and dialogue between the Churches.

In this Christian world newly taking shape, and of which only the first promontories could as yet be discerned, the old religious map seemed destined to undergo certain alterations, especially as regards the place on it of a number of smaller and less influential Christian bodies. In the case of the Christian East this applied above all to the pre-Chalcedonian or Monophysite Churches, which were themselves engaged in a historic process of unification, and to Eastern minorities separated from the ancestral stem of patriarchal Orthodoxy and grafted on to the Roman Church of the post-Tridentine era. The forward march of the ecumenical movement, which appeared to be directing Christianity into new paths, raised questions as to the purpose and prospects of these historic forms of ecclesiastical grouping.

The opening up before the Churches of so many new perspectives in such a short space of time implied a true break with a very recent past, a past which the institutional set-up still preserved and which men who had been its convinced and dedicated architects sought to perpetuate. The vital bridge linking the two eras was the Second Vatican Council. It was this which promoted the growth of a new spirit and of new institutions, so marking the beginning of a new era not only for Roman Catholicism but for all Churches definitely committed to the ecumenical path.

A chronicler who tried to keep pace with the various developments in the full range of Orthodox autocephalous Churches would soon succumb to exhaustion, so full is the material provided by a press eager to acquaint the public with all the twists and turns of an existence filled with incident and moments of suspense, with sudden reversals and with programmes half-realised, with interconfessional events pregnant with ecumenical consequences. Obviously all that can be done here is to draw attention to a few of the more noteworthy actions and try to elucidate the spirit behind them.

The gradual resumption by the ecumenical patriarch of his leading role dates from the election of Athenagoras I (3 November 1948), who arrived in Constantinople from the archbishopric of America in something of a blaze of glory and assured of the protection of the occupants of the White House. By dint of patient accommodation and collaboration with the Turkish authorities, the patriarch succeeded in regaining control (July 1949) of the Church's educational and charitable institutions, which for twenty years had been subject to close surveillance by State commissioners, and not long afterwards he was able to establish a patriarchal press and start publication of a new weekly, *Apostolos Andreas.*

In 1951 Athenagoras revived the pan-Orthodox programme of his predecessors, with the aim on the one hand of summoning a reforming pro-synod and on the other of urging the autocephalous Churches as a whole to become pan-Christian in their outlook, but the general reaction was not very encouraging. Finding Orthodoxy in no hurry to respond to his appeals, the patriarch decided on a more personal form of action. In July 1953, receiving a visit from his colleague of Antioch, Alexander III, he made manifest his desire to become acquainted with Near Eastern Christendom by going on pilgrimage to the Holy Places. He intended by this means to launch his drive for *rapprochement* between the Churches, which was to lead him to a goal very few at that time suspected. Only a year later we find a Greek theologian, B.C. Ioannidis, reviving in the review *Ekklesia* a proposal put forward as long ago as 1946 by a Greek prelate, Mgr P. K. Medawar, in a confidential communication to the Holy See. Pleading the necessity for con-tacts between the Orthodox and Roman Catholic Churches, Ioannidis wondered if it was possible to hope for a meeting between Pius XII and Athenagoras. For himself he saw no objection, but the world in general was still far from envisaging such an eventuality which, to the more shortsighted, seemed utterly utopian.

The riots in Istanbul of 6 September 1955, during which several dozen Greek Orthodox churches and institutes were ransacked, imposed a severe strain on Greek-Turkish relations and equally on Orthodox feelings with regard to the Catholic authorities. The launching of the hoped-for movement of *rapprochement* found itself postponed to better days. The unhappy situa-tion of the ecumenical patriarchate nevertheless prompted certain Orthodox leaders to consider ways in which Orthodox solidarity might be made more effective. But while the patriarch of Alexandria was recommending the crea-tion of a standing Council of Orthodox Patriarchates to give tangible and effective expression to the internal unity of Orthodoxy, pending the sum-moning at a more opportune moment of the pan-Orthodox pro-synod, the ecumenical patriarchate, paradoxically as it might seem, was turning its eyes towards the Vatican. In the issue of the journal *Apostolos Andreas* dated 13 March 1957, which conveyed greetings to Pius XII on the occasion of his eightieth birthday, a wish was expressed that at the time seemed totally un-realistic: having complimented the Roman pontiff on his political skill and farsightedness, the official organ of the Phanar looked forward to the summoning of a council representative of the whole of Christendom, for the purpose of examining the future of Christianity on the basis of 'the teaching of the Gospel, the canons of the seven ecumenical councils and the first nine centuries of Christian history'. It was given to Pius XII's successor to grant the wishes expressed by the ecumenical patriarchate and by the entire Catholic world.

As regards Moscow, the destinies of the patriarchal Church had been profoundly affected by the historic appeal issued by Metropolitan Sergius on 21 June 1941, the very day on which the Nazi armies crossed the Russian frontiers. Thinking first and foremost of the plight of his country, the metropolitan urged the faithful to defend the fatherland in the name of the Orthodox Church, 'which has always shared the lot of the people'. Two other metropolitans, Alexis of Leningrad and Nicholas of Kiev, supported this move to identify the Church with the national struggle. As the immediate upshot of a summit conference between these three hierarchs and Stalin (4 September 1943), the Church was allowed to meet in electoral synod, at which Sergius was elected to the patriarchal see. One of his first actions after his enthronement was to resume publication of the *Journal of the Moscow Patriarchate*. The outlook for a revival of religion and a return to regular church life in the Soviet Republics was now much brighter. The new patriarch was already starting to receive the submission to his regime of the various breakaway groups when he suddenly died, on 15 May 1944. His successor in the patriarchate was his closest collaborator, Alexis of Leningrad, whose election on 2 February 1945 was ratified by a national council attended in addition by an impressive number of representatives from the autocephalous sister-Churches.

Patriarch Alexis was eager right from the start to resume contact with the other autocephalies and, in so doing, to assert the role the Russian Church intended from now on to play in the pan-Orthodox concert. Hence his many journeys abroad, in particular in the Near East and the Balkans, where he found Christian communities still susceptible to the spell of Holy Russia and cherishing memories of her ancient glory, enhanced for the moment by the seeming miracle of her resurrection. This weaving together by Russia of the old strands of Orthodox solidarity culminated in the pan-Orthodox Conference held in Moscow from 9 to 17 July 1948. In the presence of representatives from nearly all the sister-Churches, the Russian hierarchy affirmed its intention of playing a determinant role in Orthodox affairs, but the violence of the criticisms levelled at the two other poles of Christianity, the Vatican and the ecumenical movement, demonstrated at the same time the extremism of Russian Orthodox positions at that period. Against the Vatican the charge was not only that it had always sided with the powerful of this world and preached a reactionary conservatism in respect of the working classes but also that, having instigated two great imperialist wars, it was even now stoking the fires for a fresh assault on the democracies. By contrast, the Conference's refusal to take part in the first plenary assembly of the World Council of Churches at Amsterdam was justified on seemingly spiritual grounds. The Orthodox Church, it was claimed, would resist 'the temptation to abandon the quest for the Kingdom of God by entering the alien domain of politics'. The political and social concerns of the ecumenical movement represented a sinful reliance on temporal measures, which was among the temptations Christ put behind him in the wilderness. Furthermore, by reducing the condition of membership of the movement to the minimum requirement of recognition of Jesus Christ as Lord, 'ecumenism was lowering Christian doctrine to that level of belief which, as Scripture tells us, is accessible even to demons'.

The anathema pronounced by the Moscow Conference did not, however, prevent Greek Orthodoxy from playing its by now accustomed part in the work of the Amsterdam assembly (August – 4 September 1948). On the other hand, it is worth noting that an ecumenist of the calibre of L. Zander, for all that he moved in the more enlightened *milieu* of the Paris diaspora, considered a return to Rome out of the question, 'for the Rome of Christian charity, the Rome of inspiration and liberty, has ceased to exist'. Slav Christianity seemed therefore to be withdrawing into isolationism, while protesting its complete loyalty to tradition.

By the time the World Council of Churches held its Second Assembly at Evanston (15–31 August 1954) this policy of abstaining from ecumenism seemed destined to prevail, even among Greek Orthodoxy's most fervent supporters of the movement. But at this point one of the most distinguished theologians of the Russian diaspora, G. Florovsky, came to the rescue with an eloquent plea for collaboration. At the same time there were signs of a thaw in Moscow, affecting several branches of ecclesiastical activity. A *rapprochement* was effected with Constantinople, thanks to the intermediary offices of the bishops of the Melkite patriarchate of Antioch. In July 1956 the editor of the Paris journal *La Croix,* Fr Wenger, was able to publish a sympathetic and revealing account of the new wind blowing through the Russian patriarchate. In the same month news was released of an exchange of letters between the World Council of Churches and the Moscow patriarchate, the object of which was to discuss the resumption of contacts and the possibility of future collaboration.

The ecclesiastical *rapprochement* with the patriarchate of Constantinople was of great assistance in bringing Slav Orthodoxy to this less isolated position. While Catholic theologians paid tribute to the beneficent presence of Orthodoxy within the ecumenical movement, which they described as 'providential', Orthodox theologians were engaged in formulating their exact position with regard to the *Una sancta,* as at the Faith and Order Conference held in Oberlin (Ohio) in September 1957. Orthodoxy, they declared, with its 'fulness of the faith and uninterrupted sacramental tradition', regarded itself as the sacrosanct part of that *Una sancta.* It therefore called on all other confessions to rediscover the full meaning of Orthodoxy, since it symbolised, beyond and because of its system of national autocephalies, enduring unity in face of 'a divided Western Christendom'. The Russian patriarchate and its satellites could scarcely do otherwise than subscribe to such a statement. The history of Orthodoxy, as of Christianity, was thus entering on a new phase.

With the election of Cardinal Roncalli to the supreme pontificate of the Roman Church, this process of re-ordering relations between Christians was to be given a fresh impetus, because of his great conciliar initiative. In the meantime, the entire Orthodox world had experienced the joy of celebrating officially the reconciliation between Constantinople and Moscow. The occasion was provided by the fortieth anniversary of the re-establishment of the Russian patriarchate. During the festivities (May 1958) Patriarch Alexander III of Antioch, who had helped to bring about the reconciliation, declared publicly to the satisfaction of the autocephalous Churches:[1]

> The sister-Church of Russia ... remembers with gratitude the source from which she received the patriarchate. She remembers she is the daughter of the Church of Constantinople; that being so, it is un-thinkable for her to supplant that Church ... The patriarch of Moscow knows himself to stand fifth in the hierarchical order. He acknowledges, recognises and honours the ecumenical patriarch as the first.... It follows that in matters pertaining to Orthodoxy he will never presume to usurp the role of head. That role belongs to the patriarch of Constantinople....'

This unanimity among the Orthodox presaged the dawning of new times in the conciliar context soon to be created by John XXIII.

2. PIUS XII AND UNION WITH THE EAST

The collapse of established institutions both in the Near East and in the European countries beyond the Iron Curtain confronted Pius XII with two very different situations. In the one case, with an Arab nationalism struggl-ing to assert its unacknowledged claims to political independence and sup-ported in the main by the indigenous Catholic hierarchy; and in the other with the complete grip of Stalinism on the new regimes installed in the people's democracies. While taking the opportunity presented by several im-

1. Quoted in *Irénikon*, XXXI (1958), 348.

portant historical anniversaries to issue somewhat abstract appeals for re-union under the aegis of Rome, the pope attempted both to limit the disasters of the liquidation of Uniate Churches as they passed under Russian control and to consolidate the position of Uniate Churches that were aspiring to greater freedom of action in the new context provided by Arab self-government; nor, finally, did he neglect the welfare of Uniate com-munities of the diaspora, in particular those settled in America.

The war made it impossible to celebrate the five hundredth anniversary of the unionist Council of Florence (1438-39), but it was clear from the academic tone of the commemorative exercise at Beirut in January 1940 how little interest the event excited even in the minds of Uniate communities.

Pius XII gave the sanction of his encyclical *Mystici corporis Christi* (23 June 1943) to a general of appeal for the unity of all Christians 'in the one community of the body of Jesus Christ', but his approach to the problem of unity found more concrete expression in the encyclical *Orientalis Ecclesiae decus* of 9 April 1944, published to mark the fifteen hundredth anniversary of the death of St Cyril of Alexandria. The homage paid to the Alexandrian doctor's collaboration with the Roman see in defence of the faith opened the way for some refreshment of the Church's vision of unity, and it was of in-terest to find a pope addressing himself for the first time explicitly to the 'anti-Chalcedon' branches of Christianity. But, in addition, the encyclical was to give rise to a number of initiatives of the 'unionist action' type, very few of which now survive. Thoughts were even entertained of launching among the faithful abandoned by the Greek hierarchy, whether in Egypt or Palestine, campaigns to promote their union *en masse* with Rome. But the extremely fluid situation at the end of the war put paid to these dreams of a bygone age, as also to the similar illusions which certain people, among them Mgr Szeptickij, had fostered during the years of German occupation regarding the Russian Ukraine.

More promising than these grandiose and unrealistic plans for re-conquest was the work undertaken by one or two more modest foundations. One can point, for example, to the Association spirituelle et fraternelle des amis de l'union, founded at Beirut in 1945, which was to produce results exceeding the hopes of its founders; or again to the strides made in France by Istina, the study centre mentioned in the previous chapter, under its direc-to Fr Dumont. The latter, sharing the perception of the Abbé Couturier, constantly stressed in his bulletin *Vers l'unité chrétienne* the need for 'changes in the traditional methods', for a searching of the unionist con-science, from which would follow a 'reciprocal avowal of faults committed against Christian unity' and positive action to make the Church 'more fitted for the re-integration of separated Christians'.

But despite these modest initiatives on the periphery, the early manoeuvrings of the cold war were far from favourable to the growth of the eirenical spirit, notwithstanding the foundation at Rome in September 1945 by Fr Boyer, S.J. of an Association pour l'unité spirituelle des peuples. The slowness and difficulty with which ecumenical ideas penetrated the Roman Church during the pontificate of Pius XII is mentioned elsewhere in this volume.[2] We shall draw attention here only to certain events and non-events which had a direct bearing on relations with the Christian East: the promulgation of the dogma of the Assumption (1 November 1950), which evoked a flood of protests from the side of Orthodoxy; the encyclical *Sempiternus Rex* (8 September 1951), published on the occasion of the fifteen hundredth anniversary of the Council of Chalcedon, in which, for all its references to 'the rich store of benefits' that would be made available, 'to the common profit of Christendom', following the return of the East to Roman unity, we seek in vain for the note of sympathy with these 'chips from an auriferous rock' sounded by Pius XI; the absence of pontifical comment on the sad anniversaries of the capture of Constantinople in 1453 or of the tragic rupture of 1054, this latter silence being all the more telling in view of the alerting of Christian opinion to the importance of the occasion by the publication of a number of authoritative works and by speeches of more than passing significance. Only at the very end of the pontificate do we find indirect evidence of sympathetic interest in the Christian East. In September 1957 the Catholic press took some notice of the seventh Week of Prayer and Study devoted to the Christian East, held at Palermo with the active participation of Cardinal Roncalli, patriarch of Venice, who in course of it paid public homage to that pioneer in the cause of union, Dom Lambert Beauduin, whose work he held up as a model of dedication and achievement. And on 2 October it was the turn of the Congregation of the Eastern Church to add its tribute to the tried and intrepid toiler in the field of Catholic unionism. This semi-official acknowledgment hinted that a change of front was imminent and that an inapposite and outdated policy towards the Christian East had finally had its day.

The reasons for Pius XII's hesitant attitude lay both in his personal ideology and in the set of diplomatic circumstances with which he willingly associated his own principles of church government. For from the very start of the cold war Catholicism had suffered disastrous setbacks and Uniatism had found itself in the front line of the attack.

The first Uniate community to be dissolved was that of the Ukraine. A 'Committee of Initiative for the Transference of the Greek Catholic Church to Orthodoxy' had been preparing for some time for the synod of Lvov which on 9–10 March 1946, less than a year after the arrest and deportation

2. See chapter 21, 605-6.

of Mgr Slipyj (11 April 1945), proclaimed the return of the Ukrainians to the Orthodox faith of their fathers and their abjuration of 'Roman errors'. The appointment of a new exarch regularised the *fait accompli*. It was with few illusions that Pius XII made his protest, in any case muted, as early as 23 December 1945 with the encyclical *Orientales omnes*.

In 1948, in the wake of the 'Prague coup' and of the publication of correspondence between President Truman and Pius XII proposing a political-religious alliance to work for Christian peace in the world, it was the turn of Rumanian Uniatism to be eliminated. The dissolution of the Rumanian Catholic Union was accomplished in successive stages between May and December of that year, with the Orthodox hierarchy, under its leader Patriarch Justinian of Bucharest, giving the political authorities a helping hand. In 1949, following the pope's exhortation to the Catholic hierarchy to guard against communist infiltrations and his warm approval of the decision of the free nations to come together in the Atlantic Pact (12 February), the Bulgarian government immediately severed diplomatic relations with the Vatican and introduced harsh measures aimed at all Churches or sects having their main seat 'abroad'. A few months later the Ruthenians of Sub-Carpathia in Czechoslovakia suffered the same fate as the Uniates of the Ukraine (28 August 1949). The decree of the Holy Office forbidding collaboration of any kind with communist parties (1 July 1949), coming as it did at the time when Slav Orthodoxy was taking the opposite course, caused the situation to deteriorate still further. To all appearances, the iron curtain had reduced the Roman Catholics of Eastern Europe to the condition of a 'Church of silence', to use the expression employed by the pope in his Christmas message of 1951, and it would be many years yet before a thaw started to set in.

Sadly disappointed in Eastern Europe, Pius XII sought to consolidate the position and status of the Eastern Catholic Churches in the Near East and of the communities of the diaspora, both in Europe and America.

In the mood of euphoria accompanying the establishment in 1947 of diplomatic relations with Egypt – the first Muslim state to make this move – the pope revived the Coptic Catholic patriarchate, which had been left vacant since the defection of the first occupant of the see, Cyril Makarios, in 1910. Nor was this all, for while the Catholic Association for Egyptian Schools reinforced at school level the missionary and parochial activities of the Franciscans in Upper Egypt, a beneficent type of missionary penetration was already starting to emanate from the Latin congregations settled in the Nile valley. Moreover, deeper reflection on the theological and aspostolic aspects was reflected in studies which owed much to ecumenical inspiration. One thinks in particular of the book, rich in matter and experience, published by an 'Easternising' missionary, Jacob Muyser, under the modest title

Face à l'apostolat copte (1950). It was followed soon after by the first appearance of the similarly orientated but unfortunately short-lived *Cahiers coptes*.

The Holy See also had reason to concern itself with the affairs of the Maronite patriarchate. In view of the likelihood that latent tensions would emerge to trouble the patriarchal election following the death of Antony Arida, Pius XII took it on himself, 'on this one occasion and by way of exception', to nominate his successor in the person of Mgr Paul Meouchi, the bishops having just assembled in the electoral synod (19 May 1955). The pope's intervention was the cause of more than internal disturbances among the Maronites but strict disciplinary measures damped down the opposition. In any case, the crisis developing in Egypt over the abolition of the confessional courts and the introduction of civil marriage (September to December 1955) was about to concentrate Catholic energies on a problem judged at the time to be vital to the future of Christianity in the East.

Lastly, the strengthening of the Uniate community in Greecē was the cause of a fresh flare-up in the quarrel which had been smouldering there since 1925. The first intimations came in August 1956 when the Holy Synod of Athens opposed the royal plan to establish diplomatic relations with the Vatican, maintaining that in so doing it remained 'loyal to the sacred traditions of the Church and the nation'. Following the death of Mgr Calavassy, exarch of the Greek Uniate Church, (7 November 1957), the professors of the faculty of theology at Athens appealed to Pius XII not to appoint a successor, declaring in justification that the Orthodox East looked on 'the *Ounia*' as a major obstacle to any *rapprochement* between the Churches because it 'poisoned relations between Orthodox Catholics and Roman Catholics'. Turning a deaf ear to this plea, the pope not only appointed a successor but arranged to have him consecrated in Athens, to the great disappointment of the most forward-looking among Greek ecumenists.

Uniate communities of Eastern rite were by now becoming established in growing numbers in lands outside the traditional boundaries of the Christian East. For the proper exercise of the ministry, these communities of the diaspora needed to be provided with structures analagous to those created for the similarly placed national communities of Latin rite scattered throughout the world. Pius XII pressed ahead therefore with a long-term programme which had been operating in a small way since 1921. Provision was made as early as 1948 for a number of Ukrainian dioceses in Canada. In 1952 the cardinal archbishop of Rio de Janeiro was named as ordinary for all the faithful of an Eastern rite living in Brazil, pending the appointment for each rite of a vicar ordinary of the appropriate rite. In 1955 the same plan was followed with respect to France, the cardinal archbishop of Paris being appointed ordinary for all Eastern Catholics living on French territory. Some of the more numerous groupings, the Armenians and Ukrainians for instance, were later to receive ordinaries of their own rite with the title pontifical exarch. Lastly, only a few weeks before his death, Pius XII instituted a full-scale Eastern hierarchy in the United States by elevating on 28 August 1958 the Ukrainian exarchate of Philadelphia to the rank of metropolitan see. The effect of these institutional measures was to provide the Ukrainians of the diaspora with a hierarchy replacing their now suppressed hierarchy in Central Europe.

The continued growth of Catholic Uniate communities in North America (a count around 1960 showed 200,000 faithful of an Eastern rite in Canada and 800,000 in the United States, of whom 600,000 were Ukranians, 125,000 Maronites and 50,000 Melkites) posed problems other than those merely of organisation. As they became acclimatised to America, many of the laity started to press for adaptations of the liturgy and of the forms of piety to suit their new surroundings, and their numbers (and their economic weight) were such that they were able to bring strong influence to bear on the Congregation of the Eastern Church. So on the American continent the threat to the authentically Eastern character of Uniate communities came no longer, as in the Near East, from the influence exerted by Latin missionaries but was the result of changes within the Uniate communities themselves.

The Arab East, it may be said, still had its vigorous centres of resistance to latinising tendencies. This was noticeably so when in 1949 the labours begun under Pius XI on the codification of Eastern canon law at last started to bear fruit with the publication by stages of the legislation common to all the Eastern Churches. Those Eastern hierarchies most conscious of their ecumenical responsibilities and at the same time most devoted to their venerable patrimony showed increasingly distinct signs of unease, and the promulgation on 2 June 1957 of the codification relating to the constitution of the Church and to the patriarchal and synodal regime in fact precipitated a serious crisis, echoes of which reverberated in the special synod of the Uniate Melkite Church held at Cairo from 6-11 February 1958. Since that time the new conciliar and ecumenical perspectives opened up by John XXIII make it seem inevitable that the codification of Eastern law will undergo the same fundamental re-examination of its juridical conception as is in progress for the law of the Roman Catholic Church as a whole.

At the conclusion of this brief survey of the destinies of Eastern Catholicism during the twenty years of Pius XII's pontificate it is important to draw attention to an aspect which in a fuller account would undoubtedly receive more mention, the fact that beneath the public happenings and the most widely noticed public pronouncements a continuous ferment was more obscurely at work preparing the way for an approach inspired to a much greater degree by the principles of ecumenism, and here we should mention in particular the action of a small band of thinkers whose confidential memoranda and discreet representations often exerted a greater influence than the more spectacular actions of personalities better known to the general public.

3. TOWARDS THE CONCILIAR SUMMITS (1958–62)

The idea of a council, once it had been put forward by the journal of the ecumenical patriarchate, *Apostolos Andreas,* began slowly to gain ground. It was echoed during 1957 in one or two Catholic journals, thus the *Palestra del clero* and the *Tablet,* but without making much impression on opinion at large. On 1 September 1958 the *Palestra del clero* returned to the theme, arguing that in mankind's present state of disarray a council of unity would direct the Churches towards a more effective examination of their mission. A month later, the death of Pius XII and the election of John XXIII initiated a period of *détente* throughout the Christian world, in particular as regards relations between Orthodoxy and Roman Catholicsm, and the announcement, on 25 January 1959, of the convocation of a Catholic council set in motion a host of ideas and initiatives, whose exact number and story are still far from being recorded. From this point on, the historian finds himself faced in fact with a mass of events, speeches, statements of attitude and inter-ecclesiastical exchanges whose importance lies above all in the way they followed on from one another and in their convergence, immediate or by stages, on a single goal: the rebuilding of Christian unity at the various confessional levels and ultimately on the universal scale.

John XXIII's conciliar initiative was undoubtedly felt as a shock to a whole firmly established tradition, even in circles most aware of the spiritual and intellectual demands made by Catholicism. But once taken, the decision gave fresh encouragement to ecumenical thought and action. In the pope's mind the idea of the council had been linked right from the start with the problem of Christian unity, in particular under its Eastern aspect. Without underrating the difficulties, he showed himself optimistic, stressing that the enterprise was not one that could be tackled unilaterally and calling on the sharers in it to cease their sterile bickering and to explore together, by means of dialogue, the paths leading to unity. An epoch-making process of inter-action was about to begin.

Echoing John XXIII, the Jacobite patriarch of Antioch, Mgr Ignatios Ja'coub III, invited his Coptic colleague of Alexandria to consider seriously the union of these two branches of the Monophysite Church, pending the extension of their sacred union to the third branch formed by the Armenian Church, and it was not long before this move to re-integrate non-Chalcedonian Orthodoxy took the more concrete form of doctrinal dialogue and arrangements of a practical nature. Patriarch Athenagoras, for his part, hastened to send to the pope as his representative the metropolitan of America, Mgr Iacovos, and for the first time a prelate from the ecumenical patriarchate paid an official visit to the Vatican (14 February 1959). Orthodoxy had taken the first step towards the Holy See. John XXIII returned the compliment through his representative in Constantinople. From now on the exchange of visits was to form a regular part of an increasingly well-defined programme for the promotion of harmony between the Churches. Hence it was possible for King Paul of Greece and Queen Frederika to call on the pope without causing undue perturbation in the Greek hierarchy: the ice was being broken, it was explained, between Greece and the Holy See.

But these hopeful signs did not prevent the airing of deeply reflected views on the difficulties of the enterprise. A series of articles commenting on the new approach to union appeared in fact in the journal *Apostolos Andreas* as early as the spring of 1959. Eirenical in spirit and careful in its weighing up of views, the series was also perceptive in its diagnosis of the situation. Attention was drawn to Rome's proselytising or expansionist proclivities, as also the 'the Vatican's baneful policy of seeking by all possible means to conclude concordats'. But the most crucial problem was Uniatism, for it was claimed that the *Ounia* was attempting through its institutions 'to undermine the spirit of Orthodoxy'. 'Far from providing a link between the Churches, the *Ounia* is the cause of a continual battle in which the Uniates are the active and aggressive party and the Orthodox are forced to defend their traditions.' The round of visits by the Melkite patriarch of Antioch to his colleagues in all the European autocephalies (July-September 1959) served to strengthen them in these opinions. And yet, when the bishops of the Uniate Melkite hierarchy met in their annual synod (24-9 August 1959) they adopted in full a series of proposals whose aim was to safeguard the 'Eastern and Orthodox patrimony' against erosion by the work of the forthcoming council.

At this same moment the Central Committee of the World Council of Churches was meeting by deliberate choice in Rhodes (19-28 August 1959), manifesting thereby the Council's desire to win support from all the Orthodox, who were both flattered and encouraged. It was proposed, in fact, to make the island a 'permanent ecumenical centre', the 'Bessey of Orthodoxy'. This initiative from Geneva made Catholics the more eager to resume their own dialogue with Orthodoxy and there was even talk, much too premature, of arranging an Orthodox-Catholic meeting in the near future in Venice. This new burst of unionist activity encouraged Patriarch Athenagoras to press ahead with the consolidation of Orthodox unity proper. Having called a pan-Orthodox conference for July 1960, the patriarch visited each of the other autocephalous Churches in turn to prepare their minds for this event, while from the presses came a number of articles and longer publications which examined the problem of reunion, in all its multiple aspects, with boldness and lucidity. The ecumenical climate was now one of optimism, despite the persistence of certain reservations.

The Roman Church continued nevertheless with systematic preparations for the council. John XXIII's intention to engage the Catholic Church in the ecumenical dialogue was made plain at Whitsun 1960 with his announcement of the setting up of a Secretariat for the promotion of Christian Unity. This move coincided with the replacement in Russia of Metropolitan Nikolas of Leningrad by the younger Nicodemus as head of the Bureau of External Affairs of the Moscow patriarchate, an indication that a change of policy over inter-Church affairs was in the wind.

In November and December of that year it was the turn of Patriarch Alexis of Moscow to make a progress through the Near East, where his appeals for peace and for unity among local Christian communities aroused marked enthusiasm. On his way he stopped in Constantinople and set the seal on the reconciliation by participating in a concelebration, a gesture he repeated in Athens. With its sights fixed on the pan-Orthodox conference of Rhodes, the whole of Orthodoxy seemed ready for collaboration.

That there was zeal for union on the Catholic side was made evident by a number of courageous statements and dramatic gestures. The Uniate Melkite patriarch, Maximos IV, speaking at Dusseldorf on 9 August 1960, referred to the special vocation of the Catholic East in the movement of *rapprochement* between Orthodoxy and Roman Catholicism, claiming for his Church a role of mediator that neither side appeared willing to acknowledge; and early in 1961 Cardinal Bea, president of the Roman Secretariat for Christian Unity, declared that the Catholic Church was under no illusions as to the obstacles in the path to unity, even admitting the validity of Orthodox objections on the doctrinal as well as on the institutional level. Shortly afterwards, however, at a ceremony in St Peter's, John XXIII acted in person to confer the office of a bishop (chirotony) on a Melkite prelate, Acacius Coussa, whom he appointed to be head of the Congregation of the Eastern Church. Gestures of this kind were not at all to the taste of the intransigent wing of Orthodoxy, which issued a reminder that 'the Uniate Church remains the Catholic Church's chosen instrument for the undermining of Orthodoxy' (16 April 1961). A month later the Moscow patriarchate began to take up a wholly negative attitude towards the forthcoming council, refusing its participation in whatever form and declaring, after advancing several considerations of a religious political character, that 'Christian unity could not have as its basis the monarchical centralisation of ecclesiastical power or hostility towards other believers'.

But in a situation so fluctuating a change of attitude was not to be ruled out. For a start, there were tangible signs from September 1961 of a *rapprochement* between John XXIII and the Soviet leaders. Next, the pan-Orthodox Conference of Rhodes (22 September-2 October 1961) permitted a calmer appraisal of the institutions of the papacy in relation to Orthodoxy, which was experimenting with a unity formally reconstituted on a synodal basis. Lastly, the admission of the Moscow patriarchate to the World Council of Churches, agreed to at the General Assembly in New Delhi (November-December 1961), furnished opportunity for candid explanations and a durable reconciliation. For example, Mgr Nicodemus of Leningrad was able to divulge to the Paris journal *Croix* the true feelings of the Russian Orthodox Church towards the Roman Church and so expunge the memory of the former's wholesale refusal to take part in the work of the Catholic council. The final months of preparation for that council were thus marked by an atmosphere of *détente*.

4. THE ACHIEVEMENT OF THE SECOND VATICAN COUNCIL (1962-5)

The many detailed reports, exhaustive commentaries and confidential reminiscences that have appeared dealing with the council make a full account of its labours unnecessary. The contribution of the Christian East to the council's deliberations, and the events taking place in the council which had a direct bearing on relations with Orthodoxy, nevertheless deserve to be recorded, if only briefly.

The tortuous history of the invitation extended to the Moscow patriarchate to send observers to the council and the circumstances attending the arrival of Russian observers in Rome are matters that still await full clarification. One thing that remains certain, and which is indicative of the equivocal character of the negotiations conducted by the Vatican's plenipotentiaries, is the bitterness and disillusionment with which the patriarchate of Constantinople reacted to the affair. Mgr Iacovos, Orthodox archbishop of America and spokesman for the Phanar, believed himself justified in asserting that the sense of grievance was due to the tactics employed, which tended to disrupt the unity of Orthodoxy and to undermine the prestige of the ecumenical patriarchate. It is a fact that that indefatigable toiler in the field of Orthodox unity and of unity between the Churches, Patriarch Athenagoras, found himself prevented, by the situation prevailing within Hellenic Orthodoxy, from sending observers to the council.

The first session of the council (11 October-8 December 1962) soon brought into the open the main currents of divergent, if not conflicting, opinions which divided the Fathers. The lengthy debate on liturgical reform seemed on the surface to concern only the Latin Church. Yet it established two points with a fundamental bearing on the authentic Catholic tradition:

that the Latin language could not claim an unassailable monopoly as the language of worship, even in the Roman Church, and that at national and local level the episcopal conferences had an important role to play in the working out and implementation of liturgical reforms. The contributions of Eastern Fathers to the debate were often enlightening and in some cases had a decisive effect on the voting. But it was when the assembly turned to the examination of the schema on Christian unity that the most convincing pleas were entered on behalf of the authenticity and permanent validity of the Eastern heritage. One of the Fathers stressed that the 'Eastern Church was as much a source-Church as the Latin Church in the West', an unaccustomed formula but one calculated to draw attention to an aspect which Latin teaching and practice had for centuries ignored.

As soon as the first session was over, an accredited representative of the Moscow patriarchate revealed the three conditions demanded and accepted for the despatch of its observers to Rome: a personal invitation directed expressly to the Russian Church; guarantees that the council would not degenerate into a political assembly (in other words, that it would refrain from the condemnation of communism); assurances that the presence of Orthodox observers would not be interpreted as an acknowledgment of the Roman primacy. The Russian observers had in fact made a genuine and useful contribution. Like their Protestant and Eastern colleagues, they followed the debates with good will and attention, invariably showing a particular interest in matters affecting the Christian East. One gratifying consequence was that the intervention from the venerable patriarch of the Melkite Uniates, Maximos IV, received a homage worthy of his dignity. The observers' favourable impression of the first session was recorded in simple and dignified fashion, with expressions of gratitude to the hosts for the fraternal warmth of their welcome and a tribute to the wisdom of the Roman pontiff, coupled with praise for the freedom of the council's deliberations.

Undoubtedly the most spectacular result of the *détente* between Moscow and the Vatican was the release of the metropolitan of Lvov, Mgr Joseph Slipyj, whose case was vigorously pressed by the Ukrainian bishops of the diaspora. Undisputed head of Uniatism in the spirit of the Union of Brest Litovsk and successor to Mgr Andrew Szeptickij, he had been in captivity since April 1945, the time when 'his' Church was dissolved and attached to the Moscow patriarchate. The action of the Soviet authorities in releasing him was further testimony to the favourable notice taken of the spirit presiding over the first session of the council.

The death of John XXIII, felt keenly by those who were anxious to maintain the spirit of *détente* and *rapprochement* between the Churches, was swiftly offset by the election of Cardinal Montini. Strongly attached like his predecessor to the spirit of *aggiornamento,* Paul VI also showed affinity with Pius XII, if not in temperament, at least by reason of his long career in the secretariat of State. In his coronation address he affirmed his intention of pursuing the dialogue with non-Roman Christians, defining the goal in an original and widely remarked formulation as 'the recomposition of unity'. And he was shortly to give proof in the conciliar and ecumenical contexts of fervent endeavours to realise the hopes of the majority of the Catholic episcopate and of his partners in other Christian confessions.

Soon after his election, in September 1963, Paul VI received a visit from Mgr Nicodemus of Leningrad, who also made a point of going to pray at the tomb of John XXIII. At the end of the audience the Russian metropolitan remarked with satisfaction that he had found the pope 'intensely eager for collaboration between the Churches and working intensively to that end'. On 1 November of that same year the Moscow patriarchate set up a Commission for Christian Unity. The Vatican maintained the same cordial relations with the ecumenical patriarchate.

At the Rhodes pan-Orthodox Conference held 26-9 September 1963, that is to say immediately before the opening of the second session of the council, a heated debate on the expediency of sending observers to the council and of engaging in dialogue with the papacy found the delegations divided in their views. The unanimous agreement of the autocephalous Churches was obtained only in respect of the dialogue, and then on condition that it was conducted 'on an equal footing'. In principle this represented an advance, and a quite considerable one in view of the state of mind that was still dominant, and that dominated in particular the official attitude of the Church of Greece, which in fact had abstained from taking part in the conference.

The second session of the Vatican Council was to prove especially fruitful from the ecumenical point of view, as also in the quality of contributions from the East. In an inaugural address pitched theologically and spiritually at a high level and which in places echoed the views of the Russian theologian Khomiakov, Paul VI affirmed his intention of committing the Church to the path of ecumenism, while at the same time respecting 'the pluralism founded on historical tradition'. He proceeded to set the tone and manner of the commitment by making a public confession calculated to dispèl all lingering mistrusts: 'If among the causes of division any fault could be imputed to us, we humbly beg God's forgiveness and ask pardon too of our brethren who feel offended by us. And we willingly forgive, for our part, the injuries the Catholic Church has suffered and forget the grief endured through the long chain of dissensions and separations.'

It was in this spirit that the Fathers debated during the second session themes of such fundamental importance as episcopal collegiality, ecumenism, the mission of the laity. The council was here touching on matters of extreme delicacy, which had a close bearing on ecclesiastical structures: the relationship between the episcopate and the Roman primacy, the patriarchal regime essential to the tradition of the Christian East, the continued existence and role of Uniate Churches in the new ecumenical perspective and, lastly, the dialogue properly so called with the other Christian confessions. The spirited and pertinent contributions from certain Eastern hierarchs did not pass unnoticed. They evoked on some occasions general approbation, on others last-ditch reactions from prelates ignorant of advances in theological research or belatedly manning the barricades against any form of ecumenical dialogue. An important contribution from the Melkite Patriarch Maximos IV deserves a special mention, since it in effect pointed the way to the creation of that symbol of episcopal collegiality in the Catholic Church, the Synod of Bishops. Basing himself on the ancient practice of Orthodoxy, Patriarch Maximos IV pleaded for 'a true sacred college of the universal Church', constituted in properly representative fashion, and he advocated the creation at Rome, on a permanent footing, of 'what is known in the Eastern Church as the *synodos endimousa*' to act as 'the supreme executive and deliberative council of the universal Church'. In justification of the proposal he offered the reflection that 'the problems of the peoples stand to be settled by the peoples themselves or in consultation with them, but never without them'.

At the end of the session Paul VI took a step of decisive importance both in furtherance of his ecumenical commitment and as a source of refreshment to the apostolic mission of the Roman Church. He announced on 4 December his intention to go on pilgrimage to the Holy Land. Within a matter of days the patriarch of Constantinople had expressed his warm approval of 'this ecumenical journey to the sources' and his desire to accompany the pope, not without drawing down on himself the wrath of the archbishop of Athens, who appealed to the monks of Athos to defend Orthodoxy from the unionist machinations of the ecumenical patriarchate. The pontifical and patriarchal pilgrims' progress (4-6 January 1964) proceeded to the accompaniment at each stage of addresses and gestures which directly opened the way to the dialogue both parties so fervently desired.

This dramatic encounter, a turning-point in the history of relations between Orthodoxy and Roman Catholicism, looked like damaging the increasingly close contacts being established between Orthodoxy and the ecumenical movement at large. At its meeting at Odessa (1-14 February 1964) the Executive Committee of the World Council of Churches had opportunity to take stock of the nature and extent of interconfessional relations. There was naturally rejoicing over 'the more open attitude of the Roman Church', in view of the fact that Christendom was entering on a new era of its ecumenical history; but at a higher level anxieties still remained regarding 'the Roman offensive on the East Christian front'. That was why Cardinal Bea, president of the Roman Secretariat for Christian Unity, took care to stress in a broadcast address delivered on Whitsunday that 'the presence of the Orthodox Churches in the World Council of Churches was undoubtedly of great benefit to the cause of union and that there seemed no reason why the Roman Church should or would seek to detach them from it'.

The work of the third session of the Vatican Council (14 September-21 November 1964) was conducted in an atmosphere of, at times, considerable tension, which by the end of the session had crystallised into a general unease. The questions debated were of an explosive nature and the Fathers became all the more acutely aware of their responsibilities. Eastern problems acquired a keener edge, especially in the debates involving theology and the role of the Holy Spirit, Uniatism as against ecumenism, the patriarchal constitution, the disposition to schism, and the true place of the Eastern Churches within the frame of the universal Church. Interventions by Eastern or pro-Eastern prelates as a rule commanded attention and even succeeded in opening up perspectives unexplored by Latin theology. It was undoubtedly during this session that Orthodoxy, in its absence, had most reason to be grateful to 'the Uniate episcopate' for making its voice heard and insisting on the better balance to be obtained in theology by giving more weight to the pneumatological tradition of the Eastern Church. In a trenchant comment on the schema on the Church, one Eastern Father declared: 'Our tradition does not recognise itself in this text. Christologically, the Latin Church is very mature; pneumatologically, it is still adolescent. But the age we live in, the modern age, the age of the latest innovation, is the age of the Holy Spirit.'

Of great value was the working partnership established by the representatives of the Uniate Eastern Church with Orthodox theologians, from which emerged the document which the strictest theological judges held to be the best contribution to the constitution on Divine Revelation.

Several speakers used the opportunity afforded by the discussion on the Eastern patriarchates to lift the entire 'Eastern debate' to heights at which, to quote an especially percipient observer, 'the council was shaken by a great gust of the spirit'. On this same occasion the 'quarrel over rites' developed into a kind of duel in which eminent members of the Eastern hierarchy vied with one another in their accounts of the divergences separating them from the rest. By contrast, the most convincing plea for open recognition of the nature and prerogatives of the traditional patriarchate of the East was entered by a Western Father, an expert in patristics: 'To omit all mention of the patriarchal constitution, not only from the decree relating to the Uniate Eastern Churches but also from the constitution on the Church and the episcopate, would be unpardonable.'

While the council was thus pursuing its labours at Rome, the autocephalous Churches were holding their third pan-Orthodox Conference of Rhodes (1–15 November 1964). Although the working sessions were all held in camera, it is known that the question of dialogue with the Catholic Church came under discussion. The thorny questions with which the Vatican Council was confronted, in particular those surrounding the 'Uniate Churches' and the question of episcopal collegiality, made the climate inauspicious for a full and fruitful dialogue. The decisions of the Orthodox summit conference were thus a reflection of the situation in the council. Dialogue was not rejected in principle, but it was decided to postpone embarking on it to a more propitious moment, since the Roman Church was 'in process of transformation', a process Orthodoxy watched with close and prayerful attention. Although this was the general policy, it would not prevent individual autocephalous Churches from discussing their particular problems with the Roman Church. Even so, the dialogue was to have as its basis the organic unity of the Church and was 'to reject the inadequate formulas for reunion represented by the Uniate Churches'. Once this hurdle had been cleared, it would remain to establish unity on the basis of unity in the apostolic tradition and in the sacramental and spiritual life. Orthodoxy thus provided itself with a common platform without ruling out individual action on the part of its members. Cautious and hedged about with limitations though they were, these decisions were not negative. The Holy See of Rome, which had sent an official representative to the conference, was in due course notified officially of the decisions the conference had endorsed (15 February 1965). But it cannot be denied that the prospect was clouded by the trying incidents which punctuated the work of the third session in each of its main stages. Both sides, however, were still intent on finding new ways of collaboration, and the Russian Church, which was taking a closer and closer interest in these supra-national ecclesiastical assemblies, went so far as to propose the creation of a 'Co-ordinating Commission', which would serve as a forum for the exchange of views on 'subjects of common interest to all the Churches . . . in the *Sobornost* spirit and on the basis of all the partners having equal rights' (December 1964).

In the non-Chalcedonian Orthodox Churches the idea of synods acting in concert was making headway. Following discussions at Aarhus (where a Faith and Order conference organised by the ecumenical movement was in progress, 11-15 August 1964) between delegates of the six Churches in question and representatives of Orthodoxy, the non-Chalcedonian Churches met on their own at Addis Abbaba (15-21 January 1965), to study the problems peculiar to their own Churches and to consider their relations with other Churches. There could be no mistaking their openness towards the Catholic

Church. They greeted the re-awakening of ecumenical awareness with optimism and pledged themselves to enter on the same path of dialogue. All the same, following the example of Rhodes, they asked the Roman Church 'to reconsider under the headings of both theory and practice the perpetuation of Uniate Churches and the proselytisation of members of our Churches'. The demand to 'clear the Uniate hurdle' thus seemed to be general, and made essential a thorough re-examination of the future destinies of Uniatism in the new ecumenical context.

While the Orthodox East was reaching quasi-unanimity on the doctrinal and practical problems presented by the Uniate patriarchates, the Roman See was reserving, from its own point of view, a quite unwonted honour for those patriarchates. At the consistory of 22 February 1965 the pope decided to elevate three Catholic patriarchs to the cardinalate. One of them, Maximos IV, accepted, in circumstances far from clear, a position he had always refused to contemplate; he thought he was entering a 'new senate' of the Roman Church, but his hopes were disappointed. The general reaction of Orthodoxy was inevitably hostile, while a profound unease and signs of unrest began to appear in the Uniate Churches. So the Uniate problem was once again in the forefront, but posed this time in the Roman setting and focused directly on the patriarchal system. The Orthodox could not but be confirmed in their apprehensions and in their stance of 'wait and see'.

This 'road block' did not prevent the ecumenical patriarchate from continuing to make contact with the Roman Church. Progress was slowly being made towards the raising of the thousand-year-old reciprocal excommunication. With the journey of Cardinal Bea to Istanbul (2-6 April 1965) the pace quickened and his visit to Santa Sophia was taken, as intended, as 'in the nature of a reparation'. On the following 6 June the London representative of Athenagoras preached a sermon in Westminster Abbey which prepared man's minds for some form of reciprocal absolution, an expectation about to be fulfilled at the last session of the Vatican Council.

The final session (12 September-21 November 1965) opened with the historic decision to create a Synod of Bishops for the Roman Church, collegial in structure and placed at the service of, and bounded by, the papal primacy. Although this new episcopally-based organ excluded the deliberative element essential to synodal meetings of the traditional type, it nevertheless testified to the desire of the Holy See to satisfy in part a general wish of the episcopate and to approach more closely the ancient constitution of the Church. In other respects, although the session witnessed no great doctrinal debate affecting the Christian East, a debate on discipline brought out a fundamental divergence between Eastern and Latin Christianity. It was an Eastern prelate, the Melkite Mgr Zoghby, who unexpectedly raised the problem of the innocent spouse and the right he should have, in certain well-defined circumstances, to remarry. The impromptu debate that followed had no chance of reaching an immediate solution, since neither side had produced supporting documents in advance. But the question it raised was echoed and re-echoed by a public opinion as ignorant of the historical and theological facts as it was disturbed, not infrequently, in its Christian conscience.

The climax, from our point of view, of this final session was beyond any doubt the reciprocal raising of the ban of excommunication between the Roman Church and the patriarchate of Constantinople. Following careful preparation by a mixed commission, this solemn and emotive act was accomplished on 7 December in the presence of the full council. And with the exchange of the kiss of peace that followed, the two Churches, separated for close on a thousand years, were set once more on the path of reunion. Having made its way slowly to this summit, the council was ending in the precise frame of mind John XXIII had desired at its inception.

This supremely important historical event was decisive for the entire future of the Eastern Church. The subsequent initiatives, the multiple statements of position, as also the encouraging reactions of the different confessions, are all to be seen against this new perspective of a reconciliation desired by both parties and having intercommunion and full unity as its goal. Even so, a little time was needed before Paul VI and Patriarch Athenagoras set the seal in person on this major act of their pontificate by visits to their respective sees. The first to act was Paul VI, who on 25-6 July 1967 made his pilgrimage to Constantinople and to Ephesus, but was unable to extend his journey as far as Antioch, St Peter's first see. The declarations of principle to which the two pontiffs now subscribed testified to the spiritual and theological distance travelled along the road to 'rediscovery as sister-Churches' and the mutual acceptance of 'diversity of customs in the unity of faith'. There next arose a new and urgent task demanding 'the sacrifice and suppression on either side, in a spirit of total abnegation, of everything which in the past had seemed to contribute to the unity of the Church but which tended in reality to create a gulf difficult to bridge'. On his return to Rome the pope reaffirmed his confident vision of the East, which he saw as 'master in its reflection on revealed truth'. It was at the conclusion of the first Catholic Synod of Bishops (29 September-28 October 1967) that the patriarch of the 'new Rome' returned the visit of the bishop of the first Rome, in course of a lengthy peregrination which took him from the Balkan capitals as far afield as London. The majesty of the pontifical ceremonies and the reiteration of the principal themes of the earlier declarations made this Roman pilgrimage a decisive stage before the joint resumption by the two Churches of their journey to the fixed goal.

The Christian East and the Christian West thus entered on a new relationship and way of life which augured 'a new history of the Church' in the making. And we are even now experiencing the first fruits of that new age of ecumenical renewal, which did not come to an end with the death of Patriarch Athenagoras (7 July 1972). Will it be given to our generation to witness the germination of the seed planted and watered by pontifical hands? As yet we can only guess in what manner the new spirit responsible for the new destinies of the Churches is at work in that Christendom renewed.

PART SIX

THE HALF–CENTURY LEADING TO THE SECOND VATICAN COUNCIL

FROM BENEDICT XV TO JOHN XXIII

BENEDICT XV was a pope misunderstood in his lifetime and one whose real merits historians have only slowly come to appreciate. He was ill-served by circumstances, starting with four years of war, which limited the scope of his activities while exposing him to criticism from both camps, and had at the finish a premature death (22 January 1922). This thwarted the accomplishment of various promising initiatives from which his successor was to reap the benefit.

The conclave of 1914 was dominated by two problems. The first of course was the war: its future dimensions were not yet foreseen, but it was recognised as placing the Holy See in an extremely delicate position which would demand from the new pope a quite exceptional skill in diplomacy. But there was also the legacy of tension inside the Church left by integrism, whose excesses, in particular in the matter of Christian trade unions, were regarded by a certain number of cardinals as so damaging to the Church that it was essential to redress the balance. It was certainly the case that at the first ballot two moderate candidates, both of them viewed with suspicion by the Vatican under the previous pontificate, took the lead, both with twelve votes: Maffi, archbishop of Pisa, and Della Chiesa, archbishop of Bologna.[1] The fact that Maffi was regarded as *italianissimo* and had the reputation of being broadminded on the social question attracted him some support, but also some powerful opposition. His votes stuck at sixteen while Della Chiesa's increased with each successive ballot: sixteen, eighteen, twenty-one. At this point the opponents of a more liberal policy, their numbers doubtless swelled by cardinals who feared that Della Chiesa did not

1. We have precise information about the conclave of 1914 thanks to the notes made by Cardinal Piffl, archbishop of Vienna, discovered by M. Liebmann. Cf. *La Revue nouvelle*, XXXVIII (1963), 34-46 and *Theologisch-praktisch Quartalschrift*, CXII (1964), 51-8. See also Gasparri's memoirs, ed. G. Spadolini (Florence 1971), 149-54.

share the intransigence towards Italy of his former chief, Rampolla, were persuaded by Cardinal De Lai to join forces in voting for Cardinal Serafini, the devout Benedictine, who rapidly amassed twenty-four votes; but Della Chiesa continued to gain ground and on the sixth ballot, 3 September, he was elected by thirty-eight votes (against eighteen for Serafini). The choice of Ferrata and then of Gasparri as Secretary of State (Ferrata having died three weeks after his appointment) provided confirmation of a return to the spirit of Leo XIII and, in a widely noted passage in the augural encyclical, [2] the integrists were given plain warning to desist from their practice of indiscriminate denunciation.

The new pope, born 21 November 1854, came of an aristocratic Genoese family. He had accompanied Rampolla to Spain during the latter's nunciature and when his master was made Secretary of State in 1887 he became his personal secretary, being greatly valued in that office for two qualities he possessed to a rare degree, a good memory and discretion. Some fifteen years later Della Chiesa was appointed under-secretary in the Secretariat of State, a post he retained during the early years of Pius X's pontificate; but the difference between his approach to politics and the new spirit prevailing in the Vatican went beyond a mere matter of degree. So in October 1907 he was made archbishop of Bologna and although the see normally carried a cardinal's hat he had to wait for his until May 1914. But if the man now ascending the throne of St Peter was a diplomat of the Rampolla school he was none the less a pastor, for during his years in Rome Mgr Della Chiesa had devoted much of his spare time to pastoral activity and as archbishop he was both zealous and well liked. He chose the name Benedict in memory of Benedict XIV, like himself a former archbishop of Bologna.

For four years the new pope had to concern himself chiefly with the war which, as it spread, confronted the Holy See with moral, legal and diplomatic problems of a different order from throse thown up by earlier conflicts. He at once set about making arrangements for military chaplaincies and took various steps, for the most part effective, to ease the lot of prisoners, refugees and deportees and to facilitate the exchange of the seriously wounded and the transmission of family news across the lines of fire. [3] Above all, he attempted to exert his moral authority in the cause of re-establishing

2. Encyclical *Ad beatissimi* of 1 November 1914 (text in *A.A.S.*, VI (1914), 565-82; the passage in question, pp. 576-7). See É. Poulat, *Intégrisme et Catholicisme intégral* (Paris-Tournai 1969), 600-2. On the running down of Mgr Benigni's *Sodalitium Pianum* and its final suppression in November 1921, see *Disquisitio circa quasdam obiectiones modum agendi [Pii X] respicientes in modernismi debellatione* (Vatican City 1950), 270-83.
3. See J. Kleyntjens in *Revue d'histoire ecclésiastique*, XLIII (1948), 536-45. It is estimated that the sums expended by the Vatican in sustaining all these charitable undertakings, described by Romain Rolland as ' a second Red Cross', amounted to around eighty-two million gold lire.

peace. His repeated exhortations to the powers to conclude a just peace (8 September and 6 December 1914; 25 May, 28 July, and 6 December 1915; 4 March and 30 July 1916; 10 January and 5 May 1917) met with no response from the authorities but stirred up lasting resentment against himself. The two camps, each convinced that its cause was just, were incensed to find the pope confining himself to general, unparticularised reprobation instead of pronouncing formal condemnation of the enemy, [4] and they accused him of undermining the morale of nations by calling for peace at a time when they needed all their energies for the struggle against the unjust aggressor. He also tried, again with totally negative results, the method of secret diplomatic approaches, in particular in the spring of 1915, in an effort to keep Italy out of the war, and in the summer of 1917, when he put a plan for mediation to the two camps. [5]

These efforts for peace were undoubtedly inspired by Christian and humanitarian motives, but they were also inspired by considerations directly affecting the Church. Because of the war, a great many priests and religious were uprooted from their ministry and sent on active service. The centralised government of the Church was greatly hampered. The unity of the Catholic world was compromised by the mutual antagonism, made worse by lying propaganda, developing between the faithful of the two camps; and the longer the war continued, the longer the trail of moral disorder it threatened to leave behind, with results likely to be disastrous for religion. In the case of Italy the Vatican had particular reasons for concern, over and above a natural desire to see a country so close to the centre of the Church remaining at peace and its fears of a socialist revolution at Rome in the event of defeat: for it was well understood that in the absence of an internationally agreed solution of the Holy See would be in a very delicate situation once it found itself lodged within a belligerent country. [6] Over and beyond all this

4. In France and Belgium, Benedict XV was reproached in particular for his failure to condemn the atrocities allegedly committed by the Germans in the occupied territories. But from discreet enquiries the pope instituted, it appeared that most of the reputed incidents were either non-existent or at least grossly exaggerated, while on the other hand the Vatican had knowledge of cruelties said to have been perpetrated by the Russians during their advance into German and Austrian territory. It was impossible to condemn the one without condemning the other.

5. This famous initiative had been preceded by others that were kept more secret. For instance, in September 1915 the pope wanted to transmit to the French Government, through the intermediary of Mgr Baudrillart, who refused to play his part, a plan for a compromise peace with Germany (cf. J. Leflon, *Benedetto XV, i cattolici e la prima guerra mondiale* (Rome 1963), 62-4). At the same time he tried to win the interest of the great Jewish associations in his attempts at mediation (cf. P. Korzek, in *Revue d'histoire moderne et contemporaine*, XX (1973), 301-33).

6. There was for example the position of the German and Austrian diplomats accredited to the Holy See. The Italian government, in conformity with the Law of Guarantees, agreed to their residing in Rome but they did not feel safe there and asked for permission to instal

was the danger that an extension of the conflict would not only prolong the war and its train of bereavement and misery but also so devastate Europe that it could no longer fulfil its traditional role as the torchbearer of Christian civilisation. Benedict XV and his advisers were particularly apprehensive of the effects of a prolongation of the conflict on Austria-Hungary, being more convinced even than the authorities at Vienna that the dual monarchy was engaged in a life and death struggle; for they had the same strong reasons as Pius X and Merry del Val for wishing to avert the break-up of this important bastion of Catholicism on its frontiers with Orthodoxy, which in their eyes had the further merit of acting as a stabilising factor in a Central Europe seething with unrest.

The question has been asked whether, in addition to these realistic considerations, which in the retrospective judgment of unbiased historians has earned him the description 'a supremely intelligent politician', Benedict XV was not also swayed by an ideological preference for the Central Powers: on the one side the dominant principles were those of authority, hierarchy and discipline, for all of which the Church had never conceded her predilection, on the other the principles of free enquiry and the liberal spirit, which the Church had always resisted. This was the charge frequently levelled against him, both during and after the war, in the English-speaking and still more in the French press; but to balance it we have the complaints in the dispatches of Austrian diplomats in Rome to the effect that the 'black sheep', that is 'the Orthodox, the Anglicans, and atheists and freemasons who set the tone in the Latin countries' received better treatment at Rome than the good 'white sheep' of the Central Powers, and the fact that although Cardinal Gasparri was viewed in France with considerable suspicion, in German circles he was regarded as pro-French. As to the prominent Germans in the pope's entourage, there is no denying that one of them, Mgr von Gerlach, was eventually expelled from Italy for espionage; but on a closer look, France and Belgium do not seem on the whole to have been so deprived of opportunities for making themselves heard as is sometimes made out. Further, although there were prelates in the curia, especially after the entry of Italy into the war, ready to accuse France of 'fighting to defend the assassins of Sarajevo',[7] or who at any rate favoured preparing the ground against the not impossible eventuality of an Allied defeat, it is known that the Vatican expressed immediate disapproval of Germany's occupation of neutral Belgium,[8] though it is true that, to avoid the appearance of taking

themselves in the Vatican. But the Secretariat of State replied that it was impossible to assume such a responsibility and the diplomats in question then withdrew to Switzerland.

7. *Benedetto XV, i cattolici e la prima guerra*, 62.
8. See in particular F. Engel-Janosi, *Oesterreich und der Vatikan*, II (Graz 1960), 275-7, and E. Vercesi, *Tre papi* (Milan 1929), 260-1.

sides, the pope refused to make public his condemnation of this violation of international law, and true also that some of Cardinal Mercier's strongly-worded attacks on Germany were regarded as excessive.

Accusations of the Vatican's partiality towards the Central Powers redoubled with the pope's offer of mediation, made in a note addressed to all the belligerents on 1 August 1917. This much-debated intervention was one of a series of peace feelers put out during the early months of 1917, the time when the apparent balance of forces between the belligerents made the chances of a purely military decision seem more and more remote. Benedict XV, long convinced that Europe's only hope of recovering her moral unity lay in a halt to the fighting on terms that left none of the belligerents completely crushed, and anxious in addition not to leave the monopoly of peacemaking efforts to international socialism, decided the moment had come to intervene and to propose not a 'white peace' but a compromise solution. From informal contacts made during the previous winter, the Vatican had gained the impression that Germany would welcome an official approach from the Holy See. In May, therefore, the Secretariat of State sent one of its most accomplished diplomats, Eugenio Pacelli, as nuncio to Munich, where he embarked on negotiations that lasted over the next three months, conducting them with exceptional finesse and determination, while the nuncio in Vienna worked at the same time on emperor Karl, who seemed particularly anxious for the deadlock to be broken. The decision to begin with an approach to the German side was dictated by the realistic consideration that concessions had to be obtained in the first instance from the parties to whom the map of war gave a temporary advantage. The chances of success were slim, but the Holy See judged that on issues of such magnitude the risk was well worth taking. At the beginning of August the Holy See despatched to all belligerents a note setting out seven detailed proposals as a basis for negotiation:[9] the evacuation of Northern France and Belgium (restoration of Belgium to full sovereignty was in fact the key to the whole plan) in exchange for the return of Germany's colonies; negotiations 'in a spirit of good will and taking into account so far as possible the wishes of the peoples affected' over territorial questions outstanding between France and Germany (Alsace-Lorraine) and between Italy and Austria (the Trentino); examination 'in the same spirit of equity and justice' of problems relating to Armenia, the Balkan States and Poland; renunciation by mutual agreement, save in a few special cases, of claims to reparations and indemnities in respect of the war; and for the future, acceptance by the powers of the principle of freedom of the seas and agreement to simultaneous disarmament and the introduction of compulsory arbitration.

9. *A.A.S.*, IX (1917), 428.

But during the summer the German attitude had changed. The Russian Revolution gave Germany new grounds for hope, and the general staff, never happy at the idea of surrendering a hostage as valuable as Belgium, had succeeded in imposing its view on the civilians. The reply from Berlin (and likewise from Vienna, which had little choice but to follow Berlin's lead) was therefore evasive in the extreme. In the absence of a good-will gesture from Germany, the pope's initiative was doomed to fail, especially since the Western Allies, made confident of their ultimate victory by the recent entry into the war of the United States, had already jumped to the conclusion that the pope's proposal for a compromise peace was a new bid by the Vatican to rescue the Central Powers. The reaction of public opinion was even more hostile than that of the chancelleries. In Italy, where it was hoped the war would lead to the completion of the Risorgimento, there was high indignation at the pope's description of it as 'a senseless massacre'; [10] in France the press fell with fury on the 'Boche pope', while Fr Sertillanges, with approval from the cardinal archbishop of Paris, declared from the pulpit of Notre-Dame: 'Holy Father, our enemies are still strong, and while they remain so we have no faith in a conciliatory peace ... Like the rebellious heir in the Gospel, we are sons who say "No" '. This reaction merely represented in extreme form a very widespread phenomenon which was observable in all the countries involved in the war: the ease with which in both camps, among the hierarchy and the theologians as much as among the faithful, fanatical patriotism triumphed over the search for a Christian solution to the problems of international justice or, it would be more correct to say, over the almost total absence of such concern, particularly during the early years of the conflict. [11] Typical is the case of Italian Catholics, who before their country intervened in the war were mostly neutralist but who then proceeded, a few rare exceptions apart, to extol the war as a moral force. This makes the gradual evolution of Erzberger in Germany and the attitude of von Hertling, the future chancellor, all the more worthy of remark. At least there was one good effect of Catholic enthusiasm for the war, the reintegration of Catholics into the mainstream of national life in those countries, France and Italy in particular, where before the war they

---

10. The expression *'inutile strage'* ('senseless massacre') had been defended by the pope himself against objections from the Secretariat of State (see the statement by G. Dalla Torre in *Benedetto XV, i catolici e la prima guerra*, 84). He had already made allusion in his message of 28 July 1915 to 'the hideous butchery which has disgraced Europe this past year'.
11. In addition to the many papers contributed to the collective work *Benedetto XV, i cattolici e la prima guerra*, see in particular H. Missala, *'Gott mit uns', Die deutsche katholische Kriegspredigt 1914-1918*, Munich 1968 (and for comparison, W. Pressel, *Die Kriegspredikt 1914-1918 in der evangelischen Kirche Deutschlands*, Göttingen 1967) and R. H. Abrams, *Preachers Present Arms*, New York 1933.

had played the part of internal *émigrés*. When the war was over, they were to find their political position substantially improved.

The pope's disappointment over the reception of his note of August 1917 caused him to keep silent thereafter on the concrete problems affecting peace between the nations.[12] Nor was he able to play a part in the negotiations leading up to the treaties of 1919. Italy had made her allies agree in 1915 that the Vatican should not be represented at the peace conference, fearing the opportunity would be taken to reopen the Roman question,[13] and the dissatisfaction that had been aroused in the Western camp by Benedict XV's policy of strict neutrality throughout the war made it impossible for him to intervene even as a moral authority, for as M. Pernot put it: 'The pope's persistent refusal during the war to judge the conduct of the belligerents made people the more wary of his claims to judge the results of the peace conference'.[14] However that may be, even if it was an exaggeration for Briand to describe the settlement as 'a Protestant peace directed against Rome',[15] there can be no doubt that the treaties of Versailles and Saint-Germain, inspired in the judgment of the Holy See by the desire for vengeance rather than justice and likely to breed a chaos productive of fresh wars, were a bitter disappointment to the pope, as he made clear in some of his pronouncements over the next few years and in particular in the encyclical *Pacem Dei munus* of 23 May 1920. As to the League of Nations, from which the Holy See was also excluded, this brought a disappointment almost as great, since the pope could not approve of the manner in which it was conceived. Yet to counter-balance these disillusionments and the many difficulties that confronted the Vatican as a result of the changed political geography of Eastern Europe[16] – with in addition a schism in Czechoslovakia[17] – the Vatican could rejoice in the

12. He did not however desist from secret diplomatic approaches. For instance, in March 1918 Cardinal Gasparri met the Italian minister Nitti for an exchange of views regarding negotiations between Italy and Austria. See G. Spadolini, *Il cardinale Gasparri e la questione Romana* (Florence 1973), 214-24.
13. On the fruitless efforts by the Vatican during the summer of 1918 to secure modification of the celebrated article 15 of the Treaty of London see R. Mosca, in *Benedetto XV, i cattolici e la prima guerra*, 401-13.
14. *Le Saint-Siège et la Politique mondiale* (Paris 1924), 38.
15. Witness the attitude of the negotiators on the subject of Catholic missions in former German colonies. Although some favoured transferring ownership of them to the Protestant missions, under article 438 of the Treaty of Versailles, ownership was attributed to the Holy See and this attribution was confirmed by a letter from Lord Balfour (cf. G. Jarlot, *Doctrine pontificale et Histoire* (Paris 1964), 440-3).
16. See A. Tamborra, 'Benedetto XV e i problemi nazionalie e religiosi dell'Europe orientale', *Benedetto XV, i cattolici e la prima guerra*, 855-84.
17. A section of the Czech clergy had been responding since the nineteenth century to the strong pull of reforming tendencies. They were now demanding the establishment of a more or less autonomous patriarchate of Prague, participation by the laity in the administration of ecclesiastical charitable undertakings, permission for the clergy to marry and the introduc-

resurrection of Poland, the setting up of the Baltic States, with their guarantee of religious liberty to Catholics in future, and, outside the scope of the peace treaties but no less a consequence of the war, the birth a year or so later of a new Catholic State, Ireland.

Furthermore, as with the Congress of Vienna a century earlier, the presence in Paris for months on end of diplomatic representatives of all the European powers enabled the Holy See, represented *sub rosa* by the astute Mgr Ceretti, to establish informal contacts which over the next few years led to the conclusion of concordats with several of the new postwar States and in France and Italy to improved relations between Church and State.

In France there signs even before 1914 that the breach was starting to heal, and the ordeals of war and the comradeship of the trenches (25,000 priests, religious and seminarists were called to the colours) helped to further the process. In the immediate postwar years the conservative outlook of the *bleu horizon* Parliament helped to make possible the re-establishment of diplomatic relations with the Vatican (1921), the continuation of the concordat regime in Alsace-Lorraine, a more conciliatory policy towards religious congregations and the rationalisation of some of the problems arising from the Separation of 1905, as achieved for example in the preliminary understanding reached by Rome and Paris on the procedure for the appointment of bishops [18] and by the statute of associations, which made it possible for churches to acquire legal status. [19] Although the negotiations were started under Benedict XV, this last affair was not finally settled until 1924, for whereas in 1906 the Holy See had condemned the law on associations for worship which the French bishops of the day (nominees of Leo XIII) had been prepared to accept, the bishops of the postwar years and their French colleagus in the curia (mostly nominees of Pius X) were unwilling to accept even the law as improved by subsequent judicial decisions (which recognised the bishop's authority as in practice overriding), although it was a law the Holy See was now prepared in principle to accept, agreeing – somewhat as in 1801 – to tolerate a certain secularity in fact so long as neutralism ceased to be so in law.

As to Italy, although Benedict XV belonged to the 'intransigent' school, he was eager from the start of his pontificate to make unofficial contact with

tion of the national language into the liturgy. Rome made some slight concessions in this last domain but refused to go any further and on 16 December 1920 condemned the movement, whose leaders then set up an independent national church of the presbyterian type, which was granted recognition by the State. It very soon numbered half a million adherents and survives into our own day; Slovakia, however, remained outside the movement. Cf. R. Urban, *Die slavisch-nationalkirchliche Bestrebungen in Tschecoslovakei*, Leipzig 1938.

18. See A. Campenhausen, *L'Église et l'État en France* (Paris 1964), 105-10.
19. See *ibid.*, 110-16 and A. Dansette, *Histoire religieuse de la France contemporaine*, II (Paris 1951), 505-10. See further, F. Renaud, *Les Diocésaines*, Paris 1923.

the government, and he was the first pope since 1870 to lay claim to the rights of the Holy See without using expressions wounding to the official Italian regime. After the war he also denied himself the one form of protest that might have caused the regime some embarrassment, refusal to receive the heads of Catholic States when they paid their respects to the king of Italy, while his Secretary of State showed willingness, in the spirit of the early years of Leo XIII, to resume the initiative in the search for a peaceful solution. Although the conversations Mgr Cerretti had with Orlando in 1920 came to nothing because of the fall of the Orlando government, there was much talk in the following year of an imminent reconciliation. But above all, overcoming the fears of his two predecessors regarding the participation of Catholics in Italian politics, and acting from the conviction that henceforward the Church had everything to gain from solid representation of her interests in the parliamentary arena, Benedict XV signified his assent late in 1918 to a plan for a new party put forward by Don Sturzo,[20] a Sicilian priest who had been remarkably successful in local government, a born leader, at once reflective and dynamic. This party, which also had backing from Count Grosoli, the last president of the Opera dei Congressi, from a journalist, Montini, and from Count Santucci, was to be non-confessional in the sense that it would not be incorporated into the diocesan framework. It was to be inspired, however, by Christian principles, and the task of organising electoral support for it was to fall in practice mainly on the presbyteries. Within a few months the Partito Popolare Italiano had succeeded in uniting Catholics of every hue, ranging from papalists who had kept strictly to the ruling *non expedit* – rescinded officially in 1919 – to former members of Murri's Lega democratica, and in the elections of November 1919, supported by the votes of a large section of the middle class and of the rural population, it scored an immediate success with the capture of 103 seats. For a couple of years it seemed on the way to becoming a model Christian democrat party, until it started to disintegrate as a result of divergences of opinion between its two constituent groups, democrats with advanced views on the one side, middle-class conservatives on the other.

The prominence given in this chapter to questions of a political and diplomatic order should not be allowed to give a false impression. Like Leo XIII, Benedict XV was much more than just a diplomat pope, as would have stood out still more clearly had his pontificate not been cut short. The creation as early as 4 November 1915 of a Congregation devoted especially to seminaries and universities was evidence of his concern to give encouragement to clerical studies after the years of integrist reaction. Nor did

20. On Luigi Sturzo (1871-1959) see F. Piva and F. Malgeri, *Vita di L. Sturzo*, Rome 1972, and G. De Rosa, *L'utopia politica di L. Sturzo*, Brescia 1972.

he share his predecessor's prejudices on the subject of trade unionism, giving frequent encouragement to the development of Christian unions and assuring their leaders that he was with them 'wholeheartedly', while exhorting the clergy 'not to regard social action, for all its economic connotations, as foreign to the sacerdotal ministry'. [21] There was nothing very startling in these positions, but by adopting them Benedict XV showed that he had turned his back on nostalgia for the past, as he had with the Roman question, and that he recognised that the trend in social action was irreversible. But it was above all in the field of missions and in his dealings with the Eastern Church that Benedict XV stood out as a pioneer, as can be seen from the chapters devoted to these topics elsewhere in this volume. The encyclical *Maximum illud* (30 November 1919), in which he criticised the 'indiscreet zeal' of many missionaries in promoting the national interests of their mother countries, manifested the wish of the Holy See to dissociate the missionary cause from colonial imperialism, and instructions were given to the Congregation of Propaganda regarding the setting up of local seminaries with a view to speeding up the establishment of an indigenous clergy. In the attitude he adopted to the Eastern Churches Benedict XV returned, as in so many other fields, to the policy of Leo XIII. With the war still raging, he took the step on 1 May 1917 of detaching from the Congregation for the Propagation of the Faith the section dealing with Churches of Eastern rite in communion with Rome which he made it into a separate Congregation headed by Cardinal Marini, a great enthusiast for the East. The same desire to pay greater heed to the individual traditions of the Uniate Churches inspired several other measures, for example the foundation at Rome in October 1917 of a Pontifical Institute for Eastern Studies and his support after the war of the efforts of the Ruthene metropolitan of Galicia, Mgr Szeptickij, to revitalise Basilian monachism. Benedict XV hoped in this way to encourage the return to Catholic unity of the separated Eastern Churches, a question given great topicality by the dissolution of Tsarist Russia and the political changes in the Middle East.

The conclave which opened on 3 February 1922 [22] resembled its immediate predecessor in that it contained two opposing schools of thought. There were those who wanted a return to the rigid ecclesiastical policy of the

21. Letter to Canon Mury of 7 May 1919, printed in *La Documentation catholique*, I (1919), 541.
22. Our knowledge of this conclave comes from the notes made by Cardinal Piffl (*La Revue nouvelle*, XXXVIII (1963), 46-52) and by Cardinal La Fontaine (see *Nuova Antologia*, CCCLXXXII (1935), 484-6). For the opposition to Cardinal Gasparri, see in addition the latter's memoirs (ed. G. Spadolini, 259-62). A detail worth noting: at the first ballot seventeen votes out of fifty-three went to non-Italian cardinals, twelve to the Spanish Merry del Val, four to the Dutch van Rossum and one to the Belgian Mercier. The two former had admittedly long formed part of the curia.

time of Pius X, and there were those who wanted the more open policy of the preceding pontificate to continue. The second group favoured the candidature of Gasparri, the former Secretary of State, whose votes mounted steadily to reach twenty-four; the first group voted initially for Merry del Val, but when his votes stuck at seventeen they transferred their votes to La Fontaine, patriarch of Venice, who in turn soon reached a ceiling of twenty-two. At the ninth ballot votes started to converge on Cardinal Ratti, who all along had attracted some four or five votes. In the course of the four ballots held on 5 February his votes rose from eleven to twenty-seven and he was elected the following day, by forty-two votes out of fifty-four. He announced he would take the name Pius in memory of Pius IX under whose pontificate he had entered clerical life and of Pius X who had summoned him to Rome.

The new pope had not made his career in the curia, but he had held an important post in Rome, occupying it for seven years. He was born in Lombardy on 31 May 1857 and although a keen mountaineer he had passed his life in scholarly occupations. Having served for twenty-five years first as librarian (appointed 1888) and then as prefect (1908) of the Ambrosian Library at Milan (coming into close contact there with Cardinal Ferrari), he had been made assistant in 1912 to Ehrle, prefect of the Vatican library, succeeding him in that office two years later. The man who followed Benedict XV was thus a scholar, as was to be made evident by many acts of his pontificate, [23] but he had also been given opportunity, as apostolic visitor and then nuncio in Poland between November 1918 and May 1921, to demonstrate his energy and skills as an organiser, his capacity for grasping the complexities of contemporary political problems and his objectivity in face of competing nationalisms (rivalry between the Latin and Ruthene clergy, clashes between Germans and Poles in Silesia). He was also a scholar with experience of governing a diocese, since after his return from Warsaw he had been appointed to the see of Milan and, although his tenure lasted only a few months, it was long enough for him to give new impetus to Catholic Action among men and to assist Fr Gemelli in the opening of the new Catholic university. He had always been a deeply devout priest, he was

---

23. Pius XI raised more than one scholar to the cardinalatial purple: Ehrle in 1922, Mercati and Tisserant in 1936. He made notable improvements to the Vatican's art gallery and still more to the library. He reorganised the Pontifical Academy of Sciences, which he opened to non-Catholic scholars. He expanded pontifical institutes for higher education such as the Gregorian University, or created new institutes such as the Pontifical Institute of Christian Archaeology. With the constitution *Deus Scientiorum Dominus* of 14 May 1931 (*A.A.S.*, XXIII (1931), 241-84) he set a higher standard for clerical studies and in 1938 he undertook in person the direction of the Congregation of Seminaries and Universities. Note will be taken, however, of the reservation made by C. Falconi, *I papi del ventesimo secolo* (Milan 1967), 227-8.

an oblate of St Charles and had a special veneration for the curé d'Ars (whom he was to have the satisfaction of canonising, along with St Teresa of the Child Jesus, in the Holy Year 1925); and he was to resemble Pius IX and Pius X in his concern for the constant betterment of the spiritual quality of the clergy and in his encouragement of the great devotional movements of modern times, in particular the cult of the Sacred Heart. He was outstandingly energetic (he found Rome's indolent ways insupportable) and inclined to be arbitrary or even authoritarian – his essential characteristic, said his secretary, C. Confalonieri, was that he possessed 'the art or rather *la virtu* to command'; he wanted to supervise and direct everything himself, rarely seeking advice and, among other things, taking a much greater part than his predecessors in the composition of his encyclicals. Lastly, his character was not of the type that could be persuaded, even in the interests of political expediency, to compromise on principles, he was a fighter whose righteous rages were a byword, and in whom discretion was perhaps not the most conspicuous of the virtues. It is thus not surprising that he left his highly individual imprint on the solution to many problems, though he also knew how to get the best out of his collaborators (for the most part people from Milan and Jesuits) and in particular from two successive secretaries of State, men of very different temperament from himself: Cardinal Gasparri, [24] who served him for eight years, and Cardinal Pacelli, who succeeded Gasparri in February 1930. [25]

Well aware that in the postwar era the problems were increasingly worldwide in their dimensions, Pius XI saw clearly the dangers for the Roman Church in appearing to be identified with Western Europe. This concern is reflected in various gestures he made to the United States and still more in his efforts to intensify missionary expansion, which have been described in detail in an earlier chapter. Among other things, he insisted that every religious order, contemplatives included, should in future maintain an establishment in a missionary country, with the result that the number of missionaries doubled in the course of his pontificate; he expanded the international organisations in support of missions and insisted on the transfer of their headquarters to Rome. He encouraged the scientific study of missiology and, above all, by recommending ways of adapting to local

24. His renewal in office, almost unprecedented, had perhaps been negotiated during the conclave. Gasparri's at times cynical brand of pragmatism made some describe him as a man 'of nobly distorted conscience' while Mgr De Luca saw him as 'the Giolitti of the Church, a man of great art, but artful'. But others have not hesitated to compare him with Consalvi. In addition to G. Spadolini, *Il Cardinale Gasparri e la questione romana*, Florence 1973, see the collective work *Il Cardinale Gasparri*, Rome 1960.
25. Gasparri's removal from office immediately following the Lateran Treaty caused him considerable distress. G. Spadolini explains it by the desire of Pius XI to have at his side for the implementation of the agreements a collaborator less involved with the opposite party and also more detached psychologically from the fascist regime (*op. cit.*, vii).

traditions and the speedier promotion of indigenous clergy, he reinforced the steps taken by his predecessor to make missions less nationalistic. In this respect the encyclical *Rerum Ecclesiae* (28 February 1926), and the subsequent consecration by the pope himself of the first six Chinese bishops marked a turning-point, signifying as it did Rome's official endorsement of ideas that a young Belgian missionary, Fr Lebbe, had succeeded in propagating in the teeth of much opposition.

But still greater than his concern for the Roman Church's extension throughout the world was Pius XI's concern to make the Church's influence penetrate more deeply. He had taken as his motto *Pax Christi in regno Christi*, thus signifying his intention of combining the programmes of Benedict XV and Pius X.

Called to the pontificate in the interwar period, he repeatedly preached peace among the nations, condemning in his inaugural encyclical 'exaggerated patriotism' and nationalism so narrow that it denied the right of other nations to exist and prosper. He did not conceal his view that the *Diktat* which had followed the surrender of 1918 and the manner in which it had since been applied, for example on the occasion of the occupation of the Rhineland, fell far short of the conditions for peace demanded by the Christian ideal. While having no great faith in the League of Nations, he supported statesmen in their efforts to set up international arbitration and to curb the arms race.[26] He encouraged Franco-German *rapprochement* during the 1920s and thought it highly regrettable that so few French Catholics supported the movement.[27] The Holy See's attitude gave encouragement to a handful of Catholic pacifist movements, for example the Catholic Council for International Relations and the Union catholique d'études internationales, but their membership never grew beyond a few thousand. After all, an interrogation conducted in 1924-5 of 160 prominent French and foreign Catholics, the findings of which were published in *L'Enquête sur le nationalisme*, had shown that 'the majority of Catholics, following the example of many of their pastors, in practice place the interests of their country before those of the Church'. This finding, equally valid ten years later, and the pope's fear of provoking in many Catholic consciences a conflict between patriotic sentiment and the duty of obedience to the Holy See, probably accounts for the pope's surprising (and to some circles scandalous) indulgence towards Italy's conquest of Ethiopia, though he may also have been influenced by his belief that Italy, a country with an expanding population, had been unjustly treated in the redistribution of the

---

26. See É. Beaupin, *Pie XI et la Paix*, Paris 1928.
27. See J. C. Delbreil, *Les Catholiques français et les tentatives de rapprochement franco-allemand, 1920-1933*, Metz 1972, and P. Delattre, 'Les Catholiques allemands et le mouvement de la paix', in *Les Études*, CXCVI (1928), 275-90.

colonial empires. By contrast, in face of the growing threat of a universal conflagration, the pope summoned up all his old energy, sending forth by turns thundering condemnations of pagan nationalism and heartfelt appeals for peace. At the same time the papal diplomatic service initiated the efforts at conciliation which the then Secretary of State was to pursue unceasingly as pope until the final outbreak of the conflict. [28]

Pax Christi in regno Christi. Like Pius IX and Pius X, Pius XI envisaged Christ presiding as king over a new 'Christendom' which had abandoned the institutional forms of the old regime but was striving by the application of more modern methods to re-create its spirit in the society of the present. He had sketched out this programme in his inaugural encyclical *Ubi arcano*[29] which, with its diagnosis of 'God's displacement from society' (Gasparri) by secularising liberalism as the chief source of contemporary evils was reminiscent of the *Syllabus,* and he returned to the theme in his encyclical on Christ the King (1925), regarded by L. Salvatorelli as the *Unam sanctam* of the twentieth century. [30]

Circumstances seemed to be propitious. In France anti-clericalism was clearly on the wane, as was shown by the failure of the religious policy of the left 'cartel' in 1925, [31] and the A.C.J.F. was starting to show results. In Germany the aspirations of an unsettled younger generation towards a less self-centred and more social way of life worked in favour of Catholicism; and thanks to the powerful Centre party, which had become one of the pillars of the Weimar republic, Catholicism was also strongly represented in the public administration. In Italy, despite sporadic outbursts of anti-clericalism at the local level, the fascist regime which had been in power since 1922 appeared to offer a more suitable setting for the Christian way of life than the bourgeois State of the prewar period (the crucifix reappeared in schools and law courts, laws were passed against divorce and blasphemy, military chaplains were reintroduced, confessional schools were given certain advantages, and so on). Relations were set fair between the Holy See and the English-speaking countries, in which Catholicism continued to make steady progress, and the general tenor of negotiations with the new States created after the war promised well, except in the case of Czechoslovakia.

28. Cf. E. Deuerlein, 'Friedensbemühungen des Hl. Stuhles 1938-39', *Stimmen der Zeit,* CLXIV (1958-59), 321-34.
29. Dated 23 December 1922. Text in *A.A.S.,* XIV (1922), 676-99.
30. *Chiesa e Stato dalla Rivoluzione Francese ad oggi* (Florence 1955), 130-1.
31. A. Dansette, *Histoire religieuse de la France contemporaine,* II, 513-24, who concludes that this failure was due not only to the disciplined cohesion of the Catholic resistance but still more to the changed outlook of the great mass of the indifferent, who for half a century had lent at least passive support to the anti-clerical policies of the Third Republic: 'For the first time an anti-religious offensive by the State met with no response from the great mass of the indifferent. Times in fact had changed. Memories of clerical interference had finally faded and *curés* and monks were no longer felt to be a threat.'

On various fronts the liberal ideal of separation between civil society and the Church seemed to be giving way to the idea of collaboration with the international moral force represented by the papacy.

Taking advantage of this favourable trend, Pius XI embarked with true Lombard energy and determination on an all-embracing and systematic campaign against the secularisation of institutions and everyday life. The constancy of this concern, which the inheritors of the liberal tradition, still more numerous one might think, persisted in attacking as a modern dress version of the old theocratic ideal, accounts for many of his attitudes and actions: his insistence on defending to the last ditch the right of the young to a Christian education (in the encyclical *Divini illius magistri* of 31 December 1929 and many of his speeches); his reaffirmation, with not the smallest concession to the modern outlook, of the Catholic teaching on marriage and his exhortations to a more sanctified family life (in the encyclical *Casti connubii* of 31 December 1930 and through the reception of countless newly-weds in Vatican audiences); his efforts to promote a more Christian view of working life and economic relationships (through the encyclical *Quadragesimo anno* of 15 May 1931 and his encouragement of Catholic 'social weeks', Christian trade unions and the J.O.C.); his encouragement of the press as a medium for presenting Catholic points of view (the encyclical *Rerum omnium* of 26 January 1923 and the international exhibition of Catholic newspapers organised at Rome in 1936); his encouragement of attempts to purify the cinema (through the encyclical *Vigilanti cura* of 29 June 1936 and his support of bodies such as the American League of Decency and the Office Catholique Internationale du Cinéma, O.C.I.C.). This same concern also accounts for the pope's tireless efforts to stimulate and defend the organisation throughout the Church of Catholic Action movements involving the laity, each striving in its own sphere to make Christian principles prevail in institutions and everyday life.

At bottom it was probably this same preoccupation that made Pius XI react with such vigour to the infatuation of a large number of French Catholics, bishops prominent among them, with Action française.[32] It can

32. The literature on this subject is considerable and often polemical. Essential is E. Weber, *Action française, Royalism and Reaction in twentieth-century France*, Stanford 1962 (French tr. Paris 1964). See in addition A. Dansette, *op. cit.*, II, 576-613 and A. Latreille, *Cahiers d'histoire*, X (1965), 389-401. L. Thomas, '*L'Action française devant l'Église de Pie X à Pie XII*, Paris 1965; V. Nguyen, 'Situation des études maurassiennes', in *Revue d'histoire moderne et contemporaine*, XVIII, 1971, 503-38. Before the war Action française had gained the ear only of a small and relatively closed group of Catholic conservatives, but after 1918, as E. Weber has well brought out, it succeeded in making inroads both in the intellectual circles of the capital, impressed by the self-confidence of Action française writing and criticism, and among lower middle-class circles throughout the country who, feeling the effects of economic stagnation, blamed their plight both on the regime and on the politicians composing it.

be granted he had other reasons for intervening: 'integral nationalism' and its champions, who constantly added fuel to the flames of Franco-German antagonism, represented a direct challenge to his desire for greater international understanding between Catholics and to his conviction that a drawing together of France and Germany offered the only hope for a securely based peace; and he was incensed that through his newspaper, with its loud insistence on the moral impossibility and political imprudence of a *rapprochement* with the republican regime, alleged to be essentially anti-clerical, Maurras should lend support to the resistance in the integrist camp to the policy of religious pacification in France initiated by Benedict XV and continued under his successor. But in addition to the tactical reasons there were issues of principle involved: not only did Action française invest the national interest with the character of an absolute value, justifying the recourse to any means, however iniquitous, it also, and this was even more fundamental, gave an absolute character to the State, contradicting with its notorious slogan 'Politics First' the Catholic principle that politics must always be subordinate to morality. The basic reasons for Pius XI's objections to Action française are clearly set out in the statement only arrived at after prolonged discussion, issued by the cardinals and archbishops of France:[33]

> This school is founded on fundamental errors which give rise, in the words of the Holy Father, to a religious, moral and social system irreconcilable with faith and morals. They (the masters) cannot teach Catholics to think rightly on matters such as God, Jesus Christ, the Church, the pope, the meaning of life, the foundations, rules and sanctions of morality, the organisation of the family, society and the State, the relations between Church and State ... They profess an integral nationalism which represents at bottom a pagan view of the polis and the State, assigning to the Church a place solely as the upholder of order and not as a divinely appointed and independent body charged with the direction of souls towards their supernatural goal.

Pius XI, who at this time was reorganising Catholic Action in a way that made it strictly subordinate to the hierarchy as sole judge of where the domain of the spiritual ended and that of political action began, kept the Action française press under close scrutiny for a couple of years and then decided, having convinced himself that the movement represented a new form of 'political and social modernism', to take a strong line. The condemnation, launched inopportunely in the summer of 1926 and followed up over

33. Statement of 9 March 1927, printed in *La Documentation catholique*, XVII (1927), cols 710-11.

the next few months with implacable severity – which the rebellious intransigence of the Action française leaders, upheld behind the scenes by certain theologians, did nothing to mitigate[34] – set up a strong emotional reaction and produced many crises of conscience; but it contributed noticeably to the success of the second *ralliement* of Catholics to the Republic[35] – under the banner first of Cardinal Dubois and then of Cardinal Verdier – and at the same time liberated forces that were to throw themselves into Catholic Action and into Christian social movements and make possible a degree of religious revival, reflected for example in the more flourishing state of voluntary associations in most dioceses and in the upward trend in the number of ordinations to the priesthood.

Pius XI's issue of solemn reminders of the principles at stake and of precise instructions regarding the conduct of the faithful in a wide variety of spheres was but one aspect of his unwearying struggle against liberal secularism;[36] he was no less ready to fight the same battle through institutional, juridical and diplomatic channels. If he continued the tradition resumed by Benedict XV of aiming at a policy of presence and a multiplication of concordats it was not, as in the case of Leo XIII, from a desire to enhance the prestige of the Holy See or to secure alliances that might contribute to the solution of the Roman question. What he sought above all from governments was legislation in harmony with Christian ideals, or if that were not possible, government neutrality in respect of Christian Action. Where he saw opportunity, he tried to go further and obtain the diplomatic guarantee of a concordat. His 'mania' for concordats has often been criticised, even in Catholic circles. Some have deplored its perspective as too human inasmuch as the Church, instead of standing up as a witness to the Gospel in the world, stooped to negotiate with terrestrial powers, placing greater reliance on their temporal self-interest than on the religious conviction of the treaty's signatories. Others, following Sforza, have suspected the

---

34. Cardinal Frühwirth, Grand Penitentiary, whom few would accuse of sympathies with the anti-German nationalism of Action française, judged this severity excessive (cf. A. Walz, *Kardinal Frühwirth* (Vienna 1950), 447). It was only after the death of Pius XI that the French episcopate's desire for conciliation succeeded in making the Holy See more understanding in its attitude.

35. On this, in addition to consulting the general works dealing with the history of French Catholicism between the wars, see H. W. Paul, *The Second Ralliement: the Rapproachement between Church and State in the 20th century*, Washington 1967. It was the 'Bloc national', in power during the years immediately following the victory of 1918, that had enabled Catholics to re-enter political life and even to aspire to ministerial office.

36. It must however be pointed out that, although Pius XI was as hostile as his predecessors to the liberal conception of society as it related to religion, his teaching marked an important step forward in the difficult evolution of a theology of religious liberty. He in effect introduced the distinction between 'freedom of conscience', which he rejected as detrimental to the divine right, and 'freedom of consciences', for which he declared himself proud to do battle (encyclical *Non abbiamo bisogno, A.A.S.*, XXIII (1931), 301-2).

pope of a naivety sometimes found in intellectuals, an excessive trust in written documents. It appears that Pius XI and his advisers, deeply impressed by the power of institutions to influence the masses, saw the concordats chiefly as an opportunity for infiltrating into civil legislation certain provisions, relating in particular to education and marriage, from the code of canon law and for guaranteeing to the Holy See the right to a free hand in the choice of bishops, a point on which the Roman curia was determined there should be no more room for compromise.

Among the many corcordats concluded by Pius XI two in particular have attracted attention and given risen to criticism, at the time and subsequently: the concordat concluded with Italy in 1929, concurrently with the final settlement of the Roman question, and the concordat concluded in 1933 with Germany, just after Hitler had come to power.

Pius XI was well aware that the actualities of the Roman question had radically altered over the past half-century and that the issue was no longer the pope's claim to temporal power but very much that of the spiritual freedom of the Holy See. Historian that he was, he was too conscious of the contingent element in ecclesiastical institutions not to commit himself more fully than his predecessors to the search for a compromise solution which would in practice concede the unity of Italy with Rome as the capital. But he held it essential that the settlement of this question of international law should go hand in hand with a satisfactory settlement of the Church's position in Italy. The negotiations which began in great secrecy in 1926 on the initiative of the fascist government were conducted on the papal side by Cardinal Gasparri and Francesco Pacelli, lawyer brother of the future pope. Although in its main outlines an agreement was quick to emerge, it was several times endangered over the next two years by serious differences of opinion over the youth movements, which the regime wanted to keep under its exclusive control. Pius XI agreed in the end to the incorporation of the Catholic Boy Scouts into the Opera Nazionale Balilla (provided chaplains were appointed) but he remained adamant on the subject of movements belonging to Catholic Action proper, on which Mussolini eventually gave away. The final stages of the negotiations were held up for several weeks by last-minute objections first from king Victor Emmanuel over the surrender of a fraction of Italian territory and then from the Ministry of Justice over the stipulations regarding marriage, 'which were inconsistent with the code of Italian civil law', but on 11 February 1929 it was at last possible to sign all three parts of the agreement, political, financial and religious.

Pius XI recognised the kingdom of Italy with Rome as the capital, Italy in return recognised the Roman Pontiff as sovereign in a minute territory of forty-four hectares (the Vatican City State) which guaranteed to him the full independence claimed since the time of Leo XIII. There was also provision for the payment of a financial indemnity, which Pius XI used among other things to equip the new State with a variety of up-to-date technical services, including a broadcasting station. In addition, the privilege of extra-territoriality was extended to a number of apostolic palaces, basilicas and ecclesiastical institutes. The concordat concluded at the same time between the Holy See and Italy satisfied the most important of the pope's expressed demands. It relied for the most part on a government scheme of 1925 for updating legislation on the Church, but in 1929 it was no longer a question of a unilateral decision by the State but of an agreement worked out in common, and one in which, not without a struggle and at the expense of some fairly substantial concessions, Pius XI succeeded in securing mention of two matters he regarded as more fundamental even than the Roman question: education and Christian marriage. Thereafter Pius XI continued to insist, to Mussolini's annoyance, that the concordat and the treaty were bound inextricably together and that any infringement of the former would be regarded in his eyes as a violation of the latter: *simul stabunt aut simul cadent*. Friction indeed soon arose: in the summer of 1929 as a result of disquieting remarks by Mussolini when ratification of the agreement was going through Parliament and in more serious form two years later, over Catholic Action and the youth movements, which led to the encyclical *Non abbiamo bisogno* of 29 June 1931.[37] But the pope stood his ground and after months of negotiation, in which Tacchi Venturi, S.J. acted as intermediary, Mussolini ended by giving way to him, at least in principle, on the essential points.[38]

The course of events in Germany took a less satisfactory turn. As was said earlier, under the auspices of the Weimar Constitution (11 August 1919) German Catholicism had made heartening progress, despite serious difficulties over the schools and despite the increasing tendency of the big towns to become 'spiritual graveyards'. Less bound up with the civil establishment than was the Protestant Church, the Catholic Church had less to lose from the introduction of a greater degree of separation between Church and State, which in fact gave to Catholics the religious freedom they had so long demanded. The period has been spoken of as a 'monastic[39] and liturgical springtime'; Catholics had begun to carry some weight in the world of science and culture; youth movements (Quickborn, Neu-

37. *A.A.S.*, XXIII (1931) 285-312.
38. On this tussle see, in addition to the general works dealing with the relations of Church and State at this period, the two relevant chapters in A. Martini, *Studi sulla questione romana*, Rome 1963.
39. The number of men and women religious rose from 72,535 in 1919 to 88,589 in 1933 and it was possible to open a number of religious houses in regions such as Saxony and Württemberg where they had previously been forbidden.

Deutschland, etc) had made a fresh start,[40] the flourishing array of German Catholic associations excited admiration in Roman circles; and in industrial regions the process of dechristianisation had perceptibly slowed or even, especially in Westphalia and Saxony, been reversed thanks to the social policies pursued by the Centre (between 1920 and 1928 a Catholic priest, H. Brauns, was Minister of Labour in twelve successive governments). All this splendid edifice, buttressed by concordats concluded with Bavaria (1924), Prussia (1929) and Baden (1932), was placed suddenly in jeopardy by the advent of Hitler to power in January 1933. The bishops had several times condemned the pagan ideology of the Nazi movement and forbidden the faithful to join the party, and it is a fact that in the elections of July 1932, with the exception of Berlin, the ten voting districts most hostile to the N.S.D.A.P. were predominantly Catholic. But many Catholics feared they would again be branded as 'bad Germans' if they opposed the one party that seemed capable of delivering their humiliated fatherland from the *Diktat* of Versailles and of restoring Austria to the bosom of 'greater Germany'. And there were Catholics who were susceptible, for economic reasons and for reasons connected with public morality, to the anti-Semitic slogans of the Nazis. This accounts for the diagnosis made as early as 1931 by Walter Dirks, a German counterpart of Emmanuel Mounier, 'of a process in German Catholicism of internal "fascisisation" which will one day make possible a coalition with National Socialism'. The process was hastened by the swing to the conservative right of the majority of Catholic politicians whose tendency, save in the case of rare exceptions such as J. Wirth, had always been to identify the democracy of the Republic with freemasonry – many of the clergy did the same –[41] and who, faced with an ever-worsening economic crisis, viewed the communist alternative with the gravest apprehension. Hoodwinked by the constitutional manner in which Nazism had come to power, Catholics in authority thought it diplomatic to run before the tide: so while Mgr Kaas, leader of the Centre since 1928 – one of many prelate politicians in Central Europe during the interwar period[42] – gave Hitler the two-thirds majority he needed to assume full powers, the bishops' conference at Fulda withdrew in cautious terms the previous censures of the party and its organisations, hoping that the presence of Catholics within the movement might strengthen the moderate forces who, on the basis of what had happened in Italy, were still thought capable of damping down its

40. On these youth movements of the Weimar period see Fr Henrich, *Die Bünde Katholischer Jugendbewegung*, Munich 1968.
41. A typical example was the attitude during the 1920s of Cardinal Faulhaber (cf. V. Conzemius, *Dictionnaire d'histoire et de géographie ecclésiastiques*, XVI, cols 696-701).
42. In 1928 there were three prelates acting in a 'prime ministerial' capacity: Mgr Seipel in Austria, Mgr Srámek in Czechoslovakia and Mgr Korosetz in Yugoslavia. Also to be noted is Mgr Nolens's position as head of the Catholic party in Holland.

anti-religious tendencies. At Rome, where the pope, a long-time admirer of German Catholicism and its vitality, and the new Secretary of State, Cardinal Pacelli, nuncio in Munich from 1917 to 1929 and like Pius XI an admirer of the sterling qualities of Catholic Germany, watched these events with anguish, it was also thought best to try to canalise the movement, which was widely regarded as likely to moderate its ideological excesses once it had come to power. This was the background to the negotiations that started as early as April, conducted on the German side by Vice-Chancellor von Papen, Mgr Kaas and Mgr Gröber, archbishop of Freiburg, with a view to concluding a concordat covering the whole Reich; it was signed on 20 July and ratified on 10 September. On the face of it this was a concordat very favourable to the Catholic Church, but Pius XI and his Secretary of State have been much criticised on its account, not only because of the success it represented for Hitler at the international level (on a par with Napoleon's in 1801) but also because it lulled Catholic consciences, and all to very little purpose, since the corcordat soon stood revealed as a confidence trick. The laws that were supposed to implement it were never passed, its clearest stipulations were consistently violated and the oppression of the Church, at first hidden but later more and more overt, worsened from year to year. The Vatican seems in fact to have had few illusions about the concordat, regarding it as a lesser evil, a means of exploiting the situation of defeat that had arisen from the capitulation by the Centre and the bishops. [43] As Cardinal Pacelli observed: 'A religious war is easy to start but very difficult to sustain and the Catholics of the country affected are entitled to know that the supreme government of the Church has done everything in its power to spare them the ordeal'. It was also thought – as things turned out with some justification – that the concordat would furnish German Catholics with a legal base for withstanding attacks on their liberty and prevent the German government from rejecting *a priori* the appeals of the Holy See for respect of the law [44] and from alleging interference in its internal affairs.

43. There has been much debate over the past two decades regarding the respective responsibility of the Holy See and the German Centre party. Some have argued (Conway for example) that it was Pius XI and his Secretary of State who, fearing a breach of the anti-communist front, put pressure on the Centre to vote Hitler full powers. According to others, Mgr Kaas played a not very creditable part in this crucial decision, sacrificing his party in return for vague promises regarding the maintenance of confessional schools. He himself declared that, had the party been given a free vote, three or four deputies at most would have refused to vote the full powers. See in particular R. Leiber, *Stimmen der Zeit*, CLXVII (1960-1), 213-23 (esp. 217), and still more important, V. Conzemius, *Revue d'histoire ecclésiastique*, LXIII (1968), 867-924, esp. 870-9.

44. Pacelli's fifty-five notes of protest to Berlin between 1933 and 1939 were his weapons in a closely-argued and vigorously contested legal battle in which the Secretary of State was not only concerned, as some have claimed, to protect the interests of Catholic institutions: 'in

The question has often been asked whether there were not other motives for Pius XI's agreeing to a step that could not fail to set a stamp of approval on the Nazi regime: the fact that the regime presented itself as the arch-foe of bolshevism, which the pope had always regarded a particularly formidable threat to religion and the Church, as noted by Pastor on several occasions;[45] and a certain sympathy he felt with regimes of the fascist type. Offspring of a conservative Lombard family, in his youth Ratti had not felt drawn to Albertario's socially orientated Catholicism, and in his early days as pope he had refused to support Don Sturzo's Popolari Party, because of the danger that it would ally with the socialists. It was this refusal that helped to bring about the rapid demise of Italian parliamentary democracy, which he appears to have viewed with little regret. He was not at all averse to the possibility of an *Anschluss* of Austria with Germany, because of the barrier it would form against Viennese socialism; and even if we leave Spain out of the picture, we know for a fact that he was sympathetic to the Salazar and Dollfuss regimes. It must also be recognised that the European fascist regimes that came to power during the interwar years presented features by no means displeasing to the Catholic Church. They were based on the ideas of authority, order and hierarchy, they advocated a society organised on the corporative pattern, they did honour to the family, they attacked freemasonry and communism.

Yet although it does indeed seem that down to 1935 Pius XI, who saw in Mussolini a 'man of destiny', looked with a not unfavourable eye on the rightward trend in many European states, failing to take sufficient account of the damage this did to the 'image' of the Catholic Church in circles on the left, it is equally clear that the increasing emphasis placed by the principal fascist regimes on their anti-Christian features – hyper-nationalism, pagan idolatry of the State (the sin condemned ten years earlier in the leader of Action française), racism (repudiated by a decree of the Holy Office as early as 1928) – in the end produced a revulsion. From then on, undeterred by the danger of head-on collision with the princes of this world, Pius XI launched a battle on two fronts, combating in the name of individual human rights the totalitarian ideologies of both left and right. The opening of this new phase of his pontificate was signalled by the simultaneous publication in March 1937 of two encyclicals, the one directed against atheistic communism, the other against Nazism. It was no novelty for Pius XI to issue warnings against communism, but with the stepping up of anti-religious propaganda in

places his memoranda read like miniature treatises on natural law' (cf. V. Conzemius, *ibid.*, 460-2).
45. In addition to his *Tagebücher*, ed. W. Wühr, Heidelberg 1950, see the extracts and analyses given of his diplomatic correspondence in F. Engel-Janosi, *Vom Chaos zur Katastroph. Vatikanische Gespräche*, Vienna 1971.

the U.S.S.R. during the 1930s, the revival in violent form since 1932 of religious persecution in Mexico, where Marxism was a patent influence, the advance of communism in China and Indo-China, the Comintern decision of 1935 to launch popular fronts wherever opportunity arose, and the tactic in France of 'the outstretched hand', and above all with the outbreak in July 1936 of the civil war in Spain,[46] which acted as a catalyst, the question had assumed an urgent topicality. The encyclical *Divini Redemptoris*,[47] published 19 March 1937, while very rudimentary in its exposition of Marxist doctrines, developed at length the Church's teaching on man, the family and society and on the means of effectively countering communism and declared in conclusion that communism, founded on atheism and regarding religion merely as an ideology developed by one social class to impose its domination on others, was 'intrinsically evil' and that 'we therefore cannot conceive any ground on which persons desirous of preserving Christian civilisation can collaborate with it'.

The encyclical *Mit brennender Sorge*,[48] published five days earlier, contrasted Catholic orthodoxy point by point with Hitlerian neo-paganism and drew attention to the multiple violations of the concordat of 1933. At Cardinal Pacelli's request the initial draft was made by Cardinal Faulhaber, the decision to issue the encyclical having been taken during discussions between the pope and his Secretary of State and the three German cardinals, augmented by Bishop von Galen and Bishop von Preysing, in the preceding January. The finishing touches were added by the pope himself. Despite the pope's powerlessness to translate or to cause others to translate his spiritual protests into temporal deeds, despite the pessimism of the Secretary of State, who felt he had no strong cards left to play, it was from now on open war, from which Italian fascism, in so far as it fell more closely into step with Hitler's Reich, ceased to be excluded. It is known that at the time of his death (10 February 1939) Pius XI was preparing a speech to be delivered to the Italian episcopate, assembled in its entirety for the first time in its history to commemorate the tenth anniversary of the Lateran treaties. In this speech, the unfinished text of which was not made public until twenty years later,[49] Pius XI gave his disillusionment full rein although not to the extent, as has sometimes been claimed, of breaking off relations. He protested once

46. On the religious position in Spain under the Republic see below, 566-7.
47. Text in *A.A.S.*, XXIX (1937), 69-106. See in particular G. Jarlot, *Pie XI, doctrine et action*, 391-416.
48. Text in *A.A.S.*, XXIX (1937), 145-67. On the drafting of the encyclical see A. Martini, *Archivum historiae pontificiae*, II (1964), 303-20. Some have regretted that the protests against the violations of the concordat (added by Pacelli) and against the persecution of priests and religious tended to blur the encyclical's condemnation of the Nazi ideology on grounds of principle.
49. In the *Osservatore Romano* of 9-10 February 1959; Cf. A. Martini, 'Gli ultimi giorni di Pio XI', *Civiltà cattolica*, (1959) Vol. IV, 236-50 (unpublished documents).

more against the Church's treatment in Italy and against 'the insane presumption of the man who believes and declares that he is omniscient, when it is transparently clear that he knows not what is the Church, the pope, a bishop, that he knows not the bond of faith and charity that unites us in the love and service of Jesus, our King and Lord'; turning to his own interventions 'In Italy, and not merely in Italy', the pope lamented that they had been denounced as meddlings in politics, 'just as Nero's persecution was accompanied by the charge of the burning of Rome'.

At the time of Pius XI's serious illness in November 1936 there were already many who regarded the Secretary of State as the man most qualified to succeed him, and in his remaining years Pius XI did not hide the fact that Pacelli was his candidate. Although a number of the Italian residential cardinals, anxious for a relaxation of tension with the regime, advocated the election of a less political pope in the person of Della Costa, archbishop of Florence, a section of the curial cardinals, headed by Canali, Pizzardo and Piazza, resembled the great majority of foreign cardinals in being committed to Pacelli even before the opening of the conclave, with the result that he was elected after only three ballots and on the first day (2 March 1939), an occurrence unknown for the past three centuries. The election was reported at the time as unanimous, but Cardinal Baudrillart, pressed in his old age by adroit questioners, inadvertently let fall the figure of forty-eight votes out of sixty-three.[50] For the first time in a long while, all the living cardinals were present at the conclave, Pius XI having arranged in advance for the opening to be delayed to allow cardinals from overseas time to arrive. The elected candidate announced he would take the name Pius XII, indicating that it was his intention, despite the differences in methods and temperament, to carry on the work of his predecessor.

Eugenio Pacelli was born in Rome on 2 March 1876 to a recently ennobled family of lawyers. After a brilliant scholastic career at the Liceo Visconti and then at the Capranica, the college for future diplomats, he entered the Secretariat of State, coming under the direct command of Cardinal Merry del Val and rising rapidly through the ranks to arrive in 1914 at the post of Secretary for Extraordinary Ecclesiastical Affairs. Benedict XV, who as Under-Secretary had had occasion to appreciate Pacelli's merits, kept him in this office until April 1917, at which date, as we have seen, he sent him as nuncio to Germany, to prepare the way for the mediation proposal of 1 August. After the war, having successfully negotiated a concordat (especially advantageous as regards Catholic schools) with the

---

50. See F. Charles-Roux, *Huit ans au Vatican, 1932-1940* (Paris 1947) 258-93, esp. 280. A rumour circulating at the time insisted that the pope-elect achieved the two-thirds majority already at the second ballot, but requested a third ballot to allow a clear-cut majority to emerge.

Bavarian government, Pacelli moved from Munich to Berlin where his tact and intelligence, combined with his understanding of Germany's problems, won him a remarkable ascendancy, both with the Catholic clergy and laity and in political circles. Created cardinal in December 1929, he succeeded the aged Cardinal Gasparri as Secretary of State and for the next ten years harnessed his powers to the dynamic efforts of Pius XI to preserve the liberty of the Church and to combat the rising threat from communism and Nazism, only attempting now and then to moderate their form.

Strongly criticised since his death, having previously been greatly admired, even outside the Roman Church, the new pope, despite one or two weaknesses that were accentuated with age (a number of blind spots, a mentality which, despite his efforts to enlarge the opportunities for laymen in the Church, persisted in being predominantly clerical, a too pronounced taste for devotions of the Mediterranean type and at times misplaced confidence in favourites who took advantage of their position, a tendency to nepotism) was undoubtedly a man of quite exceptional character and gifts. Intellectuals admired the acute intelligence which went straight to the heart of a problem, assimilating all its details with an ease much helped by a prodigious memory, his linguistic gifts, and the unusual breadth of his culture, which enabled him to dispense in his speeches, delivered at the rate of almost one a day, carefully thought out instruction on a wide variety of topics, [51] the sum of which formed a kind of practical moral code, a synthesis of the spirituality, in all its dimensions, of the modern polity. Diplomats and statesmen respected the nobility of the principles he sought to inculcate, but they respected too his sober objectivity, his realism and caution in weighing up all aspects of a problem, his characteristically Roman canniness which, in contrast with his Lombard predecessor, made him avoid reaching the point of no return and of condemnations without appeal so long as any prospect of a reasonable compromise remained. The crowds responded spontaneously to his fervent faith, which made him see everything in a supernatural perspective, as they did to the light of true priesthood that shone through the emaciated silhouette of his body. They sensed in this overburdened and solitary pontiff, cut off from the outside world by the thick wall of the Church's bureaucracy, a pastor wholly dedicated to his crushing apostolic responsibilities, a man of great sensitivity, a very human saint who was moved by a passionate fellow-feeling with themselves and who was able when occasion arose to take a sympathetic interest in their everyday concerns. And his professional colleagues were perpetually astonished at the overwhelming energy of this mystic who, after losing himself in prayer as though the exterior world had ceased to exist, tackled his paper work with a

51. The method he adopted for composing his addresses was described by Mgr Montini in the *Osservatore Romano* of 13-14 March 1957.

vigour that on some days made even the hardiest of his assistants beg for mercy. This extraordinary capacity for work and the sense, when it came to mastering problems, of being endowed by heaven with superior gifts, are no doubt the explanation, quite as much as an authoritarian temperament beneath the affable exterior, for his gradual tendency to concentrate all the government of the Church in his own hands, at some risk to the normal functioning of its institutions.[52] Not only, after the premature death of Cardinal Maglione in 1944, did he resume, with help from two devoted, and in temperament complementary, deputies, Mgr Tardini and Mgr Montini, direction of the Secretariat of State, but he also had the habit of reserving decisions to himself in very many other fields, bypassing the normal channels and not hesitating to settle questions close to his heart merely by taking the advice of a few intimates, among them a small coterie of German Jesuits whose clandestine influence was not generally appreciated in Rome.[53]

One of the reasons prompting the cardinals to depart from tradition and cast their votes for the departed pope's Secretary of State had been the conviction that at a time of extreme international tension the Church needed as its head a pope well abreast of world politics and most likely to be able to intervene as mediator with reasonable chance of success. In fact the war and its problems absorbed the major part of Pope Pius XII's energies for the first six years of his pontificate. He could draw simultaneously on three sets of experience: the unhappy experience of Benedict XV, the doctrinal grandeur of the reign of Pius XI and the embassies he had conducted in person while still cardinal. In addition, the raising of the moral prestige of the papacy in the world between 1914 and 1939 made it possible to intervene in more positive and incisive manner than had been the case twenty-five years earlier.

The efforts of the Holy See to avert the war knew two phases of intense activity: in early May 1939, with the proposal for a five-power conference to attempt the settlement of the German-Polish and French-Italian difficulties, Fr Tacchi Venturi again acting as intermediary between the Vatican and Mussolini; and in the last weeks of August, with a series of diplomatic approaches, in particular to Warsaw, which were unhappily overtaken by events. For the next few months Pius XII strove to keep Italy out of the conflict and he welcomed unreservedly the plan of a group of German conspirators to overthrow Hitler and negotiate a peace based on return to the *status quo*. Thereafter he began to be faced, like Benedict XV before him,

52. An example: traditionally the Secretariat of State, as representative of the 'hypothesis' formed a counterweight to the Holy Office; the absence of this counterweight allowed the integrist party in the Holy Office to assume by degrees a disproportionate importance.
53. Cardinal Bea, his confessor; Fr Leiber, his secretary, whom he frequently consulted on German affairs; Fr Hentrich, who marked passages in journals for him to study; Fr Hurth, for questions of family morality, Fr Gundlach for social questions.

with the question of how far the Holy See was to go in denouncing violations of international law and natural morality by the aggressor and in the issue of solemn reminders to all Catholics of their duty to obey their conscience rather than the State.

As everyone knows, the view to be taken of the Vatican's silences has been the subject of heated controversy ever since Hochhuth brought the question before the public with his play *The Representative* (1961). The Holy See is at a disadvantage in that it has not followed other governments in opening its archives to the generality of historians, but even so it must be noted that the harshest critics of the policy Pius XII pursued throughout the conflict have failed to view as a whole the evidence already available. Pius XII's policy appears to have been guided by three considerations: his belief, which in the light of present-day political theology now seems a little old-fashioned, that the Church's overriding concern was with the welfare of souls; his anxiety not to aggravate, by provoking the Nazi rulers, the situation of the Churches in occupied countries [54] and the split among German Catholics, especially since the totalitarian character of the regime made it highly unlikely that protests and appeals to public opinion could have any real effect; and lastly, arising from his obsession with the speedy ending of a conflict whose continuance he regarded as an even greater threat than the many injustices it caused, his determination to hold himself in reserve as a potential mediator, [55] from which it followed that he had to refrain from taking up a partisan position. Many have reproached Pius XII for this policy aimed at keeping the Holy See above the fray, at a time when fundamental moral principles were much more obviously under attack than in 1914; but we have to take seriously into consideration that the pope's passion for neutrality was subservient to his passion, nothing short of an obsession, for peace.

The dilemma became still more acute after June 1941, when it might appear that the war waged by the Axis powers against the U.S.S.R. was an anti-communist crusade. Some historians have argued that Pius XII, although well aware of the danger a victory for the Third Reich would represent for the Church, regarded the triumph of the Soviets as a still greater evil and that he therefore avoided weakening the chance of the former eventuality by a formal condemnation. Pius XII's obsession in regard to communism is a fact, but the historian has to pay attention first and foremost to the documents, and documents of the period 1941-2 recently published make it clear that the pope made not the slightest objection to the collaboration of the Western Democracies with the U.S.S.R. for the purpose of resisting Ger-

54. These were not merely theoretical considerations. When in October 1939 Vatican Radio began to condemn the atrocities in Poland, the bishops reported that each of the broadcasts was followed by fresh reprisals.
55. That this was not a vain hope was confirmed, in the Vatican's opinion, by certain overtures on the part of Italy and Germany during the summer of 1942 and the spring of 1943.

man aggression. Other historians have put forward the idea that Pius XII was held captive by an anachronistic conception of the relationship between the Church and the world:[56]

> For the present evil prevailed, he knew it as well as anyone and grieved it should be so, but his concern was much less with the present than with the future. He could see for the present only the impossibility of stirring up German Catholics against their government without provoking a schism (not to mention reprisals), the impossibility of undermining nazism without giving fresh scope to communism. For the future he could foresee a renewal of the Church's influence, provided the means of exercising it were not wilfully exhausted or undermined in the course of the present ordeal. On this view ... the fate of Catholics and above all of Catholic structures in war-torn Europe had an absolute priority.

There seems little doubt that we have to include among the pope's motives his concern to safeguard as fully as possible the position of Catholicism in the various European countries in order that after the war the Church might have the resources to influence the continent's future; but to reduce, as some have done, the whole of his policy to this one aspect is too limiting. Besides, we have to remind ourselves that while he was unwilling to do or say anything to indicate that the allegiance of the supreme pastor was given to one side rather than the other, Pius XII was at pains throughout the conflict, most conspicuously in his six Christmas messages, to pronounce on matters of principle in much plainer and more precise terms than had Benedict XV, calling attention not merely to the existence of a natural community of nations governed by the moral law, and to the fundamentals of a sound international order and the respect that should be given to the rights of minorities and individuals, but also to the causes of the conflict, insisting at one and the same time on the dangers of totalitarian nationalism and on the urgent need to work for the abolition of the scandalous economic inequalities between the nations.

Severest of all has been the judgment on the Vatican's silence regarding the execrable treatment of the Jews in Nazi Europe. We may dismiss as equally wide of the mark the apologists who would have us believe that Pius XII was not at least partially aware of what took place in the extermination camps and the ultra-censorious, quick to accuse him of having sacrificed the Jewish cause to the interests of the Catholic Church or to assume that he was merely an Italian diplomat like others of the fascist generation, desensitised to the Jewish plight. But the disturbing question remains. If Pius XII

56. M. Lhuiller, in *Revue d'histoire de la Deuxiéme Guerre mondiale*, XVI no. 63 (1966) 14.

yet again opted for silence, it seems indeed to have been because he judged – perhaps rightly – that a formal condemnation would bring no benefit to the Jews and that, in addition to ruling out the possibility of mediation by the Holy See between the belligerents and provoking reprisals against Catholics in Germany and in the occupied countries, it would jeopardise the undercover and circuitous operations which saved thousands of Jewish lives, in France and Italy in particular, and make it difficult for the nuncios in Rumania and Slovakia to continue their more official interventions, which produced results not to be ignored and not confined to baptised Jews. This said, we may still wonder whether a less diplomatic, a more 'prophetic' pope would not have felt it his duty, whatever the consequences, to testify more vigorously in the name of the Gospel instead of sticking to the principle of the lesser evil. Perhaps the best we can do is to concur in the conclusion of Cardinal Doepfner: 'The retrospective judgment of history makes perfectly justifiable the view that Pius XII ought to have protested more strongly. What we certainly have no right to do is to cast doubts on the complete sincerity of his motives or on the genuineness of his underlying reasons.'

Lastly, it is noteworthy that the controversy over the 'silences' of Pius XII started up only after his death. At the end of the war what people chiefly remembered were his repeated appeals for the respect of individual rights and the natural law, his many-sided efforts to humanise the conflict, and the Vatican's silent but effective help to victims of political or racial persecution. Thus no one, however ill-disposed, dreamed of accusing Pius XII – for all his undeniable admiration and compassion for German Catholics – of being pro-German or of having fascist sympathies and, as L. Salvatorelli remarks, 'at no time since 1848 had the papacy earned such favourable comment from the press throughout the world'.[57]

For the Churches of Europe without exception, the six years of war were naturally a time of severe trial, materially and morally. In France, where the episcopate as a body long continued to favour the Pétain regime, many priests and laymen had to think out afresh the problem of obedience to the hierarchy's orders, with consequences that made themselves felt for many years after the war. But the war also made Catholics more fully aware of how deeply the working classes were affected by dechristianisation, despite the successful efforts of Catholic Action movements among the select few, and this realisation led in the late 1940s to the remarkable revival of missionary activity described in the following chapter. Again, it was the war that brought recognition of the pastoral possibilities of measures adopted initially through force of circumstances, for example evening Mass. In the Netherlands, where antagonism between believers and anti-clericals had

---

57. *Chiesa e Stato dalla Rivoluzione francese ad oggi,* 138.

been particularly acute, the war marked the beginnings of a *rapprochement* that was to have important long-term consequences. Especially tragic was the wartime situation of Catholics in Germany and Poland.

The Hitler regime's covert persecution of clergy and Catholic organisations, which had already been going on for some years, did not end with the outbreak of war, and in addition German Catholics had to pay heavily for their participation, often heroic, in the various modes of resistance. Impartial history has nevertheless been obliged to add that Catholics who persisted, whether for reasons of national solidarity or out of an admiration for authoritarian regimes, in the errors of judgment of 1933 were more numerous than was generally admitted following 1945, that Catholics bold enough to expose themselves by invoking their faith in defence of human rights could not always be sure of the unequivocal support of their ecclesiastical superiors, and that there came a time when even bishops like Mgr von Galen and Cardinal Faulhaber, notable for their courageous stand in defence of the Jews, surrendered to feelings of patriotic fervour and fears of a Bolshevik victory: though these compromises with conscience, it must be added, also occurred in other confessions and so were not peculiar to Catholics. This said, which eliminates a certain over-simplified version of the picture, we must now repeat that the Catholics sincerely committed to resistance were many, ranging from Mgr von Preysing through priests such as M. J. Metzger and religious such as A. Delp and R. Mayer, both of them Jesuits, down to ordinary laymen, and that study of the police archives of the Reich, which has now begun,[58] radically contradicts any preconceived idea of an elective affinity between National Socialism and Catholicism.

As to Poland, it is hard to say which of the two occupying powers was the more ruthless, Germany or Russia:[59] priests were executed in their hundreds, religious interned, churches closed, seminaries hindered from functioning, Catholic newspapers suppressed, in some regions the Gestapo forbade the use of Polish in the confessional, and to compound their distress Catholics felt deserted by the Vatican, since from fear of provocation the bishops refrained from publishing the messages of encouragement the pope managed to smuggle through. The position of the episcopate was especially agonising, caught as it was between two fires. If it protested against the measures taken by the occupying authorities, the faithful were immediately

58. See in particular F. Zipfel, *Kirchenkampf in Deutschland, 1933-1945*, Berlin 1965. For an excellent account of the findings so far on the whole problem of the attitude of German Catholics to the Hitler regime see V. Conzemius, *Revue d'histoire ecclésiastique*, LXIII (1968), 867-924.
59. Many documents from Polish sources are published in the volumes dealing with *Le Saint-Siège et la situation religieuse en Pologne et les pays baltes, 1939-1945*, ed. P. Blet, R. Graham, A. Martini and B. Schneider, Vatican City 1967.

visited with reprisals. If it did not protest, the persecution continued. At the end of the war the Church in Poland exchanged Charybdis for Scylla, for if the measures of the communist government were less brutal, their effect was often more insidious. The same fate overtook the Churches of other countries in Central and Eastern Europe, as at varying dates between 1945 and 1948 they passed into the orbit of Moscow, no matter whether it was Czechoslovakia, where the clergy had no *a priori* objection to co-operating in the building of a more just social order, or countries such as Hungary or Yugoslavia, where the Church could fairly be accused of siding with up-holders of the old regime or of involvement during the war with anti-democratic forces. At Rome the harsh treatment of cardinals Mindzenty and Stepinac was felt as an insult, and there was especial consternation over the forced liquidation of the Uniate Churches of the Ukraine and Tran-sylvania. Then it was the turn of the Chinese missions, one of the proudest blooms of the Congregation for the Propagation of the Faith. Having just been delivered (1945) from long years of suffering under the Japanese occu-pation, they were destroyed by the communists in a matter of months.

This sum of disappointments, made all the more bitter by the accusations, part of Stalin's propaganda, that the Holy See was using its moral influence to bolster up American imperialism, accounts to some extent for the stiffen-ing of Rome's attitude to communism, but the pope seems to have been in-fluenced still more by the successes of the communist parties in France and most of all in Italy, and by the fascination Marxism exerted over 'progressive Christians'. After launching Italian Catholic Action, now head-ed by L. Gedda, into the electoral fray to keep the communists from winning power, in 1949 the Vatican issued through the Holy Office a decree of ex-communication against Catholics of whatever country who gave the com-munists their active support.[60] Even the attempts at peaceful coexistence with communist parties made by sections of the clergy in Iron Curtain coun-tries met with a bad reception at the Vatican, and it has to be said that this attitude helped to widen the rift between East and West. But it should quick-ly be added that Pius XII's concern to remain above the two opposing ideological blocs led him on several occasions to take up positions on postwar problems which caused him to be accused by one section of American public opinion of playing the neutralists' game. Another interven-tion, for all that it was much more discreet, upset people in certain socialist circles: his encouragement of the ruling Christian democrat parties in Italy, Germany, France, Belgium and the Netherlands to aim at the establishment of a united Europe, spoken of at one time as 'Vatican Europe'.[61]

60. On the significance of this decree of 1 July 1949 see *La Revue nouvelle*, X (1949), 206-9.
61. On the Vatican's attitude towards a united Europe see W. Leifer, *Stimmen der Zeit*, CLVII (1955-6), 346-61.

Of the many concordats concluded during the interwar period few survived the upheavals of the 1940s. The concordat with Italy was matter of strong opposition from the anti-fascists. Pius XII seems in the light of this experience to have become somewhat sceptical of the value to the Church of such agreements, but this did not prevent him from negotiating another concordat which created something of a stir, with Spain in 1953.[62]

Following the proclamation of the Republic in 1931 the Spanish Church had at first been faced with a wave of anti-clerical violence and with legislative measures on the model of the 'secular laws' previously introduced in France, directed in particular against religious congregations. The success in 1933 of right wing parties, backed by Catholic Action, led to an improvement in the situation, an improvement which owed much to the moderation of Cardinal Vidal, archbishop of Tarragona, at that time leader of the episcopate, but the victory of the Popular front in 1936 brought in its train a new wave of vandalism against churches and convents. Then came the civil war, with the destruction by the Republican side during the first few months of over two thousand churches and the massacre of some seven thousand priests, religious and seminarists, and on the Falangist side the enlistment of the Church, led now by Cardinal Goma (Cardinal Vidal was one of the few who held out, refusing from his exile in Switzerland to sign the joint pastoral of 1937) in the anti-bolshevik crusade with all the results in the way of privileges but also of compromises with conscience that might be expected. The Vatican granted *de facto* recognition to the nationalist government as early as 1937. The nationalist leaders regarded Catholicism as one of the essential ingredients of Hispanidad and they therefore considered it their duty, both as Catholics and as Spaniards, to promote in all possible ways the restoration of Spain's national religion. In 1941 a provisional agreement was signed with the Holy See, further details being added in 1946 and again in 1950, but the signature of a general concordat was delayed until August 1953. The stumbling-block was the strong desire of the Spanish government to recover the right formerly possessed by the king to control the appointment of bishops, and the Holy See's determination not to go back on this point. In the end a compromise was found and the treaty as a whole gave Rome great satisfaction. An expert in concordatory law judged it the most favourable of all the concordats concluded during the past twenty-five years. It turned out in practice to have defects in some areas, but there were others, education for example, in which with the able assistance of Opus Dei the Spanish Church was able to reap considerable benefit. But Spanish Catholics in circles more alive to the actualities of modern society, the

62. Text in *A.A.S.*, XLV (1953), 625-55. See R. Aubert in *La Revue nouvelle*, XVIII (1953), 434-45.

militants of Workers' Catholic Action in particular (H.O.A.C.), were less than enchanted: 'They have given us the concordat of the Church triumphant and forgotten the Church that suffers'.

The concordat with Spain is cited as a typical example of the post-Tridentine mentality prevailing at the Vatican under Pius XII. Many others could be adduced. For example, the renewed tendency, stimulated by mass tourism and television, to exalt the place of the papacy in the Church, manifested in the insertion of a common of the sovereign pontiffs, with proper preface, into the liturgy, and more materially in Pius XII's plan for the reform of the curia not put into effect for lack of time, which envisaged a more truly personal government in which new-style cardinals, like so many *missi dominici,* would have been made responsible for the execution of the sovereign pontiff's orders by the national episcopates, thus restricting still further the role played by the successors of the apostles in order to produce a monarchically governed Church, just as in his countless speeches, letters and messages Pius XII was apt to present himself as the universal doctor, implying that the rest of the Church had only to receive his teaching and pass it on.

But it would be a serious distortion to dwell only on this aspect of the pontificate. As can be seen in more detail from other chapters of this volume, Pius XII was also a reforming pope, a fact that the pontificate of John XXIII has tended to obscure. He was a reformer in liturgical matters and, though still very cautious, he made a bold and vital contribution for the future by recognising that not everything in this domain was immutable. The same pastoral concern to adapt the Church more closely to the needs of a rapidly changing world is to be seen in his efforts to make the apostolate of the religious orders more effective, in the interest he took in secular institutes and in his unsparing encouragement of the various forms of lay apostolate. Pius XII's reforming aspirations are also manifest in the steps he took to internationalise the curia and more particularly the Sacred College, in which the proportion of Italians to non-Italians was reversed, leaving Italians with only one-third of the seats. Included in the two-thirds non-Italian majority were a Chinese, an Indian and two prelates of an Eastern rite. Naturally this has been claimed as an evolutionary rather than a revolutionary process, [63] but it was none the less a striking and highly significant change.

This determination to take a global view was responsible for the pope's increasingly active interest in efforts to secure the emancipation of coloured peoples, [64] as also in the industrialisation of underdeveloped countries and in

63. See P. Andrieu-Guittrancourt, 'Les deux consistoires célébrés par S.S. Pie XII', *L'Année canonique,* II (1953), 19-33.
64. They provoked in some cases strong reactions, as in Fr Méjean's indictment *Le Vatican contre la France d'outre-Mer,* Paris 1957. For an over-all view and the principal documents

the immense pastoral problems that presented themselves in Latin America.[65] Even if we have to ascribe a fair part of this to his fear of communism, it says much for the pope's clearsightedness that, at a time when circles in the Vatican were content to indulge themselves in verbal attacks on communism, concentrating their attention almost exclusively on the current Italian political situation, he set up his defences on the true battleground, from now on as wide as the world itself, recognising that constructive measures would do more than indignant speeches or inspired press articles and make resistance effective.

The same widening of perspectives is to be seen in Pius XII's missionary directives, summed up in his encyclicals *Evangelii praecones* (11 June 1951) and *Fidei donum* (21 April 1957), which manifest his concern to hasten the formation of indigenous Churches under the control of their own bishops and his awareness of the growing part that fell to be played in this domain, as in others, by the laity. In adopting this line Pius continued, but with greater emphasis, the policies inaugurated by his two predecessors. He went even further than they in agreeing, though again not without considerable hesitation, to a more positive attitude towards the ecumenical movement.

If the elements of renewal in the pontificate of Pius XII have frequently been overlooked, the reason lies in the distinct change that set in around 1950 when Pius XII, and perhaps still more his entourage,[66] judged it their duty to place the accent more heavily on the side of caution. Warnings against ill-considered accommodations or compromises with conscience began to be sounded on the doctrinal plane (the encyclical *Humani generis,* admonitions on moral questions, the placing on the Index of several well-known works, measures against individual teachers), on the plane of political and social affairs (moves against communism, repudiation of 'progressive Christians', unsympathetic pronouncements on co-partnership in industry) as well as on the pastoral plane (greater reserve in relations with non-Catholics, halting of the worker-priest experiment and so on). The malaise engendered by this hardening of attitude during the later years of the

see *Les Églises chrétiennes et la décolonisation*, ed. M. Merle, Paris 1967.
65. In addition to encouraging the countries of Western Europe and North America to come to the aid of the South American bishops by supplying priests and militants trained by Catholic Action, Pius XII made a significant contribution in the institutional sphere: this was the setting up of CELAM (Conferentia episcoporum latino-americanorum) under the auspices of the Holy See, the first essay in bringing bishops officially together as an international body. See chapter 15, 369-71.
66. Hence A. De Gasperi's retort to someone who, detecting an increasingly reactionary trend in Roman circles, hoped there would soon be a change of pope: 'On the contrary, you have Pius XII to thank for the fact that the development you deplore is not more pronounced'. It has nevertheless been remarked that whereas during the first ten years of his pontificate the word *audacia* and exhortations to adaptation figured quite frequently in Pius XII's addresses, after that date they virtually disappeared.

pontificate is one of the main reasons for the impression retained by many that the Roman Church had to await the coming of John XXIII before there could be the beginnings of a renewal.

Few details have transpired regarding the conclave from which Cardinal Roncalli emerged as pope on 28 October 1958. Faced with a shortage of candidates – Pius XII having deliberately refrained since 1953 from filling vacancies in the Sacred College – more than one cardinal, so it is said, contemplated a choice from outside their own ranks in the person of Mgr Montini, the more progressive of the two former deputies in the Secretariat of State under the preceding pontificate, who a few years previously had been made archbishop of Milan. Among the *papabili* cardinals the name of Roncalli was high on the list of those in the know, because of his moderation and also because of the veneration in which he was held by his diocesan clergy, which weighed heavily with cardinals who had found the preceding pontificate too political for their taste and were anxious to break the tradition. But the election was not a foregone conclusion, and eleven ballots were needed to produce a decisive result. The successful candidate, whose spontaneity sometimes got the better of him, was once heard to say that for a while he was running neck and neck with the Armenian Cardinal Agagianian. Since he was already seventy-seven there was much talk of a 'transitional pope'. Most people in any case expected an uneventful pontificate and, having stood in awe for the past twenty years of a pope who by general consent was a paragon among men, not a few were content to see the throne of St Peter occupied for the time being by a 'good fellow'.

A good fellow. Such indeed had been the verdict wherever he went, with all that this expression implies of liking tinged with condescension. Born on 25 November 1881 to a family of small tenant farmers in the Bergamo district, his first position was that of secretary to the socially-concerned bishop of Bergamo, Mgr Radini Tedeschi, who took a tolerant and clear-sighted view of the social aspirations of his day and also had a keen interest in the ecclesiastical history of his own locality. After the war Roncalli was chosen by Benedict XV to superintend the centralisation in Rome of the Association for the Propagation of the Faith, but in 1925 he was sent by Pius XI, who knew him personally, as apostolic visitor to Bulgaria, a delicate mission from the point of view of resuming contacts with Eastern Orthodoxy and one that required the human qualities of tact and affability as well as an apostolic spirit. The same qualities were needed in his next post, that of apostolate delegate in Turkey and Greece and administrator of the vicariate apostolic of Istanbul (1937-44), in which he had opportunity, while deepening his knowledge of the Orthodox World, to acquaint himself with a secularised State. His somewhat surprising appointment as nuncio in Paris (1944-53) brought him yet other experiences, as much in the political sphere, where his geniality and directness made him well liked in left-wing circles, as in the pastoral, the immediate postwar years being a time when French Catholicism was in a ferment of renewal. Many aspects of this *furia francese* were of a kind to alarm Mgr Roncalli, who was not a progressive, but he was able to appreciate the serious Christian intent of the main movers and to observe the pastoral fruits of their endeavours. His sojourn in France, during which he delighted to make contact with life in the dioceses – too much so, in some people's estimation – also gave him opportunity to observe how remote, even in nominally Catholic countries and despite the splendour of her public occasions, the Church could be from wide areas of social reality and how much self-deception was inherent in certain clerical reactions which appeared to ignore that reality. The education of the future pope was completed by five and a half years spent as head of the diocese of Venice, where he again had opportunity to combine pastoral with political experience, having to deal with the presence of a communist as head of the municipal government and with pressure from local Christian democrats anxious for a *rapprochement* with Nenni's socialist party, to which the majority of bishops in the Veneto were opposed.

Believing that evangelical simplicity was to be preferred to Byzantine subtlety, Mgr Roncalli had always delighted in 'making complicated things simple' – which was taken in certain Vatican departments as a sign of his naivety – but he was also aware, more so than many intellectuals, that reality is complex, and it was this awareness that inspired his style of government, so different from that of his predecessor. His habit was 'not to issue instructions straight off about how an affair was to be settled but to wait for various proposals and estimates of their success before reaching a conclusion'. [67]

While the new style of John XXIII, less affected and more expansive, was captivating the masses, those who were hoping, after the conservative reaction of Pius XII's last years, to see the Church starting on a new path had the pleasant surprise of hearing in the coronation sermon a pastoral note struck, and by the evidence of the new pope's clear intention to take seriously his function as bishop of Rome, as bishop, that is to say, of a local church and hence 'brother to all bishops throughout the world', whereas his predecessor by contrast had stressed his function as head of the universal Church, seeing that function in terms of an ever more thoroughgoing centralisation.

But these burgeoning hopes were very soon dampened by other actions of the new pope: his appointment as Secretary of State of Cardinal Tardini, whose conservative views were well known; the marks of favour shown to

67. O. Rousseau, *Irénikon*, XXXV (1962), 280.

certain professors of the Lateran Seminary (soon to be raised to the rank of Pontifical University) notoriously hostile to a more vital theology; the creation of thirteen new Italian cardinals, which increased their representation in the Sacred College from thirty to forty per cent. It is true that by exceeding for the first time the traditional upper limit of seventy, the pope showed he was not afraid to depart from well-trodden paths.

Of this he was about to provide spectacular confirmation by announcing, after only three months, his intention of summoning an ecumenical council. The plan adopted, despite resistance from inside the curia, in respect of the council's preparatory work, was proof of the pope's desire to associate the worldwide episcopate with the responsibilities of the Holy See and also of his anxiety to set the Church on the reforming path in a pastoral direction, with the hope of encouraging in this way the reunion of the Churches. Over the next year or two the pope's frequently reiterated declarations of intent, the fraternal reception by the Vatican of prominent members of separated Churches, the creation of the Secretariat for Christian Unity, the invitation to non-Catholics to attend the council as observers, all provided pointers to the pope's earnest desire to pass from monologue to dialogue in respect of the ecumenical movement, even if there were also regular reminders that the forces of inertia and the integrist stream were throwing all their weight against the tendency to greater openness and succeeding to some extent in conveying their fears to the pope. The latter continued in fact to allow his steps to be guided by the somewhat disconcerting line he had followed as nuncio in Paris: 'a half turn to the right, a half turn to the left'. If with some of his actions he gave pleasure in reactionary quarters – not always without some distress to himself, as when he signed the decree *Veterum sapientia,* which reinforced the use of Latin – he initiated at the same time measures which pointed in an opposite direction. It could certainly be argued that he might have done more to canalise the confused aspirations that came to the surface with the announcement of the council, and that he might have guided the preparations for Vatican II and the proceedings of the first session with a firmer hand. Yet to have conceived the idea of the council, to have persevered in clearing away all obstacles in order to hasten the opening which some people, in view of his age and state of health, hoped might be postponed *sine die,* and to have contributed so signally through his discreet but effective interventions to ensuring that the council made a good start, should surely be enough to earn John XXIII a place in history. But something else has to be said if we are to take the full measure of this pontificate, brief though it was.

Renewal of the dialogue with separated Christians had been an idea uppermost in the pope's mind since it was first planted there during the distant days of his mission to Bulgaria. But although he never lost sight of this initial objective, he had found his horizon gradually enlarging. He had been distressed to discover, in Paris as much as in Turkey, that for vast sectors of contemporary society the Church was something set apart, despite the efforts of Pius XII, which today we too easily overlook, to bring Catholics out of the 'splendid isolation' in which many had sought to find protection against 'modern errors'. Throughout his career Mgr Roncalli had seized the opportunities that came his way to resume the dialogue with the non-Christian world. The success he usually had in breaking the ice was due in part to the trust inspired by his frank and friendly disposition, but still more to his natural inclination to look for the good in every man and to make this a common ground overriding ideological differences. This was still his habit after he became pope, and many were struck by the 'goodness that knew no frontiers'. But to this easy acceptance of individuals he added a more fundamental vision: that of achieving, even at the present time, despite divisions and opposing viewpoints, the beginnings of unanimity between all men of good will, on the basis of a common denominator acceptable to believers and unbelievers alike. John XXIII argued that, instead of continually harping on all the ways in which the Church's positions differed from those of others, the Church should start by explaining in simple, human and comradely language those parts of her message that coincided with what he once described as 'the primordial inheritance of all mankind'. The ideas put forward from several sides in response to the anouncement of the council, to become the basis of the message the Fathers sent out to the the world at its opening, doubtless helped to confirm the pope in his views and lent them a greater sense of urgency, but it was a direction in which he was already moving. In keeping with this was his refusal, in face of objections from influential members of the curia, to denounce the 'opening to the Left' attempted in Italy by Fanfani's government and his warm encouragement of the experiment at co-existence initiated by the Polish episcopate. Certain phrases in the encyclical *Mater et Magistra* (1961), which in its general tenor departed scarcely at all from the usual reforming line, had struck a chord with circles on the left, who interpreted them as an appeal for justice, equity, humanity and charity, and as approval for militants not only in the Christian professional associations and trade unions but in other organisations, provided the latter adhered to the normal principles of community life and respected liberty of conscience.

Realising that his end was near and hoping to offer guidance to the council in its later deliberations, John XXIII was unwilling to delay making a solemn pronouncement on these questions. He spoke it in the encyclical *Pacem in terris* (11 April 1963).[68] The encyclical's enthusiastic reception by

68. Text in *A.A.S.*, LV (1963), 257-304.

the East as well as the West was due in part to the impression John XXIII had given over the past few years of a man sincerely anxious, from no selfish or ulterior motive, to contribute to the *détente* between the two opposing blocs, but much more to the feeling that it sounded a new note. As a writer in a left-wing journal expressed it: 'John XXIII's claim to go down in history will rest not so much on his title "pope of peace" – what pope has wished to be known otherwise? – but on his merit in having matched the peace of God against the realities of our time'. This gets to the root of the matter. John XXIII openly renounced the nostalgic yearnings from which his predecessors were still not completely free, the yearnings for a Christendom on the medieval pattern in which concord between the nations was the result of their common obedience to impulses from the Vatican. Inspired by his optimistic view of the potentialities of human nature, John XXIII did not hesitate to make central to his message a theme that was only muted under Pius XII, the necessity for all members of the great human family to work together to make this world a better place. On a close look the encyclical can be seen to contain little new in principle, but with his 'good sense verging on genius' John XXIII expounded the old principles in a way that made the Church appear in the eyes of the astonished world more fundamentally preoccupied with human problems than people had imagined.

So it was that when the world learned suddenly that John XXIII was on his deathbed (he died 3 June 1963) the whole of humanity, well beyond the bounds of Catholicism and even of Christianity, felt itself stricken. A host of revealing incidents could be cited to prove it, from the lowering of the flag over the United Nations building to the demonstrations of sympathy in Moscow and the voicing of tributes by Jewish, Muslim and Buddhist leaders. The underlying reason for this unanimity in grief and praise is surely summed up in two lines from a weekly journal renowned for its anti-clericalism: 'I think John XXIII was what many Christians call a saint, I know in any case he was what we all of us call a man!'

21

THE LIFE OF THE CHURCH

THE marked trend towards centralisation in the Roman Church, which under the popes from Pius X to Pius XII became even more pronounced, and the increasingly international character of a world in which contacts outside national boundaries were becoming less and less the monopoly of a privileged social class, had as consequence a growing uniformity in the Catholic way of life, the general features of which will be described in the following pages. It would be a mistake, however, to regard this standardisation as complete. For one thing, right down to the Second Vatican Council one could still observe quite clear-cut differences between one country and another and still more between one region and another, Western Europe for example often taking up positions in advance of those of southern or Anglo-Saxon countries. For another, it must not be forgotten that a region will always have its conservatives and progressives existing side by side, though in varying proportions. And here it has to be said that although this present chapter concentrates on the new features which testify to the vitality, indeed in some departments to the rejuvenation, of a Church which in quantitative terms seemed to be slowing down, that is not to imply any disdain for the efforts of the many who kept to the traditional ways. Their contribution to the vitality of the Catholic Church during the half-century under review was by no means negligible, but in view of the limitations of space a choice has had to be made.

For the same reason it is possible to refer only in passing to the forms of devotion and of religious activity developing in other Christian communions, even though the parallels are often illuminating – for example the rediscovered sense of the Church in Reformed circles or the new trends in Christian social action – and even though the stimulus Catholics received from the influence of their separated brethren became increasingly frequent as the century advanced and the ghetto mentality of the nineteenth century started to break down. Nothing could be more untrue to history than to believe that down to the eve of the council the only fruitful contacts between Catholics, Protestants, Anglicans and Orthodox arose from the gestures each confession made towards the ecumenical movement. We need only think for example, of the Orthodox contribution to the rise of the Catholic liturgical movement or to the rediscovery of a more collegial conception of the hierarchy, and of the Reformed Churches' contribution to the birth of the biblical movement or to the greater awareness of the place of lay people in the Church.

Before taking in turn the various aspects of Catholic life during the half-century under review, attempting in each case to distinguish the most characteristic features and the general pattern of development, one final observation of a general nature may be helpful. Although for practical purposes these manifestations and movements have to be studied separately, in many cases they interacted with one another. It was the conjunction of a number of parallel discoveries that accounted in large part for the vigour of an at first sight paradoxical revival. With some shades of difference, one might apply to many countries the observation made by a Frenchman twenty-six years old in 1930: [1]

Ours is the generation that found its way back to the Bible . . . that rediscovered the liturgy . . . We were the ones on whose hearts were branded for ever the inflammatory ideas of Lord Halifax, of Cardinal Mercier . . . the ones filled with a passionate desire for Church unity. Ours is the generation that took to heart Fr Lebbe's warnings of the rise of national feeling in mission countries . . . We were the generation that read Claudel and Teilhard de Chardin and in their company were vouchsafed a vision of the world capable of satisfying the demands of the scholar and the aspirations of the poet, and we were also, alas, the generation to whom was revealed, by two hideous doctrines, the depths of inhumanity and despair that could lie in wait after centuries spent in the neglect – betrayal would not be too strong a word – of the Gospel's standards of justice and love.

The importance assumed by laymen in the life of the Catholic Church was one of the most characteristic features of its development during the pontificates of Pius XI and Pius XII. Whereas Pius X had still seen Catholic laymen as little more than adjuncts of the clergy, assisting the latter to carry out their apostolic task, after the First World War people came increasingly to realise both that the laity had a specific influence to exert, complementary

1. Bernard and Élisabeth Guyon, 'Une génération graciée', *L'Anneau d'Or*, no. 99-100 (1961), 240.

to that of the clergy and only possible to them in their capacity as laymen, and that the task was not merely something to be confided to small select groups but a universal mission devolving on all the baptised, no longer as a privilege but as a duty. Pius XI, who had already as archbishop of Milan commended Catholic Action in a circular letter to all the Lombard bishops, watched what was happening with unabated interest. Not content with encouraging movements as they arose of their own accord in various countries, he recommended that they be imitated wherever there seemed opportunity and took care to integrate such movements into the constitutional framework of diocesan life. Though alive to the role of mass movements in contemporary society, he was much less confident than Leo XIII of the efficacy of confessional political parties. What he wanted to see formed in each country, under the auspices of the hierarchy's authority, was a band of militants taking their stand on the religious ground and rallying the faithful, under the banner of Christ as universal king, to work for the reintroduction of Christian standards into private and public life, at both the national and the international level. It was this integrated Catholic Action, which he regarded as 'the apple of his eye', that he had in mind in formulating the doctrinal basis of Catholic Action,[2] defining it as 'the participation by laymen in the apostolate of the hierarchy', thus contrasting it with the Catholic social movements that his predecessors had grouped together under the heading Catholic Action, which were merely 'auxiliaries' of the hierarchy. So we find him explaining in a letter to Cardinal Segura in 1929 that Catholic Action 'is nothing less than the apostolate of the faithful who, under the direction of their bishops, lend their aid to the Church of God and in a fashion complete her pastoral ministry'. In parallel with his theoretical teaching and exhortations the pope, who rejoiced to be known as 'the pope of Catholic Action', made every effort to secure official guarantees of its

2. Expounded first in his inaugural encyclical (*A.A.S.*, XIV (1922), 693) and reiterated in the following: the consistorial allocutions of 23 May and 20 December 1923, of 14 December 1925, of 20 December 1926, of 24 December 1929 (*Ibid.*, XV (1923), 247 and 607; XVII (1925), 641; XVIII (1926), 523; XXI (1929), 766-8); the letters to Cardinal Piffl, archbishop of Vienna, of 10 June 1923 (*Ibid.*, XV (1923), 350), to the bishops of Mexico of 3 February 1926 and 28 March 1937 (*Ibid.*, XVIII (1926), 177 and XXIX (1937), 189-99), to Cardinal Gasparri of 24 January 1927 (*Ibid.*, XIX (1927), 45), to the bishops of Lithuania, to the archbishop of Malines, to the bishops of Germany and to Cardinal Bertram, dated respectively 24 June, 15 August, 17 September and 13 November 1928 (*Ibid.*, XX (1928), 256, 295-6, 356, 384-7), to the bishops of Switzerland and to Cardinal Segura, archbishop of Toledo, of 8 September and 6 November 1929 (*Ibid.*, XXI (1929), 163 and 664-8), to Cardinal Schuster, archbishop of Milan, dated 26 April 1931 and 28 August 1934 (*Ibid.*, XXIII (1931), 145-50 and XXVI (1934), 585-7), to the archbishop of Bogota dated 14 February 1934 (*Ibid.*, XXXIV (1942), 247-52), to the Brazilian episcopate of 27 October 1935 (*Ibid.*, XXVIII (1936), 159-64), to the bishops of the Philippines dated 18 January 1939 (*Ibid.*, XXXIV (1942), 252-64), and in the encyclical *Non abbiamo bisogno* of 29 June 1931 (*Ibid.*, XXIII (1931), 285-312).

status in the many concordats he negotiated, and that he would tolerate no infringement of it was proved in 1931 by the vehemence of his reaction to the threat of moves against Italian Catholic Action by the fascist government.[3]

The form of this organised lay apostolate varied with the country. Some countries long remained faithful to the unitary structure inherited from the nineteenth century, which consisted of a single national movement divided into four sections, for men, women, boys and girls. Pius XI used this form as the basis of his reorganisation of Italian Catholic Action carried out between November 1922 and October 1923, and it was also used as a model by other countries, Poland in 1923, Spain in 1926, Yugoslavia and Czechoslovakia in 1927, Austria in 1928 and several more. But there was also a developing trend towards 'specialised Catholic Action' in the form of movements aimed at a well-defined sector of the community. Here the lead was given by the Belgian young Catholic workers' movement, Jeunesse ouvrière chrétienne (J.O.C.), begun as an experiment in 1913 by a visionary young priest, the Abbé Cardijn,[4] launched officially in 1925 and introduced the next year with some not insubstantial modifications, by the Abbé Guérin into France. Pius XI encouraged the J.O.C. from the outset, ignoring the objections of those who accused it of introducing the class struggle into the Church and of 'rending the body of Christ',[5] and ten years later the cardinal Secretary of State could write that 'in the eyes of the Holy Father the J.O.C. is a perfect example of the Catholic Action he has made one of the leading themes of his pontificate'; we have it as Cardinal Garrone's opinion[6] that the J.O.C. of the early days left its mark on Catholic Action for more than a generation. What the J.O.C. did for the lower classes was often done for the middle class by Catholic scouting, and in both cases the youth movement not uncommonly extended itself into adult organisations for members who had grown up and married.

There is no denying that these organisations helped, sometimes in quite spectacular fashion, for give parish life here and there a new image. Yet the hopes entertained by Pius XI and the promoters of Catholic Action found only modest fulfilment. The causes of this partial failure were multiple: deliberate obstruction in totalitarian countries (where the timidity of the

3. For details of this clash see A. Martini, *Studi sulla questione romana* (Rome 1963), 131-73, and G. Jarlot, *Pie XI. Doctrine et action sociale* (Rome 1973), 280-315.

4. For Joseph Cardijn (1882-1967), created cardinal in 1965, see M. Fiévez and J. Meert, *Cardijn,* Brussels 1969, and the collective volume *Un message libérateur,* Brussels 1963. He set down his many ideas in his book *Laïcs en première ligne,* Brussels 1963.

5. For the clashes, some of them acute, between Cardijn and the organisers of the Association catholique de la jeunesse belge (A.C.J.B.), which represented the unitary position, see M. Walckiers, *Sources inédites relatives aux débuts de la J.O.C.* (Louvain-Paris 1970), xxx-xxxiv, 34-8, 41-3, 51-3.

6. *L'Action catholique* (Paris 1958), 13-15.

church leaders more than once restrained the more daring ardour of the young), the teething troubles that naturally beset new enterprises, the difficulty experienced by adult organisations in breaking away from methods appropriate to juveniles to discover their own proper style, the frequent tendency of the organisations to retreat into their shells, occupying themselves at best with the recovery of the negligent instead of being centres of 'conquest' (to use the terminology of the time) open on all sides to the unbelieving masses. But as causes of failure we should mention equally the apathy of most of the faithful, whose attitudes were still set in the individualist mould, and the common reluctance of the clergy to allow the laity to proceed, in their own sphere of activity, at the appropriate pace. In the period following the Second World War fresh difficulties arose, in some countries in a form so acute that the whole idea of Catholic Action as it had been conceived twenty years earlier was endangered: the universal revulsion from all forms of regimentation; objections to the artificially strict separation into masculine and feminine organisations and to the segregation of the specialised organisations from the rest; and fears on the part of those engaged in secular activities that through the back door of movements 'mandated' by the hierarchy a new form of clericalism was about to be introduced, especially since Pius XII deliberately avoided speaking as his predecessor had done of 'participation' by laymen in the hierarchy's apostolate and preferred to use more neutral expressions, 'collaboration' for example, or 'aid'.

It was in this context of challenge to the old forms that new forms of lay apostolate started to appear, whether through the infusion of a new spirit into old formulae (as with the transformation of the Marial congregations in India) or by reaching out in new directions as did certain movements aimed at the family, for example the Christian Family Movement which originated in the United States in 1948 and later captured the Far East. Special mention should be made of the Legion of Mary,[7] founded in Ireland as far back as 1921 and approved by Pius XI in 1933 but whose great expansion came only after the war, when it spread throughout Europe and to the mission countries. As a movement it differed from the classical forms of Catholic Action exemplified by the J.O.C. in that it promoted a direct and individually exercised apostolate devoted to purely religious ends, without taking on the outward social, cultural and institutional trappings of the religious society, and in drawing its members from all social classes. On the side of theory we should mention the valuable contribution of Pius XII, contained in particular in his important speech to the second Congress of the Lay Apostolate,[8] which enlarged the notion of Catholic Action as defined by

7. See F. Duff, *Miracles on Tap*, New York 1961.
8. Printed in the *Osservatore Romano* of 7-8 October 1957; French translation in *La documentation catholique*, LIV (1957), cols 1413-27. Cardinal Suenens has also drawn

Pius XI and extended it to all organised action of the Catholic laity for apostolic ends.

Although this organised action took forms which varied greatly with the country, towards the end of the pontificate of Pius XII it was possible to distinguish four main types.[9] In one group of countries Catholic Action took the form of a unitary and highly centralised national organisation working in close dependence on the ecclesiastical authorities. The most typical example was Italy,[10] but with variations this was also the system in Spain, Portugal, in much of Latin America and in some of the mission countries. In another group, represented in particular by France, Belgium, French Canada and French-speaking Africa, there was much greater stress on the movements aimed at particular social groups or professions,[11] which were left fairly free to go their own way as regards methods and objectives. In a third group of countries, which included the Netherlands, French Switzerland and Vietnam, the name Catholic Action was applied to a loosely federated assortment of organisations which continued to bear their own names and which might range, as in the Philippines, from the J.O.C. to the Knights of Columbus. There was lastly a fourth group, embracing the Anglo-Saxon world, Asia, Germany (Bavaria excepted) and German Switzerland, where the name Catholic Action was rarely used but in which there was no dearth of lay movements. Some, as the Bonifatiusverein in Germany or the Catholic Young Men's Society in Ireland, were continuations of nineteenth-century movements; but there were others of more recent origin, the Legion of Mary for example, or little *avant-garde* groups whose main interests were liturgical, biblical or ecumenical, or bodies concerned with the christianisation of the mass media (in the United States a great effort was made – as some thought in an unduly obscurantist spirit – to clean up the cinema). It should also be noted that some of the specialised movements which had originated in Western European became worldwide in extent, as happened with the J.O.C. in the decade after the war.[12]

attention (in *Nouvelle Revue théologique*, LXXX (1958), 14) to the importance of the apostolic constitution *Bis saeculari* of 27 September 1948, dealing with the Marial congregations: 'A decisive step towards a pluralistic conception of Catholic Action was taken when His Holiness Pius XII declared that the Marial congregations belonged as of right to Catholic Action'.

9. See the pamphlet *Panorama de l'apostolat organisé des laïcs dans le monde* published by COPECIAL (see p. 580) in 1963 (summary in *Civiltà cattolica*, (1963), vol. IV, 248-52).

10. See G. Poggi's distinctly critical but often illuminating *Catholic Action in Italy*, Stanford 1967.

11. Not to the total exclusion of other movements, for example the Legion of Mary; but the official status of the 'specialised movements' was sometimes a cause of tension.

12. As for J.O.C. as a worldwide influence see M. Fiévez in *Lumen Vitae*, X (1955), 434-6. For the world congress of J.O.C. at Rome in 1957, see *La Documentation catholique*, LIV (1955), cols 1157-67.

In face of this profusion of movements so greatly varying in forms and immediate objectives the need was soon felt for some kind of co-ordination at international level. Early in 1938 Pius XI had set up a central office for Catholic Action at Rome in the hope of making it an international information centre, but the project was killed by the war. After the reorganisation around 1950 of the Conference of International Catholic Organisations (O.C.I), which since the interwar period had been bringing together representatives of about a dozen organisations (ranging from Caritas Internationalis to the Office Catholique International du Cinéma and including the societies of St Vincent de Paul and the Marial congregations), the annual conferences of this body became a forum for useful exchanges. Tackling the problem from another angle, M. Veronese, the president of Italian Catholic Action, took the initiative in organising the first World Congress of the Lay Apostolate, held at Rome in October 1951.[13] Although somewhat hastily prepared and viewed with suspicion by more than one bishop, especially in Latin countries, the congress was a success, and the need was soon felt for a more continuous form of consultation. It was at this juncture that Pius XII set up the Permanent Committee for the World Congresses of the Lay Apostolate (COPECIAL), whose function is not to issue directives to the various movements and organisations but to keep track of all experiments in the field of the lay apostolate so as to derive the greatest possible mutual benefit.

Changes in the forms of Catholic Action were accompanied by an intense effort at re-thinking the doctrinal aspects, but still with a view to their practical applications. There can be no doubt that, at the beginning, Catholic Action had been sustained by false hopes of building a new Christendom, that its conception of the Church was still very post-Tridentine, placing all the emphasis on the hierarchy and the clergy, and that this outlook was coupled in many cases with a comprehensive distrust of the 'world'. But in the second generation, attitudes started to change, in response to the changing pressures of the world around. The beginnings of reaction against the 'Catholic isolation' policy so long favoured by authority had been encouraged back in the 1930s by thinkers such as Maritain[14] and Mounier,[15]

13. On this congress see R. Aubert, in *La Revue nouvelle*, XIV (1951), 576-89.
14. In particular in his book *Humanisme intégral* (1936). For Maritain's conception of the Christian's responsibilities in the State see, among others, H. Bars, *Maritain en notre temps*, Paris 1959; A. Tamosaitis, *Church and State in Maritain's Thought*, Chicago 1959; G. Forni, *La filosofia della storia nel pensiero politico di Jacques Maritain*, Bologna 1965.
15. On Emmanuel Mounier and the group associated with his journal *Esprit*, launched 1932, see ed. P. Mounier-Leclercq, *Mounier et sa génération. Lettres, carnets et inédits*, Paris 1956, and J. M. Domenach, *E. Mounier*, Paris 1972. Especially to be noted among his own works are: *L'Affrontement chrétien* (1944), *Feu la chrétienté* (1950), and the anthology entitled *L'Engagement de la foi*, Paris 1968 (in particular part II, 'Chrétien dans l'Église').

whose audience was by no means confined to France. This dissatisfaction led many minds to attempt a fundamental reappraisal of how the Christian's apostolate should be conceived in the increasingly desacralised world of the present. At one in proclaiming the 'death of the Constantinian regime' and in denouncing the illusions of the equally 'defunct' Christendom, those who wrestled with the problem were not of one mind when it came to prescribing action for the future. The advice of some was to trust in grace and to emulate the Christians of the early Church by going straight to the essentials, presenting the Gospel message in all its boldness and inviting men to enter unashamedly into the Church and to live there as obedient sons. In the opinion of others, the wall of ignorance and prejudice separating the Church from many of our contemporaries was too thick for such a method to succeed save with a number of careless Christians, who although lukewarm were still believers at heart. Instead of setting up ideals in opposition or juxtaposition, they thought it better to work alongside unbelievers without making overt efforts to convert them, trusting that by degrees the silent witness of a life filled with Christian charity would prick unbelievers into a gradual awareness that the human ideals they prized so highly could be transposed to a higher, transcendentally orientated plane. Yet a third group pointed out that this method, depending as it did on direct contact and personal friendship, restricted the field to a select few. They argued that, to reach the masses, it was necessary to rechristianise institutions and the social environment, for as long as the social climate remained unchanged, the influence exerted by individuals would very soon reach its 'ceiling'. They therefore advocated a concerted attack on what are sometimes called the temporal structures, through the extension of Catholic activity into the social and indeed the political sphere. But this raised in turn the question how far laymen engaged in such activities were to be independent of the clergy. Were the latter entitled to decide not merely the goal but even the methods to be adopted, or ought they to be content with giving 'spiritual encouragement to laymen serving in the front line'? The question gave rise to much heated debate which, in some cases, led to agonising crises within individual organisations, especially in France from 1956.

In the half-century before the Second Vatican Council, Catholic activity in secular affairs – distinguished more and more commonly from Catholic Action as such – was conspicuous most of all in the social domain.

Major happenings such as the institution of the communist regime in Russia, the consolidation of socialist parties after the First World War and the world economic crisis of the early 1930s, gave Pius XI occasion to clarify the Church's teaching in this sphere. His most important pronouncement was the encyclical *Quadragesimo anno* (1931), an extension in some respects of *Rerum novarum* but with the difference that on this occasion the critique of socialism was accompanied by a warning against the excesses of capitalism. The severity of the judgment on socialism strikes us nowadays as strangely old-fashioned, as does the encyclical's advocacy of a society on the corporatist model (which even at the time raised objections in countries such as Belgium and the Netherlands), but we can appreciate that in the perspective of 1931 the document seemed much more innovative, in places even quite daringly so. Never before had a pope taken up his pen to recommend redistribution of the national product, or indeed to recommend schemes for the better integration of the workers into their industries by means of co-partnership and profit sharing. Above all, whatever the merits of the actual solution he proposed, Pius XI showed himself much more willing than Leo XIII to contemplate the idea of far-reaching changes in the social and economic order and to dissociate himself quite openly from economic liberalism, not only as regards the relationship between workers and employers but also from the much wider standpoint of industrial life as a whole.

Pius XII did not issue a social encyclical, but he was prolix of allocutions, messages and other concisely worded documents which applied to topical issues what by now he did not hesitate to describe as 'the social teaching of the Church' (an expression not found under any of his predecessors), and he took pains to master enough of the technicalities to persuade even non-believer experts that it was to be taken seriously. Although, as mentioned in the previous chapter, he reinforced Pius XI's condemnations of communism, deeply aware as he was of the increasing fascination it held for many in the West between the end of the war and the crisis of 1956,[16] he made clear on the other hand that 'while the Church condemns existing Marxist regimes, she can neither ignore nor refuse to recognise that the worker, in his efforts to improve his lot, confronts a social system which, far from being in conformity with nature, conflicts with the order established by God and with the purposes He ordained for the fruits of the earth' (7 September 1947). Nor did he hesitate on several occasions to remind colonialist powers of their obligations and to stress the rights of peoples aspiring to independence, for all the efforts of the conventionally-minded to stifle these appeals to true justice. John XXIII's encyclical *Mater et Magistra* (1961) went still further in this direction, as also in the advocacy of co-partnership, a more collectivist society and greater intervention by the State in national economic life.

But the great difficulty for social Catholicism has always been to advance from theoretical statements to the stage of devising and implementing prac-

16. For the changing attitude of French Catholics towards communism from the time of the first *rapprochement* during the period of the 'outstretched hand' around 1935 to the resumption of the dialogue under the pontificate of John XXIII, see J. Sommet in the C.C.I.F. publication *Recherches et Débats*, no.54 (1966), 103-20.

tical measures to deal with the major problems of economic life. And here it has to be admitted that with some rare exceptions – the Centre national des jeunes agriculteurs in France is one that comes to mind [17] – Catholics continued as a whole to lack the boldness and imagination needed to take control of the social process, nowhere more so, paradoxically enough, than in countries where they formed the majority. But at least it can be said that a noticeable and growing body of Catholics gave valuable and in some instance vital support to measures of social justice initiated by others. For although the hierarchy almost in its entirety and the great mass of the faithful continued down to the eve of the Second Vatican Council to be hostile to anything that smacked of revolution, reformism by contrast was becoming more and more acceptable in Catholic circles. This was a trend that set in still more strongly after the Second World War, despite the fact that parties with the Christian democrat label were apt to be timid in embracing social reform.

We should mention here two features of the interwar period. The first is the support shown by the clergy in Mediterranean countries and in Austria for solutions of a corporatist type, a preference which often went hand in hand with sympathetic tolerance of fascist regimes. The other is the systematic extension of the efforts begun in the late nineteenth century to set up a vast network of worker-run Catholic organisations – labour unions, mutual insurance societies, co-operatives – with the aim of ensuring that the workers' struggle to defend their temporal interests and to improve their living standards, material and cultural, was pursued in a Christian spirit. After 1940 this system was often criticised, especially in France, on the ground that it kept Christians apart and prevented them from acting as a leaven in non-believing circles, but it continued to be favoured by many pastors because of its advantages in maintaining the distinctive Christian viewpoint, and great efforts were made to introduce it as a crash programme into countries of the Third world, as they became faced in turn with the social problems attendant on industrialisation.

The challenge to Christians represented by the under-development and deficiency in resources of a large part of the world gradually imposed itself during the 1950s as a major, if not the greatest, problem of our time, and Rome was much quicker to react than it had been in the case of the working class question in the nineteenth century. Stimulated by repeated appeals from the successive popes and by campaigns such as those mounted by Mgr Cardijn in an effort to shake the older Catholic countries out of their apathy,

17. This represented the extension into working life of the Jeunesse agricole catholique (J.A.C.), founded in 1929 on the model of J.O.C. and which 'was evidently to rural workers what the Communist Party was to factory workers'. See P. Houée, *Les Étapes du développement rural*, II, Paris 1972.

a number of worthwhile projects were set on foot at varying levels. They ranged from the collection of money to finance technical aid to under-developed countries – in which Germany under the auspices of the hierarchy took a notable part through bodies such as Misereor and Adveniat[18] – to study centres for research into the conditions most favourable to balanced development, having due regard to the character and particular spiritual values of the country in question. This last was a field in which the special talents of France made an original contribution, through the activity of Louis Lebret, O.P. Having launched in 1942 the group Économie et Humanisme, in 1958 he founded the research and educational institute known as IRFED whose journal, *Développement et Civilisation*, is today one of the most highly regarded in the field. Even after his death, his influence was to be a major force behind Paul VI's encyclical *Populorum progressio*.[19]

Pius X, with his exhortations to priests to devote themselves ever more wholeheartedly to the demands of their calling, had infused a new spirit into Catholic pastoral life; but, as we have seen, his pontificate was not remarkable for any great modernisation of pastoral methods. The expansion during the interwar period of Catholic Action and of socially orientated voluntary associations had the dual effect of giving a large share of respon-sibility to the priest-directors and chaplains of the latter and of causing the parochial clergy to take a more active view of their ministry, so that, in addi-tion to carrying out their normal sacramental, catechistical and sick visiting duties they found themselves devoting a growing part of their time to the organisation of study circles and of meetings of every description. In-creasing attention was also paid to the problems posed by evangelism in the big cities as they grew even larger, a field in which Germany (with men such as Karl Sonnenschein, 'the apostle of Berlin'[20]) and the Netherlands were able to make an outstanding contribution. But in fact it was only with the coming of the Second World War that a really fundamental reappraisal started to be made of the tasks facing a priest in the urban and industrial civilisation so rapidly replacing the predominantly rural civilisation around which Christianity, and Catholicism in particular, had revolved for so many centuries.

---

18. Launched by the bishops' Lenten message of 1959, Misereor, or the Bischöfliches Werk gegen Hunger und Krankheit in der Welt, had by 1961 already collected DM 127 million. Adveniat specialises in aid to Latin America.
19. See F. Malley, *Le Père Lebret, L'économie au service des hommes*, Paris 1968.
20. There are biographies of Sonnenschein by E. Thrasolt (Munich 1930: summarised in *Les Études*, CCX (1932), 738-50) and by M. Grote (Berlin 1957); see also the ten volumes of his *Notizen Weltstadtbetrachtungen*, 1925-9 (re-issued in two volumes, Freiburg-im-Breisgau 1951-2).

The questioning started in France, where the experience of mobilisation (followed in some cases by experience of the work camps in Germany) had made abundantly clear the extent of the 'apostasy of the masses', scientific confirmation of which was provided by the investigations of the school of religious sociology directed by G. Le Bras.[21] The foundation in July 1941 of the Mission de France testified to the new state of mind, in which dissatisfaction with the traditional methods mingled with hopes that recourse to some of the bolder experiments tried out by missionaries to the heathen in foreign parts might work a revival at home. But the real jolt was administered by the publication in September 1943 of the book *France pays de mission?* by two J.O.C. chaplains, after which things moved swiftly, with the foundation of the Mission de Paris and the beginnings of the worker-priest experiment.[22] Furthermore, these enterprises, which received practical support from Cardinal Suhard, whose pastoral letter *Essor ou Déclin de l'Église?* (1947) created as much stir as an encyclical, and spiritual and theological backing from the Dominican group round Fr M.-D. Chenu,[23] were but part of a wider effort to mobilise and re-deploy evangelistic resources in face of encroaching dechristianisation, an effort exemplified by the institution of the Fils de la Charité and the Missionaries des Campagnes, the reorganisation of the Prado of Lyons under the auspices of Mgr Anselme, the beginnings of the Petits Frères and Petites Soeurs of Charles de Foucauld, whose message reached a very wide audience, thanks to Fr R. Voillaume's book *Au coeur des masses* (1950). These French initiatives were watched with interest in other countries (and in the Anglican Church) and, while not escaping criticism, they helped to inspire other more modest efforts in places where the situation looked equally alarming (thus Munich, which about 1955 had 23.6 per cent practising Catholics, only 12.6 per cent working class, Geneva, with only 9.9 per cent working class, Bologna with only 7 per cent . . .)

The worker-priest crisis which broke early in 1954 – the responsibility for which rested in many quarters and not just with Rome – came to many people, again not only in France, as a bitter disappointment after the prevailing optimism of the past ten years, especially since it was accompanied by

21. For the achievement of G. Le Bras, historian of canon law and instigator of sociological research into Catholicism in France, see *Archives de sociologie des religions*, no. 29 (1970), 3-20.
22. This experiment, which aimed to ensure a continuing presence of the priesthood in industrial life, seemed at the time the product of a completely spontaneous intuition, but it was in fact the conclusion of a train of thought that had started several decades earlier, as was shown by É. Poulat, *Naissance des Prêtres-ouvriers* (Paris-Tournai 1965), 115-77 (the chapter is entitled 'Une tradition'). For a preliminary assessment of the experiment see in particular A. Dansette, *Destin du catholicisme français* (Paris 1957), 165-305 and 478-84, also M. Labourdette, *Le Sacerdoce et la Mission ouvrière*, Paris 1959.
23. See O. de la Brosse, *Le P. Chenu. La liberté dans la foi*, Paris 1969.

highly questionable measures against a number of Dominicans who had been leading lights in French Catholicism's advance guard. During those years which coincided with the dispiriting final years of Pius XII's pontificate, it might well be asked whether the Church was not indeed suffering from the sclerosis so long diagnosed by her enemies, whether she still had any zest for apostolic ventures, any interest in actively seeking the lost sheep instead of waiting in smug passivity for their return. Yet it is only fair to point out that although the Holy See put an end — as it turned out only temporarily — to the worker-priest experiment on theological grounds that are open to argument (but at bottom principally because of the drift, undeniable in some cases, of worker-priests into Marxism), it did not suppress the Mission de France: quite the contrary, the Holy See granted the Mission a new and from a canonical point of view highly original status, which went to show that the concern in high places to check apparent deviations had not stifled the will to devise new formulae to match new needs. What must also be recognised is that the crisis in France's missionary revival showed how close certain priests and religious, in their enthusiasm for greater Catholic involvement in the secular domain, had come to forgetting that Christianity is a religion, needing no doubt to be expanded into a social ethic, but providing first and foremost an answer to the problem of eternal salvation.

Nor should the dramatic character of the worker-priest formula allow us to overlook that efforts at pastoral reform were not confined to this one sector. In fact they were very varied, aimed in many instances at the reinvigoration of existing structures rather than the creation of new ones. Some remained faithful to the classical methods, as with the 'Towards a better world' movement launched in Italy in 1952 by a celebrated Jesuit preacher, Fr Lombardi, which five years later had a following in Italy of over sixty bishops and more than six thousand priests and was starting to spread to Spain and Latin America. [24] More common were efforts of a more-or-less thoroughgoing kind to adapt existing structures, in particular to infuse new life into the parish community. Force of circumstances had already made such efforts necessary in Germany during the Nazi period, when advantage was taken of the liturgical movement, to which we shall shortly return, to concentrate in the parishes the pastoral activity which up till then had tended to focus on the *Vereine*. In postwar France the parish reformers made it their great aim, following the lead of men such as the Abbé Michonneau, to inject into parochial life the community and missionary spirit that animated the extra-parochial movements. Again under the influence of the liturgical movement, there was nearly everywhere some effort to impart fresh meaning to the administration of the sacraments or to refashion preaching — too

24. Some details are given *La Documentation catholique*, LIV (1957), cols 441-4.

long converted into 'begging sermons' – into an instrument for proclaiming the word of God in the Christian congregation. Although it was not until the Second Vatican Council that acceptance of these viewpoints became general, the 1950s were a time of great progress, especially in the German-speaking countries.

Special mention deserves to be made of the advances during this period in the religious instruction of children.[25] During the late 1950s it came to be realised that it was no longer simply a question, as in the early 1900s, of resorting to modern educational methods in order to make religious instruction more comprehensible to children, for with the progressive dechristianisation not only of the working classes but also of a sizeable portion of the middle class there was no longer any guarantee that children would receive a religious upbringing in their own homes. Efforts were therefore made to provide children not only with formal instruction but also so far as possible with experience of the religious way of life. In Germany and Austria this was done chiefly through bringing children into closer contact with the liturgy, whereas in France and Belgium more store was set on the youth organisations – Croisade eucharistique, Scouting, more recently the Cœurs Vaillants or J.O.C. cadets – in which children might learn how to put the theoretical teaching of the catechism into practice in their daily lives. Improvements were also made to the formal teaching of the catechism. Although in Italy this often amounted to little more than improved training for the catechists (under the auspices of Catholic Action) and attempts to capture the children's interest by devices such as inter-parochial competitions or the institution of catechism festivals, in countries north of the Alps the reforms were at a more profound level. In Germany, where the National Catechism of 1925 had cut down the portions to be learnt by heart and simplified the language, the catechism's biblical character was emphasised by the *Katholischer Katechismus* approved by the Bishops' Conference in 1954. This new German catechism was itself inspired by a French catechism worked out by Quinet and Boyer just before the war. France subsequently plunged into a great turmoil of catechetical revision, tackling the question from all three standpoints, the biblical, the liturgical and the missionary; and although the Holy Office was obliged in 1957 to rule out some of the rasher ventures, the results of the work as a whole received on several occasions the explicit endorsement of the French

25. For some details see A. Jungmann, *Catéchèse* (Brussels 1955), 29-36, and F. Eggersdorfer, 'Die Kurve Katchesticher bewegung in Deutschland in einem halben Jahrhundert', *Katechetische Blätter* (Munich), LXXVI (1951), 10-16, 55-61. See also: A. Boyer, *Un demi-siècle au sein du mouvement catéchétique français*, Paris 1966; P. Ranwez, *Aspects contemporains de la pastorale de l'enfance*, Paris 1950; S. Riva, *Gli orientamenti attuali della pastorale catechetica*, Brescia 1965; R. Bandas, *Cinquante ans de catéchèse. Les réalisations américaines*, Paris 1961.

episcopate. Although Germany, Austria and more recently France led the way, it was not long before they had imitators, thanks to the spread of information through the written and the spoken word – a world conference, presided over by the Cardinal Prefect of the Congregation of the Council, was held at Rome in 1950, and thanks too to the work of institutes such as Lumen citae in Brussels, which attracted enquirers from all parts of the world. The conference held at Eichstatt in 1960 made clear how much the catechumenate in mission countries had in turn been influenced by the European movement for catechetical renewal.

Although in the matter of pastoral renewal nearly all the proposals made under the pontificate of Pius XII originated on the periphery and were received at Rome, in a whole series of instances, with more coolness than encouragement, in the matter of the religious orders and congregations the main impetus for renewal came from the Holy See itself. Renewal was envisaged in both senses of the term: for it was seen that the need was both for a display of fervour greater than ever, and a more intense cultivation of the spirit of the founders, and for a better adaptation, in practical terms, to economic and social conditions very different from those the founders had envisaged. In the reforming climate of the immediate postwar period the critical murmurings which had long been an undercurrent among the general public – reflected in a steady fall in vocations to brotherhoods and sisterhoods after a century and a half's uninterrupted rise [26] – were starting to be openly expressed, encouraged perhaps by comparison with the more novel forms of the religious life devised to meet the needs of our own times, for example the rule drawn up by Fr de Foucauld [27] followed by the Petits Frères and Petites Soeurs de Jésus, or some of the indigenous institutes founded in mission countries. In his *Lettere di Celestino VI agli Uomini*

26. By contrast, the number of religious priests continued in the years preceding Vatican II to show a rise: in France between 1948 and 1958 it increased by twenty-six per cent; in Germany between 1951 and 1957 religious vocations rose from 1395 to 1703 per year, whereas vocations to the diocesan clergy during that period fell by a quarter; in Spain, Great Britain and Ireland, although diocesan vocations were on the increase, the rate of increase for the orders and congregations was noticeably higher; in the United States the proportion of religious priests among the total rose from 25.6 per cent at the beginning of the century to 38.5 per cent in 1956 (see *Nouvelle revue théologique*, LXXXII (1960), 289-92).

27. Two congregations, one of men and one of women, had been founded in 1933, but experience of life in the wilds and the revelation, during the war, of the living conditions of the toiling masses, persuaded the Frères de la Solitude to make some alterations to their original rule which enabled them, while remaining faithful to Fr de Foucauld's intuition, to fit more easily into the environment of Europe's dechristianised proletariat, and subsequently into that of the 'Third World' (the first 'fraternité ouvrière' was opened in 1945). A section of the women's congregation had already started evolving in this direction as early as 1939, meeting in this new form with rapid success (in 1960 it had about eight hundred members from some fifteen different countries, many of them in Asia). See M. Carrouges, *Le P. de Foucauld et les fraternités aujourd 'hui*, Paris 1963, and J. F. Six, *Charles de Foucauld aujourd 'hui*, Paris 1966.

(1947), Papini accused a certain type of convent of being nowadays merely 'halfway between medieval museum and farmstead, half asylum and half boarding school' and he belaboured the inmates, who should have been 'watch dogs snapping at the heels of the flock' for allowing themselves to become 'fat pussies purring over memories of the past'. Much of the criticism, which although simplistic was not without a grain of truth, was levelled at 'the good Sisters': they were more scrupulous in the observance of their rules than of the Gospel; their obedience vowed them to infantilism; they did not practise charity amongst themselves; they were not poor, merely mean. Pius XII, who was to devote over two hundred documents to the religious life in the course of his pontificate – an average of twenty a year – from the outset showed himself very anxious, spurred on no doubt by his Jesuit advisers, to remedy whatever in these criticisms was justified and so enable the great army of religious – comprising three hundred thousand men and one million women – to make a more positive apostolic contribution.

The problem had been broached as far back as 1946, by a Roman canonist as renowned for his discretion as Fr Creusen, writing in the *Revue des communautés religieuses,* and two years later another Jesuit, Fr Lombardi, whose closeness to the pope was common knowledge, published in the semi-official *Civiltà cattolica* an article on 'Il rinnovamento dei religiosi' which identified certain broad principles running through the many admonitions addressed by the pope to religious in recent years (Pius XII's use of the expression *aggiornamento* in this context, a good ten years before John XXIII, is too often overlooked). At the end of 1950, as part of the programme of great congresses held in Holy Year, the Congregation for Religious organised a study week which brought together, for the first time in history, representatives of all the more important orders and congregations[28] in order that they might jointly examine under all its aspects the vast problem of adapting the orders and congregations to the modern world. The discussion ranged over the ascetic and disciplinary considerations, with special reference to poverty, problems of recruitment (with among other things a warning of the danger of apostolic schools), laying special emphasis on the training of young religious (pointing out the need for novice masters and mistresses to receive better preparation for their task and the advantages of concentrating the training of novices on a single

---

28. The acts of this first general congress of religious, comprising some 350 reports and communications, were published in full: *Acta et documenta congressus generalis de statibus perfectionis,* 4 vols, Rome 1952-3. On this congress, whose viewpoint was in many respects too exclusively Italian, see in particular A. Motte, *La Vie spirituelle,* LXXXIV (1951), 192-8 and R. Aubert, in *La Revue nouvelle,* XIII (1951), 390-8. A second congress was held in 1957 (cf. *Documentation catholique,* LV (1958), cols 115-21).

house), and lastly the apostolate, with a view to greater participation by religious in parochial and missionary work.

This great airing of views, through which superiors were familiarised with the ideas of the Holy See, prepared the way for the various legislative measures of the next few months and years. Special mention should be made of two apostolic constitutions, *Sponsa Christi* (22 November 1950), the first example of the adaptation of orders of enclosed nuns to contemporary conditions,[29] and *Sedes sapientiae* (31 May 1956), which summarised the fundamental principles to be observed in the training of novices,[30] and likewise of the various measures intended to bring greater co-ordination into the patchwork world of religious: the establishment of federal links between convents for women (most of which had previously been autonomous, looking for guidance to the bishop or the superior of a masculine order and having no organic connection with other houses, even of the same order); merging of congregations with very restricted or very similar objectives; co-ordination, achieved in large part through meeting in international congresses, between the work of orders engaged in the same type of apostolate (nursing, teaching, parochial work and so on);[31] the institution of national associations of men and women superiors (forty-seven countries had such associations by 1961) and of international unions of men and women general superiors, which had their headquarters in Rome.[32]

While efforts multiplied to adapt the lives of religious more closely to their mission, another form of the 'state of perfection' was slowly coming to maturity and acquiring juridical status: that of the secular institute. These associations of laymen, or in some cases of priests, whose members undertake to practise the precepts of the Gospel while remaining in their secular vocations, had their precursors in the emergency measures adopted by Fr de Clorivière at the time of the French Revolution and by Fr Honorat in Poland under the Tsarist persecution. First introduced in the late nineteenth century, these associations were, to begin with, especially successful in the Mediterranean countries. To this early period belong two

29. Text in *A.A.S.*, XLIII (1951), 5-24. The practical measures were inspired by three aims: to overcome the isolationism of convents by setting up federations to encourage co-operation; to lay greater stress on work as the convent's normal means of subsistence; to remind contemplatives of 'the fully and wholly apostolic' character of their vocations, since the thought of their neighbour's salvation ought always to be present in their prayers and sacrifices.

30. Text in *A.A.S.*, XLVIII (1956), 354-65.

31. See by way of example the *Atti e documenti del Primo Convegno internazionale delle religiose educatrici. Roma, settembre 1951*, Rome 1952.

32. The latter Union held a congress in Rome in 1952 at which four hundred general superiors were present and another three hundred represented. Particular topics discussed included the training of women religious for missionary work, the adaptation of their culture to modern conditions and the gradual movement towards amalgamation and federation.

Spanish foundations, the Fraternity of Diocesan Priests of the Heart of Jesus (which spread later to Italy, Germany and Latin America), and the Teresians, an association of laywomen dedicated to the Christian education of women and girls (which now has houses in all parts of western and southern Europe, in Latin America, in the Philippines and at Jerusalem); after the First World War a number of others sprang up in Milan, for example the Company of St Paul, inspired by Cardinal Ferrari, and the Missionaries of the Kingship of our Lord Jesus Christ, founded by Fr Gemelli, an association which later spread to Switzerland, the United States, Canada and Argentina. In 1928 Dom J. M. Escriva de Balaguer founded in Madrid the secular institute destined to go furthest and also, by reason of its underground activities, to arouse the greatest controversy. This was Opus Dei,[33] whose headquarters were transferred to Rome in 1946 and whose guide to spirituality, *Camino* (1939), ran in thirty years to a print of two-and-a-half million (in twenty-two languages). The juridical status of these associations had already come under discussion at the time the code of canon law was compiled, but a further twenty years were destined to elapse before it was settled. In 1938 Pius XI, who had backed Fr Gemelli and was active in defending Opus Dei against the lively attack to which it was subjected, invited the bishop of St Gallen to preside over a meeting of representatives of all secular institutes then in existence. The next few years saw two distinct schools of thought emerging. One, stressing the novel character of the vocation in question and its essentially apostolic aim, orientated itself towards the Congregation of the Council while the other, placing the accent on the ideal of perfection and foreseeing in addition the

33. Recognised in 1941 by the bishop of Madrid and in 1943 by the Holy See as a 'Community institute without public vows', Opus Dei has two branches, one for men and one for women, which in 1962 had respectively six thousand and eight thousand members, drawn principally from intellectual and middle-class circles, for the most part laymen, but receiving a philosphical and theological training similar to that of aspirants to the priesthood. There are in addition some thirty to forty thousand supernumerary members, who can be married and who are recruited in the main from the lower classes. The institute is authoritarian in structure. It nowadays has ramifications throughout the world and is especially firmly implanted in Spain and Latin America. As well as incurring reproach for the frequently secret (though not systematically so) character of its operations, which has prompted comparison with a 'Catholic freemasonry', Opus Dei has been much criticised on the following counts: that it tends to form what is virtually a 'parallel' Church, more or less independent of diocesan authority; that it is more interested in the cultivation of individual virtues (often achieving remarkable success) than in the community dimension of the faith; and its tendency, especially in Spain and Latin America, to come to terms with the established order and to mingle the crusading spirit with operations aimed at political and economic infiltration. It will be noted that similar criticism has often been levelled throughout its long history at the Society of Jesus, and also that the equivocal character, as it appears to some, of Opus Dei and its objectives does not detract from the selfless dedication of the majority of its members. See, but treat with caution, P. Artigues, *L'Opus Dei en Espagne. Son évolution idéologique et politique*, I, *1928-1957*, Paris 1968, and J.-J. Thierry, *L'Opus Dei. Mythe et réalité*, Paris 1973.

need to cater for an inter-diocesan situation, looked rather to the Congregation for Religious. The course finally adopted was in keeping with the latter view. The apostolic constitution *Provida Mater Ecclesia,* worked out in collaboration with canonist members of Opus Dei and published on 2 February 1947, at last gave canonical shape to this new form of consecrated life and laid down the conditions for official approbation.[34] Approbation of Opus Dei followed three weeks later, and over the next fifteen years thirteen other institutes of pontifical right were approved (six based on Italy, four on France, two on Spain and one on Austria) along with another fifty or so, more limited in scope, of diocesan right;[35] nor should we omit to mention the close on three hundred associations of similar type, nearly all for women, which have yet to receive official recognition.

Catholic spirituality at the dawn of the twentieth century was wanting neither in seriousness nor depth, but it presented outward features that were to meet with resistance from the rising generations. The latter, judging it perhaps rather too harshly, found the piety of their elders overloaded with sickly sentiment, to which the hymns of the period indeed bear witness, and condemned it above all for its failure to 'live', for consisting principally in exterior practices and in the observance of a code more ethical than religious. Yet a reaction had in fact already set in during the closing years of Pius IX's pontificate, the tendency of which as to focus Catholic devotion more closely on 'Christ, the life of the soul', to use the title of a book published in 1917 by Dom Columba Marmion, abbot of the Benedictine abbey of Maredsous, and translated into most European languages. Pius X's measures to encourage frequent communion quickened the pace of this rediscovery of the sacramental sources of the divine life and hastened the reaction against what has been called 'anthropocentric' piety (for which the Jesuits were often held responsible), said to pay too much attention to man himself and to his ascetic endeavours to 'work out his own salvation'.

The decade following the First World War, which was also the time when the first children to be brought up on frequent communion were reaching adult years, witnessed in Germany a rebirth of religious awareness, engendered by the liturgical movement and by the youth movements animated by the personality of Guardini.[36] It amounted to a rediscovery of

---

34. Text in *A.A.S.,* XXXIX (1947), 114-24; commentary by J. M. Perrin, *La Vie spirituelle,* LXXX (1949), 266-72. The constitution was complemented by two further documents: the *motu proprio Primo feliciter* of 12 March 1948, expounding the theology proper to this state of perfection, and an instruction from the Congregation for Religious, 19 March 1949 (text in *A.A.S.,* XL (1948), 283-6 and 293-7).

35. See *Catholicisme,* V, cols 1785-92 and *Documentation catholique,* LII (1955), cols 1059-79.

36. On Romano Guardini (1885-1968), for a quarter of a century a considerable influence on the young intelligentsia, see H. Kuhn, *R. Guardini. Der Mensch das Werk,* Munich 1961.

the fact that believers are members of a community, of a church, and that their devotional life before God and in God has to be lived within this selfsame community of the People of God. Unfortunately this new insight long remained confined to intellectual circles and penetrated only slowly to the parishes. More general and more immediate was the influence exerted throughout Western Europe by Catholic Action. Not only did it deepen spirituality among the faithful by encouraging the habit, even among the lower classes,[37] of recollections and retreats, it also fostered an active spirituality and a spirit of 'apostolic conquest', which gained additional stimulus from the institution of a feast in honour of Christ the King. The movement of which this event marked the culmination had been steadily growing in intensity since its beginnings in the preceding century. It was in 1881, at the first of the Eucharistic Congresses, that Gabriel de Belcastel had publicly proclaimed 'we are subjects of Christ before we are subjects of and civil power' and had called for Christ to be hailed as 'the Head of mankind'. Thereafter, in face of secularist claims, there was growing pressure to see 'the kingship of Christ in society' asserted with ever greater solemnity and in 1922, on the occasion of the international Eucharistic Congress at Rome, the new pope was presented with a petition from sixty-nine cardinals requesting him to institute a liturgical feast in honour of Christ the King. When the request was reiterated the following year it had the support of 340 cardinals, archbishops, bishops and religious superiors, to which was soon added the backing of twelve Catholic universities and petitions signed by hundreds of thousands of faithful. It was urged from the side of the liturgists that a feast celebrating Christ as king of all nations already existed, the feast of the Epiphany, but the eschatological perspectives of the latter presumably did not meet the requirements of those whose aim was to stress Christ's kingship here and now, and to work for the restoration of Christendom by setting over against the demands of secularism the claim of Catholicism to pervade not only the private life of individuals but the life of society as a whole. Morever, since this was the time when a decisive boost was being given to Catholic Action, it may have seemed opportune to underline by the institution of an entirely new feast the specific objective towards which Catholic Action was intended to move. So the end of Holy Year 1925 which had demonstrated that the Roman Church was still a force to be reckoned with in the world, was marked by Pius XI's institution of the new feast in the encyclical *Quas primas,* [38] to

37. On this phenomenon see *La Vie spirituelle*, LXXX (1944), 263-5. The encyclical *Mens nostra*, 1929, was to lend encouragement to this trend by stressing the fecundity of the Exercises of St Ignatius of Loyola adapted to various levels.
38. Dated 11 December; text in *A.A.S.*, XVII (1925), 593-610. The new feast was tied to a Sunday (the last in October) in order that the whole body of Christian people might be free to take part.

which he added a theological commentary (not as biblical and patristic in its inspiration as could nowadays be wished). It did not escape notice that in instituting this feast Pius XI ordained that is should be made the occasion of an annual reconsecration of mankind to the Sacred Heart of Jesus, thus underlining the link between the two devotions as they had developed in practice since the middle of the nineteenth century, following the lead in particular of the Society of Jesus.

Catholic Action influenced spirituality in yet another way, less spectacular but more lasting. In reaction against the tendency to think of spirituality only in terms of the patterns established by the religious orders there was much greater insistence on the spirituality specific to each walk of life, so that from about 1930 we hear increasingly of lay spirituality, conjugal spirituality, the spirituality of work.[39] Much in the vast literature devoted to such themes was vague and imprecise, but from it all one basic principle started gradually to emerge: the conviction that it was possible to become holy in and by means of one's state of life, whatever it might be, and that those who lived in the world could aspire not to some second-class form of spirituality, but to Christian sanctity pure and simple under the form appropriate to their lives as militant laymen or as members of a Christian family with no suggestion that this was simply a pale imitation of monastic spirituality. The example of a Teresa of the Child Jesus – canonised in 1925 and soon to have a statue in nearly every Catholic church – and more recently of Fr de Foucauld, both of whom sought sanctity outside the classical systems and drew their inspiration from the Gospel, did much to encourage this development.

Another feature of the spirituality of the interwar years which should be mentioned is the popularity around 1930 of books about Christ: in France Fr Lagrange's *L'Évangile de Jésus-Christ* (1928), Fr de Grandmaison's *Jésus-Christ, sa personne, son message* (1928), Fr Lebreton's *La vie et l'enseignement de Jésus-Christ notre Seigneur* (1931), Fr Prat's *Jésus-Christ, sa vie, sa doctrine, son oeuvre* (1933); in Germany, F. Willam's *Das Leben Jesu im Lande und Volke Israel* (1933), to which may be added Karl Adam's *Jesus Christus* (1933), the work of a theologian who had meditated deeply on the philosophical, historical and theological difficulties posed by belief in Christ and of an apostle with a profound understanding of his contemporaries, who in handling their problems showed that his mind was in tune with theirs. These lives of Jesus reaped the benefit of the detailed scholarly work which had been quietly in progress during the preceding half-century and, although their standpoint was still largely

---

39. See, *inter alia* no 99-100 (1961) of *L'Anneau d'Or*, entitled 'Pèlerinage aux sources de la spiritualité conjugale'. On the role of Fr Doncoeur, S.J. and of the J.O.C. see J. Lestavel, *Les Prophètes de l'Église contemporaine*, (Paris 1969), 93-8.

apologetic, they did much to nourish the piety of the faithful, now more than ever christocentric in character.

A parallel development of the interwar years was a renaissance in the study of spiritual theology. Much of the credit for this must go to the French Dominicans. In 1919 Fr V. Bernadot founded a new review, *La Vie spirituelle,* which gave the movement a voice. [40] It was used by one of the prime movers, Fr Garrigou-Lagrange, backed up by his colleague Fr Gardeil, to defend the proposition, contested by Fr Poulain, S.J., that all Christian souls are called to the mystical graces.

The Jesuits, although at first somewhat taken aback, were not slow to join the movement. Their own more technical journal, the *Revue d'ascétique et de mystique,* was founded as early as 1920 and over the next few years similar journals were started in Germany, Spain and Italy. Again, it was the Jesuits who in 1932 started publication of the *Dictionnaire de spiritualité,* and we should not fail to mention the valuable contribution made by the Belgian Jesuit, J. Maréchal, to the study of mystic psychology.

The Carmelites could obviously not remain aloof. In France they made their contribution through the *Études carmélitaines,* which under the editorship of Fr Bruno of Jesus Mary developed a very modern outlook, and in Spain, to even greater effect, through individuals such as Fr Ezechiel of the Sacred Heart and, above all, Fr Chrysogonus of the Blessed Sacrament. Approaching mysticism from another angle, Fr A. Stolz broke with the tradition prevalent in the West since the thirteenth century of concentrating on the psychological aspect, and in his highly original *Theologie der Mystik* (1936) returned to the objective conception found in the Fathers and in medieval spiritual authors.

But the religious orders were not alone in feeding this revival. Chief credit for the re-awakening of interest in the spiritual literature of the seventeenth century, in particular in the long-neglected Berullian tradition, must go to M. Pourrat and most of all to the Abbé H. Bremond, [41] whose monumental *Histoire littéraire du sentiment religieux* started to appear in 1916. And Bremond found an Italian emulator in Don G. De Luca, [42] founder in 1951 of that treasure-house of spiritual documents, the *Archivio italiano per la storia della pietà.* There was reason on the other hand to regret that Ger-

---

40. See the special number entitled *Les 25 ans de la Vie spirituelle* LXXI (1944), 211-496.
41. On Henri Bremond (1865-1933), see: *Dictionnaire de spiritualité,* I, cols 1928-38; *Entretiens sur H. Bremond,* ed. J. Dagens and M.Nédoncelle, Paris-Lay Haye 1967; *H. Bremond. Actes du Colloque d'Aix,* Aix-en-Provence 1967; *Revue d'ascétique et de mystique,* XLV, no. 178 (1969), 121-223.
42. On Giuseppe De Luca (1898-1962) see: H. Bernard-Maître, *Don G. De Luca et l'abbé Bremond,* Rome 1965; R. Guarnieri, *Rivista di storia della Chiesa in Italia,* XVII (1963), 15-76; I. Colosia, *Rivista di ascetica e mistica* (1962), 221-77.

many, having set the pace with men such as Guardini, Adam and Fr Lippert, showed signs of drying up as a source of spiritual literature after the Second World War. A well-qualified observer commented in 1955: 'It is characteristic, for example, that almost no more books of meditation are being produced, certainly none that provide any initiation into the spirituality of the Bible and the liturgy'.[43]

One of the spiritual phenomena most striking to the outside observer under the pontificates of Pius XI and Pius XII was the place – too obtrusive for some people's taste – assumed by devotions to the Virgin Mary. This movement, which went back to the nineteenth century, long had its epicentre in France, but it became widespread not only in Spain and Latin America, where it already had ancient roots, but also in the German countries and in the United States. Alongside Lourdes, the cult acquired in Fatima a new centre of international renown, which under the pontificate of Pius XII did not cease to grow in importance. The traditional features – exemplified by the increasing popularity of the May devotions and of pilgrimages, the holding of national and international Marian congresses and the creation of new liturgical feasts of the Virgin – were joined by some that were new, in particular the progressive institutionalisation of the cult with the founding of national institutes for Marian studies – in France in 1934, followed by institutes in Spain (1942), Canada (1947), Germany (1952) and in other countries – and with the setting up at Rome in 1939 of an international Marian centre with its own library and journal *(Marianum)* and, in 1946, of a very active international Marian academy founded on the initiative of a Croatian Franciscan, Fr Balio.

Many of these initiatives were the result of a growing concern to set the Marian movement on firmer doctrinal foundations. Even the most dedicated Mariologists had to admit that until about 1910 Marian literature was of a surpassing mediocrity. It was only after the First War that theological progress started to be made. In 1921 Cardinal Mercier initiated a line of enquiry into the mediative aspect which soon attracted attention well beyond Belgium, and from about 1926 publications of strictly theological character suddenly began to appear on all sides.

The solemn definition of the dogma of the Assumption in 1950 and the centenary of the proclamation of the Immaculate Conception in 1954 marked the apogee of the Marian movement. The movement's very flowering, which was not without its extravagances, produced some quite sharp reactions, especially in France and Germany, where many Catholics were worried about the provocative effect an unqualified exaltation of the Virgin might have on their Protestant brethren. Several Mariologists were con-

---

43. R. Scherer, in *Catholicisme allemand*, no. 45 of the *Rencontres* series (Paris 1956), 400.

scious of the possible danger of a deviation of Catholic devotion from its proper course, and sought to avert it by integrating Marian with traditional liturgical devotion, in this following the example of the Orthodox Church, and by presenting it in a more strongly biblical light which made it easier to see the Virgin in her true place in the story of salvation, fully subordinate to Christ and manifesting in its fullness the grace of which He alone is the source.

The more strongly biblical and liturgical trend of devotion in fact formed one of the characteristic features of Catholic life during the 1940s and 1950s, in parallel with the falling-off in enthusiasm for certain of the devotions popular with preceding generations, the cult of the Sacred Heart for instance,[44] or for forms of eucharistic devotion based on adoration, and in parallel also with the trend mentioned above towards forms of spirituality which restored human values to their rightful place, and which could be practised by people living in the world and going about their daily business.

Anti-Protestant considerations had long helped to deter the faithful from the regular reading of the Scriptures. The biblical revival among ordinary Catholics came about under the stimulus partly of the liturgical movement and partly of Catholic Action, which encouraged youth as a whole to a keener and keener interest in the Bible, their enthusiasm having been kindled by poets such as Péguy, Claudel, or Gertrud von Lefort, and by programmes such as those devised by Pius Parsch in Austria and the Pia Societa S. Paolo in Italy. The increased contact with Protestants during the Second World War, in particular with Protestants in Germany and the Netherlands, did much to reinforce the trend.

Among the ways in which the modern biblical movement manifested itself we should mention in particular the diffusion of biblical texts. Factors promoting this diffusion included the appearance of new translations, demonstrably superior to the old, the multiplication of biblical study circles and evening prayer-groups, the issue of leaflets by Catholic organisations suggesting readings for systematic meditation by their members, the publication of journals dealing with biblical topics and aimed not at a scholarly readership but at the mass of the clergy and faithful, and the sale of biblical recordings, one effect of which was to popularise the singing of the Psalms in the Roman Church after so many years of neglect, for anti-Protestant reasons, in favour of mediocre hymns.

---

44. See R. Graber, *Die Herz-Jesu Verehrung in der Krise der Gegenwart*, Eichstätt 1962. Devotion to the Sacred Heart had reached its peak under Pius XI, who in 1928 added further solemnity to the feast-day by instituting a new mass and a new office, and whose encyclical *Miserentissimus Redemptor* (text *A.A.S.*, XX (1928), 165-78) underlined the significance of the annual consecration of the human race to the Sacred Heart by stressing the aspect of reparation.

At first all this came about through scattered initiatives, but the movement gradually acquired a more or less official structure, which helped to make it yet more influential. Germany's Katholische Bibelbewegung came into existence as early as 1933. By 1940 Canada had its Société catholique de la Bible, an off-shoot of the J.O.C., and France soon followed suit with the Ligue de l'Évangile. In the United States the annual Catholic Bible Sunday which had been observed since 1941 was transformed ten years later into a Catholic Bible Week and placed under the auspices of the hierarchy. In 1947 Brazil started up a Liga de estudios biblicos, and so the list could continue. Furthermore, an apostolic letter of 15 December 1955 formalised biblical study circles by placing them under the supervision of the ordinary of the diocese. The clergy, at first somewhat taken aback by their flocks' enthusiasm for the Bible, were drawn increasingly into the movement and the teaching in the seminaries began in its turn to reflect this new trend, in parallel with the revival in exegetical studies after the difficult period following the anti-modernist reaction. [45]

As to the liturgical movement, Dom Lambert Beauduin's intervention in 1909 had initiated a new phase by bringing it out of the monasteries, [46] and it was around 1920 that the practice of dialogue masses was started, to be greeted at first in official quarters with considerable reserve. [47] In Belgium the torch passed from the abbey of Mont-César to that of Saint-André by Bruges, thanks to the presence there of Dom Gaspard Lefébvre, author of a *Missel des fidèles* whose circulation ran to hundreds of thousands and which was translated into several foreign languages. But the most important developments of the interwar period occurred in Germany, radiating from two centres in particular: the Benedictine order, above all the abbey of Maria Laach, and the Catholic youth movement. When, during the Nazi period, the Church was obliged to withdraw from the social field and even from organised Catholic Action, and in addition found the schools slipping from her hands, there was no choice but to retreat into the sanctuary and this gave opportunity for the popular character of the liturgical movement to assert itself, helped on its way by the recent Austrian example provided by Pius Parsch, founder of the Volksliturgisches Apostolat, whose tracts and pamphlets were broadcast far and wide. So it came about that the German liturgical movement, for so long the preserve of the select few, at last (save in Bavaria) penetrated to the parishes under the auspices of the National Liturgical Commission set up by the Fulda Bishops' Conference. A similar development took place in France during the Second World War. The im-

45. See below chapter 22, 615-16.
46. See above chapter 6, 128.
47. See for example the reaction of the Roman journal *Ephemerides liturgicae*, XXXV (1921), 308 ff.

petus in this instance came not from Solesmes, which was insufficiently attuned to the needs of the popular apostolate, but from the Centre de pastorale liturgique,[48] founded by two Dominicans with active collaboration from Dom Lambert Beauduin, Canon Martimort and Fr Doncoeur and with the twofold aim of providing the movement with a theological foundation sustainable from biblical and traditional sources, and of finding solutions to the problems posed by the dechristianisation of the masses, problems which certain liturgists, too enamoured of the archaeological aspects, tended to ignore.

As nearly always happens, the suddenness of the flowering gave rise to certain excesses and aberrations, and some people, especially in Germany, were so carried away that in the name of the transcendence and 'objective' value of the liturgical act that they minimised the importance of preaching or wanted to eliminate all modern forms of devotion. It was largely in order to restore a sense of proportion that Pius XII published in 20 December 1947 the encyclical *Mediator Dei,*[49] the first encyclical ever to be devoted exclusively to the liturgy, in which he warned against the exaggerations of certain 'liturgisers' but at the same time gave his official endorsement to the broad principles of the liturgical movement, decisively rejecting the old definition of the liturgy so long promoted by the Jesuits, which tended to reduce it to an order of ceremonies, presenting the liturgy instead as the continuation by the Church of Christ's sacerdotal office, the public offering of worship by the Christian community.

Much as there is to admire in what had been accomplished during the quarter-century preceding the encyclical, we must be careful not to see it in a deceptive or anachronistic light. All things considered, the liturgical movement of the interwar period, despite its efforts to reach out to the steadily increasing masses, kept to the ideal of 'restoration' that had inspired Dom Guéranger, in other words it attempted to satisfy a nostalgia by retracing its steps back beyond the Counter-Reformation to an *imago primitivae Ecclesiae.* Pius X, it is true, had tried to do more and embark on reform, but his two successors did little to follow his lead,[50] and outside Rome his work was felt by pioneers of the liturgical movement to be more in the nature of 'a successful restoration, analogous to the architectural restorations executed by the Romantics'.[51] The only hint of concern for accommodation with

48. P. Duployé, *Les Origines du Centre de pastorale liturgique, 1943-1949*, Paris-Mulhouse 1968.
49. Text in *A.A.S.*, XXXIX (1947), 521-95.
50. Pius XI had, it is true, created in 1930 a new section of the Congregation of Rites, whose title hinted at the possibility of reforms: 'Per le cause storiche dei Servi di Dio e l'emendazione dei libri liturgici', but the second part in fact remained in the background for the next twenty or so years.
51. J. Wagner, in *Questions liturgiques et paroissiales*, XLV (1964), 46.

present-day realities came from the discussions, and these were long confined to the German-speaking countries, regarding the use of the vernacular; but the most usual object was simply that of making it easier for the faithful to follow time-honoured ceremonies in themselves regarded as immutable. The work of reform in its true sense, which had been in abeyance since the death of Pius X, was resumed in 1948 under stimulus from Rome. In that year a confidential circular went out from the editors of the *Ephemerides liturgicae* to their contributors in all parts of the world asking them to consider five questions relating to the reform of the breviary and a sixth of more general scope. As Mgr Wagner remarks: 'Anyone at all familiar with Roman procedures knows that the despatch of a private and confidential letter of this kind from the editorial office of a Roman journal is not possible unless there is some understanding with the competent authorities' [52] and it is true that men such as the Italian Franciscan F. Antonelli and the Austrian Redemptorist J. Löw, members of the historical section of the Congregation of Rites, were to play a decisive role in the reforms of the next few years.

In response to the overture from Rome the specialists immediately set to work, to discover almost at once that a reform of the breviary could be contemplated only in the context of a much more general reform. At preparatory talks in Luxemburg in 1950 between representatives of the Centre de Pastorale Liturgique of Paris and the Liturgical Institute of Trier it was arranged, in close collaboration with the Roman dicasteries, to hold an initial international study week at the abbey of Maria Laach in 1951, and meetings of this kind, at which liturgical reform was discussed under all its aspects, scientific as well as pastoral, continued to be held at regular intervals down to the Second Vatican Council. In the meantime the Holy See introduced a series of partial measures, all of which pointed in the same direction: authorisation of sacramental rites in which the language of the country assumed an increasingly important place, as for example the German rite of 1950, in which a large place was accorded to traditions peculiar to Germany; the reshaping in 1951 of the Easter vigil and subsequently of the Holy Week liturgy in its entirety, the first important reform of the missal since 1570; the constitution *Christus Dominus* in 1953, which modified the rules governing the eucharistic fast and authorised evening Masses; simplification of the rubrics in both breviary and missal; the encyclical *Musicae sacrae* of 25 December 1955; the instruction from the Congregation of Rites dated 3 September 1958, [53] really a summing up of Pius XII's

---

52. *Ibid.*, 48.
53. On this exceptionally important decree (text *A.A.S.*, L (1958), 630-63), see the semi-official commentary provided by Fr Antonelli in the *Osservatore romano* of 2 October 1958 (French translation in *Documentation catholique*, LV (1958), cols 1425-7).

achievement in the pastoral-liturgical field and a codification of the main trends to emerge from the liturgical directories published in recent years by countless dioceses throughout the world.

Not all countries, it is true, responded with the same enthusiasm and alacrity as the countries in Western Europe in which the liturgical movement had been born. In Italy, despite a few isolated experiments, the want of a co-ordinating element at national level long remained a serious disadvantage; and in the Anglo-Saxon world, as in the Iberian peninsula, the real turning-point was the Second Vatican Council, although in Spain a Junta nacional de apostolado liturgice came into being in 1958, and in the United States precursors of the movement were to be found as far back as the 1930s[54] and active centres such as Collegeville Abbey in Minnesota were organising liturgical conferences well before the council.

The progress of the liturgical movement had its effects – which varied in degree with the region – not only on the spiritual life of Catholics but also on the development of religious art, which around 1900, after two centuries of distressing mediocrity, was starting to revive: for the liturgists' aims, which were to encourage active participation by the congregation and to highlight altar and font at the expense of adventitious elements, chimed very well with the possibilities offered by new methods of construction and this union resulted in churches that were much more functional, taking new forms in which the spaces were organised with the needs of the liturgy in mind and from which solid walls were largely eliminated, the light and colour of the glass that replaced them working in conjunction with the masses and lines to define the sacred space.

The earliest experiments date from before the First World War, but from the artistic point of view the first successful church in reinforced concrete was A. and G. Perret's Notre Dame at Raincy (1921-3), elegant in a way at once daring and traditional, an entirely new approach to the Gothic ideal of verticality, its only ornament the light flooding in through the windows. In France, however, this lead was largely ignored. It was in Germany, where as early as 1923 the Abbé J. van Acken had published a widely noticed essay on *Christozentrische Kirchenkunst, ein Entwurf zum liturgischen Gesamtkunstwerk,* and later in Switerland and Holland (countries in which some of the most original and harmonious realisations of the interwar years are to be seen) that the revival in church architecture bore its most spectacular fruit, in the work of men such as D. Böhm, [55] who in the 1920s broke away deliberately from the forms inherited from the past, R. Schwarz, who

54. For example Dom Virgil Michel (died 1938), a disciple of Dom Lambert Beauduin. See P. B. Marx, *V. Michel and the Liturgical Movement,* Collegeville, U.S.A. 1957.
55. On this precursor (1880-1955) see ed. J. Habbel, *Dominikus Böhm. Ein deutsche Baumeister,* Regensburg 1943.

through his lectures and writings helped to propagate the ideas embodied after 1930 in the church of the Blessed Sacrament at Aachen, and F. Dumas, a Swiss, one of whose aims was to design churches that harmonised with the Alpine landscape. Efforts were also made to devise modern styles for churches built in more traditional materials, for example by Dom Bellot, 'the poet in brick', a French Benedictine who worked chiefly in England (Quarr Abbey) and Holland (Oosterhout, Bloemendael, best of all Noordhoek). By contrast, churches erected in Mediterranean countries remained on the whole thoroughly banal, forced into the conventional mould by the twofold weight of academic tradition and the cowardice of the ecclesiastical authorities in not venturing off the beaten track.

Although the thirty years which separate the Raincy church from the Ronchamps chapel (1955) found France lagging behind as regards church architecture (for proof we need look no further than the distressing examples of the basilicas at Lisieux and Lourdes), in other branches of religious art – church furnishings, goldsmiths' work, sculpture, stained glass, but most of all painting – French artists were in the front rank. This revival originated with a disciple of Gauguin, Maurice Denis (1870-1943), whose earliest productions date from about 1900 (Le Vesinet) and whose work as a whole, which combined the spirit of the pre-Raphaelites with the colour techniques of the impressionists, left no doubt as to its religious and artistic authenticity. In 1919 Denis joined with Georges Desvallières (died 1950) in founding the Ateliers d'art sacré, with the aim of creating ensembles in which all the elements, stained glass, painted decoration, sacred vessels, liturgical vestments, displayed a unity of style, and his spirit could be said to pervade the religious art of the interwar period – Henri Charlier, for example, has been dubbed 'the Denis of sculpture' – even though these same years saw the emergence of other gifted artists, Rouault and Gleizes in particular, who drew their inspiration from somewhat different sources. But around 1940, just when the Denis school was in danger of falling prey to academism, another and much more radical revolution took place in religious art. The moving spirit was a pupil of Desvallières, a well-thought-of glass and fresco painter turned Dominican, Fr Couturier,[56] who with Fr Régamey founded in 1935 the journal L'Art sacré. He it was who was largely responsible for the penetration of sacred edifices first by non-figurative art and then by 'pagan painters' (the chapels at Vence and Assy, the church at Audincourt), acting on the principle that 'each generation must call on the services of its living masters', even if those masters are non-believers. But these were not innovations which could be made without arousing strong opposition. As

56. On Pierre (in religion Marie-Alain) Couturier (1897-1954) see Art sacré no. 9-10, May-June 1954, and Dieu et l'art dans une vie. Le père M. A. Couturier de 1897 à 1945, Paris 1963.

far back as 1921 the Stations of the Cross by the Flemish painter Servaes, judged to be too modern, had been the occasion of an intervention by the Holy Office and in 1947 the latter had censured a number of artists in a *Monitum* addressed to the Italian Commission of Sacred Art. The debates stirred up by the church at Assy and in particular by Germaine Richier's Crucifix were at the back of a Holy Office directive on religious art dated 30 June 1952,[57] more general in scope and, all things considered, relatively discriminating.

A final striking feature of Catholic life during the half century that preceded – and led up to – the Second Vatican Council was the change in attitude towards the ecumenical movement. Shortly after the First War the growing interest in the question of *rapprochement* between separated Christians had found concrete expression in the foundation of two movements, Faith and Order, predominantly Anglican, and Life and Work, more distinctively Protestant, which in 1948 were to fuse to form the World Council of Churches.

At the Vatican, where several unionists of Leo XIII's time, notably Cardinal Gasparri, had emerged from their eclipse under Pius X to occupy key positions, and where there was grateful recognition of the work of non-Catholic Christians in the cause of peace, the moves initiated by R. Gardiner and N. Söderblom were at first watched with sympathetic interest; but it was made plain as early as 1918 that there could be no question of the Roman Church sitting down as an equal with other confessions, still less of participation by the Roman Church in public debates on issues that in Rome's view had been settled once and for all. However, this demurrer did not prevent Pius XI from giving unofficial encouragement to the setting up of private contacts between Catholic and Anglican theologians, as in the Malines Conversations organised by Cardinal Mercier between 1921 and 1926,[58] nor a little later from supporting the efforts of Dom Lambert Beauduin and his Amay 'monks of Union' to build a bridge between Rome and the Orthodox world in a spirit of what be described as Catholic ecumenism before its time. Yet the fact remains that from 1925 Rome's attitude hardened. Hopes of *rapprochement* with Orthodox Russia seemed henceforth much more problematical, and the liberalism in doctrine evinced at the first ecumenical conference in Stockholm in 1925 had been a shock to Catholic circles (Germany excepted), whose state of mind at the time is well reflected in the writings of Abbé C. Journet. Furthermore, as far as the

---

57. *A.A.S.*, XLIV (1952), 542-6. See *Nouvelle revue théologique*, LXXIV (1952), 863-6 and 944-59.

58. On these Conversations see J. Bivort de la Saudée, *Anglicans et catholiques*, 2 vols, Brussels-Paris 1949, and as supplement R. Aubert, 'Les Conversations de Malines, le cardinal Mercier et le Saint-Siège', *Bulletin de la Classe des Lettres de l'Académie royale de Belgique*, 5th series, LIII (1967), 87-159.

Vatican was concerned, the desire of the pope and his Secretary of State to reach a negotiated settlement of the Roman question made it necessary to give certain pledges to the intransigent wing of the Sacred College, the group around Cardinal Merry del Val. The encyclical *Mortalium animos*[59] of 6 January 1928, so uncompromising, so little appreciative of the efforts of those it dismissed with scorn as 'pan-Christians', fits into this same picture, and for the next twenty years Rome was to affect indifference to the progress of the ecumenical movement, merely issuing now and then dry reminders of the earlier disavowals.

But outside Rome during those years there were noticeable advances. Under the influence of the Barthian revolution in theology and of individuals such as Dr Visser't Hooft and S. de Diétrich the ecumenical movement became firmer in its attachment to the biblical conception of the Church and there was a corresponding tendency for the pragmatic aspects and liberal Protestant influence, so noticeable at the outset, to fade into the background. In parallel, the interest in the cause of Christian unity shown by a select number of laymen and theologians on the Catholic side was steadily mounting. First awakened in France in the early days of the century by the activities of the Abbé Portal, it was given added stimulus by news of the Malines Conversations. From about 1930 small groups of Catholics specialising in ecumenical questions started to form and for the next twenty-five years these were to act, on their own responsibility, as intermediaries between Rome and Geneva, which officially were not on speaking terms. Among these farsighted and courageous pioneers three deserve a special mention. The first in order of time was the Belgian Dom Lambert Beauduin, O.S.B.,[60] founder of Amay priory, which provided from 1925 a Catholic meeting-place, unique at that time in Europe, for the ecumenical dialogue, and also founder in 1926 of the journal *Irénikon*, trail-blazer for other similarly orientated Catholic journals. The second was Fr Congar,[61] whose book *Chrétiens désunis* (1937), which established the theological foundations of an ecumenical programme in a Catholic setting, marked an advance as important in the doctrinal field as was Amay in the field of action. The third was Abbé Couturier,[62] 'prophet of spiritual ecumenism', a simple priest who in 1935 infused a new spirit into the octave of prayer inaugurated in America early in the century, central to which was the petition

59. Text in *A.A.S.*, XX (1928), 5-16.
60. On him see L. Bouyer, *Dom Lambert Beauduin, un homme d'Église*, Tournai-Paris 1964, and S. A. Quitslund, *Beauduin, a Prophet Vindicated*, New York 1973.
61. He retraced the steps of his ecumenical journey in *Une passion: l'unité. Réflexions et Souvenirs 1929-1973*, Paris 1974.
62. See M. Villain, ed., *L'Abbé Paul Couturier, Apôtre de l'unité chrétienne*, Tournai-Paris 1957 and M. Villain, *Oecuménisme spirituel, les écrits de l'abbé Couturier*, Tournai-Paris 1963.

for 'the return of heretics and schismatics to the Roman Church', by transforming it into a 'Week of Universal Prayer' asking God to 'bring about unity as He shall will, by whatever means he shall will', which made it possible in future for even non-Catholics to join in without reserve.

In Germany the same period had seen the foundation by R. Grosche of the journal *Catholica* (1932) and the formation by J. Metzger of Una Sancta, a league of prayer on the lines suggested by the Abbé Couturier, while to the discomfort of some in conservative circles a number of historians – we may also add the Czech-born F. Dvornik – were gradually disposing of certain hoary prejudices and clichés. Subsequently, Catholics and Protestants were brought into a close relationship on the existential plane by their common opposition to Hitlerism and by the dislocations of the war and of the postwar period. The organisation of communal prayers in air-raid shelters and concentration camps and the pooling of places of worship in bombed towns and evacuation areas were experiences that made for a lasting mutual comprehension between the two confessions, affecting laity and leaders alike (the position was much the same in the Netherlands). A spirit had been generated which made possible the development after the war of centres for the fostering of fraternal contacts (such as those founded by H. Hoffmann, M. Laros and J. Pinsk), as also the institution of more formal working groups, for example the Evangelische und Katholische oekumenische Arbeitskreis, which had Jäger, a Catholic archbishop, and Ställin, a Lutheran bishop, as joint presidents, and later on (1957) the J. A. Möhler-Institut at Paderborn.

In Belgium, Amay priory (transferred in 1939 to Chevetogne), although at one time threatened, now enjoyed the support of Cardinal Tisserant, currently Prefect of the Congregation of the Eastern Church, while *Irénikon*, under the editorship of Dom Clément Lialine, was emerging as the major Catholic journal for ecumenical affairs. In France several new ventures were launched, thanks to the inspiration of men such as Fr Villain and Fr Dumont, the enterprising but circumspect founder of the Dominican centre Istina. In addition, interest in the ecumenical question gradually started to assert itself during the postwar period in countries which had long remained indifferent: in England, in spite of some hesitation, thanks to Cardinal Hinsley and more recently to one or two abbeys; in Italy thanks to the work of centres such as Pro Civitate Christiana of Assisi, founded by G. Rossi in 1939, and later of the faculty of theology at Venegono in Lombardy, not to mention Unitas, founded in Rome itself in 1950 by Fr Boyer, S.J., with backing from Mgr G. B. Montini; in Spain round the university of Salamanca; in Switzerland thanks to men such as O. Karrer and the Abbé Chavaz; and in the Netherlands, where as a result of the upheavals during the war, the climate of mutual incomprehension and suspicion started to moderate, on the Catholic side even more conspicuously than on the re-formed. It was a Dutch priest, G. Willebrands, helped by his friend Fr Thyssen, who in 1952 took the initiative in setting up a Catholic Conference for Ecumenical Questions which it was intended should be the channel of communication between Catholic ecumenists and the study sections of the World Council of Churches.

By this time Roman attitudes were becoming somewhat less frigid, the thaw being assisted by representations from prelates such as Mgr Jäger of Paderborn, Mgr Gerlier of Lyons, Mgr Charrière of Fribourg and several others. Although Rome's response to the first meeting of the World Council of Churches at Amsterdam in 1948 had still been negative in the extreme, an instruction from the Holy Office eighteen months later[63] testified to a new frame of mind. At first sight the instruction might be read merely as a warning, but looked at more closely it gave encouragement to Catholics labouring in the ecumenical field and even acknowledged the operations of the Holy Spirit in the strivings of non-Catholics towards Church unity: a far cry from the taunts of *Mortalium animos*. Plainly, realisation had dawned at Rome that a major event in the religious history of the twentieth century, namely the birth and expansion of the World Council of Churches, could no longer be systematically ignored, especially since it was becoming increasingly obvious that over the past two decades the ecumenical movement had gained in theological and spiritual depth. Another milestone was passed when in 1952 the Vatican requested the vicar apostolic of Sweden to send four Catholics as observers to the Faith and Order conference due to be held that year at Lund. But the miscarriage of the affair of Catholic observers for the Second Assembly of the World Council of Churches at Evanston in 1954 showed how strong the temptation still was at Rome to draw back, and how much still remained to do when John XXIII created in 1960 the Secretariat for Christian Unity (formed essentially from members of the Catholic Conference for Ecumenical Questions and its dynamic organiser) and when he decided the next year to send official representatives to the Third Assembly of the World Council of Churches at New Delhi.[64]

63. Dated 20 December 1949, it was made public 1 March 1950 (text in *A.A.S.*, XLII (1950), 142-7.
64. For the history of the evolving relationship between the Roman Church and the Eastern Churches during this period see chapter 19 above.

22

DEVELOPMENTS IN THOUGHT

AT THE intellectual, as well as at the active and devotional levels, the half-century which preceded and led up to the Second Vatican Council – especially from the late 1930s, once the repercussions of the anti-modernist crisis had at last died away – was noticeably a time of fertility and flowering, characterised by the twofold tendency we have already noticed: return to the sources and increasingly attentive awareness of the modern world. It has to be said, moreover, that for this period the treatment of action and thought in two separate chapters seems more than usually artificial. The division was unavoidable, given the difficulty of dealing with all aspects simultaneously, but we shall do well to bear in mind the following pertinent observation by R. Rémond: 'The reason why this period will stand out in the history of the Church as a time rich in graces and as fruitful as any is precisely that during those thirty years [1930-1960] theology came to grips with the many problems presented to it by the apostolate, and because pastoral and missionary activity had the benefit in return of theology's reflection on the Church'.[1]

But there was first plenty of leeway to make up. We would search in vain on the Catholic side, during the interwar years, for the equivalent of Karl Barth's all-embracing *Dogmatik*[2] and even in more specialised fields – apart from such rare exceptions as Fr M. de la Taille's monumental treatise on the

1. In the preface to J. Lestavel, *Les Prophètes de l'Église contemporaine* (Paris 1969), 9.
2. Numerous manuals running into several volumes were published during this period, but they did no more than reiterate from a blinkered standpoint the solutions already arrived at; furthermore, although they were often presented as being composed 'ad mentem Sancti Thomae', their authors seemed scarcely aware that the work of the great medieval doctor is best regarded as a guide rather than as an end. It was only in 1938 that Mgr U. Schmaus produced the first volume of his *Katholische Dogmatik* (8 vols, 1938-55; 6th edn. 1960-9), and even this, despite its notable merits in purveying and adapting the information, only rarely ventures to tackle the difficult questions at a fundamental level.

Mass, *Mysterium fidei* (1921) – Catholic theologians tended to expend their wealth of analysis and dialectical subtlety on problems which, in comparison with the subjects dominating the religious thinking of their contemporaries, were almost peripheral. For all the great impetus that masters such as Mgr M. Grabmann and E. Gilson gave to historical research into medieval scholasticism,[3] it has to be said that the neo-Thomist revival – to which the popes of the day gave continued encouragement, from Pius XI's encyclical *Studiorum ducem* (1923) to Pius XII's exhortations in *Humani generis* (1950) – did not bear the expected fruits, at all events not in theology, where the outdated categories of neo-Thomism left it stranded against the mainstream of modern thought. The position was somewhat different in philosophy, in so far as neo-Thomism was responsible, for example, for certain new departures in the work of J. Maritain or of Fr H. D. Sertillanges, O.P. and Fr J. Maréchal, S.J., or in Germany of J. Pieper.

This failure accounts for the success enjoyed at the time by various attempts, as yet only tentative, to renovate Catholic theology by drawing on the Platonist and Augustinian tradition, or by adopting a personalist and existential standpoint. These tendencies were especially noticeable among Catholic thinkers in Germany, where the influence of Max Scheler had gone deep, but through the medium of translation the works of Karl Adam,[4] and later of Fr Lippert, S.J.[5] and of R. Guardini,[6] to name only the most prominent, were able to influence a much wider public. The same aspiration to bring theology into closer contact with devotional life was responsible for the revived interest in spiritual theology mentioned in a previous chapter, just as it accounted for the slightly later attempt, to which there was no sequel, by Fr J. A. Jungmann, S.J. and some of his Innsbruck colleagues to develop alongside academic theology a 'kerygmatic theology',[7] that is a theology capable of being preached with profit to the ordinary congregation.

It is important to mention that by contrast with the relative somnolence of dogmatic theology before the Second World War there was a marked

3. Witness the proliferation and extension of series and journals dealing with this aspect: in addition to the alteration in 1928 of the title of the celebrated *Beiträge zur Geschichte der Philosophie des Mittelalters* to include a reference to theology, the period saw the foundation of the following: the *Bibliothèque thomiste* (1921) and the *Bulletin thomiste* (1924), both associated with Mandonnet; É. Gilson's *Archives d'histoire littéraire et doctrinale du Moyen Age* (1924); the *Recherches de théologie ancienne et médiévale* (1929) published from Mont César, where Dom Lottin was laying the foundations for a revived interest in the ethical teaching of the Scholastics and lastly the *Publications de l'Institut d'études médiévales d'Ottawa* (1932), initiated by Fr Chenu, who also left his mark on the Saulchoir school.
4. See F. Hofmann's introduction (*Geleitwort*) to the collected papers of Karl Adam, *Gesammelte Aufsätze* (Augsburg 1936), 3-16 and R. Aubert, in *Tendenzen der Theologie im 20 Jht.* (Stuttgart 1966) 156-62.
5. See P. Lorson in *Études*, CCXXXVIII (1939), 465-83.
6. See chapter 21, 592, n.36.
7. For a brief critical survey with bibliography see J. Comblin, *Vers une théologie de l'action* (Brussels 1965), 32-40.

revival of interest in moral problems, as they related to the family and to society at large, in its national and international aspect. The rise of neo-Malthusianism, the appearance of totalitarian regimes of the right and of the left, the great economic crisis of the 1930s and the increasing precariousness of world peace, were bound to direct the attention of Catholic thinkers and of the Church's *magisterium* to those domains which the preceding, much more individualist, generations had barely considered. The tone was at first set not by theologians in the strict sense but by philosophers and sociologists, for example on social and economic matters by the Austrian school of Jesuits, or by a Jacques Leclercq,[8] author of a monumental treatise on natural law which rapidly became a classic. But the theologians were really obliged to follow suit, especially since Pius XI was increasingly concerned to draw attention to these problems and to present officially to the world the Church's position on controversial matters so relevant to the moulding of the Christian *polis*. The list of documents speaks for itself: *Divini illius magistri* (31 December 1929), dealing with the Christian education of the young;[9] *Casti connubii* (20 December 1930), on Christian marriage; *Quadragesimo anno* (15 May 1931), on the social question; *Nova impendet* (20 October 1931), on the economic crisis and the arms race; *Mit brennender Sorge* (14 March 1937), directed against national socialism; *Divini Redemptoris* (19 March 1937), directed against communism. Never before had the supreme teaching authority expressed itself so fully, and these documents soon came to occupy a place alongside natural law as a source of inspiration to Catholic moralists, many of whom tended in future simply to quote them as they stood, without any attempt to expand them.

So it was particularly with the question of birth control, for few indeed were the professional theologians before the council who attempted to reexamine the traditional teaching in a more discriminating light.[10] However it is only fair to mention, for all its cool reception at Rome, the thought-provoking study published by H. Doms under the title *Vom Sinn und Zweck der Ehe* (1935).

8. On this Belgian moralist (1891-1971) see G. Morin, *Introduction à l'étude de J. Leclercq*, Gembloux 1973 (with full bibliography of Leclercq's writings) and *J. Leclercq. Documents autobiographiques*, Tournai 1972.
9. The passage in which Pius XI defined the rights of the State in the matter deserves careful attention. In his anxiety to avoid breaking off relations with the fascist government the pope obviously went as far as he could in toning down his views to the limit of the concessions he regarded as permissible. On the other hand, although his views on this point seem relatively modern compared with the classical positions upheld in the nineteenth century, the encyclical still shows itself cast in the traditional mould in its attitude towards education, which it persists in viewing from in the perspective of an all-embracing Christendom (see on this topic A. Vandermeersch, in *Concile oecuménique Vatican II. Documents conciliaires*, II (Éditions du Centurion), (Paris 1965), 164-5.
10. On the relative element and the limitations of the teaching of *Casti connubii* see, among others, the remarks by G. Martelet in *Nouvelle revue théologique* XC (1968), 900-17.

Intellectual activity was greater in the field of social morality. This was a topic being developed from all sides during the interwar years, but in the writings of Catholic sociologists and theologians the forefront continued to be occupied by the injustice of the workers' condition and ways of alleviating it and by criticism of Marxist socialism. After the Second War the emphasis was to shift, in keeping with changes in the world around. For one thing, the contrast between the well-to-do and the working class in an industrial society was increasingly to seem less glaring than the contrast between rich and underdeveloped countries. For another, to Catholic criticism of unjust social conditions was to be added a more positive search for actual solutions, from which Marxist totalitarianism and capitalist anarchy were alike excluded, and a readiness to recognise the merits of the contemporary trend towards a progressively collective social life.

There were also signs of a changing outlook on questions of international morality. During the first quarter of the twentieth century the majority of Catholic writers had been more concerned to extol the virtues of patriotism than to insist on the duty of promoting world peace. They were not strong enough to withstand the rising tide of nationalism in Europe in the years preceding the First War or the whipping up of patriotic sentiment during the hostilities. Hence they tended as a rule to see more danger in the socialists' ideological rejection of patriotism than in its immoderate exaltation. Round about 1925, however, one or two courageous writers of Christian democrat inspiration started to sound a new note by harping in particular on the too-little-heeded appeals of Benedict XV and Pius XI for a peace constructed on Christian foundations. Pius XI's condemnations of pagan nationalism in the last years of his pontificate were to reinforce this trend, but there was to be no real change until the pontificate of Pius XII, when the world was faced with the terrible crisis of the Second World War.

Seeing Christianity in confrontation with Nazism, with Marxism, and indeed with scientistic humanism, which in new guises still enjoyed a great prestige, some Catholic thinkers were led to reflect on the religious significance of man's presence on earth and on what connection there might be between his temporal endeavours and his religious salvation. Though the approach varied with the author's country of origin, C. Dawson's *Progress and Religion* (1934), A. Rademacher's *Religion und Leben* (1934) and J. Maritain's *L'Humanisme intégral* (1936) were all characteristic of the thinking in this vein, and to it also belonged the work of the Jesuit palaeontologist Teilhard de Chardin,[11] not published until much later, but executed during

11. A considerable body of literature has grown up round Teilhard de Chardin (1881-1956) and is increasing every year. Among the many works that could be cited see: R. d'Ouince, *Un prophète en procès: Teilhard de Chardin*, 2 vols, Paris 1970; H. de Lubac, *La Pensée religieuse du P. Teilhard de Chardin*, Paris 1961; N. M. Wildiers, *Teilhard de Chardin* (Les

those momentous years and exercising from the start a discreet but profound influence through its circulation in mimeograph. In new terms it was the old problem of the relationship between nature and supernature that was being tackled in this way, approached in particular through debates revolving round the concept of 'Christian humanism'. But as the 1930s proceeded, thinkers who spoke of the relationship between Christianity and culture ceased to be thinking solely of artistic, literary or philosophical values and were increasingly taking into account the contribution of science and technology to the conquest of the material universe, and indeed culture in its physical aspect. In tentative fashion they began to work out a full-scale theological anthropology, which sought to consider man not simply as *animal rationale* but under all the aspects of his temporal condition: his rootedness in the universe, his technical skills, the relationships set up by his functions as worker and citizen. Theologies of the body, of work, of progress, of social reality, these and other themes were broached with increasing lack of inhibition in works that were often a diffuse *mélange* of theology, philosophy, sociology and literature, but in works as substantial and well thought-out as those by J. Mourroux (*Sens chrétien de l'homme*, 1945) and G. Thils (*Théologie des réalités terrestres*, 1946).

Hand in hand with this work of intellectual endeavour went a greater involvement of Catholics in the cultural worlds, from which at the end of the nineteenth century they had seemed virtually excluded. While on the side of unbelief it was ceasing to be fashionable to regard the religious sentiment and science as totally opposed, on the Catholic side 'the bankruptcy of science' was no longer invoked as a main plank of the apologetic and the great names, a Ternier, a Mgr Lemaître, a Whittaker, a Dessauer, a Leprince-Ringuet, were by no means the only Catholics dedicating themselves to scientific research and absorbing more and more of its outlook, stressing in particular, despite stubborn resistance in traditionalist circles, the concept of evolution, identified in the first instance in respect of the living world and seen increasingly to run through the entire universe. More noticeable still was the Catholic contribution to the human sciences: to history in particular, but also to law, psychology and even to sociology, once the perdurable suspicions of those who regarded sociology as the annihilator of particularity in ethics and religion had been overcome. But it was above all in literature that the second quarter of the twentieth century witnessed a true reversal of the previous situation. After generations of being marginal figures, Catholic novelists, poets and essayists began to show a quality that made some of them rank with the great creative artists of their

classiques du XXe siècle), Brussels 1960. See further D. Polgar, *Internationale Teilhard-Bibliographie 1955-1965*, Freiburg in Breisgau 1965.

time, a phenomenon in striking contrast to the secularisaton of society and the advance of atheistic humanism.

The phenomenon is seen at its most striking in France where alongside a proliferation of journals, book titles and writers' circles openly Catholic in affiliation there developed a body of literature profane in respect of authorship, publishers and public but which nevertheless dealt with essentially Christian themes. Claudel, whose *Le Soulier de satin* (1930) was to enjoy worldwide renown and whose *Jeanne au bûcher* (1939) was to be set to music by Honegger, was at the height of his fame during the interwar years. The Catholic novel, the foundations for which had been laid by Bourget and his school, entered its heyday with Mauriac and Bernanos, in whose novels psychological probing is constantly illumined by an implicit theology, the dialectic between sin and grace, and this heyday was to be prolonged into the beginning of the 1950s by distinguished writers ranging from Julien Green and Maxence van der Meersch to P. A. Lesort and G. Cesbron, not forgetting J. Malègue with his *Augustin ou le maître est là*. Catholic criticism was likewise growing in stature at this period and again commanded an audience well beyond the circle of *bien pensants,* thanks to writers with talents as varied as those of Henri Bremond, discoursing on poetry at its purest, Charles du Bos, bringing to the dialogue with his contemporaries an exceptional knowledge of European literature and a still more exceptional lucidity of mind, and Gabriel Marcel, whose work as drama critic was inseparable from his work as dramaturge and his work as philosopher; and to these names may be added that of the Belgian critic Charles Moeller, whose penetrating studies *Littérature du XXe siècle et Christianisme* range well beyond the frontiers of the French-speaking world.

But although France figured so prominently in the lead, the Catholic revival was in fact a European phenomenon. In varying degrees of intensity it can be observed in many other countries: in Great Britain, where the generation of Chesterton, Belloc and Baring was succeeded by best-sellers, such as the sardonic Evelyn Waugh, the entertaining Scottish writer Bruce Marshall and, in deeper vein, Graham Greene, with his oblique presentation, through fiction of a powerful realism, of a Catholic view of the human condition, a dialogue between man, frail but free, and Divine Providence, writing straight on crooked lines; in Germany, where although Catholic writers figured more as 'outsiders' in their country's literary scene, one can cite as successors to the greatest of the German Catholic novelists, Gertrud von Lefort, also author of the very fine *Hymnen an die Kirche* (1924), names such as E. Wiechert, poet of solitude and death, E. Langgässer, with his echoes of Bernanos, H. Böll, future Nobel Prize winner, among the writers to contribute most to the creation of a pre-conciliar climate in Germany, S. Andres, whose masterpiece *Wir sind Utopia* (1943) appeared in the full tide of Nazism, R. Schneider, winner in 1956 of a major peace prize awarded by German publishing houses; in the Hispanic world with the Portuguese writer M. Ribeiro, evocative of Husymans and Bloy, the Spanish writers C. Laforet, J. M. Gironella and J. L. Martin Descalzo, the Chilean author E. Barrios and the Argentinian M. Gálvez; in Italy, where Papini, the one-time atheist publicised in uncompromisingly unbridled fashion the demands of his regained faith; and as far afield as Scandinavia where the Norwegian Sigrid Unset, whose *Kristin Lavransdatter* (1920-2) has been described by Mauriac as the perfect example of the Catholic novel, found a worthy successor in the Swedish writer Sven Stolpe. One or two themes recur with particular frequency in these authors otherwise so diverse and spread out over two generations: the drama of sin, sins of the flesh to be sure but also, if less frequently, sins of the spirit; Satan's work in the world as the key to the problem of evil; conversion as a live experience; the social responsibilities of a Christian (most common in more recent authors); exemplification of the dignity of womanhood, which started with Claudel's Violaine even before 1914; and another favourite, the priest as central figure, from Bernanos's *'curé de campagne'* to Guareschi's Don Camillo.[12]

One important feature of Catholic thinking during the interwar years was its rediscovery of the Church in her true religious and supernatural dimensions. This rebirth is to be explained by a variety of factors, starting with the general reaction against nineteenth-century individualism and the growing popularity, especially in German-speaking countries of ideas of community. Equally important was the progress of the missionary movement (as also of Catholic missiology, to which J. Schmidlin and Fr Charles, S.J. gave such impetus during the interwar years) and of Catholic Action, which gave many faithful, too accustomed to think exclusively in terms of 'saving their own souls', a much clearer sense of the Church. But an important share of the credit must go to the liturgical revival, in its pastoral as much as in its historical and theological aspects, and to the whole trend of contemporary devotion, Christocentric and eucharistic, which by its very nature focused attention on the doctrine of the Mystical Body.

The standard treatise *De Ecclesia* had been composed without reference to patristic thought and in a very Western context, by men who tended to be canonists rather than theologians, for the purpose of opposing two sharply distinct programmes, Protestantism and Gallicanism. The chief stress was therefore on the visible and hierarchical, indeed on the juridical and administrative, aspect of the Church. Drawing inspiration from J. A. Möhler and nineteenth-century thinkers of the vitalist school, profiting from the

12. For this theme as treated by French novelists see J.-L. Prévost, *Le Prêtre, ce héros de roman*, Paris 1952.

lessons to be learned from Orthodox ecclesiology, relayed to the West by Russian thinkers exiled at the time of the Russian revolution, finding itself increasingly enriched by the return to the biblical and patristic sources – how enlightening to many Catholic theologians was Fr de Lubac's *Catholicisme* (1938)! – Catholic theology of the forties and fifties set itself to do greater justice to the theme of the Church as continuing the redemptive incarnation of the Son of God, mediating his divine life to mankind. The initial stimulus had been provided by Karl Adam, whose *Das Wesen des Katholizismus* (1924) was quickly translated into all the major languages. Research concentrated to begin with on the theme of the Church as the Mystical Body of Christ, expounded by Fr Tromp, S.J. in his lectures at the Gregorian, the patristic sources of which were elucidated by Fr Mersch.

This whole current of thinking and writing received a first summing up in Pius XII's encyclical *Mystici corporis Christi* (1943), which endorsed the trend in its essentials but warned against deviations that purported to erect against the visible Church of the *Credo* another and invisible Church, said to embrace all men of good will in mystical union with Christ. It was in Germany, where the movement had originated, that ideas of this type were most to the fore around 1940,[13] whereas in the French-speaking countries thinkers such as Mgr Journet, professor at Fribourg in Switzerland, and Fr Congar, O.P., youthful founder in 1937 of the collection *Unam Sanctam,* whose contribution to the contemporary ecclesiological revival can hardly be overestimated,[14] were stressing by contrast, in the Thomist tradition, the balance that must be maintained in theological thought between the two aspects of the Church: the Church as the visible, hierarchically ordered institution and the Church as the living community, within which scheme the institutional forms appear as the 'sacrament' (that which manifests outwardly and efficaciously procures) of what is inner and more vital.

So firm foundations had been laid for new advances in ecclesiology after the war. Theologians were stimulated by a concern to rethink in theological terms the problems of the apostolate[15] and by the historical research which made the contingent character of post-Tridentine ecclesiology[16] increasingly clear. The main themes were: the construction of a theology of the laity, which sought to determine the exact place assigned to laymen alongside the

13. See N. Oemen, 'L'ecclésiologie dans le crise', *Questions sur l'Église et son unité (Irénikon),* (Gembloux 1943), 1-11, and E. Przywara, 'Corpus Christi mysticum. Eine Bilanz', *Zeitschrift für Aszese und Mystik,* XV (1940), 197-215.
14. For the objects aimed at by *Unam Sanctam* see the two texts quoted in J. Lestavel, *Les Prophètes de l'Église contemporaine* (Paris 1969), 63-4.
15. See for example the remarks by O. Rousseau, 'La constitution "Lumen gentium" dans le cadre des mouvements rénovateurs de théologie et de pastorale des dernières décades', in *L'Église de Vatican II,* II (Paris 1966), 35-56.
16. See E. Ménard, *L'Ecclésiologie hier et aujourd'hui* (Paris-Bruges 1965), esp. 11 and 75-6.

priesthood in the people of God; the discovery – stimulated by fruitful theological exploration of this vein by the World Council of Churches – of the centrality of mission to the Church's function; the gradual perfection of an ecumenical theology, which attempted among other things to define exactly the theological status of Christians separated from the Roman Church; the tentative efforts to develop a theology of the episcopate, leading on the rediscovery of the collegiate character of the Church and of the importance – so much stressed by Eastern theologians – of the 'particular Church';[17] the reflections, at first sight more practical but having a profound theological and ecumenical bearing, on a theme periodically harped on by Catholic publicists, ranging from Papini to J. von Görres, which Fr Congar was brave enough to tackle as theologian under the title *Vraie et Fausse Réforme dans l'Eglise* (1950), namely the adaptation of antiquated ecclesiastical structures, carefully devised in the past to meet certain well-defined needs but unable to respond adequately to the needs of the present.

The Second World War marked no radical discontinuity in the history of Catholic thought but the profound psychological, social and cultural transformations that were its consequence did not fail to make an impact on the direction of theological researches. The latter were more than ever characterised by the twofold movement recalled at the start of this chapter: concern for the reinvigoration of theology by still more direct application to Christian sources and awareness of the continual need for reappraisal of the Christian message in its confrontation with the preoccupations of the modern world.

The desire for a 'refreshment' of theology from that never-failing fount, the word of God as proclaimed and interpreted in the Church, was made evident in the first place by the remarkable revival of biblical studies. The disheartening climate in which exegetes of the interwar years had had to work is made obvious by indications such as the very conservative tenor of the encyclical *Spiritus Paraclitus* (1920), marking a retreat from the position adopted in Leo XIII's biblical encyclical, the censure addressed to the Abbé Touzard for his articles, even though very qualified in their judgments, on the Mosaic authenticity of the Pentateuch; the placing on the Index in 1924 of Brassac's far from adventurous *Manuel biblique* and in 1929 of L. Dennefeld's good study of Messianism; the intervention of the Holy Office against H. Jenker's *Die biblische Urgeschichte* in 1932; and the very negative atitude adopted all the while by the Biblical Commission. All the more credit therefore to the exegetes for having continued to hold the fort.

In the place of honour was the École biblique of Jerusalem, dominated by

17. On this point of particular importance to the perspective of Vatican II's constitution *Lumen gentium* see C. Moeller, in *L'Église de Vatican II*, II (Paris 1966), 86-94.

Fr Lagrange (1938), who could claim the credit for training scholars such as Fr Spicq and Fr Benoît. But it is right also to mention the similarly constructive work of criticism in progress in Germany and in France, as also in Belgium where L. Cerfaux, whose *La Théologie de l'Église suivant S. Paul* (1942) was later to be hailed as a landmark in the history of Catholic exegesis, started about 1930 to apply to the study of the New Testament the *Formgeschichte* technique, ridding it of the *a priori* element which had rendered it suspect. Furthermore, it was impossible to disregard for long the many serious and constructive contributions to biblical scholarship from the Protestant and Anglican side; and in fact this was a source to which many Catholic researchers were turning for inspiration, since a shortsighted censorship so often prevented Catholic exegetes from publishing the results of their work. The late 1930s at last brought signs of a thaw, confirmed by the appointment in 1938 and 1939 of Cardinal Tisserant and Fr Vosté respectively as president and secretary of the Biblical Commission, and by the encyclical *Divino afflante spiritu* (1943), in which Pius XII gave the Holy See's official encouragement to exegetes working along prudently progressive lines; the clarifications issued in 1948 regarding interpretation of the first chapters of Genesis, and in 1955 on the exact scope of the decrees of the Biblical Commission pointed in the same liberating direction.[18]

Two features in particular of the work accomplished by Catholic exegetes during the pontificate of Pius XII need to be mentioned. We find on the one hand a more liberal use of historico-critical methods and in particular a fairly general recourse to *Formgeschichte,* and more recently, especially in Germany, an evident desire to take account of the great upheaval produced by Bultmann and his school and of the 'demythologisation' problem; and on the other, a more determined effort to draw attention to the specifically religious significance of the biblical message. The truth is that when we take a general look at the output of Catholic exegesis prior to 1940, for example the highly estimable *Études bibliques,* the series in which Fr Lagrange's Gospel commentaries appeared, we are struck in many cases by the fact that the approach is predominantly that of the archaeologist or philologist. Rare indeed is it to find scholars fastening on the doctrinal and spiritual aspects of the texts under examination. The dawn of biblical theology in the Roman Church came in the 1940s, and in 1950 M. Meinertz published his *Theologie des Neuen Testaments,* the first contribution worthy of that name to be made by a Catholic. A similar concern to lay more stress on the doc-

---

18. On this change of atmosphere see J. Levie, *La Bible, parole humaine et message de Dieu,* Part II, Paris-Louvain 1958. Text of the encyclical in *A.A.S.,* XXXV (1943), 297-325; text of the letter of 1948, addressed to Cardinal Suhard, *ibid.,* XL (1948), 45-8; and of the clarifications, by Fr A. Miller, on the scope of the decrees of the Biblical Commission, *Benediktinische Monatschrift,* XXXI (1955), 49 ff.

trinal significance of Scripture and in particular on the religious signification and christological import of the Old Testament lay at the root of a quite lively debate on the 'spiritual' meaning of Scripture and of research into typological exegesis, which seeks to establish the connections between a biblical text and parallel passages of Scripture, or between the events and personages mentioned in Scripture and subsequent events in the history of the Church of which they are the prefiguration.

The refreshment of theology from biblical sources had as its complement a patristic revival, and as the popularity of series such as *Sources chrétiennes* in France and *The Christian Fathers* a little later in the English-speaking world goes to show, this too extended well beyond specialist circles. The climate during the interwar years had been kinder to patrologists than to the biblical exegetes, although they were reminded from time to to time, by warnings from the Holy Office, of the pitfalls still ahead for those who intended to venture beyond the innocuous terrain of literary or historical research (questions of authenticity or dating) to tread the more delicate ground of doctrinal history. After the war, with so many ecclesiastics tending to turn aside from scholarly work, the future of solid research into early Christian literature seemed seriously in doubt, but in most cases the situation was saved, especially in France, where H. I. Marrou played the leading role, by the emergence of a galaxy of young lay talent. But the approach of the patrologists in the postwar years tended more and more to be in refreshing contrast with that of the preceding half-century, for developments in patristic studies were similar to those in respect of the Bible. Instead of searching the Fathers mainly for apologetic arguments with which to prove the antiquity of Catholic doctrines or practices, or at best for indications of the gradual evolution of those doctrines and practices, scholars were now more concerned to seek out what was original in the Fathers' contribution, to make their message live again in all its doctrinal and spiritual richness, and where possible to re-create the religious experience of Christian community to which those personal testimonies bore witness.

The greater emphasis on returning to the sources and the historical discoveries this movement entailed had the inevitable result of confronting theologians with the thorny question of progress in dogma. Posed in brutal fashion by the modernists, it was a question to which theologians of the interwar years had tried to find an acceptable solution. In particular, the Spanish Dominican Fr Marin-Sola began cautiously – though not cautiously enough for one or two of his fellow Dominicans – to develop Fr Gardeil's key concept of the homogeneity of theology with dogma and of dogma with the revealed data, applying it in systematic fashion to the problem of dogmatic development. While admitting that popular devotion, acting on intuition rather than reason, had done more than cold logic to demonstrate to the Church the full content of revealed propositions, he thought it possible, *post factum* at least, to show that developments of dogma or 'new dogmas' were metaphysically included in the original datum and could be deduced from it by rigorous syllogistic reasoning. Hence the title of his book, *L'Evolution homogène du dogme catholique,* (2 vols, 1923-4), in which the word *homogène* was intended to disarm the objections of those who continued to believe, like Cardinal Billot, that 'dogmas have no history'. In this Fr Marin-Sola had partially succeeded, but in exchange the trust he displayed in theological conclusions, which some even wanted to make the proper goal of theological science, came increasingly under attack from various quarters. While some critics cast serious doubt on the value of the deductive method in theology and stressed the inadequacy of philosophical concepts formulated by human intelligence to do justice to the religious wealth stored up in the revealed datum, others sought to account for the phenomenon of the development of doctrine in various other ways: by laying stress on the living tradition, in reaction against a too material conception of the function of tradition in the Church; by exploiting the wealth of subtleties in Newman's thought, which around 1940 was again very much to the forefront; [19] or indeed by stressing the role devolving at any one time on the infallible *magisterium*, which, by providing the believer with intellectual authority for advancing beyond the probability on which intuitive acceptance of a convention was founded, gives assurance that the development in question is legitimate.

This tendency to draw a contrast between a static notion of tradition and the role of the active *magisterium*, authentic interpreter of revelation, qualified to judge of its legitimate development, had at first aroused suspicion in Roman circles. But developments in Mariology, [20] among other things, helped to bring about a change of attitude, and it was in fact Roman theologians such as Fr G. Filograssi, S.J. who, when the solemn definition of the Assumption was in preparation (1951), were the most insistent on the existence of the dogma in the consciousness of the Church and on the

19. The most striking study of Newman's thought was the thesis submitted in 1942 by the Belgian Dominican H. Walgrave to the University of Louvain and subsequently published in French translation under the title *Newman. Le développement du dogme,* Tournai-Paris 1957. Among those who had helped to concentrate attention on the fund of ideas in Newman's thought that were applicable to certain tendencies in modern thought, for example the importance of historicity in the intellectual approach to religion and the role of the apprehending subject, it is only fair to mention the French philosopher J. Guitton and the German Jesuit E. Przywara.
20. Mention was made in the previous chapter (596-7) of the tendency of theological literature on the Virgin, especially after 1934, to run to excesses, and of the criticism this attracted, for example the charge that under the pontificate of Pius XII Mariology was in danger of becoming the speciality of a clique.

crucial intervention by the infallible *magisterium* as the means of sanctioning discoveries made by the *sensus fidelium* and of guaranteeing their homogeneity with the datum of revelation.

Even more than of the development of dogma, there was much talk after the war of developments of theology. A reaction against Scholastic theology had set in even before 1940: in France and Belgium, as well as in the German-speaking countries, where the Thomist revival had never caught on to the same extent as in the Latin countries, many voices were heard calling for a 'reconciliation' of Thomism with movements of modern thought, with idealism, Bergsonism, phenomenology or Marxism according to taste. After the war the reaction began to cut deeper. The rediscovery of the Fathers and better acquaintance with the medieval Augustinian tradition put new arguments at the disposal of those who rebelled against the idea that Catholic theology had to be confined to a purely Thomist framework. They insisted not only on the legitimacy but on the necessity of theological pluralism, arguing that no single system, given the limitations of human knowledge, was capable of embracing in one synthetic view all aspects of revelation. In France between 1946 and 1950 this proposition gave rise to keen controversy centred on what was unofficially known as 'the new theology'.[21]

The phenomenon just mentioned was but one manifestation among many of the theological ferment characteristic of the immediate postwar period. And that ferment, especially active in France and spreading by degrees to other countries, was itself but one aspect of a ferment affecting Catholic thought in every department, to which the success of a number of high-brow journals bears witness: for example, W. Dirks's[22] *Frankfurter Hefte*, the Belgian *Revue nouvelle*,[23] and most influential of all, because of its wide audience, *Esprit*, the organ of the very active group centred on Emmanuel Mounier.[24]

Among the multiple causes of the theological revival, which to the dismay of the licensed champions of classical theology — whose lack of historical sense caused them to identify the latter with tradition — flourished with increasing vigour, we must find space to mention the discovery, starting already in the interwar years, of the riches afforded by Orthodox and Protestant thinking: riches of content, but still more of the problems raised,

21. See G. Thils, *Orientations de la théologie* (Louvain 1958), 57-75, and J. Comblin, *Vers une théologie de l'action* (Brussels 1965), 48-58 (with detailed bibliography).
22. On W. Dirks, 'lay theologian', non-conformer, a highly controversial but also very influential figure of the postwar period, see H. T. Risse, in *Tendenzen der Theologie im 20 Jht.*, 460-5.
23. See R. Aubert, 'La "Revue nouvelle" et l'aggiornamento dans l'Église', *Revue nouvelle*, L (1969), 487-500.
24. For Mounier and his group see chapter 21, 580

very different from those tackled by the Scholastic or the purely historical schools and much more in tune with the new trends in philosophy.

While there was fairly general agreement of the need to rethink the status of theology, some theologians, influenced it might be by Newman or St Augustine, or by Scheler, Bergson or Blondel (the latter again very much in vogue after 1940), made it their concern to define more precisely the true nature of religious knowledge and to bring to the forefront the mystical element that should be one of its characteristics, affording the believer intimations here below of the divine realities that are the object of his faith. Others were most conscious of the need to make room in theology for biblical and patristic categories of thought that Scholasticism had obscured: one such category was symbolism which, when systematically employed by scholars combining a modern philosophical approach with the results yielded by minute investigation of liturgical history, made possible a remarkable revival of sacramental theology. [26] Others again, impelled by a deep desire for openness towards 'external values', set theology on new paths by studying what the Christian answer should be to the problems posed by Hegel, Marx, Kierkegaard, Heidegger, Sartre, thinkers who had the ear of their contemporaries. So, for instance, Karl Rahner, [25] whose theological writing began well before Vatican II. Brought up in this way against modern thought, theology had its attention directed to new fields for investigation, aspects of reality which theologians of previous generations had thought it pointless to dwell on.

One such was the rightful place of laymen in the Church (reference has already been made to the working out of a theology of the laity, a typical example of the interaction between life and thought); another was the interpretation to be placed by the believer on the course of human history. The revival of Hegelian philosophy and the importance attributed by Marxism to 'the movement of history' prompted many Catholic thinkers to consider what light revelation might shed in this domain, one of those which Scholastic, and still more post-Tridentine, theology, stuck fast in the contemplation of essences, had left unexplored. Hence the appearance of various attempts at a theology of history, although as yet they amounted to

25. See C. Muller and H. Vorgrimler, *Karl Rahner*, Paris 1965.
26. The revival had begun in Germany even before the Second World War and the summa by Fr Jungmann, *Missarum Solemnia* (1948) was one of its first fruits. But it developed most strongly after 1945, among other places in France around the group known as Maison Dieu. The thesis of the Belgian Dominican Schillebeeckx, part of which was written at Le Saulchoir (*De sacramenteele Heilseconomie*, Antwerp 1952), represents a remarkable advance in the theological approach to the subject, since in discussing the sacraments the theologians had long confined themselves to canonical and casuistical considerations, with possibly some reference to the historico-apologetic aspects.

little more than preliminary sketches. [27] A number of these essays, inasmuch as their chief object was to evaluate in Christian terms those temporal strivings of mankind that give rise to civilisations, were not far removed from the theology of terrestrial realities evolved in the late 1930s, although the proponents of the latter had started out with somewhat different preoccupations in mind. What had struck them in the Marxist system had been not so much its dialectical thinking on the movement of history as its rehabilitation of matter and its criticism of Christianity for its apparently disdainful attitude towards the conquest of the terrestrial world. The desire, already mentioned, of Fr Teilhard de Chardin to provide a theology of and for the present, and the growing popularity of his ideas, could only help to reinforce the interest in questions of this order. The greater attention paid in the postwar period to social and international problems subsequently widened the field still further and brought gradually to the forefront of theologians' preoccupations the elaboration of a theology of human solidarity, leaving the political theology to come later, after the council: a natural consequence of the contemporary inclination to give primacy to ethics or, in the fashionable jargon, to substitute orthopraxis for orthodoxy.

Moral theology in the strict sense could hardly fail to benefit from this willingness to take fresh stock in the light of the new perspectives opened up by contemporary philosophy. The first beginnings of a questioning of the manuals – and beyond them of an entire conception of classical ethics – went back to the interwar years. After the war the inquest was resumed, conducted at times somewhat brusquely but to the ultimate greater good of a department of fundamental importance to the Christian religion, and one that had lagged noticeably behind in the general development of religious thought. The progress of sociology and psychology, of psycho-analysis in particular, by concentrating attention on the external and internal conditioning which affects and limits human freedom, had already prompted the re-examination of certain problems. But the existentialist climate which, while not denying these aspects, emphasised by contrast the importance of spontaneity in ethical conduct, reinforced in their attitude those who even from prewar days had been troubled to find moral theology so often reduced to a set of tortuous discussions of the best way to evade the regulations of the Church and yet remain in good standing. One of the first to move in this direction was the German Redemptorist B. Häring with his book *Das Gesetz Christi* (1954). In more daring fashion, the concern with personal spontaneity was translated into a new way of regarding the Christian con-

27. For a preliminary survey see R. Aubert, 'Discussions récentes autour de la théologie de l'histoire', *Collectanea Mechliniensia*, XVIII (1948), 129-49, and G. Thils, *Théologie de l'histoire*, Bruges-Paris 1949; also the illuminating observations of J. Comblin, *Vers une théologie de l'action*, 87-109.

science. It was no longer to be thought of as a mechanism which produced by automatic syllogism a general principle to fit a particular case but as a faculty which, under the guidance of the Holy Spirit, was endowed with a certain power of intuition and invention which made it capable of arriving in each case at the appropriate and unique solution. The debate over what has been called 'situation ethics' started up in Germany around one or two laymen. It was not long before theologians began to take note in their turn of the dangers involved in always wanting 'prescriptions' and ready-made solutions, when life is made up of individual cases. In making decisions of conscience, they argued, every individual must come face to face with himself before God and make his decision in the light of his personal appraisal of an always unique situation. The censorious took fright and denounced in all this a tendency, not entirely illusory, towards a relativism which would end by reducing our moral conduct to the various sincerities at each instant, and in 1952 Pius XII himself warned against the errors lurking in an over-simplified presentation of situation ethics. But these correctives – applied at times with a want of discrimination, as in the case of the Dutch psychiatrist, A. Terruwe – did not prevent theologians from continuing to draw attention to the elements of truth in the new approach, some of which, after all, linked up with the traditional teaching on the primacy of charity in moral theology or on the role of the virtue of prudence.

Pius XII's warning, to which allusion has just been made, was no isolated measure. The last decade of the pontificate witnessed an undeniable stiffening of attitude, a reaction against the renovatory enthusiasm of the 1940s. The latter had at times been impetuous, not to say dangerous, and it was not long before authority took alarm. The best-known warning was that contained in the encyclical *Humani generis* (1950), which even at the time was compared with the anti-modernist encyclical *Pascendi* although in fact it was a more balanced document.[28] Moreover, as experience was to show, while the encyclical may have helped to make theologians more circumspect, it did not put a stop to the work of renewal, which in all fundamental respects proceeded along the same lines as before. But there were also other warnings, for example relating to biblical studies, complemented by a more insidious policy of forcing works judged to be unsettling to be withdrawn from circulation and of depriving of their teaching office theologians regarded at Rome as 'out of step'. Fr Congar, Fr Chenu, Fr de Lubac, along with others who had been the teachers of a generation, fell victim, happily only for a while, to this 'witch-hunt'.

28. Text in *A.A.S.*, XLII (1950), 513-17. For its exact bearing see, among others, *Revue nouvelle*, XII (1950), 302-9, and *Études*, CCLXVII (1950), 353-73. A list of more than eighty commentaries taking varying points of view will be found in *Bulletin thomiste*, VIII (1953), 1374-81.

Nor did the witch-hunt entirely cease with the pontificate of John XXIII, a fact too often overlooked. In 1961, for example, yet another *Monitum* was issued on biblical studies; just prior to the council, two professors at the Biblical Institute in Rome were in some obscure kind of disgrace and, even as the council opened, three Dutch-speaking exegetes found themselves under threat of penalties. It is also to be noted that the Holy See's only public pronouncement against the work of Teilhard de Chardin dates from June 1962.

All this being so, there is less reason for surprise at the unexpansive spirit in which the majority of the doctrinal schemas submitted to the Fathers of the council were first drawn up. And it is also easier to appreciate that although the roots of the Second Vatican Council can be firmly set in the intensive work of renovation accomplished during the preceding twenty-five years, the confrontations to which it gave rise were of a very different nature from mere rearguard actions. When the council opened, on 11 October 1962, the optimists were probably entitled to cherish certain hopes; but nothing had yet been conceded. The distance about to be travelled in the space of four years was all the more surprising.

23

THE SECOND VATICAN COUNCIL

ALTHOUGH the announcement by John XXIII on 25 January 1959 of his intention to summon an ecumenical council had the effect of a bombshell, the idea was not as novel as might at first sight appear. Pius XI had contemplated, almost as soon as he was elected, a resumption of the Vatican council suspended in 1870, which he thought was made desirable by the changes consequential on the war, and he had taken private soundings from the curial cardinals and from some bishops. [1] Opinions were divided: some maintained that most of the suspended business had since been dealt with through the publication of the code of canon law and by means of encyclicals, and they also thought it would be unwise to suggest, by summoning a council to Rome, that the loss of the temporal power was not a serious impediment to the Church's activity. Others welcomed the idea, arguing that a council would be of great benefit to the internal life of the Church, to the cause of world peace, and also, even at this early date, to the cause of Christian unity, while a few had stressed the need for clarification of the doctrine relating to the episcopate. A team of experts, including Fr Hugon, O.P., Fr Tacchi Venturi, S.J. and Fr Lepicier, S.M., was set to work to draw up a programme, which we know covered such items as the proposal for a dogmatic constitution on the Church and the examination of problems in the fields of international law, socialism and communism, the Eastern Churches, Catholic Action, Catholic education, and the role of women in the Church. In the event, however, the protractedness of the negotiations leading up to the Lateran agreements and the subsequent worsening of the international situation made it necessary to abandon the project. But it was revived a generation later, in 1948, by Pius XII. [2] The

1. See G. Caprile, 'Pio XI e la ripresa del Concilio Vaticano', La Civiltà cattolica, 1966, vol. III, 27-39, cont. ibid., 1969, vol. II, 121-33, concl. ibid., 563-75.
2. G. Caprile, 'Pio XII e un nuovo progetto di concilio oecumenico', La Civiltà cattolica, 1966, vol. III, 209-27.

preparatory work was entrusted to the Holy Office and a number of separate commissions (with the Belgian missiologist Fr Charles, S.J. as secretary general) worked in secret to produce schemas on a variety of topics: doctrinal dangers, the definition of the Assumption of the Virgin, communism, war, reform of canon law and of the curia, missions, Catholic Action, culture. The discussions continued down to 1951, but at that point divergences of opinion made it necessary for all activity to be suspended and this new setback seemed to confirm that the age of councils was finally past.

John XXIII, who may have been impressed by a recent article in the Italian journal *Palestra del Clero,* did not share this view, although he had only very vague ideas about the concrete programme of his proposed council, which he hoped might at one and the same time contribute to the better adaptation of the apostolate to an era of accelerated change and constitute 'encouragement to the separated Churches to join in the quest for unity'. Invitations to submit suggestions went out to the cardinals, then to all bishops and religious superiors and finally to faculties of theology and canon law — the largest organised consultation of this kind ever undertaken [3] — while in the meantime an ante-preparatory commission set to work on planning the council's agenda. Its president was Tardini, the cardinal Secretary of State, who appointed as secretary the canonist P. Felici. A year later, on 5 June 1960, ten preparatory commissions were constituted (Theology; Government of Dioceses; Discipline of Clergy; Religious; Sacraments; Liturgy; Studies and Seminaries; Eastern Churches; Missions; Apostolate of the Laity) and in addition two secretariats (Communications Media and Christian Unity). The task of co-ordination was confided to a Central Commission, which was also made responsible for drawing up standing orders for the forthcoming assembly. (This Central Commission, composed of bishops from about sixty countries, met seven times between 12 June 1961 and 20 June 1962.) The strict parallelism, with one exception, between the commissions and the corresponding Roman Congregations, each having the same cardinal at its head, made it likely that the work of the commissions would be conducted in a somewhat conformist spirit, but against that there were three signs that seemed to point to a spirit of innovation. One was the creation of a commission for the Apostolate of the Laity, the only commission not to have its counterpart in an existing Roman Congregation. The second was the establishment of the Secretariat for the Promotion of Christian Unity, [4] giving the lie to curialists who had been at pains to minimise the un-

<hr>

3. The replies, in the order of some two thousand, were in the event disappointing, the majority envisaging little more than the condemnation of errors or one or two trifling reforms, hardly likely to lead to a true renovation of the Church.

4. The creation of this new body, whose role was to be of such importance both during and after the council, is referred to above, chapter 21, 606.

ionist implications of the council. Under the leadership of Cardinal Bea and with the pope's discreet encouragement, the Secretariat revealed itself before long as an indispensable channel of communication between the Roman Church and the ecumenical movement. The last hopeful sign was the choice of members to serve on the commissions. Included were a number of bishops with diocesan responsibilities, which represented a departure from the practice of the First Vatican Council, and although the outlook of the commissions remained predominantly conservative, room was also made for other theological and pastoral viewpoints, represented by members such as Fr Congar and Fr de Lubac, who in recent years had been under attack from integrist circles.

The commissions produced seventy schemas. The Central Commission, to which the schemas had to be submitted, caused a number of them to be amended and in some cases rewritten, and a batch of the revised schemas was sent out to all the bishops three months before the council opened. Some bishops – another difference from the first council – were already aware of the lines along which the commissions were working, having been kept informed by colleagues who were members of the commissions or by one or other of the consultors. Many of these schemas were in fact mediocre or frankly inadequate, especially those emanating from the Theological Commission, which often did little more than re-state the traditional teaching in terms likely to be offensive to members of the Eastern or Reformed Churches and to provoke negative reactions in intellectual circles within the Catholic Church itself.

The standing orders of the council, dated 6 August 1962, were published at the beginning of September. As at Vatican I, three types of session were provided for, a two-thirds majority being required for a decisive vote in each case: public sessions, at which the pope presided; general congregations, steered by a committee of ten cardinals, at which the Fathers debated (normally in Latin, although the Eastern prelates often resorted to French) the texts submitted for their consideration (warned by the experience of Vatican I, the time allowed for a speech was reduced to ten minutes); and lastly the commissions, which had the task of amending the texts in the light of the Fathers' comments, aided to a much greater extent than at Vatican I by the advice of appropriate 'experts', canonists or theologians as the case might be. There were ten of these conciliar commissions, corresponding to the ten preparatory commissions, each composed of twenty-four Fathers, two-thirds elected by the assembly and one-third appointed by the pope: the president of each commission, again by papal appointment, was the prefect of the corresponding Roman Congregation, an arrangement not calculated to make the acceptance of reforming ideas any easier. Although standing orders made no provision regarding the status of the Secretariat for Christian Unity, after a brief period of indecision the latter came to be regarded as equal in status to the conciliar commissions (its composition remained as it had been during the preparatory stage). Mgr Felici, secretary of the preparatory co-ordinating commission, was appointed Secretary General to the council; very assiduous in his duties, as the sessions proceeded he became to all intents and purposes the pope's right hand man in regulating the business of the council. There was in addition a Secretariat for Extra-ordinary Affairs, presided over by the Secretary of State, whose task was to examine new problems as they arose and report on them to the pope. It played an important part at the end of the First Session but was afterwards abolished.

Vatican II consisted of four sessions, each lasting from two to three months and occupying the autumn of every year from 1962 to 1965. But no history of the council would be complete which did not reckon with the less spectacular activity which continued at Rome (and sometimes outside it) during the intervening periods. As we are told by J. Grootaers, a perspicacious and exceptionally well-informed observer: [5]

Vatican II had its knife-edge moments which usually occurred at times when the council was not in session, thus in the absence of the bishops, the army of experts and the press, at times when certain individuals in the curia had the impression that they were on the verge (temporarily) of regaining control of the situation. The Roman atmosphere of those inter-sessional periods often made it possible to isolate the representatives of the conciliar majority and to revise texts in a restrictive sense. Cardinal Cicognani, who added the functions of President of the Co-Ordinating Commission to those of Secretary of State, exerted a considerable influence in this regard, not always avoiding a confusion between his different functions.

The council opened on 11 October 1962 in the presence of some two thousand five hundred Fathers. [6] Whereas Vatican I had still been very European in complexion, Vatican II was impressively global in its weight and impressive too in the extent to which the 'Young Churches' were represented. Fathers representing Western Europe accounted for only thirty-three per cent compared with thirteen per cent from the United States and Canada, twenty-two per cent from Latin America, ten per cent from Asia,

---

5. J. Grootaers, in *Ecclesia a Spiritu Sancto edocta. Mélange théologiques. Hommage à Mgr G. Philips* (Gembloux 1970), 352.
6. The total number summoned was 2778 (eighty cardinals, seven patriarchs, 1619 archbishops and residential bishops, 975 titular bishops, 97 religious superiors). The average attendance over the four sessions fluctuated between 2100 and 2300.

ten per cent from Black Africa, three-and-a-half per cent from the Arab world and two-and-a-half per cent from Oceania. By contrast, the Catholic bishops in communist countries, over one hundred and fifty in total, were only poorly represented: from Yugoslavia, it is true, there was an attendance of twenty-four prelates out of twenty-seven, but from Poland only some twenty out of a possible sixty-five, from Eastern Germany only four out of eight, from Hungary two out of sixteen, from Czecho-Slovakia three out of fifteen, from the U.S.S.R., Rumania, China and North Vietnam none at all. In the following sessions, however, there was some improvement, especially as regards the representation of Poland and East Germany.

An even more dramatic innovation compared with Vatican I was the increasingly active presence of non-Catholic observers. The announcement of a council expressly linked by the pope with the prospective reunion of the Churches had in general been well received in the non-Catholic Churches, in particular by the patriarch of Constantinople and by the Anglican Church. A short time later the secretary of the World Council of Churches, Visser 't Hooft, was to declare: *'Nostra res agitur'*. With the setting up of the Secretariat for Christian Unity the amount of contact increased, and this led to the extension by Rome of invitations to the majority of separated Churches to send observer-delegates to the council, to whom were later added a number of individuals invited by the Secretariat to attend in their own right. For reasons internal to Orthodoxy the patriarchate of Constantinople sent no observer until the Third Session, but observers representing seven Orthodox Churches — the Soviet Russian, to the general surprise, being one — the Anglican Communion, the Old Catholics, and nine Protestant confessions were in attendance from the beginning of the First Session: at the start thirty-one, by the end of the council the number of observers had grown to ninety-three representing twenty-eight Churches and confessions. The standing of the observers was at first very uncertain, all the more since John XXIII had taken his decision against the advice of the majority in the curia, but before too long, thanks to the members of the Secretariat, acting with perspicacity and caution, but also with courage, the group of observers was accepted and took shape, to become a truly significant presence. Not only did observers attend all the sessions, more important they were invited by the Secretariat to a weekly meeting at which they had opportunity to make comments, and some were also consulted by particular commissions or by individual groups of bishops and theologians and so were able to play an essential role in the opening up of the council on the ecumenical side.

John XXIII inaugurated the council with an address which made a deep impression. He warned against the integrist temptation to pile up condemnations, and referred again to the unitive perspective that was to characterise this council summoned for pastoral ends (a perspective so much ignored by some of the preparatory commissions that they had even failed to consult the Secretariat for Christian Unity). At the first general congregation, two days later, when the Fathers were invited to elect members of the commissions from the lists prepared by the curia, the French cardinal Lienart, seconded by Cardinal Frings (Germany) and Cardinal Alfrink (Holland), called for a postponement of the voting, to give the bishops time to consult one another. Thanks to this initiative, it was possible to elect commissions much more representative of the underlying tendencies of the assembly.

The Fathers were in fact divided right from the start into what came to be known as the 'majority' and the 'minority', a division which grew more and more distinct as the council proceeded. The former group was far from monolithic and there were several occasions when differences of temperament, theological training and priorities caused other alignments. But heartened by the knowledge that this was the line desired by John XXIII, they showed themselves ready above all else to respond to the realities of the modern world and to the need for adaptation to it, willing to give ear to the ecumenical dialogue, which some of them only became aware of in the course of the council, undisguised in their preference for a pastoral theology refreshed by contact with biblical sources, more concerned with the practical effect of the decisions to be taken than with precise doctrinal definitions and on the whole suspicious of an excessive centralisation of authority in the Church. The 'minority' numbered among its leaders some of the most prominent personages in the curia, and it had a strong representation from the so-called Christian countries (Italy, Spain, Latin America). Attached above all else to the stability of the Church and the monarchical character of its government, they were alive to the risks inherent in any kind of change and very anxious to safeguard the integral deposit of faith, though they had a tendency to confuse the dogmatic formulation of revelation with revelation itself. This minority, which during later sessions coalesced into the *Coetus internationalis Patrum,* played a useful role in drawing attention to certain somewhat neglected fundamental truths and in preventing the premature promulgation of insufficiently considered texts, but there were also times when its contribution was more obstructive than helpful. Furthermore, the burden of sustaining throughout the council the running dialogue with the minority tended every now and then to thrust into second place the dialogue with the world, and the eagerness felt on both sides, and still more keenly by the pope, to minimise the gap between them and arrive at quasi-unanimity gave rise to a number of inconsistencies, both as to procedure and in the texts.

The opening formalities having been completed, on 22 October the council started on its business by debating the schema on the liturgy, one of the few to have been drafted in a spirit of renewal. Despite the voicing of criticism by speakers who dreaded change, the general principles were approved on 14 November by 2162 votes to 46, a result which confirmed on which side the general sympathies of the 'silent majority' lay.

Further confirmation was about to be provided by the debate on the schema entitled 'On the sources of Revelation', a text governed by a narrow and artificial conception of the dogmatic tradition, likely to be deeply offensive to the Reformed Churches, and showing as regards Scripture a regression from the standpoint of the encyclical *Divino afflante spiritu.* The schema had already been subjected to much criticism in private, but it was a surprise to find it attacked on such a broad front. After debating it for a week, the Fathers voted by 1368 to 822 in favour of sending it back to the drawing board with instructions to make a fresh start. Although the vote fell short of the required two-thirds majority, the pope decided to refer the schema to a mixed commission on which the Theological Commission, dominated by the Holy Office, and the Secretariat for Christian Unity, which the Theological Commission had so far ignored, would have equal representation.

After a cursory examination of two mediocre schemas, on Mass Media and on union with the Eastern Churches, on 1 December the assembly began to debate the schema on the Church. Although one of the best to emanate from the Theological Commission, the schema was still far from giving satisfaction on a number of fundamental points. It called forth not merely various proposals for re-casting, but also speeches from such notabilities as cardinals Leger, Suenens and Montini, who had been in consultation with the pope, recommending a rethinking of the entire programme of the council in the perspectives of a 'council for the world'. The occasion marked yet another defeat for the curialists who had hope, by reason of their privileged postions, to be able to impose their own outlook on a council whose summoning they had failed to prevent.

Events had rapidly taken a turn which at the opening of the council not even the most optimistic of the majority would have dared to predict. That this was so was due in large measure to the unflagging exertions throughout the First Session of a number of 'experts' *(periti),* scholars of French, German, Belgian and Dutch origin being well to the fore. As well as the consultors (about three hundred in all) officially appointed by the pope to assist the various commissions, there were present in Rome a number of theologians closely in touch with modern theological and pastoral developments who were acting as personal advisers to individual bishops, or who had come in a private capacity. Part of their contribution was the drafting of countless episcopal speeches; but more important they also made contact with individuals, gave lectures which provided for many bishops a 'retraining' in theology along lines very different from those favoured in Roman circles, and took part in 'workshops' set up of their own accord by individual groups of Fathers, and so were able to alert the Fathers to the significance of particular texts or measures and to assist in refurbishing their thinking and the formation of judgments. It could be claimed that during the first two sessions these experts, some of whom were in addition attached officially to the commissions and helped with the drafting and amendment of texts, were the council's true driving force. Furthermore, whereas during the preparatory stage the experts from Northern Europe had paid only intermittent visits to Rome while the Roman theologians were permanently *in situ,* from October 1962 the Northerners were themselves resident in Rome and could devote all their time to the task in hand, while the Romans had to continue with their routine duties as teachers or consultors to Congregations. In addition, as a distinctively conciliar viewpoint started to emerge, this in itself lent new weight to the non-Roman experts working on the commissions.

At the conclusion of the First Session it was decided to reduce the number of schemas from seventy to twenty and to refer some of the more technical questions to the commission set up under the reform of the canon law; to instruct the commissions to redraft the remaining schemas to take account of the conciliar ethos as defined by John XXIII in his opening address; and to set up a new Co-ordinating Commission, on which non-curial Fathers would this time be in the majority, for the purpose of aiding and controlling this work of revision.

The various commissions – not to mention the sub-commissions – set immediately to work. The change of pontiff caused very little disruption, since Paul VI decided as early as 22 June that the council would continue. He nevertheless took advantage of the experience gleaned during the First Session to make various changes in procedure. The most important innovation was the creation of a new body, the College of Moderators. Consisting of four cardinals, its function was to steer the debates, a task previously carried out by the Committee of Presidents whose role was now reduced to the maintenance of good order and discipline. This substitution, of great importance for the future course of the council, naturally risked giving offence, and it was subsequently to pose a delicate problem of procedure. Of the four moderators, only Cardinal Agagianian represented the curial network. The choice of the three others – Cardinal Lercaro (Bologna), one of the few Italian prelates among the *avant-garde*, Cardinal Doepfner (Munich), who enjoyed great prestige with the 'transalpine' contingent, and Cardinal Suenens (Malines-Brussels), a disciple of Dom Lambert Beauduin and like him not averse to bold measures – plainly indicated the new pope's support for the widening of perspectives which had become such a marked feature of the First Session. If there was still any doubt, his opening address confirmed that it was his desire to see Vatican II 'building a bridge between the Church and the modern world'. One could cite as concrete proof of this desire the admission of a restricted number of laymen – and from the Third Session of laywomen – to the council as auditors.[7]

The Second Session was dominated by the debate, dragging on through the whole of October, on the schema on the Church as revised by the Louvain professor G. Philips,[8] who had worked in close collaboration with an international group of experts. Several points were hotly debated: the integration of the present schema with the schema on the Virgin (which to many speakers seemed to minimise the place of the latter); the reintroduction of the permanent diaconate (which some feared would lead to a breach of clerical celibacy); above all, the sacramental character of episcopal consecration (implying that bishops occupy the place they do in the Church in virtue of their consecration and not because of the jurisdiction conferred on them by the Holy See) and 'episcopal collegiality' by divine right (which seemed to the curialist party to cast doubts on the pope's role in the Church as defined at Vatican I). To break down the stubborn resistance of the minority to the Theological Commission on this point the moderators obtained leave, after some uphill negotiation, to hold a test vote on the subject on 30 October. The result was overwhelmingly in favour,[9] but the principle of collegiality was fiercely contested by the opposition when it was pointed out a few days later that in the light of this reappraisal of the episcopate, the schema on Bishops and Government of Dioceses needed fundamental revision.

The debate on this latter schema (5-16 November) was especially notable for a rousing attack by the Melkite patriarch Maximos IV, from start to finish one of most dynamic figures of the council, on the predominating influence of the Roman curia in the Church and for a lively exchange between Cardinal Frings, archbishop of Cologne, and Cardinal Ottaviani on the sub-

7. Starting at around a dozen, this group eventually numbered thirty-six, including seven women. The idea stemmed from the personal invitation John XXIII had addressed to the French professor Jean Guitton, 21 November 1962.

8. Until obliged by his health to leave Rome at the beginning of the Fourth Session his role was considerable; among other things, he became in December 1963 joint secretary of the Theological Commission and in fact its driving force (see J. Grootaers, 'Le rôle de Mgr Philips à Vatican II', in the work cited n. 5 above, 343-80). As a member of the Belgian Senate, he knew from experience how to win a committee round to his views; more important, he was an open-minded scholar well abreast with the new trends in theology, who at the same time had a firm grasp of tradition and was able to speak the language of the Roman theologians, with whom he had long been on excellent terms.

9. Fr C. Pozo, 'Reflexiones teologicas sobre el Vaticano II', *Razon y fe*, CLXIX (1964) 129-42, pointed out that by proceeding in this way Vatican II broke with the precedent set by the Council of Trent, which had deliberately refrained from pronouncing on issues still freely under debate by the theologians. Copious literature was produced during the council and after, in an effort to prove the traditional character of the theses in question.

ject of the Holy Office. Next to be examined was the eagerly awaited decree on ecumenism. It was presented by Cardinal Cicognani, a graceful solution to a delicate question of precedence involving the Commission for the Eastern Churches, which had prepared an earlier draft rejected by the Fathers as inadequate, and the Secretariat for Christian Unity, which had stepped into the breach. The president of the Secretariat, Cardinal Bea, was nevertheless given opportunity to present the fourth chapter, on the Jews, of which he was the author. The fifth chapter, on religious liberty, was presented *con brio* by Mgr de Smedt (Bruges), who had been one of the first to utter in full council a warning against the dangers of triumphalism. Despite one or two objections raised on the first day by Spanish and Italian prelates, the debate was calm and constructive. But it dealt only with the first three chapters of the schema, the moderators having announced that the chapters on the Jews and on religious liberty, which had run into strong opposition, were to be revised with a view to re-submission at the next session. Many people feared it was intended to suppress them.

By contrast, the closing days of the session yielded the majority much ground for satisfaction. On 21 November the pope acceded to their request for the addition of five new members to each commission, four out of the five to be elected by the assembly, and for each commission to have an elected vice-president and assistant secretary. These changes would make much more difficult the obstructionist tactics employed by the curialist opposition, which up till then had monopolised most of the key positions and commanded a blocking minority. Next, in December, Paul VI announced the abolition of a number of restrictions imposed on the powers of bishops under canon law, going well beyond the proposals contained in the appendix to the schema on bishops. And on the following day the constitution on the liturgy, having undergone successive improvements in course of the session, was approved all but unanimously, the first result of the council's labours and one that came down firmly on the progressive side so often denounced in the earlier debates: a fair measure of the distance that had been travelled.

Even so, and despite the good effects of Paul VI's pilgrimage to the Holy Land and of his historic meeting with Patriarch Athenagoras, it was not long before the outlook again began to darken. The instructions given early in 1964 to condense to propositions half the schemas still awaiting examination, taken in conjunction with the fighting spirit displayed by the curial leaders of the minority during the previous session, made many fear that a 'liquidation' of the council was in the offing. Adding to the pessimism were the difficulties, this time of form and substance rather than of procedure, encountered in hammering out 'schema 13', on the Church in the World. This schema, eagerly awaited by lay public opinion, brought into play a series of new problems left virtually unexplored by the theologians and approached from angles which varied greatly from country to country. Also in dispute was the question whether the schema was to be conceived from the point of view of the faithful or of the world outside. At the end of March confidence began to revive, when it was seen that the Theological Commission, in which a constructive dialogue had at last got under way, had succeeded in reaching agreement on the theology of the episcopate and in rescuing the schema on Revelation from its impasse. In the summer, however, advised by some of his counsellors, the pope started to suggest amendments to the commission, the purpose of which was to water down the definition of collegiality and to strengthen the references to the papal primacy, at some risk to the coherence of the text. A yet further cause for misgiving, to many minds, was the opposition of the Secretariat of State to proceeding with the projected declaration on the Jews, following protests from Arab countries.

In spite of these fears, not all of which were unfounded, the Third Session, which opened with a concelebration by the pope and twenty-four Fathers – clear sign that the liturgical reform was taking effect – and which proceeded during the first few weeks in an atmosphere of unprecedented euphoria, was especially fruitful. The constitutions on the Church and on Revelation and the decree on ecumenism were all completed without much further difficulty, proving how far ideas had ripened over the past two years, and the finishing touches were put to the revised schema on the Pastoral Office of Bishops (the object early in November of a manoeuvre by the minority, scotched in the nick of time, to restrict the powers of the episcopal college) as also, though not without stormy debate, to a set of undistinguished propositions on the Uniate Eastern Churches. It was also possible to make a start, somewhat too precipitately, on debating a number of newly submitted drafts. First to come up, despite people's fears to the contrary, were the declarations on Religious Liberty, on the Jews, and on non-Christian religions. Next came the schema on the Apostolate of the Laity, the schema on the Priesthood (rejected by 1099 to 930 as being superficial and inadequate), the schema on Religious (strongly criticised as too legalistic and too Western in outlook), the schemas on Seminaries, on Christian Education, on Marriage. Last and most important was the opening of the debate on the celebrated 'schema 13', the text which to many minds should be the crowning achievement of this pastoral council but which raised a series of burning questions – birth control, limitations on the right to private property, obligations of the richer nations towards the Third World, the use of the atomic bomb – on which the 'prophets' and the 'politicians' found themselves opposed. In the end it was agreed that the schema, which was clearly not yet ripe for voting, would have to be fundamentally revised, with the help in particular of a greater number of lay experts.

Another healthy sign: it could be observed during the Third Session that

Vatican II, without any cessation of the fruitful contact between the Fathers and the experts, whose activity until now had tended to resemble the febrile and potentially harmful behaviour of pressure groups, was gradually reasserting itself as a council of bishops, at which the technical advisers reverted to their normal auxiliary role. It was, after all, still a role of capital importance, for more than once it was experts who had both the confidence of the majority and personal experience of Roman methods who finally succeeded in giving certain controversial texts an acceptable form (the service performed by Mgr Philips, but equally by Mgr Willebrands, for the schema on Ecumenism, by Fr Hamer for the declaration on Religious Liberty, by Mgr Martimort for the constitution on the Liturgy, by Mgr Onclin for the text on the Pastoral Office of Bishops).

Yet this session which had started so well ended in an atmosphere of tension and unease, all the more distressing to those who were sensitive to the ecumenical aspects of the problems under review. The pope's anxious desire to conciliate the conservative opposition induced him to take certain steps not everyone could approve of: the addition to the constitution on the Church of an explanatory note (*Nota Praevia*) defining episcopal collegiality in relation to the papal primacy; the insertion into the decree on Ecumenism, already approved by the assembly, of amendments Laurentin described as 'unfriendly' to non-Catholics; the proclamation on his own initiative of the Virgin Mary as Mother of the Church. In addition, many Fathers were deeply disappointed to discover at the last minute that voting on the declaration on Religious Liberty, which had already been the object of a shabby manoeuvre by the conservatives in mid-October, was to be postponed to the next session.

The closing meeting of the session, which from the liturgical point of view had been a success, witnessed the promulgation of the constitution on the Church and of the decrees on Ecumenism and the Eastern Churches. The pope also announced several important reforms in the central government of the Church: the setting up of commissions, with which the bishops would be closely associated, to supervise the implementation of the council's decisions; the appointment of residential bishops to the Roman Congregations, with the aim of making the latter more sensitive to the views of the 'periphery'; the creation of a synod of bishops which the pope would regularly consult.

The first five congregations of the Fourth Session were devoted to the declaration on Religious Liberty, the text of which had been completely redrafted by an American Jesuit, Fr C. Murray. Although it made important concessions to the minority viewpoint, the declaration once again met with stubborn opposition, and in the end the pope himself had to intervene to resolve the stalemate. This was the last major clash. Thereafter the council went about its business in a relaxed atmosphere, the minority abandoning its obstructionist tactics and asking nothing better than the speediest possible end to this invasion of Rome by a horde of disruptive foreigners.

The new schema on the Church in the World, in all essentials the work of the French Haubtmann and intensively revised during the intersessional period, met with a fairly favourable reception, although some speakers thought it too advanced and others too timid (a plea from the Melkite bishop Zohby on behalf of divorced persons caused a great stir, and not just in conciliar circles). At the end of a constructive debate the drafting of the final version was left to Mgr Garrone. The schema on Missions, also recast, which now stressed new doctrinal developments and the ecumenical approach, gave rise to some stormy debate but in the end was approved by an overwhelming majority. The schema on the priesthood, another text to come back noticeably improved, was treated by contrast to a somewhat listless discussion which came to life only with the pope's announcement that he was withdrawing the question of celibacy from the floor of the council.

The last month of the council was occupied with producing final versions of the texts still to be voted.[10] For the commissions this was an especially trying period, since, as well as being engaged in a race against the clock, they found themselves in some instances obliged to defend themselves against attack from two fronts, from a 'left wing' charging its former allies of the 'majority', now firmly in control, with making too many concessions for the sake of agreement, and from the conservative last-ditchers, who continued to badger the pope with their complaints. The pope intervened for example in the final drafting of the constitution on Revelation, considering he had as much right as any other member of the council to collaborate in the revision of texts. He proposed three amendments, two of which were in turn slightly amended by the commission.[11]

By 28 October five texts were ready for formal promulgation: the decree on the Pastoral Office of Bishops (which this time drew out clearly the consequences of the doctrine of episcopal collegiality and called for the establishment of bishops' conferences), the decree on Religious (noticeably improved by a volume of amendments which a commission hitherto impervious to aggiornamento had found impossible to ignore), the decree on Seminaries, an insipid declaration on Christian Education and a declaration on Non-Christian Religions, the most crucial section of which, that concerning the Jews, continued to the last to call forth stubborn opposition. This

10. During the month of November there was a brief interlude in the form of a debate on a schema presented by the Apostolic Penitentiary and containing a plan for reforming the rules for indulgences; among those offering severe criticism were Cardinals Alfrink and Koenig, and most of all Cardinal Doepfner, each speaking for their national episcopate.

11. On this affair, which created something of a stir, see G. Caprile, in La Civiltà cattolica, (1966), vol. I 214-31.

was followed on 18 November by the promulgation of the decree on the Apostolate of the Laity, which had never run into any serious opposition, and of the dogmatic constitution on Divine Revelation (*Dei Verbum*), in large part the work of Fr Betti, O.F.M., assisted by a small band of German theologians: a very impressive text, marking in the opinion of Pastor Thurian 'a decisive step along the road to Christian unity'. Finally on 7 December the four remaining documents were published: the decrees on Mission and the Priesthood, the declaration on Religious Liberty and the Constitution on the Church and the World (*Gaudium et Spes*), the longest of the Vatican II texts (eighty-two pages), part theological, part pastoral, which during the previous two weeks had again produced one or two anxious moments. Although in some ways inadequate, the constitution offers a good starting-point for further research in certain fundamental areas.

The closing days of the council were rich in spectacular and unprecedented happenings. On 4 December, there was a farewell service for the observers at St Paul's-without-the-Walls, the first occasion on which a pope had joined in worship with non-Catholics; on 6 December, the announcement of the reform of the Holy Office (to be known in future as the Congregation for the Teaching of the Faith), along lines formulated in 1963 by Cardinal Frings; on 7 December, proclamation of the 'lifting of excommunication' as between Rome and Constantinople, couched in a formula strikingly evangelical in tone; lastly the closing ceremony in St Peter's square on 8 December, majestic but devoid of triumphalism, witnessed by delegations from eighty-one governments and from nine international bodies.

Did the the council, concluding in this way on a note of great hopefulness, really mark, as many have thought, the end of the post-Tridentine era? It is still too soon to say, but what seems certain is that Vatican II will influence much more positively than Vatican I the future development of the Roman Church in a great variety of spheres, and that this will still be true even though it found only partial solutions for some of the problems. One reason for the shortfall was that the key ideas inspiring the council had not yet fully matured, another was the constraining effect of obsolescent institutions and the men inhabiting them. In this connection the re-structuring of the curia decided on by Paul VI in 1967[12] which started to come into effect the following year could well be decisive, and represents in any case an important landmark. Equally important is the Roman Church's increasingly official and organic *rapprochement,* from which there can surely be no turning back, with the World Council of Churches and the diversity of Chris-

---

12. Apostolic constitution *Regimini Ecclesiae* of 15 August 1967 (*A.A.S.*, LIX (1967), 885-928). See R. Laurentin, *L'Enjeu du Synode* (Paris 1967), 11-46.

tian confessions,[13] and by the same token the increasingly official recognition of the positive contribution of the laity to the building up of the Body of Christ. By starting to unblock a number of channels, by signalling the official abandonment of certain elements of immobilism, of triumphalism, of exclusivism, Vatican II opened up the possibility of a new surge of expansion, sustained from beneath by the profundities of the Gospel message and swept along by the combined efforts of all available Christian forces. But by calling into question so much that many people regarded as a settled part of the tradition, the council also precipitated a crisis which we see unfolding before our eyes, a crisis whose seriousness is deepened by the concomitant crisis in Western civilisation and the advent, after two centuries in gestation, of the 'secular city'. Is this crisis, as many hope is the case, simply a crisis of growth, similar to the upheavals which rocked the Church so violently at the end of the Middle Ages or again in the late eighteenth century? It will be a generation or two before historians can hope to begin to provide any meaningful answer.

13. These developments can be followed in detail in the editorial and news section of the journal *Irénikon*.

BIBLIOGRAPHY

GENERAL HISTORIES OF THE CHURCH

R. AUBERT, *Le Pontificat de Pie IX* (vol. XXI of *Histoire de l'Église*, ed. A. Fliche and V. Martin), 2nd ed., Paris, 1963 (with bibliographical supplement). The Italian translation (2nd ed., Turin, 1969, 2 vols) has useful additional matter on Italy.

DANIEL-ROPS, *L'Église des Révolutions*, Paris, 1960, 3 vols (from 1789 to 1939; with valuable insights, but also numerous errors on points of detail, and over-apologetic in tone. English translation of vol. 1, New York, 1965).

E. E. Y. HALES, *The Catholic Church in the Modern World. A Survey from the French Revolution to the Present*, London, 1958.

H. JEDIN, ed., *Handbuch der Kirchengeschichte*, vol. VI, 1 and 2, Freiburg-im-Breisgau, 1971-3 (from 1789 to 1914).

K. S. LATOURETTE, *Christianity in a Revolutionary Age. A History of Christianity in the Nineteenth and Twentieth Centuries*, 5 vols, New York, 1958-62.

A. VIDLER, *The Church in an Age of Revolution* (Pelican History of the Church no. 5), Harmondsworth, 1961.

HISTORIES OF NATIONAL CHURCHES

P. BRACHIN and L. ROGIER, *Histoire du catholicisme hollandais depuis le XVIe siècle*, Paris, 1974.

A. DANSETTE, *Histoire religieuse de la France contemporaine*, 2 vols, Paris, 1948-51.

E. DELARUELLE, A. LATREILLE and J. R. PALANQUE, eds, *Histoire du catholicisme en France*, vol. III, Paris, 1962.

A. C. JEMOLO, *Church and State in Italy, 1850-1950*, Oxford, 1960.

C. JOSET, ed., *Un siècle de l'Église catholique en Belgique (1830-1930)*, Courtrai, 1934.

E. A. PEERS, *The Church in Spain*, London, 1938.

J. ROVAN, *Le Catholicisme politique en Allemagne*, Paris, 1956.

Chapter 1
THREE POPES: PIUS IX, LEO XIII, PIUS X

Pius IX

G. MARTINA, *Pio IX, 1846-50*, Rome, 1974. Fr Martina has undertaken a critical biography of which only the first volume has been published. The quality of this augurs well for the success of the whole.

General surveys of the pontificate
R. AUBERT, in vol. XXI of Fliche and Martin, eds, *Histoire de l'Église*.
E. E. Y. HALES, *Pio IX. A Study in European Politics and Religion in the XIXth Century*, London, 1954.
J. SCHMIDLIN, in *Papstgeschichte der neuesten Zeit*, vol. II, Munich (1934-9), 1-330.

Leo XIII

R. F. ESPOSITO, *Leone XIII e l'Oriente cristiano*, Rome, 1960.
E. T. GARGAN, ed., *Leo XIII and the Modern World*, New York, 1961.
F. HAYWARD, *Léon XIII*, Paris, 1937.
O. KÖHLER, in H. Jedin, ed., *Handbuch der Kirkengeschichte*, vol. VI-2, 1-387.
F. MOURRET, *Les Directives politiques, intellectuelles et sociales de Léon XIII*, Paris, 1920.
Ch. de T'SERCLAES, *Le Pape Léon XIII*, 3 vols, Bruges, 1894-1906.
E. SODERINI, *Il pontificato di Leone XIII*, 3 vols, Milan, 1932-3, (important, as the author was able to consult the Vatican archives. Unfortunately never completed. The first volume deals with the social work of Leo XIII, the second with his relations with Italy and France, and the third with relations with Germany). The first two volumes have been translated into English, London, 1934-5.
M. SPAHN, *Leo XIII.*, Munich, 1915.
L. P. WALLACE, *Leo XIII and the Rise of Socialism*, Duke, 1966.

Pius X

L. BEDESCHI, *La Curia Romana durante la crisi modernista*, Parma, 1968.
C. FALCONI, *The Popes in the Twentieth Century*, London, 1967.
CH. LEDRÉ, *Pie X*, Paris, 1952. See the acute comments by the same author in *Revue d'histoire de l'Église de France*, XL (1954), 249-67.
J. SCHMIDLIN, *Papstgeschichte . . .*, vol. III, 1-177.
N. VIAN, *S. Pius Pp. X*, 2nd ed., Padua, 1958.

Chapter 2
THE CHURCH AND THE EUROPEAN REVOLUTIONS OF 1848

At Rome

The most recent account of the matter, the first to make systematic use of the Vatican archives, is found in the fourth and subsequent chapters of extremely fine analysis in G. Martina, *Pio nono, 1846-50*, Rome, 1974. Among earlier publications (earlier literature in G. Mollat, *La Question Romaine de Pie VI à Pie XI*, 2nd ed., (Paris, 1932), 35-7, 198-9, 215-16, 225-6, 242-3, 259-60, 268; more recent bibliography in *Handbuch der Kirchengeschichte*, vol. VI, 1, pp. 477-8), the following deserve mention (in addition to those cited in notes 1-4 of this chapter): P. PIRRI, *Pio IX e Vittorio Emanuele II dal loro carteggio privato*, vol. I, Rome, 1944.

D. DEMARCO, *Pio IX e la rivoluzione romana del 1848*, Modena, 1947.

A. M. GHISALBERTI, *Roma da Mazzini a Pio IX*, Rome, 1958.

A. de LIEDEKERKE, *Rapporti delle cosi di Roma, 1848-1849*, ed. A. M. Ghisalberti, Rome, 1949.

In France

J.-B. DUROSELLE, *Les Débuts du catholicisme social en France* (Paris, 1951), 291-490.

M. HERBERT and A. CORNEC, *La Loi Falloux et la Liberté d'enseignement*, La Rochelle, 1953.

J. LEFLON, *L'Église de France et la Révolution de 1848*, Paris, 1948.

In Germany

For a general background, see J. Droz, *Les Révolutions allemandes de 1848*, Paris, 1957.

Short survey in G. Goyau, *L'Allemagne religieuse*, vol. II (Paris, 1905), chapter V, and J. Droz, *op. cit.*, 481-503.

Chapter 3
THE CHURCH AND LIBERALISM

R. AUBERT, J.-B. DUROSELLE and A. JEMOLO, 'Le Libéralisme religieux au XIXᵉ siècle', *X Congresso internazionale di Scienze storiche. Relazioni*, vol. V (Forence, 1955), 305-83.

M. BARTHÉLEMY-MADAULE, *Marc Sangnier*, Paris, 1973.

The excellent work of E. Weber, *L'Action française*, Stanford (Cal.), 1962, may be supplemented as to the attitude of Catholics and the Vatican by that of L. Thomas, *L'Action française devant l'Église de Pie X à Pie XII*, Paris, 1965 (this gives the standpoint of Action française) and by the critical comments of A. Latreille in *Cahiers d'histoire*, X (1965), 388-401.

N. BLAKISTON, *The Roman Question. Extracts from the despatches of O. Russell, 1858-1870*, London, 1972.

L. BRIGUÉ, '*Syllabus*', *D.T.C.*, vol. XIV, cols 2877-923.

J. CARON, *Le Sillon et la Démocratie chrétienne, 1894-1910*, Paris, 1967 (fundamental; precision is given on an important point by M. Launay's article, cited in n.23).

Les catholiques libéraux au XIXᵉ siècle, Lyons, 1974. Proceedings of the international congress in Grenoble in 1971. Richly informative.

Chiesa e Statto nell' Ottocento. Miscellanea in onore di P. Pirri, 2 vols, Padua, 1962.

C. CONSTANTIN, 'Libéralisme catholique', *D.T.C.*, vol. IX, cols 506-629.

La fine del potere temporale e il recongiungimento di Roma all'Italia, Rome, 1972 (congress of 1970; in particular, a wide international survey on 'La fine del potere temporale nella coscienza religiosa e nella cultura del tempo', 41-214).

G. P. FOGARTY, *The Vatican and the Americanist Crisis, Denis J. O'Connell, American Agent in Rome, 1885-1903*, Rome, 1974.

S. W. HALPERIN, *The Separation of Church and State in Italian Thought from Cavour to Mussolini*, Chicago, 1937.

A. C. JEMOLO, *Church and State in Italy, 1850-1950*, Oxford, 1960.

T. T. McAVOY, *The Great Crisis in American Catholic History, 1895-1900*, Chicago, 1957.

D. McELRATH, *The Syllabus of Pius IX. Some Reactions in England*. Louvain, 1964

M. MOLLAT, *La Question romaine de Pie VI à Pie XI*, Paris, 1932.

J. N. MOODY, ed., *Church and Society, Catholic social and political Thought and Movements, 1789-1850*, New York, 1953.

J. C. MURRAY, '*Leo XIII· on Church and State*', in *Theological Studies*, XIV (1953), 1-30, 145-214, 551-67.

J. C. MURRAY, 'The problem of "the religion of the State" ', *American Ecclesiastical Review*, CCXXIV (1951), 327-52.

P. PIRRI, *Pio IX e Vittorio Emanuele II dal loro carteggio privato*, 5 vols, Rome, 1944-60 (texts of documents preceded by long and systematic summaries based on the Vatican archives).

A. SIMON, *L'Hypothèse libérale en Belgique*, Wetteren, 1956, and *Catholicisme et Politique, ibid.*, 1955.

W. WARD, *W. G. Ward and the Catholic Revival*, London, 1893.

W. WARD, *The Wilfrid Wards and the Transition*, 2 vols, London, 1934-6.

For the liberal Catholics of the *Rambler*, see the bibliography to chapter 11 of the present work.

G. WEILL, *Histoire du catholicisme libéral en France*, Paris, 1909.

Also the thesis of J. GADILLE, *La Pensée et l'Action politique des évêques français au début de la III ᵉ République (1870-1883)*, 2 vols, Paris, 1967; the classic work, but one systematically favourable to the liberal Catholics, is P. E. LECANUET, *L'Église de France sous la IIIᵉ République*, 4 vols, Paris 1907-30; M. PRELOT and F. GALLOUEDEC-GENUYS, *Le Libéralisme catholique* (coll. U), Paris, 1969 (documents).

Chapter 4
PROGRESSIVE CENTRALISATION ON ROME

General survey in R. Aubert, *Le Pontificat de Pie IX*, 262-310 (additions 537-41). On Vatican I the best survey is that of C. Butler, *The Vatican Council. The Story told from inside in Bp Ullathorne's Letters*, 2 vols, London, 1930; the most recent is that of R. Aubert, *Vatican I*, Paris, 1964; the most complete from the Catholic point of view is that of Th. Granderath, *Geschichte des Vaticanischen Konzils*, 3 vols, Fribourg-in-Bresgau, 1903-6 (French tr. Brussels, 1906-13), very defensive in tone; and from the point of view of the Old Catholics, that of J. Freidrich, *Geschichte des*

Vaticanischen Konzils, 3 vols, Nördlingen, 1877-87; the use of M. Ichard's Journal gives a permanent value to F. Mourret, *Le Concile du Vatican,* Paris, 1919; H. Rondet, *Vatican I,* Paris, 1962, gives particular attention to aspects that have usually been neglected (such as the preparation of the schemata, methods of procedure, suspended proposals). See also, for the diplomatic side of events, and for portraits of individuals, E. Ollivier, *L'Église et l'État au concile du Vatican,* 2 vols, Paris, 1877.

J. CWIEKOWSKI, *The English Bishops and the First Vatican Council,* Louvain, 1971.

J. GADILLE, *A. du Boijs. L'intervention du gouvernement impérial à Vatican I,* Louvain, 1968 (takes a new look at various aspects of the subject, especially those concerning the part played by Dupanloup).

J. J. HENNESEY, *The First Vatican Council. The American Experience,* New York, 1963.

M. MACCARRONE, *Il Concilio Vaticano,* 2 vols, Padua, 1966.

D. McELRATH, *Lord Acton. The Decisive Decade,* Louvain (1970), 141-83.

J.-R. PALANQUE, *Catholiques libéraux et gallicans en France face au concile du Vatican,* Aix-en-Provence, 1962.

Chapter 5

THE LOCAL CHURCHES OF CONTINENTAL EUROPE

France

Dom DELATTE, *Dom Guéranger, abbé de Solesmes,* 2 vols, Paris, 1909.

J. GADILLE, *La Pensée et l'Action politiques des évêques français au début de la Troisième République, 1870-1883,* 2 vols, Paris, 1967.

E. GRIFFITHS, *The Reactionary Revolution. The Catholic Revival in French Literature, 1870-1914,* London, 1966.

M. de HEDOUVILLE, *Mgr De Ségur,* Paris, 1957.

F.-A. ISAMBERT. *Christianisme et Classe ouvrière,* Paris-Tournai, 1960.
On Catholic life and works of charity there is the information contained in the outdated and far too exclusively favourable work of Mgr Baunard, *Un siècle de l'Église de France, 1800-1900,* Paris, 1901.

F. LAGRANGE, *Vie de Mgr Dupanloup,* 3 vols, Paris, 1883-4.

M. LARKIN, 'The Church and the French Concordat, 1891-1902', *English Historical Review,* LXXXI (1966), 717-39, and 'The Vatican, French Catholics and the Association culturelles', *Journal of Modern History,* XXXVI (1964), 298-317.

E. LECANUET, *L'Église de France sous la Troisième République,* 4 vols, Paris, 1907-30 (down to 1910; from a liberal Catholic standpoint).

E. LECANUET, *Montalembert,* 3 vols, Paris, 1896-1902 (see also A. Trannoy, *Charles de Montalembert. Dieu et la liberté,* Paris, 1970).

J. McMANNERS, *Church and State in France, 1870-1914,* London, 1972.

J. MAURAIN, *La Politique ecclésiastique du Second Empire,* Paris, 1930.

J.-M. MAYEUR, *Un prêtre démocrate, l'abbé Lemire,* Paris, 1968.

L.-V. MEJEAN, *La Séparation des Églises et de l'État,* Paris, 1959 (many unpublished documents).

X. de MONTCLOS, *Lavigerie, le Saint-Siège et l'Église, 1846-78,* Paris, 1965.

644 BIBLIOGRAPHY

X. de MONTCLOS, *Le Toast d'Alger*, Paris, 1966.
M. OZOUF, *L'École, l'Église et la République, 1871-1914*, Paris, 1963.
E. and Fr. VEUILLOT, *Louis Veuillot*, 4 vols, Paris, 1899-1913.
J. E. WARD, 'The French Cardinals and Leo XIII's Ralliement policy', *Church History*, XXXIII (1964), 60-73.

Italy

The bibliography is very abundant and, especially during the last twenty years, of high quality. It may be followed with the aid of the lists which appear regularly in the principal reviews. Here, only works of more general scope will be mentioned.

In addition to the works of wide scope mentioned above (p. 639), and the chapters relating to Italy in M. Vaussard, *L'Histoire de la démocratie chrétienne* (Paris, 1956), 199-241, there are two excellent small guides, F. Fonzi, *I cattolici e la società italiana dopo l'Unità* (coll. *Universale Studium*, no. 20) 2nd ed., Rome, 1960 (good critical bibliography), and P. Scoppola, *Dal neoguelfismo alla Democrazia cristiana* (same collection, no. 51), Rome, 1957 (augmented by a collection of texts: *Dal neoguelfismo alla democrazia cristiana. Antologia di documenti*, Rome, 1963).

Note also for a general survey of the period: A. P IOLA, *La Questione Romana nella storia e nel diritto da Cavour al Trattato del Laterano*, Rome, 1931 (reprinted Milan, 1969).

For the third quarter of the 19th century, in addition to the general survey in R. Aubert – G. Martina, *Il pontificato di Pio IX*, 2nd ed. (Turin, 1970), 119-82, 563-73 (with a very full bibliographical introduction, 14-22) and the references given (p. 641) on the Roman Question, see particularly:

Chiesa e religiosità in Italia dopo l'Unità (1861-1878), 4 vols, Milan, 1973-4 (proceedings of the La Mendola conference 1971).

See also:

A. C. JEMOLO, *La questione delle proprietà ecclesiastiche nel Regno d'Italia (1848-1888)*, Turin, 1911 (see also G. Jacquemyns, in *Revue belge de philologie et d'histoire*, XLII (1964), 442-94, 1257-91).
C. BELLÒ, *Geremia Bonomelli*, Brescia, 1961.
S. W. HALPERIN, 'Italian anti-clericalism 1871-1914', *Journal of Modern History*, XIX (1947), 18-34.
H. L. HUGHES, *The Catholic Revival in Italy, 1815-1915*, London, 1935.
G. SPADOLINI, *Giolitti e i cattolici*, 2nd ed., Florence, 1960.
G. SPADOLINI, *L'opposizione cattolica da Porta Pia al'98*, 4th ed., Florence, 1961 (with details added in *R.st. Ris.*, XLI (1954), 865-73).
P. STELLA, *Don Bosco nella storia della religiosità cattolica*, 2 vols, Zurich-Rome, 1968-9.

Germany

German studies have concentrated more than French or Italian on the politico-religious aspect (for other aspects, see also the bibliographies to the chapters that follow). This is the perspective governing the largely out-dated work of H. Bruck and J.-B. Kissling, *Geschichte der Katholischen Kirche in Deutschland im 19. Jht.*, vols III and IV, Munster, 1902-8 (with a very ultramontane outlook). To this should be added chapters 2-4 of J. Rovan, *Le Catholicisme politique en Allemagne*, Paris, 1956, and K. Bachem, *Vorgeschichte, Geschichte und Politik der deutschen Zentrumspartei zugleich ein Beitrag zur Geschichte der Katholischen Bewegung*, 9 vols, Cologne, 1926-32 (reprinted 1967; it gives the facts, but has a propagandist bias; compare K. Epstein, *Catholic Historical Review*, XLIV (1958), 2).

A. DRU, *The Contribution of German Catholicism*, New York, 1963.

E. FOERSTER, *A. Falk*, Gotha, 1927.

J. FRIEDRICH, *Ignaz von Döllinger*, 3 vols, Munich, 1899-1901.

G. GOYAU, *Bismarck et l'Église. Le Kulturkampf, 1870-1887*, 4 vols, Paris, 1911-13.

J. HECKEL, 'Die Beilegung des Kulturkampfs in Preussen', *Zeitschrift der Savigny-Stiftung für Rechtsgeschichte, Kanonistische Abt.*, XIX (1930), 215-353. This is still the best study of the dissolution of the Kulturkampf, by reason of its use of a new archival store of documents.

L. LENHART, *Bischof Ketteler*, 3 vols, Mainz, 1966-8.

R. LILL, *Die Wende im Kulturkampf*, Tübingen, 1973.

E. SODERINI, *Il pontificato di Leone XIII*, vol. III, Milan, 1933. A critical assessment of works subsequent to 1945 is given by R. Morsey in *Archiv für Kulturgeschichte*, XXXIX (1957), 232-70, and *Historisches Jahrbuch*, LXXXIII (1964), 217-45 (see also the same author's 'Bismarck und der Kulturkampf', *Archiv für Kirchengeschichte*, XXXIX (1957), 232-70.

F. VIGENER, *Ketteler*, Munich, 1924.

G. G. WINDELL, *Catholicism and German Unity*, Minneapolis, 1954.

Austria-Hungary

G. ADRIÁNYI, *50 Jahre ungarischer Kirchengeschichte, 1895-1945*, Mainz, 1974.

M. CSAKY, *Der Kulturkampf in Ungarn*, Gratz, 1967.

Fr. ENGEL-JANOSI, *Oesterreich und der Vatikan*, 2 vols, Gratz, 1958-60 (from Pius IX to Benedict XV).

A. FUCHS, *Geistige Strömungen in Oesterreich, 1867-1918*, Vienna, 1949.

E. WEINZIERL-FISCHER, *Die österreichischen Konkordate von 1855 und 1933*, Vienna, 1960.

Spain

Many aspects of politico-religious history have been treated with insight in the monographs of J. M. Cuenca. Some of these have been included in the volume *La Iglesia española ante la Revolución liberal*, Madrid, 1971, and *Estudios sobre la Iglesia española del XIX*, Madrid, 1973.

C. J. BARTLETT, 'The question of religious toleration in the XIXth century', *Journal of Ecclesiastical History*, VIII (1957), 205-16 (on the slow penetration of Protestant influence).

W. G. KIERNAN, *The Revolution of 1854 in Spanish History*, Oxford, 1966.

Belgium

There is a detailed Bibliography in *Handbuch der Kirchengeschichte*, vol. VI-1, p. 360, and vol. VI-2, p. 112.

Among published sources, note particularly those with valuable introductions that we owe to A. Simon: *Réunion des évêques de Belgique. Procès-verbaux*, 2 vols, Louvain-Paris, 1960-1 (from 1830 to 1883); *Instructions aux nonces de Bruxelles, 1835-1889*, Brussels-Rome, 1961.

M. BECQUÉ, *Le Cardinal Dechamps*, 2 vols, Louvain, 1956.

'Prêtres de Belgique, 1830-1930', *Nouvelle Revue théologique*, LVII (1930), 617-744.

A. SIMON, *Le Cardinal Mercier*, Brussels, 1960.

A. SIMON, *Le Cardinal Sterckx et son temps*, 2 vols, Wetteren, 1950.

A. SIMON, *Le Parti catholique belge*, Brussels, 1958.

Switzerland

In addition to the chapters on the period in T. Schwegler, *Geschichte der Katholischen Kirche in der Schweiz*, Stans, 1945, see:

E. DANCOURT, *Un demi-siècle de luttes religieuses dans le canton de Berne*, 2 vols, Porrentruy, 1936.

A. LINDT, *Protestanten, Katholiken, Kulturkampf*, Zurich, 1963.

W. MARTIN, *La Situation du catholicisme à Genève (1815-1907)*, Lausanne, 1909.

Russia

N. BOCK, *Russia and the Vatican on the Eve of the Revolution*, New York, 1952.

K. GÓRSKI, in *Millénaire du catholicisme en Pologne* (Lublin, 1969), 332-54, on the spiritual life.

S. OLSZAMOWSKA-SKOWRONSKA, *La Correspondance des papes et des empereurs de Russie (1814-1878)*, Rome, 1970.

Chapter 6

THE VITALITY OF THE CHRISTIAN FAITH

On the fortunes of monasticism in the 19th century see *Revue bénédictine*, LXXXIII (1973), 7-284. Also G. Penco, *Storia del monachesimo in Italia nell'epoca moderna*, Rome, 1968.

R. CHAPMAN, *Father Faber*, London, 1961.

J.-M. DERELY, 'Les décrets eucharistiques de Pie X', *Nouvelle Revue théologique* LXXIII, (1951), 897-911 and 1033-48.

R. FOURREY, *Le Curé d'Ars authentique*, Paris, 1964.

A. HAMON, *Histoire de la dévotion au Sacré-Coeur*, vol. 4, Paris, 1931. See also the same author in *Dictionnaire de spiritualité*, II, 1037-42.

R. LAURENTIN, *Thérèse de Lisieux. Mythes et réalité*, Paris, 1972.

H. du MANOIR, ed., *Maria*, vol. III, Paris, 1954.

M. NÉDONCELLE, *Les leçons spirituelles du XIXe siècle*, Paris, 1936.

O. ROUSSEAU, *Histoire du mouvement liturgique*, Paris, 1945.

Chapter 7

PASTORAL WORK AND CATHOLIC ACTION

J. ROGÉ, *Le Simple Prêtre*, Paris-Tournai, 1965 (particularly for the Latin countries).

J.-B. KISSLING, *Geschichte der deutschen Katholikentage*, 3 vols, Munster, 1920-1.

P. PIERRARD, *Le Prêtre français*, Paris, 1969.
On the development of pastoral methods, besides the indications given by M.-H. Vicaire (in G. de Plinval, ed., *Histoire illustrée de l'Église*, Paris-Geneva, 1948, vol. II, 261-326), Daniel-Rops (*L'Église des révolutions*, vol. I, 882-97) and, more briefly, by R. Aubert (*Le Pontificat de Pie IX*, 451-6), see: R. RÉMOND, *Les Congrès ecclésiastiques de Reims et de Bourges, 1896-1900*, Paris, 1964. See also the fully documented introduction by É. Poulat to the new edition of *Journal d'un prêtre d'après-demain (1902-1903) de l'abbé Calippe*, Paris-Tournai, 1961.
On the Catholic press, much information will be found in 'Catholic Press', *New Catholic Encyclopedia*, III, 283-327, also J. Morienval, *Sur l'histoire de la presse catholique en France*, Colmar, 1936.

V. BACHELET, ed., *Spiritualità e azione del laicato cattolico italiano*, 2 vols, Padua, 1969.

K. BRULS, *Geschichte des Volksvereins*, vol. I, Munster, 1960 (1890-1914).

G. FELICIANI, 'Azione colletiva e organizzazzione nazionale dell'episcopato cattolico da Pio IX a Leone XIII', *Storia contemporanea*, III (1972), 325-63 (bibliography).

A. GAMBASIN, *Gerarchia e laicato in Italia nel secondo Ottocento*, Padua, 1969.

A. GAMBASIN, *Il movimento sociale nell'Opera dei Congressi*, Rome, 1958 (important as being based on the archives of the 'Opera').

Ch. MOLETTE, *L'Association catholique de la jeunesse française, 1886-1907*, Paris, 1968.

R. OSBAT and F. PIVA, eds, *La 'Gioventù cattolica' dopo l'Unità, 1868-1968*, Rome, 1972 (11 Italian contributions, with a general survey from 1867 to 1922 by D. Veneroso, 3-137).

W. SPAEL, *Das Katholische Deutschland im 20. Jahrhundert*, Würzburg, 1964 (1st part, 1890-1918).

Chapter 8

THE BEGINNINGS OF SOCIAL CATHOLICISM

There is a large bibliography on the subject, and while enthusiastic popular accounts are noteworthy, there are also a number of publications of a scientific nature.

A first impression may be gained from R. Aubert, *Le Christianisme social*, Moscow, 1970 (report presented at the Thirteenth International Congress of Historical Sciences, which touches also the Protestant achievement). There are several general surveys.

K. H. BRÜLS, *Geschichte der Katholisch-sozialen Bewegung in Deutschland*, Munster, 1958.

R. L. CAMP, *The Papal Ideology of Social Reform. A Study in Historical Development, 1878-1967*, Leyden, 1969.

J. M. CUENCA, *El P. A. Vicent y los origenes del catolicismo social en España*, Madrid, 1972.

J.-B. DUROSELLE, *Les Débuts du catholicisme social en France, 1822-1870*, Paris, 1951.

E. FILTHAUT, *Deutsche Katholikentage 1848-1958 und Sociale Frage*, Essen, 1960.

M. P. FOGARTY, *Christian Democracy in Western Europe, 1820-1953*, London, 1957.

A. GAMBASIN, *Il movimento sociale nell' Opera dei Congressi, 1874-1904*, Rome, 1958.

G. GUITTON, *Léon Harmel*, Paris, 1930.

G. JARLOT, *Doctrine pontificale et histoire. L'enseignement social de Léon XIII, Pie X et Benoît XV vu dans son ambiance historique*, Rome, 1964.

R. KOTHEN, *La Pensée et l'Action sociale des catholiques*, Louvain, 1945.

Ch. MOLETTE, *Albert de Mun. Exigence doctrinale et préoccupations sociales chez un laïc catholique*, Paris, 1970.

J. N. MOODY, ed., *Church and Society, Catholic Social and Political Thought and Movements, 1789-1950*, New York, 1953.

É. POULAT, *Église contre bourgeoisie*, Paris, 1977, Especially chapter IV and V (very important).

R. REZSOHAZY, *Origines et Formation du catholicisme social en Belgique*, Louvain, 1958.

R. RUFFIEUX, *Le Mouvement chrétien social en Suisse romande, 1891-1949*, Fribourg, 1969.

S.-H. SCHOLL, ed., *Cent cinquante ans de mouvement ouvrier chrétien en Europe occidentale*, Brussels, 1966 (with well-informed articles, giving bibliographical information, on the Vatican, Germany, Austria, Belgium, Spain, France, Great Britain, Italy, Holland, Portugal and Switzerland).

G. SILBERBAUER, *Oesterreichskatholiken und die Arbeiterfrage*, Gratz, 1966.

Chapter 9

THE GRADUAL REVIVAL OF THE ECCLESIASTICAL DISCIPLINES

General survey, with bibliography, in E. Hocedez, *Histoire de la théologie au XIX* siècle*, vols II and III, Brussels, 1947-52. More briefly in *Handbuch der Kirchengeschichte*, vol. VI-1, pp. 672-95, and VI-2, pp. 316-41 (for the third quarter of the 19th century, see also R. Aubert, *Le Pontificat de Pie IX*, 184-223, 526-31).

R. AUBERT, 'Le grand tournant de la faculté de théologie du Louvain à la veille de 1900', in *Mélanges offerts à M.-D. Chenu* (Paris, 1967), 73-109.

H. FRIES and G. SCHWAIGER, eds, *Katholische Theologen Deutschlands im 19. Jahrhundert*, 3 vols, Munich, 1975.

L. SCHEFFCZYK, *Theologie in Aufbruch und Widerstreit. Die deutsche Katholische Theologie im 19. Jahrhundert*, Bremen, 1965.

F. TRANIELO, 'Cultura ecclesiastica e cultura cattolica', *Chiesa e religiosità in Italia dopo l'Unità*, vol. II, Milan (1973), 3-28.

For the conflict between Scholastic theology and the 'German theologians', see in particular vol. III, well documented but partisan, of J. Friedrich, *Ignaz von Doellinger*, Munich, 1901. See also:

R. LILL, 'Die deutschen Theologieprofessoren im Urteil des Münchener Nuntius', *Reformata reformanda. Festgabe für H. Jedin* (Munster 1965), 483-508.

For Günther and his condemnation:
P. WENZEL, *Das wissenschaftliche Anliegen des Güntherianismus*, Essen, 1961 (much new material on the followers and supporters of Günther).

On Döllinger:
St. J. TONSOR, 'Lord Acton on Döllinger's historical theology', *Journal of the History of Ideas*, XX (1959), 329-52.

For Christian philosophy and the rebirth of Thomism:
R. AUBERT, 'Aspects divers du néo-thomisme sous le pontificat de Léon XIII', in *Aspetti della cultura cattolica nell'età di Leone XIII* (Rome 1961), 133-227.

L. FOUCHER, *La Philosophie catholique en France au XIXe siècle*, Paris, 1955.

For Blondel and Immanentism:
P. BEILLEVERT, ed., *Laberthonnière. L'Homme et l'œuvre*, Paris, 1972.
E. LECANUET,*La Vie de l'Église sous Léon XIII*, Paris (1930), 487-583.

For Newman and the problem of belief:
A. T. BOCHRAAD and H. TRISTAM, *The Argument from Conscience to the Existence of God according to J. H. Newman*, Louvain, 1961.

For the movement of renewal in church history:
R. AUBERT, 'Un demi-siècle de revues d'histoire ecclésiastique', *Rivista di storia della Chiesa in Italia*, XIV (1960), 173-202.
H. DELEHAYE, *L'Oeuvre des bollandistes*, Brussels (1959), 149-65.
L. von PASTOR, *Tagebücher*, ed. W. Wühr, Heidelberg, 1950.

For progress in archaeology:
G. FERETRO, *Note storico-bibliografiche di archeologia cristiana*, Vatican City, 1942.

For the question of biblical criticism:
Many details in the *Mémoires* of A. Loisy (vol. I, Paris, 1930) and in *Le Père Lagrange au service de la Bible. Souvenirs personnels*, Paris, 1969.
J. COPPENS, *Le Chanoine A. van Hoonacker*, Paris, 1935.

Chapter 10

THE MODERNIST CRISIS AND THE 'INTEGRIST' REACTION

Many documents connected with the modernist crisis are still unpublished, but a great effort has been made to assemble materials, and a certain number are now available to historians, in particular the Loisy papers at the Bibliothèque Nationale in Paris, the von Hügel papers at St Andrews University, the Tyrrell papers at the British Museum, the Blondel papers at the Institut supèrieure de philosophie, Louvain, the Mignot papers in the diocesan archives of Albi and Rodez. The pace of publication of the sources has been quickening during the past ten years, and to the *Mémoires* of A. Loisy, 3 vols, Paris, 1930-1, and some of their successors (A. Houtin, *Une vie de prêtre*, Paris, 1926; J. Turmel, *Comment j'ai donné congé aux dogmes*, Paris, 1935; M. Petre, *My Way of Faith*, London, 1937), as also to those of G. Semeria, *I miei tempi*, Milan, 1929, and of E. Buonaiuti, *Pellegrino di Roma*, Rome, 1945, and to a selection of letters of Tyrrell, (edited by M. Petre, London, 1920), von Hügel (edited by B. Holland), and Fogazzaro (edited by T. Gallarati Scotti, Milan, 1940), have now been added various collections of correspondence which often supply new information or important glimpses of outlook: First, the correspondence of M. Blondel with A. Valensin (ed. H. de Lubac, 3 vols, Paris, 1957-65), J. Wehrlé (ed. H. de Lubac, 2 vols, Paris, 1969), L. Laberthonnière (ed. Ch. Tresmontant, Paris, 1961) and H. Bremond (ed. A. Blanchet, 3 vols, Paris, 1970-1).

M. BÉCAMEL, ed., Letters from Loisy to Mgr Mignot, in *Bulletin de littérature ecclésiastique*, LXVII (1966), 3-44, 81-114, 170-94, 257-86, and LXIX (1968), 241-68.

H. BERNARD-MAÎTRE, ed., 'Lettres d'H. Bremond à A. Loisy', *ibid.*, LXIX (1968), 3-24, 161-84, 269-89.

R. MARLÉ, ed., *Au coeur de la crise moderniste. Le dossier inédit d'une controverse*, Paris, 1960 (letters of Loisy, Blondel, von Hügel, etc.).

M.-Th. PERRIN, *Laberthonnière et ses amis. Dossiers de correspondance*, Paris, 1975.

Lettres de G. Tyrrell à H. Bremond, trans. by A. Louis-David, Paris, 1971.

The letters of Tyrrell published by J. H. Craham and by Th. Loome in *The Month* CCXXVI (1968), 178-85; CCXXIX (1969), 95-101, 138-49; CCXXXI (1971), 111-19.

The accounts written immediately after the crisis (noted in J. Rivière, *op. cit.*, xxi-xxv) are tendentious, but are valuable as evidence by eyewitnesses. The classic work of J. Rivière, *Le Modernisme dans l'Église*, Paris, 1929, although now superseded on certain matters, remains the best synthesis. See, however, also:

O. SCHROEDER, *Aufbruch und Missverständnis. Zur Geschichte der reformkatholischen Bewegung*, Gratz, 1969.

A. VIDLER, *The Modernist Movement in the Roman Church*, Cambridge, 1934, and *A Variety of Catholic Modernists*, Cambridge, 1970.

Modernism in France

The fundamental work is that of É. Poulat, *Histoire, dogme et critique dans la crise moderniste*, Paris-Tournai, 1962 (cf. *Revue historique*, CCXXX (1963), 262-7), with a most useful appendix on 'Pseudonymes et anonymes modernistes', 621-77.

R. BOYER de SAINTE-SUZANNE, *A. Loisy entre la foi et l'incroyance*, Paris, 1968.

A. HOUTIN and F. SARTIAUX, *A. Loisy. Sa vie, son oeuvre*, ed. É. Poulat, Paris, 1960.

On Bremond and Modernism

É. POULAT, *Une oeuvre clandestine d'H. Bremond*, Rome, 1972. See also J. Dagens, ed., *Entretiens sur H. Bremond*, Paris-Le Haye (1967), 43-98.

Modernism in England

Besides the general works, already listed, by J. Rivière and A. Vidler, see:

L. F. BARMANN, *Baron von Hügel and the Modernist Crisis in England*, Cambridge, 1972.

M. de la BEDOYÈRE, *The Life of Baron von Hügel*, London, 1951.

Th. LOOME, 'The enigma of Baron von Hügel', *Downside Review*, XCI (1973).

13-34 (excellent review of the sources), 123-40, 204-30 (very suggestive, especially for the period of intellectual adolescence).

On G. Tyrrell, in default of a good general study, the essential work remains that of M. D. Petre, *Autobiography and Life of G. Tyrrell*, London, 2 vols. 1912. M. WARD, *The Wilfrid Wards and the Transition*, vol. I, London (1937), 134-420.

Modernism in the United States
J. RATTÉ, *Three Modernists, A. Loisy, G. Tyrrell, W. L. Sullivan*, New York, 1967.

Modernism in Italy
L. BEDESCHI, *La Curia romana durante la crisi modernista*, Parma, 1968.
L. BEDESCHI, *Lineamenti dell'antimodernismo, il caso Lanzoni*, Parma, 1970.
L. BEDESCHI, in *Nuova rivista storica*, LIV (1970), 125-76; LV (1971), 90-132; LVI (1972), 389-412.
M. C. CASELLA, *Religious Liberalism in Modern Italy*, 2 vols. London, 1966.
Centro Studi per la storia del Modernismo, *Fonti e documenti*, 5 vols, Urbino, 1972-77.
T. GALLARATI-SCOTTI, *La vita di A. Fogazzaro*, Milan, 1920 (3rd ed., 1963).
M. GUASCO, *R. Murri e il modernismo*, Rome, 1968 (with bibliography).
P. SCOPPOLA, *Crisi modernista e rinnovamento cattolico*, 2nd ed., Bologna, 1969.

The Anti-Modernist Reaction
The publication by É. Poulat *Intégrisme et catholicisme intégral*, Tournai-Paris, 1969, of all the documents at present available concerning the action of Mgr Benigni, and especially the penetrating introduction and abundant notes which accompany his edition, have given new life to the issue. See also the article by the same author, ' "Modernisme" et "Intégrisme". Du concept polémique à l'irénisme critique', *Archives de sociologie des religions*, no. 27 (1969), 3-28; 'La dernière bataille du pontificat de Pie X', *Rivista di storia della Chiesa in Italia*, XXV (1971), 83-107; A. Blanchet, *Histoire d'une mise à l'Index: la 'Sainte Chantal' de l'abbé Bremond*, Paris, 1967.

Chapter 11

GREAT BRITAIN: THE REBIRTH OF A CHURCH

On Catholicism in England during the whole of this period, there is a rapid outline in D. Mathew, *Catholicism in England, the Portrait of a Minority*, 2nd ed. (London 1948), 187-278, and much information in the collective works of G. Beck, ed., *The English Catholics, 1850-1950. A Century of Progress*, London, 1950, and *Catholicisme anglais*, Paris, 1958.

For the first half of the century, Part Three of J. Bossy, *The English Catholic Community 1570-1850* is useful.

For the second half of the nineteenth century, the masterly work of O. Chadwick, *The Victorian Church*, 2 vols, London, 1966-70, provides an excellent backdrop (for matters concerning Roman Catholicism, see vol. I, 271-309 and II, 401-22). The two oldest works, by W. Ward, *William George Ward and the Catholic Revival*, London, 1893, and P. Thureau-Danguin, *La Renaissance catholique en Angleterre*, vols II and III, Paris, 1903-6, are still very useful.

E. R. NORMAN, *Anti-Catholicism in Victorian England*, London 1968, reproduces twenty texts preceded by a good hundred-page introduction on four typical cases.

Among the monographs, note particularly:

J. HICKEY, *Urban Catholicism in England and Wales from 1829 to the Present Day*, London, 1967 (sociological aspects).

D. MCELRATH, *The 'Syllabus' of Pius X. Some Reactions in England*, London, 1963.

D. MILBURN, *A History of Ushaw College*, Durham 1964 (for the development of clergy training).

On Irish Catholics in England, see the contribution by D. Gwynn in vol. VI, part 1 of P. J. Corish, ed., *A History of Irish Catholicism*, Dublin, 1968 (referring to many unpublished theses).

On the liberal Catholic trend, the tendentious book by A. Gasquet, *Lord Acton and His Circle*, London, 1906 (cf. *Cambridge Historical Journal*, X (1950), 77-105), needs supplementing and moderating by:

J. L. ALTHOLZ, *The Liberal Catholic Movement in England. The 'Rambler' and its Contributors, 1848-1864*, London, 1962.

J. L. ALTHOLZ and D. MCELRATH, eds, *The Correspondence of Lord Acton and R. Simpson*, 3 vols, Cambridge, 1971-75.

V. CONZEMIUS, ed., *I. von Döllinger, Briefwechsel mit Lord Acton*, 3 vols, Munich, 1963-71.

A. MacDOUGALL, *The Acton-Newman Relations*, New York, 1962.

D. MCELRATH, *R. Simpson. A Study in XIXth-century English Liberal Catholicism*, Louvain, 1972.

For the turn of the nineteenth to the twentieth century, see M. Ward, *The Wilfrid Wards and the Transition*, 2 vols, London, 1934-8.

On the Halifax-Portal campaign over Anglican orders, see J. J. Hughes, *Absolutely Null and Utterly Void. The Papal Condemnation of Anglican Orders*, London, 1968 (from the Anglican viewpoint see also T. A. Lacey, *A Roman Diary and Other Documents*, London, 1910); R. Ladous, *L'Abbé Portal et la Campagne anglo-romaine, 1890-1912*, Lyons, 1973.

For the last decades, S. Dayras and C. d'Haussy, *Le Catholicisme en Angleterre* (collection U²), Paris, 1970.

In Anglo-Saxon historiography, biographies occupy a particularly important place, all the more so because they often reproduce numerous documents, especially the oldest.

N. ABERCROMBIE, *The Life and Work of Edmund Bishop*, London, 1959.

L. BOUYER, *Newman. Sa vie, sa spiritualité*, Paris, 1952.

C. BUTLER, *The Life and Times of Bishop Ullathorne, 1806-1889*, 2 vols, London, 1926.

R. CHAPMAN, *Father Faber*, London, 1961.

L. COGNET, *Newman ou la Recherche de la vérité*, Paris, 1967.

C. S. DESSAIN, *John Henry Newman*, London, 1966.

C. S. DESSAIN, V. BLEHL and T. GORNALL, eds, *The Letters and Diaries of John Henry Newman*, XI-XXXI (1845-90), London, 1961-77 (to be continued).

J. FITZSIMMONS, ed., *Manning, Anglican and Catholic*, London, 1951.

J. HONORÉ, *Itinéraire spirituel de Newman*, Paris, 1964.

C. LESLIE, *Cardinal Gasquet*, London, 1953.

S. LESLIE, *Henry Edward Manning*, London, 1921.

J. G. LOCKHART, *Ch. Lindley Viscount Halifax*, 2 vols, London, 1936.

V. A. MCCLELLAND, *Cardinal Manning, His Public Life and Influence, 1865-1892*, London, 1963.

A. MCCORMACK, *Cardinal Vaughan*, London, 1966.

D. MCELRATH et al., *Lord Acton. The Decisive Decade, 1864-1874*, Louvain, 1970 (in which earlier studies, as well as partial editions of Acton's correspondence, are noted).

C. MARTINDALE, *Charles Dominic Plater, S. J.*, London, 1972.

D. MATHEW, *Lord Acton and His Times*, London, 1968.

E. OLDMEADOW, *Francis Cardinal Bourne*, 2 vols, London, 1944.

E. S. PURCELL, *The Life of Cardinal Manning*, 2 vols, London, 1896.

J. G. SNEAD-COX, *The Life of Cardinal Vaughan*, 2 vols, London, 1910.

Textes newmaniens, published by L. Bouyer and M. Nédoncelle, 7 vols planned, Bruges-Paris 1955-70 (to be continued). For Newman's doctrinal work, see the bibliographical information in part 1, chapter IX, 796.

M. TREVOR, *Newman*, 2 vols, London, 1962.

M. WARD, *Gilbert Keith Chesterton*, New York, 1943.

W. WARD, *The Life and Times of Cardinal Wiseman*, 2 vols, London, 1897.

On Catholicism in Wales:

D. ATTWATER, *The Catholic Church in Modern Wales. A Record of the Past Century*, London, 1935.

On Catholicism in Scotland, besides the out-of-date but always useful work of A. Bellesheim, *Geschichte der Katholischen Kirche in Schottland*, Mainz 1883 cf. English translation Edinburgh, 1890), see:

J. E. HANDLEY, *The Irish in Modern Scotland*, Cork, 1947.

V. A. MCCLELLAND, 'The Irish Clergy and Archbishop Manning's Apostolic Visitation of the Western District of Scotland, 1867', *Catholic Historical Review*, LIII (1967), 1-27, 229-50, and 'A Hierarchy for Scotland, 1868-1878', *ibid*, LVI (1970), 474-500.

On the Catholic Church in Ireland, the fundamental work is P. Corish, ed., *A History of Irish Catholicism*, Dublin, 1968 onwards.

There is a good deal of information up to 1869 in P. MacSuibhne, *P. Cullen and His Contemporaries with their Letters*, 4 vols, Naas, 1961-74. Equally useful is P. F. Moran, ed., *The Pastoral Letters and Other Writings of Cardinal Cullen*, 3 vols, Dublin, 1882.

On the politico-religious problems of Cullen's day, see:

C. ALIX, *Le Saint-Siège et les Nationalismes en Europe, 1870-1960* (Paris 1962), 122-40.

E. R. NORMAN, *The Catholic Church and Ireland in the Age of Rebellion, 1859-1873*, London, 1965.

C. J. WOODS, in *Irish Historical Studies*, XVIII (1972), 29-60, and in *Dublin Historical Record*, XXVI (1973), 101-10.

On the Parnellism crisis, see the articles by E. Larkin in *Victorian Studies*, IV (1960-1), 315-36, and in *Review of Politics*, XXV (1963), 157-82; *ibid.*, XXVIII (1966), 359-83; also M. Tierney, in *Collectanea hibernica*, 1968 (part 11), 111-48.

Among the biographies:

B. O'REILLY, *John MacHale, Archbishop of Tuam*, 2 vols, New York, 1890.

P. ROGERS, *Father Theobald Mathew, Apostle of Temperance*, Dublin, 1944.

P. J. WALSH, *William J. Walsh, Archbishop of Dublin*, Dublin, 1928.

Chapter 12

AUSTRALIA: THE BIRTH OF A CHURCH

As well as the older works of H. Birt, *Benedictine Pioneers in Australia*, 2 vols, London, 1911, and E. O'Brien, *The Dawn of Catholicism in Australia*, 2 vols, London, 1930, see especially the general survey by P. O'Farrell, *The Catholic Church in Australia. A Short History*, London-Melbourne, 1969 (taking account of the reservations in *Journal of Religious History*, V (Sydney 1969), 359-63, also his published collection of *Documents in Australian Catholic History*, 2 vols, London, 1969, as well as the following:

N. BRENNAN, *Dr. Mannix*, Adelaide, 1964.
R. FOGARTY, *Catholic Education in Australia, 1806-1950*, 2 vols, Melbourne, 1959.
P. FORD, *Cardinal Moran and the Australian Labor Party*, Melbourne-London, 1966 (cf. *Journal of Religious History*, IV (1967), 249-54).
J. N. MOLONY, *The Roman Mould of the Australian Catholic Church*, Melbourne, 1969 (cf. *Journal of Religious History*, VI (1970), 87-90).
T. L. SUTTOR, *Hierarchy and Democracy in Australia, 1788-1870*, London-Melbourne, 1965.
For New Zealand, see:
J. J. WILSON, *The Church in New Zealand*, 2 vols, Dunedin, 1910-26.

Chapter 13

CANADA

No systematic history of the Roman Catholic Church in Canada has yet been written. By far the most detailed work dealing directly with the Church has been done in French Canada, but here the tendency has been to concentrate on French aspects only. In 1967 a Centre for research and documentation on Canadian church history was established in Ottawa; a similar collection has been begun at St Thomas More College, Saskatoon. The best guide to recent literature on the Canadian Church, Catholic and other, is the 'Current Bibliography of Canadian Church History' compiled by M. M. Sheehan and J. Hanrahan, and published since 1964 in the annual *Report* of the Canadian Catholic Historical Association. Past issues of the C.C.H.A. *Report*, the *Canadian Historical Association Report*, the *Canadian Historical Review* and the *Revue d'Histoire de l'Amérique Française* constitute probably the best source of serious historical scholarship on many matters dealing directly or indirectly with the Canadian Catholic experience. It is becoming clear that the history of the Roman Catholic, as of any other branch of the Church of Canada, can be seen in a balanced manner only in the perspective of the total Christian and religious experience of the nation. An excellent beginning in this regard is the three-volume *History of the Christian Church in Canada* prepared under the general editorship of J. W. Grant. The first volume, by H. H. Walsh, was published in 1966, the second by J. S. Moir, and the third by J. W. Grant, appeared in 1972. These works were preceded by H. H. Walsh, *The Christian Church in Canada*, Toronto, 1956, and the Ryerson Press collection of essays edited by Grant, *The Churches and the Canadian Experience*, Toronto, 1963.

The centenary of Canadian Confederation led to a large volume of literature re-examining the movements surrounding that historic event. Perhaps the most useful for a cross-section of durable studies on the subject, including the religious dimension, is the collection entitled *Confederation* edited by Ramsay Cook, in the series *Canadian Historical Readings*, Toronto, 1967, and P. B. Waite, *The Life and Times of Confederation 1864-1867*, Toronto 1962. For religious problems in the period preceding Confederation, the best sources are F. A. Walker, *Catholic Education and Politics* in Upper Canada, Toronto, 1955, J. Monet, *The Last Cannon Shot: A Study of French-Canadian Nationalism, 1837-1850*, Toronto, 1968 and J. S. Moir, *Church and State in Canada West*, Toronto, 1963. Two quite differing points of view on the Church in French Canada before Confederation are given in H. Plante, *L'Église Catholique au Canada*, Trois-Rivières, 1970, and J. P. Bernard, *Les Rouges*, Montreal, 1971. D. G. Creighton's biography, *John A. Macdonald*, 2 vols, Toronto, 1952, 1955, is valuable for Church-State tensions both before and after Confederation, as are the biographies of other major Canadian political figures. Several biographies of individual English-speaking Canadian bishops exist, although none can be called critical history. F. A. Walker, *Catholic Education and Politics in Ontario*, Toronto, 1964, reveals the continuing concern of the Ontario episcopate with school problems. On Laurier, J. Schull, *Laurier: The First Canadian*, Toronto, 1965, is the most recent work in English. It does not replace O. D. Skelton, *The Life and Letters of Sir Wilfrid Laurier*, 2 vols, Toronto, 1921, and no definitive modern biography of the great Prime Minister yet exists in French or English. For an incisive review of what Canadians have thought about their nation, see F. H. Underhill, *The Image of Confederation*, Toronto, 1964. P. Crunican's *Priests and Politicians: Manitoba Schools and the Election of 1896*, Toronto, 1974, tells the story of Canada's most notable Church-State struggle.

Inevitably, almost every study dealing with French Canada involves the Church to some degree. In English, the most comprehensive survey of Canada's French-English dimension is R. Cook, *Canada and the French-Canadian Question*, Toronto, 1966. Unsurpassed for narrative detail and colour, although not always for balanced judgment, is R. Rumilly, *Histoire de la Province de Québec*, 35 vols, Montreal, 1940-65, as well as the same author's biographies of Bishop Laflèche, Mercier and Bourassa. On ultramontanism vs. liberalism, the studies of P. Sylvain and of P. Savard on J. P. Tardivel are valuable. Léon Pouliot's 5-vol. biography, *Monseigneur Bourget et son Temps*, Montreal, 1973-76, provides good insights. M. Wade, *The French Canadians*, 2nd ed., Toronto, 1968, has, despite criticism, continued to have a wide audience. Important for a view of response to industrialism are W. F. Ryan, *The Church and Economic Growth in Quebec, 1867-1914*, Quebec, 1966, and H. F. Quinn, *The Union Nationale: A Study in Quebec Nationalism*, Toronto, 1963. The shift in the role and appreciation of the Church in French-Canadian thinking may be seen by comparing J. Bourassa, *La Langue française et l'avenir de notre race*, Quebec, 1913, and L. Groulx, *Dix ans d'action française*, Montreal, 1926, with such recent studies as M. Brunet, *Canadians et Canadiens*, Montreal, 1954, P. E. Trudeau, *La Grève de l'amiante*, Montréal, 1956 and A. Labarrère-Paulé, *Les Instituteurs laïques au Canada français*, 1836-1900, Quebec, 1965. Although the situation has continued to change rapidly, for major points of departure in French-Canadian discontent in recent years, see F. Scott and M. Oliver, eds., *Quebec States Her Case*, Toronto, 1964. Still important for reflection on the Church in modern French-Canada is J. P. Desbiens, *Les Insolences du Frère Untel*, Montreal, 1960. Many insights can be gained from S. Trofimenkoff's *Abbé Groulx: Variations on a Nationalist Theme*, Toronto, 1973. The volumes published by the commission on the laity in the Quebec church, *L'Église du Québec: un héritage, un projet*, Montreal, 1971-2 (among which is N. Voisine, *Histoire de l'Église catholique au Québec, 1608-1970*) are important for a changed point of view, as is P. Hurtubise *et al.*, *Le Laïc dans l'Église Canadienne française de 1830 à nos jours*, Montreal, 1972. G. M. Weir, *The Separate School Question in Canada*, Toronto, 1934, C. B. Sissons, *Church and State in Canadian Education*, Toronto, 1959, and L. Groulx, *L'Enseignement français au Canada*, 2 vols, Montreal 1931-3, are older and somewhat biased surveys. And the six volumes of the report of the late 1960s Royal Commission on Bilingualism and Biculturalism are indispensable to an understanding of Canada's French-English experience.

On the West, the works of G. F. G. Stanley, and W. L. Morton are the best general sources. The most valuable studies on specifically Roman Catholic endeavours are A. G. Morice, *History of the Catholic Church in Western Canada*, 2 vols, Toronto, 1910, P. Benoît, *Vie de Monseigneur Tachê*, 2 vols, Montréal, 1904, and J. Phelan, *The Bold Heart: The Story of Father Lacombe*, Toronto, 1956. For the Maritimes, A. A. Johnston, *A History of the Catholic Church in Eastern Nova Scotia*, 2 vols, Antigonish, 1960-71, is the first part of a series projected for that area. On the Antigonish movement, see A. F. Laidlaw, *The Campus and the Community*, Montreal, 1961 and, on M. M. Coady, *The Man from Margaree*, Toronto, 1971. L. K. Shook's *Catholic Post-Secondary Education in English-Speaking Canada: A History*, Toronto, 1971, is an important survey. On the foreign missionary efforts, A. Bouffard, *Messages*, Quebec, 1959, gives a good summary, and the bulletins of the Canadian Catholic Conference publish current statistics. For positions taken by the hierarchy of Canada, see the *Joint Pastoral Letters of the Bishops of Canada*, Ottawa, 1942-75, J. Hulliger, *L'Enseignement Social des évêques canadiens de 1891 à 1950*, Montreal, 1957. Statistics and diocesan developments are well presented in *Le Canada Ecclésiastique*, Montreal, 1886-1975.

Chapter 14

THE U.S.A.

The principal works on American Catholicism published up to 1959 can be found in the annotated items in J. T. Ellis, *A Guide to American Catholic*

History, Milwaukee, 1959. The chief publications of the following decade were included, with critical comments, under the heading, 'Suggested Reading', in the revised edition of the same author's books, *American Catholicism* (Chicago, 1969), 293-307. For a collection of original documents taken from a variety of sources, see the revised and enlarged edition of J. T. Ellis, *Documents of American Catholic History*, 2 vols, Chicago, 1967, and also P. Gleason, ed., *Catholicism in America* New York, 1970. There is no entirely satisfactory history of the Church in the United States of book length. In lieu of such, the reader will find the lengthy essay of H. J. Browne, 'Catholicism in the United States', in J. W. Smith and A. L. Jamison, eds, *The Shaping of American Religion*, Princeton, 1961, a well written survey. The revised edition of Ellis's *American Catholicism* mentioned above and the same writer's article entitled, 'United States of America', in the *New Catholic Encyclopaedia*, XIV, New York (1967), 425-48, will be useful, as will T. T. McAvoy, *A History of the Catholic Church in the United States*, Notre Dame, 1969. For the last half-century the following three works, all with an emphasis on social movements and issues, are informative and perceptive: D. J. O'Brien, *American Catholics and Social Reform. The New Deal Years*, New York, 1968, the same author's *The Renewal of American Catholicism*, New York, 1972, and P. Gleason, ed., *Contemporary Catholicism in the United States*, Notre Dame, 1969, which contains fourteen essays on as many topics. A. M. Greeley, *The Catholic Experience. An Interpretation of the History of American Catholicism*, Garden City, 1967, the work of an able sociologist, is readable and provocative even if the interpretation is too subjective to satisfy the professional historian.

Obviously, it is not possible to list here all the worthwhile titles under the several categories of books into which the literature on the Church is divided. One can hope to give only a representative sample, e.g., the best general history of an American diocese is that of R. H. Lord, J. E. Sexton, and E. T. Harrington, *History of the Archdiocese of Boston*, 3 vols, New York, 1944, the first two volumes being much superior to the third, which is too eulogistic of Cardinal O'Connell, the archbishop of Boston, who commissioned the work. As background for the Church of the Middle West, which in many ways has been a pacesetter for the nation, Robert Trisco's scholarly volume, *The Holy See and the Nascent Church in the Middle Western United States, 1826-1850*, Rome, 1962, is highly informative. The three-volume work of A. P. Stokes, *Church and State in the United States*, New York, 1950, is exhaustive on a theme of perennial importance; for a critique of A. P. Stokes on those matters touching Catholicism, see J. T. Ellis, 'Church and State in the United States: A Critical Appraisal', *Catholic Historical Review*, XXXVIII (October 1952), 285-316. A significant contribution on Church-State relations is the series of essays of J. C. Murray, S. J., *We Hold These Truths. Catholic Reflections on the American Proposition*, New York, 1960. On the conciliar or canonical history of the American Church the volume of Peter Guilday, *A History of the Councils of Baltimore, 1791-1884*, New York, 1932, is still useful, and for Americans in the two last ecumenical councils, J. J. Hennesey, S.J., *The First Council of the Vatican. The*

American Experience, New York, 1963, is a first-class work, while the documents with historical introductions in *American Participation in the Second Vatican Council*, New York, 1967, edited by V. A. Yzermans, will serve historians and others well for the interval until the final record of Vatican Council II is published.

A. M. Schlesinger of Harvard (d. 1965), a ranking historian of the United States, once stated that anti-Catholicism was 'the deepest bias in the history of the American people'. That subject was well treated by R. A. Billington in *The Protestant Crusade, 1800-1860. A Study of the Origins of American Nativism*, New York, 1938, and was continued in the same competent manner by J. Higham in *Strangers in the Land. Patterns of American Nativism, 1860-1925*, New Brunswick, 1955. Three works that treated special aspects of anti-Catholicism in a thorough way were: D. L. Kinzer, *An Episode in Anti-Catholicism: The American Protective Association*, Seattle, 1964, E. A. Moore, *A Catholic Runs for President. The Campaign of 1928*, New York, 1956; the latest work in this category, although not expressly a study of anti-Catholicism, is the excellent volume of L. H. Fuchs, *John F. Kennedy and American Catholicism*, New York, 1967.

For social movements in general among Catholics, A. I. Abell, *American Catholicism and Social Action: A Search for Social Justice, 1865-1950*, Garden City, 1960, provided a good introduction. As for the issue of war and peace, J. S. Rausch, *The Family of Nations. An Expanded View of Patriotism*, Huntington, 1970, brief though the eight essays were, they showed none the less the Division of World Justice and Peace of the United States Catholic Conference, sponsor of the brochure, moving the Church's official position away from the hierarchy's super-patriotism of an earlier time criticised in D. Dohen's *Nationalism and American Catholicism*, New York, 1967. Two superior monographs that treated special phases of the social problem in the period, 1880-1900, were: H. J. Browne, *The Catholic Church and the Knights of Labor*, Washington, 1949, and C. J. Barry, *The Catholic Church and German Americans*, Milwaukee, 1953. One of the best works in the neglected field of Catholic immigration and colonisation was J. P. Shannon, *Catholic Colonization on the Western Frontier*, New Haven, 1957. The rather unhappy story of the Church and the Negro has been told by a sociologist in W. A. Osborne's *The Segregated Covenant. Race Relations and American Catholics*, New York, 1967, an informative book, although one misses the accuracy that is associated with the trained historian; the brochure of J. T. Ellis, *The Catholic Church and the Negro*, Huntington, 1968, offered an outline history of the problem. The able monograph of Robert D. Cross, *The Emergence of Liberal Catholicism in America*, Cambridge, Mass., 1958, gave an ample and sound background for the late nineteenth and early twentieth-century controversies within the Catholic community, while T. T. McAvoy, *The Great Crisis in American Catholic History, 1895-1900*, Chicago, 1957, furnished a thoroughly documented study of the so-called heresy of Americanism.

For two collections of brief interpretative essays by a professor of literature with a strong emphasis on the cultural factor. W. J. Ong, *Frontiers in American Catholicism. Essays in Ideology and Culture*, New York, 1957, and the the same author's *American Catholic Crossroads,*

.

Religious-Secular Encounters in the Modern World, New York, 1959, are thought-provoking and perceptive. For the role of Catholics in the pluralist society and in the ecumenical movement there are several helpful work such as W. Herberg, *Protestant-Catholic-Jew. An Essay in American Religious Sociology* (rev. ed., Garden City, 1960), a pioneer and almost seminal volume; *American Catholics. A Protestant-Jewish View* edited by P. Scharper, New York, 1959, and R. M. Brown and G. Weigel, S.J., *An American Dialogue. A Protestant Looks at Catholicism and a Catholic Looks at Protestantism,* Garden City, 1960. In an age when the laity are playing a more active role in the Church's life. D. Callahan's book, *The Mind of the Catholic Layman,* New York, 1963, furnished an excellent brief introduction, and the more recent volume of R. Van Allen, *The Commonweal and American Catholicism,* Philadelphia, 1974, should also be consulted.

Under the general heading of Catholic education, N. G. McCluskey, *Catholic Viewpoint on Education,* rev. ed., Garden City, 1962, offered a helpful brief introduction. The only general survey of education on all levels of recent date, with the principal emphasis on elementary and secondary schools, is H. A. Buetow, *Of Singular Benefit. The Story of Catholic Education in the United States,* New York, 1970. Higher education is better served in the seventeen essays in N. G. McCluskey, ed., *The Catholic University. A Modern Appraisal,* Notre Dame, 1970, and E. J. Power, *Catholic Higher Education in America. A History,* New York, 1972; and at a time when Catholic education had been called in question by many Catholics of the United States, Michael O'Neil's *New Schools in a New Church, Toward a Modern Philosophy of Catholic Education,* Collegeville, 1971, offered a strong and reasoned defence. The four volumes of J. T. Ellis: *Perspectives in American Catholicism,* Baltimore, 1963, *Essays in Seminary Education,* Notre Dame, 1967, *John Lancaster Spalding. First Bishop of Peoria, American Educator,* Milwaukee, 1961, and *American Catholics and the Intellectual Life,* Chicago, 1956, all contain material on the Church's educational problems. The last was the occasion for a heated controversy in the 1950s that drew forth numerous other works, e.g., T. F. O'Dea, *American Catholic Dilemma: An Inquiry into the Intellectucal Life,* New York, 1958. Institutional histories are numerous, and among them J. M. Daley, *Georgetown University: Origin and Early Years,* Washington, 1957, and J. T. Durkin, *Georgetown University: The Middle Years, 1840-1900,* Washington, 1963, treat the first of the Catholic colleges. One of the best of such histories is C. J. Barry, *Worship and Work. Saint John's Abbey and University, 1856-1956,* Collegeville, 1956. The two European schools maintained by the American hierarchy were competently treated in R. F. McNamara, *The American College in Rome, 1855-1955,* Rochester, 1956, and J. D. Sauter, *The American College of Louvain, 1857-1898,* Louvain, 1959. A recent work that contains some history but emphasises principally the problems of the American Catholic college and university today is that edited by R. Hassenger, *The Shape of Catholic Higher Education,* Chicago, 1967.

The literature on American Catholicism is especially rich in biography; indeed, too much weight has perhaps been put in that category to the neglect of interpretative studies and analytic treatment of movements

BIBLIOGRAPHY

within the Catholic community. For the years since 1850 the following biographies will prove helpful: T. W. Spalding, *Martin John Spalding, American Churchman*, Washington, 1973, gives a scholarly treatment of Baltimore's seventh archbishop; Y. F. Hoden, C.S.P., *The Yankee Paul. Isaac Thomas Hecker*, Milwaukee, 1958, brings the founder of the Paulist Fathers down to the establishment of the congregation in 1858. The German Catholicism in the Middle West which was highly significant is seen in Peter Leo Johnson's *Crosier on the Frontier. A Life of John Martin Henni*, Madison, 1959, first archbishop of Milwaukee. Of the many works on Catholic laymen, the biography of T. Maynard, *Orestos Brownson. Yankee, Radical, Catholic*, New York, 1943, is probably the best on that key convert, while W. Lewis, *Without Fear or Favor*, New York, 1965, has furnished the most up-to-date biography of Roger Brooke Taney, Chief Justice of the United States until his death in 1864. For Catholicism of a more recent period the memoirs of a laywoman and a layman are important for social reform movements and for the campaign for racial justice to the blacks, namely, D. Day, *The Long Loneliness*, New York, 1952, and *Loaves and Fishes*, New York, 1963, and on the same extraordinary laywoman, see also W. D. Miller, *A Harsh and Dreadful Love, Dorothy Day and the Catholic Worker Movement*, New York, 1973. G. K. Hunton, *All of Which I Saw, Part of Which I Was*, New York, 1967, told an equally moving story. For Catholicism on the Pacific Coast and in Hawaii, J. B. McGloin, *California's First Archbishop. The Life of Joseph Sadoc Alemany, O.P., 1814-1888*, New York, 1966, F. J. Weber, *California's Reluctant Prelate. The Life and Times of Right Reverend Thaddeus Amat. C.M., 1811-1878*, Los Angeles, 1964, and G. Daws, *Holy Man, Father Damien of Molokai*, New York, 1973, are informative.

Four leading churchmen who were closely allied in friendship and policy have been treated in J. T. Ellis, *The Life of James Cardinal Gibbons, Archbishop of Baltimore, 1834-1921*, 2 vols, Milwaukee, 1952, J. H. Monihan, *The Life of Archbishop John Ireland*, New York, 1953, P. H. Ahern, *The Life of John J. Keane, Educator and Archbishop, 1839-1918*, Milwaukee, 1955, and G. P. Fogarty, *The Vatican and the Americanist Crisis: Denis O'Connell, American Agent in Rome, 1885-1903*, Rome, 1974. Among the contemporaries of these prelates were three bishops who played important roles in the Church, but did not belong to the Gibbons-Ireland-Keane-O'Connell wing of the hierarchy, namely, F. J. Zwierlein, *The Life and Letters of Bishop McQuaid*, 3 vols, Rochester, 1925-7, D. F. Sweeney, *The Life of John Lancaster Spalding, First Bishop of Peoria, 1840-1916*, New York, 1965, and S. J. Miller, *Peter Richard Kenrick, Bishop and Archbishop of St. Louis, 1806-1896*, Philadelphia, 1973. Probably the most controversial priest of the nineteenth century has not found a scholarly biography since the journalist S. Bell's *Rebel, Priest and Prophet. A Biography of Dr. Edward McGlynn*, New York, 1937, is hardly more than a sketch, and a biased sketch as well.

Among the countless valiant figures in the American religious communities of women one was the multi-millionaire's daughter who became a ranking missionary for the Blacks and Indians, whose story was told in C. M. Duffy, *Katharine Drexel. A Biography*, Philadelphia, 1966. Two others were M. A. McArdle, *California's Pioneer Sister of Mercy, Mother*

Mary Baptist Russell, 1829-1898, Fresno, 1954, an Irish-born member of a cultivated family who came to California in 1854, and M. Synon, *Mother Emily [Power] of Sinsinawa, American Pioneer,* Milwaukee, 1955, who ruled for many years over one of the most progressive of the Dominican Sisters' congregations in the Middle West.

There have been a number of prominent social-minded priests among whom two have found able biographers, namely, M. H. Fox, *Peter E. Dietz. Labor Priest,* Notre Dame, 1953, and F. L. Broderick, *Right Reverend New Dealer, John A. Ryan,* New York, 1963. Equally socially--minded, especially in regard to racial justice, was J. LaFarge, whose memoirs, *The Manner Is Ordinary,* New York, 1954, likewise afforded insights into one of the few nationally prominent Catholic families of the late nineteenth and early twentieth centuries. Finally, C. J. Tull, *Father Coughlin and the New Deal,* Syracuse, 1965, treated the most controversial priest of the twentieth century from published sources since access to the unpublished sources was denied to the author; in the same subject, see also S. Marcus, *Father Coughlin: The Tumultuous Life of the Priest of the Little Flower,* Boston, 1973.

American Catholicism is generally weak in memoir literature, and for that reason the following representative items, in addition to those already mentioned, were all the more welcome. Maurice F. Egan, *Recollections of a Happy Life,* New York, 1924, covered the varied career in journalism, education, and diplomacy of a prominent figure on the Catholic scene in the period after 1880. Sister B. Segale, *At the End of the Santa Fe Trail,* Milwaukee, 1948, contained a series of charming letters of an Italian-born Sister of Charity who recorded her extraordinary experiences on the missions of the western frontier from 1872 to the late 1880s. The two volumes of T. Merton, *The Seven Storey Mountain,* New York, 1948, and *The Sign of Jonas,* New York, 1953, probably introduced more non--Catholic Americans to the Church than any other author, due to the vogue for Merton's writings.

A perceptive biographical essay of a leading Catholic layman was Oscar Handlin's *Al Smith and His America,* Boston, 1958. The American pioneer in the liturgical movement found a scholarly biographer in P. B. Marx, *Virgil Michel and the Liturgical Movement,* Collegeville, 1957. For the mid-nineteenth century few bishops were more colourful and controversial than Augustin Verot, S.S., who served as bishop of Savannah and later of Saint Augustine. He was fortunate in his biographer, M. V. Gannon, *Rebel Bishop. The Life and Era of Augustin Verot,* Milwaukee, 1964. The first American to serve as both an apostolic nuncio and a cardinal in curia likewise had an able biographer in C. J. Barry, *American Nuncio. Cardinal Aloisius Muench,* Collegeville, 1969. Finally, the man who in many ways was the leading churchman of the mid twentieth century had his life written five years before he died by R. I. Gannon, *The Cardinal Spellman Story,* Garden City, 1962, an informative work, and in some respects a revealing one. It has been said, not without reason, that the death of Cardinal Spellman on 2 December 1967 closed an era in the history of the Catholic Church in the United States.

Chapter 15
CATHOLICISM IN LATIN AMERICA

GENERAL WORKS

J. MACKAY, *The Other Spanish Christ*, New York, 1933. A penetrating and eloquent work by a Protestant theologian, studying various aspects of the religious spirit of Spain and Spanish America.

J. L. MECHAM, *Church and State in Latin America: A History of Politico-Ecclesiastical Relations*, Chapel Hill, N.C., 1966, revised ed. Scholarly and objective, this masterful work has come, since its first edition in 1934, to be recognised as a classic. In the revised edition the material covering the years 1934-65 is not always as meticulously researched as that for the earlier periods.

K. M. SCHMITT, ed., *The Roman Catholic Church in Modern Latin America*, New York, 1972. Covering the nineteenth and twentieth centuries, the work is distinguished by a judicious selection of essays and by a helpful, carefully annotated bibliography.

WORKS DEALING WITH SPECIFIC COUNTRIES

Argentina

J. BARAGER, 'The Historiography of the Rio de la Plata Area Since 1830', *Hispanic American Historical Review*, XXXIX (1959), 588-624. A balanced appraisal of Argentine, Paraguayan and Uruguayan historiography with many citations of works that deal with Catholicism.

J. S. CAMPOBASSI, *Laicismo y catolicismo en la educación pública argentina*, Buenos Aires, 1961. Based on careful investigation, the study reveals that there was frequent collaboration between Catholic and Liberal elements.

J. S. CAMPOBASSI, *Ataque y defensa del laicismo escolar en la Argentina, 1884-1963*, Buenos Aires, 1964. The history and some analysis of debates over secular, public education.

J. CASIELLO, *Iglesia y Estado en la Argentina*, Buenos Aires, 1948. Based on sound documentation and containing excellent bibliographical citations, the work is occasionally apologetic in tone.

J. FERNANDEZ DE LANDA, *Las relaciones entre la Iglesia y el Estado*, Buenos Aires, 1958. An extreme statement on the temporal rights alleged to inhere in the Church.

F. HOFFMAN, 'Peron and After', *Hispanic American Historical Review*, XXXVI (1956), 510-28, and XXXIX (1959), 212-33. A skilful analysis of Argentine literature dealing with the fall of Perón and the aftermath and citing several important works on Catholicism and its role in contemporary events.

J. J. KENNEDY, *Catholicism, Nationalism and Democracy in Argentina*, Notre Dame, Ind., 1958. An important intellectual history stressing the influence of several of Argentina's leading Catholic intellectuals in the nineteenth and twentieth centuries. The work is based upon extensive research.

Bolivia

C. W. ARNADE, 'The Historiography of Colonial and Modern Bolivia', *Hispanic American Historical Review*, XLII (1962), 333-84. A masterly survey with references to many works on Catholicism. Traditionally weak in its influence and not a force to excite literary passions, Catholicism in this small republic with a large Indian population has not received adequate attention from national authors.

M. BAPTISTA, *Obras completas,* 7 vols, La Paz, 1932-5. Mariano Baptista, President of Bolivia 1892-6, was the major Catholic intellectual figure of the Conservative Party in the latter part of the nineteenth century. His works are essential for an understanding of the period.

M. ROLON ANAYA, *Política y partidos en Bolivia,* La Paz, 1966. A lengthy work containing some material on mid-twentieth century Catholic reform movements.

A. ZAREÁSTEGUI, *The Catholic University in Bolivia,* in *CIF Reports,* 6, Cuernevaca, Mexico, 1967. A leading Catholic intellectual writes in the spirit of Church-State *rapprochement.*

Brazil

E. B. BURNS, 'A Working Bibliography for the Study of Brazilian History', *The Americas,* XXII (1965), 54-88. A significant section of this admirable study, characterised by its jucidious appraisals of historical literature, pertains to the Church.

E. J. de KADT, *The Catholic Church and Social Reform in Brazil,* New York, 1970. At the time of its publication, the best book-length study of the Church in contemporary Brazilian society.

S. J. STEIN, *Brazil, the Empire,* in C. C. Griffin, ed., *Latin America: A Guide to the Historical Literature,* Austin, 1971, 597-606, and J. D. Wirth, *Brazil the Republic,* in *ibid.,* 607-18. Careful bibliographical studies that touch frequently on the literature pertaining to Catholicism. *Latin America: A Guide to the Historical Literature* is an indispensable reference tool for Catholicism and virtually every other topic in Latin American history.

H. J. WIARDA, *The Brazilian Catholic Labor Movement,* Amherst, Mass., 1969. An objective, scholarly study concentrating on the period since the Second World War.

Caribbean Island Republics

L. DEWART, *Christianity and Revolution: The Lesson of Cuba,* New York, 1963. A profound study by a Canadian Catholic theologian arguing that the opposition of the Church in Cuba to basic structural changes and social reform helped drive Fidel Castro into the communist world. It is implied that the Church may have to learn to live with communism, just as it has learned to live with Protestantism.

W. MacGAFFEY, and C. BARNETT, *Cuba: Its People, its Society, its Culture,* New Haven, Conn. 1962. A penetrating social-cultural history that frequently focuses on religious factors.

A. MÉTRAUX, *Voodoo in Haiti,* New York, 1959. The indispensable source on this topic.

J. H. STEWARD, *et al., The People of Puerto Rico: A Study in Social Anthropology,* Urbane, Ill., 1956. An excellent survey with occasional references to religious customs.

H. J. WIARDA, *Dictatorship, Development, and Disintegration: The Political System of the Dominican Republic,* Chicago, 1962. Contains a sound analysis of the Catholic Church in the post-Trujillo period.

Central America

J. and M. BIEZANS, *Costa Rican Life*, New York, 1949. Chapter VIII deals effectively with religion.

M. HOLLERAN, *Church and State in Guatemala*, New York, 1947. A serious, well-documented study.

F. B. PIKE, 'The Catholic Church in Central America', *Review of Politics*, XXI (1959), 83-113. Deals with the period since independence and cites major Central American sources.

R. SCHNEIDER, *Communism in Guatemala, 1944-1954*, New York, 1957. A scholarly work that makes occasional reference to the role of the Church.

N. L. WHETTEN, *Guatemala: The Land and the People*, New Haven, Conn., 1961. One of the finest published studies on a Central American country, the work devotes considerable attention to religious practices.

Chile

J. CASTILLA, *En defensa de Maritain*, Santiago de Chile, 1949. Reveals the influence of Jacques Maritain on the ideology of Chilean Christian Democracy.

J. F. CHONCHOL, *El regimen comunitario y la propiedad*, Santiago de Chile, 1964.

J. F. CHONCHOL and J. SILVA SOLAR, *El desarrollo de la nueva sociedad en América Latina*, Santiago de Chile, 1965. The two works are important statements by leading idealogues of the left wing of Chilean Christian Democracy.

J. EYZAGUIRRE, *Fisonomía histórica del Chile*, Santiago del Chile, 1948. A thoughtful, interpretive résumé of Chilean history from the viewpoint of an extremely conservative Catholic layman-intellectual.

E. FREI MONTALVA, *Pensamiento y acción*, Santiago de Chile, 1958.

E. HALPERIN, *Nationalism and Communism in Chile*, Cambridge, Mass., 1965. A sophisticated, carefully prepared study that occasionally touches upon the Church's ideological position.

M. LARRAÍN, *La hora de la Acción Católica*, Santiago de Chile, 1956. A short but important work by a pioneer advocate among the Chilean bishops of major social reform.

F. B. PIKE, *Chile and the United States, 1880-1962: The Emergence of Chile's Social Crisis and the Challenge to United States Diplomacy*, Notre Dame, Ind., 1963. Dealing extensively with intellectual and social history, the work includes abundant citations of Chilean sources.

Colombia

Arquidiócesis [de Bogotá], Secretariado Permanente del Episcopado, *Conferencias episcopales del Colombia, 1908-1953*, Bogotá, 1956. An important source containing many of the Church's major pronouncements on political, religious and social issues.

R. H. DIX, *Colombia: The Political Dimensions of Change*, New Haven, 1967. Concentrating on the post-World War II era, this work includes a balanced treatment of the role of the Church.

G. GUZMÁN CAMPOS, O. FALS BORDA and E. UMAÑA, *La violencia en Colombia: estudio de un proceso social*, 2 vols, Bogotá, 1962-4. An exhaustive analysis of the violence that racked Colombia from the late 1940s to the early 1960s with considerable attention to its effects on the position of the Church.

B. E. HADDOX, *Sociedad y religion en Colombia*, Bogotá, 1965. A scholarly work based on extensive field research and including a useful bibliography.

M. URRUTIA, *The Development of the Colombian Labor Movement*, New Haven, 1969. Tracing the story back to the colonial period, the Colombian scholar concentrates on the period since the 1920s and deals both with the secular and Church-dominated labour movement.

Ecuador

R. W. BIALEK, *Catholic Politics: A History Based on Ecuador*, New York, 1963. Material on the 1905-37 period is particularly useful.

J. S. LARA, *Trajectoría y metas del Partido Conservador Ecuatoriano*, Quito, 1968. Reflects the attempt to up-date Catholic conservative political ideology so as to broaden its appeal to the country's youth.

A. SZÁSDI, 'The Historiography of the Republic of Ecuador', *Hispanic American Historical Review*, XLIV (1964), 503-50. Many of the works cited in this splendid historiographical analysis deal with Church-State issues and religious practices. Treatment of the literature dealing with García Moreno is outstanding.

Mexico

D. COSÍO VILLEGAS, gen. ed., *La historia moderna de México*, 5 vols, México, D. F., 1956-63. Written by Cosio Villegas and other distinguished Mexican historians, the first five volumes to appear in this series gave promise to making it perhaps the finest history of a single Latin American country. Dealing with the 1867-1911 period, the volumes include much material pertaining to the Church.

M. de la CUEVA MARIO, *et. al.*, *Major Trends in Mexican Philosophy*, trans. A. R. Caponigri, Notre Dame, Ind, 1966. Essays by some of Mexico's most eminent intellectuals shed much light on attitudes toward Catholicism.

J. L. DASSAULT, *L'Église et l'État modernes du Mexique*, Paris, 1964. An important and original study, asserting that the State has made favourable overtures to the Church and maintaining that the Church should respond by making concessions to the State. This would enable the two powers to collaborate in social justice programmes.

G. GARCIA CANTÚ, ed., *El pensamiento de la reacción mexicana: Historia documental, 1810-1962*, Mexico, 1965. A fascinating, lengthy anthology of Mexican conservative thought. This neglected topic merits extensive research.

R. POTASH, 'The Historiography of Mexico Since 1821', *Hispanic American Historical Review*, XL (1960), 383-484. In this careful study and the one cited below by Ross, there are important references to works that deal with Catholicism and Church-State issues.

S. R. ROSS, 'Bibliography of Sources for Contemporary Mexican History', *Hispanic American Historical Review*, XXXIX (1959), 234-8.

K. M. SCHMITT, 'Catholic Adjustment to the Secular State: The Case of Mexico, 1867-1911', *Catholic Historical Review*, XLVIII (1962), 182-204. The best short account of the Church in the period dominated by Porfirio Díaz.

J. VÁZQUEZ de KNAUTH, *Nacionalismo y educación en México*, México, 1970. A probing study of the guiding intellectual trends in Mexican education since the late nineteenth century, with abundant material on the clash between revolutionary ideology and traditional Catholicism.

Paraguay

P. H. BOX, *The Origins of the Paraguayan War*, Urbana, Ill., 1930. This excellent study suggests that in waging a war against Brazil and Argentina (1864-70), Paraguayan *caudillo* Francisco Solano López may have been motivated in part by the desire to protect the values of Hispanic traditions and Catholicism, introduced by the famous Jesuit *reducciones* in the early seventeenth century, against contamination by the liberalism that was felt to vitiate the regimes of the hostile countries on Paraguay's borders.

G. CABANELLAS, *El dictador del Paraguay, Dr. Francia*, Buenos Aires, 1946. This, and the Chaves work, cited next, are the two best studies of the strange autocrat who dominated politics from 1814 until his death in 1840 and who came close to establishing a national Church in line with his general policy of suspicion toward the outside world.

J. N. GONZÁLEZ, *Proceso y formación de la cultura paraguaya*, 2nd ed., Buenos Aires, 1948. A widely respected Paraguayan historian deals, among many other considerations, with the influence of Catholicism on national culture.

H. G. WARREN, *Paraguay, an Informal History*, Norman, Okl., 1949. A reliable work with occasional references to Catholicism, enhanced by useful bibliographical suggestions.

Peru

V. A. BELAÚNDE, C. CUETO FERNANDINI, R. FERRERO, E. ALAYZA GRUNDY, F. McGREGOR, *Política deber cristiana*, Lima, 1963. Essays by eminent Peruvian intellectuals dealing with the Church and the social question and revealing a cautiously progressive spirit.

T. R. FORD, *Man and Land in Peru*, Gainesville, Fla., 1955. An important contribution containing descriptions of social and economic conditions and religious practices among the masses of unassimilated Andean Indians.

F. B. PIKE, *The U.S. and the Andean Republic*, Cambridge, 1977. Devotes considerable attention to intellectual history and religious issues of the nineteenth and twentieth centuries, with extensive references to Peruvian sources.

D. SHARP, ed., *U.S. Policy and Peru*, Austin, 1972. An excellent collection of essays concerned primarily with internal Peruvian development since the 1968 military revolution and illuminating in certain sections the co-operation of the Church with the military in the attempt to carry out significant social reforms.

Uruguay

A. M. De FREITAS, *Herrera, hombre de estado*, Montevideo, 1952. A reasonably careful study of Uruguayan political history and of Luis Alberto de Herrera (d. 1959), long a leading lay figure of Uruguay's right-wing Catholic nationalism.

J. E. PIVEL DEVOTO, *Historia de los partidos y las ideas políticas en el Uruguay: la definición de los bandos, 1829-1838*, Montevideo, 1956. The standard account of the origins of Uruguay's political and ideological strife.

M. I. VANGER, *José Batlle y Ordóñez of Uruguay: The Creator of His Times*,

1902-1907, Cambridge, Mass., 1963. Close to a definitive study of a formative period in Uruguay's history, with occasional references to the prevailing agnosticism and anti-clericalism of the era.

Venezuela

P. GRASES, M. PÉREZ VILA, compilers, *Pensamiento politico venezolano del siglo XIX: textos para su estudio,* Caracas, 1960-. A multi-volume set that is the major source for Venezuelan intellectual history, dealing extensively with liberalism, conservatism, and positivism.

C. SÁNCHEZ ESPEJO, *El patronato en Venezuela,* Caracas, 1953. A careful study showing the degree to which the Church has been State controlled.

M. WATTERS, *A History of the Church in Venezuela, 1810-1930,* Chapel Hill, 1933. Scholarly and reliable, the work stresses the weakness of the Catholic Church in Venezuela and contains references to numerous Spanish-language sources.

WORKS DEALING WITH CATHOLICISM IN POST-WORLD WAR II LATIN AMERICA

Center for Intercultural Formation (CIF, Cuernevaca, Mexico), *Study No. 1, Socio-Economic Data: Latin America in Maps, Charts, Maps,* and *Study No. 2, Socio-Religious Data (Catholicism): Latin America in Maps, Charts, Tables,* both volumes compiled by Yvan Labelle and Adriana Estrada, Mexico, D. F., 1963. Indispensable sources for data relating to contemporary economic, social and religious conditions. Both studies also cite valuable references. The CIF has become an important documentation centre for Church activities and socio-economic conditions in Latin America. The Centro Intercultural de Documentación (CIDOC) dossiers which it began to publish in 1967 are invaluable sources on contemporary issues affecting Latin American Catholicism.

G. DREKONJA, 'Religion and Social Change in Latin America', *Latin American Research Review,* VI (1971), 53-72. A judicious guide to the basic literature on the subject.

Fédération Internationale de Centres de Recherches Sociales et Socioreligieuses (FERES: Brussels and Bogotá) has supported publication of various studies of Catholicism in contemporary Latin America. Not always meticulously researched and of variable quality, these studies have the advantage of being written in every instance by extremely knowledgeable individuals with vast Latin American experience. Studies in the FERES series, published in Bogotá and generally of short book length, include: I. Alonso, *La Iglesia en Brasil,* 1964; Alonso, E. Amato, A. Acha, G. Garrido, *La Iglesia en Argentina, Paraguay y Uruguay,* 1964; Alonso, Garrido, J. Dammert Bellido, J. Tumiri, *La Iglesia en el Perú y Bolivia,* 1962; Alonso, R. Poblete, Garrido, *La Iglesia en Chile,* 1962; J. M. Estepa, *La liturgia y la catequesis en América Latina,* 1963; J. L. de Lannoy, *El comunismo en América Latina,* 1964; G. Pérez, *Seminarios y seminaristas,* 1962; Pérez, J. Wust, *La Iglesia en Colombia,* 1961; R. Ramos, Alonso, D. Carré, *La Iglesia en México,* 1963; C. Torres, B. Corredor, *Las escuelas radiofónicas de Sutatenza,* 1964.

F. HOUTART, *La Iglesia latinoamericana a la hora de concilio,* Friburg, 1962. A short assessment of the status of the Catholic Church in Latin America on the eve of the Second Vatican Council. Houtart was at the time director of the FERES series.

F. HOUTART and E. PIN, *The Church and the Latin American Revolution*, New York, 1965. Expressing the opinions of two Jesuits with extensive experience in Latin America, the work is based upon sound sociological investigation as well as upon intuition. It stresses the need for the Church to play an active role in effecting significant structural changes in Latin American society.

H. A. LANDSBERGER, ed., *The Church and Social Change in Latin America*, Notre Dame, Ind., 1970. Contributed by various authorities, the essays in this volume are in general timely, but also of more than passing value.

F. C. TURNER, *Catholicism and Political Development in Latin America*, Chapel Hill, 1971. Exhaustively researched and notable for its penetrating analysis, this masterful study describes the growth of Catholic progressivism in the post-World War II era.

I. VALLIER, *Catholicism, Social Control and Modernisation in Latin America*, Englewood Cliffs, N. J., 1970. A provocative, solidly researched study that maintains an optimistic viewpoint concerning the ability of the Church to contribute to development.

Chapter 16
FROM MISSIONS TO YOUNG CHURCHES

The basic bibliographic source is the *Bibliotheca missionum* (22 volumes), Fribourg-en-Brisgau; for publications after 1933, see the *Bibliografia missionaria* (Rome) published annually.

A. SANTOS HERNANDEZ, *Misionologia III Bibliografia misional, parte historica*, Santander, 1965, gives a good but more selective bibliography.

GENERAL WORKS

W. BUHLMANN, *The Coming of the Third Church*. An analysis of the present and future of the Church, Slough 1976.

C. P. CROVES, *The Planting of Christianity in Africa*: II. *1840-1878*, III. *1878-1914*, IV. *1914-1954*, London 1954, 1956, 1958.

S. DELACROIX, *Histoire universelle des missions catholiques*, III. *Les Missions contemporaines (1800-1957)*, IV. *L'Eglise catholique en face du monde non chrétien*, Paris, 1958-1959.

K. S. LATOURETTE, *A History of the Expansion of Christianity*, New York, 1937-1945.

K. S. LATOURETTE, *The Christian World Mission in Our Day*, New York, 1954.

Alph. MULDERS, *Missionsgeschichte*, Ratisbonne, 1960 (very good bibliography).

S. NEILL, *A History of Christian Missions* (The Pelican History of the Church: 6), Harmondsworth, 1965.

J. SCHMIDLIN, *Katholische Missionsgeschichte*, Steyl, 1925.

J. SCHMIDLIN, *Manuale di storia delle missioni cattoliche*, Milan, 1929.

J. SCHMIDLIN, *Catholic Mission History*, Techny, 1933.

W. F. SHORTER, AYLWARD, *Theology of Mission*. Theology Today, No. 37, Cork, 1972.

Sylloge praecipuorum documentorum recentium Summorum Pontificum et S.C. de Propaganda Fide, Rome, 1939: complete collection of Roman documents concerning the missions from 1906 to 1938.

I. THE MISSIONARY IMPETUS OF THE 19th CENTURY

B. ARENS, *Manuel des missions catholiques*, Louvain, 1925, and supplement 1932.
A. ARNOUX, *Les Pères blancs aux sources du Nil*, Namur, 1953.
A. HUBLOU, *L'Eglise naissante au Chota-Nagpore*, Louvain, 1931.
L. LELOIR, *Les Grands Ordres missionnaires*, Namur, 1937.
MAIRE, *Histoire des instituts religieux et missionnaires*, Paris, 1930.
MARIE-AANDRE du S.C., *Ouganda, terre de martyrs*, Paris, 1963.
J. MOTT, *Five Decades and a Forward View*, New York, 1939.
I. SCHAPERA, *Livingstone's Missionary Correspondence*, London, 1961.
C. SEAVER, *David Livingstone, his Life and Letters*, London, 1957.
G. WARNECK, *Warum ist das 19 Jahrhundert ein Missionsjahrhundert?* Halle, 1880.

History of Missiology
J. GLAZIK, *50 Jahre Katholische Missionswissenschaft in Münster 1911-1961*, Münster, 1961.
A. SANTOS HERNANDEZ, "Historia de la Misionologia", in *Misionologia III* Bibliografia, parte doctrinal, pp. 47-76.
A. V. SEUMOIS, "Histoire de la missiologie" in *Introduction à la missiologie*, pp. 432-465, Schöneck-Beckenried, 1952.

II. FROM FOREIGN MISSIONS TO LOCAL CHURCHES

C. COSTANTINI, *Con I Missionari in Cina*, Rome. 1958. The first Apostolic Delegate in China, later became Secretary of Propaganda and Cardinal. He wrote these two volumes of memoirs which were published after his death. A selection of the more important parts was published in French under the title, *Réforme des missions au XXe siecle* (coll. 'Eglise vivante'), Tournai, 1960.
A. HASTINGS, *African Christianity*. An essay in interpretation. London and Dublin 1976.
L. JOLY, *Le Christianisme et l'Extrême-Orient*, Paris, 1907; and its critical analysis by M. CHEZA, *Le Chanoine Joly et la Méthodologie missionnaire*, Louvain, 1963.
J. LECLERCQ, *Vie du père Lebbe*, (coll. 'Eglise vivante') Tournai, 1955; (coll. 'Livre de Vie', Paris, 1964). A. SOHIER and P. GOFFART edited a selection of *Lettres du père Lebbe* (coll. 'Eglise vivante'), Tournai, 1960.
J. MASSON, *Vers l'Eglise indigène*, Brussels, 1944.
W. F. SHORTER, AYLWARD, *African Christian Theology: Adaptation or Incarnation?*
A. SOHIER, 'Bilan missionnaire d'un pontificat' (Pius XII), in the review *Eglise vivante*, 1948, pp. 436-443.

III. POLITICAL ASPECTS OF MISSION

J. BECKMANN, *La Congrégation de la Propagation de la foi face à la politique internationale* (coll. 'Cahiers de la Nouvelle Revue de science missionnaire'), Schöneck-Beckenried, 1963.

Protectorate in China
In addition to Costantini's work quoted above, see the well researched study by Louis Wei Tsing-Sing, *La Politique missionnaire de la France en Chine 1842-1856*, Paris, 1960, as well as three review articles: R. GERARD, 'La protection des missions catholiques en Chine et la diplomatie' in the *Bulletin de l'U.M.C.* (Belgique) October 1927, pp. 137-167, and A. SOHIER, 'La diplomatie belge et la protection des missions en Chine' in the *Nouvelle Revue de science missionnaire*, 1967, pp. 266-283; 'La nonciature pour Pékin en 1886', *ibid.*, 1968, pp. 1-14 and 94-110.

Colonial Rule
Les Eglises chrétiennes et la décolonisation (Cahiers de la Fondation nationale des sciences politiques, no. 151) Paris, 1967; collective work edited by M. MERLE.
J. PERRAUDIN, 'Le Cardinal Lavigerie et Léopold II" in the review *Zaïre*, 1957, pp. 901-932 and 1958, pp. 37-64, 165-177, 275-291, 393-408.
R. SLADE, *English-Speaking Missions in the Congo Independent State 1878-1908*, Brussels, 1959.
M. STORME, *Evangelisatiepogingen in de binnenladen van Africa gedurende de XIXe eeuw*, Brussels, 1951.

IV. MISSION AND CULTURES

Christianity in Independent Africa, a 600-page volume of selected papers. Rex Collings Ltd., 69 Marylebone High Street, London, W1M 3AQ. Edited by Adrian Hastings.
L. J. LUZBETAK, *L'Eglise et les Cultures* (with a good bibliography) Brussels, 1968.
W. F. SHORTER, AYLWARD, *African Culture and the Christian Church*: An introduction to social and pastoral anthropology, London, 1977.
Pie XII et les Cultures, collection of papal texts in *Eglise vivante*, 1958, pp. 444-452, and 1959, pp. 43-50.

V. CRISES AND NEW PERSPECTIVES

The Church in Communist China
Z. ARAMBURU, *Desterrado de China*, Bilbao, 1960.
A. T. BASSI, *Sette anni nella Cina communista*, Parma, 1960.
K. HOCKIN, *Servants of God in People's China*, London, 1964.
J. SCHUTTE, *Die Katholische Chinamission im Spiegel der Rotchinesischen Presse* (Collection 'Missionswissenschaftliche Abhandlungen und Texte', 21), Münster, 1957.
Documents of the Three-Self Movement. Source Materials for the study of the Protestant Church in Communist China, New York, 1963.

Consult, also, the excellent annual reports published by the reviews *International Review of Missions* (Protestant) and *Eglise vivante* (Catholic), as well as the *World Christian Handbook*, London, editions 1949, 1952, 1957, 1962, 1968, and *Bilan du Monde*, Tournai, 1964. The problems of missionary institutes are regularly examined in the review *Spiritus* (Paris) and especially in its no. 30, 1967: *Aggiornamento missionnaire*. See, too, J. BRULS, *Propos sur le clergé missionnaire*, Louvain, 1963; A.-M. HENRY, *Missions d'hier, mission de demain*, postscript to the French edition of the collective work *l'Activité missionnaire de l'Eglise* (collection 'Unam Sanctam' 67), Paris, 1967; Ad. de GROOT, 'La mission après Vatican II", in *Concilium* 36, pp. 151-168.
Missions: The Way Forward, The Outlook, No. 8, Vol. XIII, London.

THE EASTERN CHURCHES

Some general accounts of the Eastern Churches whether in union or not with Rome: J. Hajjar, *Christianisme en Orient. Études d'histoire contemporaine, 1684-1968*, Beyrut, 1971; G. T. Mackenzie, *Christianity in Travancore*, Trivandrum, 1901; G. Zananiri, *Catholicisme oriental*, Paris 1966; *Handbuch der Ostkirchenkunde*, ed. K. Algermissen, Düsseldorf, 1971.

Chapter 17
1848 to 1914: FROM THE CRIMEAN WAR TO THE FIRST WORLD WAR

E. BORÉ, *La Question des Lieux Saints*, Paris, 1850.

A. BOUDOU, *Le Saint-Siège et la Russie*, vol. II, Paris, 1925.

R. ESPOSITO, *Leone XIII et l'Oriente cristiano*, Rome, 1961.

G. GOYAU, *Le Protectorat de la France sur les chrétiens de l'empire ottoman*, Paris, 1895.

J. HAJJAR, *L'Apostolat des missionaires latins dans le Proche-Orient selon les directives romaines*, Jerusalem, 1956.

M. MA' OZ, *Ottoman Reform in Syria and Palestine, 1840-1861*, Oxford, 1968.

F. van STEEN de JEHAY, *De la situation des sujets ottomans non musulmans*, Brussels, 1906.

H. TEMPERLEY, *England and the Near East, The Crimea*, London, 1936.

E. WINTER, *Russland und das Papsttum*, II, Berlin, 1961.

On the fortunes of the Eastern patriarchates in union with Rome during the second half of the 19th century, see particularly the work of C. de Clerq, *Conciles des Orientaux catholiques*, 2 vols, Paris, 1949-52.

On the attempts at mutual understanding between the Churches, see chapters 4-7 of R. Rouse and S. C. Neill, eds, *A History of the Ecumenical Movement, 1517-1948*, London, 1954 (particularly G. Florowsky, 'The Orthodox Churches and the Ecumenical Movement prior to 1910', pp. 169-215).

On the rivalry between Christian Churches in the Near East: C. Crivelli, *Protestanti e cristiani orientali*, Rome, 1932; Th. G. Stavru, *Russian Interest in Palestine, 1882-1914*, Salonika, 1963.

Chapter 18
1917 to 1939: EASTERN CATHOLICISM BETWEEN THE WARS

The most useful periodicals are:
    La Documentation catholique
    Échos d'Orient
    Das Heilige Land
    Irénikon
See also:
Ch. DUMONT, 'Pio XI e i cristiani separati', in *Pio XI nel trentesimo della morte* (Milan 1969), 325-75.
J. C. HUREWITZ, *The Struggle for Palestina*, New York, 1950.
C. KOROLEVSKIJ, 'La fondation de l'Institut pontifical oriental', in *Orientalia christiana periodica*, XXXIII (1967), 5-46.
S. MINERBI, *L'Italie et la Palestine, 1914-1920*, Paris, 1970.
M. MOURIN, *Le Vatican et l'URSS*, Paris, 1965.
N. STRUVE, *Les Chrétiens en URSS*, Paris, 1964.

Chapter 19
1940 to 1968: FROM PIUS XII TO THE SECOND VATICAN COUNCIL

See the periodicals *Irénikon*, *Istina* and *Proche-Orient chrétien*. For the work of the Second Vatican Council in relation to the East, it is worth consulting the balanced and judicious accounts in A. Wenger, *Vatican II*, 4 vols, Paris, 1963-6. Also *L'Eglise grecque melkite au concile*, Beyrut, 1969; St Castanos de Medicis, *Athénagoras Ier. L'apport de l'orthodoxie à l'oecuménisme*, Lausanne, 1968.

THE HALF-CENTURY LEADING TO VATICAN II

Taking it for granted that the great Catholic histories of the Church do not as yet cover the period since 1914, it is best to make use of good textbooks such as K. Bihlmeyer-H. Tüchle, *Handbook of Church History*, III, Westminster (Md.), 1966 and G. Maron, 'Die römisch-katholische Kirche von 1870 bis 1970', in *Die Kirche in ihrer Geschichte*, ed. K. D. Schmidt, fasc. N2, Göttingen, 1972. Among the general surveys of our period, the following deserve mention:
Bilan du Monde. Encyclopédie catholique du Monde chrétien, ed. Fr. Houtart and J. Frisque, 2 vols, 2nd ed., Tournai–Paris, 1964.
J. CHEVALIER, *La Politique du Vatican*, Paris, 1969.
J. LESTAVEL, *Les Prophètes de l'Église contemporaine*, Þaris, 1969.
S. C. NEILL, ed., *Twentieth-Century Christianity*, London, 1961.

Chapter 20
FROM BENEDICT XV TO JOHN XXIII

G. FALCONI, *The Pope in the Twentieth Century*, London, 1967 (critical in spirit).

Benedict XV

There is no biography or general survey of adequate critical quality on this pontificate. The student may profit by reading the following:

F. ENGEL-JANOSI, 'The Roman Question in the First Years of Benedict XV', *Catholic Historical Review*, XL (1954), 269-85.

F. HAYWARD, *Un pape méconnu, Benoît XV.* Paris-Tournai, 1955.

H. JOHNSON, *Vatican Diplomacy in the World War*, Oxford, 1933.
The best brief account, in which is included a critical judgment on the previous literature on the subject, is the article by V. Conzemius, 'L'Offre de médiation de Benoît XV du 1 er août 1917. Essai d'un bilan provisoire', *Religion et Politique. Mélanges offerts à M. le doyen A. Latreille*, Lyons (1972), 303-26 (see also in the same volume the articles by R. Lacour and P. Renouvin, 275-302). An important symposium: *Benedetto XV, i cattolici e la prima guerra mondiale*, ed. G. Rossini, Rome, 1963.

W. H. PETERS, *The Life of Benedict XV*, Milwaukee, 1959.

M. DI PIETRO, *Benedikt XV, the Pope of Peace*, Eng. tr. London, 1941.

J. SCHMIDLIN, *Papstgeschichte . . .*, vol. III, 179-339.

G. ROSSINI (ed): *Benedetto XV, i cattolici e la prima guerra mondiale*, Rome, 1963.

Pius XI

Z. ARADI, *Pius XI. The Pope and the Man*, Garden City, 1958.

M. BENDISCIOLI, *La politica della Santa Sede 1918-1938*, Florence, 1939.

LORD CLONMORE, *Pope Pius XI and World Peace*, London, 1938.

R. FONTENELLE, *Pie XI*, Paris, 1939.

A. RHODES, *The Vatican in the Age of the Dictators, 1922-1945*, London, 1973.
On the general lines of the pontificate, besides the vol. IV of J. Schmidlin, *Papstgeschichte . . .*, Munich, 1939, the most recent work is the collection of essays *Pio XI nel trentesimo della morte*, Milan, 1969. See also:

L. SALVATORELLI, *Pio XI e la sua eredità pontificale*, Turin, 1939.

W. TEELING, *The Pope in Politics. The Life and Work of Pope Pius XI*, London, 1937 (critical in spirit).

On the Lateran Accords:

F. PACELLI, *Diario della Conciliazione*, ed M. Maccarrone, Vatican City, 1958.

On the relations of Pius XI with Nazi Germany:

W. M. HARRIGAN, 'Pius XI and Nazi Germany, 1937-1939', *Catholic Historical Review*, LI (1966), 457-86.

M. MACCARONE, *Il Nationalsocialismo e la Santa Sede*, Rome, 1947. This work has been unduly neglected by subsequent historians.

Pius XII

On the attitude of Pius XII during the Second World War, there is a very good bibliographical survey by V. Conzemius in *R.H.E.*, LXIII (1968), 437-503.

P. BLET, R. A. GRAHAM, A. MARTINI and B. SCHNEIDER, eds, *Actes et Documents du Saint-Siège relatifs à la Seconde Guerre mondiale* (9 vols have appeared), Vatican City, 1965-75 (for the years 1939-43; other volumes are in preparation).

C. N. CIANFARRA, *The Vatican and the Kremlin*, New York, 1950.

M. CLAUDIA, *Guide to the Documents of Pius XII*, Westminster (Md.), 1955.

J. CONWAY, 'The silence of Pope Pius XII', *Review of Politics*, XXVII (1965), 105-31.

A. CURVERS, *Pie XII, le pape outragé*, Paris, 1964 (apologetic).

C. FALCONI, *The Silence of Pius XII*, Eng. tr. London, 1970 (one-sided).

D. FISCHER, *Pope Pius XII and the Jews*, New York, 1963.

S. FRIEDLANDER, *Pius XII and the Third Reich. A Documentation*, Eng. tr. New York, 1966.

O. HALECKI, *E. Pacelli, Pope of the Peace*, New York, 1951.

M. MOURIN, *Le Vatican et l'URSS*, Paris, 1965.

J. NOBECOURT, *'Le Vicaire' et l'Histoire*, Paris, 1964.

A. PURDY, *The Church on the Move. The Characters and Policies of Pius XII and Johannes XXIII*, London, 1966.

A. RANDALL, *The Pope, the Jews and the Nazis*, London, 1963.

B. SCHNEIDER, *Pius XII.*, Gottingen, 1968.

M. C. TAYLOR, ed., *Wartime Correspondence between President Roosevelt and Pope Pius XII*, New York, 1947.

John XXIII

L. CAPOVILLA, *Giovanni XXIII*, Vatican City, 1963.

L. ELLIOTT, *I will be called John*, London, 1974.

E. E. Y. HALES, *Pope John and his Revolution*, London, 1965.

M. TREVOR, *Pope John*, London, 1967.

Pope John XXIII, *Journal of a Soul*, London, 1965.

Pope John XXIII, *Mission to France, 1944-1953*, London, 1966.

Pope John XXIII, *Letters to His Family*, London, 1970.

A. Roncalli, patriarcha di Venezia. Scritti e discorsi, 1953-1958, 4 vols, Rome, 1959-62.

Discorsi, messagi, colloqui del S. Padre Giovanni, XXIII, 6 vols, Vatican City, 1961-5.

See also *Encyclicals of Pope John XXIII*, Washington, 1965.

The evolution of Catholicism 1914-63

There is a store of information and texts in *La Documentation catholique*, fortnightly since 1919.

A. D. BINCHY, *Church and State in Fascist Italy*, London, 1941.

W. BOSWARTH, *Catholicism and Crisis in Modern France. French Catholic Groups at the Threshold of the Fifth Republic*, Princeton, 1961.

K. BREUNING, *Die Vision des Reichs. Deutscher Katholicismus zwischen Demokratie und Dictatur (1929-1934)*, Munich, 1969.

J. De BROUCKER, *L'Église à l'Est. I. La Pologne*, Paris, 1963.

J. S. CONWAY, *The Nazi Persecution of the Churches, 1933-1945*, London, 1968.

V. CONZEMIUS, 'German Catholics and the Nazi Regime in 1933', *Irish Ecclesiastical Record*, CIII (1967), 326-35. See also *R. H. E.*, LXIII (1968), 868-948.

A. COUTROT and F. DREYFUS, *Les Forces religieuses dans la société française* (coll. 'U'), Paris, 1965.

A. DIAMANT, *Austrian Catholics and the First Republic*, Princeton, 1960.

J. de FABRÈGUE, *Charles Maurras et son Action française*, Paris, 1966.

A. C. JEMOLO, *Church and State in Italy*, Oxford, 1960, chapters 5-8.

G. LEVY, *The Catholic Church and Nazi Régime*, New York, 1964.

J. MARTEAUX, *L'Église de France devant la révolution marxiste*, 2 vols, Paris, 1958-9 (from 1936 to 1958).

C. MARTI, 'La Iglesia en la sociedad española a partir de 1939', *Pastoral misíonera*, March-April 1972.

H. PAUL, *The Second Ralliement, the Rapprochement between Church and State in the Twentieth Century*, Washington, 1967.

J. ROVAN, *Le Catholicisme politique en Allemagne*, Paris, 1956 (general survey in chapters 5-8).

R. A. WEBSTER, *The Cross and the Fasces. Christian Democracy and Fascism in Italy*, Stanford, 1961.

G. C. ZAHN, *German Catholics and Hitler's Wars*, New York, 1962, London, 1963.

Biographies

M. R. De GASPERI, *De Gasperi uomo solo*, Milan, 1964.

J. KEMPENEERS, *Le Cardinal van Roey et son temps*, Brussels, 1971.

R. MUNTANYOLA, *Vidal y Baraquer, el cardenal de la paz*, Barcelona, 1971.

H. PORTMAN, *Kard. von Galen*, Munster, 1958.

B. SCHWERDFEGER, *Bischof Konrad von Preysing*, Berlin, 1950.

A. SIMON, *Le Cardinal Mercier*, Brussels, 1960.

L. STEVENSON, *M. J. Metzger, Priest and Martyr*, London, 1952.

Chapter 21

THE LIFE OF THE CHURCH

Pastoral Developments

O. de la BROSSE, *Vers une Église en état de mission*, Paris, 1965 (comments on pronouncements of Cardinal Suhard, preceded by a biography).

R. P. BURKE, *The Social Teaching of Pius XII*, Boston, 1965.

J. COMBLIN, *Échec de l'Action catholique?*, Paris, 1962.

G. GARRONE, *L'Action catholique, Son histoire, sa doctrine, son panorama*, Paris, 1958.

P. GLORIEUX, *L'abbé Godin*, Paris, 1946.

E. GUERRY, *Église catholique et Communisme*, Paris, 1960.

J. GUITTON, *L'Église et les laïcs, de Newman à Paul VI*, Paris, 1963.

G. NARDIN, *Il movimento d'unione tra i religiosi*, Rome, 1971.

Pastorale d'aujourd'hui. Bilan et perspectives, Fribourg congress 1961, Brussels, 1962.

S. POOLE, *Seminary in Crisis*, New York, 1965.

E. POULAT, *Naissance des prêtres-ouvriers*, Paris-Tournai, 1965.

J.-F. SIX, *Cheminements de la Mission de France*, Paris, 1967.

Spirituality

J. D. BENOÎT, *Liturgical Renewal. Studies in Catholic and Protestant Developments on the Continent*, London, 1958.

A.-M. BESNARD, 'Tendencies of Contemporary Spirituality', *Concilium*, I (November 1965), 14-24.

B. BESRET, *Incarnation ou eschatologie. Étude historique de ces thèmes dans la période 1935-1955*, Paris, 1965.

F. DEGLI ESPOSTI, *La teleologia del sacro Cuore di Gesù da Leone XIII a Pio XII*, Rome, 1967.

G. E. KIDDER SMITH, *The New Churches of Europe*, London, 1964.

R. LAURENTIN, *The Question of Mary*, New York, 1965.

SERENUS, 'The Biblical movement in the Catholic Church', *Theology*, LX (1957), 5-8.

Ecumenism

R. AUBERT, 'Stages of Catholic ecumenism from Leo XIII to Vatican II', in L. K. Shook and G. M. Bertrand, eds, *Theology of Renewal*, Toronto (1968), 183-203.

F. BIOT, *De la polémique au dialogue*, 2 vols, Paris, 1963.

D. GANNON, *Father Paul of Graymoor*, New York, 1951.

O. S. TOMKINS, 'The Roman Catholic Church and the Ecumenical Movement, 1910-1948', in R. Rouse and S. C. Neill, eds, *A History of the Ecumenical Movement*, 2nd ed., London, 1967.

Chapter 22

DEVELOPMENTS IN THOUGHT

R. AUBERT, *La Théologie catholique au milieu du XXᵉ siècle*, Tournai-Paris, 1954.

O. de la BROSSE, *Le Père Chenu. La liberté dans la foi*, Paris, 1969.

Y. M. CONGAR, *Situation et Tâches présentes de la théologie*, Paris, 1967, especially the first two chapters (11-40).

R. Van der GUCHT and H. VORGRIMLER, eds, *Bilan de la théologie du XXᵉ siècle*, 2 vols, Tournai-Paris, 1970-1 (a work of collaboration).

J.-P. JOSSUA, *Le Père Congar. La théologie au service de Dieu*, Paris, 1967.

J. MACQUARRIE, *Twentieth-century Religious Thought. The Frontiers of Philosophy and Theology, 1900-1960*, London, 1963.

E. MÉNARD, *L'Ecclésiologie hier et aujourd'hui*, Paris-Bruges, 1965.

Morale chrétienne et requêtes contemporaines, Tournai–Paris, 1954.

E. O'BRIEN, *Theology in transition. A bibliographical evaluation of the 'Decisive decade' (1954-1964)*, New York, 1965.

S. QUITSLUND, *Beauduin. A Prophet vindicated*, New York, 1973.

M. REDFERN, *Theologians Today: Hans Urs von Balthasar, Henri de Lubac*, London, 1972.

R. ROBERTS, *The Achievement of Karl Rahner*, New York, 1967.

Chapter 23

THE SECOND VATICAN COUNCIL

The text, in English, of the constitutions, decrees and declarations of the Second Vatican Council may most conveniently be found in W. M. Abbott, *The Documents of Vatican II*, G. Chapman, London, 1967 (paperback). For an account of the progress of the council, and a commentary on it, see A. Wenger, *Vatican II*, 4 vols, Paris, 1963-6 and R. Laurentin, *L'Enjeu du concile*, 5 vols, Paris, 1962-6.

F. ANDERSON, *Council Daybook: Vatican II*, 3 vols, Washington, 1965-6.

R. M. BROWN, *Observer in Rome: A Protestant Report on the Vatican Council*, Garden City, 1964.

R. CAPORALE, *Les Hommes du concile*, Paris, 1965.

H. KÜNG, *The Changing Church: Reflections on the Progress of the Second Vatican Council*, London, 1965.

M. NOVAK, *The Open Church: Vatican II Act II*, New York, 1964.

B. C. PAWLEY, *The Second Vatican Council*, Oxford, 1967 (Anglican point of view).

X. RYNNE, *Letters from Vatican City*, 4 vols, New York, 1963-6.

INDEX OF PERSONS AND PLACES

INDEX OF SUBJECTS